CAMBRIDGE LIBRA

Books of enduring

Histo_,

The books reissued in this series include accounts of historical events and movements by eye-witnesses and contemporaries, as well as landmark studies that assembled significant source materials or developed new historiographical methods. The series includes work in social, political and military history on a wide range of periods and regions, giving modern scholars ready access to influential publications of the past.

The Constitutional History of England, in Its Origin and Development

William Stubbs (1825–1901), one of the leading historians of his generation, pursued his academic research alongside his work as a clergyman. He was elected Regius Professor of Modern History at Oxford in 1866 and appointed a bishop in 1884. Stubbs was a foundational figure in medieval English history, with a special interest in the twelfth and thirteenth centuries. The three-volume study reissued here, originally published between 1874 and 1878, was one of his most influential works. Nine editions appeared during his lifetime and it was prescribed reading for generations of students. It traces the evolution of English political institutions from the early Anglo-Saxon invasions of Britain to 1485, relying mainly on primary sources. Volume 3, published in 1878, examines the developing role of Parliament during the Hundred Years' War, as well as considering the changing relationship between church and state towards the end of the Middle Ages.

The Constitutional History of England, in Its Origin and Development

VOLUME 3

WILLIAM STUBBS

CAMBRIDGE UNIVERSITY PRESS

Cambridge, New York, Melbourne, Madrid, Cape Town,
Singapore, São Paolo, Delhi, Tokyo, Mexico City

Published in the United States of America by Cambridge University Press, New York

www.cambridge.org
Information on this title: www.cambridge.org/9781108036313

This edition first published 1878
This digitally printed version 2011

ISBN 978-1-108-03631-3 Paperback

Clarendon Press Series

CONSTITUTIONAL HISTORY OF ENGLAND

STUBBS

London

MACMILLAN AND CO.

PUBLISHERS TO THE UNIVERSITY OF

Oxford

Clarendon Press Series

THE CONSTITUTIONAL HISTORY OF ENGLAND

IN ITS ORIGIN AND DEVELOPMENT

BY

WILLIAM STUBBS, M.A.

Regius Professor of Modern History

VOL. III

Oxford

AT THE CLARENDON PRESS

M DCCC LXXVIII

CONTENTS.

CHAPTER XVIII.

LANCASTER AND YORK.

CHAPTER XIX.

THE CLERGY, THE KING, AND THE POPE.

CHAPTER XX.

PARLIAMENTARY ANTIQUITIES.

CHAPTER XXI.

SOCIAL AND POLITICAL INFLUENCES AT THE CLOSE OF THE MIDDLE AGES.

CHAPTER XVIII.

LANCASTER AND YORK.

622. Character of the period.—623. Plan of the Chapter.—624. The Revolution of 1399.—625. Formal recognition of the new Dynasty.—626. Parliament of 1399.—627. Conspiracy of the Earls.—628. Beginning of difficulties.—629. Parliament of 1401.—630. Financial and political difficulties.—631. Parliament of 1402.—632. Rebellion of Hotspur.—633. Parliament of 1404.—634. The unlearned Parliament.—635. Rebellion of Northumberland.—636. The long Parliament of 1406.—637. Parties formed at court.—638. Parliament at Gloucester, 1407.—639. Arundel's administration.—640. Parliament of 1410.—641. Administration of Thomas Beaufort.—642. Parliament of 1411.—643. Death of Henry IV.—644. Character of Henry V.—645. Change of ministers.—646. Parliament of 1413.—647. Sir John Oldcastle.—648. Parliaments of 1414.—649. War with France.—650. The remaining Parliaments of the reign.—651. The King's last expedition and death.—652. Bedford and Gloucester.—653. Arrangement for the minority of Henry VI.—654. Impolitic conduct of Gloucester.—655. Quarrel with Bishop Beaufort.—656. Visit of Bedford.—657. Gloucester's attempt to govern.—658. Renewed attack on the Cardinal.—659. Henry's visit to France and change of ministers.—660. Continuation of the quarrel.—661. Bedford's second visit.—662. State of the government after Bedford's death.—663. Approaching end of the war.—664. Character of Henry VI.—665. The king's marriage.—666. Death of Gloucester and Beaufort.—667. Administration of Suffolk.—668. Fall of Suffolk.—669. Cade's rebellion.—670. Struggle of Somerset and York.—671. First rising of the Yorkists.—672. First regency of the Duke of York.—673. Results of the battle of S. Alban's.—674. Second regency of York.—675. Sole rule of Henry and Margaret.—676. The war of Lancaster and York.—677. The claim of York to the crown.—678. Accession of Edward IV.—679. Edward's first Parliaments.—680. The close of the struggle.—681. The struggle of the Nevilles.—682. Edward's supremacy.—683. Reign of Edward V.—684. Richard III.—685. Fall of Richard.—686. The claim of the house of Lancaster to the

The fifteenth century not a period of constitutional development.

622. If the only object of Constitutional History were the investigation of the origin and powers of Parliament, the study of the subject might be suspended at the deposition of Richard II, to be resumed under the Tudors. During a great portion of the intervening period the history of England contains little else than the details of foreign wars and domestic struggles, in which parliamentary institutions play no prominent part; and, upon a superficial view, their continued existence may seem to be a result of their insignificance among the ruder expedients of arms, the more stormy and spontaneous forces of personal, political, and religious passion. Yet the parliament has a history of its own throughout the period of turmoil. It does not indeed develope any new powers, or invent any new mechanism; its special history is either a monotonous detail of formal proceedings, or a record of asserted privilege. Under the monotonous detail there is going on a process of hardening and sharpening, a second almost imperceptible stage of definition, which, when new life is infused into the mechanism, will have no small effect in determining the ways in which that new life will work. In the record of asserted privilege may be traced the flashes of a consciousness that shew the forms of national action to be no mere forms, and illustrate the continuity of a sense of earlier greatness and of an instinctive looking towards a greater destiny. And this is nearly all. The parliamentary constitution lives through the epoch, but its machinery and its functions do not much expand; the weapons which are used by the politicians of the sixteenth and seventeenth centuries are taken, with little attempt at improvement or adaptation, from the armoury of the fourteenth. The intervening age has rather conserved than multiplied them or extended their usefulness.

Vast historical importance of the period of transition.

Yet the interval witnessed a series of changes in national life, mind, and character, in the relations of classes, and in the balance of political forces, far greater than the English race has gone through since the Norman conquest, greater in some respects than it has experienced since it became a consolidated, Christian nation. Of these changes the Reformation, with its attendant measures, was the greatest; but there were others which led to and resulted from the religious change. Such was that recovered strength of the monarchic principle, which, in England as on the Continent, marked the opening of a new era, and which, although in England it resulted from causes peculiar to England, from the exhaustion of all energies except those of the crown, whilst abroad it resulted from the concentration of great territorial possessions in the hands of a few great kings, seemed almost a necessary antecedent to the new conformation of European politics, and to the share which England was to take in them. Such again was the liberation of internal forces, political as well as religious, which followed the disruption of ecclesiastical unity, and which is perhaps the most important of all the phenomena which distinguish modern from medieval history. Such was the transformation of the baronage of early England into the nobility of later times, a transformation attended by changes in personal and political relations which make it more difficult to trace the identity of the peerage than the continuous life of clergy or commons. The altered position of the church, apart from Reformation influences, is another mark of a new period; the estate of the clergy, deprived of the help of the older baronage, now almost extinguished, and set in antagonism to the new nobility that is founded upon the spoils of the church, tends ever more and more to lean upon the royal power which tends ever more and more to use the church for its own ends, and to weaken the hold of the church upon the commons, whenever the interests of the commons and of the crown are seen to be in opposition. Partly parallel to these, partly resulting from them, partly also arising from a fresh impulse of its own liberated and directed by these causes, is the changed position of the commons: the third estate

Change in the position of the Commons.

now crushed, now flattered; now consolidated, now divided; now encouraged, now repressed; but escaping the internecine enmities that destroy the baronage, learning wisdom by their mistakes and gaining freedom when it is rid of their leadership; rising by its own growing strength from the prostration in which it has lain, with the other two estates, at the feet of the Tudors, all the stronger because it has itself only to rely upon and has springs of independence in itself, which are not in either clergy or baronage;—the estate of the commons is prepared to enter on the inheritance, towards which the two elder estates have led it on. The crisis to which these changes tend is to determine in that struggle between the crown and the commons which the last two centuries have decided.

Workings of modern life in the fifteenth century.

The causes which worked these changes begin from the opening of the sixteenth century to display themselves upon a lighter and broader stage, in more direct and evident connexion with their greater results. But they had been working long and deeply in the fifteenth century; and our task, one object of which is to trace the continuity of national life through this age of obscurity and disturbance, necessarily includes some examination into their action, into the relations of church and state, of the crown and the three estates, the balance of forces in the corporate body, and the growth in the several estates by which that balance was made to vary without breaking up the unity or destroying the identity of the whole. Having traced this working up to the time at which the new struggles of constitutional life begin, the point at which modern and medieval history seem to divide, we shall have accomplished, or done our best to accomplish, the promise of our title, and have told the origin and development of the Constitutional History of England.

Plan of the chapter.

Parliamentary institutions during the fourteenth century are the main if not the sole subject of Constitutional History. From this point, at which parliamentary institutions seem to have, to a great extent, moulded themselves, and parliamentary ideas have ripened, we shall have to recur to our earlier plan, and endeavour to trace more generally the workings of national life that gave substance and reality to those forms, that lay quiet under them when they seemed to be dormant, and that fought in them when the time came for it to arise and go down to the battle.

623. The object of the present chapter will be to trace the history of internal politics in England from the accession of Henry IV to the fall of Richard III: not that the period possesses a distinct political plot corresponding with its drama of dynastic history, but that from its close begins the more prominent action of the new influences that colour later history. A more distinct political plot, a more definite constitutional period, would be found by extending the scope of the chapter to the beginning of the assumed dictatorship of Henry VIII. But to attempt that would be to trench upon the domain of later history, which must be written or read from a new standing point. The battle of Bosworth field is the last act of a long tragedy or series of tragedies, a trilogy of unequal interest and varied proportions, the unity of which lies in the struggle of the great houses for the crown. The embers of the strife are not indeed extinguished then, but they survive only in the region of personal enmities and political cruelties. The strife of York and Lancaster is then allayed; the particular forces that have roused the national energies have exhausted themselves. From that point new agencies begin to work, the origin of which we may trace, but the growth and mature action of which must be left to other hands.

Plot of the History.

The history of the three Lancastrian reigns has a double interest; it contains not only the foundation, consolidation, and destruction of a fabric of dynastic power, but parallel with it, the trial and failure of a great constitutional experiment; a premature testing of the strength of the parliamentary system. The system does not indeed break under the strain, but it bends and warps so as to show itself unequal to the burden; and, instead of arbitrating between the other forces of the time, the parliamentary constitution finds itself either superseded altogether, or reduced to the position of a mere engine which those forces can manipulate at will. The sounder and stronger elements of

Importance of the Lancastrian period.

English life seem to be exhausted, and the dangerous forces avail themselves of all weapons with equal disregard to the result. It is strange that the machinery of state suffers after all so little. But it is useless to anticipate now the inferences that will repeat themselves at every stage of the story.

Good auguries for the constitution at the accession of Henry IV.

624. Although, as we have seen, the deposition of Richard II and the accession of Henry IV were not the pure and legitimate result of a series of constitutional workings, there were many reasons for regarding the revolution of which they were a part as only slightly premature; the constitutional forces appeared ripe, although the particular occasion of their exertion was to a certain extent accidental, and to a certain extent the result of private rather than public causes[1]. Richard's tyranny deserved deposition had there been no Henry to revenge a private wrong; Henry's qualifications for sovereign power were adequate, even if he had not had a great injury to avenge, and a great cause to defend. The experiment of governing England constitutionally seemed likely to be fairly tried. Henry could not, without discarding all the principles that he had ever professed, even attempt to rule as Richard II and Edward III had ruled. He had great personal advantages; if he were not spontaneously chosen by the nation, he was enthusiastically welcomed by them; he was in the closest alliance with the clergy; and of the greater baronage there was scarcely one who could not count cousinship with him. He was reputed to be rich, not only on the strength of his great inheritance, but in the possession of the treasure which Richard had amassed to his own ruin. He was a man of high reputation for all the virtues of chivalry and morality, and

[1] 'kynge Henry was admytte
Unto the croune of Englande, that did amounte
Not for desert nor yet for any witte,
Or might of him selfe in otherwyse yet,
But only for the castigation
Of king Richardes wicked perversacion,
Of which the realme then yrked everychone
And full glad were of his deposicion,
And glad to croune kyng Henry so anone,
With all theyr hertes and whole affeccion
For hatred more of kyng Richardes defection
Then for the love of kyng Henry that daye:
So chaunged then the people on hym aye.'—Hardyng, p. 409.

possessed, in his four young sons, a pledge to assure the nation that it would not soon be troubled with a question of succession, or endangered by a policy that would risk the fortunes of so noble a posterity. Yet the seeds of future difficulties were contained in every one of the advantages of Henry's position; difficulties that would increase with the growth and consolidation of his rule, grow stronger as the dynasty grew older, and in the end prove too great for both the men and the system.

Position of Henry.

The character of Henry IV has been drawn by later historians with a definiteness of outline altogether disproportioned to the details furnished by contemporaries. Like the whole period on which we are entering, the portrait has been affected by controversial views and political analogies. If the struggle between Lancaster and York obscured the lineaments of the man in the view of partisans of the fifteenth century, the questions of legitimacy, usurpation, divine right and indefeasible royalty, obscured them in the minds of later writers. There is scarcely one in the whole line of our kings of whose personality it is so difficult to get a definite idea. The impression produced by his earlier career is so inconsistent with that derived from his later life and from his conduct as king, that they seem scarcely reconcilable as parts of one life. We are tempted to think that, like other men who have taken part in great crises, or in whose life a great crisis has taken place, he underwent some deep change of character at the critical point. As Henry of Derby he is the adventurous, chivalrous crusader; prompt, energetic, laborious; the man of impulse rather than of judgment; led sometimes by his uncle Gloucester, sometimes by his father; yet independent in action, averse to bloodshed, strong in constitutional beliefs. If with Gloucester and Arundel he is an appellant in 1388, it is against the unconstitutional position of the favourites; if, against Gloucester and Arundel in 1397, he takes part with John of Gaunt and Richard, it is because he believes his old allies to have crossed the line which separates legal opposition from treason and conspiracy. On both these critical occasions he shows good faith and honest intent rather than policy or foresight. As king we find him suspicious, cold-blooded, and politic,

Difficulty of reading his character.

His character before his accession.

His character in later life.

undecided in action, cautious and jealous in private and public relations, and, if not personally cruel, willing to sanction and profit by the cruelty of others. Throughout his career he is consistently devout, pure in life, temperate and careful to avoid offence, faithful to the church and clergy, unwavering in orthodoxy, keeping always before his eyes the design with which he began his active life, hoping to die as a crusader. Throughout his career too he is consistent in political faith: the house of Lancaster had risen by advocating constitutional principles, and on constitutional principles they governed. Henry IV ruled his kingdom with the aid of a council such as he had tried to force on Richard II, and yielded to his parliaments all the power, place, and privilege that had been claimed for them by the great houses which he represented. It is only after six years of sad experience have proved to him that he can trust none of his old friends, when one by one the men that stood by him at his coronation have fallen victims to their own treasons or to the dire necessity of his policy, that he becomes vindictive[1], suspicious, and irresolute, and tries to justify, on the plea of necessity, the cruelties at which as a younger man he would have shuddered. It may be that the disease which made his later years miserable, and which his enemies declared to be God's judgment upon him, affected both the balance of his mind and the strength of his ruling hand. That love of casuistical argument which is almost the only marked characteristic which his biographer[2] notes in him, may have been a sign of the morbid consciousness that he had placed himself in a false position, and conscience may have urged that it was not by honest means that

Critical period.

[1] One stage of the transition may be seen in Arundel's speech of 1407, in which he declares that Henry has never exacted the penalties of treason from any who were willing to submit and promise to be faithful; Rot. Parl. iii. 608.

[2] 'Novi temporibus meis litteratissimos viros, qui colloquio suo fruebantur, dixisse ipsum valde capacis fuisse ingenii et tenacis memoriae ut multum diei expenderet in quaestionibus solvendis et enodandis .... Etsi sapiens fuerat, ad cumulum tamen sapientiae qui in Salomone fuerat non pervenit. Sufficiat posteriori saeculo scire quod vir iste in moralibus dubiis enodandis studiosus fuerit scrutator, et, quantum regale otium a turbinibus causarum eum permisit, liberum in his semper sollicitum fuisse;' Capgr. Ill. Henr. pp. 108, 109. He was 'sage et imaginatif;' Wavrin, p. 108.

he had availed himself of his great opportunity. We can hardly think that he was so far in advance of his age as to believe fully in the validity of the plea on which, as the chosen of the nation, he claimed the throne. If the defiance of the Percies contains any germ of truth, he had acted with more than lawful craft when he gained their assent to his supplanting of Richard; if the French chronicle of the time is to be credited, he had not refrained from gross perjury. Neither the one nor the other is trustworthy, but both represent current beliefs. If Henry were guiltless of Richard's death in fact, he was not guiltless of being the direct cause of it, and the person who directly profited by it. Although he was a great king and the founder of a dynasty, the labour and sorrow of his task were ever more present to him than the solid success which his son was to inherit. Always in deep debt, always kept on the alert by the Scots and Welsh; wavering between two opposite lines of policy with regard to France; teased by the parliament, which interfered with his household and grudged him supplies; worried by the clergy and others, to whom he had promised more than he could fulfil; continually alarmed by attempts on his life, disappointed in his second marriage, bereft by treason of the aid of those whom he had trusted in his youth, and dreading to be supplanted by his own son; ever in danger of becoming the sport of the court factions which he had failed to extinguish or to reconcile, he seems to us a man whose life was embittered by the knowledge that he had taken on himself a task for which he was unequal, whose conscience, ill-informed as it may have been, had soured him, and who felt that the judgments of men, at least, would deal hardly with him when he was dead.

Questions of conscience.

His constant difficulties and disappointments.

625. The forms observed at Henry's accession show that the greatness of the occasion was recognised by some at least of his advisers. The scene in Westminster Hall when he claimed the throne was no unpremeditated pageant; it was the solemn and purposed inauguration of a new dynasty. Archbishop Arundel, the astute ecclesiastic and experienced politician, although his zeal was quickened no doubt by the sense of the wrong done to himself and his brother, saw, more clearly than

The accession recognised as a new era.

Recognised importance of the accession.

Henry, the true justification of his proceedings. Sir William Thirning[1], the Chief Justice of the Common Pleas, had had to use argument to prevent Henry from claiming the throne by conquest. A commission of doctors had sat to inquire what fair claim he could make as rightful heir of the kingdom. The claims of the duke of Aumâle, son of Edmund of Langley duke of York, and Richard's favourite cousin, were advanced formally that they might be set aside[2]. No doubt the name of the young Mortimer was pronounced by some under their breath; for it was clear that the kingdom could fall to none but Henry. Popular superstition too was worth courting: the prophecy of Merlin was searched for an omen, and Henry was seen to be the 'boar of commerce'[3] who after days of famine, pestilence, and desolation, 'should recall the dispersed herds to the lost pastures; whose breast should be food for the needy and his tongue should quiet the thirsty, out of whose mouth should proceed streams to moisten the dry jaws of men.' Turning to more hallowed sources of authority, Henry was found to be

[1] 'Proposuerat Henricus de Darby vendicare regnum per conquaestum, sed Guillelmus Thirning justitiarius Angliae dissuasit;' Leland, Coll. i. 188; Ann. Henr. p. 282.

[2] Creton, an utterly untrustworthy writer, makes the archbishop ask the parliament whether they will have the duke of York, the duke of Aumâle or his brother Richard; Archaeol. xx. 200. According to Hardyng the debate in which Henry alleged the false pedigree took place on September 21. If there were any such debate, it must have been there that the bishop of Carlisle protested against Richard's deposition; but it is more probable that the discussion on Henry's hereditary title took place in the meeting of the commission of doctors, one of whom was Adam of Usk the chronicler, who reports that it was held on that day. (Chron. ed. Thompson, p. 29.)

[3] 'Superveniet aper commercii, qui dispersos greges ad amissa pascua revocabit.' Geoff. Mon. vii. § 3. Several pretended prophecies of Merlin were in vogue at the time on both sides, in one of which Henry is described as the mole who should reign after the ass; 'post asinum vero talpa ore Dei maledicta, superba, misera et turbida,' &c. See Mr. Webb's note on the subject, Archaeologia, xx. 258; Hall, Chr. p. 26. Froissart says that when he was at the court of Edward III, he heard an old knight who mentioned a prophecy contained in a book called Brut, that the descendants of the duke of Lancaster would be kings of England. He also heard a prophecy to the same purport on the day of Richard's birth. The stories, if true, tend to prove that John of Gaunt was suspected as early as that date of aspiring to the succession. (Froissart, iv. 121.) Adam of Usk has other prophecies, one by John of Bridlington, in which Henry is represented as a dog; and one taken from Merlin in which he is described as an eaglet; Chron. p. 24.

a new Judas Maccabeus to whom Northumberland was the Mattathias[1]. The sword which he had drawn on landing was to be preserved as a part of the regalia, the sword of Lancaster by the side of the sceptre of the Confessor. The glories of the line of Lancaster were crowned by the discovery of the golden eagle and cruse of oil which were to give to the new dynasty that miraculous unction that the house of Clovis had received from the holy dove; the blessed Virgin had confided it to S. Thomas of Canterbury at Sens, and it had lain concealed at Poictiers until under divine directions it had been delivered to duke Henry of Lancaster, the grandfather of the new king[2]. It may be feared that the same hand may be traced here that drew up the claim of legitimate descent through Edmund Crouchback as elder son of Henry III, if such a claim were really made. Wiser men were satisfied with the threefold title established by Henry's formal claim, the ready consent of the estates and the resignation of Richard in his favour[3]: 'Henry,

The Lancaster sword.

The sacred oil.

[1] So the earl calls himself in his letters to Henry; Ordinances of the Privy Council, i. 204, 205.

[2] The story of the ampulla is given in full in the Annales Henrici Quarti, pp. 297–298; Eulog. iii. 380; Capgr. Chr. p. 273. It is examined by Mr. Webb in the notes on Creton, Archaeol. xx. 266.

[3] Froissart, iv. c. 116, states the three reasons as conquest, inheritance and Richard's resignation. Cf. Chronique de la Trabison, p. 220. Capgrave (Ill. Henr. p. 107) says 'primo ex propinquitate sanguinis, quam probavit ex antiquis quidem gestis quorum veras copias nec dum vidi;' secondly by election, and thirdly by Richard's assignment. It is a curious thing that neither chronicles nor records preserve the exact form of the pedigree which was alleged at the time of Henry's challenge. Hardyng, the chronicler, who was brought up in the household of the earl of Northumberland, says that it was based on a story invented by John of Gaunt, that Edmund of Lancaster, from whom his wife Blanche was descended, was the elder son of Henry III, but was set aside in favour of Edward I, who was his younger brother. The earl had told Hardyng that on the 21st of September this claim had been laid before the lords, tested by the Chronicles of Westminster, and rejected; but notwithstanding was alleged by Henry. (Chron. pp. 352, 353.) Adam of Usk, whose chronicle has been lately discovered and edited by Mr. Maunde Thompson, says that on that day the subject was broached in the commission of doctors who were inquiring into the question of succession, and quotes the chronicles by which it was refuted; p. 30. This is no doubt the true account of the matter. See Hall, Chron. p. 14. Probably other stories were told. It was said in the controversy on the Yorkist title, that Philippa of Clarence was illegitimate; Fortescue, Works, i. 517. But the words of Henry's challenge do not necessarily imply that he meant to assert the forged pedigree; they need imply no more than that succession through females

Henry's solemn claim, Sept. 30, 1399.

duke of Lancaster, stood forth and spoke in English'—here also we may discern a deliberate and solemn formality—'"In the name of Father, Son, and Holy Ghost, I Henry of Lancaster challenge this realm of England and the crown with all the members and the appurtenances, as I that am descended by right line of blood, coming from the good lord king Henry Third, and through that right that God of his grace hath sent me with help of my kin and of my friends to recover it, the which realm was in point to be undone for default of governance and undoing of the good laws[1]." After which challenge and claim, the lords spiritual and temporal, and all the estates there present, being singly and in common asked what they thought of that challenge and claim, the said estates with the whole people, without any difficulty or delay, with one accord agreed that the said duke should reign over them.' Then immediately the king showed to the estates the signet of king Richard which he had delivered to him as a sign of his good-will. Thereupon Arundel took him by the right hand and led him to the throne. Henry kneeled down before it and prayed a little while; then the two archbishops Arundel and Scrope seated him upon it. By a strange and ominous coincidence, the close kinsmen of the two murdered earls joined in the solemn act. Arundel had avenged his brother; Scrope had yet to perish in a hopeless attempt to avenge his old master and the cousin who had laid down his life for Richard. When Henry had taken his seat, Arundel preached a sermon contrasting Henry's manliness with

was regarded as strange to the customs of England. It is on the exclusion of females that Fortescue urges the claim of the king's brother as against the grandson by a daughter, in the treatise 'de Natura Legis Naturae;' and if that were accepted, Henry might fairly call himself the male heir of Henry III. It was, moreover, on this principle probably that he excluded his own daughters from the succession in 1404 and 1406. Hardyng's story that John of Gaunt procured the insertion of the forged pedigree in several monastic chronicles is not borne out by any known evidence. If true, it must be referred to the year 1385, when it is said that he tried to obtain Henry's recognition as heir, and when the Earl of March was preferred; Eulog. iii. 361.

[1] Rot. Parl. iii. 422, 423; Mon. Eves. p. 209; Ann. Ric. p. 281; Raine, Northern Registers, p. 429. There are some slight variations in the wording as given by these authorities. See also Otterbourne, p. 219; Eulog. iii. 384; Capgrave, Chron. p. 273.

Richard's childishness [1], and after the king had expressly disavowed any intention of disinheriting any man on the plea that he had won England as a conqueror [2], he nominated the ministers and officers of justice, received their oaths, and fixed the day for his coronation. The session broke up; the members were to meet again on the 6th of October under the writ of summons already prepared [3], and the king was to be crowned on the feast of S. Edward the Confessor, October 13. The proceedings of the deposition were completed on the 1st of October, when Sir William Thirning, in the name of the commissioners appointed to convey to Richard the sentence of the Estates, declared his message to the unhappy king and renounced his homage and fealty. Richard replied 'that he looked not thereafter, but he said that after all this he hoped that his cousin would be good lord to him [4].' So the record ends; but it was known at the time that Richard, when he was further pressed to renounce all the honours and dignity pertaining to a king, refused to renounce the spiritual honour of the royal character impressed upon him, or his unction [5]. When the judge read to him the terms in which he had confessed himself unworthy, insufficient, and unfit to govern, and had allowed that he was deposed on account of his demerits, he corrected him, saying 'not so, but because my governance pleased them not [6].' Thirning insisting on the form, Richard gave way, and said with a smile that he

Parliament summoned.

Richard's acquiescence in his deposition.

[1] The text was 'Vir dominabitur populo'; 1 Sam. ix. 17. Rot. Parl. iii. 423.

[2] 'It is not my will that no man think that by way of conquest I would disinherit any man of his heritage'; Rot. Parl. iii. 423; Raine, Northern Registers, p. 429; Otterbourne, p. 220. Cf. Adam Usk, p. 32.

[3] The parliament which met on the 30th of September under Richard's writ was supposed to be dissolved by his deposition; the new parliament was summoned on the same day for October 6; but although it was obviously impossible for elections to be held in the six days intervening, no intimation is contained in the writs that the same members should attend; see the Lords' Report, iv. 768. The king, however, apologised for the short notice, and declared that it was intended to spare labour and expense; Rot. Parl. iii. 423.

[4] Rot. Parl. iii. 424.

[5] 'Respondit quod noluit renunciare spirituali honori characteris sibi impressi et inunctioni quibus renunciare non potuit nec ab hiis cessare'; Ann. Henr. p. 286; Capgr. Ill. Henr. p. 107.

[6] Ann. Henr. p 286.

trusted they would provide him with such means that he would not be destitute of an honourable livelihood. To the last he is a problem; we cannot tell whether they are words of levity or of resignation.

Meeting of parliament.

The meeting of the parliament on the 6th of October was merely formal[1]. The king took his seat; the lords and commons with a great company of spectators were in attendance. Arundel explained the circumstances which had rendered the new writ of summons necessary, and repeated the substance of his sermon.

Arundel's discourse.

'This honourable realm of England, the most abundant angle of riches in the whole world,' had been reduced to destruction by the counsels of children and widows; now God had sent a man knowing and discreet for governance, who by the aid of God would be governed and counselled by the wise and ancient of his realm. Having thus struck the keynote of the Lancastrian policy, he took another text, 'the affairs of the kingdom lie upon us,' from which he deduced the lesson that Henry was willing to be counselled and governed by the honourable, wise, and discreet persons of his kingdom, and by their common counsel and consent to do his best for the governance of himself and his kingdom, not wishing to be governed of his own will nor of his own 'voluntary purpose or singular opinion,' but by common advice, counsel and consent. After praising England as the land which most of all lands might trust to its own resources, and pointing out the requisites of good government, he declared the king's purpose of conserving the liberties of the Church, of the lords spiritual and temporal, and the commons; and with the consent of the assembly the parliament was adjourned to the day after the coronation.

The coronation.

That solemn act was celebrated on the appointed day with all the pomp and significance that befitted the beginning of a new dynasty. The Lancaster sword was borne before the king by the earl of Northumberland as sovereign of the Isle of Man; the golden eagle and cruse were used for the first time, and from the knighting of forty-six candidates for the honours of chivalry, the heralds date the

[1] Rot. Parl. iii. 415.

foundation of the order of the Bath[1]. The king had already begun to reward his friends; Ralph Neville, the earl of Westmoreland, had been made marshal and received the honour of Richmond; Henry Percy, the father, had been made constable and lord of Man; his son received the isle of Anglesey; his brother, the Earl of Worcester, was made admiral[2]; Arundel had been of course recognised as archbishop without waiting for the pope's reversal of his translation[3]. John Scarle, the chancellor, and John Northbury, the treasurer, were probably men who had stood aloof from politics and were trusted as officers who knew their own business[4].

Appointment of ministers.

626. On the 14th of October the parliament met for despatch of business; four dukes, one marquess, ten earls, and thirty-four barons, with the regular number of prelates, composed the house of lords; the house of commons numbered seventy-four knights, and somewhat over two hundred representatives of boroughs. The clergy had met under Arundel in their provincial synod on the 6th, and had in preparation the measures for which they reckoned on the grateful co-operation of the king.

Composition of parliament.

It is in the house of lords of course that the changes and chances of the preceding century have made the deepest mark. Edward I, in 1300, had summoned eleven earls and ninety-eight barons. Of the eleven earldoms, three were now vested in the king, who, besides being earl of Lancaster, Lincoln, and Hereford, was also earl of Derby, Leicester, and Northampton[5].

Changes among the earls.

[1] See Froissart, book iv. c. 116; Ann. Henrici, p. 291; Chronique de la Trahison, p. 225 note; Fabyan, Chr. p. 565; Taylor, Glory of Regality, p. 259; Favine, Theatre of Honour, tome ii. p. 65; Selden, Titles of Honour, pp. 819, 820.

[2] Rymer, viii. 91, 95.

[3] The temporalities were restored Oct. 21; Rymer viii. 96.

[4] Northbury had been Richard's minister, but in the discussions on the king's guilt declared that he had resisted his attempts at tyranny; and when Bagot asked what man in parliament would have ventured to do so, 'Vere, inquit, ego, etsi perdidissem omnia bona mea, una cum vita'; Ann. Henr. p. 305.

[5] So he styles himself in a deed dated 1399, printed by Madox, Formulare Angl. p. 327; see also Rymer, viii. 90; and Rot. Parl. iv. 48. The earldom of Northampton was afterwards conceded by Henry V to the Staffords as coheirs of Bohun.

Changes in the peerage.

One had become the regular provision for the prince of Wales. The earldoms of Arundel and Surrey were united in the son of the murdered earl, who was a minor, and suffering under his father's sentence. The heir of the Bigods had just died in exile[1]: the heirs of Umframville were no longer called to the English parliament; the house of Valence was extinct. Gloucester was for the moment held by Thomas le Despenser. Oxford and Warwick survived. Of the ninety-eight baronies twenty[2] were represented by the descendants of their former possessors, five were in the hands of minors, fourteen were altogether extinct, twenty-one had fallen into what the lawyers have termed abeyance among coheiresses and their descendants; thirty-three had ceased to be regarded as hereditary peerages from the non-summoning of their holders; one had been sold to the crown; besides extinction and abeyance some had suffered by attaint. Of the new lords, the four dukes and the marquess represented younger branches of the royal house; of the earls three represented the ancient earldoms; three had been created or revived by Edward III, four were creations of Richard II[3]. Of the fourteen newer baronies ten date from the early years of the preceding century; three, the two Scropes and Bourchier, from the reign of Edward III; one, that of Lumley, from 1384. The chief political results of this attenuation had been to lodge constitutional power in far fewer hands, to accumulate lands and dignities on men who were strong rather in personal qualifications and interests than in their coherence as an estate of the realm, to make deeper and broader the line between lords and commons, and to concentrate feuds and jealousies in a smaller circle in which they would become more bitter and cruel than

[1] The duke of Norfolk died at Venice Sept. 22, 1399.

[2] These numbers are derived from a collation of the writs for March 6, 1300, with the statements in Nicolas' Historic Peerage, Dugdale's Baronage, and Banks' Dormant Peerage. The barony sold to the king was that of Pinkeni, in 1301. The minors were Latimer, Clifford, Grey of Wilton, l Estrange, and Mortimer.

[3] The dukes were York, Aumâle, Surrey and Exeter; the marquess, Dorset; the three ancient earldoms were Gloucester, Warwick and Oxford. Edward III had created Devon, Salisbury and Stafford; Richard II, Northumberland, Westmoreland and Worcester.

they had been before. The quarrels of the last reign had already proved this, and Henry, when he looked round him, must have seen many places empty which he had once seen filled with earnest politicians. Of the appellants of 1388, only himself and Warwick survived; of the counter-appellants of 1397, Nottingham and Wiltshire were dead; the rest were waiting with anxious hearts to know whether Henry would sacrifice them or save them. Could he have looked forward a few months only he would have seen four more noble heads from among them laid low; a few years farther, and he would have seen the very men who had placed him on the throne perish as the victims of treason and mistrust.

Diminution of the peerage.

The strong men of the peerage now were the Percies, who shared with the house of Arundel the blood of the Karolings, and had risen by steady accumulations of office and dignity to a primacy in power and wealth; the earl of Northumberland was that Henry Percy who had disappointed the hopes of the Good Parliament, who had stood by John of Gaunt when he defended Wycliffe at S. Paul's, who had been afterwards his bitter enemy, and whose desertion of the cause of Richard had, more than any other single event, ensured the success of Henry. His brother Thomas had been steward to Richard II and had received from him the earldom of Worcester. Ralph Neville, the earl of Westmoreland, was brother-in-law of Henry Percy, and had risen in the same way; he was son of the lord Neville who had been impeached in the Good Parliament, and he had married, as second wife, Johanna Beaufort, a daughter of John of Gaunt. The blood of the house of Lancaster ran also in the veins of the Hollands and the Arundels; and such lords as were not cousins to the king through his parents, were ranked in the affinity of the Bohuns. The vast estates of the house of Lancaster lay chiefly in the north and midland shires; and the great names of the Percies, Nevilles, Scropes, Lumley, Roos, Darcy, Dacre, Greystock and Fitzhugh, show that the balance of political strength in the baronage lay northwards also.

The Percies.

The Nevilles.

The northern lords.

The first parliament of Henry IV sat from October 6 to November 19. It despatched a great deal of work. There

The king's difficulties at the beginning of the reign.

were, notwithstanding the great popularity of the king, grounds for alarm at home and abroad; how to obtain recognition by the pope and foreign princes, how to equip an army without having recourse to heavy taxation, how to deal with the Wycliffites, how to reconcile the feuds, how to punish the destroyers of Gloucester and Arundel, what was to be done with king Richard. Henry had made great promises to the clergy, and to Arundel he owed scarcely less than he owed to the Percies. At Doncaster, and again at Knaresborough castle, soon after he landed, he had promised not to tax the clergy with tenths or the laity with tallages[1]; Arundel was aware that any moment the knights of the shires in parliament might demand the seizure of the temporalities of the clergy. Sir John Cheyne, the speaker chosen by the commons, was known to be inclined to the Wycliffites; on the plea of ill-health he declined the election, but not until the archbishop had moved the synod of the clergy against him[2]. Sir John Doreward was chosen in his place[3].

Proceedings of the parliament.

The speaker was admitted on the 15th of October; and the same day all the proceedings of Richard's last parliament, in accordance with a petition of the commons, were annulled, and the acts of that of 1388 reinstated in their validity; the sufferers of 1397 were restored, so far as they could be restored, in blood and estate; the king undertook that the powers of parliament should not be again delegated to a committee such as Richard had manipulated so cleverly; the blank bonds which he had used to tax the counties illegally were cancelled; and the king's eldest son, Henry of Monmouth, was made prince of Wales, duke of Cornwall, and earl of Chester[4].

[1] The oath at Doncaster is mentioned by Hardyng in the Percy Challenge, Chron. p. 352. That at Knaresborough by Clement Maidstone: 'quod nunquam solveret Ecclesia Anglicana decimam nec populus taxam'; Ang. Sac. ii. 369.

[2] Ann. Henr. p. 290. Walsingham says that Cheyne was an apostate deacon; ii. 266. He was member for Gloucestershire and had been implicated in the designs of duke Thomas.

[3] Rot. Parl. iii. 424.

[4] Ib. iii. 425, 426, 436; cf. Adam of Usk, p. 35. The blank charters were burned by the king's order of Nov. 30; Rymer, viii. 109.

Challenges and recriminations among the appellants of 1397.

The next day the knights of the shire demanded the arrest of the evil counsellors of King Richard[1]. Sir William Bagot, the only survivor of the luckless triumvirate who had managed the parliament of 1397, made a distinct charge against the duke of Aumâle as the instigator of the murder of Gloucester. He repeated a conversation in which Richard had spoken of Henry as an enemy of the church, which called forth from the king himself a most distinct asseveration of his faithfulness; and Aumâle, who saw that he was to be represented as Richard's intended successor[2], challenged the accuser to single combat. The dukes of Surrey and Exeter, alarmed by Bagot's words, followed Aumâle's example; and the king, fearing that the informer would do more harm than good, remanded him to prison. The next day the lords, on the advice of lord Cobham, agreed that the three dukes should be arrested; the unhappy Warwick, who still survived to his own shame, attempted to excuse his confession of treason, and finally denied that he had made it, calling forth from the king a summary command to be silent. Lord Fitzwalter loudly proclaimed the innocence of Gloucester. Henry, remembering the part which he had himself played in the events of the last parliament, must have felt very miserable; he seems however to have determined that matters should not be driven to extremities, and put off the proceedings as well as he could from day to day. Every step in the transaction seemed to make the guilt of Aumâle more probable. On the 18th of October lord Fitzwalter formally impeached him[3]; Surrey

[1] 'Die Jovis,' Ann. Henr. p. 303; where a graphic account of the whole proceedings will be found, supplementing the meagre record in the Rolls of Parliament. See also Archaeologia, xx. 275–281.

[2] The story was that Richard had once expressed a wish to resign the crown to the duke of Aumâle, as the most generous and wisest man in the kingdom. The duke of Norfolk had urged that Henry stood nearer to the succession. Then Richard had said, 'Si ipse teneret regni regimen destruere vellet totam ecclesiam sanctam Dei'; Ann. Henr. p. 304; Fabyan, p. 566. Henry now allowed that he had wished to see more worthy men promoted than had been in Richard's time; and thus to some extent admitted that the subject had been discussed. According to Hall, Henry had been heard by the abbot of Westminster to say, when he was quite young, 'that princes had too little and religions had too much'; Chron. p. 15.

[3] Otterbourne, p. 222; Ann. Henr. p. 310.

Richard condemned to imprisonment.

alone stood by him; the loud challenges of the lords and the shouts of the commons threatened a civil war, and Henry only succeeded by personal exertions in rescuing his cousin from imminent death. During the lull that followed this storm, archbishop Arundel, on the 23rd of October, determined to raise the question what was to be done with Richard[1]. He charged the lords and all who were present to observe strict secrecy; and Northumberland put the question at once[2]. Twenty-two prelates, eight earls, including the prince of Wales and the duke of York, and twenty-eight barons and counsellors, declared their mind, that the late king should be kept in safe and secret imprisonment; and on the 27th, Henry himself being present, the sentence of perpetual imprisonment was passed on him[3]. The commons, on the 3rd of November, protested that they were not judges of parliament, but petitioners[4], thus guarding themselves against the consequences of a possible reaction. In consequence of this sentence Richard was, on the 29th, at midnight, removed from the Tower[5].

Protest of the commons.

Proceedings renewed against the dukes.

As soon as the sentence on Richard was declared, the outcry was again raised against the appellants of 1397; and on the 29th the proceedings were continued more quietly and formally. The six survivors pleaded their own cause severally; and bishop Merks took courage to present himself and disavow all participation in the murder of Gloucester[6]. The lords admitted different degrees of complicity in the appeal; Aumâle declared

[1] Rot. Parl. iii. 426.

[2] 'Coment leur semble que serroit ordeignez de Richard nadgairs roy, pur luy mettre en saufe garde, sauvant la vie quele le roy voet que luy soit sauvez en toutes maneres?' Rot Parl. iii. 426.

[3] Rot. Parl. iii. 427. The version of the sentence given in the Chronique de la Trahison as pronounced by the recorder of London, must be a fabrication; John of Bourdeaux, who had been called king Richard, was condemned to be imprisoned in a royal castle, and if any one rose in his favour, he was to be the first who should suffer death for the attempt; Chron. &c. p. 223; cf. Archaeol. xx. 274.

[4] Rot. Parl. iii. 427.

[5] Ann. Henr. p. 313.

[6] Ib. p. 313. The formal proceedings are in the Rot. Parl. iii. 449-453; they are deficient in dates, but it would seem from them that the debate was renewed on Wednesday the 29th; the answers of the accused were discussed on the Thursday; on the Friday the king consulted the prelates. The date of the judgment is given by the annalist.

that he had acted under constraint; Surrey was a boy at the time and had complied in fear for his life; Exeter had done what the others had done; Dorset had been taken by surprise, and had not dared to disobey the king; Salisbury had acted in fear; Despenser did not know how his name had got into the bill, but when it was there he dared not withdraw it. Other charges were included in the accusation; the death of Gloucester, the banishment of Henry, the repeal of the patent which secured the Lancaster inheritance, and the other sentences of the parliament. These were distinctly disavowed with various degrees of assurance. On the 3rd of November Sir William Thirning pronounced the judgment of the lords[1]; the excuses of the appellants were to some extent a confession of guilt; but the circumstances of the case were exceptional; the common law did not furnish adequate machinery for deciding the questions at issue, and to attempt to treat the matter as treason, as usually treated, would be to stir up elements most dangerous and disastrous to the realm; mercy and judgment were to be commingled in the decision; the dukes of Aumâle, Surrey, and Exeter were to be reduced to their former rank as earls of Rutland, Kent, and Huntingdon; the marquess of Dorset was to become earl of Somerset again, and le Despenser to cease to be earl of Gloucester. Salisbury's fate was not decided by the sentence; his confession was somewhat more damaging than those of the others, and he had not been admitted to state his case to the king. He was left to prove his innocence in a trial by battle with the lord Morley his accuser[2]. Hall, the person who was regarded as one of the actual murderers of Gloucester, had been sentenced to death on the 17th, and executed the same day[3]. The proceedings exhibit Henry as a somewhat temporising politician, but not as a cruel man. The offence against Gloucester

Pleas of the accused.

Sentence pronounced.

The dukes degraded.

[1] Rot. Parl. iii. 451; Ann. Henr. pp. 315–320; Wals. ii. 241.

[2] Froissart (iv. 116) says that Salisbury, who had been imprisoned, was received into favour on Rutland's intercession. Preparation was made for the trial by battle, but Salisbury's fate was decided before it could take place (see Williams' note on the Chronique &c., p. 224; Lingard, Hist. Eng. iii. 200); and lord Morley the challenger recovered costs from the earl's sureties; Adam Usk, pp. 44, 45.

[3] Rot. Parl. iii. 452, 453; Adam Usk, p. 36.

and Arundel in which he had participated was mixed up with the offence against himself; and he might have availed himself of the popular outcry to revenge his own wrongs. His conduct was condemned as weak and undecided, and he was threatened in an anonymous letter with an insurrection if the guilty were not more severely punished[1]. The lords and the knights of the shire denied on oath their knowledge of the writer; but subsequent events gave a sad corroboration to its threat, and popular fury completed the task which the king had mercifully declined.

Henry threatened with insurrection.

Formal protest of the commons.

It was probably as a direct consequence of these proceedings that the commons, on the 3rd of November, made the protest already referred to: 'that as the judgments of the parliament belong solely to the king and lords, and not to the commons, except in case that it please the king of his special grace to show to them the said judgments for their ease, no record may be made in parliament against the said commons, that they are or will be parties to any judgments given or to be given hereafter in parliament. Whereunto it was answered by the archbishop of Canterbury at the king's command, how that the same commons are petitioners and demanders, and that the king and the lords have of all time had, and shall of right have, the judgments in parliament, in manner as the same commons have shown; save that in statutes to be made, or in grants and subsidies, or such things to be done for the common profit of the realm, the king wishes to have especially their advice and assent. And that this order of fact be kept and observed in all time to come[2].'

The revival of the Acts of 1388 and the repeal of those of 1397 involved some readjustment of personal claims, which formed an important part of the work for the remainder of the session. The earls of Suffolk[3], Arundel, and Warwick[4], re-

[1] 'Quasi illi (the King, Arundel and Percy) caecati muneribus salvassent vitam hominum quos vulgus sceleratissimos et morte dignissimos reputabat'; Ann. Henr. p. 320. Hardyng at a later period recommends to Edward IV the example of Henry in favour of clemency as a piece of sound policy; Chron. p. 409.

[2] Rot. Parl. iii. 427.

[3] Ann. Henr. p. 312; Rot. Pat. Cal. p. 238; Rot. Parl. iii. 668.

[4] Rot. Parl. iii. 435, 436; Chron. Henr. ed. Giles, p. 5.

quired restitution; the three persons[1] excepted from the pardon of 1388 had to be secured by a royal declaration of their loyalty. The sentence against Haxey, already set aside by Richard, had to be again annulled[2]; and the pardons granted by Richard in 1398 to be confirmed. The king refused however to restore the heirs of the condemned judges, or to replace the heir of Vere as high chamberlain. Archbishop Arundel was allowed to demand reparation from Walden, whom Richard had forced into the primacy; and the prince of Wales was empowered to bear the titles of duke of Aquitaine and Lancaster[3]. Reparation for past losses.

The necessary work of the parliament was soon despatched; a subsidy on wool was granted for three years, and a fifteenth and tenth already granted to Richard was confirmed to Henry[4]. The king rejected the proposal that, for fear of the plague, he should not go abroad, and obtained the consent of the lords that he shou d go in person against the Scots[5]. Time was found for the passing of a statute of twenty clauses, and more than sixty important petitions were heard and answered. Of the legislative acts the most significant were those which restricted the definition of treason to the points defined in the statute of Edward III, and forbade appeals of treason to be made in parliament; another prohibited the delegation of the powers of parliament to a committee like that abused to his own destruction by Richard II[6]. Taxation and legislation.

It is in the treatment of petitions that the king shows the most strength of will. There were no doubt about him some counsellors who wished for reconciliation and concord at any cost, and were content to wipe out summarily all the sad history of the late reign. There were others who had private as well as public wrongs to avenge, and some to whom the opening of the new Petitions in parliament.

[1] The three were Richard Clifford now Privy seal, Richard Metford now bishop of Salisbury, and Henry Bowet afterwards bishop of Bath and Wells and archbishop of York; the latter was the king's confidential agent. Rot. Parl. iii. 428.

[2] Rot. Parl. iii. 430, 434.

[3] Ib. iii. 427, 441, 442.

[4] Ib. iii. 425. A half tenth and fifteenth payable at the preceding Michaelmas is not confirmed to Henry.

[5] Ib. iii. 427, 428, 434. The king himself spoke in full parliament on the expedition to Scotland.

[6] Ib. iii. 426, 434, 442.

Henry obtains an acknowledgment of his prerogative.

era seemed to give an opportunity for urging at once fundamental changes. Henry found that he must take his own line. He obtained from the commons a declaration that he, like Richard, was entitled to all the royal liberty that his predecessors had enjoyed[1], undertaking however not to follow the example of Richard in overthrowing the constitution. He freely exercised the right of rejecting petitions even when strongly urged by the commons; in some instances showing more policy than equity. He had already discovered that he would be far from a rich sovereign, and that the relations with France and Scotland were likely to involve him immediately in a great expenditure. Richard had thrown the whole finance of the kingdom into confusion; and were Richard's obligations to be reviewed the confusion would be worse confounded. To the petitions that the sums borrowed by Richard should be repaid, that the sums due for purveyances should be discharged, and that the acquittances which he had granted should be revoked, he returned the same answer, le roi s'avisera[2]; but he authorised a careful inquiry into the effects of Richard[3]. He refused to order the repayment of the money paid as ransoms by the adherents of Gloucester and Arundel. He had to refuse to submit to the judgment of his council the great donations of land by which he had already provided for his servants, or to agree to a general resumption of crown lands[4]. His last act in the parliament was to except from all the benefits of the national pacification the estates of Scrope, Bussy, and Green, whom he regarded as guilty of all the evil that had come upon the land: yet even here he would try to be just; he would not lay hand on the estates with which those culprits were enfeoffed to the use of others, and he would do nothing that would endanger or disgrace the venerable lord le Scrope of Bolton who had been so faithful to his father and grandfather, and who was in no way answerable for the sins of his unhappy son, the earl of Wiltshire[5].

Treatment of petitions.

Question of a resumption.

[1] Rot. Par. iii. 434.

[2] Ib. iii. 437, 438, 440. In the case of the purveyances the king promised to take the advice of his council and do what was reasonable.

[3] Ib. iii. 439. [4] Ib. iii. 433. [5] Ib. iii. 453.

The convocation or provincial synod of Canterbury, which sat contemporaneously with this parliament, made no grant of money but contented itself with drawing up articles directed against the Lollards and the continual encroachments of the royal courts[1]. Henry had dealt carefully with them, and as early as the 7th of October had sent Northumberland to tell them that he wanted no money, but prayers, promising to do his best to suppress heresy. Although this assembly seems to have been summoned by the chapter of Canterbury, as if in a vacancy of the see, and although Boniface IX did on the 19th of October issue letters restoring Arundel to the primacy[2], neither king nor archbishop, parliament nor synod, had thought it necessary to wait for the formal act. The archbishop had taken his place in both the assemblies, had crowned the king and had been restored to his temporalities long before the papal letter could have reached England. This conduct seemed to promise that however strenuously orthodox Henry might be, his relations to Rome would not be marked by servility, and that the house of Lancaster would act up to the spirit of the constitution in both Church and State. Henry's dealings with convocation.

627. The reign of peace lasted for a little more than a month. Henry, perhaps, had done either too much or too little. An eastern potentate would have struck off the heads of the Hollands and extinguished the house of Mortimer, regardless of the infant innocence of the little earl of March. But Henry does not seem to have cast a thought on Mortimer, and the ready acquiescence of the Hollands in his assumption of the crown either deceived him or left him without a plea for crushing them. Yet he had in the two degraded dukes, in Salisbury and in le Despenser, four very determined enemies; and his cousin Short reign of peace.

[1] Ann. Henr. pp. 290, 291; Wilkins, Conc. iii. 238, sq.
[2] Wilkins, Conc. iii. 246. Adam of Usk thus describes the position of the rival archbishops during the interval, 'Thomas et Rogerus, si fas est dicere, duo archiepiscopi in una ecclesia, quasi duo capita in uno corpore, Rogerus scilicet tunc per papam in possessione juris, et dominus Thomas, quia necdum per papam restitutus, per seculi tamen potestatem in possessione facti, quae praevaluit in omnibus, quia sibi soli crucis Cantuariensis, sibi a dicto Rogero remissae, paruit in omnibus delatio'; Chron. p. 37.

Conspiracy of the earls.

Rutland was not beyond suspicion. Whether the degraded lords were goaded into desperate action by their own fears, or whether they really miscalculated national opinion so far as to hope for Richard's restoration, cannot be determined. They formed a plot to seize the king on Twelfth Night, and replace Richard on the throne. The conspiracy was discovered, whether betrayed by Rutland or suspected by his father, and foiled. Kent and Salisbury were seized and murdered by the mob at Cirencester; le Despenser fled and fell a victim to the hereditary hatred of the citizens of Bristol; Surrey was taken in Essex, and notwithstanding the intervention of the countess of Hereford, Henry's mother-in-law, was beheaded at Pleshey[1]. Of these cruelties Henry was no wise guilty, but he did not punish the murderers, and shortly afterwards increased the number of victims by more legal executions at Oxford and London[2]. The failure of the attempt sealed the fate of Richard; whether he was murdered at Pomfret, or starved himself to death, or escaped to live in Scotland an idiot and a prisoner, he had already quitted the stage of history[3]. We may believe that Henry spoke the truth when he declared that he had no hand in his death. A solemn funeral was celebrated for the unhappy victim at Langley on the 14th of February; and although the king rewarded the services of the men and women of Cirencester with an annual present[4] of venison, he proclaimed on the 24th that accused persons were not again to be beheaded without trial.

Its failure and punishment.

Fate of Richard.

628. Meanwhile the political difficulties which overshadowed the whole reign were looming at no great distance. France would not recognise the new king, or accept his proposals for an

[1] Ann. Henr. p. 327. Hardyng says that the countess ordered the execution; p. 356. She was a sister of archbishop Arundel.

[2] Otterbourne, p. 228; Ann. Henr. pp. 329, 330; Leland, Coll. ii. 484; Adam Usk, p. 41. Lord Lumley was taken and killed at Cirencester, Sir Thomas Blount and Sir Benedict Shelley and twenty-seven or twenty-eight others at Oxford; Richard Magdalene, and John Feriby clerks, Thomas Schevele and Bernard Brocas knights, in London. On Feb. 24 the king issued a proclamation against beheading traitors without trial; Rymer, viii. 124; Ordinances, i. 107 sq., 113.

[3] On the evidence about Richard's death see Webb, in Archaeol. xx. 282 sq.; Amyot, ibid. pp. 424–442.

[4] Rymer, viii. 150.

alliance by marriage, and demanded the restoration of Richard's child-widow. The Scots were stirring at the instigation of the French; the Welsh were preparing to rise under Owen Glendower. Invasion was imminent. Richard's treasures, if they had ever existed, had been spent or stolen. The year 1400 was a very busy year for Henry. In the summer he marched north to insist on the homage of Scotland [1]: he reached Leith as a victorious invader, but returned home without gaining his object. In September he heard that Owen Glendower was at war with lord Grey of Ruthyn, and he had to make an expedition to Wales in the autumn. The money for the Scottish expedition was provided by the contributions of the lords, granted in a great council; the prelates giving a tenth and the lords temporal giving an aid under specified conditions [2], but the king had no success in his attempt to borrow from the Londoners; and at Christmas the emperor of Constantinople [3], to whom Richard had made large promises, arrived to claim the fulfilment. A truce had been patched up with France, but peace was not to be looked for. New allies must be sought; a project of marriage was started, to secure the alliance of the new king of the Romans, who had supplanted Wenzel as Henry had supplanted Richard; and there could be no marriage without money.

Foreign difficulties.

Invasion of Scotland.

War in Wales.

Supply of money.

Although on the view of the whole year Henry's position had become stronger, the dangers ahead were greater. The clergy, although the king had surrendered the alien monasteries and had not pressed the demand for money, were clamouring against the Wycliffites; the Percies who were bearing the burden of defence on both the Scottish and the Welsh marches, were discovering that the change of ruler was bringing them more cost than honour. Money was wanted everywhere and for every one. Henry knew

Complaints of the want of money.

[1] Otterbourne, p. 230; Ann. Henr. p. 333; Eulog. iii. 387; Wals. ii. 246; Chron. Giles, p. 20.

[2] The great council was held on 9th of February by writ under the Privy Seal; Rymer, viii. 125, 153; Ordinances of the Privy Council, i. 102-106. According to the annalist the clergy were asked by letter for a tenth, which it was thought uncivil to refuse; Ann. Henr. p. 332. The commons were not asked; Adam Usk, p. 43.

[3] Ann. Henr. p. 334; Ad. Usk, p. 55.

that when once the financial alarm began to spread, constitutional difficulties would arise. He had already too few friends, and ministers of scarcely average experience. The parliament must meet again. It had already been summoned to meet at York in October 1400; but the day was postponed and the place changed. It met at Westminster on the 20th of January, 1401 [1], and sat until the 10th of March.

New parliament called.

Statement of finance laid before the parliament.

Sir William Thirning, the chief justice, who made the opening speech, had no easy task. The financial report which had been laid before the council showed that, besides the expenses of the royal household, more than £130,000 [2] was required for the defence and administration of the realm. The £350,000 at which Richard's accumulations were estimated had disappeared, and the king had already incurred a debt of £16,000 [3]. No figures, however, were laid before the commons; the expenses of the coronation, the suppression of the conspiracy, the expeditions to Scotland and Wales, the defence of Calais and Guienne, were dwelt upon, and the commons in particular were urged to give more attention than was usually given to public business, and less to matters of private interest. The result of this exhortation was a long and specially important session.

The commons seize their opportunity.

629. The commons, although they may, in the first instance, have required a spur, now saw their advantage at once. It was not the weakness of the king's title, as has sometimes been said, but their knowledge of his necessities that gave them their vantage ground. With the utmost apparent loyalty and with no little liberality they began to put in form the claims which they conceived themselves to possess. They chose as speaker Sir Arnold

[1] Lords' Report, iv. 770–775; Rot. Parl. iii. 454.

[2] The estimate is printed in the Ordinances of the Privy Council, i. 154. ii. 56; but the document is mutilated. Among the items are Calais £13,320 6*s*. 8*d*; Ireland £5333 6*s*. 8*d*.; Guienne £10,000; Queen Isabella £8242 0*s*. 10*d*.; the last loan £16,000; the wardrobe £16,000; annuities and grants £24,000: all together including lost items, but not including the household, £130,908 14*s*. 2*d*. These items agree with the particulars of Thirning's Speech; Rot. Parl. iii. 454.

[3] On the amount of treasure left by Richard see Chronique de la Trahison, p. 263; Fabyan, p. 569, from the Polychronicon, estimates it at £700,000; the Chronique at 900,000 nobles, or £300,000.

Savage[1], one of the members for Kent, a man who showed by the length and ingenuity of his speeches, that he was capable of rivalling the curious orations with which the parliaments were usually opened by chancellor, archbishop or justice. Thirning had directed that no one should leave the parliament until the business of the session was completed. Savage, after making the usual protest on being presented to the king, recounted the principal points of the justice's speech, and expressed a hope that the commons might have good advice and deliberation, and not be pressed suddenly with the most important matters at the very close of parliament. The king, through the Earl of Worcester, replied that he imagined no such subtilty. Not satisfied with this, three days after, the commons again presented themselves, and again returned thanks for Thirning's speech, and administered another reproof[2]. It might happen, the speaker said, that some of their body, out of complaisance to the king, might report their proceedings before they were completed, a course which might exasperate the king against individuals; he prayed that the king would not listen to any such tales. Henry made the requisite promise. The speaker then proceeded to expatiate in a set speech on the course to be adopted with respect to a number of lords who had been challenged by the French as traitors to King Richard. Henry thanked them for their advice. On the occasion however of a third address on the 31st of January, the king, tired of Savage's eloquence, declined to hear any more petitions by word of mouth, and requested the commons to put all their requests in writing[3]. The object of the whole proceeding was no doubt that which was stated in one of the petitions so delivered, that the king's answer to their requests might be declared before the grant of money was made. This petition was presented on the 26th of February;

Arnold Savage's speeches.

Discussions of the king and speaker.

Redress to precede supply.

[1] Rot. Parl. iii. 455: Otterbourne, p. 232. 'Qui tam diserte, tam eloquenter, tam gratiose, declaravit communitatis negotia, praecipue ne de cetero taxis gravarentur aut talliagiis, quod eandem ab universis promeruit ea die'; Ann. Hen. p. 335. Sir Arnold Savage, of Bobbing near Sittingbourn, had been sheriff of Kent in 9 Rich. II, and gone with John of Gaunt to Castille. He was constable of Queenborough castle in 1393 and died in 1410. Hasted's Kent, ii. 635, 636.

[2] Rot. Parl. iii. 455

[3] Ib. iii. 455, 456.

Henry's refusal.

the king in reply promised to confer with the lords on the point, and on the last day of the session refused the demand as unprecedented[1]. This petition and its answer involve one of the most distinct statements of constitutional theory that had been ever advanced.

Another speech of Savage.

Savage no doubt was capable of formulating so much and more; in another of his speeches he compares the estates to a Trinity, that is to say 'the person of the king, the lords spiritual and temporal, and the commons. But the crowning instance of his ingenuity is found in the closing address, in which he draws an elaborate parallel between the parliamentary session and the Mass; the office of the archbishop at the opening of the session is compared to the reading of the epistle, gospel, and sermon; the king's declaration of a determination to maintain the faith and the laws is compared with the propitiatory offering; the closing words 'Ite missa est' and 'Deo gratias' are equally appropriate in both cases[2]. The 'Deo gratias' of the commons was expressed in their money grant, for which the king thanked them and then dissolved the parliament. The grant made was a fifteenth and tenth, for a year, with tunnage of two shillings and poundage of eightpence for two years[3].

The commons force their demands on the king.

The claims of the commons were not confined to matters of theory; the king was obliged to comply with their petition that he would revoke the assignment of certain pensions charged on the subsidy of wool which in the last session had been granted for a special time and purpose. They further prayed him to institute a careful examination into the inventory of king Richard's jewels[4], a petition which, according to the historian of the time, Henry met with a declaration that he had received none of Richard's property, but was in reality poor and needy. They urged that the record of parliamentary business should be engrossed before the departure of the justices, whilst the facts were still present in their memory[5], no indistinct hint that the record was not always trustworthy; the answer was that the clerk of the

[1] Rot. Parl. iii. 458. [2] Ib. iii. 466.
[3] Ib. iii. 455; Dep. Keeper's Rep. ii. App. ii. p. 181.
[4] Rot. Parl. iii. 457; Ann. Henr. p. 335. [5] Rot. Parl. iii. 457, 458.

parliament should do his best with the advice of the justices and subject to the advice of the king and lords.

Sentences and restorations.

The lords were otherwise employed, partly in the work of pacification, partly in the work of retribution. The conspiracy of the earls had ruined many and endangered more. Sentence of forfeiture was declared against the earls of Kent, Huntingdon, and Salisbury and the lords Lumley and le Despenser. Rutland and Fitzwalter agreed to refer their quarrel to the king's decision; the earls of Rutland and Somerset were, on the petition of the commons, declared loyal. The king's clemency looked even farther back; the heirs of the judges Holt and Burgh were restored; the bishop of Norwich, the valiant Henry le Despenser, the only man who had ventured in arms to oppose Henry's march in 1399, was reconciled to the king; the proceedings against Sir Simon Burley were reversed. All these were wise and politic measures, although they were too late to heal the evils caused by the exceptional misgovernment of the late reign[1].

The statute against the Lollards.

The mark however by which the parliament of 1401 is chiefly known in history is the action taken against the Lollards. This was prompted no doubt by archbishop Arundel, who throughout his career was their unflinching enemy. He had a double opportunity. The popular hatred of Richard's court and courtiers was still strong; and among Richard's courtiers the chief protectors of the Lollards had been found. The earl of Salisbury had been a noted and powerful heretic, closely connected with Thomas Latimer, Lewis Clifford, William Neville, the Cheynes, and the Clanvowes, who were the leaders of the party. Advantage might be taken of the unpopularity of the old court to destroy the Lollards. Henry again was fervently orthodox, all the more so perhaps for the dislike that as an honest man he must have felt at his father's intrigues with the Wycliffites; he had made very weighty promises to the clergy, and Arundel might well demand that those promises should be now fulfilled: a calumny had been breathed against Henry himself; this would be the easiest way of repelling it.

[1] Rot. Parl. iii. 456, 459, 460, 461, 464.

Petition of the clergy.

The clergy had shown a dislike to contribute money, and had made no grant since the reign began; they might be inclined to be more liberal if they saw themselves secured against their enemies. With this intention Arundel had called together the clergy on January 26th, and told them that the great object of their meeting was to put down the Lollards[1]. The royal commissioners, Northumberland, Erpingham, and Northbury, promised the king's aid, and prayed for some decisive measure. The result was a long and bitter petition[2], and the immediate initiation of proceedings against William Sawtre, a Lollard priest. The petition was granted by the king with the assent of the lords; and a petition of the commons, conceived in shorter terms but in the same sense, conveyed the assent of the lower house[3]. It was then framed into a clause of the statute of the year, and by it the impenitent heretic, convicted before the spiritual court, was to be delivered over to the officers of the secular law to be burned; all heretical books were to be destroyed[4]. The exact date of the petition is not given. Sawtre's trial, however, lasted from the 12th to the 24th of February[5]; on the 26th the royal writ for his execution was issued[6]. On the 11th of March the convocation granted a tenth and a half-tenth to supplement the contribution of the laity[7]. The whole proceeding, grievous as it is to the reputation of all persons concerned in it, seems to show that there was already in the country, as in the court, a strong reaction against the Wycliffites. Doubtless it was in the House of Commons that the widest

Petition of the commons.

Sawtre burned.

[1] Wilkins, Conc. iii. 254.

[2] Rot. Parl. iii. 466, 467; Wilkins, Conc. iii. 252.

[3] Rot. Parl. iii. 473. 'Item priount les Communes qe qant ascun homme ou femme, de quel estat ou condition qu'il soit, soit pris et emprisone pur Lollerie, que maintenant soit mesne en respons, et eit tel juggement come il ad desservie, en ensample d'autres de tiel male secte, pur legerement cesser lour malveis predications et lour tenir a foy Cristien.'

[4] 2 Hen. iv. c. 15; Statutes, ii. 123; Chr. Giles, p. 22; Wilkins, Conc. iii. 328.

[5] Ann. Henr. pp. 336, 337; Eulog. iii. 388; Chr. Giles, p. 22; Adam Usk, p. 57; Wilkins, Conc. iii. 254.

[6] Rymer, viii. 178; Rot. Parl. iii. 459. We gather from Adam Usk, p. 4, that there was during the session an alarm of a Lollard rising.

[7] Wilk. Conc. iii. 262; Ad. Usk, p. 59. The clergy of York granted a tenth, July 26: Wilk. Conc. iii. 267.

divergence of opinion would be looked for; a year and a half before the commons had chosen a suspected Lollard as their speaker. But the fall of Salisbury, and the desertion of Sir Lewis Clifford[1], who formally renounced Lollardy in 1402, must have weakened them. Sir John Cheyne no longer represented Gloucestershire, and Sir John Oldcastle had not yet been elected for Herefordshire. It must not however be supposed that the revival of doctrinal zeal affected the relations of the national church to Rome in other points. The same parliament that passed the statute of Lollardy urged the exact execution of the statute of provisors[2], and shewed no reluctance to confiscate the property of the alien priories which Henry had restored in the previous year[3]; it was no time for sparing either the property or the labour of the clergy, as the king had shown by directing them to arm to repel a French invasion. The policy which Arundel dictated seemed still to combine the maintenance of orthodoxy with great zeal for national welfare.

Probable objects of Arundel's policy regarding the Lollards.

Possibly to some of the questions thus raised was owing the change of ministry which occurred at the close of the session. Scarle on the 9th of March resigned the great seal, which was given to bishop Stafford[4], the very prelate who had been chancellor during the last years of Richard; and on the 31st of May Northbury was removed from the treasury, and Lawrence Allerthorp succeeded him. Allerthorp was an old baron of the Exchequer, who after holding office as treasurer for a year was sent to Ireland with Thomas of Lancaster, the king's son. It seems more probable that both ministers were chosen for their practical qualifications, than that any political change had taken place. It was no doubt acceptable to the clergy that a bishop should again preside in the chancery, and the restoration of

Change of ministers.

[1] Ann. Henr. p. 347.
[2] Rot. Parl. iii. 459, 465, 470. The king had been empowered in the last parliament to dispense with this statute in particular cases; the commons now pray that it may not be dispensed in favour of cardinals or other aliens; another petition alleged that the enactment of the last parliament had been wrongly enrolled, but this on examination was proved untrue; ibid. p. 466. Cf. Statutes. ii. 121, 122.
[3] Rymer, viii. 101; Rot. Parl. iii. 456.
[4] Rymer, viii. 181.

Stafford may have been part of the plan of reconciliation which four years later placed the deposed archbishop Walden in the see of London.

Henry's difficulties increase.

630. The year thus begun was not less busily employed than that which preceded it. It was a year of increasing labours and increasing difficulties. The king himself spent a month in Wales in the summer, trying in vain to bring Owen Glendower to a decisive engagement. After returning to Westminster for a great Council in August[1], he again mustered his forces at Worcester in October to renew his efforts. But the season was by that time too far advanced, and he returned to London without having entered Wales. The younger Percy, Hotspur as he was called, who had been acting as commander on the Welsh march, was, in repeated letters to the council, complaining of the expenses of the war. On the 17th of May he wrote to say that he could not retain his command beyond the end of the month, and on the 4th of June he repeated the warning[2]. The apprehensions of attack from France were again becoming formidable. At a council held probably in June, a division of opinion manifested itself: should war be declared at all, should it be declared without the consent of parliament, or should parliament be immediately summoned. The great lords saw that the financial difficulty would be great; Rutland especially deprecated a new war whilst money was so scarce, and the earls of Northumberland, Westmoreland, and Suffolk thought with him. The lord Grey of Ruthyn thought it well to wait until the negotiations which were still pending had broken down, and then to refer the whole matter to parliament[3]. The momentary alarm passed over, and the little queen was restored to her parents. But money did not become more

The Welsh war in 1401.

Discussion in the council on a war with France in June.

[1] Henry was at Evesham June 3, at Worcester June 8, and spent four weeks on the border 'parum proficiens'; Mon. Evesh. p. 174. On the 21st he was back at Wallingford; and on the 25th at London. Cf. Ordinances, &c. ii. 56.

[2] See the letters in the Ordinances and Proceedings of the Privy Council, i. 150, 151, 152.

[3] Ordinances, &c. i. 143–145; cf. p. 165.

plentiful. Another great council was held in August[1], and attended by a very large number of knights and esquires severally summoned by letters of privy seal. In this assembly the king is said to have resolved on going to war with France and Scotland. In the winter the king ordered the collection of an aid on the marriage of his daughter Blanche to the count palatine Lewis, son of the king of the Romans[2].

Great council on the war, August 1401.

Henry's popularity was on the wane; he had not been successful in Wales; the exactions of his purveyors were a bitter source of complaint among the people[3]; an attempt was made upon his life. The next year, 1402, was one of still worse omen. In Lent the lord Grey of Ruthyn was captured by Owen Glendower. In June, Edmund Mortimer, the brother of the late earl Roger of March who had been declared heir-presumptive by Richard, fell into the hands of the rebel chief, and after a short imprisonment married his daughter, proclaimed himself his ally, and declared that he was in arms to maintain the right of his nephew to the throne[4]. The king's invasion of Wales, now become an annual event, was more than ever unsuccessful and calamitous; it lasted for three weeks, during which the army was nearly starved and nearly drowned[5],

In 1402 Edmund Mortimer joins Owen Glendower.

[1] Ordinances, &c. i. 155. Adam of Usk mentions this council and the determination to go to war, p. 67.

[2] The letters for collecting the aid were issued Dec. 1, 1401, and Feb. 16, 1402; Rymer, viii. 232, 242; Dep. Keeper's Rep. ii. App. ii. p. 181; the amount was 20s on the knights' fee held immediately of the king, and the same on every twenty pounds rental of land held of the king in socage, according to Stat. 25 Edw. III. But the grant of the aid was not yet made; it was to be discussed in a great council in January 1402. See p. 36, note 4, below.

[3] Ann. Henr. p. 337; Eulog. iii. 387; Rot. Parl. iii. 473. An exaction on the sale of cloth produced loud complaints and riots in Somersetshire where the king was regarded as having broken his promise about taxation; Ad. Usk, p. 61.

[4] Ord. i. 185; Chron. Henr. ed. Giles, pp. 27, 30. In a letter to his tenants dated Dec. 13, 1402, Mortimer announces that he has joined Glendower in a scheme to restore Richard if he is alive, or if he is dead to place the earl of March on the throne; Ellis, Original Letters, 2nd series, i. 24; Tyler, Henry of Monmouth, i. 135. On the 28th of Feb. 1405 is dated the agreement between Glendower, Mortimer, and Northumberland, for a division of England and Wales between the three; ib. p. 150; Chron. Henr. ed. Giles, pp. 39 sq.; Hall, p. 28.

[5] Ann. Henr. p. 343.

Rumour that Richard is alive.

nothing being done against the foe. As Henry's failures lessened his popularity, a mysterious reaction in favour of Richard began to set in. It was currently reported that he was alive in Scotland. Franciscan friars went up and down the country organising conspiracy. In May Henry had to charge the bishop of Carlisle and the earl of Northumberland to arrest all who were spreading the false news[1]; and a number of executions followed[2], showing that the king's patience was exhausted and his temper embittered. Walter Baldock, an Augustinian canon, and another priest who had engaged in conspiracy, were hanged. Eight Franciscans underwent the same fate, without any show of ecclesiastical remonstrance. Sir Roger Clarendon, a son of the Black Prince, with his esquire and page, perished in the same way and for the same cause. A popular rising was expected in London; Owen Glendower and the Scots were believed to hold the strings of a secret league, and the sorceries of the friars were supposed to be the causes of the ill success of the king[3]. In one quarter only there was light. The earl of Northumberland and Hotspur defeated the Scots at Homildon in September, and in that victory crowned the series of their services to Henry with a success which seems to have led to a final breach with him. The victory of Homildon was the one piece of good news which could be reported to the next parliament.

Executions.

Battle of Homildon Hill.

Parliamentary history of 1402.

631. The last instalment of the tenth and fifteenth granted in March 1401 was due in the following November, and as a renewal of the grant would be immediately required, the parliament was summoned for January 29, 1402; but if such an assembly was ever held it left no traces whatever of its action[4]; there are no statutes, no rolls of proceedings, no writs

[1] Rymer, viii. 255; cf. p. 261, 262, 268.

[2] Ann. Henr. pp. 309, 340; Wals. ii. 249; Eulog. iii. 389–394; Chr. Giles, p. 28.

[3] 'Arte magica,' Otterb. p. 236; 'mala arte fratrum minorum,' Ann. Henr. p. 343; Wals. ii. 251. 'All men trowed witches it made that stounde'; Hardyng, p. 360.

[4] The writs for such a parliament at Westminster were issued on the 2nd of December; Lords' Report, iv. 776; and for convocation to be held the first Monday in Lent; ib. p. 778. The Rolls of Parliament contain a

of expenses, or of prorogation. The working parliament of the year met on the 30th of September[1]; Henry Bowet, the king's old chaplain, being treasurer, and bishop Stafford still chancellor. The latter in his opening speech said what could be said for the king, but did not attempt to conceal the distress of the country. True, Henry had been, as the mightiest king in the world, invited by the king of the Romans to attempt to heal the schism in the church, and the victory over the Scots was an almost miraculous proof of divine favour. Still the realm was enduring punishment at God's hand[2]. The commons in reply gave a proof of their earnest desire to work for the public good, that awoke the suspicions of the king; they desired, as they had done in the evil days of King Richard, to have 'advice and communication' with certain of the lords on the matters to be treated. Henry granted the request with a protest that it was done not of right, but of special favour; and four bishops, four earls, and four lords were named[3]. The most important business despatched was the grant of supplies. The subsidy on wool was continued for three years, tunnage and poundage for two years and a half; and protesting that the grant should not be made an example for taxing except by the will of lords and commons, the poor commons by assent of the lords granted a tenth and fifteenth for the defence of the realm[4].

Parliament meets in September.

Conference of lords and commons.

Grants of money.

few petitions of the third year of Henry which might be referred to such a parliament if it were really held; but one of them speaks of the parliament as sitting at Coventry, so that probably they belong to 1404. The bishop of Norwich was directed to attend a *council* to be held Jan. 27, 1402, on Aug. 24, 1401; Ordinances, i. 167; and we know from the minutes of the council held in November, that both a great council and a parliament were to be held; the aid for the marriage of Blanche was to be discussed at the council on Jan. 27; Ordinances, i. 179. One short minute of such a council is preserved; ib. p. 180.

[1] Rot. Parl. iii. 485; Eulog. iii. 395.

[2] 'Dieux ad mys punissement en diverse manere sur ceste roialme'; 'le roi de Rome, pur appaiser et ouster cel schisme ad escript a notre dit seigneur le roi come a le pluis puissant roi du monde.' Rot. Parl. iii. 485.

[3] Rot. Parl. iii. 486.

[4] Dep. Keeper's Rep. ii. App. ii. p. 182; Rot. Parl. iii. 493; Ann. Henr. p. 350. Great sums were borrowed in anticipation of the first instalment of the grants; letters asking for loans to the amount of 22,200 marks were issued April 1, 1403; Ordinances, &c. i. 199–203. The clergy of Canterbury met, Oct. 21, and on Nov. 27 granted a tenth and a half. Wilkins, Conc. iii. 271.

Proceedings of the commons. The most important statute of the session is one which confirms the privileges of the clergy; and the majority of the petitions concern private suits. The commons seem however to be fully aware of the character of the king's difficulties; they pray that the king will abstain from fresh grants, and retain the alien priories in his hands; that Northumberland may be duly thanked, Grey of Ruthyn ransomed, and Somerset restored to his dignity of marquess, an offer which he wisely declined. George of Dunbar, earl of March, whose adhesion to the king had led to the victory over the Scots, entreated Henry to recover for him his lost estates. The increase in the number of petitions, the revival of old complaints, the demand for the enforcement of old statutes, show a great increase of uneasiness. The session ended on the 25th of November[1].

In February 1403 Henry married his second wife, Johanna of Navarre, the widowed duchess of Brittany, an alliance which gave him neither strength abroad nor comfort at home[2]. The same month Stafford resigned the great seal, which was intrusted by the king to his brother, Henry Beaufort, bishop of Lincoln. The appointment of Beaufort, coupled with the nomination of the prince of Wales as lieutenant in Wales, and Thomas of Lancaster, the king's second son, as lieutenant of Ireland, perhaps implies that Henry was severing himself from his old friends. Beaufort and Arundel do not seem to have acted well together, and the proud independence of the Percies was becoming, if not intolerable to the king, at least a source of danger to him as well as to themselves.

Henry Beaufort chancellor.

The Percies. 632. Northumberland and Hotspur had done great things for Henry. At the outset of his reign their opposition would have been fatal to him; their adhesion ensured his victory. He had rewarded them with territory[3] and high offices of trust, and they had by faithful service ever since increased

[1] Rot. Parl. iii. 487, 488, 491, 495.

[2] 'Utinam fausto pede'; Otterbourne, p. 239; Ann. Henr. p. 350.

[3] The earl, as late as Mar. 2, 1403, had a grant of the Scottish lands of Douglas, which however could scarcely be a profitable gift so long as they were in Scottish hands; Rymer, viii. 289.

Growing discontent of the Percies.

their claims to gratitude and consideration. The earl was growing old; he was probably some years over sixty; Hotspur was about the same age as the king. Both father and son were high-spirited, passionate, suspicious men, who entertained an exalted sense of their own services, and could not endure the shadow of a slight. Up to this time not a doubt had been cast on their fidelity. Northumberland was still the king's chief agent in parliament, his most valued commander in the field, his Mattathias. It has been thought that Hotspur's grudge against the king began with the notion that the release of his brother-in-law, Edmund Mortimer, had been neglected by the king, or was caused by Henry's claim to deal with the prisoners taken at Homildon; the defenders of the Percies alleged that they had been deceived by Henry in the first instance, and only needed to be persuaded that Richard lived in order to desert the king[1]. It is more probable that they suspected Henry's friendship, and were exasperated by his compulsory economies. For two or three years Hotspur had been engaged in a service which exhausted his own resources, and he could get no adequate supplies from king or council. A less impatient mind might have been driven to discontent, and when it was once known

[1] 'Comes Northumbriae rogavit regem ut solveret sibi aurum debitum pro custodia marchiae Scotiae, sicut in carta sua continetur; Egomet et filius meus expendimus nostra in custodia illa: rex respondit; 'aurum non habeo, aurum non habebis. Comes dixit Quando regnum intrastis promisistis regere per consilium nostrum; jam multa a regno annuatim accipitis et nihil habetis, nihil solvitis et sic communitatem vestram irritatis. Deus det vobis bonum consilium'; Eulog. iii. 396. Other reasons are given: Henry's demand that Hotspur should surrender his prisoner Douglas (see Wavrin, p. 56; Rymer, viii. 292; Hardyng p. 360), whilst Hotspur insisted that the king should ransom Mortimer. Hardyng gives the formal challenge made by the three Percies, embodying most of the charges made in 1405; and also makes them fight for the right of the little earl of March (p. 361). The challenge is made by the three Percies as 'procuratores et protectores reipublicae,' and charges Henry with (1) having sworn falsely at Doncaster that he was come only to recover his inheritance, in spite of which he had imprisoned Richard and compelled him to resign; (2) he had also broken his promise to abstain from tallages; (3) contrary to his oath he had caused the death of Richard; (4) he had usurped the kingdom which belonged to the earl of March; (5) he had interfered with the election of knights of the shire; (6) he had hindered the deliverance of Edmund Mortimer and had accused the Percies of treason for negotiating for his release. Hardyng, pp. 352, 353; Hall, Chr. pp. 29, 30. See also Lingard, iii. 212.

that he was discontented, the same crafty heads that were maintaining the strife on the Welsh and Scottish borders would know how to approach him. Yet Henry seems to have conceived no suspicion. In April he was employed in raising money by loan to send to Scotland. Northumberland and Hotspur were writing for increased forces. The castle of Ormeston was besieged; a truce made with its defenders was to end on the 1st of August; the king was to collect all the force of the country and to join in the invasion. Henry started on his journey: still the old earl was demanding the payment of arrears, and the king was fencing with him as well as he could; on the 30th of May[1] he wrote for both help and money; on the 26th of June[2] he told the king that his ministers were deceiving him; it was not true that he had received £60,000 already; whatever he had received, £20,000 were still due. On the 10th of July Henry had reached Northamptonshire on his way northwards; on the 17th he had heard that Hotspur with his uncle the earl of Worcester were in arms in Shropshire[3]. They raised no cry of private wrongs, but proclaimed themselves the vindicators of national right: their object was to correct the evils of the administration, to enforce the employment of wise counsellors, and the proper expenditure of public money[4]. The king declared in letters to his friends that the charges were wholly unfounded, that the Percies had received the money of which the country was drained, and that if they would state their complaints formally they should be heard and answered[5]. But it was too late for argument. The report ran like wildfire through the west that Richard was alive, and at Chester. Hotspur's army rose to 14,000 men, and not sus-

Henry suspects nothing.

Northumberland presses for money.

Rebellion of Hotspur.

His professions.

Henry's answer.

[1] Ordinances &c., i. 203.

[2] Ib. i. 204; this letter is signed 'Votre Mathathias,' in the old man's own hand.

[3] Ib. i. 206, 207.

[4] 'Ut personae suae possent gaudere indemnitatis securitate et corrigere publicas gubernationes, et constituere sapientes consiliarios ad commodum regis et regni. Scripserunt insuper quod census et tallagia concessa regi sive donata pro salva regni custodia non sunt conversa in usus debitos sed devorata nimis inutiliter, atque consumpta'; Annales Henr. pp. 361, 362. Cf. Otterbourne, p. 240; Wals. ii. 255; Capgr. Chr. p. 282.

[5] Ann. Henr. p. 362; cf. Eulog. iii. 395.

pecting the strength and promptness of the king, he sat down with his uncle and his prisoner, the earl of Douglas, before Shrewsbury. Henry showed himself equal to the need. From Burton-on-Trent, where on July 17 he summoned the forces of the shires to join him [1], he marched into Shropshire, and offered to parley with the insurgents. The earl of Worcester went between the camps, but he was either an impolitic or a treacherous envoy, and the negotiations ended in mutual exasperation. On the 21st the battle of Shrewsbury was fought; Hotspur was slain; Worcester was taken and beheaded two days after. The old earl, who may or may not have been cognisant of his son's intentions from the first, was now marching to his succour. The earl of Westmoreland, his brother-in-law, met him and drove him back to Warkworth. But all danger was over. On the 11th of August he met the king at York, and submitted to him [2]. Henry promised him his life but not his liberty. He had to surrender his castles [3]; his staff as constable was taken from him, and given to John of Lancaster; but Henry did not bear malice long; the minor offenders were allowed to sue for pardon [4], and within six months Northumberland was restored to his liberty and estates.

Hotspur at Shrewsbury.

Battle of Shrewsbury, July 21, 1403.

Northumberland submits.

633. Although Hotspur's demands for reform were a mere artifice, and his connexion with the Welsh proved his insurrection to be altogether treasonable, subsequent events showed that the reform was really wanted and that the spirit of discontent was becoming dangerous in each of the estates. The cry was everywhere what had become of the money of the nation? The king had none, the Percies had received none, the people had none to give, the clergy were in the utmost poverty. Yet war was everywhere imminent. The Bretons were plundering the coast; hostilities with France were only staved off by ill-kept truces; the Welsh were still in full force. When Henry returned southwards and had gathered his forces at Worcester early in September, it was found that he could not

Reality of the king's difficulties.

Want of money.

[1] Rymer, viii. 314.
[2] Otterbourne, p. 244; Annales Henr. p. 371.
[3] Ordinances, i. 211.
[4] Rymer, viii. 338; Ordinances, i. 212.

The clergy threatened. move for want of supplies[1]. To an application which was made for a grant from the clergy Arundel replied that they were utterly exhausted; and when, after an insolent demand from the courtiers that the prelates should be stripped of their equipages and sent home on foot, he had succeeded in assembling the synod of his province and obtained a grant of half a tenth, only £500 could be raised immediately on the security of the grant[2]. Such a fact proves that all confidence in the stability of the government was at an end. Complaints were becoming louder, suspicions graver and more general. The parliament summoned to Coventry in December was afterwards ordered to meet at Westminster in January[3]; a great council was held preparatory to the parliament, and when it met, every accusation of misgovernment, and every proposal for restraint on the executive, which had been heard since the days of Henry III, were repeated.

Weakness of the government.

Parliament of January, 1404.

In this parliament bishop Beaufort was chancellor, the lord Roos of Hamlake treasurer, and Sir Arnold Savage again speaker of the commons. The election of Savage was in itself a challenge to the king; his long speeches invariably contained unpalatable truths. As was generally the case, the minister spoke chiefly of foreign dangers, the commons thought and said most about domestic mismanagement, the sudden diminution of the revenue, the lavish grants of the king, the abuses of liveries, the impoverishment of the royal estates, the extravagant administration of the household. A demand for a conference of advisers resulted in a formal array of such complaints; if those complaints were satisfied, the commons would show themselves liberal and loyal[4]. An unexpected amount of favour was shown to the earl of Northumberland; the peers refused to find him guilty of treason; it was not more than trespass:

[1] Ann. Henr, p. 373; cf. Eulog. iii. 398. A council was held at Worcester; Rot. Parl. iii. 525.

[2] Ann. Henr. p. 374. The clergy of Canterbury met October 7, and granted a half tenth; Wilkins, Conc. iii. 274.

[3] Lords' Report, iv. 785–790: it met Jan. 14, Rot. Parl. iii. 522; and sat until Mar. 20, Lords' Report, i. 496; the great council was held before Christmas, Rot. Parl. iii. 525.

[4] Rot. Parl. iii. 523, 524.

Lenity of the parliament.

he was admitted to pardon and took the oath of fealty. The struggle in the north was, it seemed, to be regarded as a case of private war rather than of rebellion. The earls of Westmoreland and Northumberland were prayed to keep the peace; the commons returned thanks to the king for Northumberland's pardon, and showed the extent of the public suspicions by a petition that the archbishop of Canterbury and the duke of York might be declared guiltless of any complicity in Hotspur's rising[2]. But the most significant work of the session was the attack on the household.

Attack on the royal household.

On a petition of the commons four persons were removed from attendance on the king, his confessor, the abbot of Dore, and two gentlemen of the chamber; the king excused his servants but complied with the request, and undertook to remove any one else whom the people hated[3]. The same day, February 8, it was determined that an ordinance should be framed for the household, and the king was asked to appoint his servants in parliament, and those only who were honest, virtuous, and well renowned. Nor did the attack stop here:

Outcry against aliens.

the old cry against aliens was after so many years revived; the king's second marriage might, like the second marriage of Richard, be a prelude to constitutional change. The commons demanded the removal of all aliens from attendance on either king or queen; a committee of the lords was appointed to draw up the needful articles, and they reported three propositions: all adherents of the antipope were to be at once expelled from the land; all Germans and orthodox foreigners were to be employed in garrisons and not made chargeable to the household; all French, Bretons, Navarrese, Lombards and Italians were to be removed from court, exception being made in favour of the two daughters of the queen, with one woman and two men servants. Henry yielded so graciously that the commons relaxed their rigour and allowed the queen to retain ten other friends and servants. On the 1st of March a fundamental change was introduced into the administration of the household, and a sum of £12,100 arising

[1] Rot. Parl. iii. 324.
[2] Ib. iii. 525, 526.
[3] Ib. iii. 525.
[4] Ann. Henr. p. 379; Rot. Parl. iii. 527; Eulog. iii. 400.

Payment to the charge of the household.

from various specified sources was set apart from the general revenue of the crown to be devoted to this purpose[1]. The archbishop of Canterbury declared the king's consent to this, and made in his name a repeated declaration of his purpose to govern justly and to maintain the law. A further condescension to public feeling was made by the publication of the names of the persons whom the king had appointed to act as his great and continual council. The list contains the names of six bishops, Edward of Rutland, who had now succeeded his father as duke of York, the earls of Somerset and Westmoreland, six lords, including the treasurer and privy seal, four knights, and three others[2]. Sir John Cheyne and Sir Arnold Savage are among the knights, and their presence shows that neither the Wycliffite propensions of the one nor the aggressive policy of the other was regarded as a disqualification for the office of counsellor. A petition and enactment on the abuse of commissions of array show that the king's poverty was leading to the usual oppressive measures for maintaining the defence of the country[3], and the number of private petitions for payment of annuities proves that the plea of poverty was by no means exaggerated. Yet the commons refused to believe that it was true. If we may trust the historians, the argument on the subject led to personal altercations between the king and the commons. It was not the expenses of defence, they told him, that troubled England; if it were so, the king had still all the revenues of the crown, and of the duchy of Lancaster, besides the customs, which under king Richard had so largely increased as far to exceed the ordinary revenues[4]. He had too the wardships of the nobles; and all these had been granted that the realm might not be harassed with direct taxation. Henry replied that the inheritance of his fathers should not be lost in his days; and he must have a grant of money.

Declaration of the names of the council.

Petitions.

Personal discussion between the king and the commons.

[1] Rot. Parl. iii. 528. Of this sum £2000 arose from ferms, £1300 from the small custom, £2000 from the hanaper, £500 from escheats, £2000 from alien priories, £300 from the subsidy on wool, and £4000 from the ancient custom. See Chr. Henr. ed. Giles, pp. 36, 37; Ann. Henr. p. 380.

[2] Rot. Parl. iii. 530.

[3] Ib. 526.

[4] 'Isti non inquietant Angliam multum'; Eulog. iii. 299. Neither the discussion nor the grant of the tax are noticed in the Rolls of the Parliament.

The speaker answered that if he would have a grant he must reduce the customs; the king insisted that he must have both. The customs were indeed safe, having been granted for more than a year to come. The commons held out until March 20, when they broke up after discussing a somewhat novel tax on the land; it was proposed that a shilling should be paid on every pound's worth of land, to be expended, not by the ministers, but by four treasurers of war, three of whom were citizens of London[1]. The grant was probably voted in this session, but the final enactment was postponed to the next parliament; possibly that the constituency might be consulted meanwhile. The settlement of the succession on the prince of Wales and his heirs, and in default on the other sons of the king in order[3], completed the important business of a session which must have been exceedingly unsatisfactory to the king, especially as another parliament must be called within the year to renew the grant of the customs. The influence of the archbishop, which the details of this session prove to have been still very great, obtained an increased grant from convocation in May[4]; a measure which, viewed in connexion with the later history of the year, seems to have the air of precaution. Possibly the commons were meditating, probably Arundel was anticipating, an attack on the church, to follow the attack on the royal administration.

Proposal for a new tax on the land.

Settlement of the succession.

In other respects the year was one of preparation and anticipation. The French were threatening the coast; the fleet, under Somerset, was vindicating at great cost the national

[1] Eulog. iii. 400; Otterbourne, p. 246; Ad. Usk, p. 83; Ann. Henr. pp. 379, 380.

[2] 'Carta scripta sed non sigillata'; Eulog. iii. 400. The subject, although circumstantially discussed by the annalists, does not appear in the Rolls until the next session. The persons, however, nominated as treasurers were recognised as such by the Council, and the subsidy is spoken of as granted in this parliament; Ordinances, i. 220. Stowe, Chr. p. 330, says that the record was destroyed lest it should make a precedent.

[3] Rot. Parl. iii. 525.

[4] The convocation of Canterbury met April 21, and granted a tenth and a subsidy (Wilk. Conc. iii. 280) on condition that their rights should be respected. Ann. Henr. p. 388; Dep. Keeper's, Rep. ii. App. ii. p. 182. The subsidy was a grant of 2s on every 20s of every benefice or office ecclesiastical untaxed, over 100s per annum.

Transactions of 1404. reputation at sea; the Welsh were gaining strength and forming foreign alliances; the sinister rumours touching Richard were obtaining more and more credit. In the summer Northumberland visited the king at Pomfret, and surrendered the royal castles which had been in his charge. Serle, a confidential servant of Richard, was given up to Henry, and executed[1]. But little was done. In October at Coventry the 'Unlearned Parliament' met.

The Unlearned Parliament. 635. This assembly acquired its ominous name from the fact that in the writ of summons the king, acting upon the ordinance issued by Edward III in 1372[2], directed that no lawyers should be returned as members. He had complained more than once that the members of the House of Commons spent more time on private suits than on public business; and the idea of summoning the estates to Coventry, where they would be at a distance from the courts of law, was perhaps suggested by his wish to expedite the business of the nation[3]. In the opinion of the clergy the Unlearned Parliament earned its title in another way, for, although the rolls of parliament contain no reference to the fact, a formidable attempt was made to appropriate the temporalities of the clergy to the necessities of the moment. The estates met on the 6th of October; the chancellor reported that the grant of the last parliament was entirely inadequate, and Money grants. the commons replied with a most liberal provision; two tenths and fifteenths, a subsidy on wool, and tunnage and poundage for two years from the following Michaelmas, 1405, when the grants made in 1402 would expire; lords and commons confirmed the land-tax voted in the last parliament, and lord Furnival and Sir John Pelham were appointed treasurers of the war instead of the persons then nominated[4]. The bold proposition that the land of

[1] Otterbourne, p. 248; Ann. Henr. p. 390; Rymer, viii. 364.

[2] Rot. Parl. ii. 310; Statutes, i. 394.

[3] Ann. Henr. p. 391; Otterbourne, p. 249, 'nomen parliamenti laicalis.' Cf. Eulog. iii. 402; Wals. ii. 265. The writ runs thus—'nolumus autem quod tu seu aliquis alius vicecomes regni nostri praedicti apprenticius sive aliquis alius homo ad legem aliqualiter sit electus'; Lords' Report, iv. 792. On Coke's denial of this fact see Prynne, Second Register, pp. 123 sq.

[4] The grant was made Nov. 12; Dep. Keeper's Rep. ii. App. ii. p. 182;

the clergy should for one year be taken into the king's hands for the purpose of the war[1] was brought forward by certain of the knights of the shires[2]; but the archbishop in a spirited speech turned the tables on the knights, and pointed out that they had by obtaining grants of the alien priories robbed the king of any increased revenue to be obtained from that source. The bishop of Rochester declared that the proposition subjected its upholders, ipso facto, to excommunication as transgressors of the great charter, and the knights succumbed at once. A formal proposal that the king should be enabled to live of his own by the resumption of all grants and annuities given since 1367 was accepted by Henry but referred to a commission of lords to ascertain how it could be executed[3]. The session passed off quietly; the clergy supplemented the parliamentary grants as good subjects[4], and the archbishop, feeling himself perhaps all the stronger for his victory, urged the king to more vigorous measures against the Lollards[5]. The death of William of Wykeham in the autumn of 1404 enabled the king to transfer his brother Henry Beaufort from Lincoln to Winchester, a promotion which probably caused him to resign the great seal for a

Attack on the clergy.

Proposed resumption.

Henry Beaufort made bishop of Winchester.

Rot. Parl. iii. 546; Eulog. iii. 402. The grant of the land-tax is made by the lords temporal 'pur eux et les dames temporelx, et toutz autres persones temporelx,' a departure from the now established form; it was 20s on every £20 of land over 500 marks per annum.

[1] Ann. Henr. pp. 393, 394; cf. Wals. ii. 265.

[2] Walsingham makes Sir John Cheyne speaker of this parliament; but he was not present as a knight of the shire in it. Sir William Esturmy, member for Devon, was speaker. Capgrave translates Walsingham, Chr. p. 287. See also Stow, Chr. p. 330.

[3] Rot. Parl. iii. 547–549.

[4] The convocation of Canterbury granted a tenth and a half on the 25th of November; the York clergy granted a tenth, Oct. 5; Wilkins, Conc. iii. 280; Ann. Henr. p. 394: but the king was not satisfied, and asked for a grant from the stipendiary clergy. Archbishop Arundel wrote to tell him that the proctors of the clergy had refused this; that convocation had no such power, and that there was no machinery for obtaining a representative body of chaplains. He advised that the bishops should be asked to press it on the stipendiaries by opportune ways and means; Royal Letters, i 413; Wilkins, Conc. iii. 280. The matter was referred to the Chancellor, Treasurer, and Privy Seal, who were ordered to issue letters under Privy Seal to the bishops; they replied that the letters had betters be sealed with the King's own signet; Ordinances, ii. 100, 101.

[5] Ann. Henr. pp. 396.

Longley chancellor.

time. He was succeeded by Thomas Longley, who a year afterwards was made bishop of Durham.

Critical year, 1405.

635. The following year, 1405, was perhaps the critical year of Henry's fortunes, and the turning point of his life. Although in it were accumulated all the sources of distress and disaffection, it seemed as if they were now brought to a head, to be finally overcome. They were overcome, and yet out of his victory Henry emerged a broken-down unhappy man; losing strength mentally and physically, and unable to contend with the new difficulties, more wearisome though less laborious, that arose before him. Henceforth he sat more safely on his throne; his enemies in arms were less dangerous; but his parliament became more aggressive, his council less manageable; his friends and even his children divided into factions which might well alarm him for the future of his house.

Attempt to seize the Mortimers.

The difficulties of the year began with an attempt made in February to carry off the two young Mortimers from Windsor[1]. The boys were speedily retaken, but it was a matter of no small consequence to discover who had planned the enterprise. On the 17th the lady Despenser, daughter of Edmund of Langley and widow of the earl of Gloucester, a vicious woman who was living in pretended wedlock with the earl of Kent, informed the king's council that her brother, the duke of York, was the guilty person, and that he had planned the murder of the king. Her squire, William Maidstone, undertook to prove her accusation in a duel, and the duke accepted the challenge. He was however immediately arrested[2]. As usual, the first charge gave rise to a large number of informations. Thomas Mowbray, the earl-marshal, was unable to deny that he had some inkling of the plot, and archbishop Arundel had to purge himself from a like suspicion. The king forgave Mowbray and thanked the archbishop for the assurance of his faithfulness, but the sore

Accusation against the duke of York.

Great men implicated.

[1] Ann. Henr. pp. 398, 399.

[2] He was arrested on the 6th of March; Rymer, viii. 386; imprisoned at Pevensey; Eulog. iii. 402; Wals. ii. 274; Otterbourne, p. 260. After seventeen weeks he begged to be released; Rymer, viii. 387: he was in full employment again in June; Ordinances, i. 270.

rankled still; and in two meetings of the council held at London and at S. Alban's the king found himself thwarted by the lords[1]. On the 1st of March a dispute about precedence took place in council between the earl of Warwick and the earl marshal, the son of the king's old adversary Norfolk; it was decided in favour of Warwick, and Mowbray left the court in anger[2]. Whilst this was going on in the south, Northumberland and Westmoreland were preparing for war in the north. Possibly the attitude of Northumberland may have been connected with the Mortimer plot, and Mowbray was certainly cognisant of both. The lord Bardolf, who had opposed the king strongly in the recent councils, had joined Northumberland, and Sir William Clifford had associated himself with them[3]. Unfortunately for himself and all concerned, the archbishop of York, Richard le Scrope, placed himself on the same side. These leaders drew up and circulated a formal indictment against the king, whom they described as Henry of Derby. Ten articles were published by the archbishop[4]; Henry was a usurper and a traitor to king and church; he was a perjurer who on a false plea had raised the nation against Richard; he had promised the abolition of tenths and fifteenths and of the customs on wine and wool; he had made a false claim to the crown; he had connived at Richard's murder; he had illegally destroyed both clerks and prelates; and without due trial had procured the deaths of the rebel earls, of Clarendon and of Hotspur; he had confirmed statutes directed against the pope and the universities; he had caused the destruction and misery of the country: the tenth article was a protest that these charges were not intended to give offence to the estates of the realm. Another document stated the demands of the insurgents in a less precise form[5]. They demanded a free parliament, to be held at London, to which the knights of the shire

Quarrel of Mowbray.

Archbishop Scrope publishes articles against the king.

[1] Ann. Henr. p. 399; Stow, Chr. p. 332.
[2] Eulog. iii. 405; Chr. ed. Giles, p. 43; Ordinances, ii. 104.
[3] Ann. Henr. p. 402; Otterbourne, p. 254.
[4] Anglia Sacra, ii. 362–368. Another form, drawn up as a vindication of the archbishop after his death, by Clement Maidstone, is given in the same work, p. 369. See also Foxe, Acts and Monuments, iii. 230 sq.
[5] Ann. Henr. pp. 403–405; Wals. ii. 422.

The rebels propose to lay their complaints before parliament.

should be duly elected, without the arbitrary exclusion which the king had attempted in the Parliament of Coventry. Before this assembly four chief points were to be laid: the reform of government, including the relief of church and nation from the unjust burdens under which both were groaning; the regulation of proceedings against delinquent lords, which had been a fruitful cause of oppression; the relief of the third estate, gentlemen, merchants, and commons, to be achieved by restricting the prodigality of the crown; and the rigorous prosecution of war against public enemies, especially against the Welsh[1]. These demands, which were circulated in several different forms, certainly touched all the weak points of Henry's administration, and although it must ever remain a problem whether the rising was not the result of desperation on the part of Northumberland and Mowbray rather than of a hope of reform conceived by Scrope, their proposals took a form which recommended itself to all men who had a grievance.

Military operations.

As soon as it was known that the lords were in arms Henry hastened to the north, and having reached Derby on the 28th of May summoned his forces to meet at Pomfret[2]. The contest was quickly decided. The earl of Westmoreland, John of Lancaster, and Thomas Beaufort, at the head of the king's forces, encountered the rebels on Shipton moor and offered a parley. The archbishop there met the earl of Westmoreland, who promised to lay before the king the articles demanded.

Arrest of the lords.

The friendly attitude of the leaders misled the insurgent forces; they dispersed, leaving Scrope and Mowbray at the mercy of their enemies, and they were immediately arrested. In spite of the earnest pleading of archbishop Arundel[3] and the refusal of the chief-justice, Sir William Gascoigne, to sanction the proceedings, the king allowed his better judgment to be overruled by the violence of his followers[4]. On the advice of Thomas Beaufort and the young earl of Arundel, he determined to sacrifice them: he obtained the assistance of Sir William Fulthorpe, who acted as

[1] Another form occurs in the Eulogium, iii. 405. See also Capgrave, Chr. p. 289; Chron. Henr. ed. Giles, p. 44.
[2] Ordinances, i. 264; Rymer, viii. 400.
[3] Ann. Henr. p. 408; Eulog. iii. 407.
[4] See his account as given to the pope, in Raynaldi, Ann. Eccl. viii. 143.

president of the tribunal of justices assigned[1], and on the 8th of June the archbishop and the earl marshal were beheaded. That done, the king followed the earl of Northumberland and Bardolf to the north. They fled to Scotland, and Henry, having seized the castles of the Percies, returned to the task of defence against the Welsh.

Execution of Scrope and Mowbray.

It was no wonder that the body of the murdered archbishop began at once to work miracles[2]; he was a most popular prelate, a member of a great Yorkshire house, and he had died in the act of defending his people against oppression. Nor is it wonderful that in popular belief the illness which clouded Henry's later years was regarded as a judgment for his impiety in laying hands on the archbishop. English history recorded no parallel event; the death of Becket, the work of four unauthorised excited assassins, is thrown into the shade by the judicial murder of Scrope. Looked at apart from the religious and legal question—and the latter in the case of Mowbray is scarcely less significant than the former in the case of Scrope—these executions mark a distinct change in Henry. Much blood had been shed formally and informally since he claimed the throne; but in no one case had he taken part in direct injustice, or allowed personal enmity or jealousy to make him vindictive. Here he had cast away every scruple; he had set aside his remembrance of the man who had placed him on the throne on

Effect of Scrope's execution.

[1] It seems improbable that Fulthorpe should under any circumstances have ventured to try Scrope and Mowbray, and it is far more likely that the annalist is right in saying that they were formally condemned by the earl of Arundel and Beaufort, although Beaufort was not one of their peers; Ann. Henr. p. 409. Sir William Fulthorpe is mentioned in the Rolls of Parliament as trying the minor offenders; Rot. Parl. iii. The statement, however, that Gascoigne refused to pass sentence on Scrope, and that Fulthorpe did it, is made very circumstantially by Clement Maidstone; Ang. Sac. ii. 369 sq. The Chronicle edited by Dr. Giles, p. 45, maintains Gascoigne's refusal, and adds that Randulf Everis and Fulthorpe passed sentence by special commission. Hardyng says that Sir John Lamplugh and Sir William Plumpton were beheaded near York, and that the lords Hastings and Fauconberg, Sir John Colville of the Dale, and Sir John Ruthyn were beheaded at Durham (p. 363); Stow, Chr. p. 333.

[2] A list of the offerings at his shrine is given in the Fabric Rolls of York, pp. 225, 226; letters from archbishop Arundel, bishop Longley, the king, and John of Lancaster, urging the dean and chapter to prevent pilgrimages, are also given there, pp. 193 sq.

Imprudence of the act. the day of Richard's deposition; he sinned against his conviction of the iniquity of laying hands on a sacred person; he disregarded the intercessions of archbishop Arundel, his wisest friend; he shut his eyes to the fact that he was giving to his enemies the honour of a martyr; he would not see that the victory which he had won had removed all grounds for fear. He allowed his better nature to be overcome by his more savage instinct. The act, viewed morally, would seem to be the sign of a mind and moral power already decaying, rather than a sin which called down that decay as a consequence or a judgment.

New attack on the prelates. In August the king went into Wales, where the French were assisting Glendower, and where he was, as in 1402, prevented by the floods from doing any work. On his return, at Worcester, the proposal to plunder the bishops was repeated, as it had been in 1403, and sternly repelled by the archbishop. But continued ill-luck produced its usual effect; from every department of the state, from every minister, from every dependency, from Wales, Great want of money. Ireland, Guienne and Calais, from army and fleet, came the same cry for money[1]; and in answer the king could only say that he had none and knew not where to procure any. The year 1405 was a year of action, the next year was almost entirely occupied with discussions in parliament, the longest hitherto known and, in a constitutional point of view, one of the most eventful.

Parliament of 1406. 636. It opened on the 1st of March[2]; the chancellor in his speech announced that the king wished to govern himself by the advice of his wise men, and Sir John Tibetot was chosen speaker. The cause of the summons was announced to be the

[1] In the parliament of 1404, John of Lancaster is described as being in great dishonour and danger for want of money for his soldiers on the North Marches; Rot. Parl. iii 552.

The prince of Wales is in great distress for the same cause; Ord. i. 229.

Thomas had been crying out for supplies for Ireland since 1401; Royal Letters of Henr. IV. pp. 73, 85.

The tradesmen of Calais were in despair (Aug. 17, 1404); ib. p. 290.

In 1405 lord Grey of Codnor the governor of South Wales could get no wages; Ord. i. 277.

As late as 1414, the duke of Bedford sold his plate to pay the garrison of Berwick, where wages were £13,000 in arrear; ib. ii. 136.

In the parliament of 1406, when the associated merchants applied to the king for £4000, he replied that 'il n'y ad de quoy'; Rot. Parl. iii. 570.

[2] Rot. Parl. iii. 567.

defence of the king's subjects against their enemies in Wales, Guienne, Calais, and Ireland; but the deliberations of the parliament almost immediately took a much wider scope. On the 23rd of March the speaker, after a protest and apology, announced that the commons required of the king 'good and abundant governance,' and on the 3rd of April explained the line of policy which they recommended for the national defence; the prince of Wales should command in person on the Welsh Marches; and the protection of the sea should be entrusted to a body of merchants who were ready to undertake the task on condition of receiving the tunnage and poundage and a quarter of the subsidy on wool. After a supplementary demand that the Bretons should be removed from court, and that the king should retain in his hands, at least for a short time, the estates forfeited by the Welsh rebels, the houses adjourned until after Easter[1].

Proceedings in parliament.

The merchants undertake the defence at sea.

The estates met again on the 30th of April; and it was at once manifest that a brisk discussion of the administration was impending. On the 8th of May the day was fixed for the departure of the aliens[2]; on the 22nd the king was prevailed on to nominate a council of seventeen members, two of whom were Sir John Cheyne and Sir Arnold Savage[3]. Archbishop Arundel having stated that the councillors would not serve unless sufficient means were placed in their hands to carry into effect the 'good governance' that was required, the commons addressed a formal remonstrance to the king on the condition of the coasts and dependencies of England. To this Henry could only reply that he would order the council to do their best[4]. On the 7th of June the speaker followed up the attack with still plainer language. The king, he said, was defrauded by the collectors of taxes; the garrison of Calais was composed of sailors and boys who could not ride; the defence of Ireland was extravagantly costly, yet ineffective; but above all, the king's household was less

Expulsion of aliens.

Nomination of council.

Complaints against the king's servants.

[1] Rot. Parl. iii. 569–571; Rymer, viii. 437, 438. The merchants nominated Nicolas Blackburn their admiral April 28; Rymer, viii. 439; cf. pp. 449. The plan failed and the king stayed the supply of money Oct. 20; Rymer. viii. 455; Rot. Parl. iii. 610.

[2] Rot. Parl. iii. 571; Ann. Henr. p. 419.

[3] Rot. Parl. iii. 572.

[4] Ib. iii. 573.

Complaints against the household.

honourable and more expensive than it had ever been, and was composed, not of valiant and sufficient persons, but for the most part of a rascally crew; again, he urged, the state of affairs required good and abundant governance[1]. Under this show of remonstrance and acquiescence—for the king agreed to all that the commons proposed—there was going on, as we learn from the annalist, a struggle about supplies. The commons had demanded that the accounts of Pelham and Furnival should be audited; the king declared that kings were not wont to render accounts; the ministers said that they did not know how to do it; the commissioners appointed to collect the taxes imposed in the last parliament did not venture to execute their office from a doubt of their authority[2]. At last, on the 19th of June, when the commons were about to separate[3], the question of account was conceded, the commons were allowed to choose the auditors, and the speaker announced that they had granted a supply of money for current expenses[4]. the king might have an additional poundage of a shilling for a year and a certain fraction of the produce of the subsidy on wool, but the aliens must be dismissed at once, and the council must before Michaelmas ascertain what economies could be made in the annuities granted by the king and in the administration of the alien priories. They also insisted on the king's abstaining from bestowing any gifts until the debts of the household had been paid and regulations made for putting an end to the outrageous and excessive expenditure. The parliament then adjourned to the 13th of October.

Struggle for the audit of accounts.

Restriction on the king's gifts.

Henry's illness.

During the recess, it would appear, Henry's health showed unmistakeable signs of failure. He had been ill ever since his journey into the north in 1405; whether his disease were leprosy, as the chroniclers say, or an injury to the leg aggravated by ague, as we might gather from records, or a complication of diseases ending in epilepsy, as modern writers have inferred[5], he had before the meeting of parliament become far

[1] Rot. Parl. iii. 577.
[2] Eulog. iii. 409.
[3] Rot. Parl. iii. 577.
[4] Ib. iii. 578.
[5] On the 28th of April 1406, the King had hurt his leg and was so ill with ague that he could not travel; Ordin. i. 290.

too weak to resist the pertinacious appeals of the commons. The second session lasted until the 22nd of December. On the 18th of November the speaker again came before the king with the old complaint, and begged that he would charge the lords on their allegiance to take up the work of reform[1]; but the conclusion of the complicated transactions of the year is recorded on the 22nd of December. On that day the king empowered the auditors to pass the accounts of Pelham and Furnival[2]; a grant of a fifteenth and tenth, tunnage and poundage, was made by the commons 'for the great confidence which they had in the lords elected and ordained to be of the continual council[3];' and the other acts of the session were ordered to be engrossed under the eye of a committee elected by the commons[4]. The same day a body of articles was presented, which the counsellors at the king's command swore to obey[5]. These articles comprise a scheme of reform in government, and enunciate a view of the constitution far more thoroughly matured than could be expected from the events of late years. It had pleased the king to elect and nominate counsellors pleasing to God and acceptable to his people, in whom he might have good confidence, to advise him until the next parliament, and some of them to be always in attendance on his person; he will be pleased to govern in all cases by their advice, and to trust it. This preamble is followed by thirty-one articles, which forbid all gifts, provide for the hearing of petitions, prohibit interference with the common law, enforce regularity and secrecy, and set before the members as their chief aim the maintenance of economy, justice, and efficiency in every public department. The records of the rivy council contribute some further articles[6] which were either withdrawn or kept private; a good controller was suggested for

Second session of 1406.

Vote of confidence in the council.

Scheme of reform in government.

[1] Rot. Parl. iii. 579.
[2] Ib. iii. 584.
[3] Ib. iii. 568. A list of the council nominated Nov. 27 is in the Ordinances, i. 295; it is somewhat different from the lists of May 15 and Dec. 22; Rot. Parl. iii. 572, 585; but the three commoners, Hugh Waterton, John Cheyne, and Arnold Savage, appear both in May and in November.
[4] Rot. Parl. iii. 585.
[5] Ib. iii. 585–589.
[6] Ordinances, i. 283–286.

Scheme of reform mooted in council.

the household, Sir Arnold Savage or Sir Thomas Bromflete; ten thousand pounds of the new grant might be devoted to the expenses of that department; but, most significant of all, it was desired that the king should after Christmas betake himself to some convenient place where, by the help of his council and officers, might be ordained a moderate governance of the household, such as might be for the future maintained to the good pleasure of God and the people[1]. The demands of the commons and the concessions of the king almost amounted to a supersession of the royal authority. This done, the parliament broke up, after a session of 159 days. The expenses of the knights and borough members nearly equalled the sum bestowed on the royal necessities: £6000 were granted to Henry on the last day of the parliament; the wages of the representatives amounted to more than £5000[2].

Length and cost of the session.

Acts of succession to the crown.

The whole time of the parliament was not, however, occupied in these transactions; one most important legislative act was the resettlement of the succession. On the 7th of June the crown was declared to be heritable by the king's sons and their male heirs in succession; this measure involved a repeal of the act of 1404, by which the crown was guaranteed to the heirs of the body of the sons in succession. It was no doubt intended to preclude a female succession. Such a restriction was, however, found to entail inconvenient consequences; and on the 22nd of December it was repealed and the settlement of 1404 restored[3]. A new statute against the Lollards, founded on a petition of the commons and supported by the prince of Wales,

Legislation against the Lollards.

[1] Ordinances, i. 296. Henry V in the first year of his reign was advised by the council to stay in the neighbourhood of London that he might be within reach of news from all sides; ib. ii. 125.

[2] The returns from thirty-seven counties and seventy-eight boroughs are known. The wages of the knights (knites-mete, Capgr. Chr. p. 293) amounted to £2595 12*s.* 0*d.* Those of the other members calculated on the same principle would make £2854 16*s.* 0*d.*; all together £5450 8*s.* 0*d.* See Prynne, Fourth Register, pp. 477–481.

[3] Rot. Parl. iii. 574–576, 580–583; Statutes, ii. 151; Rymer, viii. 462–464. The act asserts that the reason for the change was 'quod statutum et ordinatio hujusmodi jus successionis eorundem filiorum suorum et liberorum eorum, sexum excludendo femininum, nimium restringebat, quod aliquo modo diminuere non intendebant, sed potius adaugere.'

was likewise enacted in December[1]. Sentence of forfeiture was passed against Northumberland and Bardolf, but the lords avoided giving a positive opinion as to the guilt of archbishop Scrope[2]. One most important statute of the year introduced a reform into the county elections, directing that the knights should be chosen henceforth, as before, by the free choice of the county court, notwithstanding any letters or any pressure from without; and the return was to be made on an indenture containing the names and sealed with the seals of all who took part in the election[3].

Reform in county elections.

The liberality of the parliament was, as usual, supplemented by a grant of a tenth from the clergy in convocation and by an exaction from the stipendiary priests of a noble, six and eightpence, a head[4]. The parliament of 1406 seems almost to stand for an exponent of the most advanced principles of medieval constitutional life in England.

Importance of the parliament of 1406.

The foreign relations of England during the year were comparatively easy. The civil war which broke out in Scotland on the death of Robert III prevented any regular warfare in the north; and against Owen Glendower, with whom Northumberland and Bardolf sought an asylum, nothing great was attempted. The intestine troubles of France, where the dukes of Burgundy and Orleans were contending for supremacy, made it unnecessary for Henry to do more than watch for his opportunity. Notwithstanding then a certain amount of disaffection at home, and in spite of the somewhat impracticable conduct of the parliament, the political position of the king was probably stronger at this time than it had been since the beginning of the reign.

Foreign relations.

637. It is, however, from this point that may be traced the growth of those germs of domestic discord which were in process of time to weaken the hold of the house of Lancaster upon

[1] Rot. Parl. iii. 583, 584. The exact purport of this act will be found discussed in another chapter. It is not enrolled as a statute.

[2] Rot. Parl. iii. 593, 604–607.

[3] Ib. iii. 601; Statutes, ii. 156.

[4] The convocation, which sat from May 10 till June 16, granted a tenth and a subsidy; Wilk. Conc. iii. 284. The subsidy was the 'priests' noble'; Record Report, ii. App. ii. p. 183. The York clergy followed the example, Aug. 18; Wilk. Conc. iii. 303; cf. Stow, Chr. p. 333.

The king's sons.

England, and ultimately to destroy the dynasty. Henry himself was now a little over forty; and his sons were reaching the age of manhood. The prince of Wales was in his nineteenth year; Thomas, the second son, was eighteen; John, the third, was seventeen; and Humfrey, the youngest, fifteen. Besides these, the family circle included the king's three half-brothers, John Beaufort, who now bore the title of earl of Somerset, and was high chamberlain; Henry, bishop of Winchester; and Sir Thomas Beaufort, knight. The sons were clever, forward, and ambitious boys; the half-brothers accomplished, wary, and not less ambitious men. The act by which Richard II had legitimised the Beauforts placed their family interest in the closest connexion with that of the king; for although that act did not in terms acknowledge their right of succession to the throne, in case of the extinction of the lawful line of John of Gaunt, it did not in terms forbid it[1]; and as heirs of John of Gaunt they would, even if the crown went off into another line, have claims on the duchy of Lancaster. But such a contingency was improbable; the four strong sons of Henry gave promise of a steady succession, and in the act of 1406, by which the crown was entailed on them successively, it was not thought necessary to provide for the case of the youngest son's death without issue. Still the Beauforts had held together as a minor family interest; they seem to have acted in faithful support of the king under all circumstances, and they possessed great influence with the prince of Wales. Henry Beaufort is said to have been his nephew's tutor, and he certainly was for a long time his confidential friend and adviser. The three brothers were the king's friends, the old court party revived in less unconstitutional guise; maintaining the family interest under all circumstances, opposing the parliament when the parliament was in opposition, and opposing the archbishop when the clergy were supporting the cause of the parliament. The archbishop to a great extent embodied the traditions, dynastic and constitutional, of the elder baronage. The Beauforts were the true

His half-brothers.

Political position of the Beauforts.

[1] On this subject see Sir Harris Nicolas's article in the Excerpta Historica, pp. 152 sq.

successors to the policy of John of Gaunt, and seem to have inherited both his friendships and his jealousies, in contrast, so far, with the king, who throughout his life represented the principles, policy, and alliances of the elder house of Lancaster. If the Beauforts were a tower of strength to the king, their very strength was a source of danger.

Employment of the king's sons.

The young lords of Lancaster had been initiated early in public life. Henry had been an eyewitness of the revolution of 1399, and had retained some affection and respect for his father's victim. At a very early age he had been entrusted with command in Wales, and fought at the battle of Shrewsbury; he was popular in parliament, and had now become an important member of the council. Thomas, the second son, high admiral and lord high steward of England, had been employed in Ireland, where he was made lieutenant in 1401, and where he had early learned how utterly impossible it was to carry on government without supplies. John, the third son, was made constable in 1403, and remained for the most part in England assisting his father in command of the north[1]. He, like Henry, was a good deal under the influence of the Beauforts, whilst Thomas, who possibly was somewhat jealous of his elder brother, was opposed to them. Between Arundel and the Beauforts, the court, the parliament, the mind of the king himself, were divided.

Family division.

Arundel again chancellor, 1407.

One result of the parliamentary action of 1406 was the resignation of the chancellor, Longley, who on the 30th of January, 1407, was succeeded by archbishop Arundel, now chancellor for the fourth time[2]. Ten days later the king confirmed the act by which Richard legitimised the Beauforts, but in doing so, he introduced the important reservation 'excepta dignitate regali[3].' These words were found interlined in Richard's grant on the Patent Rolls, although they did not occur in the document laid before parliament in 1399, which alone could have legal efficacy. Such an important alteration the Beauforts must have regarded

Legitimation of the Beauforts confirmed with a limit.

[1] He was made warden of the East March, Oct. 16, 1404; Ordinances, i. 269.

[2] Rymer, viii. 464.

[3] Excerpta Historica, p. 153.

The Beaufort adhere to the prince of Wales.

as a proof of Arundel's hostility; their father had had no love for either the archbishop or the earl; one at least of the brothers must have felt that he had little gratitude to expect from the Arundels. They drew nearer to the prince of Wales and away from the king. The increasing weakness of Henry gave the prince a still more important position in the council; and the still undetermined question of the loyalty of the duke of York, in whom the prince seems to have reposed a good deal of confidence, probably complicated the existing relations. There was too, no doubt, some germ of that incurable bane of royalty, an incipient jealousy of the father towards the son.

Parliament of 1407.

638. A terrible visitation of the plague desolated England in 1407. The rumours that Richard was alive were renewed. The prince of Wales found employment in both marches, for since the rebellion of Northumberland he had taken work on the Scottish border also. The parliament of the year was held in October at Gloucester, and being under the influence of Arundel, showed itself liberal and forbearing[1]. On the 9th of November the archbishop announced that the accounts of the recent grants had been spontaneously submitted by the council to the inspection of the commons; that the council had been obliged to borrow large sums[2], and wished to be relieved from the oath drawn up in the preceding year. On the 2nd of December a grant was made of a fifteenth and tenth, and a half of the same[3]; of the subsidy on wool and tunnage and poundage for two years; the king undertaking not to ask the nation for money for two years from the next March[4]. The statutes and petitions of the session were mostly devoted to the reduction and pacification of Wales. The merchants were relieved from the defence of the sea, and severe measures were taken against

Money grants.

[1] Oct. 20 till Dec. 2; Rot. Parl. iii. 608 sq. Arundel preached on 'Regem honorificate.' Thomas Chaucer was speaker.

[2] A loan of £10,900 was contracted for the payment of the Calais garrison, on the credit of the lords of the council, June 27, 1407; Rymer, viii. 488.

[3] Dep. Keeper's Rep. ii. App. ii. p. 184; Rot. Parl. iii. 612 sq. The clergy of York voted a tenth in December 1408; Wilk. Conc. iii. 319.

[4] On the 1st of February, 1408, the king by letters patent undertook to retain for the expenses of the household all proceeds of the alien priories,

extortionate purveyors [1]. It was enacted that foreigners should be compelled to contribute to the fifteenths and tenths [2]. One discussion, and that historically an important one, disturbed the harmony of the session.

The commons claim the right to declare all grants of money by the mouth of their speaker.

The principle that money grants should be initiated in the house of commons, involved the reasonable doctrine that the poorest of the three estates should be left to state the maximum of pecuniary exaction, and that the representatives of the great body of payers should fix the amount of taxation. That principle had grown into practice but had not yet received authoritative recognition. This session saw a long step taken towards that recognition. On the 21st of November the king in consultation with the lords put to them the question what amount of aid was necessary for the public defence; the lords in reply mentioned the sums that were subsequently granted; the king then summoned a number of the commons to hear and report to the house the opinion of the lords. Twelve of the commons attended and reported the message. The house at once took alarm; 'the commons were thereupon greatly disturbed,' saying and affirming that this was in great prejudice and derogation of their liberties. Henry, who had certainly no object in derogating from the rights of the commons, and who had probably acted in mere inadvertence, as soon as he heard of the commotion, yielded the point, and with the assent of the lords gave his decision to the effect that it was lawful for the lords to deliberate in the absence of the king on the state of the realm and the needful remedies; that likewise it was lawful for the commons to do the same; provided always that neither house should make any report to the king on a grant made by the commons and assented to by the lords, or on any negotiations touching such grant, until the two houses had agreed; and that then the report should be made through the speaker of the commons [3]. This decision has its important relations to earlier and later history; here it appears

vacant sees, wardships, marriages, forfeitures, escapes and fee farms; Rymer, viii. 510.

[1] Rot. Parl. iii. 609.

[2] Statutes, ii. 161.

[3] Rot. Parl. iii. 611.

as a significant proof of the position which the house of commons had already won under the constitutional rule of Lancaster.

Rebellion and death of the earl of Northumberland.

639. For two years Arundel retained the great seal, and the country, as it had desired, remained without a parliament. The great event of 1408 was the final effort of the old earl of Northumberland to unseat the king: an attempt more desperate than the last[1]. In February, in company with lord Bardolf, the abbot of Hales, and the schismatic bishop of Bangor, he advanced into Yorkshire, and on the 19th was defeated by Sir Thomas Rokeby, at the head of the forces of the shire, on Bramham moor. The old earl fell in battle; Bardolf died of his wounds; the bishop was taken. In the spring the king went to York and hanged the abbot of Hales. The Welsh war went on without any show of spirit on either side; France had her own troubles to attend to. The king and the archbishop were chiefly employed in negotiations for the healing of the great schism, and for the holding of the Council of Pisa; and in the numerous councils of the clergy, for which this business gave occasion, Arundel saw his opportunity of sharpening the edge of the law against the Lollards. In 1408 councils were held both at London and at Oxford[2], where the Wycliffite party was strong and where another strong party that was not Wycliffite resented the interference of the archbishop. In January, 1409, Arundel published a series of constitutions[3]; one of which forbade the translation of the Bible into English until such a translation should be approved by the bishop of the diocese or a provincial synod; whilst another prohibited all disputations upon

Foreign and ecclesiastical affairs.

Constitutions on Lollardy.

[1] 'Infausta hora, nempe conceperant tantum de odio vulgari contra regem, et tantum praesumpserunt de favore populi penes se quod omnis plebs illis concurreret et adhaereret relicto rege, ita quod, cum pervenerunt ad Thresk, fecerunt proclamari publice quod ipsi venerunt ad consolationem populi Anglicani et iniquae oppressionis subsidium qua noverant se jam longo tempore oppressum;' Otterbourne, p. 262. From Thirsk they marched to Grimbald bridge near Knaresborough, where they were forbidden to cross the Nidd, and so passed round Hay Park to Wetherby, the sheriff continuing in Knaresborough. The next day, Sunday, the earl went to Tadcaster, and on the Monday the battle took place. Ib. pp. 262, 263; cf. Eulog. iii. 411; Wals. ii. 278.

[2] Wilkins, Conc. iii. 306.

[3] Ib. iii. 314-319. The seventh constitution forbids the translation.

points determined by the church. Great efforts were made to enforce these orders at Oxford, and Richard Courtenay, who was chancellor of the university in 1406 and 1410, seems to have engaged the good offices of the prince of Wales in defence of the liberties of the university[1]; thus helping to widen the breach between him and Arundel. As was inevitable in the present state of opinion, Arundel's oppressive measures roused both the Wycliffite and the constitutional opposition, and he did not venture to meet another parliament[2]; he resigned in December, 1409[3]. A month afterwards Henry gave the seals to his brother, Sir Thomas Beaufort, a layman not perhaps beyond suspicion of an alliance with the anti-clerical party which his father had led thirty years before.

Disputes at Oxford.

Arundel resigns.

640. The session of 1410[4] was opened on January 27, with a speech by Bishop Beaufort, his brother having not yet assumed his office. Thomas Chaucer, of Ewelme, himself a cousin of the Beauforts[5], was speaker. The Lollards must have been strongly represented, as on the 8th of February the commons prayed for the return of a petition touching Lollardy, which had been presented in their name, requesting that nothing might be enacted thereon[6]. No such petition accordingly appears on the roll, but we learn from the historian Walsingham that it was intended to obtain a relaxation of the recent enactments against the heretics[7]. If we may believe the same writer, the

Parliament of 1410.

Proceedings about Lollardy.

[1] Wilkins, Conc. iii. 323; Chr. Henr. ed. Giles, p. 58; Wood, History and Antiquities of Oxford, p. 205; Anstey, Munimenta cademica, i. 251.

[2] In a council held Nov. 21, 1409. the king assigned £6899 6s. 8d. from the subsidies to the expenses of the household; Rymer, viii. 610.

[3] December 21; Rymer, viii. 616. The Lord le Scrope of Masham was made treasurer at the same time; Otterb. p. 267; Wals. ii. 282.

[4] Eulog. iii. 416; Rot. Parl. iii. 622 sq.

[5] Thomas Chaucer of Ewelme in Oxfordshire, son of a sister of Katherine Swinford. The king warned him when he admitted him as speaker, that nothing should be said but what was honourable and likely to produce concord; Rot. Parl. iii. 623.

[6] Rot. Parl. iii. 623.

[7] Wals ii. 283; they petitioned for an alteration of the statute of heresy, and that clerks convicted might not be committed to the bishops' prison. The Rolls contain a petition that persons arrested under the statute of 1401 may be bailed in the county where they are arrested, and that such arrests may be made by the sheriffs regularly: but 'le roy se voet ent aviser;' Rot. Parl. iii. 626. The Eulogium (iii. 417) mentions a statute made in this

Petition of the Lollards.

party was so powerful as to attempt aggressive measures; the knights of the shire sent in to the king and lords a formal recommendation that the lands of the bishops and religious corporations should be confiscated, not for a year only, as had been suggested before, but for the permanent endowment of fifteen earls, fifteen hundred knights, six thousand esquires, and a hundred hospitals, £20,000 being still left for the king[1]. The extravagance and absurdity of such a demand insured its own rejection: the lords did not wish for a multiplication of their rivals; the commons in a wiser moment would scarcely have desired to give strength to the element which, as represented by the Percies and their opponents, had nearly torn the kingdom to pieces. The prince of Wales stoutly opposed the proposal and it was rejected. The king asked to be allowed to collect an annual tenth and fifteenth every year when no parliament was sitting[2]. This was refused, but he obtained a gift of 20,000 marks and grants of tenths, fifteenths, subsidies, and customs which lasted for two years[3]. Notwithstanding the Lollard movement, two years of steady government had benefited the country. Still the petitions of the commons testify much uneasiness as to the governance, both internal and external, of the realm[4], and the economy of the court which they tried to bind with stringent rules. It was remembered that in Richard's time the subsidy on wool

Henry asks a revenue for life.

parliament allowing friars to preach against the Lollards without licence from the bishops. In a convocation held Feb. 17, 1409, the statute 'de heretico' of 1401 was rehearsed at length; Wilk. Conc. iii. 328.

[1] Wals. ii. 282, 283. Fabyan, p. 575, gives a full account of the scheme: the temporalities are estimated at 322,000 marks per annum. It is described more fully in Jack Sharp's petition in 1431. It is added that £110,000 might be secured for the king; £110,000 for a thousand knights and a thousand good priests, and still there would be left to the clergy £143,724 10*s*. 4½*d*. And all this without touching the temporalities of colleges, chantries, cathedrals, or canons secular, Carthusians, Hospitallers, or Crouched Friars. Amundesham (ed. Riley), i. 453–456.

[2] Wals. ii. 238; cf. Otterbourne, p. 268.

[3] A fifteenth and a half, and a tenth and a half; Dep. Keeper's Rep. ii. App. ii. p. 184; Rot. Parl. iii. 635; Eulog. iii. 417; Wals. ii. 283. The clergy of Canterbury met to grant an aid, Feb. 17, 1410; Wilk. iii. 324. The York clergy granted a tenth May 23; ib. p. 333. A tenth and a half tenth is mentioned in the Ordinances, i. 342. Commissions were issued for raising a great loan the same year; ib. p. 343.

[4] Rot. Parl. iii. 623–627.

had brought up the national income to £160,000; although the subsidy on wool could not now be calculated at more than £30,000, there were hopes that it might rise again[1]. Half the tenth and fifteenth granted in 1410 reached the sum of £18,692, and although the charges upon it amounted to more than £20,000, still the sum was not much smaller than it had been in the prosperous days of Edward III[2]. A statute of this session directed a penalty to be exacted from the sheriffs who did not hold the elections in legal form, and made the conduct of the elections an article of inquiry before the justices of assize[3]. On the 2nd of May the king's counsellors were named, and all except the prince took the oath required[4]. The national income.

641. The administration of Thomas Beaufort, like that of his predecessor, lasted only two years; and during this time it is very probable that the prince of Wales governed in his father's name. From the month of February, 1410, he appears as the chief member of the council[5], which frequently met in the absence of the king, whose malady was increasing and threatening to disable him altogether. The chief point of foreign policy was the maintenance of Calais, which was threatened by Burgundy, and had thus early begun to be a constant drain on the resources of England. At home the religious questions involved in the suppression of The prince of Wales takes the lead in council.

[1] Rot. Parl. iii. 625. The statement made is that the subsidy on wool in the fourteenth year of Richard brought in £160,000 over and above other sources of revenue. It was estimated at £30,000 in 1411; Ordinances, ii. 7.

[2] The half tenth and fifteenth is £18,692 19*s*. 8¾*d*.; Ordinances, i. 344, 345. The charges, £20,639 15*s*. 2*d*.; ib. p. 347: these include the sea-guard, the East March, the West March, Wales, Guienne, and Roxburgh. The estimate for Calais in time of peace was £18,000, in time of war £21,000 a year; that of Ireland about £4500; ib. p. 352.

[3] Statutes, ii. 162; Rot. Parl. iii. 641.

[4] Rot. Parl. iii. 632.

[5] The prince's name appears as first in the council from December 1406. Ordinances, i. 295; cf. p. 313. A petition is addressed by Thomas of Lancaster to the prince and other lords of the king's council, June 1410; ib. 339. A council was held at the Coldharbour Feb. 8, 1410; ib. i. 329. The Coldharbour was given to the prince, Mar. 18, 1410, and he was made captain of Calais the same day; Rymer, viii. 628. He had the wardship of the heirs of Mortimer; ib. pp. 591, 608, 639.

Arundel again at Oxford. the Lollards and the reconciliation of the schism were complicated by a renewed attack of archbishop Arundel on the university of Oxford[1]. In an attempt to exercise his right of visitation, he was repulsed by the chancellor Courtenay and the proctors. The archbishop, availing himself of his personal influence with the king, compelled these officers to resign; but, as soon as the university could assert its liberty, they were re-elected, and it was only after a formal mediation proffered by the prince that the conflicting authorities were reconciled. It is more than probable that Arundel's conduct led to a personal quarrel with the prince, who was his great-nephew; he does not seem to have attended any meeting of the privy council during this period, or to have lent any aid to the ministers in their attempts to raise money by loan.

Jealousies in the royal family. Long afterwards, in the reign of Henry VI, it was remembered how there had been a great quarrel between the prince and the primate, and how the etiquette observed in consequence constituted a precedent for time to come[2]. A new cause of offence appears in the conduct of the king's second son. John Beaufort, the quondam marquess of Dorset, died in April 1410, and, notwithstanding their relationship, Thomas of Lancaster obtained a dispensation for a marriage with his uncle's widow. The bishop of Winchester refused to divide with him a sum of 30,000 marks which he had received as his brother's executor, and a quarrel ensued between Thomas and the Beauforts, in which the prince of Wales took the side of his uncle[3].

The expedition of 1411 to France. It was at this juncture that the duke of Burgundy, finding himself hard pressed by the Orleanists, requested the aid of England. The prince of Wales[4] supported his application; a matrimonial alliance between him and the duke's daughter was set on foot; and the king furnished the duke with a considerable force[5], which defeated the Orleanists at S. Cloud in November 1411, and

[1] Wals. ii. 285.

[2] Ordinances, iii. 186.

[3] Chron. Henr. ed. Giles, p. 62; Rot. Pat. Cal. p. 259.

[4] Hardyng, p. 367; Rymer, viii. 698 sq.; Ordinances, ii. 19 sq.

[5] The expedition was under the command of the earl of Arundel, Sir John Oldcastle and Gilbert Umfraville, called the earl of Kyme; Chron. Henr. ed. Giles, p. 61.

having received their pay returned home. On the 3rd of November the parliament met again [1].

642. This assembly no doubt witnessed scenes which it was not thought prudent to record; but on the evidence of the extant rolls it is clear that it was not a pleasant session; and it is probable that the king, under the influence of Arundel or of his second son, made a vigorous effort to shake off the Beauforts. On the third day of the parliament, when Thomas Chaucer, the speaker, made the usual protestation and claimed the usual tolerance accorded to open speaking, the king bluntly told him that he might speak as other speakers had spoken, but that he would have no novelties in this parliament [2]. Chaucer asked a day's respite, and made a very humble apology. The estates showed themselves liberal, granting the subsidy on wool, tunnage and poundage, and a new impost of six and eightpence on every twenty pounds' worth of income from land [3]. Yet, notwithstanding their complaisance, they were obliged to petition the king for a declaration that he esteemed them loyal: so great was the murmuring among the people that he had grounds of enmity against certain members of this and the last parliament. Henry declared the estates to be loyal [4]: but, in reference apparently to some restrictive measure adopted in the last

Parliament of 1411.

The speaker has to apologise.

The estates declared loyal.

[1] Rot. Parl. iii. 647. The council had been busy with the estimates as early as April; there was a deficit of £3,924 6*s*. 5*d*. The household expenses are £16,000; Ordinances, ii. 11, 12, 14.

[2] Rot. Parl. iii. 648.

[3] Dep. K. Rep. ii. App. ii. p. 184; Rot. Parl. iii. 648, 671; Eulog. iii. 419. On the 20th of November, 1410, the king ordered all persons holding forty librates of land to receive knighthood before Feb. 2; Rymer, viii. 656. The order to collect the fines thus accruing was issued May 20, 1411; ib. p. 685. The Canterbury clergy on the 21st of December granted a half tenth; Wilk. iii. 337. The York convocation followed, Ap. 29, 1412; ib. p. 338.

[4] Rot. Parl. iii. 658. The language of the roll is mysterious. The king sent the chancellor to show the commons an article passed in the last parliament. The speaker asked the king to say what he wanted to do with it. Henry replied that he wished to enjoy the liberties and prerogatives of his predecessors. The commons agreed and the king cancelled the article. The same day he declared the estates loyal. The article was possibly one of the two (Rot. Parl. iii. 624, 625) which compelled the king to devote all his windfalls to the payment of his debts, and forbade gifts. A letter of the earl of Arundel to the archbishop, complaining of having been misrepresented, probably belongs to the same business; Ord. ii. 117.

At the end of the session the ministry is changed.

parliament, he announced that he intended to maintain all the privileges and prerogatives of his predecessors. The parliament broke up on the 19th of December; on the 22nd a general pardon was issued[1]; and on the 5th of January Beaufort resigned the seals[2]. The annalists of the period supply an imperfect clue to guide us through these obscurities. We are told that the Beauforts had advised the prince to obtain his father's consent to resign the crown, and to allow him to be crowned in his stead[3]; that the king indignantly refused; and that in consequence the prince retired from court and council, his brother Thomas taking his place. It is to be observed that many years later, when Bishop Beaufort was charged by Humfrey of Gloucester with having conspired against the life of Henry V, and having stirred him up to assume the crown

The prince retires.

The Beauforts support him.

[1] Rymer, viii. 711. Owen Glendower, and Thomas Ward of Trumpington, who personated Richard II, were excepted.

[2] Rot. Parl. iii. 658.

[3] 'In quo parliamento Henricus princeps desideravit a patre suo regni et coronae resignationem, eo quod pater ratione aegritudinis non poterat circa honorem et utilitatem regni ulterius laborare. Sed sibi in hoc noluit penitus assentire, immo regnum cum corona et pertinentiis dummodo haberet spiritus vitales voluit gubernare. Unde princeps quodammodo cum suis consiliariis aggravatus recessit et posterius quasi pro majori parte Angliae omnes proceres suo dominio in homagio et stipendio copulavit.' Chron. ed. Giles, p. 63. 'Interea dominus Henricus princeps offensus regis familiaribus qui ut fertur seminaverunt discordiam inter patrem et filium scripsit ad omnes regni partes, nitens repellere cunctas detractorum machinationes. Et ut fidem manifestiorem faceret praemissorum, circa festum Petri et Pauli venit ad regem patrem cum amicorum maxima frequentia et obsequentium turba qualis non antea visa fuerit his diebus. Post parvissimi temporis spatium gratulabunde susceptus est a rege patre, a quo hoc unum petiit ut delatores sui si convinci possent punirentur, non quidem juxta meritum sed post compertum mendacium citra condignum. Rex vero postulanti videbatur annuere, sed tempus asseruit expectari debere parliamenti, videlicet, ut hii tales parium suorum judicio punirentur.' Otterbourne, p. 271. According to the Chronicle of London Henry came to London with a great retinue in July 1412 and attended council on Sept. 23, 'with a huge people'; Chron. Lond. p. 94; Stow, Chr. p. 339. 'Eodem autem anno facta fuit conventio inter principem Henricum primogenitum regis, Henricum episcopum Wintoniensem et alios quasi omnes dominos Angliae, uter ipsorum alloqueretur regem ut redderet coronam Angliae, et permitteret primogenitum suum coronari, pro eo quod erat ita horribiliter aspersus lepra. Quo allocuto ad consilium quorundam dominorum cedere noluit sed statim equitavit per magnam partem Angliae non obstante lepra supradicta'; Eulog iii. 421. Some other authorities are given in Mr. Williams' Preface to the Gesta Henrici V. Cf. English Chronicle, ed. Davies, p. 37; Elmham, ed. Hearne, p. 11.

during his father's lifetime, he solemnly denied the former charge, but was much more reticent as to the latter[1]. It can scarcely be doubted that the matter had been broached, and possibly had been proposed in parliament on the first day of the session, which seems to have been opened whilst the king was absent through illness, although on the third day he was able to receive and rebuke the speaker. But whatever were the circumstances, the result is clear; Beaufort resigned the seals, Arundel returned to power; very soon afterwards the prince ceased to attend the council[2]; almost immediately the king transferred his friendship from the duke of Burgundy to the duke of Orleans, and sent an army to his assistance under Thomas, who in preparation for his command was made duke of Clarence. The dates of these transactions are tolerably clear. On the 5th of January Arundel took the seals; on the 18th of February the prince received payment of his salary for the time that he had served on the council: negotiations were still pending with Burgundy. On the 18th of May the king concluded his league with Orleans, the prince withholding his consent for two days longer. On the 9th of July Thomas was made duke of Clarence. Money for the expedition was raised by loan[3]. The result of Clarence's enterprise was neither honourable nor fortunate; finding that the contending parties had united against him, he ravaged Normandy and Guienne, and was bought off at last by Orleans. It would appear that the enemies of the prince of Wales were not content with dislodging him from power; a slanderous charge was brought against him for receiving large sums for the wages of the Calais garrison, and

Arundel returns to power, and the foreign policy is changed.

Second expedition to France.

Attack on the prince of Wales.

[1] Rot. Parl. iv. 298; see below, pp. 103, 104; Hall, Chr. p. 133.

[2] 'Then the king discharged the prince of his counsayle, and set my lord syr Thomas in his stede.' Hardyng, p. 369.

On the 18th of Feb. 1412, Henry received 1000 marks as his wages 'tempore quo fuit de consilio ipsius domini regis'; Pell Rolls; Tyler, Henry of Monmouth, i. 298.

For the story of Henry carrying off his father's crown, see Wavrin, p. 159.

[3] Rymer, viii. 757. Archbishop Arundel lent 1000 marks for the expedition, July 12; ib. p. 760; Ordin. ii. 32. The bishop of Winchester was not asked to lend.

not paying them. The matter came before the council, and the charge was disproved[1].

Illness of the king.

643. In the autumn of 1412 the king became so ill that his death was expected; he had periods of insensibility, and was much troubled in mind as well as in body. It is even possible that the action of an ill-informed conscience, working upon a diseased frame, made him look back with something like remorse on the great act of his life. He had intended too to go once more on crusade[2], and had made great preparations, hoarding perhaps for the purpose even when money was most scarce. If his illness were to result in death, it would be a sign that his great atonement was not accepted. It was said that he professed that he would have resigned the crown to the right heirs but for fear of his sons, who would not part with their inheritance[3]: anyhow he must have shuddered when he thought of the bloodshed with which his throne had been secured. After a very dangerous attack, however, at Christmas, 1412, he rallied, and even called his parliament to meet on the 3rd of February[4]. The parliament met on that day, but it is not certain that it was formally opened; no record of its action is preserved; and on the 20th of March the king died. He was buried in Canterbury, the great sanctuary of the English nation, near his uncle the Black Prince.

He calls a parliament and dies.

This summary survey of the reign opens some important questions for which it furnishes no adequate answer. There

[1] Ordinances, ii. 34, 35; Elmham, ed. Hearne, p. 11.

[2] Nov. 20, 1412, a council was held at Whitefriars to prepare for the crusade; Fabyan, p. 576; Hall, Chron. p. 45; Rastall, p. 244; Leland, Coll. ii. 487.

[3] John Tille the king's confessor moved him to do penance for the murder of Richard, the death of Scrope, and the pretended title to the crown; he replied that on the first two points he had satisfied the pope and been absolved; 'as for the third point it is hard to set remedy, for my children will not suffer that the regalia go out of our lineage.' Capgr. Chr. p. 303. The author, however, who tells this story of Edward IV, in an earlier work puts some very pious advice to his son in the dying king's mouth, and says nothing about penance; Capgr. Ill. Henr. p. 111. Hardyng (p. 369) gives a dying speech, but says that the king said nothing about either repentance or restitution. Stow, p. 340, on the other hand, has a speech full of penitence, especially warning Henry against the ambition of Clarence.

[4] Lords' Report, iv. 813.

are two hostile and most dangerous influences at work during the first half of it; the extraordinary poverty of the country, and, partly resulting from it, the singular amount of treason and insubordination which reached its highest point in the rebellion of the Percies. Of the first of these it is now impossible to say how far it was real or how far fictitious: it is possible that the country was now beginning to realise fully the result of the long-continued drain caused by the wars of Edward III and the extravagance of Richard II: it is possible that the public feeling of insecurity had led men to hoard their silver and gold, instead of contributing to the support of a government which they did not believe to be stable. Whichever be the true hypothesis, the king's poverty and the national distress served to augment disaffection: the hostile action of the Percies was unquestionably caused by financial as well as political disputes. The second evil influence was in great measure the result of Henry's ill luck, his inability to close the Welsh war, and the tardiness of his preparations against France and Scotland. The moment his personal popularity waned, the popular hatred of Richard began to diminish also; the mystery of his death gave opening for a semi-legendary belief that he was still alive; and that faith, whether false or genuine, became a rallying point for the disaffected, the last cry of desperate men like Northumberland and Bardolf. Welcome as Henry's coming had been, violence had been done to the conscience of the nation, and it needed only misfortune to stimulate it into remorse for the past and misgiving for the future. And there were physical evils to boot, famines and plague. There was the religious division to complicate matters still more; for Richard's court had been inclined to Lollardy, while Henry, under whatever temporary influence he acted, was hostile to the heretics. Yet on the whole Henry left behind him a strongly founded throne, and a national power vastly greater than that which he had received at his coronation. And some portion of the credit is due to him personally: he was not fortunate in war; he outlived his early popularity; he was for years a miserable invalid; yet he reigned as a constitutional king; he governed by the help of his

Causes of the difficulties of the reign.

Poverty of the country.

Disaffection and treason.

Work of Henry IV.

Strength of the commons. parliament, with the executive aid of a council over which parliament both claimed and exercised control. Never before and never again for more than two hundred years were the commons so strong as they were under Henry IV; and in spite of the dynastic question, the nation itself was strong in the determined action of the parliament. The reign, with all its mishaps, exhibits to us a new dynasty making good its position, although based on a title in the validity of which few believed and which fewer still understood; notwithstanding extreme distress for money, and in spite of much treachery and disaffection. All the intelligent knowledge of the needs of the nation, all the real belief in the king's title, is centered in the knights of the shire; there is much treason outside, but none within the walls of the house of commons. Power of archbishop Arundel. The highest intelligence, on the whole, however, is plainly seen to be Arundel's, and next to his, although in opposition for the time, that of the prince of Wales. The archbishop knows how to rule the commons and how to guide the king; he believes in the right of the dynasty, and, apart from his treatment of the heretics, realises the true relation of king and people. If his views of the relation of Church and State, as seen in his leading of the convocation, are open to exception, he cannot be charged with truckling to the court of Rome.

Character of the reign of Henry IV, 644. The reign of Henry IV had exemplified the truth, that a king acting in constitutional relations with his parliament may withstand and overcome any amount of domestic difficulty. He had known when to yield and when to insist, and thus, in spite of the questionable character of his title, much ill success, harassing poverty, unwearied and unsuspected treasons, bad seasons, and bad health, he had laid the foundations of a strong national dynasty. His parliamentary action was one long struggle, but it was a struggle fairly conducted, and he, as well as the parliament, stood by the constitutional compromise, maintained the constitutional balance. in relation to that of Henry V. The history of Henry V exhibits to us a king acting throughout his reign in the closest harmony with his parliament, putting himself forward as the first man of a nation fairly at one with itself on all political questions, a leader in heart and soul worthy of England, and crowning his leadership with ample signal successes. Henry IV striving lawfully had made his own house strong; Henry V leading the forces with which his father had striven made England the first power in Europe. There were deep and fatal sources of weakness in his great designs, but that weakness was not in his position at home; it was not constitutional weakness, although the result which it precipitated went a long way towards destroying the constitution itself.

It is one of the penalties which great men must pay for their greatness, that they have to be judged by posterity according to a standard which they themselves could not have recognised, because it was by their greatness that the standard itself was created. Henry V may be judged and condemned on moral principles which have emerged from the age in which he was a great actor, but which that age neither knew nor practised. He renewed a great war, which according to modern ideas was without justification in its origin and continuance, and which resulted in an exhaustion from which the nation did not recover for a century. To modern minds war seems a terrible evil, to be incurred only on dire necessity where honour or existence is at stake; to be justified only by the clearest demonstration of right; to be continued not a moment longer than the moral necessity continues. Perhaps no war ancient or modern has been so waged, justified, or concluded; men both spoke and thought otherwise in earlier times, and in times not so very far distant from our own. For medieval warfare it might be pleaded, that its legal justifications were as a rule far more complete than were the excuses with which Lewis XIV and Frederick II defended their aggressive designs; for the kings of the middle ages went to war for rights, not for interests, much less for ideas. But it must be further remembered, that until comparatively late times, although the shedding of Christian blood was constantly deplored, war was regarded as the highest and noblest work of kings; and that in England, the history of which must have been Henry's guide, the only three unwarlike kings who had reigned since the Conquest had been despised and set aside by their subjects. The war with France was

Henry V as a warrior.

Changes in the estimate of war.

War with France an hereditary doctrine.

not to him a new war, it had lasted far beyond the memory of any living man, and the nation had been educated into the belief that the struggle was one condition of its normal existence. The royal house we may be sure had been thoroughly instructed in all the minutiae of their claims; the parliament insists as strongly on the royal rights as on its own privileges, and the fall of Henry VI shows how fatal to any dynasty must have been the renunciation of those rights. The blame of continuing the war when success was hopeless, if such blame be just, does not fall on Henry V, who died at the culminating point of his successes, and whose life, if it had been prolonged, might have consolidated what he had won. Judged by the standard of his time, judged by the standard according to which later ages have acted, even whilst they recognised its imperfection, Henry V cannot be condemned for the iniquity or for the final and fatal results of his military policy. He believed war to be right, he believed in his own cause, he devoted himself to his work and he accomplished it.

Henry V as a religious persecutor.

A similar equitable consideration would relieve him from the imputation of being a religious persecutor. He lived in an age in which religious persecution was rife; in which it was inculcated on kings as a duty, and in which it was to some extent justified by the tenets of the persecuted; for one of the miseries of authoritative persecution is that it arrays the rebel against both spiritual and temporal authority. Besides the germs of social and political destructiveness which were inherent in the Lollard movement, the persecution regarded the Lollards not merely as heretics but as traitors, and not only regarded them as such but made them so, leagued them with the Welsh and Scots, and implicated them in every conspiracy against the reigning house. This may be lamentable, but it is a consideration which equity cannot disregard. Posterity may well condemn all persecutors who have loved persecution; it cannot without reservation condemn those who have persecuted merely as a religious or as a legal duty. Henry V persecuted, as his father had done, but even when he persecuted on religious and not on political grounds, he did it with a singular reluctance to undertake the vindictive part of the work[1]. To his mind it was as a correction for the soul of the sinner, and a precaution against evils to come, not as mere exercise of justice. There is proof enough of this in the way in which he personally attempted to convert the heretic Badby[2], and in the impolitic delay which encouraged Oldcastle.

Greatness of Henry's character.

If we set aside the charges of sacrificing the welfare of his country to an unjustifiable war of aggression, and of being a religious persecutor, Henry V stands before us as one of the greatest and purest characters in English history, a figure not unworthy to be placed by the side of Edward I. No sovereign who ever reigned has won from contemporary writers such a singular unison of praises[3]. He was religious, pure in life, temperate, liberal, careful and yet splendid, merciful, truthful, and honourable; 'discreet in word, provident in counsel, prudent in judgment, modest in look, magnanimous in act;' a brilliant soldier, a sound diplomatist, an able organiser and consolidator of all forces at his command; the restorer of the English navy, the founder of our military, international and maritime law[4]. A true Englishman, with all the greatnesses and none of the glaring faults of his Plantagenet ancestors, he stands forth as the typical medieval hero. At the same time he is a laborious man of business, a self-denying and hardy warrior, a cultivated scholar, and a most devout and charitable Christian. Fortunately perhaps for himself, unfortunately for his country, he was cut off before the test of time and experience was applied to try the

[1] Henry was reproved by Thomas Walden for his great negligence in regard to the duty of punishing heretics: Tyler, ii. 9, 57, quoting Von der Hardt, i. 501 and L'Estrange, ii. 282; Goodwin, App. p. 361.

[2] Wals. ii. 282.

[3] For Henry's character see Walsingham, ii. 344; 'le plus vertueus et prudent de tous les princes Christiens rengnans en son temps'; Wavrin, p. 167. He was severe, 'et bien entretenoit la disciplene de chevallerie comme jadis fasoient les Rommains'; ib. p. 429. See Aeneas Sylvius, De Viris Illustribus; Pauli, v. 175. Elmham and Titus Livius are professed panegyrists.

[4] Henry's Ordinances for his armies may be found in Excerpta Historica, p. 28; Nicolas' Agincourt, Appendix, pp. 31 sq.; his dealings with the navy in the Proceedings of the Privy Council, vol. v. pref. cxxviii sq.; and in Sir H. Nicolas' History of the Navy; Black Book of the Admiralty, vol. i. pp. 282, 459, &c. See also Bernard's Essay on International Law, in the Oxford Essays.

Advantages of his position compared with that of Henry IV.

fixedness of his character and the possible permanence of his plans. In his English policy he appears most distinctly as a reconciling and uniting force. He had the advantage over his father in two great points: he was not even in a secondary degree answerable for the difficulties in which Henry IV had been involved by the very circumstances of his elevation; and he had, what Henry IV perhaps had not, an unshaken confidence in his own position as a rightful king. He could afford to be merciful; he loved to be generous; he saw it was his policy to forgive and restore those whom his father had been obliged to repress and punish. The nobility and the wisdom of this policy not only made him supreme as long as he lived but ensured for his unfortunate son thirty years of undisputed sovereignty, a period of domestic peace which ended only when the principles on which it was based were, by misfortune, impolicy, and injustice, themselves subverted.

He immediately displaces Arundel.

645. Henry IV died on the 20th of March, and on the 21st Henry V removed archbishop Arundel from the chancery and put bishop Beaufort in his place; on the same day he made the earl of Arundel treasurer in the place of lord le Scrope; on the 29th he removed Sir William Gascoigne the chief justice of the bench[1]. In the two former appointments nothing more was done than was reasonably to be expected. Beaufort was Henry V's minister as distinctly as Arundel was Henry IV's; the earl of Arundel had supported him as prince contrary to the wishes of his uncle the archbishop, and it was important to the new king not to offend the Arundel interest, although he could not act cordially with its most prominent representative. The dismissal of Sir William Gascoigne can by itself be easily accounted for; Gascoigne was an old man, who had been long in office, and a great country gentleman, who might fairly claim to rest in his later years. But tradition has attached to the name of Gascoigne a famous story, which, were it true, would have its bearing on the character of Henry V. Gascoigne had probably, for the evidence is not very clear, refused to join in the judicial murder of archbishop Scrope: popular tradition, more than a hundred

Dismissal of justice Gascoigne.

[1] Foss, Tabulae Curiales, p. 32; Dugdale, Origines, ad ann.

years later, made him the hero of a scene in which Henry, when prince of Wales, was represented as striking the judge upon the bench in defence of an accused servant, and as obeying the mandate of the same judge when he committed him to prison for the violence done to the majesty of the law[1]. It is not only highly improbable, but almost impossible that such an event could have taken place: the story was one of a series of traditions which represented Henry V as a wild dissolute boy at the very times when either at the head of his father's forces he was repressing the incursions of the Scots and Welsh, or at the head of his father's council was leading high deliberations on peace and war and national economies. The story of Gascoigne must be taken at its true value. The legends of the wildness of Henry's youth are so far countenanced by contemporary authority that the period of his accession is described as a point of time at which his character underwent some sort of change; 'he was changed into another man' says Walsingham, 'studying to be honest, grave, and modest[2].' If the words imply all that has been inferred from them, Henry may at least plead that his wild acts were done in public; his follies and indiscretions, for vice is not laid to his charge, were the frolics of a high-spirited young man indulged in the open vulgar air of town and camp; not the deliberate pursuit of vicious excitement in the fetid atmosphere of a court. The question however concerns us here only as connected with the change of ministers. If there had been any real change in Henry's character, manifested on the occasion of his father's death, it would have been more likely to make him retain than remove his father's servants. One difficulty immediately resulted from the measure: the removal of Arundel from the chancery at once enabled him to renew his attack on

Legend of Gascoigne.

Traditional reformation of Henry V at his accession.

[1] On this and the points of chronology connected with it, see Foss, Biographia Juridica, pp. 290 sq. Recent investigation has thrown no new light upon the story, which first turns up in Elyot's Governour, Book II. c. 6, written in 1534; cf. Pauli, Gesch. v. Engl. v. 71.

[2] Wals. ii. 290; Capgr. Chr. p. 303. Hardyng's words (p. 372) read like a translation of Walsingham. Fabyan, p. 577, charges Henry before his father's death with all vice and insolency, after it 'sodaynly he became a newe man.' Cf. Hall, Chr. p. 46; Elmham (ed. Hearne), p. 12; and Pauli, Gesch. v. Engl. v. 70 sq.

the Lollards, and emboldened the Lollards to more hopeful resistance.

Henry's first parliament.

646. The parliament which had met before the death of Henry IV continued to sit as the first parliament of his successor; but it was not called on for despatch of business until after the coronation, which took place on the 9th of April, 1413. On the 15th of May the session opened with a speech from Beaufort, and the assembly sat until the 9th of June[1]. Ample provision was made for the maintenance of the government; the subsidy on wool was granted for four years for the defence of the realm, tunnage and poundage for a year, and a fifteenth and a tenth for the keeping of the sea: and the king was allowed a 'preferential' claim on the public revenue, to the amount of £10,000, for the expenses of his household, chamber, and wardrobe[2]. The commons spoke their minds plainly as to the weakness of the late reign and the incompleteness of national defence[3]. The law of 1406 on elections of knights was confirmed and amended with a clause ordering that residents only should be chosen[4]; the measures taken against the aliens were enforced, the king granted a general pardon, and the usual anti-papal petitions presented and accorded. Another significant event of the year was the translation of the body of Richard II from Langley to Westminster; an act by which Henry no doubt intended to symbolise the burial of all the old causes of enmity[5].

Taxes and statutes.

Arundel attacks the Lollards.

647. Archbishop Arundel had lost no time in proceeding against the Lollards. The convocation which had met on March 6

[1] Rot. Parl. iv. 3-14. The members had their wages from Feb. 3 to June 9; ib p. 9.

[2] Rot. Parl. iv. 5, 6; Dept. K. Rep. ii. App. ii. p. 185.

[3] 'Reherçant qu'en temps notre seigneur le roy son pier, qui Dieux assoile, y feust pluseurs foitz requis par les ditz Communes de bon governance et lour requeste grauntee. Mes coment y feust tenuz et perfourne en apres mesme notre seigneur le roy en ad bone conisance'; Rot. Parl. iii. 4. 'Bon governance' is defined as 'due obeissance a les lois deins le roialme'; ib.

[4] Rot. Parl. iv. 8; Statutes, ii. 170.

[5] December; Chr. Lond. p. 96: 'Non sine maximis expensis regis nunc, qui fatebatur se sibi tantum venerationis debere quantum patri suo carnali'; Wals. ii. 297; Otterbourne, p. 274. He had been knighted by Richard. Hardyng says also that he gave licence for offerings to be made at the tomb of archbishop Scrope; p. 372.

had sat by prorogation until the end of Juno, and had voted a tenth to the king. Before this body Arundel had laid a proposition to attack Lollardy in the high places of the court. It was resolved that there was no chance of preventing the schism imminent in the English church unless those magnates who protected the heretics were recalled to due obedience[1]. Of these the chief was Sir John Oldcastle, a Herefordshire knight, who had sat in the house of commons in 1404, and who by a subsequent marriage with the heiress of the barony of Cobham had, in 1409, obtained summons to the house of lords as lord Cobham. Oldcastle was a personal friend of the king, and had been joined with the earls of Arundel and Kyme in command of the force sent at Henry's instigation to France in 1411. He was an intelligent and earnest Lollard, and had taken pains to spread the influence of the sect, by the preaching of unlicensed itinerants, in his Herefordshire and Kentish estates. Against him a formal presentment was made by the convocation, and after consultation with the king, who tried by personal argument to bring him over, he was summoned to appear before the archbishop and the bishops of London, Winchester, and Bangor[2]. Having refused to receive the first citation he received a second summons to appear at Leeds on the 11th of September; not presenting himself there he was called once more by name and declared contumacious. In consequence of this he was arrested by the king, and appeared before the archbishop in custody of the keeper of the Tower on the 23rd of September. A long discussion ensued, during which Oldcastle proffered an orthodox confession; but, being pressed by the archbishop with distinct questions on the main points of Lollard doctrine, refused to renounce them. He was therefore condemned as a heretic on the 25th, and returned to the Tower, a respite of forty days being allowed him in hopes of a recantation. Almost immediately, however, he effected his escape, and the country, which had been already alarmed by the declaration that a hundred

Sir John Oldcastle, lord Cobham.

His trial and perseverance.

His condemnation and escape.

[1] Wilkins, Conc. iii. 353.

[2] On Oldcastle's trial see Walsingham, ii. 291–297; Otterb. p. 274; Fascic. Zizan., pp. 433–450; Capgr. Ill. Henr. p. 113; Wilkins, Conc. iii. 351–357; Rymer, ix. 61–66, 89, 90; Hall, Chr. pp. 48 sq.

Alarm of a Lollard rising.

thousand Lollards were prepared to rise, was thrown into a panic. The sentence of excommunication and the rewards offered for his capture were alike ineffectual, and it was found that at Christmas an attempt was to be made to seize the king at Eltham. Henry defeated this by coming up to London, but the conspirators were not discouraged, and a very large concourse was called to meet in S. Giles's fields on the 12th of January, 1414. Henry, by closing the gates of London, prevented the disaffected citizens from joining in the proceedings, and with a strong force took up his position on the ground. Some unfortunate people were arrested and punished as heretics, but Oldcastle himself escaped for the time. He was then summoned before the justices and declared an outlaw. He failed in an attempt to excite a rebellion in 1415 in connexion, it was said, with the Southampton plot. In the year 1417 however, when Henry was in France, he was captured on the Welsh marches, brought up to London, and cruelly put to death [1]. With this abortive attempt the politico-religious schemes of the Lollards disappear for many years, although the effects of the alarm were very considerable. Archbishop Arundel died in the following February, and his successors were more moderate, and more politic in the ways they took to repress the evil. It may be questioned

Henry prevents it.

Death of Arundel.

[1] There is no doubt that Oldcastle's proceedings, overt and secret, added to Henry's difficulties in the opening of the second French campaign. When Thomas Payn, Oldcastle's secretary, was captured, Henry V declared that the taking pleased him more 'than I had geten or given him £10,000, for the great inconveniences that were like to fall in his long absence out of his realm'; Ordinances, v. 105; Exc. Hist. p. 146. The writings of the Lollards were spread through the country; Oldcastle either was, or was said to be, in league with the Scots and with the Mortimer party in Wales, and to have relations with the pseudo-Richard even at the last; Elmham (ed. Cole), p. 151; Wals. ii. 307. Capgrave says that he ventured to propose to the king a bill for confiscating the temporalities of the church, which was presented by Henry Greyndore; Ill. Henr. p. 121; Sir John Greyndore was a tenant of the Mortimers; Ellis, Orig. Letters, 2nd Series, i. 26. See also Elmham (ed. Cole), p. 148. Oldcastle was captured towards the end of 1417; brought to London on a warrant of the council dated Dec. 1; and taken before the parliament as an outlaw for treason and as excommunicated for heresy. On the 14th the commons petitioned for his execution; the sentences of the justices and of the archbishop were read the same day; the lords, with the consent of the duke of Bedford the guardian of the kingdom, sentenced him to execution; and he was drawn, hanged, and burned, Dec. 14; Rot. Parl. iv. 107–110.

whether the movement which is thus connected with the name of Oldcastle has any very definite analogy with the popular commotions of 1381 and 1450; but it is obvious that if the prompt and resolute policy adopted by Henry V had been taken in those years, the tumults then raised might have been effectually prevented; if Richard II or Henry VI had had to deal with Oldcastle, the meeting at S. Giles's fields might have assumed the dimensions of a revolution. The character of Oldcastle as a traitor or a martyr has long been a disputed question between different schools; perhaps we shall most safely conclude from the tenour of history that his doctrinal creed was far sounder than the principles which guided either his moral or his political conduct.

Strong policy of Henry V.

648. The alarm had scarcely subsided when the parliament met, April 30, at Leicester[1]; and the chancellor in his opening speech declared that one of the causes of the summons was to provide for the defence of the nation against the Lollards; the king did not ask for tenths or fifteenths, but for advice and aid in good governance. A new statute was accordingly passed against the heretics, in which the secular power, no longer content to aid in the execution of the ecclesiastical sentences, undertook, where it was needed, the initiative against the Lollards[2]. Judged by the extant records the session was a quiet one; the estates granted tunnage and poundage for three years, and obtained one great constitutional boon, for which the parliaments of Edward III and Richard II had striven in vain; the commons prayed, that 'as it hath been ever their liberty and freedom that there should no statute or law be made unless they gave thereto their assent,' 'there never be no law made' on their petition 'and engrossed as statute and law, neither by addition nor by diminution, by no manner of term or terms the which should change the sentence and the intent asked.' The king, in reply, granted that 'from henceforth nothing be enacted to the petitions of his commons that be contrary to their asking, whereby they should be bound without their assent; saving

Parliament at Leicester in 1414.

New law against Lollardy.

Statutes to be made without altering the words of the petitions on which they are based.

[1] Rot. Parl. iv. 15–33.
[2] Ib. iv. 24; Statutes, ii. 181; Wilkins, Conc. iii. 358.

alway to our liege lord his prerogative to grant and deny what him list of their petitions and askings aforesaid[1].' In this session the king created his brothers John and Humfrey dukes of Bedford and Gloucester, and his cousin Richard of York, earl of Cambridge. The duke of York was declared loyal and relieved from the risks which had been impending since 1400; and Thomas Beaufort was confirmed in the possession of the earldom of Dorset[2]. The possessions of the alien priories, which had, since the beginning of the war under Edward III, retained a precarious hold on their English estates, were, on the petition of the commons, taken for perpetuity into the king's hands[3].

Promotion of the king's brothers and other kinsmen.

Confiscation of the alien priories.

Negotiations with France.

Although the rolls of parliament are completely silent on the subject, it may be fairly presumed that the question of war with France was mooted at the Leicester parliament; for soon after the close of the session, on the 31st of May, the bishop of Durham and lord Grey were accredited as ambassadors to Charles VI with instructions to negotiate an alliance, and to debate on the restoration of Henry's rights—rights which were summed up in his hereditary assumption of the title of King of France[4]. It is not improbable that the design of a great war was now generally acceptable to the nation. The magnates were heartily tired of internal struggles, and the lull of war with Scots and Welsh gave them the opportunity of turning their arms against the ancient foe. The king himself was ambitious of military glory and inherited the long-deferred designs of his father, his alliances, and his preparations. The clergy were willing to further the promotion of a national design which at the same time would save the church from the attacks of the Lollards[5]. The people also were ready, as in prosperous times they always were, to regard the dynastic aims of the king as the lawful and indispensable safeguards of the nation. The historians who in

Prospect of war.

[1] Rot. Parl. iv. 22.

[2] Ib. iv. 17.

[3] Ib. iv. 22; Mon. Angl. vi. 1642; Rymer, ix. 280, 281.

[4] Rymer, ix. 131. The parliament broke up May 19; the ambassadors were accredited May 31.

[5] See Fabyan, p. 578; Leland, Coll. ii. 490. 'It was concluded by the said council, and in especial by the spiritualty, that he should go and get Normandy, and they should help him to their power. It is said that the spiritualty feared sore, that if he had not had to do without

the later part of the century looked back through the obscurity of the civil war and the humiliation of the house of Lancaster, and still more the writers of the next century, who visited the sins of the clergy upon their predecessors, asserted that the war was precipitated by the line of defence taken up by the bishops against the Lollards; and according to the chronicler Hall the parliament of Leicester saw the first measures taken[1]. The story runs that the petition of 1410 was introduced again by the Wycliffite knights, and that in reply archbishop Chichele suggested and argued for a French war, the old earl of Westmoreland answering him and recommending instead a war with Scotland. These exact particulars cannot be true; Chichele did not sit as archbishop in the Leicester parliament, and the speeches bear manifest tokens of later composition[2]. But it is by no means improbable that, the project of war once broached, the bishops promoted it and promised their assistance: nor does it follow that in so doing they, any more than the king or the barons, should be deemed guilty of all the misery that ensued. It is possible too that the resumption of the alien priories may have been the result of some larger proposition of confiscation. However broached, the

Share of the clergy in promoting the war.

the land, that he would have laboured for to have take fro the church the temporal possessions, and therefore they concluded among themself that they should stir him for to go and make war over sea in France, for to conquer his rightful inheritance'; Cont. Polychr. (ed. 1527) f. 329. The advice given by the council (Ordinances, ii. 140) seems sound enough; the lords know well that the king will attempt nothing that is not to the glory of God, and will eschew the shedding of Christian blood; if he goes to war the cause will be the refusal of his rights, not his own wilfulness. They recommend him to send ambassadors first; if that is done, and the peace of the realm provided for, they are ready to serve him to the utmost of their power. The council in which this was done is not dated. Cf. Tyler, Henry of Monmouth, ii. 72.

[1] Hall, Chr. p. 49.

[2] The parliament sat from April 30 to May 19; Lords' Report, i. 497. Chichele had the royal assent to his election March 23; but he was not provided by the pope until April 27, and received the temporalities only on May 30. His name does not occur either as archbishop or as bishop of S. David's in the parliamentary roll. Hall (Chr. p. 49) says that he was newly made archbishop, having before been a Carthusian (!) But the speeches abundantly supply the refutation of the story in this form; the earl of Westmoreland quotes John Major the Scottish historian who was born in 1469. Whether Hall or some contemporary writer composed them, we cannot decide; there is an outline or abridgment of them in Redmayne's Life of Henry V, composed about 1540. Hall died in 1547.

Delay of the war.

design was not immediately prosecuted. Negotiations for peace with France continued; the council of Constance occupied the minds of men a good deal, and the king employed himself chiefly in the foundation of his new monasteries of Sheen and Sion.

Second parliament of 1414.

But in November, when, on the failure of the negotiations, the parliament was called together[1], bishop Beaufort opened the session with a sermon on the text 'Strive for the truth unto the death,' supplementing the exhortation with the suggestion 'while we have time let us do good unto all men.' It was clearly the king's duty to strive for the truth; and now the time was come. The estates saw the matter with the king's eyes, and, having recommended him to exhaust the power of negotiation first, granted two tenths and fifteenths for the defence of the realm[2]: the clergy had already granted their two tenths[3].

Measures of conciliation at home.

Henry saw that the initiation of a great national effort should be marked by a great act of reconciliation. Measures were taken for the restoration of the heir of Hotspur, now a prisoner in Scotland, to the earldom of Northumberland[4]; the young earl of March was received into the king's closest confidence; the heir of the house of Holland was encouraged to hope for restoration to the family honours[5]. Military preparations and diplomatic

War resolved on.

negotiations were pressed on all sides. A great national council determined that war should begin. In April 1415 Henry laid formal claim to the crown of France[6]; on the 16th the chancellor announced to the council his resolve to proclaim war[7];

[1] Nov. 19. Rot. Parl. iv. 34. A great council was held Sept. 22; in which probably the advice to go to war was given. Chron. Lond. p. 98.

[2] Ordinances, ii. 150; Dep. Keeper's Rep. ii. App. ii. p. 185; Rot. Parl. iv. 35.

[3] The convocation of Canterbury was opened Oct. 1; Wilkins, Conc. iii. 358: it broke up Oct. 20, after granting two tenths; Wake, p. 351.

[4] Wals. ii. 300; Hardyng, pp. 372, 373. Henry Percy was restored to the earldom Nov. 11, 1414. See Rot. Parl. iv. 35; Rymer, ix. 242, 244, 324; Ordinances, ii. 160 sq. 188. He was exchanged and liberated early in 1416.

[5] John Holland was restored to the lands of the earldom of Huntingdon in 1416; Rot. Parl. iv. 100. He came of age March 29, 1417, or would have been restored earlier. He is called earl of Huntingdon in April 1415; Rymer, ix. 223; and was made admiral of England in 1416; Ordinances, ii. 155, 198, 199; Rymer, ix. 344.

[6] Rymer, ix. 222.

[7] Ib.; Ordinances, ii. 155.

the duke of Bedford was to act as lieutenant of the kingdom in his absence; in June he went down to the coast to watch the equipment of the fleet; on the 24th of July he made his will; on the 10th of August he embarked[1]. But before this he had to deal with a signal, short, but most dangerous and ominous crisis. The young earl of March, the legitimate heir of Edward III, had, by his reception into the king's good graces, become again a public man. The earl of Cambridge, a weak and ungrateful man, was the godson of Richard II and brother-in-law of the earl of March: he, together with Henry lord le Scrope of Masham and Sir Thomas Grey of Heton[2], concocted a design of carrying off the earl of March to Wales as soon as Henry sailed, and there proclaiming him heir of Richard II. Henry, it was said, on the information of the young earl himself[3], was made acquainted with the plot; the traitors were arrested, a commission of special justices was appointed to try them, and the verdict of a local jury presented against them. Cambridge and Grey confessed themselves guilty. Grey suffered on the 2nd of August. Scrope denied his guilt and demanded trial by his peers. A court was formed under Clarence, which passed sentence of death on Scrope and Cambridge; they were executed on the 5th of August[4]. This was the only blood shed by Henry V to save the rights of the line of Lancaster; and for the time his prompt and stern action had its effect. His anger went no further; March was not disgraced, the duke of York retained his confidence, the heir

Henry's preparations.

The Southampton plot.

Execution of the conspirators.

[1] On all the details of the expedition see Sir Harris Nicolas's History of the Battle of Agincourt and the notes to Mr. Williams's edition of the Gesta Henrici V. There is a statement of the revenue, June 24, 1415—June 24, 1416, in the Ordinances, ii. 172. It amounts, exclusive of the tenths and fifteenths, to £56,966 13*s*. 4*d*.

[2] 'Francorum munere corrupti'; Otterb. p. 276; cf. Wals. ii. 305, 306. 'Prece conducti Gallorum'; Capgr. Ill. Henr. p. 114; Elmham (ed. Cole), p. 105.

[3] Wavrin, p. 178. The earl received a general pardon Aug. 7; Rymer, ix. 303.

[4] Wals. ii. 305, 306; Gesta Henrici, p. 11; Rot. Parl. iv. 64 sq; Rymer, ix. 300. The confession of the earl of Cambridge exonerates Scrope but implicates the earl of March, or rather his confessors who had refused to absolve him unless he claimed his right, and proves the guilt of Grey. Rymer, ix. 301; Nicolas, Battle of Agincourt, App. pp. 19, 20; Ellis, Original Letters, 2nd Series, i. 45.

of the unhappy Cambridge was brought up in his household. But the evil tradition of bloodshed was continued, and the heir of Cambridge and Mortimer was nourished for the time of vengeance which forty years later was to destroy the dynasty.

Tradition of bloodshed.

Henry's first French war.

The wars of Henry V do not enter much into our general view of the internal history of England, except as a cause for results which are scarcely to be traced during his life. The expedition sailed on the 11th of August: Harfleur was taken on the 22nd of September; the battle of Agincourt was won on the 25th of October; on the 23rd of November the king entered London in triumph. The parliament which met on the 4th of November[1] under Bedford signalised its gratitude by granting the custom on wool, tunnage and poundage for life, by anticipating the payment of the money grant of 1414, and a gift of another tenth and fifteenth[2]. The proceedings against Cambridge, Scrope and Grey were recorded, confirmed, and completed, by a decree of forfeiture[3].

Parliament after Agincourt.

Henry's stay in England.

650. From Nov. 17, 1415, to July 23, 1417, Henry devoted himself to the task of preparing the means of continuing the war. He remained, except for a few days, in England[4], building ships, training men, reconciling enmities at home, and strengthening alliances abroad. The victory at Agincourt had made him, as it were in an instant, the arbiter of European politics. Sigismund of Luxemburg, king of the Romans, a man whose better qualities placed him in general sympathy with Henry[5], arrived at Dover in April 1416, purposing to close the schism in the church and to make peace between England and France; on the 15th of August he departed, after a vain

Visit of Sigismund.

[1] Rot. Parl. iv. 62.

[2] Ib. iv. 63, 71; Dep. Keeper's Rep. ii. App. ii. p. 186. The clergy of Canterbury granted two tenths in a convocation held Nov. 18-Dec. 3; ib.; Wake, p. 352.

[3] Nov. 4-12; Rot. Parl. iv. 64 sq.

[4] He went to Calais Sept. 4. 1416, completed his negotiations with Burgundy Oct. 8, and returned Oct. 16. See Rymer, ix. 385; Gesta Henr. pp. 94, 95, 100-104; Lenz, König Sigismund, &c., pp. 123 sq.

[5] Wals. ii. 316; Gesta Henrici, pp. 76 sq.; Ordinances, ii. 193. The history of the transactions between Sigismund and Henry, with their various results, is worked out by Dr. Max Lenz, in his 'König Sigismund und Heinrich V' (Berlin 1874).

attempt to procure a truce for three years, having concluded an offensive and defensive alliance with Henry against France. In October the king, during a short visit to Calais, made a league with the duke of Burgundy, whom he had convinced of his right to the crown of France. With the minor powers of the continent, the Hanse towns, Cologne, Holland, and Bavaria, with the northern courts and Spain, negotiations for alliance were set on foot with general success. The relations with France were of course hostile in fact, although truces and armistices were concluded so as to make any general attack or defence unnecessary, whilst both powers were preparing for a decisive struggle. At home the reconciliation of Percy was accomplished; the earl of March was attached still more closely to the king; the heir of the Hollands was restored to his father's earldom; envoys were accredited for negotiating the release of James of Scotland, and powers were bestowed on Gilbert Talbot to receive the remains of Owen Glendower's party to pardon [1]. Henry's success in obtaining money, men, and ships, seems after the story of the late reign little less than miraculous. The expedition of 1415 had involved the raising of 11,000 men and 1300 vessels large and small; the money required had been raised largely by loans secured on the grants of the parliament. The expedition of 1417 was to be on a much larger scale; an army of 25,000 men and a fleet of 1,500 vessels, of which a much greater proportion were to be vessels of war, worthy of an English navy [2]. Two parliaments sat during the season of preparation. In March 1416 the commons accelerated the grant of a tenth and a fifteenth due at Martinmas [3]; in October they

League with the continental powers.

Peace at home.

Expedition of 1417.

Supplies granted.

[1] Rymer, ix. 283, 330, 417; Ordinances, ii. 221; Gesta Henr. p. 81.

[2] Sir Harris Nicolas estimates the total number of Henry's army in 1415, when it started, at 30,000; Battle of Agincourt, p. 48. 11,500 men-at-arms each with his servant, and the persons of higher rank with two or three servants, might make up this number. A Muster Roll of 1417 is printed in Williams' notes to the Gesta Henrici V, pp. 265 sq.; this contains 8000 men-at-arms and archers; but forms only one third of the entire list. The Gesta (p. 109) give 16,400 as the number of men-at-arms; the total calculated on the basis given above, must thus have reached nearly 50,000.

[3] Mar. 16–Apr. 8; Rot. Parl. iv. 71; Gesta Henrici, pp. 69, 73.

granted two similar aids, payable in the February and November following; and empowered the king to raise a loan on the security thus created[1]. The bishop of Winchester lent the king 21,000 marks on the security of the customs; the city of London lent 10,000 on the crown jewels. The clergy of the two provinces granted their tenths in proportion to the liberality of the commons. To the building of ships Henry devoted himself with special ardour; although a great part of the naval service was still conducted by pressed ships, the royal navy was so much increased as to be henceforth a real national armament. In February 1417 the king possessed six great ships, eight barges, and ten balingers[2]; the ships were built under his personal superintendence at Southampton and in the Thames. Following the example of Richard I he issued ordinances for the fleets and armies, which may, far more safely than earlier fragments of legislation, be regarded as the basis of the English law of the admiralty, and as no unimportant contribution to international jurisprudence[3]. Surgeons were appointed for the fleet and army[4]. The minutest details of victualling went on under the king's eye. The parliaments forgot to grumble, the earls felt themselves too weak or too safe to make it wise to quarrel; the duke of York, whose name, rightly or wrongly, had been mixed up with every conspiracy of the last reign, had fallen at Agincourt; Thomas Beaufort was made duke of Exeter in the parliament of October, 1416. Even Lollardy was on the wane. No untoward omen like the plot at Southampton threw a shadow over the second epoch of the war. Coincidently with the king's departure bishop Beaufort resigned the great seal[5], and set out by way of Constance to Palestine. The duke of Bedford stayed

Bishop Beaufort's loans.

Ships built.

Cessation of domestic dangers.

Bedford lieutenant of the realm.

[1] Dep. Keeper's Rep. ii. App. ii. p. 187; Rot. Parl. iv. 95. The parliament sat Oct. 19 to Nov. 20; Gesta Henr. p. 105, 107. The convocation of Canterbury granted two tenths, York one; Wake, p. 352; Wilkins, Conc. iii. 377, 380. The commissions for loans were issued July 23, 1417; Rymer, ix. 499. The commission for Hertfordshire reported that they could get no money, Oct. 6; ib. p. 500.

[2] Nicolas, Agincourt, App. p. 21; Ellis, Original Letters, 3rd Series, i. 72; 2nd Series, i. 68: cf. Ordinances, ii. 202.

[3] Nicolas, Agincourt, App. p. 31.

[4] Rymer, ix. 363.

[5] Ib. ix. 472.

at home as the king's lieutenant, with bishop Longley as chancellor. The successes of the king in his second expedition, although less startling than those of 1415, were amply sufficient to keep up the national ardour; the earl of Huntingdon was victorious at sea, Henry himself secured Normandy by a series of tedious sieges in 1417 and 1418, gaining however even more from the miserable discord of his adversaries. Early in 1419 Rouen was taken, and in July Pontoise surrendered, opening the way to Paris. In August the murder of John of Burgundy by the dauphin threw the weight of that important but vacillating power decisively on the side of Henry; duke Philip determined to avenge his father and to make common cause with England. The crime of the dauphin placed France at Henry's feet. The unhappy king was brought to terms, and in May 1420, by the peace of Troyes, he accepted Henry as his son-in-law, regent and heir of France. On the 24th of June the peace was proclaimed in London, and on the 1st of February, 1421, the king returned to England[1].

Henry's conquest of France.

Peace of Troyes.

In the meanwhile Bedford was learning how to rule a free people; a lesson which, if he had been allowed to practise it in after years, might have even now saved the house of Lancaster from utter destruction. He presided in the parliament of 1417, which granted two fifteenths and tenths[2], and sealed the fate of Oldcastle, who was executed on the 14th of December[3]. With the funds so provided the government was carried on without a parliament until October, 1419[4], when another fifteenth and

Bedford's government.

Parliament of 1417.

[1] Rymer, ix. 895 sq. The king reported the conclusion of the treaty to the regent, May 22; ib. p. 906; it was approved by the three estates of France Dec. 6; ib. vol. x. p. 33; and by those of England May 2, 1421; ib p. 110.

[2] The parliament met November 16; Roger Flower was speaker; the grant was made Dec. 17; Dep. Keeper's Rep. ii. App. ii. p. 187; Rot. Parl. iv. 107. The convocation of Canterbury (Nov. 26–Dec. 20) granted two tenths, that of York one (Jan. 20. 1418); Wilkins, Conc. iii. 381, 389. A loan by bishop Beaufort of 21,000 marks, made July 18, 1417, was now secured by act of parliament; Rot. Parl. iv. 111.

[3] Wals. ii. 327, 328; Rot. Parl. iv. 107.

[4] The parliament of 1419 met Oct. 16; Roger Flower was again speaker; the grant was made Nov. 13; Dep. Keeper's Rep. App. ii. p. 188; Rot. Parl. iv. 117. On Oct. 30, 1419, the convocation granted a half tenth and a noble from stipendiary priests; Wake, p. 354; Wilkins, Conc. iii. 396.

Parliaments of 1419 and 1420.

tenth, with a supplementary grant of a third of the same sum, was voted and authority given for a new loan secured on the grant of this third and the tenth of the clergy[1]. The queen dowager was accused in this session of an attempt to destroy the king by sorcery, and was deprived of the power of conspiring in other ways by being relieved from the task of administering her income[2]. The parliament of December, 1420, in which the duke of Gloucester[3] represented the king, was held in daily expectation of his return[4]; Gloucester did not ask for money. Matters were not looking so prosperous as they had been; money was scarce; the peace was badly kept in the north. True, the Lollards, as the chancellor said, were decreasing, but it was time that the king came home[5]. Petitions were not to be engrossed until they had been sent over sea for the royal assent[6]; the statute of Edward III, which secured that English liberties should not be diminished by the king's assumption of a new title was re-enacted[7]. A pressing invitation was sent for the king and his bride to visit England[8]. Henry was glad enough to return. He landed in February and, after having the queen crowned and making a grand progress through the country, on the 2nd of May opened parliament in person[9]. A new expedition was already necessary; the duke of Clarence had fallen in battle against the dauphin in March.

Gloucester lieutenant.

Return of the king.

Treaty of Troyes confirmed.

The joy felt at the king's return seems to have prevented the asking of any inconvenient questions; the treaty of Troyes was laid before the three estates and solemnly confirmed. No gloom was thrown over the session by a dispute about money. So

[1] Rot. Parl. iv. 117. Commissions for collecting the loan were issued Nov. 26; Rymer, ix. 815.

[2] Wals. ii. 331; Rot. Parl. iv. 118. She was arrested and sent to Leeds castle; Leland, Coll. ii. 489.

[3] Gloucester was made lieutenant Dec. 30, 1419, when Bedford joined the king in Normandy; Rymer, ix. 830.

[4] The parliament opened Dec. 2; Roger Hunt was speaker; Rot. Parl. iv. 123.

[5] Rot. Parl. iv. 123.

[6] Ib. iv. 127.

[7] Ib. iv. 128.

[8] Ib. iv. 125.

[9] The parliament of 1421 opened May 2; Thomas Chaucer was speaker; Rot. Parl. iv. 129. On the 6th a statement of the revenue was made: it amounted to £55,743; the charges on which reached the sum of £52,235; leaving only £3,507 for extraordinary expenditure; Ordinances, ii. 312; Rymer, x. 113. The convocations granted a tenth; Wake, p. 358.

great indeed was the confidence of the nation in its leader that the parliament empowered the council to give security for the payment of all debts contracted by the king for the present expedition[1]; and a proof of private confidence even more signal than any which the parliament could give was seen in the conduct of bishop Beaufort, who, although he had as yet recovered only a third of his former loan, was ready to lend the king £14,000 more[2]. In these monetary transactions the bishop probably acted as a contractor on a large scale, and deserved the thanks of the country far more than the odium which has been heaped upon him as a money-lender. It can scarcely be supposed that the very large sums which he lent were his own, for although he held a rich see he had not inherited any great estate, and he kept up a very splendid household. It was probably his credit, which was unimpeachable, more than any enormous personal wealth, that enabled him to pour ready money, when ready money was very scarce, into the king's coffers. In this session the Bohun inheritance was divided between the king and the countess of Stafford, his cousin, as coheirs of the earldoms of Essex, Hereford, and Northampton[3].

Security for the king's debts.

New loans by Beaufort.

651. Thus provided with money, Henry on the 10th of June left England, never to return. He spent the rest of his life in attempts to secure the remaining strongholds of the unhappy country which he desired to reform and govern. The need of further supplies brought together the parliament in December[4] under the duke of Bedford. A fifteenth and tenth was granted, but little else was done[5]; the scarcity of money was already alarming, and received some slight attention in the way of

Henry's last expedition, June 1421.

Supplies granted.

[1] Rot. Parl. iv. 130. The king had issued commission for raising a loan, at York, April 7; Rymer, x. 96; and at Westminster April 21; ib. p. 97.

[2] Rot. Parl. iv. 132; Ordinances, ii. 298.

[3] Rot. Parl. iv. 135.

[4] This parliament met December 1; Richard Banyard was speaker; the grant was made apparently on the day of the meeting; the speaker however was elected on the 3rd; Rot. Parl. iv. 151; Wals. ii. 332.

[5] Dep. Keeper's Rep. ii. App. ii. p. 189; Rot. Parl. iv. 151. The clergy granted two half tenths. The Ordinances (ii. 312) contain a statement of the revenue of 1421, amounting to £55,743, charged with regular burdens amounting to £52,235, and thus leaving £3,507 to provide for the household and extraordinary expenditure.

Death of Henry V.

His last arrangements and wishes.

Record of his death.

legislation. On the 6th of December the unhappy Henry of Windsor was born. In May the queen joined her husband, and on the 31st of August he died. His last wishes were that Bedford should be the guardian of both realm and heir, and that the earl of Warwick should be the boy's preceptor. A strong command was laid on his brothers not to make peace with the dauphin and never to quarrel with Burgundy or to allow the duke of Orleans to go free. In a sad foreboding he warned his youngest brother not to be selfish or to prefer his own personal interests to those of the country which he would have in part to govern. The duke of Exeter was also charged with the care of the kingdom of England[1]. With his last breath Henry professed himself a crusader[2]. His death is recorded in the book of the acts of his son's council thus: 'Departed this life the most Christian champion of the church, the beam of prudence and example of righteousness, the invincible king, the flower and glory of all knighthood[4], Henry, the fifth since the Conquest, king of England, heir and regent of the realm of France, and lord of Ireland, at the castle of Bois de Vincennes near Paris on the last day of August in the year of our Lord 1422 and of his

[1] See Wavrin, p. 423; Monstrelet, liv. i. c. 264. According to the account in the Gesta, p. 159, Bedford was to rule France, Gloucester England; and Exeter, Warwick, and bishop Beaufort, to be governors of the young prince. Elmham joins Sir Walter Hungerford and Sir Henry Fitz Hugh to the duke of Exeter (ed. Hearne, p. 333). Hardyng likewise says that the duke of Exeter was to be guardian to the young Henry—

> 'Thomas Beauforde his uncle dere and trewe
> Duke of Excester, full of all worthyhode,
> To tyme his soone to perfect age grewe,
> He to kepe hym, chaungyng for no newe,
> With helpe of his other eme then full wise
> The bishop of Winchester of good advise.'—p. 387.

He adds that it was on the duke of Exeter's death that the earl of Warwick became tutor; p. 394. See also Hall, Chr. p. 115; Tit. Liv. For. p. 95.

[2] His last words were 'Good Lord thou knowest that my mind was to re-edify the walls of Jerusalem'; Leland, Coll. ii. 489; cf. Wavrin, p. 424; Hardyng, p. 388. The report of Gilbert de Lannoy on the ports of Egypt and Syria, ordered by Henry V in contemplation of his expedition to the East is in the Archaeologia, xxi. 312–348.

[3] 'The good and nobylle Kyng Harry the V aftyr the Conqueste of Inglonde, floure of chevalrye of crysten men'; Gregory, p. 148: cf. Chron. London, p. 110.

reign the tenth: whom succeeded his illustrious son Henry VI, on the 1st day of September, in the first year of his age and reign.' The unhappy Henry of Windsor was destined to lose all and more than all Henry of Monmouth had won.

Great possibilities of Henry's career.

Henry V was by far the greatest king in Christendom, and he deserved the estimation in which he was held, both for the grandeur and sincerity of his character and for the greatness of the position which, not without many favouring circumstances on which he could not have counted, he had won. It was very much owing to his influence that the great schism was closed at Constance; it was the representative of the English church who nominated pope Martin V[1], the creator of the modern papacy: and although the result was one which ran counter to the immemorial policy of kings and parliaments, of Church and State, the mischief of the consequences cannot be held to derogate from the greatness of the achievement. It is not too much to suppose that Henry, striking when the opportunity came and continuing the task which he had undertaken without interruption, might have accomplished the subjugation and pacification of France, and realised the ambition of his life, the dream of his father and of his Lancastrian ancestors, by staying the progress of the Ottomans and recovering the sepulchre of Christ. This was not to be; and he had already done more than on ordinary calculations could have been imagined, compassed more than it was in England's power alone to hold fast or to complete. England was nearly exhausted; it could only have been at the head of consolidated France and united Europe that he could have led the Crusade. In him then the dying energies of medieval life kindle for a short moment into flame; England rejoices in the light all the more because of the gloom that precedes and follows: and the efforts made by England, parliament, church, and nation, during the period, are not less remarkable than those made by the king. They prove that the system of government was capable of keeping pace with the great

[1] The bishop of London nominated him; Wals. ii. 320. See Lenz, König Sigismund, p. 184. Whoever was the nominator the election was the result of the league between Henry and Sigismund.

mind that inspired it, although the mass of the nation was, as it soon proved to be, not sufficiently advanced to maintain the system when the guiding hand was taken away.

John duke of Bedford and Humfrey duke of Gloucester.

652. The two men into whose hands the administration of Henry's dominions now fell were in singular contrast with one another. The two brothers were but a year apart in age, John was thirty-three, Humfrey thirty-two. There was perhaps as little personal jealousy between them as could exist between two brothers so situated. Bedford was never jealous of Gloucester; Gloucester, if during his brother's absence he acted with little regard to his wishes, and aimed at power for himself irrespective of the national interest, was always amenable to Bedford's advice when he was present, and never ventured to withstand him to his face. In character however, and in the great aim and object of life, there was scarcely anything in common between them. They seem, as it were, to have developed the different sides of their father's idiosyncrasy, or to have run back to a previous generation. Humfrey has all the adventurous spirit, the popular manners, the self-seeking and ambition that marked Henry IV; he is still more like the great-uncle whose title he bore, and to whose fate his own death was so closely parallel, Thomas of Woodstock. John has all the seriousness, the statesmanship, the steady purpose, the high sense of public duty, that in a lower degree belonged to his father. He, although with a far higher type of character, in some points resembled the Black Prince. Bedford again has all the great qualities of Henry V without his brilliance; Gloucester has all his popular characteristics without any of his greatness. The former was thoroughly trusted by Henry V, the latter was trusted only so far as it was necessary. The Beauforts were no doubt intended by Henry to keep the balance steady. He knew that while to the actual wielders of sovereign power their personal interests are apt to be the first consideration, to a house in the position of the Beauforts the first object is the preservation of the dynasty. He had confided in them and had found them faithful; Bedford trusted them and also found them faithful. Gloucester, as Clarence had been, was opposed to them, and the jealousy

Contrast between the two brothers.

Their relations with the Beauforts.

which he missed no opportunity of showing was one cause of the destruction of his house. Gloucester was the evil genius of his family; his selfish ambition abroad broke up the Burgundian alliance, his selfish ambition at home broke up the unity of the Lancastrian power; he lived long enough to ruin his nephew, not long enough to show whether he had the will or the power to save him. Yet the reaction provoked by his competitors for power invested him with some popularity whilst he lived, and won for him the posthumous reputation of being the pillar of the state and the friend of the commons[1]. Clever, popular, amiable, and cultivated[2], he was without strong principle, and, what was more fatal than the want of principle, was devoid of that insight into the real position of his house and nation which Henry IV, Henry V, and Bedford undoubtedly had; he would not or could not see that the house of Lancaster was on its trial, and that England had risked her all on that issue.

Mischievous character of Gloucester.

The uncertainty that still rests on the exact form in which Henry's last wishes were expressed compels us to content ourselves with supposing that they were duly carried into execution, and that he intended Bedford to govern France, Gloucester to act as his vicegerent in England. But the arrangement was not adopted at home without misgivings. The lords, the council, the parliament, all had something to say before the final

Question about the late king's intentions.

[1] According to Hall he had abroad the reputation of being 'the very father of his country and the shield and defence of the poor commonalty'; Chron. p. 212. Hall however knew better.

[2] Capgrave (Ill. Henr. p. 109) calls him 'inter omnes mundi proceres litteratissimus.' He took special pains to stand well with learned men, whereby his reputation has no doubt largely benefited. Duke Humfrey's benefactions to the Oxford Library are detailed in Munimenta Academica, i. 326; ii. 758–772. See also Macray, Annals of the Bodleian, pp. 6–12. Among the scholars promoted by him the best known are bishops Beckington and Pecock, and Titus Livius Forojuliensis. Peter de Monte dedicated to him a work 'De Virtutibus et Vitiis'; Beckington, i. 34. Aeneas Sylvius (p. 64) speaks of him as 'clarissimo et doctissimo, qui . . poetas mirifice colit et oratores magnopere veneratur.' 'Iste dux Humfredus inter omnes mundi principes excellebat in scientia et speciositatis ac formae decentia; tamen vecors cordis et effaeminatus vir ac voluptati deditus'; Chr. Giles, p. 7; cf. Tit. Liv. For. p. 2. His constitution was weakened by his excesses as early as 1424. See the advice of his physician Gilbert Kymer in Hearne, Lib. Nig. Scaccarii, vol. ii. pp. 552 sq.

Mutual jealousies.

adjustment was made, and Gloucester himself was never satisfied with the position allotted him. The lords were jealous of their own rights; the influence of Bedford and the Beauforts, and the constitutional power already wielded by the council, were sufficient to limit the power of the protector in that body; and the parliament contained men who were watchful of any attempt to diminish the liberties or control the powers to which the last two kings had allowed free exercise.

The council undertakes the work of government.

653. Gloucester, who was in England at the time of Henry's death, at once took the place which belonged to him, and on the 28th of September in the name of his nephew received the great seal from Bishop Longley[1]. But the council acted as administrators of the executive power, and with this he did not venture to interfere. It was by the advice of the council that he was on the 6th of November appointed to open the ensuing parliament[2]. The words of the commission were sufficient to tell him that he would have no unrestricted power; he was authorised to begin, carry on, and dissolve the parliament, by the assent of the council. Gloucester objected to the last words[3]; and the lords replied that considering the tender age of the king, they neither could, ought, or would consent to the omission of the words, which were as necessary for the security of the duke as they were for that of the council. Thus pressed he gave a reluctant consent, and on the 9th of November opened the parliament simply as the king's uncle acting by virtue of that commission[4]. Archbishop Chichele announced the causes of summons,—the good governance of the king's person, the maintenance of peace and law, and the defence of the realm; for all which purposes it was

Attitude of duke Humfrey.

Parliament of 1422.

[1] Rymer, x. 253; Rot. Parl. iv. 170.

[2] Ordinances, iii. 6, 7; Rot. Parl. iv. 169.

[3] 'Ad parliamentum illud finiendum et dissolvendum de assensu consilii nostri plenam commisimus potestatem'; Ord. iii. 7. It certainly seems probable that 'de assensu consilii nostri' should be read with the words that follow rather than with the preceding words, that Gloucester misconstrued the sentence, and that the council took advantage of his misconstruction to force that interpretation upon him. The words do not occur in the commission given by Edward III to Lionel in 1351; Rot. Parl. ii. 225; or to Richard in 1377; ib. p. 360.

[4] Rot. Parl. iv. 169; Rymer, x. 257; Wals. ii. 345. Roger Flower was speaker. The session closed Dec. 18.

necessary to have provision of honourable and discreet personages of each estate of the realm. Before determining the form of regency, the parliament examined the list of the ministers; the commons asked to know their names, and on the 16th letters patent were produced in which the king by advice of his council in the present parliament re-nominated his father's chancellor and treasurer[1]. It was not until the twenty-seventh day of the session that Gloucester's position was definitely settled. He claimed the regency as next of kin to the young king and under the will of Henry V[2]: the lords, having searched for precedents, found that he had no such claim on the ground of relationship, and that the late king could not without the assent of the estates dispose of the government after his death; they disliked too the names of regent, tutor, governor, and lieutenant[3]. He had to submit, and on the 5th of December the king[4], by assent and advice of the lords spiritual and temporal and by assent of the commons, constituted the duke of Bedford protector and defender of the realm and of the church of England and principal counsellor to the king, whenever and as soon as he should be present in England, the duke of Gloucester in that event being the chief counsellor after him; he further ordained that the duke of Gloucester should occupy the same position so long as Bedford was absent, should be the protector and defender of the kingdom and church, and chief counsellor to the king. These letters were confirmed by an act of parliament; and Gloucester at once accepted the responsibility. By a further act the protector was empowered to exercise the royal patronage in the administration of the forests, and the gift of smaller ecclesiastical benefices; the greater prizes being reserved for him to bestow only by advice of the council[5]. The members of the council were then

Question of regency considered in parliament.

Gloucester made protector in the absence of Bedford.

[1] Rot. Parl. iv. 171, 172.

[2] Ib. iv. 326.

[3] According to Hardyng, Beaufort led the opposition, p. 391, 'for cause he was so noyous with to dele'; 'the bishop of Winchester by perlyament was chaunceller and hiest governour of the kynghis persone and his greate socour; his godfather and his father's eme, and supportour was moost of all this realme'; p. 392.

[4] Rot. Parl. iv. 174, 175; Rymer, x. 261; Wals. ii. 346.

[5] Rot. Parl. iv. 175; Ordinances, iii. 14.

The names of the council. named: Gloucester as chief; five prelates, the primate, the bishops of London, Winchester, Norwich, and Worcester; the duke of Exeter; the earls of March, Warwick, Marshall, Northumberland, and Westmoreland; the lords Fitz Hugh, Cromwell, Hungerford, Tiptoft, and Beauchamp[1]. This body, in which every interest was represented and every honoured name appears, accepted office under five conditions, which still further limited the powers of the protector; they were to appoint all officers of justice and revenue; they were to have the disposal of the wardships, marriages, ferms, and other incidental profits of the crown; nothing at all was to be done without a quorum of six or four at least, nothing great without the presence of the majority; whilst for business on which it was usual to ask the king's opinion the advice of the protector was required: the fourth article secured secrecy as to the contents of the treasury, and the fifth provided that a list of attendances should be kept. The commons added an article to prevent the council from encroaching on the patronage belonging to existing officers of state[2]. On the 18th of December the grant of the subsidy on wool and of tunnage and poundage was made[3]. It was agreed that all Lollards imprisoned in London should be handed over to the ordinaries to be tried[4]: no important legislation was attempted, and neither parliament nor convocation was troubled by anything like direct taxation. The arrangements for the regency were completed by the council in the following February; the protector was to receive an annual salary of 8000 marks[5].

Powers of the council.

Supplies granted.

Gloucester's foreign intrigues. 654. From the very first months of the new reign appeared symptoms of divided counsels. Bedford was hard at work on the fabric of alliances which Henry had founded; Gloucester was intriguing and aspiring to make a principality for himself. In April, 1423, Bedford at Amiens[6] concluded an offensive and defensive alliance with the dukes of Burgundy and Brittany, cementing the league by a double marriage, and himself espous-

[1] Rot. Parl. iv. 175; Ordinances, iii. 16.
[2] Rot. Parl. iv. 176.
[3] Ib. iv. 173.
[4] Ib. iv. 174.
[5] Ordinances, iii. 26, 27; Rymer, x. 268.
[6] April 17; Rymer, x. 280, 281.

ing a sister of duke Philip. In March[1] Gloucester had celebrated his marriage with Jacqueline of Hainault, the half divorced wife of the duke of Brabant, and an heiress whose claims were irreconcileable with the interests of the house of Burgundy. All that was to have been gained by the one marriage was thrown to the winds by the other; the strongest injunction of Henry V was disregarded by Humfrey, and the alienation of the Duke of Burgundy began at the moment when his friendship might have been secured for ever. With the same insolent impolicy Gloucester undertook to recover in arms the estates to which Jacqueline was entitled. The year 1423 saw Burgundy delivered from the French by the aid of an English force at Crevant; and in August, 1424, Charles VII was reduced to the lowest point of degradation by the great victory won by Bedford at Verneuil. In October, 1424, Gloucester invaded Hainault, drawing off the duke of Burgundy from France and putting an end to the cordiality of the national alliance[2]. In this attempt he failed even to show the military skill and perseverance that became an English prince: he challenged the duke of Burgundy to single combat; he assumed the title of count of Hainault and Zealand; he persisted in spite of the reproaches of Bedford, who was obliged to purchase the continuance of the alliance at great sacrifices of territory in France. Then he returned to England and left his young wife behind him. When he was once in England Bedford did his best to keep him there, but he soon began to do worse harm still.

He marries Jacqueline of Hainault, and alienates Burgundy.

He invades Hainault.

His return to England.

The government of England whilst Gloucester was thus employed had rested in the hands of the council. A parliament which sat from October, 1423, to February, 1424[3], continued the grants of the year 1422[4]; the members of the council were most of them continued in office, and additional rules framed for

Parliament of 1423-4.

[1] Stevenson, Wars in France, i. p. lii.

[2] Chron. Angl. ed. Giles, p. 7; Monstrelet, liv. ii. c. 22.

[3] Rot. Parl. iv. 197. It opened Oct. 20; John Russell was speaker. The little king was brought into parliament on Nov. 18. The chronicler tells how 'he schriked and cryed and sprang' before he would leave his lodging at Staines; Chron. Lond. p. 112.

[4] The grants were made Feb. 28, the last day of the session; Rot. Parl. iv. 200.

Sir John Mortimer.

council business[1]. Sir John Mortimer, who was charged with a treasonable design in favour of the earl of March, was declared guilty by both lords and commons, and sentenced to death[2]. Peace was made with Scotland and the long-imprisoned king released in January 1424[3]. In the following July bishop Beaufort was again made chancellor[4], either as a check put by Bedford on the vagaries of his brother or as a compromise with Gloucester himself before he started on his expedition. The government remained in his hands during the protector's absence, and he received an additional salary of £2000 for his services[5]. The parliament of 1425[6] was opened by the little king in person; the chancellor in his opening speech inferred the good qualities of a counsellor from the wonderful physical fact that the elephant has no gall, is of inflexible purpose and of great memory. The work of this session was chiefly financial[7]: Beaufort received security for his loans[8]; Gloucester, who had returned from his inglorious expedition, was allowed to borrow 20,000 marks on security given by the council[9]; the subsidies were continued for three years[10]. The three estates condescended further to inhibit the duke from continuing his quarrel with Burgundy, and referred it for arbitration to the queens of

Beaufort chancellor during Gloucester's absence.

His speech at the opening of parliament in 1425.

Parliament forbids war with Burgundy.

[1] Rot. Parl. iv. 201, 202; Rymer, x. 310.

[2] Hall, p. 128; Rot. Parl. iv. 202; Amundesham, i. 6, 7. The earl of March attended this parliament with so large a retinue that the council in alarm sent him to Ireland, where he died soon after; Chron. Giles, p. 6.

[3] Rymer, x. 302–308. On the 13th of February, 1424, King James was released from the payment of 10,000 marks, out of the £40,000 due for his ransom, in consideration of his marriage with Johanna Beaufort, the bishop's niece; ib. p. 322.

[4] July 16; Rymer, x. 340.

[5] Ordinances, iii. 165.

[6] Rot. Parl. iv. 261. It began April 30; Sir Thomas Wauton was speaker; the grant was made on the last day of the session, July 14; ib. p. 75. The convocation granted a half tenth in July; Wilk. Conc. iii. 438.

[7] 'In that parlyment was moche altercacyon bytwyne the lordys and the comyns for tonage and poundage. And at that parlyment was grauntyd that alle maner of alyentys shuld be put to hoste as Englysche men benne in othyr londys, and ovyr that condyscyon was the tonage grauntyd; the whyche condyscyon was brokyn in the same yere by the Byschoppe of Wynchester as the moste pepylle sayde, he beyng chaunseler the same tyme, and therefore there was moche hevynesse and trowbylle in thys londe'; Gregory, p. 157.

[8] Rot. Parl. iv. 275, 277.

[9] Ib. iv. 289.

[10] Ib. iv. 275.

England and France and the duke of Bedford[1]. A dispute for precedency between the earl of Warwick and the earl Marshall was settled by the promotion of the latter to be duke of Norfolk[2]. Although duke Humfrey seems to have escaped animadversion in parliament, he was severely taken to task in council[3]. Beaufort, it may be safely assumed, was unsparing in his strictures; Gloucester seems to have retaliated by an attack on the bishop's administration during his absence: and the result was an open quarrel between uncle and nephew, which peremptorily recalled Bedford to England.

Gloucester quarrels with Beaufort, in 1425.

655. Duke Humfrey had come home deep in debt, as was to be expected, and the council had treated him with unwise liberality: in May they had given him the wardship of the Mortimer estates during the minority of the duke of York[4], and in July had allowed him to borrow the large loan just mentioned. But he was not satisfied. The Tower of London had been garrisoned by Beaufort[5] during the absence of the duke. Gloucester, on the 29th of October, ordered the Lord Mayor of London to prevent him from entering the city[6]. A riot followed on the 30th, in which the Archbishop of Canterbury and the Duke of Coimbra had to mediate between the conflicting parties. It was finally resolved that Bedford should arbitrate, and on the 31st the chancellor wrote to him imploring him to return if he would save the state[7]. On the 5th of November, at Guildford, the council, acting on the order of the last parliament, allowed the protector to borrow £5000 of the king, to be repaid when Henry should reach the age of fifteen. This was charged on the tenth last granted by the clergy, although the government was at the very time being carried on by the voluntary loans of the lords of the council[8]. Probably this was done in Beaufort's absence.

Riot in London.

Beaufort sends for Bedford.

Loans by the council to Gloucester.

[1] Rot. Parl. iv. 277.
[2] Ib. iv. 262–274.
[3] Ordinances, iii. 174; Monstrelet, liv. ii. c. 32.
[4] Ordinances, iii. 169. The duke was allowed further to borrow 9000 marks of the king on July 9, 1427; Rymer, x. 374.
[5] Beaufort's force was from Cheshire and Lancashire. Cf. Monstrelet, liv. ii. c. 36.
[6] Chron. London, p. 114.
[7] The letter, dated Oct. 31, is given by Hall, p. 130.
[8] Ordinances, iii. 179. The loan of July 1427 was assigned on the customs, the duchy of Lancaster, and the proceeds of wardships; Rymer, x. 375; Ordinances, iii. 271.

Bedford returns.

It was time that Bedford should return; he left France on receipt of his uncle's letter, and landed at Sandwich on the 20th of December[1].

Treaty of alliance between the two brothers.

656. The two brothers had not met since the death of Henry V, and Gloucester was not able to resist the personal influence of Bedford. It is probably to this period that we should refer an interesting document, preserved among the letters of bishop Beckington, duke Humfrey's chancellor[2]. In this treaty of alliance, as it professes to be, the duty of fraternal unity is solemnly laid down, and a contract published which is to disarm for the future the tongues of meddlers and detractors. Seven articles follow, by which the dukes undertake to bear true allegiance to the king; next to the king to honour and serve each other, to abstain from aiding each other's enemies, to reveal to each other all designs that are directed against either, to refuse belief to calumnious accusations, to form no alliances without common consent or in prejudice of their common alliances. These latter articles were no doubt called for by Gloucester's treatment of the duke of Burgundy. Queen Katharine also appears to have joined in the contract. On the 7th of January was issued[3] a summons for parliament to meet on the 18th of February at Leicester: the intervening weeks were spent in an attempt to reconcile duke Humfrey with the chancellor. On the 29th of January, archbishop Chichele, the earl of Stafford, lords Talbot and Cromwell, and Sir John Cornwall, were sent to the duke, with elaborate instructions from Bedford and the council, which had met at St. Alban's[4]. It was proposed that the council should reassemble at Northampton on the 13th of February to prepare business for the parliament; at this council Gloucester was first invited and then urged to attend, as he valued the unity of the land and the common good of the subject; the enmity between the duke and his uncle must of necessity come before parliament, it were well that it should be ended before the day of meeting: the duke had

Parliament summoned.

Gloucester invited to attend council.

[1] Bedford came to London, Jan. 10; Gregory, p. 160.

[2] Beckington's Letters, ed. Williams, i. 139–145.

[3] Lords' Report, iv. 863.

[4] Ordinances, iii. 181–187.

refused to come to Northampton if he should there meet the chancellor; he was implored to set that feeling aside; there would be no fear of a riot; the bishop had undertaken to keep his men in order, and the peace would be duly kept: it was unreasonable in Gloucester, and even if he were king it would be unreasonable in him, to refuse to meet a peer; the king and council were determined that Gloucester should have his rights; he could not insist on Beaufort's removal from office, but if anything were proved against Beaufort, he would of course be dismissed. If Gloucester refused to attend the council, he must come to the parliament, and in that assembly the king would execute justice without respect of persons. Whether the duke complied with the request does not appear; but the matter was not settled when the parliament, which is called by the annalists the parliament of bats or bludgeons, met. The chancellor opened the proceedings with a speech, in which he made no reference to the quarrel; for ten days the two parties stood face to face, nothing being done in consequence of their hostile attitude. On the 28th of February the commons sent in an urgent prayer that the divisions among the lords should be reconciled[3], and Bedford and the peers solemnly undertook the arbitration; on the 7th of March Gloucester and Beaufort consented to abide by that arbitration, and to make peace on the terms which should be prescribed. The charges of Gloucester against his uncle were stated; he had shut the Tower of London against him, had purposed to seize the king's person, had plotted to destroy Gloucester when visiting the king, had attempted the murder of Henry V when prince of Wales, and had urged him to usurp his father's crown. The bishop explained his conduct as impugned in the first and third charges, and denied the truth of the rest. The arbitrators determined that Beaufort should solemnly deny the truth of the charges of treason against Henry IV, Henry V, and Henry VI,

Arguments addressed to him.

The Parliament of Bats.

Bedford and the lords mediate.

[1] Gregory, p. 160.

[2] Rot. Parl. iv. 295. The speaker was Sir Richard Vernon; the grant was made June 1. Cf. Amundesham, i. 9, 10; Chron. Giles, pp. 8, 9. The clergy, April 27, granted a half tenth and a farthing in the pound; Wilk. Conc. iii. 461, 462.

[3] Rot. Parl. iv. 296; Ordinances, iii. 187.

Pacification and resignation of Beaufort.

whereupon Bedford should declare him loyal: he should then disavow all designs against Gloucester, who should accept the disavowal; and they should then take each other by the hand[1]. This was done and recorded on the 12th of March[2]; on the 14th, Beaufort resigned the great seal, and the treasurer, bishop Stafford, prayed to be discharged of the treasurership. John Kemp, bishop of London, became chancellor, and Walter lord Hungerford treasurer[3]. On the 20th the parliament was prorogued, to meet again on the 29th of April. In the second meeting, grants of tunnage, poundage, and the subsidy on wool were granted[4], extending to November, 1431; the council had been already empowered to give security for loans amounting to £40,000. On the 1st of June the parliament separated. The king had during the latter days of the session received from his uncle Bedford the honour of knighthood.

Money grants.

Beaufort trusts in the council.

Bedford stayed sixteen months in England, and Beaufort, before he left, appeared from time to time at the council board[5]; at the end of the year he lost his brother the duke of Exeter, and he probably thought that he might bide his time. He had undergone a personal discomfiture, but the council might be trusted not to allow duke Humfrey to have his own way. The chancellor Kemp too, now archbishop of York, was a resolute defender of constitutional right. In contemplation of his return to France, Bedford held a council in the Star Chamber on the 28th of January[6]. The chancellor, as spokesman of the council, addressed him in a speech probably pre-arranged in order to produce some effect on Gloucester. He reminded him of the great responsibility which lay on that body during the king's minority. The king, child as he was, centered in his person all the authority that could belong to a grown-up king,

Address to Bedford by archbishop Kemp.

[1] The articles are given by Hall, Chr. pp. 130, 131; and Beaufort's answers, pp. 131–134; then the arbitrament, pp. 135–138; they are not stated in the rolls of parliament. See also Arnold, Chr. pp. 287, 300.

[2] Rot. Parl. iv. 297.

[3] Ib. iv. 299; Amundesham, i. 9; Rymer, x. 353.

[4] Rot. Parl. iv. 302.

[5] Beaufort was a member of the council Nov. 24, and Dec. 8, 1426, and March 8 and 10, 1427; Ordinances, iii. 213, 221, 226, 255.

[6] Ordinances, iii. 231–242.

but the execution of that authority stood 'in his lords, assembled either by authority of his parliament, or in his council, and in especial in the lords of his council,' who might be called to account for their administration; 'not in one singular person, but in all my lords together,' except where the parliament had given definite powers to the protector; the council therefore asked for the duke's opinion on the present state of affairs, and the feasibility of the present system of government[1]. Bedford replied that it was his wish to act in all things under advice and governance of the council, and then, with tears in his eyes, swore on the gospels that he would be counselled and ruled by them. On the following day the chancellor and council, thus fortified with a precedent, visited Gloucester, who was lying ill at his lodgings, and administered a formal remonstrance; it was impossible for them to carry on the government if he continued to claim the position which on several occasions he had claimed. He had said more than once that 'if he had done anything that touched the king in his sovereign estate, he would not answer for it to any person alive save only to the king when he came to his age;' he had also said, 'Let my brother govern as him list whilst he is in this land, for after his going over into France I will govern as me seemeth good.' The council hoped that he would give them the same answer that they had had from Bedford; and in fact Gloucester, after some words of apology, repeated his brother's declaration. Bedford now prepared to return to France; on the 25th of February[2] the council resolved that it had been the late king's intention that he should devote himself to the maintenance of the English hold on Normandy; and the little king, now five years old, was made to understand

The authority of the council defined.

Bedford undertakes to respect it.

Gloucester asked to make the same promise.

Bedford takes leave.

[1] There are two copies of the minute, in which this statement is worded somewhat differently; the words occur as in the text in Ord. iii. 238; at p. 233 the sentence stands thus: 'the execution of the king's said authority, as toward that that belongeth unto the politique rule and governaille of his land, and to the observance and keeping of his laws, belongeth unto the lords spiritual and temporal of this land at such time as they be assembled in parliament or in great council, and else, them nought being so assembled, unto the lords chosen and named to be of his continual council.'

[2] Ordinances, iii. 247.

that his uncle must leave him. On the 26th, the crown, which had been kept by bishop Beaufort as a pledge, was placed in the custody of the treasurer[1]; on the 8th of March, the king, with Bedford, Beaufort, and the council, were at Canterbury. Immediately afterwards Bedford left. Beaufort accompanied him. On the 14th of May, 1426, he had applied for leave to go on pilgrimage[2]. He did not return until September, 1428, having in the meanwhile been made a cardinal, legate of the apostolic see, and commander of a crusade against the Hussites[3].

Departure of Bedford and Beaufort.

657. The conduct of Gloucester, when thus relieved from the pressure of his brother and uncle, was what might have been expected. He resumed his designs against Burgundy, and attempted to sow discord in his brother's council. A very summary threat from Bedford was required before he would desist[4]. In July he obtained the consent of the council to raise men and money to garrison Jacqueline's castles and towns in Holland; no further conquests were however to be attempted without the consent of parliament[5]. Parliament was summoned for the 13th of October[6], but Gloucester was not allowed to open it; the little king presided in person. Little was done in the first session, and on the 8th of December it was prorogued. In the second session, which began on the 20th of January, Gloucester began to show his hand again. On the 3rd of March he demanded of the lords a definition of his powers as 'protector and defender of the realm of England and chief counsellor of the king.' He quitted the assembly that the lords might consider the question at their ease. They returned a written answer, in which they reminded him that

Gloucester resumes his designs against Burgundy.

Parliament of 1427-8.

[1] Ordinances, iii. 250.
[2] Ellis, Originals Letters, 2nd Series, i. 101; Ordinances, iii. 195; Rymer, x. 358.
[3] On Beaufort's expedition to Bohemia, where he was in the autumn of 1427, see Æneas Sylvius, Hist. Bohem. c. 48; opp. p. 116; Raynald, A. D. 1427, § 5; Palacky, Gesch. v. Böhmen, iii. 438-467.
[4] Monstrelet, liv. ii. c. 38.
[5] Ordinances. iii. 271; see above p. 101.
[6] Rot. Parl. iv. 316. John Tyrell was speaker. In this parliament a number of women presented themselves with a letter complaining of duke Humfrey's behaviour to his wife; Amund. i. 20.

at the beginning of the reign he had claimed the governance of the land in right of his blood and of the late king's will; that thereupon the records of the kingdom had been searched for precedents, and the claim refused as grounded neither on history nor on law, the late king having no power to dispose of the government of England after his death without the consent of the estates. Notwithstanding this, in order to maintain the peace of the land, he had been declared chief of the council in his brother's absence; but to avoid the use of the title of Tutor, Lieutenant, Governor, or Regent, the name of Protector and Defender was given him; 'the which importeth a personal duty of intendance to the actual defence of the land,' with certain powers specified and contained in the act. If the estates had intended him to have further powers, they would have given them in that act. On those terms he had accepted the office. The parliament however knew him only as duke of Gloucester, and saw no reason why they should recognise in him more authority than had been formally given him. They therefore prayed, exhorted, and required him to be content, and not desire, will, or use any larger power. By this reply they were determined to stand, and they subscribed it with their own hands, eleven bishops, four abbots, the duke of Norfolk, three earls, and eight barons[1]. The consent of the commons was not asked, but they showed their confidence in the council by making liberal grants; they were empowered to give security for a loan of £24,000; tunnage and poundage was granted for a year, and a new complicated form of subsidy was voted[2]. Such a very decided rebuff would have quelled the spirit of a braver man than Gloucester; but the council did

The lords, at Gloucester's request, define the powers of the protector.

Grants of money in parliament.

[1] Rot. Parl. iv. 326, 327.

[2] Ib. iv. 317, 318: the grants were made on March 25, the last day of the parliament; Amund. i. 20.

The subsidy was very curious; all parishes the churches of which were taxed above ten marks, were to pay 13*s*. 4*d*.; below that sum 6*s*. 8*d*.; parishes containing ten inhabited houses, with the parish church assessed up to 20*s*, paid 2*s*.; every knight's fee paid 6*s*. 8*d*. The tax was to be paid by the parishioners; Amund. i. 21; Rot. Parl. iv. 318; Dep. Keeper's Rep. iii. 9. The clergy in convocation also granted a half tenth and a graduated tax on stipendiaries; ib. p. 11. See below, p. 109.

Warwick acts as tutor to the king.

not stop there. Henry V had directed that the earl of Warwick should be the preceptor of his son. On the 1st of June Warwick was summoned by the chancellor to perform his office; special instructions are given him[1]; he is to do his devoir and diligence to exhort, stir, and learn the king to love, worship, and dread God, and generally nourish him and draw him to virtue by lessons of history; he is further to teach him 'nurture, literature, language, and other manner of cunning as his age shall suffer him to comprehend such as it fitteth so great a prince to be learned of.' He shall have power to chastise him if he does amiss, to dismiss improper servants, and to remove the king's person in case of any unforeseen danger. Warwick, who lived to attend on Henry until he was eighteen, discharged his duties faithfully, and made his pupil a good scholar and an accomplished gentleman. He could not make him a strong or a happy man.

Beaufort's error in accepting the cardinal's hat.

Beaufort had made the great mistake of his life in 1426, in accepting the cardinalate[2]. He may well be excused for grasping at what was the natural object of clerical ambition in his time, an object which ten years before he had foregone at the urgent entreaty of Henry V, and which now seemed all the more desireable when he saw himself ousted for a time from his commanding position in the English council. But it was not the less a blunder; it involved him immediately in the great quarrel which was going on at the time between the church

His legation.

and state of England and the papacy; it to some extent alienated the national goodwill, for the legation of a cardinal

[1] Ordinances, iii. 296; Rymer, x. 399; further instructions were given in 1432; Ordinances. iv. 132.

[2] He was nominated to the cardinalate as early as Dec. 28, 1417, (Wharton, Ang. Sax. i. 800) by Martin V at the council of Constance. Chichele addressed a strong protest on the matter to Henry V; this is printed by Duck in his life of Chichele (ed. 1699, pp. 115–131). According to Gloucester's letter of accusation written in 1440 (Stevenson, Wars in France, ii. 441) Henry refused him leave to accept the dignity, saying that 'he had as leef sette his coroune beside hym as to se him were a cardinal's hatte, he being a cardinal.' The second nomination was made on the 24th of May 1426 (Panvinius, Epitome Pontificum, p. 291), the title being that of S. Eusebius; on the the 25th of the next March he received the cardinal's hat at Rouen. See Gregory, Chron. p. 161; Chron. Lond. p. 115; Hall, p. 139; Amund. i. 11.

was inextricably bound up in the popular mind with heavy fees and procurations, and it gave Gloucester an opportunity for attack which he had sought for in vain before. His share in the ecclesiastical struggle forms part of a very intricate episode in our church history which cannot be touched upon here. The bearings of his promotion on popular opinion and on his relations to Gloucester were immediately apparent. He returned to England in 1428, and was solemnly received at London by the lord mayor and citizens on the 1st of September. Gloucester in the king's name refused to recognise his legatine authority[1]. He had already forwarded to Chichele the papal bull under which he was commissioned to raise money for the Hussite crusade. On the 23rd of November two papal envoys informed the convocation of Canterbury[2] that the pope had imposed the payment of an entire tenth for the Bohemian war. Some similar proposition had been made to the council in the preceding May, but little notice was taken of the subject until the cardinal returned. The alarm of a new impost, on a nation already bearing its burdens somewhat impatiently, gave Gloucester his opportunity. The cardinal was treated with great respect, and allowed to go on his mission to Scotland[3], but on the 17th of April, 1429, a question was raised in council which involved his right to retain the bishopric of Winchester; ought he, being a cardinal, to be allowed to officiate as bishop of Winchester and prelate of the Order of the Garter at the approaching feast of S. George. The lords being severally consulted refused to determine the point, but begged the bishop to waive his right[4]. Notwithstanding this indication of his weakness, Beaufort, on the 18th of June, obtained leave from the king and council to retain 500 lances and 2500 archers for his expedition[5]. On the same day was fought the battle of Patay,

Beaufort's legation.

Alarm at his proceedings in connexion with the Hussite crusade.

Gloucester attacks him.

He is allowed to enlist forces.

[1] Gregory, p. 162; Amund. i. 26; Foxe, Acts and Monuments, iii. 719.

[2] The convocation opened July 5, and closed about Nov. 30, after granting a half tenth to the king, and making some ordinances against the Lollards; Amund. i. 24, 32; Wilkins, Conc. iii. 493 sq. 496 sq. 503.

[3] Amund. i. 33, 34; he passed through S. Alban's on his way Feb. 12, and on his return about April 11; ib.; Ordinances, iii. 318.

[4] Ordinances, iii. 323; Rymer, x. 414.

[5] Ordinances, iii. 330-332; Rymer, x. 419-422.

Beaufort's forces lent to Bedford.

in which Talbot the English general was taken[1], and this, coupled with the relief of Orleans by the Maid of Orleans in the preceding month, had a marked effect on the council. On the 1st of July, at Rochester, the council agreed with the cardinal that his forces should be allowed to serve in France under Bedford for half a year[2]. He yielded the point graciously; the approaching parliament would have to decide whether he had bettered his position.

Parliament of 1429.

658. The parliament met on the 22nd of September[3]. The condition of France was such that the council of that kingdom had strongly urged the coronation of the young king[4]. Before he could be crowned king of France he must be crowned king of England; preparations were accordingly made somewhat hurriedly, and the ceremony was performed at Westminster on the 6th of November[5]. As soon as England had a crowned king the office and duty of the protector terminated, and the lords spiritual and temporal voted that it should cease; on the 15th of November Gloucester was obliged to renounce it, retaining only the title of chief counsellor, but leaving it open to Bedford to retain or surrender it as he pleased[6]. This stroke told in favour of the cardinal, who seems to have retained more power in parliament than in the council. The question of his position had been raised in a new form; was it lawful for him, a cardinal, to take his place in the king's council; the lords voted not only that it was lawful, but that the bishop should be required to attend the councils on all occasions on which the relations of the king with the court of Rome were not in question. He

Henry's coronation.

End of the protectorate.

Failure of the attempt to exclude Beaufort from council.

[1] Monstrelet, liv. ii. c. 61.

[2] Ordinances, iii. 339. On June 22 the cardinal had set out for Bohemia, but remained in France with the regent, and returned for the coronation. Gregory, p. 164; Hall, p. 152; Amund. i. 38, 39, 42; Rymer, x. 424, 427; Chron. Giles, p. 10. He lost his legation on the death of Martin V in 1431, and the whole project came to an end.

[3] Rot. Parl. iv. 335; Amund. i. 42. William Alyngton was speaker.

[4] Rymer, x. 413, 414; letters to this effect were laid before a great council on April 15, 1429; Ordinances, iii. 322; and the king announced his intention of going to France, Dec. 20; ib. iv. 10.

[5] The ceremonies are detailed in Gregory's Chronicle, pp. 165 sq. The amnulla was used; Ordinances, iv. 7.

[6] Rot. Parl. iv. 336; Rymer, x. 436.

graciously accepted the position on the 18th of December[1], and used his influence with the commons to such purpose that on the 20th they voted a fifteenth and tenth to the king in addition to a like sum granted on the 12th, with tunnage and poundage until the next parliament[2]. The same day parliament was prorogued to the 14th of January; in the second session the subsidy on wool was continued to November, 1433; the council had already been empowered to give security for loans to the amount of £50,000[3], and the payment of the second fifteenth was hastened[4]. The nation was awaking to the necessity of a great effort to save the conquests in France. The most important statute of this parliament was one which further regulated the elections of knights of the shire, and fixed the forty shilling freehold as the qualification for voting[5]. The county elections had been a subject of intermittent legislation since the beginning of the century, but it is difficult to connect the successive changes which were introduced with any political or personal influences prevailing at the time: the matter must be considered in another chapter, and it may be sufficient to say here that as the changes in the law scarcely at all affected the composition of the House of Commons, the particular steps of the change probably resulted from local instances of undue influence and violence. It must not, however, be forgotten that the historians under Richard II had complained of the exercise of crown influence, and that the cry was repeated by the malcontents under Henry IV.

Financial measures.

Second session, Jan. 1430.

Law of county elections.

It is a wearisome task to trace the continuance of the fatal quarrel between Beaufort and Gloucester, but it is the main string of English political history for the time. Lollardy was smouldering in secret; the heavy burdens of the nation were wearily borne; Bedford was wearing out life and hope in a struggle that was now seen to be desperate. The Maid of

[1] Rot. Parl. iv. 338.

[2] Ib. iv. 336, 337; Amund. i. 44. The clergy in October 1429, granted a tenth and a half; Wilk. Conc. iii. 515; and in March 1430, another tenth; Wilk. Conc. iii. 517.

[3] Rot. Parl. iv. 339, 341, 342. Commissions for raising a loan on this security were issued May 19, 1430; Rymer, x. 461.

[4] Rot. Parl. iv. 342; Amund. i. 46, 48.

[5] Rot. Parl. iv. 350.

The Maid of Orleans. Orleans was captured on the 26th of May, 1430, and burned as a witch on the 31st of May, 1431; Bedford might perhaps have interfered to save her, but such an exercise of magnanimity would have been unparalleled in such an age, and the peculiarly stern religiousness of his character was no more likely to relax in her favour than it had in Oldcastle's. On the 17th of December, 1431, Henry was crowned king of France at Paris by Beaufort.

Beaufort goes to France. 659. Henry's absence in France gave Gloucester a chance in his turn. Long deliberations in council were needed before the expedition could be arranged; on the 16th of April, 1430, the cardinal agreed to accompany his grand nephew[1]; on the 21st Gloucester was appointed lieutenant and custos of the kingdom[2]. Gloucester remains as lieutenant of the kingdom. On the 23rd Henry sailed with a large retinue, and remained abroad for nearly two years. During this time the duty of maintaining the authority of the council devolved on archbishop Kemp, who, although he managed to act with Gloucester in his new capacity as custos, had on more than one occasion to oppose him, and was made as soon as the court returned to pay the penalty of his temerity. Jack Sharp's plot. The year 1431 witnessed a bold attempt at rebellion made by the political Lollards under a leader named Jack Sharp, who was captured and put to death at Oxford in May[3]. The parliament of 1431[4] was chiefly occupied with the financial difficulties. The country was becoming more convinced of its own exhaustion, and debt was annually increasing[5]. New methods of taxation were tried and failed. This year, besides fifteenths and tenths, tunnage and poundage, and the continued

[1] Ord. iv. 35–38; Rymer, x. 456. [2] Ord. iv. 40 sq.; Rymer, x. 458.

[3] Jack Sharp's petition for the confiscation and appropriation of the temporalities of the church, being the same proposition as that put forth in 1410 (above, p. 64) is printed from the MS. Harl. 3775 in Amundesham (ed. Riley), i. 453; cf. Hall, Chr. p. 166; Amund. i. 63; Gregory, p. 172; Chron. Lond. p. 119; Ellis, Orig. Lett. 2nd Series, i. 103; Ordinances, iv. 89, 99, 107; Chron. Giles, p. 18.

[4] The parliament, called in pursuance of a resolution of the great council held Oct. 6, 1430, opened Jan. 12, 1431; Rot. Parl. iv. 367; Amund. i. 57; Ordinances, iv. 67. John Tyrell was again speaker. The grants were made on the 20th of March.

[5] In a great council, Oct. 9, 1430, the bishops and abbots lent large sums, and soon after a fifteenth was levied; Amund. i. 55. On the 12th of July, 1430, orders were issued for constraint of knighthood; Ord. iv. 54.

subsidy, a grant was made of twenty shillings on the knights' fee or twenty pounds rental[1]; and security authorised for a loan of £50,000[2]. The payments for Beaufort's services were a large item in the national account; Gloucester was still more rapacious, and he did not, like his uncle, hold his stores at the disposal of the state. On the 6th of November the duke again mooted in council the removal of the cardinal[3], this time directly. The king's serjeant and attorney laid before the lords in general council a series of precedents by which it was shown that every English bishop who had accepted a cardinal's hat vacated his see; the duke of Gloucester asked the bishop of Worcester whether it was not true that the cardinal had bought for himself an exemption from the jurisdiction of his metropolitan; and the bishop, when pressed to speak, allowed that he had heard this stated by the bishop of Lichfield who had acted as Beaufort's proctor. The bishops and other lords present professed that their first object was the good of the kingdom, and said that, considering the cardinal's great services and near relationship to the king, they wished justice to be done on a fair trial, and ancient records to be searched. The bishop of Carlisle voted that nothing be done until the cardinal's return[4]. Notwithstanding this, on the 28th of November the council ordered letters of praemunire and attachment upon the statute to be drawn up, the execution of them being deferred until the king's return. The same day there was a brisk debate on the question of the protector's salary, in which the chancellor and treasurer were outvoted by Gloucester's friends[5] led by the lord Scrope. Before the king's return additional offence was given by the seizure of the cardinal's plate and jewels when they were landed at Dover[6]. Beaufort was still abroad, and Gloucester took the opportunity which his absence offered, and which perhaps an

Grants of money.

Discussions in council on Beaufort's position;

and on the protector's salary.

Beaufort's jewels seized.

[1] Rot. Parl. iv. 368, 369; Amund. i. 58.
[2] Rot. Parl. iv. 374.
[3] Ordinances, iv. 100.
[4] Ib. iv. 103; Rymer, x. 497.
[5] Kemp and Hungerford were supported by the bishop of Carlisle, lords Harrington, De la Warr, Lovell, and Botreaux; Ordinances, iv. 103.
[6] Beaufort had returned to England Dec. 21, 1430, and attended the parliament of 1431, but went back to France after Easter; Amund, i. 56, 58, 62; Rymer, x. 491.

Change of ministers on the king's return.

increasing personal influence over the king helped him to seize, to remove the ministers and make a great alteration in his nephew's surroundings. The king landed on the 9th of February; on the 26th Hungerford had to resign the treasurership to Scrope; on the 1st of March lord Cromwell the chamberlain was dismissed, and lord Tiptoft was relieved from the stewardship of the household[1]; on the 4th of March, the great seal, which the archbishop of York had resigned on February 25, was confided to John Stafford, bishop of Bath[2]; other minor changes followed.

Parliament of 1432.

As might be expected, the cardinal speedily returned home and the next parliament was a stormy one.

660. It met on the 12th of May at Westminster before the king in person[3], and was opened by the new chancellor with a speech on the text 'Fear God, honour the King;' the three points of application being the defence of religion, the maintenance of law, and the relief of the national poverty; the last a new feature in such addresses, but probably introduced now in consequence of a real pressure. On the second day Gloucester spoke, in the idea, he said, of assuring the commons that the lords were agreed among themselves[4]: he was, it was true, the king's nearest kinsman, and had been constituted by act of parliament his chief counsellor, but it was not his wish therefore to act without the advice and consent of the other lords; he accordingly asked their assistance and promised to act on their advice; the lords signified their agreement, and this pleasing fiction of concord was announced by the chancellor to the commons. The duke had by this assertion of his intentions thrown down the gauntlet. Beaufort took it up and made a successful appeal to the estates. He declared that, having with due licence from the king set out for Rome, he had, when in Flanders, been recalled to England by the report that

Gloucester professes his desire of concord.

Formal complaint of the cardinal.

[1] Rymer, x. 502; Ordinances, iv. 109. Hardyng speaks highly of lord Cromwell's wisdom, perhaps referring to his money-getting craft, p. 395.

[2] Rymer, x. 500, 501.

[3] Rot. Parl. iv. 388. John Russell was speaker; the grants were reported July 17. The council had on the 7th addressed writs to the duke of Norfolk, the earls of Suffolk, Huntingdon, Stafford, Northumberland, and lord Cromwell, forbidding them to bring up more than their ordinary retinue; Ordinances, iv. 112.

[4] Rot. Parl. iv. 389.

he was accused of treason. He had returned to meet the charge: let the accuser stand forth and he would answer it. The demand was debated before the king and Gloucester, and the answer was that no such charge had been made against him, and the king accounted him loyal. Beaufort asked that this proceeding might be recorded, and it was done[1]. In the matter of the jewels he was easily satisfied: they were restored to him, and he agreed to lend Henry £6000, to be repaid in case the king within six years should be convinced that the jewels had been illegally seized, and £6000 more as an ordinary loan. At the same time he respited the payment of 13,000 marks which were already due to him[2]. The victory, for it was a victory, was thus dearly purchased; but Beaufort probably saw that the choice of alternatives was very limited, and that it was better to lend than to lose. His sacrifice was appreciated by the commons. On their petition a statute was passed which secured him against all risks of praemunire[3]. Encouraged by the cardinal's success, lord Cromwell, on the 16th of June, laid his complaint before the lords; he had, contrary to the sworn articles by which the council was regulated, been removed from his office of chamberlain: he recounted his services, producing Bedford's testimony to his character, and demanded to be told whether he had been removed for some fault or offence. Gloucester refused to bring forward any charge against him. He was told that his removal was not owing to his fault, but was the pleasure of the duke and the council; and this formal acquittal was enrolled at his request among the records of parliament[4]. On the 15th of July the supplies were granted; half a tenth and fifteenth was voted, with tunnage and poundage for two years; and the subsidy on wool was continued until November 1435[5]. Of the

The king declares him loyal.

A compromise.

Lord Cromwell asks to be told the reason of his dismissal.

He is answered.

Grant of supplies.

[1] Rot. Parl. iv. 390, 391; Rymer, x. 517.

[2] Rot. Parl. iv. 391; Rymer, x. 518. In 1434 Henry promised that the £6000 should be repaid and then Beaufort lent £10,000 more; Ordinances, iv. 236–239.

[3] Rot. Parl. iv. 392; Rymer, x. 516.

[4] Rot. Parl. iv. 392.

[5] Ib. iv. 389. The Canterbury clergy granted a half tenth, the York clergy a quarter of a tenth; Wilk. Conc. iii. 521,

Minor transactions in parliament.

minor transactions of the parliament some were important; Sir John Cornwall, who had married the duchess of Exeter, daughter of John of Gaunt, was created baron of Fanhope in parliament[1]; the duke of York was declared of age; and the statute of 1430 was amended by the enactment that the freehold qualification of the county electors must lie within the shire[2]. The complicated grant of land and income tax of 1431, which it was found impossible to collect, was annulled[3]. Two petitions of the commons, one praying that men might not be called before parliament or council in cases touching freehold[4], the other affecting the privileges of members molested on their way to parliament[5], were negatived. The result of the proceedings was on the whole advantageous to Gloucester; he had failed to crush the cardinal, but he retained his predominance in the council. He was not to retain it long.

Proceedings of Bedford in France.

661. The hopes of the English in France were rapidly waning. The duke of Burgundy was growing tired of the struggle, Bedford's health and strength were rapidly giving way. The death of his wife in November 1432 broke the strongest link that bound him to duke Philip, and a new marriage which he concluded early in 1433 with the sister of the count of S. Pol, instead of adding to the number of his allies, weakened his hold on Burgundy. Negotiations were set on foot for a general pacification. Gloucester spent a month on the continent, trying his hand at diplomacy[6]; and immediately on his return summoned the parliament to meet in July. In the interval Bedford and Burgundy met at S. Omer, and the coolness between them became a quarrel, although they had still so great interests in common that they could not afford to break up their alliance.

[1] Rot. Parl. iv. 400; '17mo die Julii ultimo die praesentis parliamenti, in trium statuum ejusdem parliamenti praesentia de avisamento ... dominorum spiritualium et temporalium in parliamento praedicto existentuum, praefatum Johannem in baronem indigenam regni sui Angliae erexit praefecit et creavit.' Cf. Rymer, x. 524. The Chronicle published by Dr. Giles, p. 9, states that Cornwall was made baron of Fanhope, and the lords Cromwell, Tiptoft, and Hungerford were created at Leicester in 1426.

[2] Rot. Parl. iv. 409; Statutes, ii. 273.

[3] Rot. Parl. iv. 409.

[4] Ib. iv. 403.

[5] Ib. iv. 404.

[6] April 22 to May 23; Rymer, x. 548, 549.

At the end of June Bedford visited England once more, and he was present at the beginning of the session[1]. Whether he had seen or heard anything that led him to suspect his brother's friendship, it is not easy to say; but on the sixth day of the parliament he announced that he had come home to defend himself against false accusations. It had been asserted, as he understood, that the losses which the king had sustained in France were caused by his neglect; he prayed that his accusers might be made to stand forth and prove the charges[2]. After mature deliberation the chancellor answered him: no such charges had reached the ears of the king, the duke of Gloucester, or the council. The king retained full confidence in him as his faithful liegeman and dearest uncle, and thanked him for his great services and for coming home at last. A sudden alarm of plague broke up the session in August, to be resumed in October[3]; but the effect of Bedford's visit on the administration was already apparent; lord Cromwell before the prorogation was appointed treasurer of the kingdom[4], and in the interim prepared an elaborate statement of the national accounts. Money was so scarce that the parliament authorised him to stay all regular payments until he had £2000 in hand for petty expenses. Cromwell's statement of the national finances[5] was brought up on the 18th of October, and was alarming if not appalling. The ancient ordinary revenue of the crown, which in the gross amounted to £23,000, was reduced by fixed charges to £8,990; the duchy of Lancaster furnished £2,408 clear, the indirect taxes on wine, and other merchandise brought in an estimated sum of £26,966 more. The government of Ireland just paid its expenses; the duchy of Guienne, the remnant of the great inheritance of queen Eleanor, furnished only £77 0*s.* 8¾*d.*: the expenses of Calais, £9,064 15*s.* 6*d.*, exceeded the whole of the ordinary revenue of the crown. The sum

Parliament of 1433.

Bedford defends himself against false charges.

Change of Treasurer.

Lord Cromwell's financial statement.

[1] Parliament opened July 8; Roger Hunt was the speaker; Rot. Parl. iv. 419, 420; Stow, p. 373; Fabyan, p. 607. Bedford reached London June 23; Chr. Lond. p. 120.

[2] Rot. Parl. iv. 420.

[3] The parliament was prorogued Aug. 13, to meet again Oct. 13; Rot. Parl. iv. 420.

[4] Aug. 11; Ordinances, iv. 175.

[5] Rot. Parl. iv. 432–439.

Financial statement.

available for administration, £38,364, was altogether insufficient to meet the expenditure, which was estimated at £56,878, and there were debts to the amount of £164,814 11*s.* 1½*d.* It is probable that the accounts of the kingdom had been in much worse order under Edward III and Richard II, but the general state of things had never been less hopeful. All expenses were increasing, all sources of supply were diminishing. But there could not have been much maladministration; a single annual grant of a fifteenth would be sufficient to balance revenue and expenditure and would leave something to pay off the debt.

Bedford's proposal to economise.

There was reason for careful economy; Bedford determined to make an effort to secure so much at least, and the discussion of public business was resumed on the 3rd of November[1]. On that day the commons, after praying that a proclamation might be issued for the suppression of riotous assemblies, which were taking place in several parts of England, requested that the duke of Bedford would make, and the duke of Gloucester and

Declaration of concord.

the council would renew, the promise of concord and mutual co-operation which had been offered in the last parliament. This was done, and the two houses followed the example[2]. On the 24th the speaker addressed the king in a long speech, extolling the character and services of Bedford, and stating

The Commons pray Bedford to stay in England.

the belief of the commons that his continued stay in England would be the greatest conceivable security to the well-being of the king and his realms: he besought the king to request the duke to abide still in the land. The lords, on being consulted by the chancellor, seconded the prayer of the commons, and the proposal was at once laid before the duke. Bedford, in a touching speech, full of modesty and simplicity, declared

His self-denying offer.

himself at the king's disposal. The next day, giving a laudable example of self-denial, he offered to accept a salary of £1000 as chief counsellor instead of the 5000 marks which Gloucester had been receiving[4], and on the 28th Gloucester in council

[1] A very peremptory summons was issued on Nov. 1 for the immediate attendance of several lay lords and abbots; Lords' Report, iv. 887.

[2] Rot. Parl. iv. 421, 422.

[3] Ib. iv. 423.

[4] The wages of the councillors are a constantly recurring topic in all the records of the time; see especially Rymer, x. 360; Ordinances, iii. 156,

agreed to accept the same sum[1]. At the close of the session the archbishops, the cardinal, and the bishops of Lincoln and Ely agreed to give their attendance without payment, if they were not obliged to be present in vacation[2]. This simple measure effected a clear saving of more than £2000 a year. The good-will of the commons followed on the good example of the council; a grant of one fifteenth and tenth, minus the sum of £4000 which was to be applied to the relief of poor towns, was voted, and tunnage and poundage continued[3]. The fifteenth would bring in at least £33,000, and the clerical grant voted in November[4] would give about £9,000 more. The council was empowered to give security for 100,000 marks of debt[5], and it was agreed, on the treasurer's proposal, that the accounts should be audited in council[6]. On the 18th of December Bedford produced the articles of condition on which he proposed to undertake the office of counsellor; he wished to know who would be the members of the continual council; he demanded that without his advice and that of the council no members should be added or removed, that the opinion of the council should be taken as to the appointments to great offices of state, that he should, wherever he was, be consulted about the summoning of parliament and the appointment to bishoprics, and that a record should be kept of the names of old servants of the king, who should be rewarded as occasion might offer. All these points were conceded, and the duke entered upon his office[7].

Economics in the council.

Grants in parliament.

Bedford undertakes the office of chief counsellor.

But he was destined to no peaceful or long tenure. It was soon seen that even with Bedford at home duke Humfrey could

202, 222, 265, 278; iv. 12; Rot. Parl. v. 404. Cardinal Beaufort when attending the king in France had £4000 per annum; Rymer, x. 472. Gloucester was to receive 4000 marks as lieutenant during the king's absence; 2000 when he was in England; Ord. iv. 12: to this sum 2000 marks were added, ib. p. 103; and 5000 marks fixed as his ordinary salary, ib. p. 105.

[1] Rot. Parl. iv. 424; Ordinances, iv. 185.

[2] Rot. Parl. iv. 446.

[3] Ib. iv. 425, 426.

[4] Dep. Keeper's Rep. iii. App. p. 15. It was three quarters of a tenth; Wilk. Conc. iii. 523.

[5] Rot. Parl. iv. 426.

[6] Ib. iv. 439.

[7] Ib. iv. 423, 424.

Uneasy relations between Gloucester and Bedford.

not long be kept quiet. Signs of uneasiness and mistrust between the two brothers at last appeared. It was proposed that Gloucester should go to France, where the earl of Arundel was tasked beyond his strength in the defence of Normandy. The country was not altogether indisposed to peace, and an order had been passed in the parliament of 1431 that Bedford, Gloucester, Beaufort, and the council might open negotiations[1]. On the 26th of April, 1434, a large council was held at Westminster[2], a considerable number of lords and knights who were not of the privy council being summoned by writs of privy seal. Gloucester offered to go to France, and reviewed the conduct of the war there in such terms that Bedford, conceiving himself to be attacked, demanded that the words should be written down, in order that he might defend himself before the king.

Gloucester's futile proposition.

The council deliberated on Gloucester's proposition and found that it would involve an expenditure of nearly £50,000, which they saw no means of raising[3]. Gloucester, who as usual dealt in generalities, was pressed to explain how the money was to be secured. Bedford and the council severally appealed to the king, who declared that the matter must go no further.

Henry makes peace between his uncles.

The poor lad, now only thirteen, consulted the council, and probably under the advice of Beaufort, told the dukes that they were both his dearest uncles, that no attack had been made on the honour of either, and that he prayed there should be no discord between them. The discord indeed ceased, but Bedford immediately began to prepare for departure. On the 9th of June he addressed three propositions to the king; the revenues of the duchy of Lancaster should be applied to the war in France; the garrisons in the march of Calais should be put under his command; and he should be allowed to devote for two years the whole of his own Norman revenue to the war[4]. The king and council gratefully agreed: on the 20th he took his

Bedford goes back to France.

leave of them[5], and about the end of the month he sailed for France. His game there was nearly played out. After a

[1] Rot. Parl. iv. 371.
[2] Ordinances, iv. 210–213
[3] Ordinances, iv. 213 sq.
[4] Ib. iv. 222–226; Rot. Parl. v. 435–438.
[5] Ordinances, iv. 243–247.

conference with the duke of Burgundy at Paris at Easter 1435, he was obliged, by the pressure of the pope and his conviction of his own failing strength, to agree to join in a grand European congress of ambassadors which was to be held at Arras in August, for the purpose of arbitrating and if possible making peace. The French offered considerable sacrifices, but the English ambassadors demanded greater; they saw that Burgundy was going to desert them, and on the 6th of September withdrew from the congress. Burgundy's desertion was the last thing required to break down the spirit and strength of Bedford. He died on the 14th at Rouen. Duke Philip, relieved by his death from any obligation to temporise, made his terms with Charles VII, and a week later renounced the English alliance. Bedford must have felt that, after all he had done and suffered, he had lived and laboured in vain. The boy king, when he wept with indignation at duke Philip's unworthy treatment, must have mingled tears of still more bitter grief for the loss of his one true and faithful friend.

Congress of Arras.

Defection of Burgundy.

Bedford's death.

662. With Bedford England lost all that had given great, noble, or statesmanlike elements to her attempt to hold France. He alone had entertained the idea of restoring the old and somewhat ideal unity of the English and Norman nationalities, of bestowing something like constitutional government on France, and of introducing commercial and social reforms, for which, long after his time, the nation sighed in vain. The policy on which he acted was so good and sound, that, if anything could, it might have redeemed the injustice which, in spite of all justificative argument, really underlay the whole scheme of conquest. For England, although less directly apparent, the consequences of his death were not less significant. It placed Gloucester in the position of heir presumptive to the throne; it placed the Beauforts one step nearer to the point at which they with the whole fortunes of Lancaster must stand or fall. It placed the duke of York also one degree nearer to the succession in whatever way the line of succession might be finally regulated. It let loose all the disruptive forces which Bedford had been able to keep in subjection. It left cardinal

Results of Bedford's death.

Beaufort's policy after Bedford's death.

Beaufort the only Englishman who had any pretension to be called a politician, and furnished him with a political programme, the policy of peace, not indeed unworthy of a prince of the church, a great negotiator, and a patriotic statesman, but yet one which the mass of the English, born and nurtured under the influences of the long war, was not ready heartily to accept.

Irritation against Burgundy.

For the moment perhaps both king and nation thought more of Burgundy's desertion than of Bedford's death, of revenge more than of continued defence. Peace with France would be welcome; it would be intolerable not to go to war with Burgundy. The chancellor, in opening parliament on October 10, dilated at length on the perjuries of duke Philip; if he said a word about Bedford, it was not thought worth recording: the only thought of him seems to have been how to raise money on the estates which he and the earl of Arundel, who also had laid down his life for the English dominion, had left in the custody of the crown. The commons, who had grown so parsimonious of late, granted not only a tenth and fifteenth, a continuance of the subsidy on wool, tunnage and poundage, but a heavy graduated income-tax, of novel character now[2], though it became too familiar in later times. They empowered the council too to give security for £100,000, a larger loan than had ever been contemplated before[3]. Gloucester was appointed for nine years captain of Calais[4], and at last he was to have the chance of showing his mettle; for the cardinal himself had nothing better to propose. The session closed on the 23rd of December; war was to be resumed early in the next year; the garrison of Calais

Parliament of 1435.

Great effort of the commons.

[1] Rot. Parl. iv. 481. John Bowes was speaker. It was called in pursuance of a resolution of council held July 5; Ord. iv. 304; Lords' Report, iv. 888.

[2] Rot. Parl. iv. 486, 487. Incomes of 100*s.* paid 12*s.* 6*d.*, and 6*d.* in the pound up to £100; over £100 they paid 20*s.* 8*d.*, and 8*d.* in the pound up to £400; over £400 2*s.* in the pound. A similar grant was made in convocation Dec. 23; Dep. Keeper's Rep. iii. App. 16; Wilk. Conc. iii. 525.

[3] Rot. Parl. iv. 482. Writs were issued for a loan, Feb. 14, 1436, the treasurer to give security for repayment from the fifteenth granted in the last parliament; Ordinances, iv. 316, 329. Cf. pp. 352 sq.

[4] Rot. Parl. iv. 483.

ravaged the Flemish provinces, and the Burgundians prepared to besiege Calais. Yet, before anything was done by Gloucester, Paris had been recovered by the French king. Calais was succoured by Edmund Beaufort[1] and enabled to repel its besiegers before Gloucester would set sail for its relief or the duke of York, the new regent, who entered on his office in April, could complete his equipment[2]. Gloucester's Flemish campaign occupied eleven days[3], and he returned, after this brief experience of marauding warfare, to receive from his nephew the title of Count of Flanders, an honour scarcely less substantial than the royal title which its bestower continued to bear. This was the work of 1436. In 1437 the parliament, which sat from January to March, renewed the grants of 1435, except the income-tax, and did little more[4]. This year negotiations were set on foot for the release of John Beaufort, earl of Somerset, who had been a captive in France since 1421; he was exchanged for the count of Eu and returned home to strengthen the party of the cardinal[5]. After a year's experience the duke of York refused to serve any longer in France, and the earl of Warwick, Henry's tutor, was appointed to succeed him as regent[6]. Bedford's widow had

Paris taken, April 13.

Calais relieved by Edmund Beaufort.

Gloucester's short campaign in 1436.

Parliament of 1437.

Warwick regent of France.

[1] Now count of Mortain and Harcourt, 'wise and sage,' Hardyng, p. 388; he was made earl of Dorset in 1441, marquess in 1442, and duke of Somerset in 1448. Hardyng ascribes to him all the credit of relieving Calais, p. 396; as for Gloucester, 'he rode into Flanders a litle waye and litle did to count a manly man.' 'The earl of Mortayne went to Calys sone aftyr Estyr'; Gregory, p. 178. This chronicler gives the credit of the repulse of the Burgundians to Beaufort and Camoys. Cf. Leland, Coll. ii. 492; Engl. Chron. (ed. Davies), p. 55; Chron. Giles, p. 15.

[2] According to Hall, p. 179; Stow, p. 375, the earl of Mortain was so jealous of the duke of York that he prevented him from leaving England until Paris was lost. He had wished, it was said, to marry queen Katharine, but was prevented by Gloucester; Chron. Giles, p. 17.

[3] Aug. 1–15; see Stevenson, Wars in France, ii. pp. xix, xx.

[4] The parliament of 1437 began Jan. 21; Sir John Tyrell was speaker. The grants were made on the last day of the session; Rot. Parl. iv. 495, 496, 501, 502. The security given was for £100,000; p. 504. The clergy granted a tenth; Wilk. Conc. iii. 525.

[5] Rymer, x. 664, 680, 697.

[6] The duke's indentures expired and he was not willing to continue in office, April 7, 1437; Ordin. v. 6, 7. The earl of Warwick was nominated lieutenant July 16, 1437; Rymer, x. 674. He died in April, 1439. After his death the lieutenancy seems to have been in commission: but the earl of Somerset is found calling himself, and acting as, lieutenant until after

Death of the queen.

already forgotten him and married one of his officers; queen Katharine had long ago set the example, although the public revelation of her imprudence was deferred during her life. She died on the 3rd of January, 1437, leaving the young king more alone than ever. Warwick died in April, 1439, after no great successes. Such credit as was gained in France at all fell to the share of the two Beauforts. The zeal of the nation died away quickly; and in October, 1439, a truce for three years with Burgundy was concluded at Calais[1]; negotiations for a peace with Charles VII going slowly on in parallel with the slow and languishing war[2]. The cardinal's schemes for a general pacification were ripening. Gloucester showed neither energy nor originality, but contented himself with being obstructive. The parliament, in a hopeless sort of way, voted supplies and sanctioned the granting of private petitions, trying from time to time new expedients in taxation and slight amendments in the commercial laws. In the session of 1439[3] the renewed grants of subsidies for three years—a fifteenth and tenth and a half—were supplemented by a tax upon aliens, sixteen pence on householders, sixpence a head on others[4]; and the unappropriated revenues of the duchy of Lancaster were devoted to the charge of the household[5].

Truce with Burgundy.

Parliament of 1439.

York's reappointment; see Appendix D to the Foedera, pp. 443-447; Stevenson, Wars in France, ii. 304. Cf. Ordinances, v. 16, 33; Chr. Giles, p. 18. It could however only be for a few months, as he was in England in December 1439; Ordinances, v. 112.

[1] Rymer, x. 723-736.

[2] The journal of the ambassadors sent to negotiate with France on the mediation of cardinal Beaufort and the duchess of Burgundy, who was Beaufort's niece, is printed in the Ordinances, v. pp. 335-437.

[3] The parliament began Nov. 12; on Dec. 21 it was prorogued to meet at Reading, Jan. 14; William Tresham was speaker; measures were taken against dishonest purveyors. Convocation granted a tenth; Wilk. Conc. iii. 536; Rot. Parl. v. 3; Chron. Lond. pp. 126, 127. Hall commends the commercial policy of this parliament, p. 187; see Rot. Parl. v. 24; Statutes, ii. 302. One act forbade alien merchants to sell to aliens, put their sales under view of the Exchequer, and ordered them within eight months to invest the proceeds in English goods. Cf. Stow, p. 377.

[4] Rot. Parl. v. 4-6; 3rd Report of Dep. Keeper, App. p. 17. 'Alyens were putte to hyr fynaunce to pay a certayne a yere to the kynge'; Gregory, p. 182.

[5] The Lancaster inheritance had been preserved as a separate property of the crown, apart from the royal demesne, by Henry IV; and Henry V had added to it the estates inherited from his mother. Great part of it

663. The next year the projects of peace began to take a more definite form, and Gloucester's opposition assumed a more consistent character. On the 2nd of July [1] the duke of York was again made lieutenant-general in France, in the place of Somerset, who had been in command since Warwick's death, and who, with his brother Edmund, achieved this year the great success of retaking Harfleur [2]. At the same time the duke of Orleans, who had been a prisoner in England since the battle of Agincourt, obtained the order for his release, on the understanding that he should do his best to bring about peace with France. This was done notwithstanding the direct opposition and formal protest of Gloucester. In this document, which was addressed to Henry [3], the duke embodied his charges against the cardinal and archbishop Kemp, and vents all the spite which he had been accumulating for so many years: the letter assumes the dimensions of a pamphlet, and is sufficient by itself to establish the writer's incapacity for government. Beaufort, according to his nephew's representation, had obtained the cardinalate to satisfy his personal pride and ambition, and to enable him to assume a place to which he was not entitled in the synods of the church and in the council of the king: he had illegally retained or resumed the see of Winchester and deserved the penalties of praemunire; he and the archbishop of York, his confederate, had usurped undue influence over the king himself, and had estranged from him not only the writer but the duke of York

The duke of York regent in France.

Release of the duke of Orleans.

Violent attack of Gloucester on Beaufort and Kemp.

had however by charters of enfeoffment been put in the hands of trustees for the payment of his debts, charitable endowments, and trusts of his will. Of these trustees cardinal Beaufort was the most influential, and he retained the administration of the lands, according to the belief of parliament, much longer than was necessary. See Rot. Parl. iii. 428; iv. 46, 172; 138, 139, 301, 488; v. 6.

[1] Rymer, x. 786. The appointment was for five years. He had not set out on May 23, 1441; Ordinances, v. 146. Hardyng's statements about the regency of France and Normandy are peculiar; he says that the duke of Burgundy governed for a year after Bedford's death; the earl of Warwick succeeded, p. 396; then the earl of Stafford for two years, the earl of Huntingdon for two, and then the duke of York for seven.

[2] July to October, Appendix D to Foedera, pp. 453-459; Stow, p. 376.

[3] Rymer, x. 764-767; Stevenson, Wars in France, ii. 440; Hall. Chr. pp. 197-202; Arnold, Chr. pp. 279-286.

Gloucester's charges against Beaufort.

and the earl of Huntingdon, to say nothing of the archbishop of Canterbury; he had moreover, in his money-lending transactions, sacrificed the king's interest to his own; he had provided extravagantly for Elizabeth Beauchamp[1] and his nephew Swinford; he had defrauded the king of the ransom of king James of Scotland by marrying him to his niece; he had mismanaged affairs at the congress of Arras in 1435 and at Calais in 1439; in the former case he had allowed Burgundy and France to be reconciled, in the latter he had connived at an alliance between Burgundy and Orleans. The release of the duke of Orleans simply meant the renunciation of the kingdom of France; Beaufort and Kemp had even gone so far as directly to counsel such a humiliating act. Public mismanagement, private dishonesty, and treachery both private and public, are freely charged against both the prelates.

Reply of the council.

The duke's protest, which must have been very mischievous, was answered by a letter of the council[2], in which, not caring to notice the personal charges, they defended the policy of the act: it was an act of the king himself, done for the desire of peace; a desire fully justified by the great cost of bloodshed, the heavy charges, the exhaustion of both countries: it was a bad example to doom a prisoner of war to perpetual incarceration; or by vindictively retaining him to lose all the benefit of his cooperation in the obtaining of peace. The answer is full of good sense and good feeling, but it could never have commanded the same success as the manifesto of duke Humfrey obtained. That document helped to substitute in the mind of the nation, for the wholesome desire of peace which had been gradually growing, a vicious, sturdy, and unintelligent hatred to the men who were seeking peace: a feeling which prejudiced the people in general against Margaret of Anjou, and which, after having helped to destroy Gloucester himself, caused the outbreak of disturbances which led to civil war. It is curious

[1] Henry V had left this lady '300 marks worth of lyvelode,' if she should marry within a year. She had waited two years and more; notwithstanding Beaufort, as his nephew's executor, had paid the money.
[2] Stevenson, Wars in France, ii. 451.

to note how Gloucester tries to represent the duke of York and the earl of Huntingdon as sharers in his feelings of resentment. Either he was too much blinded by spite to see the real drift of the cardinal's policy, or else those deeper grudges of the royal house, which had cost and were still to cost so much bloodshed, were at the time altogether forgotten in the personal dislike of the Beauforts. Notwithstanding the protest, the duke of Orleans obtained his freedom.

Mischief done by Gloucester.

The next year witnessed a miserable incident that served to show that Gloucester was either powerless or contemptibly pusillanimous[1]. After his separation from the unfortunate Jacqueline, which was followed by a papal bull declaring the nullity of their marriage, he had consoled himself with the society of one of her ladies, Eleanor Cobham, whom he had subsequently married. Eleanor Cobham, early in 1441, was suspected of treasonable sorcery, and took sanctuary at Westminster. After appearing before the two archbishops, cardinal Beaufort, and bishop Ascough of Salisbury, she was imprisoned in Leeds castle; and subsequently, on the report of a special commission, consisting of the earls of Huntingdon and Suffolk and several judges, she was indicted for treason. After several hearings, she declined to defend herself, and submitted to the correction of the bishops, and did penance; she was then committed to the charge of Sir Thomas Stanley and kept during the remainder of her life a prisoner. The object of her necromantic studies was no doubt to secure a speedy succession to the crown for her husband. He does not seem to have ventured to act overtly on her behalf; whether from cowardice or from a conviction of her guilt. It was not forgotten that queen Johanna had in the same way conspired against the life of Henry V; and when both accusers and accused fully believed in the science by which such treasonable designs were to be compassed, it is as difficult to condemn the prosecutor as it is to acquit the accused. The people, we are told, pitied the duchess. If the prosecution were dictated

Eleanor Cobham, Gloucester's wife, tried for witchcraft.

[1] Chron. Lond. pp. 129, 130; Engl. Chron. (ed. Davies) pp. 57-60; Stow, p. 381; Fabyan, p. 614; Rot. Parl. v. 445.

by hostility to her husband, the story is disgraceful to both factions alike.

During the years 1441 and 1442 the duke of York won some credit in the north of France; the power of Charles VII was increasing in the south. The English parliament met on the 25th of January in the latter year[1]; granted the subsidies, tunnage and poundage, for two years, a fifteenth and tenth, and the alien tax. The vote of security for £100,000 had now become an annual act. A petition, connected doubtless with the duchess of Gloucester's trial, that noble ladies should, under the provisions of Magna Carta, be tried by the peers, was granted[2]; Sir John Cornwall, the baron of Fanhope, was created baron of Milbroke. The statute of Edward III was ordered to be enforced on the royal purveyors: there were few general complaints, as what little legislation was attempted was connected with the promotion of trade and commerce, which from the beginning of the Lancastrian period had been so prominent in the statute-book. A demand was made for the examination of the accounts of the duchy of Lancaster, which was still in the hands of the cardinal and his co-feoffees for the execution of the will of Henry V[3]. The young king was busy with his foundations at Eton and Cambridge.

Parliament of 1442.

Trials of peeresses regulated by statute.

Henry comes of age.

664. On the 6th of December, 1442, Henry reached the age of legal majority, and must then have entered, if he had not entered before, into a full comprehension of the burden that lay upon him in the task of governing a noble but exhausted people,

[1] Rot. Parl. v. 35; William Tresham was again speaker; the grants were made March 27; ib. pp. 37–40. 'At which parliament it was ordained that the sea should be kept half a year at the king's cost, and therefore to pay a whole fifteenth, and London to lend him £3000'; Chr. Lond. p. 130. The force so ordered included eight great ships of a hundred and fifty men each; each ship attended by a barge of eighty men, and a balynger of forty: also four 'spynes' of twenty-five men; it was to keep the sea from Candlemas to Martinmas; Rot. Parl. v. 59. Convocation granted a tenth, April 16; Wilk. Conc. iii. 536. A general pardon was granted at Easter 1442, from which remunerative returns were expected, Ordinances, v. 185.

[2] Rot. Parl. v. 56.

[3] Rot. Parl. v. 56–59. The appropriation of the duchy revenue to the household, ordered in 1439, was continued for three years; ib. p. 62.

and of setting to right the wrongs of a hundred years[1]. He had been very early initiated in the forms of sovereignty. Before he was four years old he had been brought into the painted chamber to preside at the opening of parliament, and from that time had generally officiated in person on such occasions. Before he was eight he was crowned king of England, and as soon as he was ten king of France. At the age of eleven he had had to make peace between his uncles of Bedford and Gloucester, and at thirteen had shed bitter tears over the defection of Burgundy. Whilst he was still under the discipline of a tutor, liable to personal chastisement at the will of the council, he had been made familiar with the great problems of state work. Under the teaching of Warwick he had learned knightly accomplishments; Gloucester had pressed him with book learning; Beaufort had instructed him in government and diplomacy. He was a somewhat precocious scholar, too early taught to recognise his work as successor of Henry V. It is touching to read the letters written under his eye, in which he petitions for the canonisation of S. Osmund and king Alfred, or describes the interest he takes in the council of Basel, and presses on the potentates of east and west the great opportunity for ecclesiastical union which is afforded by the councils of Florence and Ferrara[2]. Thus at the age of fifteen he was hard at the work which had overtasked the greatest kings that had reigned before him, and which is undone still. In the work of the universities, like duke Humfrey himself, he was as early interested; his foundations at Eton and Cambridge were begun when he was eighteen, and watched with the greatest care as long as he lived. The education of his half-brothers Edmund and Jasper Tudor[3] was a matter of serious

Early training of the king.

He was overtasked in his youth.

His interest in education.

[1] A panegyric on Henry VI, written by John Blakman, S.T.B., afterwards a monk of the Charterhouse, furnishes some of the most distinct traits of his character; it is edited by Hearne, at the end of his Otterbourne, i. 287 sq.

[2] Beckington's Letters, ed. Williams, i. 134, &c. 'Nonnullis etiam solebat clericis destinare epistolas exhortatorias, caelestibus plenas sacramentis et saluberrimis admonitionibus'; Blakman, p. 290.

[3] 'Quibus pro tunc arctissimam et securissimam providebat custodiam'; Blakman, p. 293. The same writer records his habit of saying to the Eton

His weak health.

thought to him whilst he was a child himself. Weak in health,—for had he been a boy of average strength he would have been allowed to appear in military affairs as early as his father and grandfather had appeared,—and precocious rather than strong in mind, he was overworked from his childhood, and the overwork telling upon a frame in which the germs of hereditary insanity already existed, broke down both mind and body at the most critical period of his reign. Henry was perhaps the most unfortunate king who ever reigned; he outlived power and wealth and friends; he saw all who had loved him perish for his sake, and, to crown all, the son, the last and dearest of the great house from which he sprang, the centre of all his hopes, the depositary of the great Lancastrian traditions of English polity, set aside and slain. And he was without doubt most innocent of all the evils that befel England because of him. Pious, pure, generous, patient, simple[1], true and just, humble, merciful, fastidiously conscientious, modest and temperate, he might have seemed made to rule a quiet people in quiet times. His days were

Unrivalled misfortunes.

boys 'sitis boni pueri, mites et docibiles et servi Domini'; ib. p. 296. His answer to the petition for the restoration of grammar schools is in Rot. Parl. v. 137. Beckington's Letters are full of illustrations of his zeal for the universities. Yet Hardyng describes him as little better than an idiot when a child:

> 'The Erle Richard in mykell worthyhead
> Enfourmed hym, but of his symplehead
> He could litle within his brest conceyve;
> The good from evill he could uneth perceive'; p. 394.

He was so tired 'of the symplesse and great innocence of King Henry' that he resigned his charge and went to France; p. 396. Henry's tendency to insanity may have come from either Charles VI or Henry IV.

[1] 'Vir simplex sine omni plica dolositatis aut falsitatis, ut omnibus constat'; Blakman, p. 288. 'Veridica semper exercuerat eloquia'; p. 288. 'Fuerat et rectus et justus . . . nulli vero injuriam facere voluit scienter'; ib. p. 288. His early attempts at the exercise of power were checked; in 1434 the council advised him not to listen to suggestions about important matters, or about the changing of his governors; Ord. iv. 287; Rot. Parl. v. 438. In 1438 they tell him that he gives too many pardons, and has thrown away 1000 marks by giving away the constableship of Chirk; Ordin. v. 89. The executions which followed Cade's rebellion may be alleged against his merciful disposition; but although cruelty would be by no means wonderful in the case of a panic-stricken, nervous invalid, Henry's horror of slaughter and mutilation is so well attested that those acts must be charged on Somerset and his other advisers, rather than on the king. See Blakman, pp. 301, 302.

divided between the transaction of business and the reading of history and scripture[1]. His devotion was exemplary and unquestionably sincere; he left a mark on the hearts of Englishmen that was not soon erased: setting aside the fancied or fabled revelations, a part perhaps of his malady, and the false miracles that were reported at his tomb, it was no mere political feeling that led the rough yeomen of Yorkshire and Durham to worship before his statue, that dictated hymns and prayers in his honour, and that retained in the Primer down to the Reformation the prayers of the king who had perished for the sins of his fathers and of the nation. It is needless to say that for the throne of England in the midst of the death-struggle of nations, parties, and liberties, Henry had not one single qualification. He was the last medieval king who attempted to rule England as a constitutional kingdom or commonwealth.

Henry's piety, and sanctity.

665. His coming of age did not much affect his actual position. He had long been recognised as the depositary of executive powers which were to be exercised by the council; he continued under the influence of the cardinal, from whom he had learned the policy of peace, though he had not learned the art of government. That which was a policy in Beaufort was in Henry a true love and earnest desire. He must have longed for peace as a blessing which he and living England had never known. Gloucester, powerless for good, stood aloof from government, sometimes throwing in a cynical remark in council, but chiefly employed in cultivating popularity and that reputation as a lover of literature which has stood him in so good stead with posterity. The parallel lines of war and negotiation run on for three years more: the war kept alive by the emulation of the duke of York and the Beauforts, a rivalry which, whilst it prevented anything like concerted action, saved the reputation of English valour abroad. The duke's term of office lasted until 1445; in 1442 a great expedition under Somerset was

The cardinal continues to be the king's chief adviser.

Rivalry between York and the Beauforts.

[1] 'Aut in orationibus, aut in scripturarum vel cronicarum lectionibus assidue erat occupatus'; Blakman, p. 289. 'Dies illos aut in regni negotiis cum consilio suo tractandis . . . aut in scripturarum lectionibus, vel in scriptis aut cronicis legendis non minus diligenter expendit'; ib. p. 299.

Beaufort supplies money for Somerset's expedition to France in 1443.

contemplated[1]; the want of money delayed it until the summer of 1443; funds were at last provided by the cardinal, who pledged his jewels and plate and furnished £20,000; insisting, however, that security should be given in a special form submitted to the council, which called forth from Gloucester the sneering remark that as his uncle would lend on no other terms it was little use reading the special form[2]. Before the expedition started distinct assurances were given that Somerset's authority should not prejudice the position of the duke of York as regent[3]; but the provision was almost neutralised by his promotion to the rank of duke. John Beaufort was made duke of Somerset in August 1443. His campaign was marked by no great success, and in the following May he died, leaving as his heiress the little lady Margaret, and as the representative of the family his brother

Edmund Beaufort.

Edmund, now marquess of Dorset and count of Mortain and Harcourt. Archbishop Stafford was still chancellor. Lord Cromwell resigned the treasurership in July 1443, and was succeeded by Ralph Boteler, lord Sudeley[4]. No parliament was held between 1442 and 1445, but a great council was ordered for the third week after Easter in 1443, to which in ancient fashion all freeholders were to be called, and possibly a new tax propounded[5]. It is uncertain whether it was ever summoned, and if summoned it either did not meet or effected nothing.

Council called in 1443.

Political action of the earl of Suffolk.

The year 1444 was occupied with negotiation. The earl of Suffolk, William de la Pole, grandson of Richard II's chancellor, and closely connected by marriage with the Beauforts, was the head of the English embassy to France; and he, whether pressed by the court in defiance of his own misgivings, or deliberately

[1] Sept. 8, 1443, the duke of Somerset went to France; 3700 men were slain or taken during the expedition; Gregory, p. 185. The preparations for the expedition formed a considerable part of the deliberations in council for nearly a year before; Ordinances, v. 218–409.

[2] Ordinances, v. 279, 280.

[3] Ib. v. 261.

[4] Ib. v. 299, 300; Rymer, xi. 35. Sudeley retained office until Dec. 18, 1446, when bishop Lumley of Carlisle succeeded him.

[5] All the king's freemen and the great council were to be summoned to meet at Westminster a fortnight after Easter, May 5, 1443; Ordinances, v. 236, 237. No records are in existence that show this assembly to have met, but it is possible that some financial expedients which are described in the Ordinances, v. 418 sq., may belong to this date.

pursuing the policy which, whilst it was the best for the country, he felt would be ruinous to himself[1], concluded on the 28th of May a truce which was to last till the 1st of April, 1446[2]. During the truce negotiations were briskly pushed for a marriage, or number of marriages, which might help to secure a permanent peace. Henry, it was proposed, should marry Margaret, daughter of René of Anjou, the titular king of Naples and count of Provence; and the duke of York might obtain a little French princess for his baby son Edward[3]. The former match was pressed and concluded by Suffolk, who, having been created a marquess on the 14th of September, 1444, was sent to Nancy to perform the ceremonies of betrothal. Margaret was brought to England early in the following year and married on the 22nd of April; on the 30th she was crowned. She was sixteen at the time.

Negotiations for peace.

A truce concluded, 1444.

The king's marriage, April, 1445.

Henry, in contemplation of the ceremony, had on the 25th of January opened a parliament, which sat, with several prorogations, until April 9, 1446[4]. This parliament, in March 1445, granted a half fifteenth and tenth[5], and in April, 1446, a whole fifteenth and tenth and another half[6]: it also continued the subsidy on wool until Martinmas, 1449. The peace and the young queen were as yet new and popular, and the restoration of commerce with France was a great boon. On the 2nd of June, 1445, Suffolk gave an account of his labours to the lords, and on the 4th repeated it to the commons; both houses thanked him and recommended him to the king for his special favour; the record of his services and the votes of thanks were entered on the rolls of parliament[7]. On the last day of the session the chancellor addressed Henry in the name of the lords, in

Parliament of 1445-6.

Suffolk thanked for his services.

[1] See below, p. 140.
[2] Rymer, xi. 59-67; Rot. Parl. v. 74.
[3] Stevenson, Wars in France, i. 79, 80, 160, 168.
[4] Rot. Parl. v. 66. William Burley was speaker.
[5] Mar. 15; Rot. Parl. v. 68. Convocation granted a tenth in Oct. 1444, and another in 1446; Wilk. Conc. iii. 539 sq, 554. The pope had also imposed a tenth on the clergy for a crusade, and sent the golden rose to Henry; ib. p. 551. The king and clergy refused the papal tenth. Cf. Stow, p. 385. The golden rose was delivered Nov. 29, 1446.
[6] Rot. Parl. v. 69; Hall, Chr. p. 206.
[7] Rot. Parl. v. 73; Stow, p. 385.

Project of a lasting peace.

contemplation of the king's visit to France for the purpose of completing the pacification. The thought of peace had come, he said, not by the suggestion of the king's subjects but by direct inspiration from God: if the king would declare that his purpose of peace was thus spontaneous, the lords would do their best to make it a reality. The words, somewhat ominous, betray a misgiving and, read by the light of later events, look like a protest [1]. The article of the peace of Troyes, which had bound the king not to make peace with Charles without the consent of the three estates of both realms, was however annulled by act of parliament [2]. All seemed to promise a speedy end to the long trouble and the opening of a new era of happiness for England.

Gloucester's dislike to the policy and advocates of peace.

It was the crowning victory of Beaufort's life, and it was the most galling defeat for Gloucester: not that he cared to continue the war or would have much preferred the daughter of the count of Armagnac to the daughter of the count of Provence [3], but that still whatever Beaufort aimed at he tried to hinder. But the end of the long rivalry was near.

Rise of Suffolk.

In the earl of Suffolk Gloucester had a rival, perhaps an enemy, who cared less about the blood of Lancaster than the Beauforts did; who had devoted himself heart and soul to the service of the young queen, and looked with no special love on the man who, until she should bear a son, stood in the relation of heir presumptive to the king. At once he took the leading place in the counsels of the young couple; Gloucester was scarcely consulted [4]. In the event

[1] Rot. Parl. v. 102. [2] Ib. v. 102, 103.

[3] The Armagnac marriage had been proposed in 1442 (Rymer, xi. 7; Negotiations, &c., in Beckington, Letters, ii. 178–248): but if Gloucester had preferred it, he had reconciled himself to the Angevin match before Margaret's arrival, and had met her with great pomp. On the last occasion too in parliament he had put himself forward in commending Suffolk; Rot. Parl. v. 73.

[4] 'Incepit rex Henricus graves et ingratas occasiones et querelas contra avunculum ducem Glocestriae ministrare, renuens ejus praesentiam et ab ipso se muniens cum custodibus armatis non paucis, tanquam ab ejus aemulo et inimico mortali'; Chron. ed. Giles, p. 33. Whethamstede's Register, drawn up by one who was well acquainted with duke Humfrey's history, says that his enemies so prejudiced the king, 'ut crederet rex eum illius esse inimicum adeo grandem quod moliretur assidue media quibus posset jura coronae sibi surripere illique clam procurare necem ac sic in se regni regimen usurpare'; i. 179. Hall, Chron. p. 209, says that the duke was summoned before the council and accused of maladministration during the king's

of queen Margaret being childless, Suffolk had, as was suspected, a deep design of his own; he obtained the wardship of the little lady Margaret[1], on whom the representation of the title of John of Gaunt devolved at her father's death. Child as she was, he projected for her a marriage with his son John: it might come to pass that the great-great-grandson of the merchant William de la Pole would sit on the throne of England. The obscure story of the arrest and death of Gloucester will, it may be safely assumed, never be cleared up: and the depth of the darkness that covers it has inevitably been made the occasion of broadcast accusations and suspicions of every sort. The ostensible events were simple enough.

Design imputed to him.

666. It is by no means improbable that before the end of 1446 an attempt was made to bring the duke to account for his administration as protector, and that a somewhat stormy session of parliament was to be expected when it next met. Overt action however was reserved for 1447.

Threatened attack on Gloucester.

England had been in 1445 and 1446 devastated by the plague. It was not at all unreasonable to hold a parliament, under the circumstances, away from London; and the parliament of 1447 was summoned to meet at Cambridge. By a second writ it was transferred to Bury S. Edmund's, a place where Suffolk was strong and Gloucester would be far away from his friends the Londoners. There it met on the 10th of February[2]. The archbishop announced the cause of summons—to provide the king with money for a visit to France which was in contemplation[3]. William Tresham, knight of the shire for Northamptonshire, and a friend of the duke of York, was chosen speaker. A large force was encamped in the neighbourhood, and it was perhaps known that some proceedings in parliament relating to the duke's conduct were to be expected. Neither the duke nor the cardinal seems

Parliament of Bury.

Forces collected on the spot.

minority, of illegal executions and extra-legal cruelties; from which charges he freed himself in a clever speech and was acquitted. There are no traces of this in the extant authorities.

[1] Cooper's Lady Margaret, p. 5; Excerpt. Hist. pp. 3, 4.

[2] Rot. Parl, v. 128. The last day of the session was March 3; ib. p. 135. The credit for £100,000 was given on that day.

[3] This visit which never took place occupies a prominent place in the negotiations of these years, as 'Personalis Conventio'; Rymer, xi. pp. 87 sq.

Arrest of Gloucester.

to have been present at the opening of the session. On the 18th of February Gloucester arrived with about eighty horsemen and was met a mile out of the town by the treasurer and controller of the king's household, who bade him retire at once to his lodgings. As soon as he reached the North Spital, where he was to lodge, and had supped, he was arrested by the viscount of Beaumont, who appeared attended by the duke of Buckingham, the marquess of Dorset, and the earl of Salisbury. Several other persons were arrested at the same time; and on the following days a large number of the duke's servants were imprisoned[1].

His death.

On the 23rd duke Humfrey died in his lodging, called St. Saviour's, outside the north gate[2]: the next day his body was viewed by the members of the parliament, after which it was taken to be buried at S. Alban's. Such little business as could be done in parliament was hurried through; no grants were asked for; and in March the king went down to Canterbury.

Obscurity of the question.

It would be vain to attempt to account positively for Gloucester's death; it may have been a natural death, produced or accelerated by the insult of the arrest; it may have been the work of an underling who hoped to secure his own promotion by taking a stumbling-block out of his master's path: if it were the direct act of any of the duke's personal rivals, the stain of guilt can hardly fall on any but Suffolk. It is impossible to

[1] See an account by a contemporary writer in English Chron. ed. Davies, pp. 116–118.

[2] 'Fecit eum rex . . arestari, ponique in tam arcta custodia quod prae tristitia decideret in lectum aegritudinis, et infra paucos dies posterius secederet in fata'; Regist. Whethamstede, i. 179. Cf. Gregory, p. 188; Chr. Giles, p. 34; Fabyan, p. 619. The French contemporary historian Mathieu de Coussy asserts that he was strangled, ap. Buchon, xxxv. p. 102; the same writer (xxxvi. 83) says that the murder was ascribed by some to the duke of York, who indeed was the only person who was likely to profit by it. But this is most improbable. Hardyng, who wrote in the Yorkist interest, says, p. 400:—

'Where in parlesey he dyed incontinent
For hevynesse and losse of regiment;
And ofte afore he was in that sykenesse
In poynt of death, and stode in sore distress;
. . he so dyed in full and hole creaunce
As a christen prince of royall bloude full clere,
Contryte in herte with full greate repentaunce.'

Cf. Stow, p. 386.

suppose that Henry himself was cognisant of the matter, and it is hard to suspect Margaret, a girl of eighteen, although she had already made herself a strong partisan, and there may have lurked in her that thirst for blood which marked more or less all the Neapolitan Angevins. It cannot be supposed that the cardinal would in the last year of his life reverse the policy on which he had acted for fifty years and deal such a fatal blow to the house of Lancaster; or that the marquess of Dorset, who had more to fear from the duke of York than from the duke of Gloucester, would connive at a deed so contrary to the interest of the Beauforts. It is just possible that the council, which must have ordered the arrest, may, by some division of responsibility which would blunt the edge of individual consciences, have connived at the murder. It is almost as probable that the duke was really guilty of treason and was put out of the way to save the good character of others who would be implicated if he were brought to trial. It is most probable that Suffolk knew more of the secret than any other of the lords. The keeper of the privy seal, Adam Moleyns, bishop of Chichester, must have sealed the warrant for the arrest; and in his confession, made shortly before his death, he stated some matters which Suffolk had to disavow, although the name of duke Humfrey was not mentioned. Yet there is nothing in the history of either of these men that would give the least probability to such a charge as this. The commons, when in 1451[1] they petitioned for sentence of forfeiture against Suffolk, did not go beyond terming him the cause and labourer of the arrest, imprisonment, and final destruction of the duke; the accusation in its complete form was the work of the triumphant Yorkists long after. On the whole, the evidence both of direct statement and silence among contemporary writers tends to the belief that Gloucester's death was owing to natural causes, probably to a stroke of paralysis; his arrest to some design in which all the leading lords were partakers. The charges made against his servants, who were arrested at the same time, were definite enough; they had conspired to make the duke king of England and Eleanor

Impossibility of the cardinal's guilt.

The council responsible for the arrest.

The secret of it kept by Suffolk.

Yet Suffolk was never legally charged with murder.

The death probably natural.

[1] Rot. Parl. v. 226.

Charges brought against Gloucester's servants.

Cobham queen; they had falsely and traitorously imagined the death and destruction of the king, and had conspired together for the purpose; they had raised an armed force and set out for Bury S. Edmund's to kill the king[1]. On the 8th of July Thomas Herbert and four others were tried by a special commission, of which Suffolk was the head, and convicted by a Kentish jury at Deptford; but a week later they were pardoned by the king; and in the month of October their reputed accomplices received a similar pardon. We may infer from this that Henry could scarcely have believed the story of his uncle's treason; but the favours which were afterwards showered on both Suffolk and Moleyns show equally clearly that he did not believe them responsible for the duke's murder.

They are pardoned.

Death of cardinal Beaufort.

On the 11th of April, six weeks after the death of Gloucester, the cardinal of England passed away; not, as the great poet has described him, in the pangs of a melodramatic despair[2], but with the same business-like dignity in which for so long he had lived and ruled. As he lay dying in the Wolvesey palace at Winchester he had the funeral service and the mass of requiem solemnised in his presence; in the evening of the same day he had his will read in the presence of his household, and the following morning confirmed it in an audible voice; after which he bade farewell to all, and so died; leaving, after large legacies,

[1] Rymer, xi. 178. Thirty-eight of the duke's servants were arrested. On Friday, July 14, five were condemned to the penalties of treason and brought to the gallows. At the last moment Suffolk produced the pardon and they were released; Gregory, p. 188. A list of forty-two is given by Ellis, Original Letters, 2nd Series, i. 108, 109; cf. Leland, Coll. ii. 494. Gregory says that the arrested persons never 'ymagenyd no falseness of the that they were put upon of.' The pardon is granted in consideration of the approaching festival of the Assumption, on which day the pope had granted indulgences to those visiting the king's college at Eton: it is dated July 14, and was no doubt the king's independent act. See Blakman, p. 301.

[2] Hall, Chr. p. 210, on the authority of John Baker, a counsellor of the cardinal, gives a last speech, which contains nothing positively unnatural, but much that is improbable. It is asserted that the bulk of the cardinal's wealth fell to Edmund Beaufort, the marquess of Dorset, his nephew, who was one of his executors. This does not appear from the will; £4000 is left to the Bastard John of Somerset, and to the king the jewels pledged by the parliament to the cardinal and in his hands at his death. His last loan to the king seems to be one of 2000 marks in 1444; Rymer, xi. 55: but he had provided £20,000 in 1443.

the residue of his great wealth to charity. He had been indeed too rich for his own fame; Henry when the bishop's executors offered him a sum of £2000 from the residue put them aside, saying, 'My uncle was very dear to me and did much kindness to me whilst he lived; the Lord reward him. But do ye with his goods as ye are bounden; I will not take them[2].' Henry spoke the truth; Beaufort had been the mainstay of his house; for fifty years he had held the strings of English policy, and done his best to maintain the welfare and honour of the nation. That he was ambitious, secular, little troubled with scruples, apt to make religious persecution a substitute for religious life and conversation; that he was imperious, impatient of control, ostentatious and greedy of honour,—these are faults which weigh very lightly against a great politician, if they be all that can be said against him. It must be remembered in favour of Beaufort that he guided the helm of state during the period in which the English nation tried first the great experiment of self-government with any approach to success; that he was merciful in his political enmities, enlightened in his foreign policy; that he was devotedly faithful and ready to sacrifice his wealth and labour for the king; that from the moment of his death everything began to go wrong and went worse and worse until all was lost[3]. If this result seems to involve a condemnation of his policy, it only serves to enhance the greatness of his powers and fidelity. But his policy, so far as it was a policy of peace and reconciliation, is not condemned by the result. It was not the peace, but the reopening of the strife that led directly to ruin. It is probable that he foresaw some part of the mischief that followed; certainly the words on his tomb, 'tribularer si nescirem misericordias Tuas[4],' may be read as expressing a feeling that,

His wealth.

His political skill.

Character of his administration.

[1] Cont. Croyland, ap. Gale, p. 582.

[2] Blakman, de Virtutibus Henrici VI., p. 294.

[3] There are among the ordinances of the privy council some good illustrations of Beaufort's character. On one occasion it was proposed to appropriate for the payment of debt some fund that was already assigned to a similar purpose; the whole council approved, but the cardinal protested against the deception; 'so by this mean no man hereafter should trust none assignment, whereto he wol in no wyse consent.' The treasurer agreed with the cardinal; Ordinances, v. 216.

[4] Godwin de Praesulibus, p. 232.

humanly speaking, there was little hope for his country under Henry VI.

Suffolk left chief minister.

The death of Gloucester, followed so closely by the death of the cardinal, left Suffolk, the queen's minister, without a rival; Edmund Beaufort was ordered to undertake the lieutenancy in France and Normandy, thereby increasing the jealousy between him and York[1]; and under their joint misfortune and mismanagement all that remained to England in France, save Calais, was lost.

His policy of peace.

667. Suffolk was an old and experienced soldier, and if it were not for the cloud that rests on him in relation to Gloucester's death, might seem entitled to the praise of being a patriotic and sensible politician[2]. The policy of peace which Beaufort had nursed, had been carried into effect by him; and it was pursued by him when he became the most powerful man at court. It was a bold policy, for it was sure in the long run to ruin its supporter even in the estimation of the class which was to gain most by the result[3]. Suffolk saw that England could not retain her hold on France, and he tried by surrendering a part of the conquest to maintain possession of Normandy and Guienne. He knew well how dangerous

Surrender of Maine and Anjou.

[1] The duke of York had left Normandy in the autumn of 1445, and the country was governed by commissioners appointed during his absence, until 1447. According to Whethamstede (i. 160) Henry had reappointed him for five years more, but had at Somerset's instigation cancelled the nomination. In July 1447 York was appointed lieutenant of Ireland (Wars, &c. i. 478), but he still retained the title of lieutenant-governor of France in November 1447. In December 1447 it had been determined to appoint Edmund Beaufort, and he was acting as full lieutenant in May 1448. See Appendix D to Foedera, pp. 509–538; Ordin. vi. 90.

[2] Suffolk was born in 1396; Dugd. Bar. p. 186. He became a member of the council in 1431; Ordin. iv. 108. His wife was Alice, widow of the earl of Salisbury and daughter of Thomas Chaucer of Ewelme, whose mother was sister to Katharine Swinford.

[3] On the 1st of February, 1444, Suffolk's mission was discussed in council; he said that he had been too intimate with the duke of Orleans and other prisoners to be trusted by the nation, and he was very unwilling to go; but the chancellor overruled the objections. Ordinances, vi. 32–35. Accordingly, on February 20, the king wrote to Suffolk promising to warrant all that he might do in the way of obtaining peace, and overruling his scruples at undertaking the task; Rymer, xi. 53. This shows that Suffolk was throughout open and straightforward in his behaviour. The council knew what his policy was, and was warned of the dangers which ultimately overwhelmed him.

Policy and impolicy of the surrender.

a part he had undertaken, and openly warned the council of the results which really followed. He had promised, probably by word of mouth, that, on the completion of the marriage scheme, the remaining places which the English held in Maine and Anjou should be surrendered to king René. If by such a sacrifice peace could be obtained it would be cheaply purchased; and it might be, for Charles VII had more than once offered terms that would leave Henry in possession of more than he now retained. But affairs had materially changed; Charles was gaining strength, England was more and more feeling her exhaustion. Anjou and Maine were now the keys of Normandy, no longer the gate by which England could march on France. The project of peace languished, the surrender of Maine was urged more imperiously. The cessation of warfare was maintained only by renewal of short truces, until in March 1448[1] the coveted province was actually given up, and then a truce for only two years was granted. The high spirit of Edmund Beaufort chafed against the delays and irritations of diplomacy, and unfortunately his strength, whether of mind or of armaments, was not equal to his spirit. He was made duke of Somerset in March 1448[2], and in company with bishop Moleyns commissioned to treat for a perpetual peace. But before the end of the year the French were complaining that the truce was broken: early in 1449 it was really broken by the capture of Fougères by a vassal of Henry[3];

Breach of the truce.

[1] The negotiations may be traced in the collections of William of Worcester, published by Stevenson, Wars in France, vol. ii. pp. [634] sq. The final surrender took place March 11; Rymer, xi. 210, 214.

[2] Somerset's creation as duke was on March 31, 1448 (not 1447: see Nicolas, Hist. Peerage, p. 437); Lords' Reports, v. 258, 259. The commission to him and Moleyns is dated April 6, 1448. See Stevenson, Wars in France, ii. 577; Hardyng, p. 399.

[3] Mar. 24; Blondel, p. 5. The conduct of Francis L'Arragonois, who broke the truce, with the connivance of Suffolk and Somerset, as he tried to prove, and possibly with that of Henry, is the subject of a long discussion in the letters of the time. Stevenson, Wars in France; Stow, p. 386. The chronicler however (Giles, p. 36) represents the true state of the case when he says that the French were eagerly watching for the first breach of truce in order to overwhelm the English, 'imputantes omnem causam rebellionis.' See also Æneas Sylvius, opp. p. 440. According to M. de Coussy (Buchon, xxxv. 133 sq.) Somerset professed himself unable to control the English forces or to restore Fougères.

Loss of Normandy in 1449 and 1450.

and in April war began again. Somerset saw all the strongholds of Normandy slip from his grasp with appalling rapidity: the English ascribed it to treachery, but against strong armies without and a hostile population within, it was impossible to retain them. In May Pont l'Arche was taken; Conches, Gerberoi, Verneuil followed; in August Lisieux surrendered; on the 29th of October Rouen. In January 1450 Harfleur and Dieppe fell; in May the English were defeated in a battle at Formigny, and Bayeux was taken; Caen surrendered on the 23rd of June, Falaise on the 10th of July; on the 12th of August Cherbourg, the last stronghold in Normandy. Not content with recovering Normandy, Charles was threatening descent on England, and the Isle of Wight was expecting invasion. In the meanwhile England was suffering the first throes of the great struggle in which her medieval life seems to close.

Unpopularity of the court.

No parliament was held in 1448; the year was occupied in peace negotiations; nothing is known of the proceedings of the council; and as the surrender of Maine became known in the country, the popularity of the court and of Suffolk waned.

Suffolk vindicates himself.

As early as May 1447 he had been allowed at his own request to defend his conduct before the council, and the king in the following month had declared that the charges brought against him by public report were mere scandals and that he was guiltless of any real fault[2]. On the 2nd of June, 1448, he was made a duke, and although he must have been aware that his policy found no favour with the people, he bore himself as an innocent man to the last. In February 1449 the parliament met at Westminster[3], and granted a half-tenth,

[1] Hardyng, p. 399.

[2] Rot. Parl. v. 447; Rymer, xi. 172–174. The duke had heard that he was reported to have acted faithlessly in the matter; and it had come also to the king's ears; the duke had desired a hearing, and May 25 was appointed: there were present the chancellor, treasurer, the queen's confessor, the dukes of York and Buckingham, lords Cromwell, Sudeley and Say, with some others. The king regarded the vindication as complete, declared Suffolk innocent, and ordered the reports to be silenced, issuing letters to that effect on the 18th of June.

[3] Rot. Parl. v. 141. It met Feb. 12; John Say was speaker. On the 4th of April it was prorogued to May 7, and on May 30, to June 17, at Winchester. The grants were made April 3 and July 16, the last day of

fifteenth, and continued tunnage and poundage for five years. After two prorogations in consequence of the plague, it met in June at Winchester, and there continued the wool subsidy for four years and renewed the tax on aliens; the commons attempted also to tax the clergy by granting a subsidy of a noble from each stipendiary priest in consideration of a general pardon. Henry sent the bill to convocation, telling the clergy that it was for them to bestow the subsidy; if they would grant the noble, he would issue the pardon[1]. The clergy accepted the compromise and voted the tax. An urgent appeal for help for Normandy was made by Somerset's agents[2]; but matters were already too far gone to be helped; still to the last we see the king and council toiling in vain to send over men and munitions. At home too the prospect was becoming very threatening. A second parliament was called in November. War had broken out with Scotland and the earl of Northumberland had suffered an alarming defeat[3]. Parliaments of 1449.

The session was opened on the 6th of November, and continued at Westminster or at Blackfriars, by prorogation until Christmas, when it was again prorogued to the 17th of January[4]. Little is known of the proceedings during these weeks, but they were probably stormy; for on the 9th of December bishop Moleyns, who next to the duke of Suffolk was regarded as responsible for the surrender of Maine, resigned the Privy Seal[5]. Bishop Lumley of Carlisle, who had been treasurer since 1446, had in October made way for the lord Say and Sele, who immediately became unpopular. The dissatisfaction of the country would no doubt have resulted in a rebellion, if there had Parliament of 1449-50. General disaffection.

the session; ib. pp. 142, 143. Security was given for £100,000; p. 143. In July the clergy voted a tenth and *6s. 8d.* on chaplains; Wilk. Conc. iii. 556. Another tenth was voted in November, ib. p. 557.

[1] Rot. Parl. v. 152, 153; 3rd Report Dep. Keeper p. 27.

[2] Rot. Parl. v. 147.

[3] Henry was charged with conniving at the breach of the truce with the Scots, when visiting Durham in 1447; Chr. Giles, p. 35.

[4] Rot. Parl. v. 171. John Popham was speaker. The parliament met at Westminster, and was adjourned at once to Blackfriars, returning Dec. 4, to Westminster. On the 17th it was adjourned to Jan 22; and on March 30 adjourned to Leicester for April 29. It sat until May 17.

[5] Rymer, xi. 255.

Financial ruin.

been any one to lead it: the cession of Maine and Normandy had produced a violent reaction against Suffolk; the finances of the country had gone to ruin; the king's debt, the debt of the nation, had since Beaufort's death gone on increasing, and now amounted to £372,000; his ordinary income had sunk to £5000; the household expenses had risen to £24,000[1]. Stafford, who was growing old, might be expected to give way under the circumstances; he had been eighteen years in office, and if he had done little good he had done no harm: as soon as the parliamentary attack on Suffolk began, he resigned, and archbishop Kemp, the faithful coadjutor of Beaufort, now a cardinal[2], was called again into the chancery, too late however to restore the falling fortunes of his master. Suffolk had not acted cordially with Kemp, and the cardinal's return to office was one sign that the duke's influence over the king was already weakened.

Archbishop Kemp again chancellor.

Obscure history of Suffolk's trial.

668. The history of the trial and fall of Suffolk, although more fully illustrated by documentary evidence, is scarcely less obscure, in its deeper and more secret connexion with the politics of the time, than is that of the arrest and death of Gloucester. Looked at in the light of the parliamentary records, the attack seems to be a spontaneous attempt on the part of the commons to bring to justice one whom they conceived to be a traitorous minister; and if it were indeed so, it would be the most signal case of proper constitutional action by way of impeachment that had occurred since the days of the Good Parliament. That it was not so is sufficiently proved by the fact, recorded by a strong anti-Lancastrian par-

[1] Rot. Parl. v. 183.

[2] Kemp was made cardinal, with the title of S. Balbina, by Eugenius IV, Dec. 18, 1439 (Panvin. Ep. Paparum. p. 300), and cardinal bishop of S. Rufina July 21, 1452 (Ang. Sac. i. 123). There is a high panegyric upon him in a letter of Henry VI to the pope on the occasion of his promotion, Beckington, i. 39. It is possible that Kemp had, although attached to Beaufort, opposed himself to the influence of Suffolk. In 1448, when the see of London was vacant, Henry applied for the appointment of Thomas Kemp, the nephew of the cardinal; Suffolk, however, procured letters in favour of Marmaduke Lumley, the treasurer, and called the earlier application surreptitious. The pope administered a serious rebuke to the king and appointed Kemp; Beckington, Letters, i. 155 sq. It will be observed that Lumley's resignation of the treasurership just preceded the attack on Suffolk.

tisan, that the commons were urged to the impeachment by a member of the council[1] who was a personal enemy of Suffolk, and by the circumstances of the duke's death, which proved that bitterer enemies than the commons were secretly at work against him. Yet there is no difficulty in understanding the causes of the great ruin which befel him. The loss of Maine and Anjou had been followed by the loss of great part of Normandy. Maine and Anjou had been surrendered by the policy of Suffolk. Normandy was being lost by the incapacity or ill luck of Somerset. Both were in the closest confidence of the king and queen. It was not easy for the rough and undisciplined politicians of the country to discriminate between the policy of Suffolk and the incapacity or ill luck of Somerset. The easiest interpretation of the phenomena was treason, and there were not wanting men like lord Cromwell to guide the commons to that conclusion. Cromwell represented possibly a small minority in the council; possibly he stood alone there; he was an old servant of Henry, whom the cardinal had been able to keep in his place, and who was personally hostile to Gloucester[2]. Now that the cardinal and the duke were both gone, he may have envied the rise of a new minister like Suffolk, or he may thus early have been connected with the band of men who later on undertook the overthrow of the dynasty.

Prosecution of Suffolk, occasioned by his ill-success,

prompted by lord Cromwell.

[1] Lord Cromwell a few days before Christmas charged William Taillebois with an attempt to assassinate him at the door of the Star Chamber. Suffolk defended Taillebois, who notwithstanding was sent to the Tower; 'et postea dominus de Cromwelle reddidit duci Suffolchiae vices suas in malo anno ipsi duci.' During the parliament Cromwell obtained damages for £1000 against Taillebois from a Middlesex jury; and then 'domino de Cromwell secrete laborante dux Suffolchiae per communes in parliamento de alta et grandi proditione appellatus est'; W. Worcester, pp. [766-769].

[2] Cromwell had been, as we have seen, chamberlain to Henry VI and treasurer from 1433 to 1443; he became chamberlain again in 1450. It was at the marriage of his niece to Thomas Neville that the quarrel of Egremont and the Nevilles broke out, W. Worc. pp. 770, 771. The duke of Exeter sided with Egremont, and the duke of York with the Nevilles. Cromwell in 1454 exhibited articles in parliament against the duke of Exeter, and no doubt was then in the York interest. He was accused of treason in 1455; and on bad terms with Warwick, the two charging on each other the guilt of the battle of S. Alban's. He died however in 1456. See Paston Letters, i. 293, 344, 345, 376; cf. Ord. vi. 198.

Bishop Moleyns murdered, Jan. 1450.

The mischief began during the Christmas holydays. Bishop Moleyns had gone down to Portsmouth to pay the soldiers who were going to France, and was there on the 9th of January[1] murdered by the sailors, the soldiers looking on. In his last moments he was heard to say something about the duke of Suffolk, which was understood as a confession of their common delinquency. Suffolk, probably aware that a formal charge would be preferred against him, attempted to anticipate it and, as he had done before the council in 1447, to put himself at once on his defence. Accordingly, on the first day of the session, January 22, 1450, he made a formal protest before the king and lords. He declared in simple and touching language his services and sacrifices, denied the slander that was publicly current against him in consequence of the bishop's supposed confession, and prayed that, if any one would charge him with treason or disloyalty[2], he would come forth and make a definite accusation, which he trusted to be able to rebut. The commons at once took up the gauntlet. On the 26th they petitioned that, as he had acknowledged the currency of these infamous reports, he might be put in ward to avoid inconvenient consequences; on the 27th the lords, acting on the advice of the chief justice, resolved that he should not be arrested until some definite charge was made; on the 28th the commons made the definite charge, and the duke was sent to the Tower. This first charge was based on the report that he had sold the realm to Charles VII, and had fortified Wallingford castle as headquarters for a confederacy against the independence of England[3]. Ten days later the first formal and definite impeachment was made;

Suffolk anticipates the charges laid against him.

The commons demand his arrest.

General charges of treason.

[1] Gregory, p. 189, 'for his covetysse as hyt was reportyde.' 'Through the procurement of Richard duke of York,' Stow, p. 387. 'Et pacem sitiens cum morte recessit atroci,' Chr. Giles, p. 58. 'Inter quos et amicus noster Adam Molines secreti regii signaculi custos et litterarum cultor, amisso capite truncus jacuit'; Æneas Sylvius, Opp. p. 445. Æneas had addressed Moleyns as the king's first favourite or next to the first; Epist. 18, p. 514: in another letter, Epist. 64, he congratulates him on his style. See also Epist. 80. There is a letter of Moleyns to Æneas, Epist. 186.

[2] Rot. Parl. v. 176.

[3] Ib. v. 176, 177. 'And also for the dethe of that nobylle prynce the duke of Gloucester'; Gregory, p. 189.

the chancellor having been changed in the meantime[1]; and on the 7th of February cardinal Kemp, attended by several of the lords, was sent by the king to the commons to hear the charge. This elaborate accusation contained eight counts of high treason[2] and misprision of treason: he had conspired with the king of France to depose Henry and place on the throne his own son John de la Pole as husband of the little heiress of the Beauforts[3]; he had advised the release of the duke of Orleans, and had conspired with him to urge Charles VII to recover his kingdom; he had promised the surrender of Anjou and Maine, had betrayed the king's counsel to the French, had disclosed to them the condition of the king's resources, and had by secret dealing with Charles prevented the conclusion of a lasting peace, even boasting of the influence which he possessed in the French court[4]; he had likewise prevented the sending of reinforcements to the army in France, had estranged the king of Aragon and lost the friendship of Brittany. On the 12th of February these articles were read and referred to the judges, and the discussion was adjourned at the king's discretion. The delay gave time for a fresh indictment to be drawn up.

First set of formal charges; also of treason.

Referred to the judges.

On the 7th of March the lords resolved that Suffolk should be called on for his answer; and on the 9th eighteen additional articles were handed in by the commons. These, which may be regarded as a second and final indictment, chiefly comprised

Second set of charges.

[1] The chancellor resigned Jan. 31: the charges were brought forward on the 7th of February; Rot. Parl. v. 177.

[2] Rot. Parl. v. 177–179; Hall, Chr. pp. 212, 213; Paston Letters (ed. Gairdner) i. 99–105.

[3] The marriage of the two children was celebrated after the arrest; Rot. Parl. v. 177.

[4] This was possibly a reference to the language which he had used in the Privy Chamber, when attempting to excuse himself from acting as ambassador in 1444; above, p. 140; 'I have had great knowledge among the parties of your adversaries in France,' &c.; Ord. vi. 33. Here, however, the speech is said to have been made in the Star Chamber. 'He declared openly before the lords of your council here being, that he had his place in the council house of the French king as he had here, and was there as well trusted as he was here, and could remove from the said French king the priviest man of his council if he would'; Rot. Parl. v. 179.

Charges of malversation.

charges of maladministration, malversation, misuse of his power and influence with the king, the promotion of unworthy persons, and the sacrifice of the English possessions in Normandy by a treacherous compact with the king of France[1]. Suffolk was then brought from the Tower and received copies of both the bills. On the 13th he stated his own case in parliament: he denied with scorn the charge that he had or could have planned the king's deposition; as for the matters of fact contained in the eight articles, the rest of the council were as much responsible as he; his words had been perverted to a meaning which they would not bear. The next day the chief justice asked the lords to advise the king; but the question was again deferred, and it was not until the 17th that the compromise was effected which would, as it was supposed, save the duke and satisfy the commons. All the lords 'thenne beyng in Towne' were called into the king's chamber; Suffolk was admitted and knelt before the king. The chancellor reminded him that he had not put himself on his peerage in regard to the first bill of impeachment, and asked whether he had anything further to say in that matter. The duke replied by a forcible repetition of his denial and protestation of innocence, and then placed himself entirely at the king's disposal, thus not acknowledging any fault but showing himself unwilling to stand a regular trial. The chancellor then declared the king's mind: as to the greater and more heinous charges included in the first bill, the king held Suffolk 'neither declared nor charged'[2]; as to the second bill the royal intention was to proceed not by way of judgment, but on the ground of the duke's submission: accordingly the king, by his own advice, 'and not reporting him to the advice of his lords, nor by way of judgment, for he is not in the place of judgment,' ordered him to absent himself from the king's dominions for five years from the 1st of May following. The lords lodged

Suffolk asserts his innocence.

Compromise.

He does not put himself on his trial, but submits.

The king sends him abroad.

[1] Rot. Parl. v. 179-182.

[2] The expression is obscure, but it seems to signify that the king regarded these charges as prima facie groundless, that he in fact 'ignored' or threw out the indictment.

a protest against this way of dealing with an accused person, insisting that the royal act done without their advice and counsel should not be construed to their prejudice in time to come; this protest, however, which was presented by the viscount of Beaumont, one of Henry's faithful friends, was itself part of the scheme of compromise[1]. It was clear that Suffolk could not be tried formally unless the king and council were prepared to face the storm of popular indignation which, however undeservedly, had been aroused against the policy of peace; nor, if the matter were allowed to run its course in the parliament, could the king have there interfered to rescue him from the uncertain issue[2]. He had therefore declined to be tried by his peers, and sacrificed himself to save the king and the council, or that part of it which followed the same policy. He had six weeks given him to prepare for his departure; after settling his affairs and writing a beautiful letter of farewell to his infant son, he sailed on the 30th of April. On the 2nd of May he was beheaded by the crew of a ship which had been waiting to intercept him[3]. There is no evidence to determine whether the act was prompted by the vindictiveness of political rivalry or by the desire of vengeance for the death of Gloucester, or was the mere result of the hatred felt by the sailors of the fleet, which had been fatal to bishop Moleyns, or was part of a concerted attempt against the dynasty[4]. Anyhow it robbed Henry of his most

Protest of the lords.

Possible clue to this proceeding.

Suffolk murdered at sea.

[1] Rot. Parl. v. 182, 183; cf. Paston Letters, i. 115. Mr. Gairdner's new edition of these letters, and his prefaces, which furnish an absolutely invaluable sketch of the history of this period, leave scarcely anything to be added, and comparatively little to be cleared up.

[2] The proceedings at the councils preliminary to the Leicester parliament of 1426 may be compared with this: so long as the matter was before council a compromise might be effected; if parliament were appealed to, such justice must be done as parliament willed. See above, p. 102; and Ordinances, iii. 185, 186.

[3] The letter is printed among the Paston Letters, ed. Gairdner, i. 121, 122; and the account of the duke's death is given in the same collection, vol. i. pp. 124, 126.

[4] Æneas Sylvius (Opp. p. 442), representing perhaps foreign opinion, regards the death of Suffolk as connected with the attempt of the duke of York to change the government: his account of Suffolk is hostile; 'qui leges pro suo arbitratu et populis in principibus dixit. Suppressit quos odivit et iterum quos amavit erexit.'

faithful and skilful adviser, and left him for a time dependent on the counsel of the aged archbishop of York.

Parliament of April, 1450, at Leicester.

The parliament, which met again at Leicester on the 29th of April and granted a graduated tax on incomes arising from lands and offices, completed its work by making a special provision for the royal household; the fee farms of the crown were to be applied to this purpose to the amount of £5522 0s. 7*d.*; and the revenues of the duchy of Lancaster, so far as they were not already appropriated, were devoted to the same object[1]. A general act of resumption was passed, by which all the grants made since the king's accession were annulled; a great number however of exceptions and reservations were made, and the act became a precedent which many subsequent parliaments thought it wise to follow[2]. Immediately after the death of the duke of Suffolk the rebellion of Cade and the Kentish men broke out.

Act of Resumption.

Helplessness of Henry after Suffolk's death.

669. This event, which more than anything else in Henry's reign proves his utter incapacity for government, serves also to show how helpless the removal of Suffolk had left him. Of the two men who would most naturally have taken the lead in council, the duke of Somerset was in France, the duke of York was in Ireland. The lord Say and Sele, who was one of the special objects of popular hatred, was the king's treasurer. Cardinal Kemp the chancellor was scarcely fitter than Henry himself to deal with an armed mob. The condition of the country would have tasked much stronger and more unscrupulous men[3]. The nation was exhausted by tax-

[1] Rot. Parl. v. 172–176.

[2] Ib. v. 183–200. Whethamstede remarks that the necessity for these acts was caused by the king's extravagant liberality; the politicians in parliament remembered 'quo modo pauperiem regis subsequitur spoliatio plebis'; i. 249. Hardyng says that taxes and dymes ceased in consequence of the relief; p. 401. 'The kyng hath sumwhat graanted to have the resumpsion agayne in summe, but nat in alle'; J. Crane to J. Paston, May 6, 1450; Paston Letters, i. 127; Arnold's Chronicle, pp. 179–186.

[3] Some changes were made at this time; lord Beaumont is said to have been made chamberlain, and lord Rivers (Richard Wydville) constable; Paston Letters (May 13), i. 128. If this were done, changes were made soon after, for in July lord Beauchamp was treasurer (in Say's place) and lord Cromwell chamberlain; W. Worc. p. 769.

ation, impatient of peace, thoroughly imbued with mistrust. Cade and the party which used him—for there were not wanting signs and symptoms of much more crafty guidance—based their complaints and demands on the existence of grievances, political, constitutional and local, which could not be gainsayed[1]. They united in one comprehensive manifesto the loss of Normandy, the promotion of favourites, the exclusion of the lords of the blood royal from council, the interferences with county elections, and the peculiar oppressions of the commons of Kent. The leader took the name of John Mortimer, and declared himself to be cousin of the duke of York. He found means to collect round him, from Kent, Surrey and Sussex, a force to which he gave a semblance of order and discipline, and which was arranged very much as it would have been if called on to serve under the regular local administration. He proclaimed that he came to correct public abuses and remove evil counsellors. On the 1st of

Rebellion under Jack Cade.

Proclamation by the rebels.

[1] 'It was for the weal of him our sovereign lord and of all the realm and for to destroy the traitors being about him, with other diverse points that they would see that it were in short time amended'; Gregory, p. 190. 'This attempt was both honourable to God and the king and also profitable to the commonwealth; promising them that if either by force or policy they might once take the king, the queen, and other their counsellors into their hands and governance, that they would honourably entreat the king and so sharply handle his counsellors that neither fifteens should hereafter be demanded, nor once any impositions or tax should be spoken of'; Hall, p. 220.

'They chesse them a captayne, the whyche captayne compellyd alle the gentellys to arysse whythe them'; Gregory, p. 190. Stow, pp. 388, 399, gives the manifesto of Cade in fifteen articles of complaint and five of redress. The complaints include the threatened devastation of Kent in revenge for Suffolk's death, the heavy taxation, the exclusion of the lords of the royal blood from the king's presence and the promotion of upstarts, the abuse of purveyance, the false indictments by the king's servants who coveted the estates of the accused, false claims to land promoted by the king's servants, the treasonable loss of France, the expense of suing for the allowance of the barons of the Cinque ports, extortion of sheriffs in farming offices, excessive fines and amercements of the green wax, the usurpations of the court of Dover castle, undue interference with elections, illegal appointment of collectors of taxes, and the burden of attending the county court. The articles demanded are (1) a resumption of demesne, (2) the banishment of the Suffolk party and the return of the duke of York to court, (3) the vindication of the fame of duke Humfrey; (4) Suffolk and his party are made answerable for the death of Gloucester, cardinal Beaufort, and the duke of Warwick, as well as for the loss of France; the fifth article is a demand for the abolition of the abuses noted in the complaint.

Encounter of the royal forces with the rebels.

June he encamped at Blackheath. On the 6th Henry reached London. On the 11th, with 20,000 men, he marched on Blackheath, from whence Cade had retreated[1]; on the 18th a part of the royal force was cut to pieces at Sevenoaks: but the spirit of mutiny broke out in the rest[2]; the king was obliged to send the treasurer to the Tower, either to appease the mutineers or to save the minister. Deserted by his army the unhappy king retired to Kenilworth; the mayor and citizens of London offered to stand by him, but Henry had no confidence either in them or in himself. On his departure the rebels returned; Cade entered London on the 3rd of July, and on the 4th the treasurer was seized and beheaded. On the 5th, in a battle on London bridge, the rebels were defeated and the city freed from their presence. The chancellor then offered pardons already sealed to Cade and his followers. The pardons were accepted; the rebels dispersed; Cade to plunder and ravage, the more honest followers to their own homes. His subsequent conduct was not such as to justify his pardon, and no pardon could have a prospective validity to cover his new crimes. A reward[3] was set on his head, and soon after he was killed in Kent. The disturbances did not end here. Anarchy was spreading from the moment that Henry was seen to be incompetent. In Wiltshire bishop Ascough of Salisbury had been murdered in June. The malcontents in Kent elected a new captain after Cade's death; but the government speedily recovered from the panic into which they had fallen, and the severe executions which followed attested the sincerity of the alarm[4].

Henry retires to Kenilworth.

Cade in London

He is killed in Kent.

Other disturbances.

[1] At Blackheath the king ordered all his liege men should 'avoid the field'; whereupon the rebel army dispersed. The next day he went in pursuit to Greenwich, and Stafford was killed at Sevenoaks; the king slept at Greenwich but the lords went home soon after. Then, according to Gregory, another captain, who had taken the name of the former, led his force up to Blackheath and forced their way into London, where, on the 4th of July, they beheaded lord Say. Gregory, pp. 192, 193.

[2] Chron. ed. Giles, p. 40; Fabyan, p. 623.

[3] Rymer, xi. 275.

[4] On Cade's rebellion see Gairdner, preface to Paston Letters, vol. i. pp. lii.–lvi. sq.; and Sussex Archaeological Collections, vols. xviii, xix.

670. It is now that Richard duke of York first comes prominently on the stage. He was about forty years of age, and had been for fifteen years in public employment as regent of France or lieutenant of Ireland[1]. In both capacities he had shown good ability; and in France especially his administration, which came to an end shortly after Henry's marriage and before the loss of Normandy, had been fairly successful. Whatever credit it really deserved, it shone conspicuously in contrast with the luckless administration of Somerset: and York's popularity was in some measure the result of the mistrust inspired by his rival. For the two dukes were rivals in more ways than one. They were the nearest kinsmen of the king; the male line of Edward III had run into two branches; of the posterity of John of Gaunt, Somerset, after the king himself, was the male representative, the duke of York represented the descendants of Edmund of Langley. It is true that York, as representing the Mortimers, and through them the line of Lionel of Clarence, had a prior claim to the crown, and, in case of the king dying childless, the question of the rights of that line would have to be decided. But precedent was by no means clear; and the claim, ascribed to Henry IV, to succeed as heir of the house of Lancaster, complicated a question which was obscure enough already. If the inheritance after Henry VI belonged to the male heir of Edward III, it would be difficult to set aside Somerset; if it belonged to the heir general of John of Gaunt, the lady Margaret was not without real pretensions; but the Beauforts had no claim through Henry IV and the elder house of Lancaster, and, although their legitimation by pope and parliament was complete, they were excluded from the succession by Henry IV so far as he had power to do it. If on the other

The Duke of York.

Rivalry between him and Somerset.

Uncertainty of succession to the throne.

[1] 'Regent was of all that longed to the kyng.
And kept full well Normandy in specyall,
But Fraunce was gone afore in generall;
And home he came at seven yere ende agayne
With mekell love of the lande certayne.' Hardyng. p. 399.
He had been a good and popular ruler in Ireland, where the house of Mortimer had long cultivated popularity; ib. The duke's mission to Ireland was regarded by his friends as an exile; Gregory, pp. 189, 195.

Questions of succession.

hand the right of an heiress to transmit her claim to the crown to her descendants were admitted, York had no doubt the prior right: but no such case had yet occurred in English history[1]. Henry IV had entailed the crown on his sons to the exclusion of heiresses; the recognition of the earl of March as heir of Richard II in 1385 had little more significance than the recognition of Arthur of Brittany by Richard I. If then the Beauforts were excluded, York might claim as heir of Edmund of Langley; if the claims of the line of Clarence were admitted he might inherit as heir of Lionel. But so long as the house of Lancaster was on the throne, it was a delicate matter to urge a claim which, on the only principle on which it could be urged, was better than their own. And the conduct of the Mortimers had been such as to lead to the conclusion that their claim would not be urged. Edmund Mortimer, the ally of Owen Glendower, had indeed broached the rights of his nephews, and Richard of Cambridge had conspired to place his brother-in-law the young earl of March on the throne; the name of Mortimer had twice been mingled with deeds of treason and insurrection; but the heads of the house had been loyal and faithful, even to self-sacrifice. The last earl had been on the closest terms of friendship with Henry V, and Richard of York himself had been educated and promoted by the Lancastrian kings, as if they had no suspicion that he would ever think of supplanting them. But now that Henry had been married for five years without issue, the question of the succession could not fail to be constantly before the minds of both competitors. With Somerset it was more than a question of succession, it was a question of existence. The house of York would not be likely to tolerate the continued influence of the bastard line; personal emulation added another element to the causes of mutual mistrust; for Somerset had shown a signal contempt for the first military aspirations of duke Richard, and his own early brilliancy had paled before

Double claim of York.

Position of the Mortimers.

Position of Somerset.

[1] The right of Henry II, as successor of Henry I, is the only similar case, and in it there were so many points of difference as to destroy any real analogy.

Popularity of the Duke of York.

the more substantial glories of his rival, until it was entirely forgotten in the loss of Normandy. Now that Somerset and the policy which he supported had become odious, the nation looked kindly on the one sound administrator left, and the more so perhaps when they saw in him the rightful heir to the throne.

His constitutional position.

Yet Richard of York had no such claim as Henry IV to the character of a constitutional deliverer. He had none of the great traditions which, however illusory, had hung round the early Lancasters, earl Thomas and earl Henry. His father had suffered death as a traitor, and it was only by an act of impolitic equity that his blood had escaped the taint of legal corruption. His uncle, under the titles of Rutland, Aumâle, and York, had been connected with every conspiracy that was framed against Henry IV, and had been more than once imprisoned. His grandfather Edmund, the most worthless of the brood of Edward III, had been little else than a self-indulgent courtier. Any prince moreover who should come to the throne as the mere heir of Richard II would be likely to claim it free from all the constitutional restrictions on prerogative, which had been accepted and acted on by the three Henries. Nor, finally, was the kingdom at all in the condition to need a deliverer like Henry IV. It was exhausted, impoverished, and in disorder, but it was not unconstitutionally ruled. It was weakness, not tyranny, that lay at the root of the national distress. The administration of justice was sound, but the power of enforcing justice was to some extent wanting; the constant occurrence of local riots, the predatory bands which kept whole districts in alarm, the difficulty of collecting taxes, the general excitement of popular feeling arising on the national disgrace abroad, all called for a strong administration. Henry himself connived at no injustice; Somerset's incapacity was shown only by his misadventures abroad; and there is no reason to suppose that he wished to play the despot at home. But York's position was too full of danger to the crown to make it possible to lodge the administration in his hands; whilst in his own estimation it was such as entitled him to nothing lower

Weakness of the government.

Comparison of Somerset and York.

than the first place in court and council. It is not for the historian to attempt too minutely to adjust the balance between the two parties on moral or political grounds; neither York nor Somerset was a monster of vice nor a paragon of virtue; neither was endowed with much political skill or showed paramount ability in administration: the constitutional position indeed of Somerset was more defensible than that of York; but Somerset was thoroughly unpopular, and York, from that unpopularity, gained the character of a popular champion, the representative of legitimate succession and administrative reform.

Somerset comes from France and York from Ireland.

The death of Suffolk had left Henry without a minister, and Cade's rebellion had proved not only that he could not act for himself, but that there were troubles ahead which might task a strong man. York was tired of Ireland, where his friends thought him an exile, Somerset had let France slip out of his hands. It was a race who should come home first and take the kingdom in hand. York seems to have reached England before his rival, but Somerset had a strong ally in the queen, and he was not far behind. The capture of Cherbourg on the 12th of August set him free from all duty in Normandy; on the 11th of September he was made High Constable of England[1]. Before this the duke of York had visited the king. His return was not unexpected, and measures had been taken, justified no doubt by the belief that he was implicated in Cade's rebellion, to intercept him and to prevent him from collecting his friends[2]. Notwithstanding these precautions he forced his way to London, made his formal complaint to the king and obtained an apology for the mistrust that had been shown him, with a declaration of the king's confidence in him[3]. After a further remonstrance,

Visit of York to the king.

His complaint.

[1] Rymer, xi. 276.

[2] Chr. Giles, p. 42. See the duke's letter referred to in the following note.

[3] The bill of complaints presented to Henry is given in Stow, pp. 353, 354. The duke complains of the attacks on himself and his servants, and of a proposal to indict him for treason; the king in reply tells him how much appearances have been against him, how he was implicated in the murder of Moleyns and commonly reputed to be hostile to Henry himself; concluding however with the admission that he regarded him as his faithful

in which he embodied some of the complaints of the rebels and urged the legal trial of persons indicted, a complaint which the king met with a promise to appoint a sad and substantial council, of which the duke was to be a member[1], he urged the calling of a new parliament; and on the 5th of September a summons was issued convening it on November 6. He then went to Fotheringay, whence he conducted negotiations with his friends, and attempted to influence the elections in the counties[2]. His chief allies were the Nevilles, the earl of Salisbury his brother-in-law, and the earl of Warwick his nephew; the duke of Norfolk[3] also was inclined to support him in his attempt to make himself influential in the council.

He obtains from Henry a promise to appoint a new council; and a parliament is called.

How far his designs really went it is impossible to say: no doubt the court believed that he was an accomplice of Cade, who had asserted his claim to be one of the chief councillors; he too was the only person who had had anything to gain by the death of Gloucester and Suffolk; but there was little evidence as to the latter crime, and he was not even suspected of conniving at the former. He was himself throughout his career very cautious in stating any claims of his own. At this moment he appeared only as the guardian of order and demanded reform of abuses in the government.

The alarm felt by Henry and the court as to the duke's ulterior designs.

subject. These documents are placed by Stow under the year 1452, but they belong, as Mr. Gairdner says (Past. Lett. i. p. lx), to 1450.

[1] The remonstrance is in Stow, p. 385, and among the Paston Letters, i. 153; the answer is given (after Holinshed) by Mr. Gairdner; ib. introd. p. lxii. The duke tells the king that there is a common complaint that justice is not duly ministered to offenders, especially those indicted for treason; promises to aid the king in remedying this, and urges that the king's officers may be instructed to arrest and commit to the Tower all such persons as are so noised or indicted, of whatever estate, degree, or condition soever they be, there to abide without bail until they can be tried in court of law. Henry declined to take the advice of the duke without consulting the council.

[2] W. Worc. p. 769. The dukes of York and Norfolk chose the persons who were to be elected in Norfolk; Paston Letters, i. 160, 161, 162.

[3] John Mowbray succeeded his father in 1432 and was confirmed in the dukedom in 1444. His mother, Katharine Neville, was sister to the earl of Salisbury, and his wife, Eleanor Bourchier, was sister to archbishop Bourchier and half-sister to the duke of Buckingham. He died in 1461.

Parliament of November 1450.

The parliament met on the 6th of November[1], and cardinal Kemp in his opening speech stated the urgent necessity of national defence, and of putting down the local tumults. The French were threatening invasion; Calais was in imminent danger. The election of speaker at once showed that York's attempt to influence the elections had been successful[2]; the choice of the commons fell on Sir William Oldhall, his chamberlain and counsellor, one of the allies who had been only prevented by arrest from meeting him when he landed. The proceedings of the session were begun by an altercation between the two dukes, the one supported by the commons, the other by the court and council[3]. During the session parliament was supreme; Somerset was arrested on the 1st of December, his equipage being plundered by the mob[4]. On the 18th the parliament was prorogued[5]; and immediately after Christmas Somerset was made captain of Calais[6]. On the meeting of parliament, January 20, 1451, the struggle was renewed. Henry plucked up spirit to reject a petition that Suffolk might be declared a traitor[7]; but he was obliged to receive another[8] in which the commons demanded that he should remove from court the duke of Somerset, the duchess of Suffolk, the lord Dudley, the bishop of Lichfield, and the abbot of Gloucester[9], with several knights and gentlemen.

Disputes between York and Somerset.

Petition for the removal of the king's friends.

[1] Rot. Parl. v. 210. 'A parliament wherein all the commons were agreed, and rightfully elected him (York) as heir apparent of England, nought to proceed in any other matters till that were granted by the lords, whereto the king and lords would not consent nor grant but anon brake up the parliament'; Chron. Lond. p. 137.

[2] Rot. Parl. v. 210; Paston Letters, i. 163.

[3] W. Worc. p. 769.

[4] Dec. 2; Gregory, p. 195; Chr. Giles, p. 42. Dec. 1; Fabyan, p. 626.

[5] Rot. Parl. v. 213.

[6] W. Worc. p. 770. Henry was at Greenwich at Christmas. Gregory says that in February 1451 the king, and the dukes of Somerset and Exeter were at Canterbury 'where were dampnyde many men of the captayne ys men for hyr rysyng, and for hyr talking agayne the kynge, havynge more favyr unto the duke of Yorke thenne unto the kynge'; Gregory, p. 196. Henry punished the 'stubborn heads' but spared the poor people; Hall, p. 222. The judges, however, commissioned for Kent were the duke of York, lord Bourchier, Sir John Fastolf, and others; Paston Letters, i. 19. A general pardon was issued May 18; Rymer, xi. 286.

[7] Rot. Parl. v. 226.

[8] Ib. v. 216.

[9] Reginald Bowlers was an old servant of Henry, of great piety and learning. He became abbot in 1437, had refused the bishopric of Llandaff

The king refused to dismiss the lords, but consented to the removal of the rest for a year. This was itself no small triumph; Dudley and the abbot of Gloucester were excluded from the council; and Somerset's position became still more critical. Thomas Yonge, the member for Bristol, ventured to propose that the duke of York should be declared heir to the crown[1]. Little was done however in the parliament, which sat until April 19 and met again on May 5[2]. The act of resumption passed in the last session was again enacted[3]; Jack Cade and his followers were attainted[4]: an order was given for the enforced payment of the subsidy granted at Leicester; and the exigencies of the government were met by assigning to the king a preferential payment of £20,000 on the subsidies, to be expended on the defence of the realm, after the maintenance of Calais was secured[5]. The result of the deliberations was to shake but not to overthrow Somerset. He retained his influence with both king and queen; the unpopular abbot of Gloucester had already in December been made bishop of Hereford; Thomas Yonge was sent to the Tower[6].

Henry's partial concession.

Proposal to declare the duke of York heir to the crown.

Supplies.

Somerset remains in power.

There was still one chance open for the recovery of England's proud position on the continent. Normandy was lost, but Guienne was not yet conquered; and some show of energy and promptness abroad might have saved the dynasty at home. But the opportunity was lost. The French overran Gascony in the summer of 1451; Bourdeaux fell in June; Bayonne was taken on August 25; before the winter all the country was in their hands, and Calais was again threatened. The duke of York believed himself fully warranted in making this a ground of his renewed attack on the minister. He

Loss of Guienne and Gascony in 1451.

ii. 1440, and had been a member of the council since 1443. Mon. Angl. n 536; Beckington's Letters, i. 31; Ordinances, v. 269 sq. The bishop of Lichfield, William Booth, was the subject of a satirical poem printed in Exc. Hist. p. 357; Wright, Pol. Songs, ii. 225.

1 W. Worc. p. 770; Chr. Lond. p. 137.

2 Rot. Parl. v. 213, 214.

3 Ib. v. 217.

4 Ib. v. 224.

5 Ib. v. 211, 214.

6 W. Worc. p. 770; Rot. Parl. v. 337.

Movements of the duke of York. had failed to overcome him by the constitutional procedure of parliament. He determined now to follow up the formal remonstrance by such a display of force as would bring the king to his senses[1].

He declares his loyalty, 671. On the 9th of January, 1452, the duke wrote a formal declaration of his loyalty, and offered to swear it on the Blessed Sacrament before any two or three lords whom Henry should appoint[2]. and attacks Somerset. On the 3rd of February he published a letter to the men of Shrewsbury in which he attacked the duke of Somerset, accusing him of the loss of Normandy and Guienne, and complaining of his constant attempts to prejudice the king against him, labouring for his undoing, endeavouring to corrupt his blood and to disinherit him and his heirs[3]. For these reasons, which involved the speedy ruin of the nation, he declared himself to be about to proceed against Somerset, and begged the men of Shrewsbury to take measures for the maintenance of order in the contingent which they were to contribute to the expedition. He marches to London. He was joined by the earl of Devonshire and lord Cobham[4], and marched on London. Henry was not unprepared; he no doubt saw in the duke's proceedings full confirmation of the designs which had been imputed to him in 1450; he could no longer believe that the untoward events of that year were unconnected with the policy of York, and Somerset was by his side to keep all suspicions alive. On Henry goes to meet him. the 16th Henry marched against his cousin[5]; and on the 17th summoned lord Cobham to his presence[6]. The duke avoided an engagement, but was prevented by the royal orders from entering the city, and, expecting aid from Kent, moved

[1] 'That year' (1451), says Gregory, 'was competent well and peaceable as for any rising among ourself, for every man was in charity, but somewhat the hearts of the people hung and sorrowed for that the duke of Gloucester was dead, and some said that the duke of York had great wrong, but what wrong there was no man that durst say; but some grounyd and some lowryd and had disdain of other'; Chron. p. 198.

[2] Stow, p. 393.

[3] Cf. Hall, p. 225. The letter is printed in Ellis, Original Letters, 1st Series, i. 11–13; Paston Letters, i. pp. lxxi, lxxii.

[4] English Chron. ed. Davies, p. 69.

[5] Fabyan, p. 626.

[6] Ordinances, vi. 116.

on to Dartford with a force of not less than seventeen thousand men[1]. The king thereupon marched to Blackheath and encamped there, probably with a still larger force. A battle was prevented by the negotiation of the bishops and other lords, among whom the chief were bishops Waynflete and Bourchier, the earls of Salisbury and Warwick and the lords Beauchamp and Sudeley[2]. The duke found that his cause was not so popular in Kent as he had expected; the earls of Salisbury and Warwick had not yet declared themselves on his side, and he was willing to treat. He was anxious only as yet to prove his own loyalty and to overthrow Somerset. The king offered him pardon for himself, a general amnesty, and full opportunity of obtaining justice in the ordinary process of law[3]. It was now, possibly, that he laid before the king his formal charges against Somerset, in a bill of accusation similar to that which had proved fatal to Suffolk. According to this statement, Somerset was directly responsible for the loss of Normandy, where he had removed the good officers whom his predecessor had left, and let out their places to the highest bidder; he had alienated the king's friends by imprisonment and fines, he had connived at the breaches of the truce in 1449; he had weakened the garrisons, had neglected to succour besieged places, had surrendered Rouen in a way that was treacherous and treasonable, had allowed Calais to fall into a state in which it was barely defensible, and had embezzled the money paid by way of indemnity for private losses on the surrender of Maine and Anjou[4]. Here was a sufficiently formidable bill of indictment; yet there are no charges of tyranny or maladministration at home, nothing that on the most liberal interpretation could justify the attempt to coerce the king. And so the lords seem

Meeting at Blackheath.

Charges made by the duke of York against the duke of Somerset.

[1] Whethamstede estimates the duke's force at ten thousand; and the king's at three times that number; i. 160, 161. See however, Paston Letters, i. p. cxlviii.

[2] Fabyan, p. 627; Paston Letters, i. p. lxxiv.

[3] Whethamstede, i. 162.

[4] The full text of the accusation is printed for the first time by Mr. Gairdner, Paston Letters, i. pp. lxxvii sq., it was known to Stow, Chr. p. 393.

Misunderstanding and reconciliation.

to have thought. It was agreed that Somerset should remain in custody until he had answered the accusation, and on this understanding the duke of York dismissed his forces[1]. On the 1st of March he presented himself in the king's tent, and, to his great disgust, found Somerset in his accustomed place. He himself was sent under guard to London where, on the 10th of March[2], a reconciliation with the king was effected. The duke of York, at S. Paul's, swore fealty to Henry and promised for the future to sue for remedy in legal form, whenever he should be aggrieved. But no mention was made of Somerset, and the duke returned to his home disappointed of his more immediate aim. England was not yet ready for the civil war, and did not regard an armed force as the constitutional expedient for getting rid of a minister in whom the king trusted. The king himself, too ready to believe in the sincerity of the pacification, issued in the following month a general pardon[3] and spent the autumn in a royal progress the object of which was to reconcile all parties. But the policy and influence of Somerset were still supreme. Archbishop Kemp was transferred in July from York to Canterbury; bishop Booth of Lichfield, one of those against whom the commons had petitioned in 1451, was promoted to York. The treasury however was committed to Tiptoft earl of Worcester, a friend of the duke of York. One good effect followed the rising; an expedition was sent in September[4] to Guienne under the earl of Shrewsbury, who recovered Bourdeaux and gave hopes

The duke of York is unsupported.

Change of ministers.

[1] The duke of York yielded 'on condition that his petitions before asked for the weal of the king and of all his realm might be granted and had, and his enemies to be committed to the Tower to abide the law, and so the lords were agreed and granted that it should be and were sworn to each other and forthwith the duke sent his men home again and he meekly came and submitted himself at the Blackheath to the king, his adversaries there standing present contrary to the appointment and their oaths'; Chr. Lond. p. 138; cf. Stow, p. 385. Whethamstede says nothing about the arrest of Somerset, i. 163. Hall states the matter as uncertain; the king 'caused the duke of Somerset to be committed to ward as some say, or to keep himself privy in his own house, as others write'; p. 226. Cf. Fabyan, pp. 627.

[2] Cf. Chron. Giles, p. 43. Stow gives the form of the duke's submission, p. 395. Whethamstede (i. 163), says that the duke obtained papal absolution from this oath before he imprisoned Somerset in 1453.

[3] Whethamstede, i. 85, 86 sq.

[4] Rymer, xi. 313.

of glorious vindication of English renown[1]. In January 1453 the king called a parliament to meet at Reading on the 6th of March[2]. The place was probably selected as one free from the York influence, which was strong in London, and the election of the speaker showed that the duke was not likely to have his own way in the assembly. The choice fell on Thomas Thorpe, a knight of the shire for Essex, and a baron of the Exchequer, who was strongly opposed to him[3]. The session was short; little was done beyond granting supplies, the liberality of which seems to show that the pacification was regarded as satisfactory. A grant of a tenth and fifteenth was voted; the other taxes, tunnage and poundage, the subsidy on wool and the alien tax, were continued for the king's life. A force of twenty thousand archers was moreover granted, to be maintained by the counties, cities and towns according to their substance. These grants were made on the 28th of March[4], and the parliament was then prorogued to April 25, when it was to meet at Westminster. The second session was occupied with financial business, and closed on the 2nd of July after an additional half-tenth and fifteenth had been granted, and the number of archers reduced to thirteen thousand. On the 22nd of June Sir William Oldhall, the speaker of the last parliament, was attainted for his conduct at Dartford in 1452 and for his alleged complicity with Cade[5]. The parliament was not yet dissolved, but ordered to meet again at Reading on the 12th of November[6].

Parliament at Reading, March, 1453.

Thorpe speaker.

Grants of money and men.

Second session.

Prorogation to Reading.

672. In the interval the storms gathered more heavily and

[1] Mem. de J. du Clercq (Buchon, xv.) liv. 2. cc. 2 sq. liv. 3, cc. 1–5.

[2] Rot. Parl. v. 227.

[3] Ib. v. 228. Thorpe was a faithful Lancastrian, who had been Remembrancer of the Exchequer and removed from office by Tiptoft, when he became treasurer in 1452. He was made a baron of the exchequer in 1453; was at the battle of S. Alban's in 1455, and was saved from condemnation in parliament that year by the king refusing the petition against him. He was taken prisoner at the battle of Northampton in 1460, and beheaded by the Yorkists in 1461. Foss, Biog. Jurid. p. 658.

[4] Rot. Parl. v. 228–232. The convocation of Canterbury granted two tenths in Feb. 1453, Wilk. Conc. iii. 562; about the same time the York clergy granted half a tenth, ib. p. 563; and a whole tenth at Michaelmas, p. 564.

[5] Rot. Parl. v. 265, 266.

[6] Ib. v. 236.

Shrewsbury killed.

more fatally than ever. On the 23rd of July the earl of Shrewsbury was killed at Castillon[1] and the whole of the recent conquests were shortly recovered by the French. During the autumn[2] the king was attacked by illness, which very soon produced a total derangement of his mental powers and made him for the time an idiot. On the 13th of October queen Margaret bore her unfortunate son Edward. The coincidence of the three events was strangely important. The final loss of Guienne destroyed all the hold which the government still had on the respect of the country; the king's illness placed the queen and the duke of York in direct rivalry for the regency; the birth of the heir of Lancaster cut off the last hope which the duke had of a peaceful succession to the crown on Henry's death.

Illness of the king; and birth of an heir.

The speaker arrested.

The duke was not idle during the vacation; he procured the arrest and imprisonment of Thorpe the speaker on an action of trespass, and in contempt of the privilege of parliament[3]; a quarrel between the Percies and the Nevilles caused the latter to draw closer to their kinsman, and he secured the assistance of the duke of Norfolk for a renewed attack on Somerset. The parliament met at Reading in November, only to be prorogued to the following February[4]. The king's illness increased, and it was the urgent business of the council to provide for the interrupted action of the executive. On the 21st of November a great council was held for the purpose of securing peace in the land, and to this the duke of York, who seems at first not to have been properly summoned, was called up by special letters[5]. In this invitation Somerset did not join, and

Schemes of Duke Richard.

Council in November, 1453.

[1] Du Clercq, iii. c. 2 (Buchon, xxxviii. 130).

[2] July 6, at Clarendon; Chr. Giles, p. 44; W. Worc. p. 771. So great was Somerset's unpopularity that he was regarded as accountable for Henry's sickness, for having taken him to Clarendon. Gregory, p. 198.

[3] The duke of York had collected certain harness and other habiliments of war in the bishop of Durham's house in London. These Thorpe had seized and carried off, possibly under the orders of the court. At the beginning of Michaelmas term the duke brought an action against him in the court of exchequer, and got damages to the amount of £1000, and costs £10; for the non-payment of which he was thrown into the Fleet prison; Rot. Parl. v. 239.

[4] Rot. Parl. v. 238.

[5] Ordinances, vi. 163, 164.

the invitation itself probably implies that the council was now inclined to accept the services of his rival. The duke attended and made a formal protest against the proceedings of the government in depriving him of the advice of his personal counsellors[1]. It is not improbable that the queen on this occasion proposed to assume the regency during her husband's illness[2]; and the duke of Norfolk perhaps took the same opportunity of presenting his charges against Somerset; the arrest and imprisonment of the luckless minister followed early in December[3]. He was not friendless, and both parties prepared to appear with armed force at the ensuing parliament[4]. The influence however of the duke of York had already made itself felt in the council. The place of meeting was altered; the earl of Worcester on the 11th of February, 1454, prorogued the assembly to the 14th at Westminster[5]; and on that day the duke of York opened the proceedings under a commission from the king and council. He was already in possession of supreme power, although not yet nominally regent; the influence of Somerset in the council was paralysed by his arrest; an indictment against the earl of Devonshire for high treason in consequence of his action in 1452 failed, and the duke of York, conceiving himself to be attacked, claimed and received from the lords an assurance of their belief in his loyalty[6]. The house of commons in vain demanded the release of their speaker. He

Complaints of the duke of York.

Possible design of the queen.

New attack on Somerset.

Parliament meets in February, 1454.

York declared loyal.

[1] See the curious document printed by Mr. Gairdner, Paston Letters, i. cxlviii, from the Rot. Pat. 32 Hen. VI, m. 20.

[2] One of the Paston Letters (i. 265) mentions a bill of five articles in which the queen claimed the regency, the patronage in church and state, and the expenditure of the sum allowed to the king for livelihood.

[3] The petition of Norfolk against Somerset is in the Paston Letters, i. 259. He had delivered some charges before; to these Somerset had replied, and Norfolk had answered the reply. He contends that the duke's acts have justified the charges; he has used bribery to prevent the charges being brought home, 'some saying that the cases by him committed be but cases of trespass, and other taking a colour to make universal peace'; but he is guilty of the loss of Guienne and Normandy; he demands a full inquiry.

[4] Paston Letters, i. 264, 265.

[5] Rot. Parl. v. 238, 239. The duke of Norfolk had attempted to influence the elections in Suffolk, and the sheriff made a return that he dared not proceed on account of the menaces of the duke's servants; on which account the duke afterwards had him summoned before the council. Ord. vi. 183.

[6] Rot. Parl. v. 249.

Question of privilege.

had been arrested at the suit of the duke; the privilege of the commons was asserted on his behalf; the question of privilege was referred to the judges, who denied that they had power to decide such high matters, and the lords determined that he should remain in prison[1]. The commons had to make the best of it, and elected a new speaker, Sir Thomas Charlton, member for Middlesex[2]. Through him on the 19th of March they addressed the lords with a request that measures might be taken for the defence of Calais, for which an outlay of £40,000 was required, and that the promise which the chancellor had made at Reading, to appoint a sad and wise council, might be fulfilled. Cardinal Kemp replied to the address, promising a good and comfortable answer[3]. That answer he did not live to furnish. He died three days after, on the 22nd of March. He was about seventy-four, a man of great experience, moderation, and fidelity; the friend and coadjutor of Beaufort, and yet thoroughly respected by the opposite party. He knew however that he himself must be the next victim; the duke of Norfolk, the pliant agent of the duke of York, had already begun to threaten him, and his death may have been hastened by the alarm and excitement[4]. He left the two most important posts in church and state vacant, and removed the most powerful influence that might have curbed the ambition of the duke of York.

A new speaker. Address of the commons. Death of Cardinal Kemp.

Continued illness of the king.

A message sent by the lords, to inquire the royal pleasure as to the appointment of a new archbishop and a new chancellor, revealed unmistakeably the present condition of the king. It was impossible to attract his attention or to get a word from him. On the 23rd a committee of the lords visited him at Windsor; on the 25th they reported the failure of their mission[5]. Nothing now could be done without the appointment of a regent. On the 27th the lords chose the duke of York to be protector and defender of the realm[6]. The duke accepted the election with a protest that he undertook the task only in obedi-

The duke of York chosen protector.

[1] Rot. Parl. v. 239, 240. [2] Ib. v. 240. [3] Ib. v. 240.

[4] 'Eo quod noluit in aliquo a veritate declinare, sic ab aliquibus dominis et specialiter a duce Norfolkiae minatur, quod citius elegit mori quam vitam ducere mortis'; Chron. Giles, p. 45.

[5] Rot. Parl. v. 240–242. [6] Ib. v. 242.

ence to the king and the peerage of the land, in whom, by reason of the king's infirmity, 'resteth the exercise of his authority.' He requested further the advice and assistance of the lords, which was graciously promised, and a definition of his functions and commission. These were described as constituting him chief of the king's council, and as comprised under the title of protector and defender, 'which importeth a personal duty of intendance to the actual defence of this land, as well against the enemies outward, if case require, as against rebels inward, if any hap to be, that God forbid, during the king's pleasure and so that it be not prejudice to my lord prince[1].' Precedents were to be searched to determine the amount of the protector's salary. The resolution of the lords was embodied in an act, which received the assent of the commons and passed on the 3rd of April; by this the duke was constituted protector until the prince came of age, or as long as the king pleased[2]. On the previous day he had placed the great seal in the hands of his brother-in-law, the earl of Salisbury[3]; on the 9th the monks of Canterbury had a licence to elect the primate, and their choice, directed by the protector and confirmed by the pope, fell on Thomas Bourchier, bishop of Ely, a grandson of duke Thomas of Gloucester and half-brother of the duke of Buckingham[4]. The same day the council recommended George Neville, the chancellor's son, a young man of twenty-three, for the next vacant bishopric[5]. Although these appointments indicate a determination in the victorious faction to strengthen, wherever it was possible, their hold on power, their position was not by any means assured, and their administration, whether it were guided by policy or by an honest wish to be fair, was one of compromise. The appointment of the archbishop, although he afterwards showed himself a faithful Yorkist, was one to which no objection could be raised on the ground of incompetency or

Conditions of acceptance.

Salisbury chancellor;

Bourchier archbishop.

Policy of this appointment.

[1] Rot. Parl. v. 242; above, p. 107. [2] Ib. v. 242, 243; Rymer, xi. 346.

[3] Rymer, xi. 344, 345; Rot. Parl. v. 449.

[4] On the 30th of March the council determined to nominate Bourchier for the primacy; Ordinances, vi. 168, 170. He was elected April 23; Ang. Sac. i. 123.

[5] Ordinances, vi. 168; Rot. Parl. v. 450.

No extreme measures attempted.

partisanship, and was perhaps intended to secure the support of the Staffords and Bourchiers[1]. Tiptoft was not removed from the treasury. The mixed composition of the parliament prevented any extreme measures. No attempt was made in parliament to bring Somerset to trial; a fact which perhaps his near relationship to the Nevilles[2] might account for. He was, as a matter of course, deprived of the government of Calais, which the duke of York took upon himself[3], and he remained in prison, as did the Lord Cobham, who was in disgrace as a partisan of York's[4].

Other transactions in parliament.

The provision which had been made by the king for his two half-brothers was confirmed, and the rights of the queen and the little heir apparent were scrupulously guarded wherever they were supposed to be affected. Owing to the confused way in which the acts of this long parliament have been enrolled, it is difficult to assign to the particular session the several financial acts to which no date is appended; but it may be presumed that they formed part of the closing business of the parliament. The act of 1450, which assigned £20,000 to the king, was repealed[5], and a new provision was made for the expenses of the household; the subsidies appropriated to Calais were vested in the earls of Salisbury, Shrewsbury, Wiltshire, and Worcester, and the Lord Stourton[6]. On the 28th of February a graduated fine was imposed on the lords who absented

[1] Anne of Gloucester, daughter of duke Thomas of Woodstock, married first Edmund earl of Stafford who died in 1403, and secondly William Bourchier earl of Eu who died in 1420. By her first husband she had Humfrey earl of Buckingham, Hereford, Stafford, Northampton, and Perche, lord of Brecon and Holderness, who was in 1444 created duke of Buckingham; by her second husband she had Henry Bourchier, created viscount in 1446, Thomas archbishop of Canterbury 1454–1486, and other sons. The duke of Buckingham had married Anne Neville, sister of the earl of Salisbury. He attempted, as we shall see, to mediate in the first years of the struggle. His eldest son, the earl of Stafford, fell at the first battle of S. Alban's, and he himself at Northampton in 1459.

[2] The earl of Salisbury was, it will be remembered, son of Ralph Neville earl of Westmoreland, by Johanna Beaufort, Somerset's aunt.

[3] Rot. Parl. v. 254.

[4] Ib. v. 248.

[5] Rot. Parl. v. 247. The amount assigned to the household was £5183 6*s*. 8*d*.

[6] Rot. Parl. v. 243. These lords were relieved from their office in the next Parliament; ib. p. 283. The duke of York was made captain of Calais July 17; Rymer, xi. 351. Councils were held for the purpose of raising money for Calais in May and June; Ordinances, vi. 174–180, &c.

themselves from parliament[1]; on the 15th of March the infant prince was created prince of Wales[2]; on the 9th of March the Lord Cromwell demanded security of the peace against Henry Holland, the duke of Exeter[3]. An act of resumption, which was now becoming a part of the regular business of parliament, was likewise passed[4]. Several statutes were enrolled.

Doings in parliament.

The parliament probably broke up a week before Easter, April 21[5]; and the government devolved upon the protector and the council, which he no doubt was able to form at his own discretion. The first task which he undertook was the pacification of the north, where the quarrel between the Nevilles and the Percies was spreading[6]; the duke of Exeter had joined the latter party and had attempted, by the use of the king's name, to stir up Yorkshire and Lancashire against the duke of York. The protector's presence in the north served to disperse the forces of the two factions, but not to reconcile them; the duke of Exeter came to London and took sanctuary at Westminster, whence he was taken by force and confined at Pomfret. The Percies remained at large. A second question was how to dispose of the duke of Somerset. In a meeting of the great council on the 18th of July, his friends attempted to obtain his release on bail, but on the appeal of the protector it was determined to ask the advice of the judges and of the absent lords; and the 28th of October was fixed as the day on which the charges of the duke of Norfolk were to be brought forward[7]. What was then done is not known; Somerset, however, was not released.

Administration of the duke of York.

Somerset kept in prison.

[1] Rot. Parl. v. 248; Ordinances, vi. 181–183.
[2] Rot. Parl. v. 249. [3] Ib. v. 264. [4] Ib. v. 267 sq.
[5] The last dated transaction is one of April 17; ib. p. 247.
[6] The duke of Exeter and lord Egremont rose against the Nevilles in 1453. The duke was summoned before the council on June 25, 1454, Ordinances, vi. 189; arrested and imprisoned at Pomfret July 24, ib. vi. 217; and at Wallingford, ib. vi. 234; but released on the king's recovery. The earl of Devon also, who had a private war with lord Bonneville, was arrested during York's regency; Chr. Giles, p. 46. Bonneville had a quarrel with the earl of Huntingdon, father of the duke of Exeter, in 1440; Beckington, i. 193; Paston Letters, i. 264, 290, 296, 350; Ordinances, vi. 130, 140, 217, 234.
[7] Ordinances vi. 207, 218.

The king recovers early in 1455.

673. The king recovered his senses a few weeks later. He was sane at Christmas, and recognised his little son for the first time on the 30th of December; on the 7th of January he admitted bishop Waynflete to an interview. The dismissal of the protector and his ministers was imminent[1]. On the 5th of February Somerset was released; the duke of Buckingham, the earl of Wiltshire, and the lords Roos and Fitzwarin undertaking that he should present himself for trial on the 3rd of the following November[2]. On the 4th of March he appealed to the king in council and was declared loyal; he and the duke of York were bound over to accept an arbitration[3]; on the 6th Somerset was restored to the captaincy of Calais[4]. On the 7th the great seal was taken from the earl of Salisbury and given to archbishop Bourchier[5], no doubt to secure Buckingham's support; on the 15th James Butler earl of Wiltshire was made treasurer[6]. A great council was then called, to meet at Leicester, to provide for the safety of the king[7], and the partisans of York were no longer summoned to attend the ordinary councils. The duke could scarcely allege that such measures were unconstitutional or unprecedented, for they were in close analogy with his own policy of the previous year. He saw that they must be met by a resistance backed with armed force. With the Nevilles he collected his forces in the north[8], and marched towards London. On the 20th of May, in conjunction with Salisbury and Warwick, he addressed the archbishop in a letter dated at Royston, and followed it up with an appeal to the king on the 21st from Ware[9]; in both the lords declared their loyalty, and affirmed that their forces were intended only to secure their own safety against their enemies who surrounded the king, and to enable them to prove their good will towards him. The letter to the king was, as they afterwards said, intercepted by Somerset, but

Somerset released.

Bourchier chancellor.

York is not satisfied and marches on London.

His letter to the king intercepted.

[1] Paston Letters, i. 315.
[2] Rymer, xi. 361; see J. du Clercq, iii. c. 10.
[3] Rymer, xi. 361, 362.
[4] Ib. xi. 363.
[5] Ordinances, vi. 365.
[6] Dugdale, Origines Juridiciales.
[7] Rot. Parl. v. 280.
[8] Whethamstede, i. 164.
[9] Rot. Parl. v. 281; Paston Letters, i. 325. The letter to the king is given in Latin by Whethamstede, i. 184.

if it had been delivered it could have made little difference. Henry, with his half-brother the earl of Pembroke, the dukes of Somerset and Buckingham, the earls of Northumberland, Devonshire, Stafford, and Wiltshire, and a force of two thousand men, advanced to S. Alban's, and there on the 22nd the two parties met. Negotiation was tried in vain; the Yorkists demanded an interview with the king and the arrest of the counsellors whom they hated. The royal party replied with threats which they must have known that they were too weak to execute; and Henry was himself moved to declare that he would be satisfied only with the destruction of his enemies. A battle followed, in which the duke of Somerset, the earl of Northumberland, the earl of Stafford. son of Buckingham, and the lord Clifford, on the king's side, were slain, and he himself was wounded. Although in itself little more than a skirmish which lasted half an hour, and cost comparatively little bloodshed, the first battle of S. Alban's sealed the fate of the kingdom; the duke of York was completely victorious; the king remained a prisoner in his hands, and he recovered at once all the power that he had lost.

First battle of S. Alban's, May 22, 1455.

Somerset slain.

The battle of S. Alban's had one permanent result: it forced the queen forward as the head of the royal party. Suffolk first and Somerset after him had borne the brunt of the struggle, and enabled the duke to say that it was against the evil counsellors, not against the king himself, that his efforts were directed. The death of Somerset left her alone; the duke of Buckingham, although loyal, was not actuated by that feeling towards the house of Lancaster which moved the Beauforts, and which drew down upon them in successive generations the hatred of the opposition. The young duke of Somerset was too young to have more than a colourable complicity with his father's policy, although he was not too young to inherit the enmities which his very name entailed upon him. Nor could the royal party under Margaret's guidance be said to have any longer any policy but that of resistance to the duke of York. She had been taught to

Political result of the battle, in forcing queen Margaret into the foreground.

[1] Whethamstede i. 167; Stow, pp. 390–400; Archaeologia, xx. 519; Paston Letters, i. 327–333; J. du Clercq, iii. c. 23.

believe, and no doubt believed, that he was accessory to Cade's rebellion and to the murder of Suffolk; he was directly answerable for the death of Somerset. York himself made scarcely any pretence to the character of a reformer of the state; it was to vindicate his own position, to dislodge the enemies who poisoned the king's mind against him, that he rose in arms; and the charges against them, by which he tried to justify his hostility, were such as tended rather to involve the accused in popular odium than to indicate a treacherous intent. Still it may be questioned whether the design of claiming the crown had distinctly formed itself in his mind before this period. That he regarded himself and was regarded by his party as the fittest man to rule England, under a king so incapable as Henry VI, could only be a justification of his proceedings in the eyes of those who believed that such a sense of fitness gives by itself a paramount claim to office. Under these circumstances the struggle henceforth loses all its constitutional features; the history of England becomes the history of a civil war between two factions, both of which preserve certain constitutional formalities without being at all guided by constitutional principles. Such principles neither actuate the combatants nor decide the struggle: yet in the end they prove their vitality by surviving the exhausted energies of both the parties, and maintaining the continuity of the national life in the forms which its earlier history had moulded.

Apparent incompleteness of the duke's designs.

Change in the constitutional action of the period.

Changes in the ministry.

674. Immediately after the battle the unhappy king admitted his victorious enemies to reconciliation: on the 26th of May he summoned the parliament to meet in July[1]; and on the 29th he removed the treasurer, replacing him with the viscount Bourchier, the archbishop's brother[2]: the government of Calais was given to Warwick, and the duke of York himself became high constable. But the royal party was not yet intimidated; the private feuds which divided the lords were not merged in the public quarrel; lord Cromwell was at enmity with Warwick: the elec-

[1] Lords' Report, iv. 936; by another letter he directed certain lords to bring up only their household servants and avoid setting a dangerous example; Ordinances, vi. 244.

[2] Paston Letters, i. 334.

tions even required careful attention on the part of the new government, and the duke had some trouble in obtaining a parliament which would be likely to warrant his proceedings[1]. The circumstances, however, of the session bore some analogy with those of the last parliament. The estates met on the 9th of July; on the 10th the chancellor declared the causes of the summons: the sustenance of the royal household, the defence of Calais, the war against the French and Scots, the employment of the thirteen thousand archers voted in 1453, the preservation of peace in the country, the procuring of ready money, the protection of the sea, and the pacification of Wales[2]. Five committees of the lords addressed themselves to the several points[3]: the next day Sir John Wenlock was chosen speaker; the duke of York presented a schedule giving his account of the recent struggle, and the king declared him and the Nevilles to be loyal[4]. On the 24th the lords took an oath of allegiance to Henry, and ordered it to be taken by the absent members[5]. On the 31st the parliament was prorogued, and before the day of meeting, November 12, the king was again insane. The formalities observed in 1454 were again adopted: on the 13th the commons asked for the nomination of a protector: on the 15th they repeated the request, and the chancellor undertook to consult the lords; the lords agreed and nominated the duke of York: on the 17th, in answer to the speaker's inquiry as to the result of the proposal, it was announced that the royal assent was given to the nomination made by the lords[6]. The duke under protest accepted the office; and the king by letters patent on the 19th made the formal appointment, to continue until

Preparations for parliament.

It meets, July, 1455.

York and the Nevilles declared loyal.

Oath of allegiance taken.

Second illness of Henry and second protectorate of duke Richard.

[1] The duchess of Norfolk wrote to John Paston praying him to vote for her candidates; Letters, i. 337: the Norfolk nominees were returned; ib. 339, 340. On the 5th of July the king wrote to the sheriff of Kent about the 'busy labour' which had been spent in that county in order to influence the elections, and ordered him to proclaim that the election was free according to the laws; Ordinances, vi. 246; Rot. Parl. v. 451.

[2] Rot. Parl. v. 278; Stow, p. 400.

[3] Rot. Parl. v. 279.

[4] Ib. v. 280.

[5] Ib. v. 282. It was taken by the two archbishops, the dukes of York and Buckingham, eleven bishops, six earls, two viscounts, eighteen abbots, two priors, and seventeen barons.

[6] Rot. Parl. v. 284–289, 453; Rymer xi. 369, 370.

the duke should be relieved of his charge by the sovereign himself in parliament, or the prince should come of age. On the 22nd the king vested the 'politique rule and governance' in the hands of the council, of which the duke was chief[1]. On the 13th of December the parliament was again prorogued to January 14, 1456; on which day it met[2]. On the 25th of February the king had recovered[3] and at once relieved the duke from his office as protector[4]. What little else was attempted in the session may be learned from the petitions; Warwick's appointment as captain of Calais was completed[5]; duke Humfrey was declared to have been loyal[6]; the questions arising on the imprisonment of Thomas Young were referred to the council[7], and provision was made for the household[8]; no taxation seems to have been asked for; a new act of resumption was passed[9]. The few statutes enrolled are important only as being the last attempts at legislation made during the reign. Probably the king's sudden recovery brought to a precipitate end both the session of the parliament and the supremacy of the protector. Before he was formally relieved from his office he and Warwick had come up with a large guard to parliament; he had not strengthened his political position during his short term of office; and he went out leaving affairs in worse confusion than that in which he had found them.

The government vested in the council.

Henry's recovery, February, 1456.

Petitions in parliament.

The duke of York had not mended matters.

675. Two years of comparative quiet followed the king's restoration to health. Henry made a sustained effort to keep

[1] Rot. Parl. v. 289, 290. He ordains 'that his council shall provide, commyne, ordain, speed and conclude all such matters as touch and concern the good and politique rule and governance of this his land'; he is himself to be informed of all matters that concern his person. The council accept, protesting that the sovereignty must always remain in the royal person.

[2] Rot. Parl. v. 321; Ordinances, vi. 274.

[3] Feb. 9, John Bocking wrote to Sir John Fastolf, that the king was inclined to continue the duke as chief counsellor, but the queen was opposed to it; Paston Letters, i. 378.

[4] Rot. Parl. v. 321, 322; Rymer, xi. 373.

[5] Rot. Parl. v. 341.

[6] Rot. Parl. v. 335. This was proclaimed on the 31st of July, 1455, having been for seven years opposed by the king and council; Whethamstede, i. 181; Stow, p. 400.

[7] Rot. Parl. v. 337.

[8] A sum of £3934 19*s*. 4¾*d*. was assigned; Rot. Parl. v. 320.

[9] Whethamstede, i. 250; Paston Letters, i. 377; Rot. Parl. v. 300 sq.

peace between the parties which were gathered round the queen and the duke of York. They watched one another uneasily, but neither would strike the first blow [1]. The death of Somerset had deprived the duke of his main grievance, and the queen of her ablest adviser: the chief object of each seems to have been to prevent the other from gaining supreme influence with the king. Henry was willing to listen to the duke, but could scarcely be expected to trust him. He showed no vindictive feeling towards the Nevilles; in March 1456 he assented to the promotion of George Neville to the see of Exeter. He retained for several months the ministers whom the duke had appointed, and probably gave his confidence chiefly to the duke of Buckingham, who was constantly called in to take the part of a mediator. But a state divided against itself is not secured by the most skilful diplomacy against attacks from without; and Margaret of Anjou had little scruple about employing the services of foreign foes to overthrow her foes at home. The king of Scots, whose mother was a Beaufort, made the death of Somerset an opportunity of declaring that he would not be bound by the truce which had been concluded in 1453 [2]; the duke of York, acting in the king's name, accepted the challenge; the king found himself obliged to repudiate the action of the duke; the nation was taught that the court was in league with the Scots, and as a matter of fact Scotland became the refuge of the defeated Lancastrians. The French in the same way were courted by the queen, who, intent upon the victory of the moment, would not see that a national dynasty cannot be maintained by the forces of foreign enemies. The duke of York, on the other hand, was intriguing with the duke of Alencon, who was conspiring against Charles VII [3]. In October 1456 the king called a council at Coventry, in hopes of turning this political armistice into such a peace as might make concordant action possible. The lords attended in arms, and the duke of Buckingham had to make peace between Warwick and the

Pacific exertions of Henry.

Influence of the duke of Buckingham.

Intrigues with Scotland and France.

Council at Coventry, Oct. 1456.

[1] See Paston Letters, i. 386, 387, 392.
[2] See Beckington, Letters, ii. 139–144; cf. Rymer, xi. 383.
[3] Cont. Monstr. liv. iii. c. 77.

Change of ministers, Oct. 1456.

young Somerset[1]. The council had no other result than a change of ministers; the Bourchiers, whose leaning towards the duke of York was becoming more decided, were removed; bishop Waynflete became chancellor[2], and the earl of Shrewsbury treasurer[3]. The removal of the Bourchiers perhaps indicates that the mediating policy of the duke of Buckingham was exchanged for a more determined one, and that the duke of York was henceforth to be excluded from the royal councils.

Alarm of war.

In 1457 the alarm of war on the side of France became more threatening; Calais was known to be in the utmost danger[4]; Sandwich and Fowey were taken by the French fleets, and no power of resistance seems to have been forthcoming[5]. Henry travelled through the country making ineffectual attempts at reconciliation, and received again at Coventry the oath of the duke of York[6]; the queen negotiated with the national enemies and weakened more and more the hold which the king had on the people. The duke and the Nevilles either plotted in secret or waited until she had ruined her husband's cause. Norfolk received licence to go on pilgrimage. The clergy, under the guidance of Bourchier, were employed in the trial of bishop Pecock of Chichester[7], a learned and temperate divine, who was trying to convert the heretics by argument

Pacifications and intrigues.

Bishop Pecock.

[1] Paston Letters, i. 408.

[2] Oct. 11; Ordinances, vi. 360; Rymer, xi. 383.

[3] Oct. 5; Paston Letters, i. 403, 407.

[4] Mathieu de Coussy ascribes the attack on the English coast by Pierre de Brezé in 1457 to an agreement between Margaret and Charles VII; and gives an account of an alliance with Scotland to be cemented by the marriage of two sons of Somerset with two daughters of James II (Buchon, xxxvi. 295, 296). Du Clercq, who recounts the invasion, does not mention the agreement with Margaret; liv. iii. c. 28. Both parties had the idea of strengthening themselves by French alliances; Cont. Monstr. liv. iii. cc. 77, 89. But of course York's intrigues with Alençon would be regarded as justified by the fact that Charles VII was the national enemy.

[5] Eng. Chron. ed. Davies, p. 74.

[6] Such seems to have been the object of a great council called to meet at Coventry Feb. 14, 1457; in which the duke swore that he would seek redress only by legal means, and was warned that he was pardoned for the last time; Rot. Parl. v. 347; Gregory, p. 203; Ordinances, vi. 433. Mr. Gairdner (Paston Letters, i. cxxviii sq.) traces the king's movements by the dates of privy seals. Cf. Fabyan, p. 631.

[7] Wilkins, Conc. iii. 576; Eng. Chr. p. 75; Whethamstede, i. 279 sq.; Fabyan, p. 632.

rather than by force, and who in the strength of his own faith had made admissions which recommended him to neither the orthodox nor the heterodox. At the close of the year Henry called a great council with his usual intention of making peace: on the 27th of January all the lords met in London and the neighbourhood, the Yorkist party within the city, the Lancastrian lords outside. As might be expected, both hard words and hard blows were heartily interchanged; but the king, with the aid of archbishop Bourchier, succeeded at last. A grand pacification took place in March, and on Lady Day at S. Paul's[1], after an imposing procession in which the duke led the queen by the hand, the high conflicting parties swore eternal friendship. The ministers who had contrived this happy result remained in office. The command of the fleet and the captaincy of Calais were allotted to Warwick[2], and the duke of York and other lords who had conquered at S. Alban's, by paying for masses for the souls of the slain, appeased the hostility of their sons. The victories won by Warwick as soon as he had assumed his command were sufficient to vindicate the wisdom of employing him as admiral, but they increased his popularity and made the queen more than ever apprehensive of his predominance.

Meeting at London in January 1458.

Great pacification at S. Paul's, March 25.

676. The eternal friendship sworn in March 1458 served for about a year and a half to delay the crisis, whilst it gave both parties time to organise their forces for it. But long before they came to blows all pretence of cordiality had vanished. In October the king held a full council and recalled the earl of Wiltshire to the treasury[3]. In November[4] a riot occurred at Westminster in which the earl of Warwick was implicated, and which caused him to leave England and establish himself at

During the peace both parties prepare to renew the struggle.

Warwick goes to Calais, November 1458.

[1] Ordinances, vi. 290 sq.; Fabyan, p. 633; Political Songs, ii. 254; Hall, p. 238. Cf. Paston Letters, i. 424–427; Stow, Chr. pp. 403, 404; Whethamstede, i. 295–308.

[2] Ordinances, vi. 294, 295.

[3] The council was summoned for Oct. 11; Ordinances, vi. 297: the treasurer was appointed Oct. 30.

[4] Nov. 9; Engl. Chron. (ed. Davies) p. 78; Stow, Chr. pp. 404, 405. Fabyan, p. 633, places it on Feb. 2.

Divisions and rumours.

Calais, which henceforth became the head quarters of disaffection. The country returned to the condition in which it had been the year before: it was divided as it were between two hostile camps, all regular government was paralysed; the queen devoted herself to organising a party for her son; the Yorkists spread the evil report that the royal boy was a bastard or a changeling. The treasurer was said to be amassing untold wealth[1]; yet the taxes were uncollected, and the king's debts unpaid. Everything was going wrong, and everything, wrong or right, was represented in its worst colours. The grant of the taxes to the king for life made it unnecessary to call a parliament; but this abeyance of constitutional forms, whilst it seemed to confine personal altercations within the walls of the council chamber, left the nation at large without an opportunity of broaching its grievances or forcing them on the notice of the king. At last, in the month of September 1459[2], the final breach occurred. The earl of Salisbury, who seems to have been, notwithstanding his years and experience, more inveterately hostile to the king than either York or Warwick, collected a force of 5000 men at Middleham and marched towards Ludlow castle, where he was to join the duke of York, and with him to visit the king at Coleshill. The queen, mistrusting the object of the visit, sent lord Audley with an insufficient force and a royal warrant for the earl's arrest. The two lords met at Bloreheath on the 23rd; Salisbury refused to obey the warrant, defeated Audley, who was killed on the field, and made his way to Ludlow, where Warwick also joined him. Henry was better prepared than they expected. He marched on Ludlow: the opposing force, after attempting to surprise him at Ludford, melted before him; and, unable to face him, the duke and his companions fled. York took refuge in Ireland; the two earls went to Calais[3], after writing to the king a formal protest in which they proclaimed their own loyalty, complained of the misrepresentations of their enemies and the oppression of their vassals, and alleged that the cause of their flight was not dread

Cessation of parliaments.

Salisbury marches southwards with a large force.

Battle of Bloreheath Sept. 23, 1459.

Flight of the Yorkist lords.

[1] Eng. Chron. p. 79.
[2] Ib. p. 80; Whethamstede, i. 338.
[3] Whethamstede, i. 345.

of those enemies but fear of God and the king[1]. This letter was written on the 10th of October; the king, on the 9th of the same month, called a parliament to meet at Coventry on the 20th of November. No summons was addressed to the three delinquents or the lord Clinton, but all the rest of the barons were cited. No time was given for the earls to pack the house of commons; the knights of the shire were chosen on the nomination of the Lancastrian leaders, and, as the result showed, the king had it all his own way[2].

Parliament called at Coventry.

The bishop of Winchester opened the proceedings with a discourse on the text 'Grace be unto you, and peace be multiplied[3].' The speaker was Thomas Tresham, the member for Northamptonshire. The business of the session was the attainder of the duke of York and his friends. The bill which contained the indictment is an important historical manifesto; for whether its statements are true or not they furnish a proof of what the king and the Lancastrian party believed to be true. The duke's connexion with Cade's rebellion, his conduct in forcing himself on the king's councils, his disloyal practices in parliament, his attempt at rebellion in 1452, his breach of the oath taken at S. Paul's in the same year, his attack on the king at S. Alban's, his breach of the oath taken at Coventry in 1457, and at S. Paul's in 1458; his responsibility for the battle of Bloreheath and continued resistance to the king at Ludlow, Ludford, and Calais;—all are rehearsed in order[4]. Besides the duke and the Nevilles, the young earls of March and Rutland, lord Clinton, two of the Bourchiers, Sir John Wenlock, the speaker of 1455, Sir William Oldhall, the speaker of 1450, the countess of Salisbury, and several other persons of less note were attainted on these charges[5]. Lord Powys and two other knights who had

Parliament of Coventry Nov. 20.

The Yorkist lords attainted.

[1] Stow, pp. 405, 406; Eng. Chr. pp. 80, 81.

[2] Hall, p. 243; Eng. Chr. p. 83. The sheriffs petitioned for indemnity in consequence of the haste with which the elections were held; Rot. Parl. v. 367; and the charge was made in the parliament of 1460 that the members were returned without due election, and in some cases without even the form; Rot. Parl. v. 374.

[3] Rot. Parl. v. 345; cf. Whethamstede, i. 345.

[4] Rot. Parl. v. 346–350.

[5] Ib. v. 350; Eng. Chron. ed. Davies, pp. 83, 84.

Sentences of the parliament of Coventry.

submitted after the skirmish at Ludford had their lives spared, but forfeited their lands[1]. The others were adjudged to suffer the penalties of high treason: the king reserving however his prerogative of pardon[2]. A petition for the attainder of Lord Stanley was rejected by him, although presented by the commons. A very solemn oath of allegiance was then taken by the lords, who swore further to defend the queen and the prince, to accept the latter as his father's successor, and to do their best to secure the crown to the male line of the king's descendants. The latter article shows that although the right of the duke of York to the crown had not been formally stated, it was sufficiently well known to require some such precautions. The oath was recorded, signed and sealed by the two archbishops, three dukes, sixteen bishops, five earls, two viscounts, sixteen abbots and priors, and twenty-two barons[3]. Of these only a small number appeared later on as Yorkist partisans, but the list does not furnish a complete roll of the Lancastrian lords. It is signed by the duke of Norfolk and the lords Bonneville and Stourton, who were Yorkists; the names of the duke of Somerset, the earls of Devonshire, Oxford, and Westmoreland, the lords Hungerford, Lovell, and Moleyns, all Lancastrians, are not attached to it. There can be no doubt that the king had a large majority of supporters among the lords, independently of the influence which the prelates consistently exercised on behalf of peace. The commons cannot be so distinctly classified, but it would seem that parties in most of the counties were so nearly balanced as to enable either faction by a little exertion to influence the elections in their own favour. The north of England, notwithstanding the influence of the Nevilles, was loyal; the old feud between the first and second families of earl Ralph made the head of the house, the earl of Westmoreland, at least half Lancastrian; the estates of the Percies and Cliffords, and of the duchy of Lancaster, gave great influence in Yorkshire to the same party; the queen had succeeded in raising a strong feeling of affection in the western counties. In the east,

Oath of allegiance taken by the lords,

notwithstanding party divisions.

Local distribution of the two parties.

[1] Rot. Parl. v. 349. [2] Ib. v. 350; Whethamstede, i. 356. [3] Rot. Parl. v. 351.

Norfolk, Suffolk[1], and Kent seem generally to have been inclined to the duke of York, who was also strong on the marches. The south-western counties did not witness much of the military action of the time, and bore their share in the common burden quietly; no politician sufficiently prominent to be chosen speaker represented any western county during the whole struggle.

The parliament of Coventry sat only for a month, and attempted nothing further. On the 20th of December it was dissolved by the lord chancellor in a speech abounding with gratitude[2]. In this short campaign Henry had shown energy, decision, and industry, which earlier in his reign might have insured him a happy career. Moderation, mercy, and readiness to forgive he invariably showed. If he seems to have been unwise just now in driving his formidable antagonists to extremities, it must be remembered that he had borne and forgiven very much already, that he must have earned the scorn of the nation if he endured the defiance of his subjects, however powerful, and that he was fully awake to the jeopardy in which his son's inheritance stood.

The parliament dissolved Dec. 20, 1459.

The king's behaviour and policy.

The sentence passed against the rebellious nobles served only to confirm them in their purpose. They were out of the king's reach; the duke of York in Ireland and the Nevilles at Calais were able to concert measures for an invasion of England; the king had neither politic counsel, nor military skill, nor sufficient resources to dislodge them. The queen's efforts to stir up the native Irish and the French against their strongholds served only to increase her unpopularity; the successive attempts made by the lord Audley, lord Rivers, Sir Baldwin Fulford, and the duke of Somerset, to seize Calais, or to neutralise its importance by occupying Guisnes, to clear the channel from Warwick's cruisers, or to guard against his landing at Sandwich, proved ludicrously ineffectual. The treasurer, by severe requisitions from the Yorkist towns, and by the exercise of the

The Yorkist lords plan a descent on England.

The royal forces fail to seize Calais.

[1] John de la Pole, the young heir of the duke of Suffolk, was a Yorkist, and married a daughter of the duke; he was restored to the dukedom in 1463.

[2] Rot. Parl. v. 370.

Unpopularity of the Treasurer.

right of purveyance, which, in the abeyance of all administrative order, was the only means left for raising supplies from day to day, drew down popular hatred on the cause which was reduced to such expedients. The first half of the year 1460 passed away whilst the clouds were thus gathering. In March[1] Warwick passed over to Ireland, whence, having arranged his plan of operations with the duke, he returned to Calais in June[2] and immediately prepared for the attack. On the 26th of that month, Salisbury, Warwick, and Edward earl of March, the eldest son of the duke of York, crossed over to Kent; they had a papal legate in their company and were immediately joined by archbishop Bourchier and a host of Kentish men[3].

Warwick and York concert an invasion.

Landing of the earls.

Manifesto issued by the Yorkist lords against the king's friends.

In the document[4] which now or a little earlier was addressed by the duke and the three earls to the archbishop and commons of England may be read their formal indictment against the government of Henry VI. It contains many points which are mere constitutional generalities, statements that have no special reference to the circumstances of the times, and charges which had been from time immemorial part of the stores of political warfare; but they comprise other points which, whilst they evince the unscrupulous hostility of the accusers, at the same time reveal the causes of the king's fall and explain his helplessness in the great crisis. First come the oppressions of the church, offences which least of all could be laid to Henry's charge; then follow, as notorious grievances, the poverty of the king, which has compelled the practice of purveyance; the perversion of the law, whereby all righteousness and justice is exiled from the land; the waste of royal revenue on men who are 'the destroyers of the land,' so that the king cannot live of his own as his ancestors did, but is obliged to plunder the commons; the heavy taxation which had enriched the very men who had lost Anjou, Maine, and Normandy; the recent demand of a force to be maintained by the townships for the king's guard; the attempts made to stir up the Irish against the duke

[1] W. Worc. p. 772; Eng. Chr. p. 85. [2] W. Worc. p. 772.
[3] Ib. p. 772; Eng. Chr. p. 86.
[4] Stow, pp. 407, 408; Eng. Chr. pp. 86, 87. See Gregory, p. 206.

and the French against Calais, attempts which show that the ministers are ready to betray the realm into the hands of foreigners; the murder of Gloucester and attempted murder of the duke of York and the earls; the influence of the earls of Shrewsbury and Wiltshire and the lord Beaumont, who have prevented the king from showing grace to them, hoping to escape the penalty due to them for causing the misery of the kingdom 'whereof they be causes and not the king, which is himself as noble, as virtuous, as righteous, and blessed of disposition as any prince earthly;' and the acts of the parliament of Coventry which were really the acts of the same lords. In expectation of a French invasion, the writers pray the archbishop and the commons to assist them in gaining access to the king, and call on God, the Virgin, and all saints to witness the sincerity of their profession of fealty. In another memorial, circulated among the Kentishmen, all these charges are repeated and the king's friends are accused of teaching that his will is above the law[1]. Having thus prepared the way the lords marched on London, where the citizens received them on the 2nd of July[2], the lords Scales, Vescy, Lovell, and de la Warr, holding out against them in the Tower. Convocation was sitting at the time, and Warwick took the opportunity of stating his grievances before the clergy, and swearing faith and allegiance on the cross of Canterbury. Then, leaving the earl of Salisbury as governor of London, they set out to meet the king.

Charges against the royal advisers.

Kentish memorial.

The lords enter London.

Henry, who was with his council at Coventry, marched, when he heard of the landing of the earls, for Northampton; Margaret was gathering forces in the north. At Northampton the earls arrived with 60,000 men, and, after Warwick had made three separate attempts to force himself into the king's presence, in which he was foiled by the duke of Buckingham, the battle of Northampton was fought on the 10th of July[3]. Like the first battle of S. Alban's it was marked by a great slaughter of the

Battle of Northampton July 10, 1460.

[1] Chr. White Rose, p. lxxv.

[2] W. Worc. p. 773; Eng. Chr. p. 94. With March and Warwick were the lords Fauconberg, Clinton, Bourchier, Audley, Bergavenny, Say, and Scrope.

[3] Eng. Chr. pp. 95–97; Gregory, p. 207; W. Worc. p. 773; Whethamstede, i. 372 sq.

Slaughter of the Lancastrian lords.

Lancastrian lords; the duke of Buckingham, the earl of Shrewsbury, the lords Beaumont and Egremont, were slain beside the king's tent. It is a miserable sign of Warwick's vindictiveness that those against whom he had private grievances like Egremont, or public rivalries like Beaumont and Shrewsbury, were the special victims. He had given orders that no man should lay hand on the king or on the commons, but only on the lords, knights, and squires, and the command was so far faithfully obeyed[1]. The lord Grey of Ruthyn, who led the king's vanguard, went over to Warwick, and the battle lasted only half an hour. Henry was taken in his tent and obliged to accept the profession of devotion which the earls consistently proffered[2]. On the 16th of July he was brought to London[3]. On the 19th the defenders of the Tower surrendered, and lord Scales, on his way to sanctuary, was murdered by the boatmen on the Thames[4]. On the 25th George Neville, bishop of Exeter, brother of the earl of Warwick, was made chancellor[5]. On the 30th a parliament was summoned in the king's name to meet at Westminster on the 7th of October[6]. The queen fled to Scotland; the duke of York returned to England before the day of meeting.

Desertion of Grey of Ruthyn.

The king taken and brought to London.

Flight of Margaret.

Parliament of Oct. 7, 1460.

677. The duke of York saw that his hour of triumph was now come: regardless of the oaths which he had so often sworn, and of the mercy which had been, until the parliament of Coventry, so constantly extended towards him, he determined to make his claim to the crown. The parliament was opened by the new chancellor in due form: John Green, member for Essex, was chosen speaker[7], and on petition of the commons the acts of the last parliament were repealed at once[8]. On the third day of the session the duke, having previously dislodged Henry from his apartments in the palace[9], appeared in the chamber of the lords, and going up to the royal seat, laid his

The Coventry acts repealed.

[1] Eng. Chron. p. 97. [2] Ib. p. 97. [3] Ib. p. 98.
[4] W. Worc. pp. 773, 774; Eng. Chr. p. 98.
[5] Rymer, xi. 458. On the 5th of August Warwick was recognised as captain of Calais; ib. p. 459. On the 8th the rebel lords were declared loyal; ib. 460. Cf. Ordinances, vi. 303.
[6] Lords' Report, iv. 945. [7] Rot. Parl. v. 373, 374.
[8] Ib. v. 374. [9] Eng. Chron. p. 99.

hand on the cushion as if about formally to take possession. The gesture was viewed by the assembled lords with more wonder than approval. Archbishop Bourchier asked what he wanted, and whether he wished to go in to see the king. The duke replied, 'I do not bethink me that I know of any within the realm for whom it were not more fitting that he should come to me and see me than for me to attend on him and visit him[1].' This outspoken boast did not procure him any distinct support, and it was clear that the royal position could not be stormed[2]. On the 16th of October therefore the duke's counsel laid before the lords his pedigree and the formal claim to the crown, as heir of Edward III, through Lionel of Clarence[3]. The next day the claim was reported to the king, who was probably well prepared for it. He replied by requesting the lords to search for materials by which the claim might be refuted, and they appealed to him as a diligent student of chronicles to do the same[4]. On the 18th the judges were consulted; but, although Sir John Fortescue the chief justice afterwards wrote a treatise on the question, they were not now prepared to answer; they replied that the question was not for them but for the lords of the king's blood to decide. The king's counsel, sergeants, and attorney-general, sheltered themselves under the same excuse. Thus left to themselves the lords drew up five articles of objection to the duke's claim; they could not recognise it without breaking the solemn oaths which they had so often taken; the acts of parliament by which the succession was settled were still the law of the land and were of such 'authority as to defeat any manner of title made to any person;' it was a serious question whether the right of the crown did not pass by the entails so often made upon the heirs male; the duke did not even bear the arms of Lionel of Clarence, but those of Edmund of Langley his younger brother; lastly, king Henry IV had claimed the crown by hereditary descent from Henry III, not by conquest or unrighteous entry,

The duke of York asserts his right to the throne;

and puts in his pedigree.

The king is informed; the judges decline to give an opinion.

Five objections drawn up by the lords.

[1] W. Worc. p. 774; Eng. Chr. p. 99; Fabyan, p. 637. Hall gives a long speech, Chr. pp. 245, sq.

[2] Whethamstede. i. 377–380; W. Worc. p. 774.

[3] Rot. Parl. v. 375.

[4] Ib. v. 375, 376.

Answer of the duke to the objections of the lords.

as the duke's counsel had asserted [1]. The first three arguments were sound, the other two worse than useless. The duke presented a formal reply; the allegation of the oath he met by the assertion that oaths made contrary to truth, justice, and charity, are not obligatory; that the oath of allegiance binds no man to that which is inconvenient and unlawful, and that he was prepared to defend himself at the due time in the spiritual court against the charge of perjury; to the second and third articles he replied that the succession rested only on the act of 1406 which by itself afforded conclusive proof that Henry IV had no valid claim by descent; as for the heraldic question, although he had not assumed the arms of Clarence, he might have assumed them or even those of Edward III; he had abstained, and the country well knew why he had abstained, from making either claim before now. As for the descent of the house of Lancaster as stated by Henry IV, it was in no wise true, and should be thoroughly disproved [2]. On Saturday, the 25th of October, the chancellor informed the lords that a way of compromise had been devised which, as the title of the duke was indefeasible, would save the king's dignity, would satisfy the duke, and enable the lords themselves to escape from the guilt of perjury: the king was to 'keep the crowns and his estate and dignity royal during his life, and the said duke and his heirs to succeed him in the same.' This proposal was approved by the lords, who determined to leave to the king the choice of acceptance or refusal. Henry received the chancellor graciously, and heard his tale, and then, as the record continues, 'inspired with the grace of the Holy Ghost [3], and in eschewing of effusion of Christian blood, by good and sad deliberation and advice had with all his lords spiritual and temporal, condescended to accord to be made between him and the said duke, and to be authorised by the authority of the parliament.' The agreement was drawn up; the duke and his sons were not to molest the

A compromise devised.

Henry is to be king for life, and the duke is to succeed him.

[1] Rot. Parl. v. 376.

[2] Ib. v. 377.

[3] 'The kynge for fere of dethe graunted hym the crowne, for a man that hathe by lytylle wytte wylle soone be aferyd of dethe, and yet I truste and beleeve there was no man that wolde doo him bodely harme'; Gregory, Chr. p. 208.

king; he was declared heir to the crowns; any attempt on his life was made high treason; the principality of Wales and the earldom of Chester were made over to him; an income of 10,000 marks was assigned to him and his sons, and they swore to the lords, and the lords to them, oaths of mutual defence[1]. The unfortunate king, unable to make even a protest for the rights of his son, was prevailed on to ratify the agreement; the act of 1406 was repealed, and on the 31st of October the transaction was completed. It was said that the duke had chosen the 1st of November for his coronation in case the lords had accepted him as king.

Oaths taken.

Henry submits.

Although the decision of the question of succession was thus made to be the king's personal act, and the lords present availed themselves of the compromise to save themselves from the guilt of perjury, there can be little doubt that the parliament contained hardly any of the king's partisans; and but few of the lay lords who had taken the oath of allegiance a year before. Of those lay lords the duke of Buckingham, the earl of Shrewsbury, lords Beaumont, Scales, and Egremont were dead, and many others stayed away. The dukes of Somerset and Exeter, the earls of Devonshire and Northumberland, and the lords Clifford, Dacre, and Neville were in the north. Lords Grey and Audley had changed sides. The list of the triers of petitions contains only the names of Warwick and Salisbury among the earls, and Grey de Ruthyn, Dacre, Fitz-Warin, Scrope, Bonneville, Berners, and Rougemont-Grey among the barons[2]. The commons had little to do with the business, save by assenting to the decision of the lords. If betrayal or tergiversation is to be imputed to any under the very difficult circumstances in which they found themselves, the blame must lie most heavily on the spiritual lords; on Bourchier and Neville, now the avowed partisans of the duke. Yet it was probably owing to their reluctance to incur the blame of perjury that Henry was secured in possession of the throne for life. The whole baronage was summoned to this parliament, but it can scarcely be regarded

Question as to the composition of the parliament of 1460.

The clerical element.

[1] Rot. Parl. v. 377–381; Engl. Chr. pp. 100–106. According to the last authority the duke was made protector, prince of Wales, and earl of Chester.

[2] Rot. Parl. v. 373.

as so free or full an assembly of the estates as even the parliament of Coventry had been. Its work lasted but a few weeks, and already the march of events was too rapid to wait on the deliberations of any such assembly.

Battle of Wakefield, Dec. 29, 1460.

678. The battle of Wakefield enabled the Lancastrian party to avenge the blood of Suffolk, Somerset, and Buckingham. York and Salisbury had gone northwards to thwart the designs of the queen, who had collected a considerable force by letters issued in the king's name[1]. On the 21st of December they had lost a part of their force in a struggle with the duke of Somerset at Worksop[2]; on the 29th they were overwhelmed at Wakefield by the united forces of Somerset, Northumberland, and Neville. The duke was killed in the battle, his son the earl of Rutland was slain by lord Clifford; the earl of Salisbury was taken prisoner and beheaded at Pomfret by the Yorkshiremen whom he had offended when administering the duchy of Lancaster[3]. The indignities offered to the slain testify at once to the lack of moderation in the victorious party, and to the cruel embitterment of public feeling by personal and private antipathies.

Death of York and Salisbury.

The earl of March wins a battle at Mortimer's Cross, Feb. 2, 1461.

Whilst the duke of York and Salisbury were thus perishing in the north, the young earl of March was raising forces on the Welsh marches, and Warwick remained in the neighbourhood of London with the captive king. Against the earl of March Jasper Tudor earl of Pembroke, the king's half-brother, and the earl of Wiltshire pitted themselves. They were defeated at Mortimer's Cross near Wigmore on the 3rd of February[4]. Against Warwick queen Margaret and the northern lords advanced southwards the same month; the second battle of S. Alban's, on the 17th, restored the king to liberty, and proved that Warwick was not invincible[5]. The victorious earl of

Second battle of S. Alban's, Feb. 17.

[1] Whethamstede, i. 381; Eng. Chr. p. 106.

[2] W. Worc. p. 775.

[3] 'The commune peple of the cuntre whiche loved him nat'; Eng. Chr. p. 107. According to William of Worcester the Bastard of Exeter killed him; W. Worc. p. 775; cf. Whethamstede, i. 382.

[4] Eng. Chr. p. 110; W. Worc. pp. 775, 776. On the 12th of February Edward had the king's commission to raise forces against the queen, although her name is not mentioned; Rymer, xi. 471; Ordinances, vi. 307–310.

[5] Engl. Chr. p. 107, 108; W. Worc. p. 776; Whethamstede, i. 390 sq.

March and the defeated earl of Warwick met at Chipping-Norton, and hastened to London[1]. Henry and Margaret, in order to prevent their followers from sacking the capital, had moved from S. Alban's[2] to Dunstable, and lost their chance of seizing the city, where, although the common people were as usual bitter against the court, they would have met with no organised resistance. On the 28th the earls of March and Warwick entered London; on the 1st of March the chancellor, bishop Neville, called a general assembly of the citizens at Clerkenwell, and explained to them the title by which Edward now duke of York, claimed the crown. The mob received the instruction with applause, and proclaimed that he was and should be king. On the 3rd a council of the party was held at Baynard's castle. Archbishop Bourchier, bishop Beauchamp of Salisbury, bishop Neville, the duke of Norfolk, the earl of Warwick, the lords Fitzwalter and Ferrers of Chartley, and Sir William Herbert, with their friends, there took upon themselves to declare Edward the rightful king. On the 4th he was received in procession at Westminster, seized the crown and sceptre of the Confessor, and was proclaimed king by the name of Edward IV[4]. From that day the legal recognition of his royal character begins and the years of his reign date. The fact is important as illustrating the first working of the doctrine by virtue of which he assumed the royal character. Although there was no formal election, no parliamentary recognition, and a mere tumultuary proclamation, the character of royalty was regarded as complete in virtue of the claim of descent, and as soon as that claim was urged. Parliamentary recognition followed; but Edward's reign was allowed to begin from the day

Henry and Margaret retire to the North.

Edward claims the crown.

He is acknowledged king, Mar. 4. 1461.

[1] W. Worc. p. 777.

[2] Towards York for fear their forces should sack London; Gregory, Chr. p. 214; Eng. Chr. p. 109; W. Worc. p. 776.

[3] W. Worc. p. 777.

[4] 'By counsaill of the lords of the south'; Hardyng, p. 406. 'By the advice of the lords spiritual and temporal and by the election of the commons'; Gregory, Chr. p. 215; cf. Hall, Chr. p. 254; Eng. Chr. p. 110; Whethamstede, i. 405–407; Fabyan, p. 639. Pius II wrote to congratulate Edward on his accession, March 22, 1462; Rymer, ix. 489. George Neville bishop of Exeter was made chancellor Mar. 10, Rymer, xi. 473; and lord Bourchier became treasurer on the 18th.

Character of the usurpation.

on which he declared himself king. The nation, by its action in the next parliament, sanctioned the proceeding, but the whole transaction is in striking contrast with the revolution of 1399; and even with the proceedings taken a few weeks before, when the duke of York made his claim. To anticipate the language of later history, the accession of the house of York was strictly a legitimist restoration.

Battles at Ferrybridge and Towton; Mar. 28 and 29.

The struggle was not even now fought out; although Edward was king in London, Henry and Margaret still possessed a large and hitherto undefeated army. Feeling however the insecurity of their position in the south, they had returned to Yorkshire[1] whither Edward at once pursued them. On the 28th of March a battle was fought at Ferrybridge, in which lord Clifford on the one side, and Lord Fitzwalter on the other, fell[2]. The next day the two hosts met at Towton, and in a bloody battle Edward was victorious. Of the Lancastrian lords, the earl of Northumberland, and lords Wells, Neville, and Dacre were slain; the earls of Devonshire and Wiltshire were taken and executed, the former at York, the latter at Newcastle. The dukes of Somerset and Exeter escaped[3]. Margaret carried off her husband and son to Scotland. By the surrender of Berwick to the Scots, in April, the fall of the house of Lancaster was recognised as final[4]. Edward, after securing his conquests, returned to London, and was crowned at Westminster on the 28th of June[5].

Berwick surrendered to the Scots.

Edward IV crowned.

[1] With them were the dukes of Somerset and Exeter, the earls of Devon and Wiltshire, the lords Moleyns, Roos, Rivers, and Scales; Hardyng, p. 405.

[2] W. Worc. p. 777. Lord Fitzwalter was John Radcliffe, husband of the heiress of Fitzwalter, and a titular lord only: see Nicolas, Hist. Peerage, p. 199.

[3] Gregory, p. 216, gives a list of the lords who were at Towton on the king's side; the prince of Wales, the dukes of Exeter and Somerset; the earls of Northumberland and Devonshire; the lords Roos, Beaumont, Clifford, Neville, Wells, Willoughby, Harry of Buckingham, Rivers, Scales, Mauley, Ferrers of Groby, Lovell, and the young lord of Shrewsbury; Sir John Fortescue, Sir Thomas Hammys, Sir Andrew Trollope, Sir Thomas Tresham, Sir Robert Whittingham, Sir John Dawney. Henry and Margaret had been left at York; Hall, p. 254. The slain lords were Northumberland, Clifford, Neville, Wells, and Mauley. Cf. Paston Letters, ii. 6; Hardyng, p. 407.

[4] Hall, p. 256.

[5] Gregory, p. 218.

The cause of the fall of Henry VI.

The overthrow of the house of Lancaster was not in itself a national act. The nation acquiesced in, approved and accepted it, because it had no great love for the king, because it distrusted the queen and the ministers and policy which she represented, because it had exhausted its strength, and longed for peace. The house of Lancaster, although practically, was not put formally upon its trial. Henry was not deposed for incompetency or misgovernment, but set aside on the claim of a legitimate heir whose right he was regarded as usurping. But such a claim would not have been admitted except on two conditions; the house of York could not have unseated the house of Lancaster unless the first had been exceedingly strong, and the second exceedingly weak. The house of York was strong in the character and reputation of duke Richard, in the early force and energy of Edward, in the great popularity of Warwick, in the wealth and political ability of the family party which he led: but its great advantage lay in the weakness of the house of Lancaster. That weakness was proved in almost every possible way. The impulse which had set Henry IV on the throne, as the hereditary champion of constitutional right, and as personally the deliverer from odious tyranny, had long been exhausted. The new impulse which Henry V had created in his character of a great conqueror, a national hero and a good ruler, had become exhausted too; its strength is proved by the fact that it was not exhausted sooner. Since the death of Gloucester and Beaufort, in 1447, everything had gone wrong; the conquests of Henry V were lost, the crown was bankrupt, the peace was badly kept, the nation distrusted the ministers, the ministers contemned, although they did not perhaps deserve, the distrust of the nation. Henry himself never seems to have looked upon his royal character as involving the responsibility of leadership; he yielded on every pressure, trusted implicitly in every pretended reconciliation, and, unless we are to charge him with faults of dissimulation with which his enemies never charged him personally, behaved as if his position as a constitutional monarch involved his acting as the puppet of each temporary majority. Without Margaret, he might have reigned as long as

Strength of York.

Weakness of Lancaster.

Personal weakness of the king: false strength of the queen.

Fatal preponderance of Margaret.

he lived, and perhaps have outlived the exhaustion under which the nation after the struggle with France was labouring. He might with another wife have transmitted his crown to his posterity as Henry III had done, who was not less despised, and much more hated. But in Margaret, from the very moment of her arrival, was concentrated the weakness and the strength of the dynastic cause; its strength in her indomitable will, her steady faithfulness, her heroic defence of the rights of her husband and child; its weakness in her political position, her policy and her ministers. To the nation she symbolised the loss of Henry V's conquests, an inglorious peace, the humiliation of the popular Gloucester, the promotion of the unpopular Beauforts. Her domestic policy was one of jealous exclusion: she mistrusted the duke of York, and probably with good cause: she knew the soundness of his pedigree, and looked on him from the first as a competitor for the crown of her husband and son. She was drawn to the Beauforts and to Suffolk by the knowledge that their interests were entirely one with the interests of the dynasty. She supported them against all attacks, and when they perished continued the policy which they had shared. The weight of their unpopularity devolved on her, and she was unpopular enough already. Still she might have held out, especially if she had known how to use the pliancy and simplicity of her husband. But when the nation began to believe that she was in league with the national enemies; when she began to wage a civil war, pitting the north against the south, and it was believed that her northern army was induced to follow her by the hope of being allowed to plunder the rich southern farms and cities; when she stirred up, or was believed to have stirred up, the Irish against the duke of York, the French against Calais, and the Scots against the peace of England, she lost all the ground that was left her. The days were long past when the English barons could call in French or Scottish aid against a tyrant; no king of England had yet made his throne strong by foreign help. It was fatal here. Men began to believe that she was an adulteress or her son a changeling. Her whole strength lay henceforth in the armed forces

Her unpopularity.

Her strong partisanship.

Her foreign connexion.

Calumnies about her.

she was able to bring into the field, and a defeat in battle was fatal and final. Warwick saw his advantage, prepared his forces, grasped success at the critical moment, and triumphed in the field over a foe whose whole strength was in the field. Thus the house of Lancaster fell without any formal condemnation, without any constitutional impeachment. Henry had not ruled ill, but had gradually failed to rule at all. His foreign policy was not in itself unwise, but was unpopular and unfortunate. His incapacity and the failure of the men whom he trusted, opened the way for York and the Nevilles: and the weaker went to the wall. National exhaustion and weariness completed what royal exhaustion and weakness had begun. Spirit and ability supplanted simple incapacity; the greater force overcame the smaller, national apathy cooperated with national disgust; and the decision which the fortune of war had adjudged, the national conscience, judgment and reason accepted. The present decision of the struggle neither depended on constitutional principles nor was ascertained by constitutional means. In the general survey of history, the justification of the change is to be found in this—that England, as at the Norman Conquest, needed a strong government, and sought one in the house of York; but the deep reasons, which in the economy of the world justify results, do not justify the sins of the actors or prove the guilt of the sufferers.

Fall of the house of Lancaster.

Edward IV came to the throne with great personal advantages. He was young and handsome; he had shown great military skill, and won a great victory; he brought the prospect of peace; he had no foreign connexions; he was closely related to the most powerful of the old houses of England. In many points his personal position was like that of Henry IV at the beginning of his reign; but he was younger, less embarrassed by previous obligations, more buoyant and hopeful. His character developes its real nature as his reign goes on, and it is seen how personal fitness adapted him to be the exponent of despotic theory. Whilst he was learning and practising the lessons which Richard II might have taught him, but which kings learn only too well without accredited instructors, the other

Position of Edward IV at the beginning of his reign.

Edward of Lancaster, the pupil of Fortescue.

Edward, an exile and wanderer in France or in Scotland, was learning from Sir John Fortescue the principles of constitutional government, by which the house of Lancaster rose; on which they always believed themselves to act, and in spite of which they fell. But Edward IV was too young, and his advisers too wary, to violate more than was absolutely necessary the forms of the constitution; so long as they were supreme they could use it for their own ends; they were popular, the commons would need no pressure; they were powerful, their rivals dared not lift their heads in parliament. Warwick could manage the lords, Bourchier the clergy[1]. One parliament, prepared to take strong measures, could make the new king safe, and they had no scruples of conscience about the strength of any measure that might be conclusive.

Popularity and power of Edward of York.

Parliament of November 1461.

679. Edward's first parliament, called on the 23rd of May to meet on the 6th of July, was delayed by the condition of the Scottish border, and did not meet until the 4th of November[2]. Summons was issued to but one duke, Norfolk, to four earls, Warwick, Oxford, Arundel, and Westmoreland, to the viscount Bourchier, and to thirty-eight barons, of whom seven were now first summoned; the whole number of lay peers was forty-four[3], which, when contrasted with the number of fifty-six summoned to the parliament of 1453[4], the last which was called before the great struggle, shows perhaps a smaller falling off than might have been expected. Many, especially in the higher ranks of the peerage, had fallen; many were in exile; some were willing to temporise. The fourteen who were attainted in the parliament itself were either dead or in arms against the new dynasty. The king too was already taking measures for replacing the missing dignities with new creations; on the 30th of June lord Bourchier was made earl of Essex, and William Neville, lord Fauconberg, was raised soon after to

Number of lords.

New creations.

[1] The king by letters patent issued Nov. 2, 1462, granted to the clergy a confirmation of privileges which probably disarmed a good deal of opposition. See Rymer, xi. 493–495; Wilk. Conc. iii. 582. On the 25th of November the convocation granted a tenth; ib. iii. 580.

[2] Rot. Parl. v. 461; Paston Letters, ii. 15, 22, 31.

[3] Lords' Report, iv. 950 sq.

[4] Ib. pp. 931 sq.

the earldom of Kent; the king's brothers were made dukes, George of Clarence and Richard of Gloucester; of the seven new barons, one was a Stafford and one a Bourchier[1]. Bishop Neville, as chancellor, opened the parliament with a discourse on the text 'Amend your ways and your doings[2].' The speaker was Sir James Strangeways, knight of the shire for Yorkshire, who was founding a new family on his connexion with the Nevilles.

New earls and dukes.

On the 12th of November the serious business began with an address of the commons to the king. Strangeways in their name thanked God for the king's victories, and the king for his exertions; not content with that, he expatiated on the iniquities of the late period of disorder, all of which were laid to the charge of Henry, and demanded the punishment of offenders[3]. The address was followed by a petition, presented nominally by the commons, embodying the claim made by the counsel of the duke of York in the last parliament, and praying for the declaration of the king's title. After rehearsing the pedigree it proceeded to recount the circumstances under which Edward had assumed the title of king, and to recognise its validity according to the law of God, the law of man, and the law of nations, praying that it might be affirmed by act of parliament, and that, in consequence, the alienations of royal territory under the late dynasty might be cancelled, and an act of resumption passed. Then, recurring to recent events, it recapitulated the history of the compromise made in 1460, charged the breach of that agreement upon Henry, and demanded its repeal. Edward is thus regarded as succeeding to the rights of Richard II, and Henry as both a usurper and a traitor[4]. The king's advisers, wiser than the commons, modified the petition before it became an act of parliament, by

The commons demand the punishment of the king's enemies, and the declaration of his title.

Henry charged with breach of the compact of 1460.

[1] The seven are William lord Herbert, Humfrey Stafford of Southwick, Humfrey Bourchier of Cromwell, Walter Devereux of Ferrers, John Wenlock of Wenlock, Robert Ogle of Ogle, and Thomas Lumley; but of these Bourchier, Devereux, and Lumley held old baronies.

[2] Rot. Parl. v. 461.

[3] Ib. v. 462.

[4] Rot. Parl. v. 463-467; Whethamstede, i. 416, 417.

numerous clauses saving the rights which had been created during the Lancastrian reigns and since Edward's accession [1].

Discussion on the validity of the acts of the Lancaster kings.

Another roll of petitions, that the judicial acts of the late dynasty might be declared valid [2], formed the basis of a statute which was absolutely necessary if civil society was to be held together. In his answers the king undertook to confirm such proceedings, to renew the creation of the disputed peerages and to allow others to stand good, to allow confirmations of charters to be issued by the chancellor, and to recognise the validity of all formal acts of the kind, carefully excluding from the benefit of the concession the victims attainted in the present session [3]. Neither petition nor statute ventures to touch the question of the validity of laws passed under the Lancastrian kings; perhaps the subject was too difficult to be attempted, perhaps the public interests were lost sight of in the anxiety to preserve individual rights. The other branch of the work of the session was the punishment of the opposing party. A bill of attainder was presented to the king in the form of an act of parliament [4], and with his approval laid before the commons, who assented to it; it was then by advice and assent of the lords spiritual and temporal returned to the king to receive the royal assent, which was given in the usual form 'le roy le voet.' By this act Henry VI is attainted of high treason, and condemned to forfeit the duchy of Lancaster, his patrimonial estate, which is henceforth attached as a separate provision to the crown; Margaret likewise is attainted for high treason, and with her son suffers forfeiture; the attainder is shared on diverse counts by the fourteen lords, living or dead, who had most vigorously supported them [5], and by a large

Bill of attainder passed, against Henry, Margaret, and their friends.

[1] Rot. Parl. v. 467–475.

[2] Ib. v. 489 sq.

[3] Statutes, ii. 380 sq.

[4] Rot. Parl. v. 476–483; W. Worc. p. 778.

[5] Henry duke of Somerset, Thomas Courtenay earl of Devon, Henry late earl of Northumberland, Thomas lord Roos, John late lord Neville, Henry duke of Exeter, William viscount Beaumont, John late lord Clifford, Leo late lord Wells, lord Rougemont Gray, Randolf late lord Dacre, Robert lord Hungerford, Jasper earl of Pembroke, James late earl of Wiltshire; Rot. Parl. v. 480. Hardyng wrote to press on Edward the example of Henry IV, in favour of clemency; Chr. p. 409. The Yorkists were dissatisfied with his moderation; Paston Letters, ii. 30.

number of knights, squires, clerks, merchants, and others, the most notable of whom are Sir John Fortescue, the late chief justice, and John Morton, afterwards archbishop of Canterbury. Parallel with the attainder of the dead lords is the act restoring the reputation and legal position of the early victims of Henry IV; the attainder of the earl of Salisbury and lord le Despenser, who perished in 1400, was reversed, that the earl of Warwick and his mother might have their inheritance; the heirs of lord Lumley were restored, and the sentence against Richard of Cambridge, the king's grandfather, was annulled[1]. Some obdurate commoners were summoned to submit or incur the penalties of treason[2]; the defenders of Harlech, which still held out for Margaret, were condemned to forfeiture[3]. An ordinance directed against liveries, maintenance, and gambling, was proclaimed by the king, and a statute referring indictments taken in sheriff's tourn to the justices of the peace, completed the legislative work of the session[4].

Restoration of the victims of the Revolution of 1399.

Statutes of this parliament.

On the 21st of December the parliament was prorogued after a speech addressed by the king to the commons, in which, in modest and manly language, he thanked them for their share in what he regarded as a restoration, and for helping him to avenge his father, promising to devote himself heartily to the national service, and asking for a continuance of their good will[5]. The parliament met again in the following May only to be dissolved[6]. Its work ended here, and seemed to promise better days to come; no money had been asked for, no barbarous severities were perpetrated; many of the attainted lords were dead, the way for reconciliation was open for the living. The royal success had been so great as almost to dispense with new cruelties. It would have been well if the policy thus foreshadowed could have been carried into effect. It must be remembered that Edward was not yet twenty, and that he had been fairly well educated and trained; he was not the voluptuary that he afterwards became, and he was under

Royal speech in prorogation.

Favourable omens.

[1] Rot. Parl. v. 484.
[2] Ib. v. 483.
[3] Ib. v. 486.
[4] Ib. v. 487 sq.; Statutes, ii. 389.
[5] Rot. Parl. v. 487.
[6] Ib. v. 488.

the influence of the Nevilles, who, whatever their faults may have been, were wise enough to see the importance of moderation. The king's character did not stand the test to which it was from this time subjected, but he need not be regarded as intentionally false now because in after life he became a tyrant.

Margaret maintains a warfare on the border.

680. The Lancastrian cause might have seemed desperate, but Margaret knew no despair. In Scotland first, and then in France, she enlisted some sympathy for her wrongs; and on the northern border, where the Percies were strong, she maintained a stout resistance, to the final ruin of her friends. In February 1462 the earl of Oxford, on suspicion of intriguing with her, was arrested, tried before the high constable, the earl of Worcester, and beheaded[1]. In March Somerset arrived in Scotland, and undertook the command whilst the queen went to France[2]. In the summer the border castles fell; in the autumn Margaret recovered them; in November and December the king retook them again, and admitted Somerset to peace and favour[3]. Early in 1463 the politicians of both parties went abroad to canvass for new allies. The duke of Burgundy was courted by both, and in his magnificent way listened to both. To Margaret he gave money, with bishop Neville he negotiated a truce. In the meantime money was required for the maintenance of the government, and a new parliament met on the 29th of April, 1463, which sat by virtue of several prorogations, at Westminster and York, until the year 1465[4]. The Rolls preserve little record of its transactions beyond a few trade petitions, an act of resumption, and the attainder of those enemies who incurred the guilt of treason during its continuance[5]. It showed however towards Edward an amount of confidence which must have been based either on fear or on hope, for it could not have been the result of experience. A grant of £37,000 was made for the defence of the realm, to be levied in the way in

The earl of Oxford put to death, Feb. 1462.

Somerset submits.

Foreign intrigues in 1463.

Parliament of 1463-5.

[1] The earl, his son Aubrey, Sir Thomas Todenham, and two esquires were beheaded; Gregory, p. 218; Chron. Lond. p. 142; W. Worc. p. 779.
[2] Gregory, Chr. p. 219, 221; W. Worc. p. 779; Paston Letters, ii. 113.
[3] W. Worc. p. 780.
[4] Rot. Parl. v. 496–570. John Say was speaker.
[5] Rot. Parl. v. 511.

which the fifteenth and tenth were levied, and to be subject to the usual deduction of £6000 for the relief of decayed towns; this grant seems to show that £37,000 was the ordinary produce of a fifteenth and tenth [1]. This was done in the first sitting which closed in June 1463. On meeting again in November the commons changed the form of the grant and ordered it to be levied under the name of a fifteenth and tenth [2]. In another meeting tunnage and poundage and the subsidy on wool were granted to the king for his life [3]; but this was after the battle of Hexham had made him practically supreme. By these grants the commons probably obtained the royal assent to several commercial statutes, which show that with a strong government the interests of trade were reviving, and the national development following the line which it had taken in the better days of Henry V and Henry VI. But the interest of the drama still hangs on the career of Margaret [4], which drew near its close.

Money grants in 1463.

Grant for life in 1465.

Having obtained some small help from Lewis XI, she returned to England at the close of 1463, and early in the next year, having recalled Somerset to his allegiance [5], entered Northumberland and retook the castles. John Neville, lord Montague, brother of Warwick, was sent to meet her, and defeated her in two battles; at Hedgley Moor on the 25th of April, and at Hexham on the 15th of May. At Hexham the duke of Somerset, the lords Roos and Hungerford, and Taillebois, titular earl of Kyme, were taken. Somerset was beheaded at once, the others two days later at Newcastle [6]. Other prisoners were carried to York, where the

Renewal of warfare in 1464.

Battle at Hexham.

[1] Rot. Parl. v. 497; Warkworth, p. 3. Convocation granted a tenth, July 23, 1463; Wilk. Conc. iii. 585, 587; and in 1464 a subsidy of sixpence in the pound for the crusade, p. 598.

[2] Rot. Parl. v. 498; Nov. 4.

[3] Jan. 21, 1465; Rot. Parl. v. 508.

[4] In June 1462, at Chinon, Margaret borrowed 20,000 livres of Lewis XI to be repaid within a year after the recovery of Calais: in default of payment Calais was to be delivered to Lewis; App. D, to Foed. p. 86.

[5] Gregory, p. 223; W. Worc. p. 781.

[6] Gregory gives a synopsis of the executions: May 15, Somerset and four others at Hexham; May 17, Hungerford, Roos, and three others, at Newcastle; May 18, Sir Philip Wentworth and six others at Middleham; May 26, Sir Thomas Hussey and thirteen others at York. Sir William Taillebois was beheaded at Newcastle. Chr. pp. 225, 226; cf. Warkworth, notes, pp. 39, 40.

Rewards and punishments. king was, tried before the constable and executed. Montague, as a reward for his prowess, was made earl of Northumberland and endowed with the Percy estates in that county. In July Sir Ralph Grey, who had defended Alnwick against Warwick, was beheaded at Doncaster[1], in Edward's presence. In September bishop George Neville became archbishop of York. The point at which the fortunes of the Nevilles thus reach their zenith almost exactly coincides with the moment at which the political relations of the king and court are totally altered by his marriage. For on the 29th of September Edward proclaimed that he had been for some time married to Elizabeth, the lady Grey, or Ferrers, of Groby, a widow, and daughter of a Lancastrian lord, Richard Wydville lord Rivers, who had been steward to the great duke of Bedford and had married Jacquetta of Luxemburg his widow.

George Neville made archbishop of York.

The king's marriage announced Sept. 1464.

Disappointment of the Nevilles on Edward's marriage.

681. Edward's marriage was signally distasteful to the Nevilles. Warwick had planned a great scheme[2], according to which the king should by a fitting matrimonial alliance, connecting him with both France and Burgundy, secure the peace of Western Europe, at all events for some years. Even if that scheme failed he might fairly have looked for a politic marriage, perhaps with a daughter of his own, by which the newly founded dynasty might be strengthened against the risks of a counter-restoration. All such hopes were rendered futile by the art of a woman or the infatuation of a boy. But the earl knew that he must endure his disappointment, and continued to support Edward with his counsels until his own position became intolerable. The failure of his foreign scheme did not prevent the king from securing the expulsion of the Lancastrians from France. This was one of the conditions of a truce with Lewis XI in 1465[3]; they were too much dis-

Warwick continues to support him.

[1] W. Worc. p. 782; Warkworth, notes, p. 38.

[2] On Warwick's policy see Kirk, Charles the Bold, i. 415, ii. 15; where it is shown that negotiations were on foot for the king's marriage with a sister of the queen of France, by which a final peace was to be secured, in 1463 and 1464, on the principle on which Suffolk had negotiated in 1444. See also Hall, Chr. p. 263; Rymer, xi. 518 sq.; Warkworth, p. 3.

[3] W. Worc. p. 785; cf. Rymer, xi. 566, 568. The chronicler refers the truce to 1465, but the documents belong to 1466.

heartened to move again yet. The year 1465 passed away without disturbance; in July the unfortunate Henry was arrested whilst wandering about among his secret friends in Lancashire[1]. The Scots had already forsaken him, and in 1464 concluded a truce for fifteen years with Edward[2]. He was committed to the Tower, only for a few months again to be restored to light and liberty. His mind, never strong, was probably weakened by suffering, and it is only very occasionally that a gleam of light is cast on his desolate existence. He was allowed now and then to receive visitors in the Tower. When pressed by some impertinent person to justify his usurpation, he used to answer, 'My father had been king of England, possessing his crown in peace all through his reign; and his father my grandfather had been king of the same realm. And I, when a boy in the cradle, had been without any interval crowned in peace and approved as king by the whole realm, and wore the crown for wellnigh forty years, every lord doing royal homage to me, and swearing fealty as they had done to my forefathers; so I may say with the Psalmist, "The lines are fallen unto me in a pleasant place, yea I have a goodly heritage;" "My help cometh of God, who preserveth them that are true of heart[3]."'

Capture of king Henry.

His imprisonment in the Tower.

From this moment began the contest between the earl of Warwick and the Wydvilles; a struggle which in some degree resembles the former struggle with the Beauforts, but which involves fewer points of political principle and more of mere personal rivalry. Edward was tired of the domination of the Nevilles, who, like the Percies sixty years before, seemed to be overvaluing their services and undervaluing their rewards. Warwick, like Hotspur, was a man of jealous temper and high spirit. The king, unwilling to sink into the position of a pupil or a tool, had perhaps conceived the notion, common to Edward II and Richard II, of raising up a counterpoise to the Nevilles in a circle of friends devoted to himself. From the time of the declaration of his marriage he seems to have

Rivalry between the Nevilles and the Wydvilles.

[1] W. Worc. p. 785; Warkworth, p. 5.
[2] Rymer, xi. 525.
[3] Blakman, pp. 303, 305.

Advancement of the queen's relations.

laboured incessantly for the promotion of his wife's relations. Her father, a man of years and experience, already a baron, became in March 1466 lord treasurer[1], in the following May an earl, and in 1467 high constable of England; his eldest son Antony was already a baron in right of his wife, the heiress of lord Scales; another, John, was married in 1465 to the aged duchess of Norfolk. Of the daughters, one was married in 1464 to the heir of the Arundels, another in 1466 to the duke of Buckingham, another to the lord Grey of Ruthyn, and another to the heir of lord Herbert, the king's most confidential friend[2]. The same year the queen's son, by her first husband, was betrothed to the heiress of the duke of Exeter, the king's niece.

Warwick plans a marriage for his daughter with Clarence.

These marriages, especially those which connected the upstart house with the near kindred of the royal family, the Staffords and the Hollands, were very offensive to Warwick, who did not scruple to show his displeasure, and began a counter-intrigue for the marriage of one of his daughters with the duke of Clarence, the heir-presumptive to the throne[3]. The appointment of lord Rivers as treasurer was even more offensive, since he had been a warm partisan of the Lancastrian cause, for which also the queen's first husband had fallen.

Conflicting foreign policy.

In foreign policy too the aims of Edward and Warwick were now diverging, the king making approaches to Burgundy, the earl trying to negotiate an alliance with France. On this errand Warwick was absent when Edward next met the parliament, in June 1467.

Parliament meets in June 1467.

The session was opened on the 3rd with a discourse from the bishop of Lincoln, in the absence of the chancellor[4]. On the 6th the king made a declaration of his intention 'to live of his own,' and only in case of great necessity to ask the estates for an aid; and the declaration was followed up with an act of resumption, in which, although provision was made for Clarence and Warwick, archbishop Neville was not spared[5]. On the 8th the absence of the chancellor was explained; the king and lord Herbert visited archbishop Neville in his house at Westminster,

[1] W. Worc. p. 785. [2] Ib. pp. 783, 785, 786. [3] Ib. p. 788.
[4] Rot. Parl. v. 571. [5] Ib. v. 572–613; W. Worc. p. 786.

and took from him the great seal[1]; it was given the next day to Robert Stillington, bishop of Bath. On the day of Warwick's return, July 1, the parliament was prorogued, and did not meet again till the 12th of May, 1468[2]. Before that time Warwick's influence over the king's mind was entirely lost and his own position seriously imperilled.

Neville removed from the chancery. Prorogation to 1468.

The French ambassadors whom he brought over in July 1467 were treated by the king with scant civility; the negotiations with Burgundy, where duke Charles had in June succeeded his father Philip, were busily pressed; and in a great council held in October it was agreed that Charles should marry the king's sister, Margaret of York[3]. Warwick, perhaps as a counter-move, urged on the project for Clarence's marriage with his daughter. Just at the same time a courier of queen Margaret was arrested by lord Herbert, and to save himself laid information against several persons as favouring the intrigues of his mistress[4]. Warwick's name was in the list, possibly placed there by Herbert and the Wydvilles; although it was possible, and indeed not improbable, that in the disappointment of his foreign policy he had opened communication through Lewis XI with Margaret. Having declined to accept an invitation from the king, he was examined at Middleham by a royal messenger, and the charge was declared frivolous. But the accusation, whether based on fact or not, sank deep into his soul. Edward, feeling that there was cause for mistrust, surrounded himself with a paid body-guard. Clarence drew off from his brother, and, following the policy of heirs presumptive, took on every possible occasion a line opposed to that of the king. The widening of the breach was not stopped by a formal reconciliation which took place at Coventry at Christmas[5]. Archbishop Neville and lord Rivers having first adjusted their own differences, acted as mediators, and brought the king and Warwick together; Herbert and the Wydvilles were included in the pacification.

Alliance of Edward with Burgundy.

Warwick charged with intrigue with the Lancastrians.

He is acquitted but offended.

Clarence adheres to Warwick.

General pacification at Coventry in 1467.

In the following May Edward conceived himself strong

[1] W. Worc. p. 786; Rymer, xi. 578, 579; Warkworth, p. 3.
[2] Rot. Parl. v. 618; W. Worc. p. 787.
[3] W. Worc. p. 788. [4] Ib. p. 788. [5] Ib. p. 789.

Session of parliament in 1468.

enough to declare his hostility to France; and the chancellor[1], in opening the parliamentary session, was able to announce the conclusion of treaties with Spain, Denmark, Scotland, and Brittany; the close alliance with Burgundy, which was to be cemented by the marriage of Margaret; and the king's intention and hopes of recovering the inheritance of his fore-fathers across the Channel.

Proposed war with France.

Edward himself spoke his mind to the lords[2]; if he could secure sufficient supplies he would lead his army in person. The commons welcomed the idea of a foreign war, which might, as in the days of Henry V, result in internal peace; and voted two tenths and fifteenths[3].

Money grants. The war delayed.

This done, the parliament, on the 7th of June, was dissolved. The next month the Burgundian marriage was completed[4], and the alarm of treason and civil war revived. Seven years were to elapse before Edward could fulfil his undertaking; and before the end of the year 1468 duke Charles and king Lewis had concluded a truce[5].

Margaret's continued efforts.

The spirits of the Lancastrians were now reviving, notwithstanding the fact that the seizure of Margaret's letters had ruined several others of her partisans, and that the lord Herbert, after defeating Jasper Tudor, earl of Pembroke, had succeeded at last in taking Harlech. On both occasions some few executions followed. Herbert was made earl of Pembroke in the place of the defeated Tudor. Earl Jasper's rising was probably part of a scheme in accordance with which Margaret, with the forces she had raised in France, was to land on the south coast.

Threatened attack on the south coast.

To repel this attack the lords Scales and Mountjoy were sent to the Isle of Wight with a fleet and five thousand men. The threat of invasion was a mere bravado; the expedition of lord Scales cost £18,000, one quarter of the grant made for the French war. Edward's devotion to the advancement of the Wydvilles took

[1] After several formal prorogations the parliament met at Reading, May 12; Rot. Parl. v. 622. Convocation, May 12, 1468, granted a tenth and a subsidy of the priests' noble; Wilk. Conc. iii. 606; Chron. Abbrev. p. 12.

[2] W. Worc. p. 789.

[3] Rot. Parl. v. 623; Chron. Abbrev. p. 12.

[4] W. Worc. p. 789; Paston Letters, ii. 317–319.

[5] W. Worc. p. 792.

this year the curious form of an attempt to force his brother-in-law Richard into the office of prior of S. John's, Clerkenwell, the head of the Knights Hospitallers of England[1].

Renewal of war in 1469.

The next year witnessed the renewal of the civil war. The Lancastrian party in the north had been suffered to gather strength, and had been more than encouraged by the attitude of Warwick. Since 1466 the relics of earl Thomas of Lancaster had been sweating blood and working miracles[2]. Margaret and her agents had been active abroad. The king's popularity was gradually vanishing, as the more active politicians found every prize lavished on the Wydvilles, and the more apathetic mass of the nation discovered that the peace and security of life and property were no better cared for under the new dynasty than they had been under the old[3]. But there was not yet any concert between the two sections of the disaffected; the struggle of 1469 was by the Nevilles and Clarence for their own ends; in 1470 the Lancastrians took advantage of the situation to ally themselves with them for the purpose of a restoration. The rebellion of Robin of Redesdale was an attempt to employ against Edward IV the weapons used in the Kentish rising of 1450 under Jack Cade. The insurrection had begun in Yorkshire in consequence of a quarrel about tithes, and the leader, Robert Huldurn or Hilyard, had been defeated and put to death by Montague. A knight of the house of Conyers then assumed the name of Robin of Redesdale and placed himself at the head of the discontented commons of the north. He collected forces and began to traverse the country as an agitator in the summer of 1469; possibly at the suggestion, certainly with the connivance, of Warwick. The outbreak seems to have taken the king altogether by surprise, but he was not long left in doubt as to its importance. Soon after midsummer the earl of Warwick, archbishop Neville, and Clarence, went over to Calais, and the archbishop married the duke to his niece, Isabella Neville. Early in July the commons, to the number of sixty thousand, rose under Robin of

General discontent.

Rising of the commons of the north under Robin of Redesdale.

Marriage of Clarence.

[1] W. Worc. pp. 791, 792.
[2] Chron. Abbrev. (Camb. Antiq. Soc.) p. 10.
[3] See Warkworth, p. 12.

Manifesto of the commons under Robin of Redesdale.

Redesdale and published a manifesto in the form of an address to the king[1]. In this document, after recounting the mistakes which had proved fatal to Edward II, Richard II, and Henry VI, the alienation of the near kinsmen of the king from his councils and the promotion of favourites, the heavy taxation, and the maladministration of the law, they enumerate the great estates in the royal hands and charge the king with extravagant gifts made to the Wydvilles, dishonest dealing with the coinage, excessive taxation, extortion by purveyance, and perversion of the law of treason; they add that he has by the bad advice of the same counsellors embezzled the papal dues, forbidden the due execution of the laws, and removed his wisest advisers from the council. They therefore pray for the punishment of the evil counsellors, the regulation of the royal expenditure and revenue, the prohibition of gifts of crown lands, the devotion of tunnage and poundage to the defence of the seas, and the maintenance of the laws of king Edward III.

The Nevilles support the demand for reform.

This comprehensive bill of articles was circulated among the lords; Clarence and the Nevilles vouchsafed their approval, and on the 12th of July proclaimed that they would be at Canterbury to meet their friends on the following Sunday[2]. The king had three days before sent them orders from Nottingham to come to him at once[3].

Battle of Edgecote, July 26, 1469.

On the 26th of July William Herbert, earl of Pembroke, and Humfrey Stafford of Southwick, the newly created earl of Devonshire, were beaten by Robin of Redesdale, at Edgcote, near Banbury; Pembroke was taken and sent to Northampton, where he was soon after beheaded by the order of Clarence; lord Rivers and his son John, who were captured in Gloucestershire, shared the same fate; and the earl of Devonshire, who was captured by the commons in Somersetshire, was also beheaded.

Edward a prisoner.

Edward, left alone in the midst of a hostile country, surrendered himself as a prisoner to archbishop Neville, who carried him off first to

[1] Warkworth, notes, pp. 47–51; Chronicles of the White Rose, pp. 222–224; Chron. Abbrev. p. 13.

[2] The manifesto of Clarence and Warwick against Edward is in the Chronicles of the White Rose, p. 219; Warkworth, notes, p. 46. See also Chr. Abbrev. p. 13.

[3] July 9; Paston Letters, ii. 360 361. The marriage of Clarence took place on the 11th.

Coventry, and then to Middleham[1]. The victorious lords do not seem to have known what to do with their prisoner. After making some conditions with the Nevilles, he was allowed to resume his liberty, and returned to London[2], where before Christmas he issued a general pardon, in which they were included[3]. The effort of the commons was only a spasmodic undertaking; like the other risings of the kind, it subsided as quickly as it had arisen, and if Robin of Redesdale's host were to any extent composed of Lancastrians, they had risen too soon. The too sudden reconciliation of the lords was an evil sign, and whilst Warwick and Clarence were pardoned, Robin of Redesdale vanished altogether. But the throne was not secure; and Warwick had perhaps yielded only to gain time. In March, 1470, Sir Robert Welles rose in Lincolnshire, and Edward, after cruelly and treacherously beheading lord Welles, father of the rebel chief, by a sudden display of craft and energy summarily overthrew him near Stamford. After the battle the king found unmistakeable proof that Warwick and Clarence, whom he seems still to have trusted[4], were implicated in the transactions. Sir Robert, before he was executed, confessed that the object of the rebels was to make Clarence king[5]. He was beheaded on the 13th of March; on the 23rd[6] Edward issued a proclamation against his brother and Warwick, who, having failed to find help in Lancashire, and to effect a landing at Southampton, had fled to France. In France they were brought into communication with queen Margaret, and Warwick in all

He makes terms with Warwick.

Pardon at Christmas 1469.

Rebellion in Lincolnshire in March, 1470.

Warwick and Clarence fly to France.

[1] The dates of these transactions are very obscure. The king's detention must have covered the month of August. On August 17 he appointed Warwick chief justice of South Wales; Rymer, xi. 648; and he was at Middleham on the 25th and 28th; on Michaelmas day he was at York; and on the 27th of October, Henry Percy heir of Northumberland swore fealty to him at Westminster; Rymer, xi. 648; Cont. Hardyng, p. 443; Hall, p. 275; cf. Warkwork, p. 7; Cont. Croyland, p. 555.

[2] Paston Letters, ii. 389; and Mr. Gairdner's notes, ib. p. xlix.

[3] Warkworth (p. 7) states that a fifteenth was collected at the same time.

[4] Paston Letters, ii. 394, 395; Rymer, xi. 652.

[5] The confession of Sir Robert Welles is printed in the Excerpta Historica, pp. 283 sq.

[6] Rymer, xi. 654; Warkworth, notes, pp, 53-56; see also Rot. Parl. vi. 233.

Design of Margaret and Warwick.

sincerity undertook to bring about a new revolution; Clarence probably contemplating his chance of recovering his brother's good-will by betraying his father-in-law.

Warwick lands, Sept. 1470. Flight of Edward and restoration of Henry VI.

The design was rapidly ripened. On the 13th of September Warwick landed at Dartmouth; Edward, finding himself forsaken by the marquess of Montague, Warwick's brother[1], fled to Flanders on the 3rd of October; on the 5th archbishop Neville and bishop Waynflete took Henry VI from the Tower; queen Elizabeth took sanctuary at Westminster; the earl of Worcester, Edward's constable and the minister of his cruelties, was taken and beheaded[2]. The nation without regret and without enthusiasm recognised the Lancastrian restoration. On the 9th of October writs for the election of coroners and verderers, and on the 15th the summons for parliament, were issued in Henry's name[3]. On the 26th of November Henry was made to hold his parliament; no formal record of its proceedings is preserved, but the writs of summons show that thirty-four lords were called to it, and one historian has preserved the text of the opening sermon. Archbishop Neville, who had been made chancellor, preached on the words 'Turn, O backsliding children[4].' The crown was again settled on Henry and his son, with remainder, in case of the extinction of the house of Lancaster, to the duke of Clarence[5]. The attainders passed in Edward's parliaments were then repealed, and in consequence, early in 1471, the dukes of Somerset and Exeter and the earls of Pembroke and Richmond returned to England.

Henry's parliament, November.

Acts of the parliament.

[1] John Neville, who had been made earl of Northumberland in 1465, had had to restore the Percy estates in 1470, and was then made marquess of Montague.

[2] Paston Letters, ii. 412. Tiptoft hanged the prisoners taken at Southampton in 1470, and impaled their bodies; Leland, Coll. ii. 502; cf. Warkworth, p. 9.

[3] Lords' Report, iv. 976; Rymer, xi. 661 sq.; the period of restoration, 'readeptio regiae potestatis,' or forty-ninth year of Henry VI, extended from October 9, 1470, to the beginning of April 1471.

[4] Warkworth, p. 12.

[5] This act of the parliament is known only by the rehearsal in the act of 1478 which repealed it; Rot. Parl. vi. 191–193. Warwick was made governor of the realm with Clarence his associate; Hall, p. 286. The writer of the account of Edward's return (White Rose, p. 36) speaks of him as 'calling himself lieutenant of England by pretended authority of the usurper Henry and his accomplices.'

No great enthusiasm for either king.

The collapse of Edward's power was so complete, that for some weeks neither he nor his enemies contemplated the chance of a restoration. The Nevilles disbanded their forces, and Edward scarcely hoped for more than the recovery of his paternal estates. For Henry it was impossible to excite any enthusiasm; he had never been popular: five years of captivity, calumny, squalor, and neglect had made him an object of contempt. Yet the royal name had great authority, and whoever claimed it seemed to have the power of calling large forces into the field; and men fought as if to preserve their own lives or to satiate their thirst for blood, with little regard to the banner under which they were marshalled. As for the maintenance of the common weal, the nation was now fully persuaded that there was little to choose between the weak government of Henry and the strong government of Edward; both alike allowed the real exercise of power to become a mere prize for contending factions among the nobles: the laws were no better administered, the taxes were no lighter, under the one than under the other. They accepted Henry as their king at Warwick's behest; they would accept Edward again the moment he proved himself the stronger. There were local attachments and personal antipathies no doubt, but the body politic was utterly exhausted, or, if beginning to recover from exhaustion, was too weak and tender to withstand the slightest blast or to endure the gentlest pressure. Margaret and her son too were absent, and did not arrive until the chances were decided against them.

Edward's return in March 1471.

In March 1471 Edward, who had obtained a small force from his brother-in-law of Burgundy, sailed for England and, after being repulsed from the coast of Norfolk, landed in Yorkshire on the 14th, at the very port at which Henry IV had landed in 1399. As if the name of the place suggested the politic course, he followed the example of Henry IV, solemnly declaring that he was come to reclaim his duchy only. At York he acknowledged the right of Henry VI and the prince of Wales[1]. But at Nottingham he proclaimed himself king; and moved on by Leicester

[1] Warkworth, p. 14; Fleetwood, Chr. White Rose, p. 40–42.

to Coventry, where Warwick and Montague were. Deceived by a letter from Clarence[1], they allowed him to pass by without a battle, and he advanced, gathering strength at every step, to Warwick, where Clarence joined him. On the 11th of April he reached London. Henry, under the guidance of archbishop Neville, had attempted to rouse the citizens to resistance, but had completely failed. Edward, on the other hand, was received with open arms by archbishop Bourchier and the faithful Yorkists. On the 13th he marched out of London, with Henry in his train, to meet Warwick. He encountered him at Barnet the next day, Easter day, and totally defeated him. Warwick himself and Montague were killed in the battle or in the rout.

He gains London.

Battle of Barnet.

Margaret lands.

The same day Margaret and her son landed at Weymouth, and as soon as the fate of Warwick was known, she gathered the remnant of her party round her and marched towards the north. On the 4th of May Edward encountered her ill-disciplined army at Tewkesbury, and routed them with great slaughter. No longer checked by the more politic influence of Warwick, the king both in the battle and after it gave full play to his lust for revenge. The young prince, Thomas Courtenay the loyal earl of Devonshire, and lord Wenlock were killed on the field; the duke of Somerset, the prior of the Hospitallers, and a large number of knights were beheaded after the battle, in spite of a promise of pardon. Queen Margaret, the princess of Wales, and Sir John Fortescue were among the prisoners[2].

Battle of Tewkesbury.

The bastard of Fauconberg.

Edward's danger was not yet quite over. On the 5th of May the bastard of Fauconberg, who had landed in Kent, reached London, and, having failed to force an entrance, passed on to cut him off on his return. But his force, although large, was disheartened by the news from Tewkesbury; and, persuaded by the promises of immunity, he deserted them and fled. Edward, with thirty thousand men under his command, re-entered London on the 21st of May in triumph[3]. The same night king Henry died in the Tower, where he had been replaced after the battle

Death of Henry VI.

[1] Paston Letters, ii. 4213; Warkworth, p. 15; Fleetwood, p. 50.
[2] Warkworth, pp. 18, 19.
[3] Ib. p. 21; Fleetwood, pp 86-92.

of Barnet. Both at the time and after, the duke of Gloucester was regarded as his murderer; and although nothing certain is known of the circumstances of his death, it is most probable that he was slain secretly. So long as his son lived, his life was valuable to his foes; the young Edward might, as claimant of the crown, have obtained from the commons an amount of support which they would not give to his father, whom they had tried and found wanting. Now that the son was gone, Henry himself was worse than useless, and he died. On Wednesday, the 22nd of May, his body lay in state at S. Paul's and Blackfriars, and on Ascension day he was carried off to be buried at Chertsey[1]. Almost immediately he began to be regarded as a saint and martyr[2]. In Yorkshire especially, where he had wandered in his desolation, and where the house of Lancaster was immemorially regarded as the guardian of national liberties, he was revered with signal devotion, a devotion stimulated not a little by the misrule that followed the crowning victory of Edward. For this was the last important attempt made during his life to unseat the new dynasty. The seizure of S. Michael's Mount by the earl of Oxford in September 1473 was a gallant exploit, but led to nothing; he had to surrender in February 1474. In 1475 Margaret was ransomed by her father and went home. The existence of the son of Margaret Beaufort, the destined restorer of the greatness of England, was the solitary speck that clouded the future of the dynasty, and although Edward saw the importance of getting him into his power, he was too young and insignificant to be a present danger. The birth of a son, born to queen Elizabeth in the Sanctuary in 1470, was an element of new promise. Edward had no more to fear and everything to hope.

Honour shown to him after death.

Exploit of the earl of Oxford.

Present security of Edward IV.

Warwick, whose death afforded the real security for these anticipations of better times, has always occupied a great place in the view of history; and his character, although in some respects only an exaggeration of the common baronial type, certainly

Warwick's character.

[1] Warkworth, p. 21; Fleetwood, pp. 93 sq.

[2] 'Unde et agens tyranni, patiensque gloriosi martyris titulum mereatur'; Cont. Croyl. p. 566.

Character of Warwick.

contained some elements of greatness. He was greedy of power, wealth, and influence; jealous of all competitors, and unscrupulous in the measures he took to gain these ends. He was magnificent in his expenditure and popular in consequence. He was a skilful warrior both by land and by sea, and good fortune in battle gave him another claim to be a national favourite. He was a far-seeing politician too, and probably, if Edward had suffered him, would have secured such a settlement of the foreign relations of England as might have anticipated the period of national recovery of which Henry VII obtained the credit. He was unrelenting in his enmities, but not wantonly bloodthirsty or faithless: from the beginning of the struggle, when he was a very young man and altogether under his father's influence, he had taken up with ardour the cause of duke Richard, and his final defection was the result of a profound conviction that Edward, influenced by the Wydvilles, was bent on his ruin. He filled however for many years, and not altogether unworthily, a place which never before or after was filled by a subject, and his title of King-maker was not given without reason. But it is his own singular force of character, decision and energy, that mark him off from the men of his time. He is no constitutional hero; he comes perhaps hardly within the ken of constitutional history, but he had in him the makings of a great king.

Results of Edward's triumph.

682. The cruelties and extortions which followed Edward's victory need not detain us, although they fill up the records of the following years. By executions and exactions he made the nation feel the burdens of undivided and indivisible allegiance. 'The rich were hanged by the purse and the poor by the neck.' What forfeiture failed to secure was won by extorted ransoms.

Fate of archbishop Neville.

In April 1472 archbishop Neville, who had made his peace after the battle of Barnet, was despoiled of his wealth; he spent the rest of his life in captivity or mortified retirement. The estates, which were not called together until October 1472[1], were in too

[1] Parliament met Oct. 6, and sat till Nov. 30; sat again Feb. 8, 1473, to April 8; Oct. 6 to Dec. 13; in 1474, Jan. 20 to Feb. 1; May 9 to May 28; June 6 to July 18; and in 1475, Jan. 23 to March 14; when it was dissolved. William Alyngton was speaker; Rot. Parl. vi. 1–166. See Cont. Croyl. pp. 557, 558.

great awe of the king to venture on any resistance to his commands. They granted him a force of thirteen thousand archers, to be paid at the rate of sixpence a day for a year; and the commons and lords, in two separate indentures, directed that a new and complete tenth of all existing property and income should be collected to defray the cost[1]. In 1473, when they met again after a prorogation, they found that the tax could not be easily got in, and voted a fifteenth and tenth of the old kind, on account[2]. The same year Edward began to collect the contributions which were so long and painfully familiar under the inappropriate name of Benevolences[3]; a method of extortion worse than even the forced loans and blank charters of Richard II. In the following October an act of resumption was passed[4]; in July 1474 the same parliament, still sitting by prorogation, voted a tenth and fifteenth, with an additional sum of £51,147 4*s*. 7¾*d*., to be raised from the sources from which the tenth and fifteenth were levied[5]; the payment was accelerated in the following January, and in March 1475, after another grant of a tenth and fifteenth, this long parliament was dissolved[6]. Besides the details of taxation, the parliamentary records have little to show but mercantile enactments, private petitions, acts of settlement of estates, attainders and reversals of attainders, and a few points of parliamentary privilege. Of the restorations the most significant are those of Sir John Fortescue[7], who was pardoned in 1473 on condition that he should refute his own arguments for the title of the Lancastrian kings; and that of Dr. John Morton[8], a faithful Lancastrian partisan who had been attainted in 1461, and who in 1472

Parliamentary history.

Benevolences.

Large grants in parliament.

Mercantile legislation.

Fortescue and Morton.

[1] Rot. Parl. vi. 4–8.
[2] Ib. vi. 39–41.
[3] Cont. Croyl. p. 558; 'nova et inaudita impositio muneris ut per benevolentiam quilibet daret id quod vellet, immo verius quod nollet.' 'This year the king asked of the people, great goods of their benevolence'; Chr. Lond. p. 145: 'he conceived a new device in his imagination'; Hall, p. 308, where an amusing account is given of Edward's selling his kisses for a benevolence of twenty pounds.
[4] Rot. Parl. vi. 71 sq.; Cont. Croyl. p. 559.
[5] Rot. Parl. vi. 111–119; Warkworth, p. 23.
[6] Rot. Parl. vi. 120, 149–153.
[7] Ib. vi. 69.
[8] Ib. vi. 26.

obtained not only the annulment of his sentence but the office of master of the rolls, and in 1473 was even made keeper of the great seal. The court was disturbed by the jealousies of the king's brothers, who were scarcely more jealous of the Wydvilles than of each other; Richard with great difficulty obtained the hand and part of the inheritance of the lady Anne Neville, Warwick's daughter and prince Edward's widow. The great seal, after some unimportant changes, rested in the hands of Thomas Rotherham, afterwards archbishop of York[1]; in the treasury the earl of Essex, Henry Bourchier, retained his position from 1471 until the close of the reign. The period is otherwise obscure; the national restoration was impeded by a severe visitation of the plague; and the king's attention, so far as it was not engaged by his own pleasures and the quarrels of his brothers, was devoted to the preparation for his great adventure, the expedition to France in 1475.

Jealousy of Clarence and Gloucester.

The chancellor and treasurer.

Expedition to France.

This expedition, which had been contemplated so long and came to so little, was intended to vindicate the claim of the king of England to the crown of France,—the worn-out claim of course which had been invented by Edward III. The policy of alliance with Burgundy had culminated in July 1474 in a league for the deposition of Lewis XI. In July 1475 Edward and his army landed at Calais. It was the finest army that England had ever sent to France, but it found the French better prepared than they had ever been to receive it. The duke of Burgundy was engaged in war on the Rhine; Lewis knew an easier way of securing France than fighting battles. Instead of a struggle, a truce for seven years was the result; this was concluded on the 29th of August. The two kings met, with a grating of trellis-work between them, on the bridge of Pecquigny[2]; and Edward returned home richer by a sum

[1] Bishop Stillington was chancellor from 1467 to 1473; Morton and the earl of Essex were keepers in June and July, 1473; Laurence Booth, bishop of Durham, July 27, 1473, to May 25, 1474; after which date Thomas Rotheram became chancellor, and held the seal until the end of the reign. See Cont. Croyl. p. 557; Rymer, xi. 782.

[2] Cont. Croyl. p. 558; Rymer, xii. 14-20. The prince of Wales was left at home as custos.

of 75,000 crowns and a promised pension of 50,000. And England, which had allowed a dynasty to be overthrown because of the loss of Maine and Anjou, bore the shame without a blush or a pang[1].

Lewis buys off Edward.

The history of 1476 is nearly a blank; the jealousy of Clarence and Gloucester probably increased; the king failed to obtain the surrender of the earl of Richmond by the duke of Brittany; the duke of Burgundy was ruining himself in his attack on the Swiss. In 1477 Clarence, unable to endure the ascendancy of Gloucester, quitted the court. He had lost his wife in 1476, as he suspected, by poison, and had gone beyond the rights of his legal position in exacting punishment from the suspected culprits[3]. A series of petty squabbles ended in a determination of the ruling party at court to get rid of him. In a parliament which met on the 16th of January, 1478, Edward himself acting as the accuser, he was attainted, chiefly on the ground of his complicity with the Lancastrians in 1470[5]; the bill was approved by the commons; and on the 7th of February order was given for his execution, the duke of Buckingham being appointed high steward for the occasion[6]. How he actually perished is uncertain, but he was dead before the end of the

Behaviour of Clarence.

He is accused and attainted in 1478.

His death.

[1] The Crowland annalist attributes to Edward a great show of vigorous justice at this time, adding that but for his severity there would have been a rebellion, so great was the discontent felt at the waste of treasure: 'tantus crevisset numerus populorum conquerentium super male dispensatis regni divitiis, et abraso de omnium scriniis tanto thesauro tam inutiliter consumpto, ut nesciretur quorum consiliariorum capita incolumia remanerent, eorum praesertim qui familiaritate muneribusve Gallici regis inducti pacem modis supradictis initam persuasissent'; p. 559. See Davies, Municipal Records of York, pp. 50–52.

[2] Charles the Bold fell at Nancy, Jan. 5, 1477. There was a great council, 'to whyche alle the astats off the londe shall com to,' begun Feb. 13, 1477; it seems to have been employed on foreign affairs; Paston Letters, iii. 173.

[3] Rot. Parl. vi. 173.

[4] Ib. vi. 167. The chancellor's text was 'The Lord is my shepherd'; the application 'He beareth not the sword in vain.' William Alyngton was again speaker. The writs for the parliament are lost, but we know from the York Records that it sat from Jan. 16 to Feb. 26; the representatives of that city receiving wages for forty-two days of session and twelve more going and returning; Davies, York Records, p. 66.

[5] Rot. Parl. vi. 193-195; Cont. Croyl. p. 560.

[6] Rot. Parl. v. 195.

Fate of Clarence.

month, and the Wydvilles received a large share of the forfeitures. Clarence was a weak, vain, and faithless man; he had succeeded to some part of Warwick's popularity, and had, in the minds of those who regarded the acts of the Lancastrian parliament of 1470, a claim to be the constitutional king. If his acts condemn him, it is just to remember that the men with whom he was matched were Edward IV and Richard III. The particular question of his final guilt affects his character as little and as much as it affects theirs.

Parliament of 1478.

The parliament had probably been called for this express purpose; the chancellor, who had opened it with a discourse on the first verse of the twenty-third Psalm, had illustrated his thesis with examples drawn from both Testaments of the punishments due to broken fealty. Besides the formal declaration of the nullity of the acts of the Lancastrian parliament which was now made [1], two or three exchanges of estates were ratified and some few attainders reversed. George Neville, son of the marquess of Montague, who had been created duke of Bedford, and was intended to marry the king's eldest daughter, was deprived of his titles on the ground that he had no fortune to maintain them [2]; his father's estates had been secured to the king's brothers. The statutes which were passed were of the usual commercial type. The session must have been a very short one, and no money was asked for. The convocation, which under the influence of archbishop Bourchier was more amenable to royal pressure, was made to bestow a tenth in the following April [3]. Edward was growing rich by mercantile speculations of his own; and complaisant as the parliament might have proved, there was a chance that the military failure of 1475 might be subjected to too close inspection if any large demand had been made from the assembled estates [4]. No parliament was called for the next five years, and the intervening period, so far as constitutional history is concerned, is absolutely without incident.

Edward grows rich.

[1] Rot. Parl. vi. 191, 192.
[2] Ib. vi. 173.
[3] Wilkins, Conc. iii. 612.
[4] Cont. Croyl. p. 559.

The quarrels of the court did not extend beyond the inner circle around the king. He continued to heap favours on the Wydvilles, and to throw military and administrative work on Gloucester. Considerable efforts were made during the time to enforce the measures necessary for internal peace; frequent assizes were held, and as of old, when the sword of justice was sharpened[1], the receipts of the Treasury increased; obsolete statutes and customs were made to produce a harvest of fines, and ancient debts were recovered. But neither the rigour of the courts nor the extortions which the rising prosperity of the country was well able to bear, seem to have damaged Edward's popularity. He remained until his death a favourite with the people of London and the great towns; and his reign, full as its early days had been of violence and oppression, drew to its close with no unfavourable omens for his successor. The troubled state of Scotland furnished employment for Gloucester from 1480 onwards; Edward had undertaken the cause of the duke of Albany against his nephew James III; and Albany had promised, if he were successful, to hold Scotland as a fief of the English crown[2]. The great exploit of the war, the seizure of Edinburgh in 1482, was the joint work of Gloucester and Albany; the funds were raised by recourse to benevolences[3]; the establishment of relays of couriers to carry despatches between the king and his brother is regarded as the first attempt at a postal system in England, and as one of the main benefits

Edward's judicial activity.

He retains his popularity.

Gloucester engaged in Scottish warfare.

[1] In his nineteenth year Edward 'began more than he was before accustomed, to search out the penal offences, as well of the chief of his nobility as of other gentlemen . . . by reason whereof it was of all men adjudged . . . that he would prove hereafter a sore and an extreme prince amongst his subjects . . . he should say, that all men should stand and live in fear of him and he to be unbridled and in doubt of no man'; Hall, p. 329.

[2] Rymer, xii. 156–158.

[3] Cont. Croyl. p. 562. The York records furnish some indications that other methods of exaction were practised. The king had issued letters for the collection of a force to join in the expedition to Scotland; forty persons were to be maintained by the Ainsty, eighty by the city; the money required was to be collected in each parish by the constables, the portion unspent to be returned; Davies, pp. 115, 116, 128. This seems very like the worst form of commission of array. See also Rymer, xii. 117, and p. 279 below.

which entitle the house of York to the gratitude of posterity[1]. With France the king's relations continued to be friendly, but the cordiality of the newly formed alliance quickly cooled; Lewis found that he did not need Edward; Edward tried hard to think that he was not duped. Towards the close of 1482 the marriage between the king's daughter Elizabeth and the dauphin, which had been one of the articles of the peace of Pecquigny, was broken off by Lewis himself; who on the 22nd of January 1483[2] ratified the contract for the betrothal of his son to Margaret of Austria. Edward felt this as a personal insult, and the failure of all his negotiations for the marriage of his children with foreign princes contributed no doubt to his mortification, if they did not suggest that, great as his power and prosperity were, he was regarded by the kings of Europe as somewhat of an outlaw. It was probably with some intention of avenging himself on Lewis XI that on the 15th of November 1482 he called together his last parliament. It met on the 20th of the following January[3]. The chancellor's sermon, the text of which was 'Dominus illuminatio mea et salus mea,' has not been preserved; so that it is impossible to say whether the renewal of the war with France was distinctly proposed to the estates. The truce of 1475 had been in 1477 changed into a truce for life[4]; but both the amount and character of the money grants now made in parliament prove that a speedy outbreak was expected. For the hasty and necessary defence of the realm, the commons voted a fifteenth and tenth[5], and on

Lewis cajoles and disappoints the king.

Edward's last parliament, in 1483.

Preparation for war.

[1] Cont. Croyl. p. 571.

[2] Ib. p. 563; Commines, liv. 6, c. 9.

[3] Rot. Parl. vi. 196; John Wood was the speaker. See Davies, York Records, p. 138; Cont. Croyl. p. 563.

[4] Rymer, xii. 46. The truce was to last during the joint lives of Edward and Lewis and for a year after the death of the one who died first.

[5] Rot. Parl. vi. 197. The Crowland historian says, 'nihil adhuc tamen a communitate subsidii pecuniarii expetere ausus, erga praelatos necessitates suas non dissimulat, blande exigendo ab eis prae manibus decimas quae proximo concedentur, quasi, semel comparentibus praelatis et clero in convocatione, quicquid rex petit id fieri debeat'; p. 563. A tenth was granted by the clergy in 1481, and another in April 1483, after the king's death. Wilk. Conc. iii. 614; Wake, pp. 380, 381.

the 15th of February, three days later, they re-imposed the tax on aliens[1]. In the expectation of war the commons seem to have attempted to make their voices heard; they prayed for the enforcement of the statutes which maintained the public peace, the statutes of Westminster and Winchester, and the legislation on liveries, labourers and beggars[2]. It was possibly to disarm opposition, possibly to secure the provision for his sons and brother and the Wydvilles, that the king agreed to pass an act of resumption[3] and to accept an assignment of £11,000 for the maintenance of the household. A few months however were to show how little foresight he possessed, and to break up all his schemes. His constitution was ruined with debauchery: whether the failure of his foreign policy, as foreign writers believed, or the natural consequences of dissipation, as the English thought, finally broke him down, he died somewhat suddenly on the 9th of April, leaving his young family to be the prey of the contending factions which had long divided the court.

Petitions for maintenance of order.

Death of the king.

Edward IV was not perhaps quite so bad a man or so bad a king as his enemies have represented: but even those writers who have laboured hardest to rehabilitate him, have failed to discover any conspicuous merits. With great personal courage he may be freely credited; he was moreover eloquent, affable, and fairly well educated. He had a definite plan of foreign policy, and although he was both lavish in expenditure and extortionate in procuring money, he was a skilful merchant. He had, or professed to have, some love of justice in the abstract, which led him to enforce the due execution of law where it did not interfere with the fortunes of his favourites or his own likes and dislikes. He was to some extent a favourer of learned men; he made some small benefactions to houses of religion and devotion, and he did not entirely root up the collegiate foundations of his predecessors of the house of Lancaster. But that is all: he was as a man vicious far beyond anything that England had seen since the days of John; and more cruel and bloodthirsty than any king she had ever known: he had too a conspicuous

Character of Edward IV.

[1] Rot. Parl. vi. 197. [2] Ib. vi. 198. [3] Ib. vi. 198, 199.

Cruelties and bloodshed.

talent for extortion[1]. There had been fierce deeds of bloodshed under Edward II and Edward III; cruel and secret murder under Richard II and Henry IV; the hand of Henry V had been heavy and unrelenting against the conspirators of Southampton; and at S. Alban's the house of York, and at Wakefield the house of Lancaster, had sown fresh seeds for a fatal harvest. But Edward IV far outdid all that his forefathers and his enemies together had done. The death of Clarence was but the summing up and crowning act of an unparalleled list of judicial and extra-judicial cruelties which those of the next reign supplement but do not surpass.

State of the court at the time of Edward's death.

683. Edward IV, by the strength of his popularity, the force of his will, and his ruthless extinction of every kind of resistance, had been able for the last few years to keep his court at peace. The Wydvilles were not more beloved by the elder nobility than they had been by the Nevilles, and had done little to secure the position to which Edward had raised them. The queen's brothers, Antony earl of Rivers, Lionel bishop of Salisbury, and Edward and Richard Wydville, with her sons, Thomas Grey marquess of Dorset, and Sir Richard Grey, formed a little phalanx, strong in union and fidelity, in the support of the queen and in the influence which Edward's favour had won for them, but to any cause that might depend on them alone a source of danger rather than a safeguard. The lords of the council, among whom the chief were the lords Hastings, Stanley and Howard, were personally faithful to the king and the house of York, but were kept on friendly terms with the Wydvilles only by the king's influence. Somewhat outside these parties were the duke of Gloucester, whose interests up to this point had been one with Edward's; Henry Stafford duke of Buckingham, the head of the line which represented Thomas of Woodstock; and the duke of Suffolk, who had married the king's sister. Of these lord Hastings

The Wydvilles and Greys.

The council.

The great officers of state.

[1] 'Tantam omnium memoriam esse ut omnium pene hominum per comitatus regni dispersorum, si in patriis ubi degebant etiam in conditione valecti alicujus compoti erant, nomina et fortunae sibi tanquam eos quotidie prospicienti innotescerent'; Cont. Croyl. p. 564.

was the captain of Calais, lord Stanley steward of the household, the duke of Gloucester great chamberlain and lord high admiral, Dorset constable of the Tower; archbishop Rotherham was chancellor; the earl of Essex the treasurer died a few days before the king[1]. There was at the time of Edward's death no great public question dividing the nation; the treasury was well filled, and as against France and Scotland England was of one mind. The king's death at once broke up the unity of the court, the peace of the country and the fortunes of the house of York.

The ministers.

The young Edward was keeping court at Ludlow, surrounded by his mother's kinsfolk, and the council which his father had assigned him as prince of Wales[2]; the queen was at Westminster in the midst of the jealous council of the king; the duke of Gloucester in Yorkshire. At once the critical question arose, into whose hands the guardianship of the king and supreme influence in the kingdom should fall. The queen naturally but unwisely claimed it for herself; her brother, the marquess of Dorset, seized the treasure in the Tower[3], and Sir Edward Wydville attempted to secure the fleet[4]. The council, led by lord Hastings and supported by the influence of the duke of Buckingham, would have preferred to adopt the system which had been adopted in the early days of Henry VI, and to have governed the kingdom in the king's name, with Gloucester

The young king.

Question of guardianship.

[1] April 4. Sir John Wood was appointed treasurer of the exchequer, May 16; Nichols, Grants, &c. p. 13.

[2] His governor was lord Rivers, appointed Sept. 27, 1473; bishop Alcock of Worcester was the president of his council; bishop Martin of S. David's his chancellor; Sir Thomas Vaughan chamberlain; Sir William Stanley steward; Sir Richard Croft treasurer; Richard Hunt controller: Nichols, Grants of Edw. V, p. viii. Lord Rivers was an accomplished man and the patron of Caxton; and the boy's education was carefully attended to. Ordinances were drawn up by Edward IV for his son's household in 1473, which are printed among the Ordinances of the Household, pp. 25–33; and others were issued as late as 1482; Nichols, Grants &c., pp. vii, viii.

[3] On the 27th commissions were issued for collecting the alien tax; the marquess of Dorset being among the commissioners, but not Gloucester. See the 9th Report of the Deputy Keeper, App. ii. p. 7.

[4] Nichols, Grants &c. pp. ix, 2, 3. Orders were given to take Sir Edward and to receive all who would come in except him and the marquess, on May 14.

as president or protector. The course of the deliberations is obscure, but the action of the parties was rapid and decisive. The king from Ludlow, the duke of Gloucester from York, set out for London; the council knowing that Edward was in the hands of the Wydvilles, forbade him to bring up with him more than two thousand men; he was to be crowned on the first Sunday in May[1]. When Gloucester reached Northampton he met the duke of Buckingham and concerted with him the means of overthrowing the Wydvilles. Fortune played into their hands; lord Rivers and Sir Richard Grey, who had been sent to them by the king, accompanied them as far as Stony Stratford where they were to meet the king; but before they entered the town they were arrested and sent into the north[2]. The news travelled rapidly, and the queen on the 1st of May fled into sanctuary. Dorset and Edward Wydville took to flight. On the 4th the king and the dukes entered London; after a long session of the council, in which Hastings vainly flattered himself that he was securing the safety of the realm by supporting the claim of Gloucester, duke Richard was proclaimed protector of the kingdom[3]. On the 13th of May, a summons was issued for parliament to meet on June 25[4]; on the 16th the duke of Buckingham was made chief justice of Wales. About the same time, archbishop Rotherham was made to surrender the great seal, which was entrusted to bishop Russell of Lincoln. The coronation had already been deferred to the 22nd of June[5].

The king and Gloucester go to London.

Rivers and Grey arrested.

Richard made protector.

Parliament called.

Russell chancellor.

[1] Cont. Croyl. p. 565.

[2] Ib. p. 565; More's Edward V (Kennet, Complete History, vol. i), p. 482.

[3] The writ for convocation was issued on the 16th; see Nichols, Grants &c. p. 13; on the 20th the abbot of S. Mary's York, was excused attendance in parliament; ib. p. 18.

[4] The writ to the archbishop of Canterbury, dated May 13, is in Bourchier's Register at Lambeth, and printed in Nichols, Royal Wills, p. 347. York was ordered to elect four citizens, who were chosen on the 6th of June. The writ of supersedeas was received there on the 21st; Davies, York Records, pp. 144, 154. On the 14th of May the commissions of justices of the peace were issued, one of them addressed to Richard as protector. See the 9th Report of the Dep. Keeper of the Records, App. ii. p. 3; Nichols, Grants &c. p. 13; Cont. Croyl. p. 566.

[5] Rymer, xii. 185.

Richard wins the duke of Buckingham to his plans.

Whether Richard had been long laying his schemes for a usurpation, or yielded to the temptation which was suddenly put before him, and how he won over the duke of Buckingham to support him, are among the obscure questions of the time. Buckingham, who on the 16th of May was made justiciar of Wales[1], must even then have placed himself at Gloucester's disposal. Some time elapsed before the plot, if it were a plot, reached completeness. During this time most probably was concocted the claim which Richard was about to advance, and the petition on which he grounded his acceptance of the crown. A writ of supersedeas was issued to prevent the meeting of parliament[2], and the city was filled with the armed followers of the duke[3]. When all was ready, on the 13th of June, he seized lord Hastings, who had been summoned to the Tower to attend the king, and beheaded him at once. The two strongest prelates in the council, Rotherham and Morton[4], were then arrested and committed to the Tower, whence Morton was soon after sent off to prison in Wales. Archbishop Bourchier, now nearly eighty, proved once more his faithfulness to the stronger party, by inducing the queen to allow her younger son to join his brother in the Tower, on the 16th. On the 22nd, Richard's right to the crown was publicly declared by a preacher at S. Paul's cross, and on the 24th the duke of Buckingham propounded the same doctrine at Guildhall[5]. On the 25th, at

Parliament deferred.

Hastings beheaded.

Richard's claim to the throne.

[1] Rot. Pat. Edw. V (Report of the Deputy Keeper, ix. App. ii.) p. 2. The same day he had a commission of array for the western counties; ib. p. 9; Foed. ii. 180. The grant was renewed July 15; Rot. Pat. Ric. III. p. 12.

[2] It is quite clear that the parliament was never held. See Nichols, Grants &c. pp. 12, 13. But before the writ was issued the new chancellor had prepared his speech, which is printed by Nichols, pp. xxxix–l.

[3] Twenty thousand of Gloucester's and Buckingham's men were expected in London on the 21st of June; Exc. Hist. p. 17. See also Paston Letters, iii. 306.

[4] Exc. Hist. p. 17. Sir Thomas More (p. 485) says that Rotherham left the Great Seal in the queen's hands in the sanctuary at Westminster, and had to demand it again owing to the disturbances in London before the king's arrival.

[5] More gives, among many other speeches composed for this eventful drama of history, the speech of the duke of Buckingham, which contains several interesting points against Edward IV: e.g. the hanging of Burdett for a jesting word, and the deprivation of the judge who refused to

The crown is offered to Richard.

Baynard's castle, the protector received a body of lords and others, 'many and diverse lords spiritual and temporal, and other nobles and notable persons of the commons,' who in the name of the three estates, presented to him a roll of parchment, with the contents of which he was no doubt already familiar. The roll contained an invitation to accept the crown; it rehearsed the ancient prosperity of England, its decay and imminent ruin owing to the influence of false counsellors; since the pretended marriage of Edward IV the constitution had been in abeyance, laws divine and human, customs, liberties and life, had been subjected to arbitrary rule, and the noble blood of the land had been destroyed; that marriage was the result of sorcery, was informally celebrated, and was illegal, Edward being already bound by a pre-contract of marriage to the lady Eleanor Butler: the children of the adulterous pair were illegitimate; the offspring of the duke of Clarence were disabled by their father's attainder from claiming the succession; the protector himself was the undoubted heir of duke Richard of York and of the crown of England; by birth and character too he was entitled to the proffered dignity. Accordingly, the petitioners proceed, they had chosen him king, they prayed him to accept the election, promised to be faithful to him and implored the divine blessing upon the undertaking[1]. The petition was favourably received; resistance, if it were thought of, was impossible, for the city was full of armed men brought up from the north in Gloucester's interest. On the 26th he appeared in Westminster Hall, sat down in the marble chair, and declared his right as hereditary and elected king[2]. Edward V ended his reign on the 25th, and with his brother Richard then disappears from authentic history. How long the boys lived in captivity and how they died is a matter on which legend and conjecture have been rife with no approach to certainty. Most men believed, and still believe, that they

Illegitimacy of Edward's children.

Clarence's had suffered attaint.

Richard III declares himself king.

sentence him; the illtreatment of alderman Cook; the influence of Jane Shore, &c. But the speech, although worthy of study as a composition of More, is not historical.

[1] See Rot. Parl. vi. 258, 239.

[2] Cont. Croyl. p. 566; Letters of Rich. III. i. 12.

died a violent death by their uncle's order. The earl of Rivers[1] and Sir Richard Grey had been executed at Pomfret a few days after the usurpation, and the new king was not strong enough to afford to be merciful.

Execution of Rivers.

684. It is unnecessary to attempt now anything like a sketch of Richard's character; the materials for a clear delineation are very scanty, and it has long been a favourite topic for theory and for paradox. There can however be little doubt of his great ability, of his clear knowledge of the policy which under ordinary circumstances would have secured his throne, and of the force and energy of will which, put to a righteous use, might have made for him a great name. The popularity which he had won before his accession, in Yorkshire especially, where there was no love for the house of York before, proves that he was not without the gifts which gained for Edward IV the lifelong support of the nation. The craft and unscrupulousness with which he carried into effect his great adventure, are not more remarkable than the policy and the constitutional inventiveness with which he concealed the several steps of his progress. Brave, cunning, resolute, clear-sighted, bound by no ties of love or gratitude, amenable to no instincts of mercy or kindness, Richard III yet owes the general condemnation, with which his life and reign have been visited, to the fact that he left none behind him whose duty or whose care it was to attempt his vindication. The house of Lancaster, to be revived only in a bastard branch, loathed him as the destroyer of the sainted king and his innocent son. The house of York had scarcely less grievance against him as the destroyer of Clarence, the oppressor of the queen, the murderer, as men said, of her sons. England, taken by surprise at the usurpation, never fully accepted the yoke. The accomplices of the crime mistrusted him from the moment they placed him on the throne. Yet viewed beside Edward IV he seems to differ rather in fortune than in desert. He might have reigned well if he could have rid himself of the entanglements under which he began to

Richard's character for ability.

His popularity,

and political craft.

Hatred of his memory.

Distrusted and suspected in his lifetime.

[1] Lord Rivers made his will on the 23rd of June; Excerpta Historica, p. 246: his obit was kept on the 25th; ib. p. 244.

reign, or have cleared his conscience from the stain which his usurpation and its accompanying cruelties brought upon it.

Coronation of Richard III, July 6, 1483.

The story is not a long one, for the shadows begin from the moment of his accession to deepen round the last king of the great house of Anjou. He was crowned with his wife, the surviving daughter of the king-maker, on the 6th of July[1]. Archbishop Bourchier, who was to crown his successor, placed the diadem on his head. Rotherham too had already submitted and been released. Of his chief advisers, Buckingham had received his reward, and was made on the 15th of July lord high constable; Howard on the 28th of June had been made duke of Norfolk and earl marshal, the earldom of Nottingham being bestowed on lord Berkeley[2], another of the coheirs of Mowbray; the earl of Northumberland had been made warden of the Scottish marches[3]; Edward the king's only son was made lieutenant of Ireland, earl of Chester, and prince of Wales. The royal party made a grand progress during harvest, and at York on the 8th of September the heir to the crown was knighted with great pomp[4]. That event seems to have been the last glimpse of sunshine. The next month the duke of Buckingham was in open rebellion, and Henry of Richmond the heir of the elder line of Beaufort was threatening an invasion.

His adherents promoted.

Rebellion of Buckingham.

The duke of Buckingham was but a degenerate representative of the peacemaking duke who fell at Northampton. He had betrayed his great position and become a tool of Richard; but his position was still too great to suffer his ambition or Richard's

[1] Cont. Croyl. p. 567; Exc. Hist. pp. 379–383.

[2] Bishop Russell of Lincoln was made chancellor June 27; Rymer, xii. 189; having, according to More, p. 486, been appointed to the same office under Edward V, early in the month. On the 15th of July Buckingham was made constable for life, and the same day had his patent and commission renewed. John Howard was made duke of Norfolk and earl marshal June 28, and had a commission of array for the eastern counties July 16; he was made admiral of England, Ireland, and Aquitaine, July 25; Rot. Pat. pp. 12, 13.

[3] Northumberland's commission was issued May 20; Nichols, Grants, p. 20: it was renewed July 24, 1484; Rot. Pat. p. 85.

[4] Ross, p. 217; Fabric Rolls of York, p. 212; on the story of a second coronation see Davies, York Records, pp. 282, sq.; Cont. Croyl. p. 567.

suspicions to sleep. The house of Lancaster and its share in the house of Bohun being extinguished, the heir of the Staffords was sole heir of the earldom of Hereford. This, under the crafty advice, it was said, of bishop Morton[1], he ventured to claim, and Richard did not hesitate to refuse. Whilst the king was in the north, Buckingham was planning treason; the Wydvilles and the Greys were helping; three bishops, Wydville of Salisbury, Courtenay of Exeter, and Morton of Ely[2], were active in promoting the rising: negotiations were opened with the earl of Richmond, and he was promised, in case of success, the hand of the lady Elizabeth, eldest daughter of the late king, and the succession to the crown. The design was premature; Richard was not yet unpopular, and the conspirators were not in full concert with one another. The struggle accordingly was short: on the 18th of October the conspirators rose in Kent, Berkshire, Wiltshire, and Devonshire[3]. Richard was already on the watch; he had taken precautions to prevent Buckingham, whose head-quarters were at Brecon, from crossing the Severn. On the 23rd from Leicester he proclaimed pardon to the commons, and set a price on the heads of the leaders[4]. When the duke arrived at Weobly he found that the game was lost, and fled in disguise. He was taken, brought to the king at Salisbury on November 2, and beheaded forthwith[5]. The three bishops escaped to the continent. Many of the minor conspirators were taken and put to death, among them Sir Thomas Saint Leger, the king's brother-in-law, who had married the duchess of Exeter. The attempt of Henry of Richmond to land at Plymouth was delayed by weather, until the chances of

Extent of the conspiracy.

Its failure.

Buckingham taken and beheaded.

Executions.

[1] More, ap. Kennett, i. 502.

[2] Cont. Croyl. p. 568; Rot. Parl. vi. 250.

[3] On the 11th of October Richard wrote from Lincoln announcing Buckingham's treason and asking for men; Davies, York Records, p. 177–181. The proclamations against the rebels are dated Oct. 23; Rot. Pat. p. 31; Rymer, xii. 204.

[4] Lord Stanley was appointed constable in his place Nov. 18, and Dec. 16; Rot. Pat. pp. 16, 36: Sir William Stanley justice of North Wales, Nov. 12; and the earl of Northumberland great chamberlain, Nov. 12; ib.

[5] Cont. Croyl. p. 568.

Great danger avoided.

success were over. The extent of the danger may be estimated by the great exertions which Richard made to obviate it, and by the fact that the expense of the army which he had on foot made a very heavy drain on the great treasure that Edward IV had left behind him.

Richard's parliament, January, 1484.

After Christmas Richard held his parliament on the 23rd of January[1]: it is probable that preparations had been made for an earlier meeting, which had been prevented by the outbreak of the revolt[2]. Two dukes, seven earls, two viscounts, and twenty-six barons were summoned. The chancellor preached on the text, 'We have many members in one body,' and especially exhorted the estates to search diligently for the piece of silver that was lost, to secure that perfection in government which was the one thing wanted to make England safe and happy. On the 26th William Catesby, one of Richard's most unscrupulous servants, was presented and approved as speaker[3]. One of the first matters which was discussed was the king's title. The bill which was introduced on the subject rehearsed the proceedings by which Richard had been induced to assume the crown, and contained a copy of the petition of invitation, all the statements of which it was proposed to ratify, enrol, record, approve, and authorise, in such a way as to give them the force of an act of the full parliament. The title of the king was, the bill continues, perfect in itself, as grounded on the law of God and nature, the customs of the realm and the opinion of the wise; yet in condescension to the ignorance of the people, and because they are of such nature and disposition that the declaration of any truth or right made by the three estates of the realm in parliament, and by authority of the same, 'maketh

Proceedings touching the king's title.

[1] Rot. Parl. vi. 237; Cont. Croyl. p. 570.

[2] On the 22nd of September summons was issued for Nov. 6; Wake, State of the Church, p. 382. On the 24th of October the election of members of parliament was held at York; Davies, pp. 181, 182. As the chancellor's speech prepared for the occasion has for its text a portion of the gospel for S. Martin's day, there can be little doubt that the parliament was to have been opened on that day. See Nichols, Grants of Edward V, p. liv. Another summons was issued Dec. 9; Wake, p. 382. The election for the parliament of January 1484, was held at York on the 16th of January, the members started on the 24th, and returned February 26; Davies, pp. 184, 185.

[3] Rot. Parl. vi. 238.

before all other things most faith and certainty,' it is decreed that Richard is king as well by right of consanguinity and inheritance as by lawful election, consecration and coronation. The crown is accordingly secured to him and the heirs of his body. The bill, having been introduced before the lords in the king's presence, was carried down to the commons, and received their approval, after which, with the assent of the lords, all the statements contained in it were pronounced to be true and undoubted, and the king gave his assent[1]. By such an extraordinary and clumsy expedient was the action of the June council made the law of the land, and the parliament bound to the truth of certain historical statements which many of the members, if not all, must have known to be false.

Completeness of his right alleged.

Next in importance as a matter of deliberation, was the punishment of the conspirators in the late revolt. An act of attainder was passed against the duke of Buckingham, the earls of Richmond and Pembroke, the marquess of Dorset, and an immense number of knights and gentlemen, who were condemned to the penalties of treason[2]. Another act for the punishment of the three bishops declared them worthy of the same punishment, but from respect to their holy office contented itself with confiscating their temporalities[3]. The lady Margaret of Richmond[4] was attainted in a separate act, the grants made to the duke and duchess of Exeter were resumed, and the king was empowered to make grants from the property of the attainted[5]. On the 20th of February, the last day of the session, the king obtained a grant of tunnage, poundage, and the subsidy on wool for his life[6].

Punishment of the recent offenders.

Grant of revenue for life.

The statutes of this parliament, fifteen in number, and many of them enacted on petitions of the commons, are of great significance, and have been understood to indicate more certainly than any other part of Richard's policy the line which he would have taken if he had ever found himself secure on the throne. With one exception, however, they are of small constitutional importance, and unless more were known about the influence under which they were passed, it would be rash to suppose that

Legislation of this parliament.

[1] Rot. Parl. vi. 240–242. [2] Ib. vi. 244–248. [3] Ib. vi. 250.
[4] Ib. [5] Ib. vi. 242, 249. [6] Ib. vi. 238–240.

Legislation of 1484.

Richard had any definite scheme of policy in assenting to them. Six of them concern trade and commercial relations: by one the grants made to queen Elizabeth are annulled[1]; another exempts the collectors of the clerical tenths from vexatious proceedings in secular courts[2]; four are intended to remedy or regulate legal proceedings in the matters of bail, juries, fines, and the action of the court of pie-powder; by another legal chapter the king is divested of the property in lands of which he is enfeoffed or seized to uses, and the estate is vested in the co-feoffees or in the cestui que use[3]—a piece of legislation which anticipates the general action of the statute of uses; by another, secret feoffments, a natural and necessary outgrowth of the civil wars, are forbidden[4]. The great act of the session is the second chapter of the statute[5], which abolishes the unconstitutional practice of exacting benevolences, stigmatising them as new and unlawful inventions, and dilating on the hardships to which many worshipful men had been subjected by them. One or two private acts were passed, and after a solemn oath taken to ensure the succession of the prince of Wales, the parliament was dissolved. On the 23rd of February the king by charter confirmed the privileges secured by Edward IV to the clergy in 1462. The gratitude of convocation was shown by liberal votes of money[6].

Abolition of benevolences.

Management of convocation.

Richard's precautions against attack.

The rest of Richard's reign was employed in attempts, made by way of diplomacy, police, and warlike preparations, to detect, anticipate and thwart the machinations which his enemies at home and abroad were planning against him. To this end he negotiated in September a truce for three years with Scotland, throwing over the duke of Albany, and promising one of his nieces as wife to the king[7]. With the duke of Brittany, whose

[1] 1 Ric. III, c. 15; Statutes, ii. 498.
[2] 1 Ric. III, c. 14; Statutes, ii. 497.
[3] 1 Ric. III, c. 5; Statutes, ii. 480.
[4] 1 Ric. III, c. 1; Statutes, ii. 477.
[5] 1 Ric. III, c. 2; Statutes, ii. 478; Cont. Croyl. p. 571.
[6] Wilkins, Conc. iii. 616; 4th Rep. Dep. Keeper, App. ii. p. 45. The convocation sat from Feb. 3 to Feb. 24, 1484 and from February 10 to March 11, 1485. A tenth was granted in 1484, and two tenths in 1485.
[7] Rymer, xii. 230, 232, 235–247; Gairdner, Letters of Richard III,

court afforded a refuge for the remnant of the Lancastrian party, he concluded an armistice to last until April 1485; he even undertook to send over a force to defend the duke against his neighbours, and finally prolonged the truce to Michaelmas, 1492[1]. To secure the papal recognition he empowered the bishops of Durham and S. David's to perform that 'filial and catholic obedience which was of old due and accustomed to be paid by the kings of England to the Roman pontiffs[2].' These measures had a certain success; Henry of Richmond quitted Brittany, and sought for refuge in other parts of France less amenable to Richard's influence. The king devoted much attention also to the improvement of the fleet, with which, notwithstanding some mishaps, he secured the final superiority of the English over the Scots at sea. By disafforesting certain lands which Edward IV had enclosed, he gained some local popularity[3]; and in the north of England he was certainly strong in the affection of the people[4]. Calamity, however, never deserted the royal house; the prince of Wales died on the 9th of April, 1484, and the queen fell into ill health, which ended in her death in March, 1485. Richard had to recognise as his heir presumptive John de la Pole, earl of Lincoln, his nephew, son of the duke of Suffolk[5].

Foreign negotiations of Richard.

His policy at home.

Death of the prince of Wales.

Notwithstanding the constant exertions of the king, the submissive conduct of his parliament, and the success of his foreign negotiations, the alarm of invasion from abroad never for an instant subsided. At Christmas it was known that the earl of Richmond was preparing for an invasion at Whitsuntide, and the king without hesitation betook himself to the

Threatened invasion by Richmond.

i. 51 sq. 55. Some fragments of the deliberations of the council on Scottish affairs are preserved; ib. pp. 63-67.

1 Rymer, xii. 226, 229, 255, 261, 262; Letters of Richard III, i. 37 sq.

2 Rymer, xii. 253, 254; a similar act of Henry VI in 1459 is in Rymer, xi. 422.

3 Ross, Hist. Reg. Ang. p. 216.

4 The number of Yorkshiremen employed by Richard, and the immunities bestowed on towns and churches in the north, is a sufficient proof of this.

5 The prince had been appointed lieutenant of Ireland July, 19, 1483; the earl of Lincoln was nominated to succeed him Aug. 21, 1484; Rot. Pat. pp. 50, 96.

Proposed marriage of Richard and his niece.

collection of benevolences[1]; notwithstanding the recent act by which such exactions were proscribed. As soon as the queen died—and her death was, according to Richard's enemies, the result of his own cruel policy—he began to negotiate for a marriage with his own niece, whose hand the queen Elizabeth had held out as a prize for Richmond. He even succeeded in inducing that vain and fickle woman to agree to the incestuous bargain[2]. This proposition was opposed by his most faithful advisers, and, under a threat that they would desert him, he was obliged, in a council held before Easter, to renounce it[3]. But the very rumour had served to promote union among the opposing parties, and to inspirit the earl of Richmond to greater exertions. The earl of Oxford had escaped from Hammes and joined him.

Richmond's preparations.

He had no doubt promises of aid from England, and secret as well as open help afforded him abroad. But it must ever remain a problem how he was enabled to maintain his position on the continent so long as he did; the extent and permanence of his resources seem even a greater mystery than his subsequent success.

He lands at Milford Haven, Aug. 7, 1485.

685. The time was come at last: on the 1st of August Henry of Richmond, now twenty-seven years old, but a man of experience and caution far beyond his years, sailed from Harfleur[5], and, having eluded the fleet which Richard had sent to intercept him, landed at Milford Haven on the 7th. He had with him at the most two thousand men, but he depended chiefly on the promises of assistance from the Welsh, among whom his father's family had taken pains to strengthen his interest, and he himself roused a good deal of patriotic feeling. The lord Stanley, the present husband of Henry's mother, was

[1] Cont. Croyl. p. 572. Fabyan (p. 672) says that the king gave pledges for the loans borrowed in the city of London. Orders issued for the more hasty levy of money are in Gairdners's Letters of Rich. III, i. 81–85; but they contain nothing that bears on this point. Another set of instructions however (ib. pp. 85–87) shows that the commissions of array were again used as an instrument of taxation as in 1482. See above, p. 217.

[2] Cont. Croyl. p. 572; Hall, pp. 406, 407.

[3] Hall, p. 407.

[4] Richard's proclamation against 'Henry Tydder,' dated June 23, 1485, is in the Paston Letters, iii. 316–320.

[5] Aug. 1; Cont. Croyl. p. 573.

indeed one of Richard's trusted servants, and Sir William Stanley his brother was in command in Wales; but the king had alienated them by his mistrust, and had confined the lord Strange, son of lord Stanley, as a hostage for his father's fidelity. Scarcely believing the formidable news of Henry's progress, the king moved to Nottingham, where he expected to be able to crush the rebellion as soon as it came to a head. Henry marched on, gathering forces as he went, and securing fresh promises of adhesion. As he came nearer, the king removed to Leicester, whence he marched out to meet the invader at Market Bosworth, on the 21st of August. On the 22nd the battle of Bosworth was fought. The Stanleys and the earl of Northumberland went over to Henry, and Richard was killed. Treachery, on which he could not have counted, and which nothing but his own mistrust, his tyranny and vindictiveness could palliate, closed the long contest[1]. The crown was left for the successful invader to claim on a shadowy title, and to secure by a marriage of convenience. By a strange coincidence the heir of the Beauforts was to be wedded to the heiress of the houses of York and Clarence; the grandson of Queen Katharine to the granddaughter of the duchess Jacquetta. The result reveals at once the permanence of the old family jealousies, and the gulf in which all the intervening representatives of the house of Plantagenet had been submerged. With the battle of Bosworth the medieval history of England is understood to end. It is not, however, the distinct end of an old period, so much as the distinct beginning of a new one. The old dividing influences subsist for half a century longer, but the newer and more lasting consolidating influences come from this time to the front of the stage. The student of constitutional history need not go twice over the same ground; he may be content to wait for the complete wearing out of the old forms, whilst he takes up the quest of the new, and dwells more steadily on the more permanent and vital elements that underlie them both.

Advance of Richmond.

Battle of Bosworth, Aug. 22, 1485.

Mark of an epoch.

686. Any attempt to balance or to contrast the constitutional claims and position of the houses of Lancaster and York, is

[1] Cont. Croyl. pp. 573, 574.

Comparison of the constitutional position of the Lancaster and York dynasties.

embarrassed by the complications of moral, legal, and personal questions which intrude at every point. The most earnest supporter of the constitutional right of the Lancastrian kings cannot deny the utter incompetency of Henry VI.; the most ardent champion of the divine right of hereditary succession must allow that the rule of Edward IV and Richard III was unconstitutional, arbitrary, and sanguinary. Henry VI was not deposed for incompetency; and the unconstitutional rule of the house of York was but a minor cause of its difficulties and final fall. England learned a lesson from both, and owes a sort of debt to both : the rule of the house of Lancaster proved that the nation was not ready for the efficient use of the liberties it had won, and that of the house of York proved that the nation was too full grown to be fettered again with the bonds from which it had escaped. The circumstances too by which the legal position of the two dynasties was determined, have points of likeness and unlikeness which have struck and continue to strike the readers of history in different ways. It may fairly be asked what there was in the usurpation of Edward IV that made it differ in kind from the usurpation of Henry IV; whether the misgovernment of Richard II and the misgovernment of Henry VI differed in nature or only in degree; what force the legal weakness of the Lancastrian title gave to the allegation of its incompetency, to what extent the dynastic position of the house of York may be made to palliate the charges of cruelty and tyranny from which it cannot be cleared.

Such questions will be answered differently by men who approach the subject from different points. The survey which has been taken of the events of the period in the present chapter, rapid and brief as it appears, renders it unnecessary to recapitulate here the particulars from which the general impression must either way be drawn. The student who approaches the story from the point of view at which these pages have been written, will recognise the constitutional claim of the house of Lancaster, as based on a solemn national act, strengthened by the adherence of three generations to a constitutional form of government, and not forfeited by any distinct breach of the understanding

Constitutional character of the Lancaster rule.

upon which Henry IV originally received the crown. He will recognise in the successful claim of the house of York a retrogressive step, which was made possible by the weakness of Henry VI, but could be justified constitutionally only by a theory of succession which neither on the principles of law nor on the precedents of history could be consistently maintained. The Yorkist usurpation.

But he may accept these conclusions generally without shutting his eyes to the reality of the difficulties which from almost every side beset the subject—difficulties which were recognised by the wisest men of the time, and knots which could be untied only by the sword. There are personal questions of allegiance and fealty, broken faith and stained honour; allegations and denials of incapacity and misgovernment; a national voice possessing strength that makes it decisive for the moment, but not enough to enable it to resist the dictation of the stronger; giving an uncertain sound from year to year; attainting and rehabilitating in alternate parliaments; claiming a cogency and infallibility which every change of policy belies. The baronage is divided so narrowly that the summons or exclusion of half a dozen members changes the fate of a ministry or of a dynasty; the representation of the commons is liable to the manipulation of local agencies with which constitutional right weighs little in comparison with territorial partisanship: the clergy are either, like the baronage, narrowly divided, or, in the earnest desire of peace, ready to acquiesce in the supremacy of the party which is for the moment the stronger. Even the great mass of the nation does not know its own mind: the northern counties are strong on one side, the southern on the other: a weak government can bring a great force into the field, and a strong government cannot be secured against a bewildering surprise: the weakness of Henry VI and the strength of Richard III alike succumb to a single defeat: the people are weary of both, and yet fight for either. The history contains paradoxes which confused the steadiest heads of the time, and strained the strongest consciences. Hence every house was divided against itself, and few except the chief actors in the drama sustained their part with honesty and consistency. Oaths too were taken only to be broken; recon-

Complication of personal and political questions.

Relations of the three estates.

Local parties.

Domestic divisions.

Ebb and flow in national life.

ciliations concluded only that time might be gained to prepare for new battles. The older laws of religion and honour are waning away before the newer laws are strong enough to take their place. Even the material prosperity and growth of the nation are complicated in the same way; rapid exhaustion and rapid development seem to go on side by side; the old order changes, the inherent forces of national life renew themselves in diverse ways; and the man who chooses to place himself in the position of a judge must, under the confusion of testimony, and the impossibility of comparing incommensurable influences, allow that on many, perhaps most, of the disputed points, no absolute decision can be attempted.

Proposed treatment of the question.

Without then trying to estimate the exact debt which England owes to either, it will be enough, as it is perhaps indispensable, to compare the two dynasties on the level ground of constitutional practice, and to collect the points on which is based the conclusion already more than sufficiently indicated, that the rule of the house of Lancaster was in the main constitutional, and that of the house of York in the main unconstitutional. It might be sufficient to say that the rule of the house of Lancaster was most constitutional when it was strongest; and that of the house of York when it was weakest: that the former contravened the constitution only when it was itself in its decrepitude, the latter did so when in its fullest vigour. Such a generalisation may be misconstrued; the administration of Henry V may be regarded as constitutional because he was strong enough to use the constitutional machinery in his own way, and that of Edward IV as unconstitutional because he was strong enough to dispense with it. If however it be granted, as for our purpose and from our point of view it must, that the decision of the quarrel was not directly affected by constitutional questions at all,—if it be admitted, that is, that the claim of York and the Nevilles to deliver the king and kingdom from evil counsellors was neither raised nor prosecuted in a constitutional way, and was in reality both raised and resisted on grounds of dynastic right,—there is no great difficulty in forming a general conclusion. Nor need any misgivings be suggested by the mere forensic difficulty that

Possible generalisation.

Dynastic forces decide the struggle.

the claim of the house of York, based on hereditary right of succession, is in itself incompatible with the claim of the baronage, or the nation which it represented, to use force in order to compel the king to dismiss his unpopular advisers.

The three Lancaster kings in relation to their parliaments.

687. The first point upon which a comparison can be taken is that of parliamentary action. The reign of Henry IV is one long struggle on points of administrative difference between a king and a parliament that on all vital points are at one: Henry V leads and impersonates national spirit, and so leads the action of parliament; Henry VI throughout the earlier and happier part of his reign is ruled by a council which to a great extent represents the parliament, and during the later years he retains such a hold on the parliament as to foil the attempt made by the duke of York to supplant him; nor is his deposition recognised by the parliament until Edward has claimed, won, and worn the crown. We may set aside, however, the question of the constitutional title, the reality of which was more completely recognised in later times than in the age in which it was practically vindicated, and which, as we have seen, was imperfectly realised by Henry IV himself, in consequence of the oaths by which he was bound to Richard, and the conviction which compelled him to advance a factitious hereditary claim. The questions that arise upon this subject will always be answered more or less from opposite points of view. It will be more instructive if we attempt first to collect and arrange the particular instances in which the theory of parliamentary institutions was advanced and accepted by the different factors in the government, then to show that that theory was acted upon to a very great extent throughout the first half at least of the fifteenth century, and to note as we proceed the points in which the accepted theory went even beyond the practice of the times, and anticipated some of the later forms of parliamentary government. This view will enable us summarily to describe the character of the legislative, economical, and administrative policy pursued by the two rival houses, and so to strike the balance between them upon a material as well as a formal issue.

The question of their title always debateable.

Their professions of constitutional rule.

Statements of the kings and ministers, as to their wish to rule with consent of the nation.

Archbishop Arundel's declaration, made on behalf of Henry IV in his first parliament, was a distinct undertaking that the new king would reign constitutionally. Richard II had declared himself possessed of a prerogative practically unlimited, and had enunciated the doctrine that the law was in the heart and mouth of the king, that the goods of his subjects were his own [1]. Henry wished to be governed and counselled by the wise and ancient of the kingdom for the aid and comfort of himself and of the whole realm; by their common counsel and consent he would do the best for the governance of himself and his kingdom, not wishing to be governed according to his proper will, or of his voluntary purpose and singular opinion, 'but by the common advice, counsel, and consent,' and according to the sense and spirit of the coronation oath [2]. Again, when in the same parliament the commons 'of their own good grace and will trusting in the nobility, high discretion and gracious governance' of the king, granted to him 'that they would that he should be in the same royal liberty as his noble progenitors had been,' the king of his royal grace and tender conscience vouchsafed to declare in full parliament 'that it was not his intent or will to change the laws, statutes, or good usages, or to take any other advantage by the said grant, but to guard the ancient laws and statutes ordained and used in the time of his noble progenitors, and to do right to all people, in mercy and truth according to his oath [3].' Nor did this avowal stand alone. In the commission of inquiry into false rumours, issued in 1402, Henry ordered that the counties should be assured 'that it always has been, is, and will be, our intention that the republic and common weal, and the laws and customs of our kingdom be observed and kept from time to time,' and that the violators of the same should be punished according to their deserts, 'for to this end we believe that we have come by God's will to our kingdom [4].' It is true that these and many similar declarations owe some part of their force to the fact that they presented a strong contrast to Richard's rash utterances, and that they were at the

[1] Vol. ii. p. 505.
[2] Above, p. 14.
[3] Rot. Parl. iii. 434; above, p. 24.
[4] Rymer, viii. 255.

Declarations of constitutional theory.

time prompted by a desire to set such a contrast before the eyes of the people. But as time went on and the alarm of reaction passed away, they were repeated in equally strong and even more elaborate language. Sir Arnold Savage in 1401 told the king that he possessed what was the greatest treasure and riches of the whole world, the heart of his people; and the king in his answer prayed the parliament to counsel him how that treasure might be kept longest and best spent to the honour of God and the realm, and he would follow it[1]. In 1404 bishop Beaufort, in his address to parliament, compared the kingdom to the body of a man; the right side answered to the church, the left to the baronage, and the other members to the commons[2]. Archbishop Arundel declared the royal will to the same assembly, that the laws should be kept and guarded, that equal right and justice should be done as well to poor as to rich, and that by no letters of privy seal, or other mandates, should the common law be disturbed, or the people any way be delayed in the pursuit of justice; that the royal household should be regulated by the advice of the lords, and the grants made in parliament should be administered by treasurers ordained in parliament[3]. In 1406 bishop Longley announced that the king would conform to the precept of the son of Sirach, and do nothing without advice[4]. In 1410 bishop Beaufort quoted the apocryphal answer of Aristotle to Alexander on the surest defence of states: 'The supreme security and safeguard of every kingdom and city is to have the entire and cordial love of the people, and to keep them in their laws and rights[5].' The same sound principle pervades even the most pedantic effusions of the successive chancellors in the following reigns; everywhere the welfare of the realm is, conjointly with the glory of God, recognised as the great end of government; the king's duty is to rule lawfully, the duty of the people to obey honestly; the share of the three estates in all deliberations is fully recognised; the duty as well as the right to counsel, the limitations and responsibilities, as well as the prerogatives, of royal power. In all these may be

[1] Rot. Parl. iii. 456. [2] Ib. iii. 522. [3] Ib. iii. 529.
[4] Ecclus. xxxii. 24; Rot. Parl. iii. 567. [5] Rot. Parl. iii. 622.

Illustrations to be found in the works of Sir John Fortescue.

traced not merely a reaction against the arbitrary government of former reigns, but the existence of a theory more or less definite, of a permanent character of government. Not to multiply however verbal illustrations of what, so long as they are confined to mere words, may seem mere arguments *ad captandum*, it is more interesting to refer to the language of Sir John Fortescue, the great Lancastrian lawyer, in whose hands Henry VI seems to have placed the legal education of his son. Fortescue, in drawing up his account of the English constitution, had in his eye by way of contrast, not the usurpations of Richard II, but the more legal and the not less absolute governments of the continent, especially that of France, and, although in some passages it is possible that he glanced at the arbitrary measures of Edward IV, the general object of his writing was didactic rather than controversial; one moreover of the most interesting of his treatises was written after his reconciliation with Edward. Taken all together, his writings represent the viev of the English constitution which was adopted as the Lancastrian programme and on which the Lancastrian kings had ruled.

Fortescue's division of governments.

688. Fortescue, taking as the basis of his definition the distinction drawn by the medieval publicists under the guidance of S. Thomas Aquinas and his followers[1], divides governments into three classes, characterised as *dominium regale, dominium politicum,* and *dominium regale et politicum*[2]. These institutions differ in origin; the first was established by the aggressions of individuals, the other two by the institution of the nations[3]. England belongs to the third class. The king

[1] The tract used by Fortescue was the 'De Regimine Principum' of which Thomas Aquinas wrote only the first and part of the second book. The distinction of governments is drawn in the third book, which was probably written by Ptolemaeus Lucensis.

[2] Fortescue, de Natura Legis Naturae, i. 16; Opp. (ed. Clermont) i. 77; Monarchy, c. i; ib. p. 449. The division is primarily between the dominium regale and the dominium politicum; then is added a third class, the dominium regale et politicum, to which England belongs.

[3] De Nat. Leg. Nat. i. 16. quoting Aegidius Romanus de Regimine Principum; see lord Carlingford's note, p. 360*; de laudibus legum Angliae cc. 12, 13, pp. 345, 346.

Statements of Fortescue as to the nature of the royal power.

of England is a 'rex politicus'[1]; the maxim of the civil law, 'what has pleased the prince has the force of law,' has no place in English jurisprudence[2]; the king exists for the sake of the kingdom, not the kingdom for the sake of the king[3]; 'for the preservation of the laws of his subjects, of their persons and goods, he is set up, and for this purpose he has power derived from the people, so that he may not govern his people by any other power'[4]: he cannot change the laws or impose taxes without the consent of the whole nation given in parliament. That parliament, including a senate of more than three hundred chosen counsellors, represents the three estates of the realm[5]. Such a government deserves in the highest sense the title of 'politic,' because it is regulated by administration of many; and the title of 'royal' because the authority of the sovereign is required for the making of new laws, and the right of hereditary succession is conserved[6]. The righteous king maintains his sway not from the desire of power, but because it is his duty to take care of others[7]. But the politic king has a right to use exceptional means to repress rebellion or to resist invasion[8]; he has likewise prerogative powers which are not shared with his people, the right, for instance, of pardon and the whole domain of equity[9]. The judgments of the courts of justice are his, but he does not sit personally in judgment[10]. The limitations of his power are a glory rather than a humiliation to him, for there is no degradation deeper than that of wrongdoing[11]. Although the

[1] De Nat. Leg. Nat. i. 16, p. 77.

[2] Ib. i. 28, p. 90; De Laudibus Legum Angliae, c. 9, p. 344; c. 35, p. 365.

[3] De Nat. Leg. Nat. i. 25, p. 86; ii. 4, quoting the De Regimine, lib. iii. Opp. p. 118.

[4] De Laudibus, c. 13, p. 347. 'Ad tutelam namque legis subditorum ac eorum corporum et bonorum rex hujusmodi erectus est, et hanc potestatem a populo effluxam ipse habet, quo ei non licet potestate alia suo populo dominari.'

[5] De Nat. Leg. Nat. i. c. 16, p. 77; De Laudibus, c. 18, Opp. p. 350.

[6] De Nat. Leg. Nat. i. c. 16, p. 77.

[7] Ib. i. c. 34, p. 97, quoting Aug. de Civitate Dei, xix. c. 14.

[8] De Nat. Leg. Nat. i. 25, p. 86.

[9] Ib. i. c. 24, p. 91.

[10] De Laudibus, c. 8, p. 344.

[11] De Nat. Leg. Nat. i. c. 26, p. 88. 'Non jugum sed libertas est politice regere populum, securitas quoque maxima nedum plebis sed et ipsi

Statements of Fortescue as to the excellence of the English system.

origin of politic kingship is in the will of the people, and its conservation is secured by hereditary succession, righteous judgment is its true sustaining power and justification. 'If justice be banished,' says S. Augustine, 'what are kingdoms but great robberies or bands of robbers?' Yet kingdoms acquired by conquest may be established by four things, 'acceptation of God, approving of the church, long continuance of possession, and the assent of the people[1].' The proof of the excellence of politic royalty is seen in the comparison of England with France, where, although kings like S. Lewis could make good laws and administer sound justice by God's special grace, bad government under absolute sovereignty had produced general impoverishment, oppression, and degradation[2]. Not only were the laws of England better than the laws of France, as was shown by the absence of any legal system of torture[3], by the institution of trial by jury[4], by the careful provisions for provincial administration of justice[5], and other points in which the English law excels the civil; but the financial system of government was better. There were no such oppressions of the nature of purveyance, forced impressments, taxes on salt, octroi on wine, levies of money for wages and for a force of archers at the king's will[6]: the administration of justice was better, there were no secret executions done without form of law, nor any like abuses by which the rich were crushed and the poor trampled on[7]. And still more distinct was the result in the happiness of the English, as a nation in which property was not concentrated in a few hands, but the commons as well as the baronage were rich, and had a great stake in public welfare[8]. Nothing

The excellent results.

regi, allevatio etiam non minima solicitudinis suae'; De Laudibus, c. 34, p. 363.

[1] Of the Title of the House of York, Opp. i. 501. S. Augustine's words are 'Remota itaque justitia quid sunt regna nisi magna latrocinia?' De Civitate Dei, iv. c. 4.

[2] On the Monarchy of England, c. 3; Opp. i. 451.

[3] De Laudibus, c. 22. p. 352.

[4] Ib. c. 20, p. 350; cc. 29–32, pp. 359–363.

[5] Ib. cc. 24 sq. pp. 354 sq.

[6] Ib. c. 35, p. 364.

[7] Ib. c. 29. p. 359; c. 35, pp. 364, 365; Monarchy, c. 3. p. 452.

[8] De Laudibus, c. 29, p. 359. 'In ea (sc. Anglia) villula tam parva reperiri non poterit in qua non est miles armiger vel paterfamilias qualis

was so great security to England as the wealth of the commons; if they were impoverished, they would at once lay the blame on the government and rise in revolt. But their very boldness in rising was a point of superiority; for the French had lost the spirit to rise: in England there were it was true many robbers, in France many thieves; but there is more spirit and a better heart in a robber than in a thief[1].

Spirit of the commons.

England, notwithstanding the advantages of politic royalty, had fallen into trouble, as Fortescue was obliged to allow, and in one of the latest of his works he sketches, perhaps as advice to Edward IV, a system of reform, many points of which are a mere restoration of the system that was in use under the Lancastrian kings. Some of these may be noticed as illustrating the preceding sections of this chapter as well as tending to a general conclusion. The politic royalty of England, distinguished from the government of absolute kingdoms by the fact that it is rooted in the desire and institution of the nation, has its work set in the task of defence against foreign foes and in the maintenance of internal peace[2]. Such a work is very costly; the king is poor; royal poverty is a very dangerous thing, for the king can contract loans only on heavy interest; he is liable to be defamed for misgovernance; he is driven to make ruinous assignments of revenue and to give extravagant gifts of land, and he is tempted or compelled to use oppressive means for raising funds[3]. His expenses are of two sorts: ordinary charges are those of the household and wardrobes, the wages of public functionaries, the keeping of the marches and of Calais, and the maintenance of public works. The expenses of the navy are not counted here, for they are provided for by tunnage and poundage[4]. The extraordinary charges are those for the maintenance and reception of embassies, the rewarding of old

Fortescue's scheme of Reform.

The king's poverty and great expenses.

ibidem Frankelayn vulgariter nuncupatur, magnis dilatus possessionibus, nec non libere tenentes alii et valecti plurimi suis patrimoniis sufficientes ad faciendum juratam.' Cf. Monarchy, c. 12, p. 465.

[1] Monarchy, c. 12, p. 464.

[2] Ib. c. 4, p. 453. 'A king's office stondith in two things, one to defend his realme ageyn their ennemyes outward by sword, another that he defendith his people ageyn wrong doars inwarde.'

[3] Ib. c. 5, pp. 454, 455.

[4] Ib. c. 6, pp. 455, 456.

Obligation of the nation to help the king.

servants, the provision for royal buildings, for the stock of jewels and plate, for special commissions of judges, royal progresses for the sustentation of peace and justice, and above all the resistance of sudden invasion[1]. The nation is bound to support the king in all things necessary to his estate and dignity; his ordinary revenue may suffice for the household, but the king is not only a sovereign lord, but a public servant; the royal estate is an office of ministration, the king not less than the pope is *servus servorum Dei*[2]. He should for his extraordinary charges have a revenue not less than twice that of one of his great lords[3]. The question is how can such a revenue be raised. There are among the expedients of French finance some that might with parliamentary authority be adopted in England[4], but the real source of relief must be sought in the retention and resumption of the lands which the kings were so often tempted to alienate. The king had once possessed a fifth part of the land of England; this had been diminished by the restoration of forfeited estates, by the recognition of entails and other titles, by gifts to servants of the crown, by provision for the younger sons of the king, and most of all by grants to importunate suitors. The further diminution of the crown estates might be prevented; the king might content himself with bestowing estates for life; if he were economical the commons would be ready to grant subsidies[5]. If however he wished to restore national prosperity and to live of his own, he must be prepared to go further; a general resumption of gifts of land made since a certain period must be enforced[6]. To do this and to secure that for the future only due and proper grants should be made, it was necessary to constitute or reform the royal council[7]. This important body, before which all questions of difficulty might be brought, should not henceforth consist, as it had done, of great lords who were prone to devote themselves to their own business

Diminution of the royal estates to be stopped.

A resumption of gifts of land to be enforced.

[1] Monarchy, c. 7, pp. 457, 458.
[2] Ib. c. 8, pp. 458, 459.
[3] Ib. c. 9, p. 459.
[4] Ib. c. 10, p. 461.
[5] Ib. cc. 10, 11, pp. 462–464.
[6] Ib. c. 14, p. 467.
[7] In the Rules of Council drawn up in 1390, Ord. i. 18, the business of the king and kingdom is made to take precedence of all other matters.

more than to the kings, but of twelve spiritual and twelve temporal men, who were to swear to observe certain rules, and constitute a permanent council, none of whom was to be removed without consent of the majority. To these should be added four spiritual and four temporal lords to serve for a year; the king should appoint the president or chief councillor. The wages of the members should be moderate, especially those of the lords and the spiritual councillors; if the charges were very great the number might be reduced[1]. This body might entertain all questions of state policy, the control of bullion, the fixing of prices, the maintenance of the navy, the proposed amendments of the law, and the preparation of business for parliament. The great officers of state, especially the chancellor, should attend on its deliberations, and the judges if necessary; and a register of its proceedings should be kept[2]. Chosen counsellors were much better than volunteers[3]. One of the first things to be done after the resumption was to consolidate and render inalienable or, so to speak, amortize the crown lands, a measure which would entitle the king who should enact it to the confidence of his subjects and the gratitude of posterity. Then from lands otherwise accruing, gifts might be made; grants for a term of years might be given with consent of council, life estates and greater gifts only with the consent of parliament[4]. Except the exact determination of the selection and number of the councillors, Fortescue's scheme contains nothing which had not been in principle or in practice adopted under Henry IV and Henry V. The example for 'amortizing' the crown lands had been given in the consolidation of the estates of the duchy of Lancaster; the

Fortescue proposes the remodelling of the privy council.

Business allotted to them.

[1] Monarchy, c. 15, pp. 468–470. The office of chief or president of the council had been held by William of Wykeham under Edward III; Rot. Parl. iii. 388: but the post was not a fixed one, and the title of consiliarius principalis had belonged to Gloucester and Bedford as a part of the protectorship. Coke says (4 Inst. p. 54) that John Russell, bishop of Lincoln, was *praesidens consilii*, in the 13th Edward IV. He was then keeper of the privy seal.

[2] Monarchy, c. 15, pp. 468–470.

[3] 'Good Counsayle,' Opp. pp. 475, 476.

[4] Monarchy, c. 19, p. 473; see Rot. Parl. iii. 479, 579.

Fortescue's plan had been in use under the Lancastrian kings.

scheme of resumption broached so often, and accepted in principle by Henry IV, had been put into force under Henry VI. The powers of the council had been freely exercised during all the three reigns, and although the direct influence of parliament on the council had been less under Henry VI than under Henry IV, the theory of the relation of the two bodies subsisted in its integrity; it is only in the latter years of the last Lancastrian reign that the king attempts to maintain his council in opposition to the parliament, and then only in the firm belief that his council was faithful to him, his parliament actuated by hostile motives or prompted by dangerous men.

National consciousness of the king's position.

689. It is true that neither in the vague promises of Henry IV nor in the definite recommendations of Sir John Fortescue are to be found enunciations of the clear principles or details of the practice of the English constitution. But the constitution did not now require definitions. The discipline of the fourteenth century, culminating in the grand lesson of revolution, had left the nation in no ignorance of its rights and wrongs. The great law of custom, written in the hearts and lives and memories of Englishmen, had been so far developed as to include everything material that had been won in the direction of popular liberties and even of parliamentary freedom. The nation knew that the king was not an arbitrary despot, but a sovereign bound by oaths, laws, policies, and necessities, over which they had some control. They knew that he could not break his oath without God's curse; he could not alter the laws or impose a tax without their consent given through their representatives chosen in their county courts. They knew how, when, and where those courts were held, and that the mass of the nation had the right and privilege of attending them; and they were jealously on the watch against royal interference in their elections. And so far there was nothing very complex about constitutional practice: there was little danger of dispute between lords and commons; the privilege of members needed only to be asserted and it was admitted; there was no restriction on the declaration of gravamina, or on the impeachment of ministers or others who were suspected of exercising a malign

influence on the government. When the king promised to observe their liberties, men in general knew what he meant, and watched how he kept his promise. They saw the ancient abuses disappear; complaints were no more heard of money raised without consent of parliament, or of illegal exaction by means of commissions of array; the abuses of purveyance were mentioned only to be redressed and punished, and if legal decisions were left unexecuted, it was for want of power rather than from want of will[1].

The constitution as understood by the nation.

690. To recapitulate then the points in which the Lancastrian kings maintained the constitution as they found it, would be simply to repeat the whole of the parliamentary history, which from a different point of view we have surveyed in this chapter. It will be sufficient to mark the particulars in which constitutional practice gains clearness and definiteness under their sway. And of these also most have been noticed already.

Previous illustration of Lancastrian rule.

Perhaps the feature of the constitution which gains most in clearness and definiteness during the period is the institution of the royal council, the origin and varying conditions of which have been already traced down to the close of the fourteenth century[2]. That body, however constituted at the time, has been seen, from the minority of Henry III onwards, constantly increasing its power and multiplying its functions; retiring into the background under strong kings, coming prominently forward when the sovereign was weak, unpopular, or a child. At last, under the nominal rule of Richard II, but really under the influence of the men who led the great parties in the parliament and in the country, it has become a power rather coordinate with the king than subordinate to him, joining with him in all business of the state, and not merely assisting but restricting his action. And as the council has multiplied its functions and increased its powers, the parliament has endeavoured to increase the national hold over the council by insisting that the king should nominate its members in parliament, and by more than once taking the nomination of the consultative

Importance of the privy council.

Its growth and development.

[1] See below, p. 269.

[2] Vol. ii. pp. 255–264.

The council. body out of his hands, superseding for a time by commissions of reform both the royal council and the royal power itself. Such an act it was which, in 1386, brought about the crisis of the reign and the subsequent reactions which ended in Richard's fall[1].

Henry IV accepted this constitution of the council: Henry V acted consistently upon the same principle; it forms the key to guide us in reading the reign of his son: the manipulation of the system by Edward IV supplies one of the leading influences of the Tudor politics; and the council of the Lancastrian kings is the real, though perhaps not strictly the historical, germ of the cabinet ministries of modern times. When in 1406 the house of commons told the king that they were induced to make their grants, not only by the fear of God and love for the king, but by the great confidence which they had in the lords then chosen and ordained to be of the king's continual council[2], they seem to have caught the spirit and anticipated the language of a much later period.

Vote of confidence in 1406.

Council nominated in parliament.

The demand that the members of the king's continual council should be nominated in parliament and should take certain oaths and accept certain articles for their guidance, was one which was sure to be made whenever a feeling of distrust arose between the king and the estates[3]. It was accordingly one of the first signs of the waning popularity of Henry IV after Hotspur's rebellion. In the parliament of 1404, at the urgent and special request of the commons, the king named six bishops, a duke, two earls, six lords, including the treasurer and privy seal, and seven commoners, to be his great and continual council[4]. In 1406, under similar pressure, he named three bishops, a duke, an earl, four barons, three commoners, the chancellor, treasurer, privy seal, steward, and chamberlain[5]. In 1410 the king was requested to nominate the most valiant, wise, and discreet of the lords, spiritual and temporal, to be of his council, in aid and support

[1] Vol. ii. p. 476.
[2] Rot. Parl. iii. 568; above, p. 55.
[3] Vol. ii. 343, 368, 432, 444.
[4] Rot. Parl. iii. 530; Ordinances, i. 237, 243; above, p. 44.
[5] Rot. Parl. iii. 572; Ordinances, i. 295.

of good and substantial government; after a good deal of discussion the request was granted on the last day of the session[1]. During the reign of Henry V the perfect accord existing between the king and parliament made any question of the composition of the council superfluous; but the minority of Henry VI gave the council at once a commanding position in the government. In the first year of his reign it was constituted, not by a mere nomination, but by a solemn act of the parliament; the king, at the request of the commons and by the advice and assent of the lords, elected certain persons of state as well spiritual as temporal to be counsellors assisting in government[2]. This council consisted of the protector and the duke of Exeter, five bishops, five earls, two barons, and three knights; a few names were added in 1423, and again in 1430[3]. In addition to its ordinary functions, this council was a real council of regency, and by no means a mere consultative body in attendance on the protector. It defined its own power in the statement that upon it during the king's minority devolved the exercise and execution of all the powers of sovereignty[4]. It may therefore be regarded as superseding or merging in its own higher functions the ordinary powers of the continual council, but it was really the same body. The result, however, of the union of the two functions seems to have been that, after Henry came of age and the executive power of the council ceased, the parliament either forgot or did not care to exercise any influence in the selection of the council; as early as 1437 the king had begun to nominate absolutely[5]; it became again a mere instrument in the hands of the king or the court, and was often in opposition to the parliament or to the men by whom the parliament was led. The removal of the old council then became a measure of reform, and

Concord of council and parliament under Henry V.

Under Henry VI the council increases in power.

It acts as a council of regency.

The parliament loses its connexion with council after 1437.

[1] Rot. Parl. iii. 623, 632.
[2] Ib. iv. 175.
[3] Ib. iv. 201, 344.
[4] Above, p. 105.
[5] Nov. 12, 1437, at S. John's Clerkenwell, the lords of the council were reappointed and new names added; 'and the king wol that after the fourme as power was gyve by king Henry IV to his counsaillers, that the kyng's counsaillers that now be, that they so do, after a cedule that was rade there the which passed in the parlement tyme of K. H. the iiij.' Ordinances, &c. v. 71; Rot. Parl. v. 438.

Council holds executive power during one of the York regencies.

Henry's promise to nominate a sad and grave council was one of the means by which he proposed to strengthen a general pacification[1]. During the protectorship of the duke of York, the council again assumed the character of a regency for a short time, the king, although he admitted the authority of a protector, preferring to lodge the executive power in the council[2]. No thorough reconstitution of the council was however made during the reign, and to the last it contained only the great lords who were on Henry's side, with the great officers of state and other nominees of the court. Edward IV, following perhaps the advice of Sir John Fortescue, or the plan adopted by Michael de la Pole under Richard II, mingled with the baronial element in the council a number of new men on whom he could personally rely, and who were in close connexion with the Wydvilles. It may be questioned whether the position which the privy council henceforth occupied was directly the result of an arbitrary policy on the part of the crown, or of the weakness of the parliament; but, however it gained that position, it retained it during the Tudor period, and became under Henry VII and Henry VIII an irresponsible committee of government, through the agency of which the constitutional changes of that period were forced on the nation, were retarded or accelerated.

Change in the character of council under Edward IV and the Tudors.

Parliament imposes oaths on the council, and regulates the wages of councillors.

Not content with securing such a public nomination of the privy council as gave the estates a practical veto on the appointment of unpopular members, the parliament attempted, by the imposition of oaths or rules of proceeding and by regulating the payments made to the councillors, to retain a control over their behaviour. In 1406 the commons prayed that the lords of the council might be reasonably rewarded for their labour and diligence[3]; in 1410 the prince of Wales, for himself and his fellow councillors, prayed to be excused from serving unless means could be found for enabling them to support the necessary charges[4]; in the minority of Henry VI the salaries of the members

[1] See above, pp. 157, 166; Rot. Parl. v. 240.
[2] Above, p. 174; Rot. Parl. v. 289, 290.
[3] Rot. Parl. iii. 577.
[4] Ib. iii. 634.

were very high; in 1431 they were secured to them according to a regular tariff[1]; and in 1433 the self-denying policy of the duke of Bedford enabled him, by obtaining a reduction of this item of account, to secure a considerable economy[2]. The duke of York, when he accepted the protectorship in 1455, insisted on the payment of the council[3]. The provision for the wages of the permanent council was one of the particular points of Fortescue's scheme; but by that time the parliament had ceased to possess or claim any direct control over the payment. Payments to councillors.

It was not so with the rules which were prescribed for the conduct or management of business, and the oaths and charges by which those rules were enforced. Several codes of articles, running back to the days of Edward I, still existed[4]; and various attempts were made throughout the fifteenth century to improve upon them. The rolls of parliament for 1406, 1424, and 1430 contain such regulations, which are constantly illustrated by the proceedings of the council. Those of 1406 were enacted in parliament and enrolled as an act[5]; those of 1424 were contained in a schedule annexed to the act of nomination[6]; those of 1430 were drawn up in the council itself, approved by the lords and read in the presence of the three estates, after which they were subscribed the councillors[7]. Copies of these documents are preserved also among the records of the privy council; especially one drawn up at Reading in December 1426[8]. The object of these regulations was in general to prevent the councillors from accepting or sanctioning gifts of land, from prosecuting or maintaining private suits, from revealing the secrets of the body, or neglecting the king's business[9]. Others prescribe rules for the removal of Rules and regulations for the councillors. Object of these rules.

[1] Rot. Parl. iv. 374. The archbishops and cardinal Beaufort had 300 marks, other bishops 200; the treasurer 200; earls 200; barons and bannerets £100, esquires £40. Cf. Ordinances, iii. 155–158, 202, 222, 266.

[2] Rot. Parl. iv. 446; above p. 118.

[3] Rot. Parl. v. 286.

[4] See vol. ii. p. 258; Foed. i. 1009; Fleta, i. c. 17; Coke, 4 Inst. p. 54; Rot. Parl. i. 218, iii. 246, iv. 423; Ordinances (1390) i. 18.

[5] Rot Parl. iii. 585–589; Ordinances, i. 297.

[6] Rot. Parl. iv. 201 sq.; Ordinances, iii. 148–152.

[7] Rot. Parl. iv. 343, 344; Ordinances, iv. 59–66.

[8] Rot. Parl. v. 407; Ordinances, iii. 213–221. See also one of 1425; Ordinances, iii. 175.

[9] Ordinances, i. 18.

Valid exercise of parliamentary influence over the council.

unworthy members, and guard against the usurpations of individuals by fixing a quorum [1]. The anxiety of the councillors to avoid the oath and to be released from it after the expiration of their term of office [2], and the strict conditions [3] on which they insist before accepting office, seem to show that the method adopted was sufficiently stringent to be effectual. There can be little doubt that the council thus nominated, regulated, and watched by the parliament was a substantive and most valuable feature of the Lancastrian system of government: not new, not uniform in its composition, powers, or policy at different times, but always forming a link between the king and the parliament, responsible to both, and, during at least fifty years, maintaining the balance of force between the two.

Powers of the council defined.

The powers of the council thus formed and guided were very great; and the definition which was laid down in 1427, by which they claim to have the execution of all the powers of the crown during the king's minority, needs perhaps but a slight alteration to make it applicable to their perpetual functions. Their work was to counsel and assist the king in the execution of every power of the crown which was not exercised through the machinery of the common law. It was in the matter of judicial proceedings only that their action was restricted; and as the king had long ceased to act as judge in person in the courts, his council had no place there. The petitions against their assumption of jurisdiction in matters cognisable at common law, which had been frequent under Richard II [4], did not wholly cease under his successor [5]; but few cases, if any, of judicial oppression by the council can be adduced during the period; and in the year 1453 by an act of parliament the chancellor was empowered to enforce the attendance of all persons summoned by writ of privy seal before the king and his council in

Objections to their judicial acts.

[1] Rot. Parl. iv. 343, v. 408.

[2] Ib. iv. 176, 423. See also the important articles addressed to Richard II by the council, protesting against his interference; Ordinances, i. 84 sq.

[3] Ib. iii. 609, 632.

[4] See above, vol. ii. p. 606.

[5] Rot. Parl. iii. 471.

all cases not determinable by common law[1]. Beyond the region of the common law the council retained the right of advising the king in knotty cases and appeals, in which the opinion of the judges was likewise asked. As to powers of legislation and taxation, the parliament was more liberal; the power of ordaining relaxations of the statutes of the staple or of provisors was formally entrusted to the king and council[2]; they were watched, and when the result was bad were requested to abstain from or suspend proceedings. Financial business was also expressly entrusted to them, almost from the beginning of the Lancastrian reigns; a fact which, while it shows the confidence felt by the nation in the honesty of the king and his ministers, proves unmistakeably the great difficulty of obtaining supplies, the poverty of the crown, and the scarcity of money. To go through the particular expedients adopted by the council itself would be to write the whole financial history of the time; it was by the advice of the council that the king was able to borrow money by writs of privy seal[3]; more than once the members contributed gifts or loans from their private purses to meet an emergency[4], or gave personal security, or wrote letters of personal application to lords or merchants[5]. In the most important junctures, however, they received power from parliament, either to stop the outgoings of money[6], or to give security for the large loans by which the accruing taxes were anticipated. In the year 1421 the lords of the council were empowered by parliament to give security for the king's debts incurred in the proposed expedition to France[7]. Up to this time the loans had generally been obtained by assigning to the creditor

Powers of the council.

Legislative authority.

Financial authority.

Variety of financial expedients.

[1] 31 Hen. VI, c. 2; Statutes, ii. 361, 362. The court of Star Chamber, as the judicature of the council in special cases, was organised by the Act 3 Hen. VII. c. 1, which appointed the chancellor, treasurer, privy seal, a bishop, a lord temporal of the council, and the two chief justices, as judges. The privy councillors however retained their places: hence the dispute whether this was a new court or an old one; Coke, 4 Inst. p. 61.

[2] Rot. Parl. iii. 428, 491.

[3] Ordinances, ii. 31, 280, 281.

[4] As in 1400, see above, p. 27; Ordinances, i. 104, 105: in 1425, ib. iii. 167.

[5] See Ordinances, i. 200 sq. (1403); 343, 347 (1410).

[6] Ordinances, iii. 348.

[7] Rot. Parl. iv. 130.

Council empowered to give security for loans.

certain portions of the revenue[1]; thus bishop Beaufort's great loans had been recovered by him from the customs[2]; sometimes the credit of the lords was pledged, as in 1419[3]. From 1421, however, the more prudent practice was followed with some regularity; the sums for which the council were authorised to give security increased from £20,000 in 1425[4] to £40,000 in 1426, £24,000 in 1427[5], £50,000 in 1429 and 1431[6], 100,000 marks in 1433[7], and £100,000 in 1435, 1437, 1439, 1442, and 1447[8]. After the death of cardinal Beaufort these acts of security disappear and other expedients were adopted, which illustrate both the exigences of the court and the waning confidence placed by the country in the privy council.

Petitions heard in council.

The office of the council in hearing petitions addressed to the king continues during the period before us much the same as it had been under Edward III and Richard; the chamberlain being the officer to whose care such documents were intrusted. The jealousy of the commons was not aroused by the quasi-judicial character of the proceedings, as it was against the summons by letter of privy seal, and the writ of subpoena. The diversity of petitions which appear on the rolls of parliament, variously addressed to the king, the lords, the commons, the king and the lords, the lords and the commons, or the council, must have given employment to a large class of lawyers, whose action in the parliament itself was occasionally deprecated. It could only be after much urgency that such petitions reached either king or council. Nor was the correspondence of the council at all confined to petitions and their answers; letters, reports from every department of state, and applications for money were addressed to them as commonly and as freely as to the king himself[9].

Variety of forms of petition.

Correspondence of council.

[1] Rot. Parl. iv. 95, 96; Ordinances, ii. 170.

[2] Ib. iv. 111, 132, 210, 275, &c., 496.

[3] Ib. iv. 95, 96, 117; and in 1434, Ordinances, iv. 202. So too in 1423 the feoffees of the duchy of Lancaster lent the king £1000 on the personal security of the lords of the council; Ordinances, iii. 135.

[4] Rot. Parl. iv. 277. [5] Ib. iv. 300, 317. [6] Ib. iv. 339, 374.

[7] Ib. iv. 426. [8] Ib. iv. 482, 504; v. 7, 39, 135.

[9] On the minute points of practice in matters of petitions, see besides the Rolls of Parliament, passim, and the Proceedings of the Privy Council, the

It is hardly possible to specify particularly the less definite functions of the council; they are coextensive on the one hand with royal prerogative, all exercise of which was a matter for advice in this assembly; every sort of ordinance, pardon, licence, and the like, which the king could authorise, was passed through the council; and where on the other hand, special powers were, as we have seen, vested in the king by parliament, they were exercised with the advice of the council.

Large share of the council in executive business.

Besides its relation to the king and the parliament, the privy council had a direct relation to the great councils which were often called by the Lancastrian kings on occasions on which it was not necessary or desireable to call a parliament. These great councils, the constitution of which was very indefinite, were essentially deliberative rather than executive, but they very often appear rather as enlarged and 'afforced' sessions of the privy council, than as separate assemblies. It is probable that the theory which gives to all the peers of the realm the right of approaching the king with advice was thus reduced to practice; and that, as volunteer advisers, any of the lords who chose might occasionally attend the council. But the more formal sessions of the great council were attended by persons summoned by writs of privy seal, sometimes in large numbers[1]; and thus was formed an assembly of notables whose advice, though welcome, was not conclusive. As these assemblies had no regular constitution or place in the parliamentary system, it is only now and then that a record of their proceedings has been preserved. They may, however, on all important occasions of their sitting, be regarded either as extra-parliamentary sessions of the house of lords or as enlarged meetings of the royal council. In both characters they are found acting, as we have seen, in questions of the regency after the death of Henry VI, in the disputes between Beaufort and Gloucester, and in the preliminary

Relation of the privy council to the great councils.

Loose constitution of the great council.

remarks of Sir Harris Nicolas in the prefaces to the latter work; i. p. xxv; ii. pp. xii. xxxi; vi. pp. xc sq.

[1] See for example the list of persons summoned in 1401, Ordinances. i. 155 sq.; and others, ib. 179, 180; ii. 73, 80, 85; iii. 322; iv. 191; v. 237, 238; vi. 163, 206, &c. Most of the great councils here indicated have been noticed already.

work of parliament, as had been usual before parliament became a full representation of the three estates.

Relations between the crown and the parliament.

691. The relations of the council to the king and the parliament had thus gained definiteness and recognition. Scarcely less was this the case with the direct relations between the crown and the parliament. The period before us witnessed some very important exemplifications of the matured action of the constitution in this respect also. The house of lords, for so the baronage may be now called, underwent under the Lancastrian kings none but personal changes, and such formal modifications as the institution of marquessates and viscounties; their powers remain the same as before, and in matters where they attempt a separate action, as for instance in the arrangement of the regency or protectorate, their action, which is in itself as much the action of the great council as of the baronage *eo nomine*, is generally confirmed by an act of the whole parliament. Such minor particulars as are worth recording may be noted in another chapter, in which the antiquities of parliament may be examined in regular order. The history of the house of commons, on the other hand, furnishes some valuable illustrations of constitutional practice. These illustrations, many of which have been noted already, and many of which must be recapitulated again, may be for our present purpose arranged in their natural order under the heads of organisation of the house of commons, including election, privilege, freedom of conference and freedom of debate, and the powers of the house of commons as a part of the collective parliament, exercised in general deliberation, legislative action, taxation, and control of the national administration.

The house of lords.

Questions touching the house of commons.

County elections.

The regulation of the county elections with a view to securing not merely a fair representation but the choice of competent counsellors for the national senate, was a point upon which some consideration had been spent under Edward III, whom we have seen rejecting all propositions made for limiting the electoral body and diminishing the powers of the old county courts[1].

[1] Vol. ii. pp. 425, 433.

Much jealousy of the right of the full county court to elect had been evinced on more than one occasion; Edward's ordinance against the choice of lawyers had remained a dead letter[1]; Richard had been obliged to withdraw from his writs in 1388 the words which directed the election of persons who had taken no part in the recent quarrels[2]; his interference in the elections of 1397 was one of the grounds of his deposition[3], and Henry IV had been taken to task for excluding lawyers from the parliament of Coventry in 1404[4]. Yet there can be little doubt that the right, however jealously watched, was sparingly exercised; that, under the influence of the crown or of the great lords, the sheriffs often returned their own nominees; and that neither the composition of the county court, the regularity of its proceedings, nor the way of ascertaining its decisions, was very definitely fixed. Sometimes a few great men settled the elections, sometimes a noisy crowd failed to arrive at any definite choice, sometimes the sheriff returned whom he pleased. It was to remedy this uncertainty that Henry IV in 1406 enacted on the petition of the commons that, in the first county court held after the reception of the writ, proclamation should be made of the day and place of parliament, and that all persons present, whether suitors duly summoned for the purpose or others, should attend the election; they should then proceed to the election freely and indifferently, notwithstanding any request or command to the contrary, and the names of the persons chosen should be written in an indenture under the seals of the persons choosing them: this indenture should be tacked to the writ and considered to be the sheriff's return[5]. This act, so far as the electoral body was concerned, only declared the existing custom; but the notice, the prohibition of undue influence and the institution of the indenture, took from the sheriff all opportunity of making a false return. An act of 1410 vested in the justices of assize the power of inquiring into the returns, fining the sheriffs in the sum of £100 where the law had been broken, and condemning

Maintenance of the right of the county court to elect knights of the shire;

evaded by the sheriffs, or great men.

Regulations enacted in 1406.

Penalties for infringement of these.

[1] Vol. ii. p. 425.
[2] Vol. ii. p. 479.
[3] Vol. ii. p. 504.
[4] Above, p. 46.
[5] 7 Hen. IV, c. 15; Stat. ii. 156.

Residents to be chosen.

the members unduly returned to forfeit their wages[1]. The first parliament of Henry V restricted both the electoral vote and the choice of the electors to residents within the county, city, or borough for which they were to elect members[2]. In 1427 the effect of the act of 1406 was so far modified as to allow the accused sheriffs and knights to make answer and traverse before any justices of assize, so that they should not be fined unless they had been duly convicted[3]. Three years afterwards, in the eighth year of Henry VI, was passed the restrictive act which, in consequence of the tumults made in the county courts 'by great attendance of people of small substance and no value, whereof every of them pretended a voice equivalent, as to such elections, with the most worthy knights and squires resident,' established the rule that only resident persons possessed of a freehold worth forty shillings a year should be allowed to vote, and that the majority of such votes should decide the election[4]. In 1432 it was ordered that the qualifying freehold should be within the county[5]. These regulations received further authority by an act of the twenty-third year of the same king, which, after recounting several abuses that had recently revived, gave minute rules for the enforcement of these and the preceding statutes, and prescribed that the knights henceforth to be chosen should be notable knights, esquires, or gentlemen able to be knights, and not of the degree of yeoman or under[6]. The restriction of the electoral franchise to the class which was qualified to serve on juries commended itself to moderate politicians of the fifteenth century. There is no evidence to show that the allegations of the statute with respect to the disorders of the county court are untrue. But the history of the particular years in which the changes were made throws no light upon the special circumstances that called for legislation, and what is more curious, the acts seem to have produced no change whatever in the character or standing of the persons returned; they were all, however, passed at the

Forty shilling freeholders to elect.

Freehold to lie within the county.

Knights, not yeomen, to be chosen.

[1] 11 Hen. IV, c. 1; Stat. ii. 162.
[2] 1 Hen. V, c. 1; Stat. ii. 170.
[3] 6 Hen. VI, c. 4; Stat. ii. 235.
[4] 8 Hen. VI, c. 7; Stat. ii. 243.
[5] 10 Hen. VI, c. 2; Stat. ii. 273.
[6] 23 Hen. VI, c. 14; Stat. ii. 340 sq.

request of the commons and in orderly times. Henry V had not the will, and the council of Henry VI had not the power, to reject a proposal of amended practice in favour of an ill-defined and abused prescription. The key to the question is probably to be found in the social changes which had been at work since the days of Edward III, and which belong to another part of our subject. We have seen how during the struggle of parties in the latter years of Henry VI the forms of election were evaded and dispensed with.

Result of social changes.

692. Next to purity of election the great requisite of the national council was freedom of action; and this, whether exemplified in the maintenance of the privilege of members, of the right of conference with the lords, of the freedom of the Speaker, or of freedom of debate, was sufficiently strengthened by practice under the three Henries. The most signal examples have been noticed already; the case of the speaker Thorpe being the most important instance of disputed privilege[1], and the discussions of Henry IV with Savage and Chaucer the most significant occasions on which the privilege of the Speaker was asserted[2]. The right of conference with the lords, which had been conceded as a matter of grace by Edward III and Richard II, was claimed from and allowed by Henry IV, under protest, in 1402[3] and 1404[4]; in 1407 the king was obliged to concede the whole question so far as money grants were concerned. The last occasion secured to the two houses perfect freedom of debate, and deserves special notice.

Freedom of action in parliament, increased under the Lancaster kings.

Henry IV, no doubt instructed by his parliamentary experience as duke of Lancaster, had more than once shown irritation at the conduct of the commons, and they in return had been somewhat tedious. In 1401 they had requested that they might have good advice and deliberation without being called upon suddenly to answer on the most important matters at the end of the parliament, as had been usual. The king was affronted at the request, and commissioned the earl of Worcester to disown any such subtlety as was imputed to him. A day or two

The increase of liberty in the commons.

[1] Above, p. 164.
[2] Above, pp. 29, 67.
[3] Rot. Parl. iii. 486; above, p. 37.
[4] Ib. iii. 523; above, p. 42.

Henry IV promises not to interfere in deliberations.

after they begged the king not to listen to any report of their proceedings before they themselves informed him of them; and Henry acquiesced[1]. In 1407 however, in the parliament of Gloucester, the king, without reference to the commons, inquired of the lords what aid was required for the exigences of the moment, and, having received their answer, sent for a certain number of the commons to hear and report the opinion of the lords. Twelve members were sent, and their report greatly disturbed the house; the king saw fit to recall the impolitic measure and to recognise the rule that on money grants he should receive the determination of the two houses by the mouth of the speaker of the commons[2]. The leaving of the determination of the money grant to that estate which being collectively the richest was individually the poorest of the three was consonant to common sense; where taxation fell on all in the same proportion, the commons might safely be trusted not to vote too much: sparing their own pockets, they spared those of the lords. But the importance of the event is not confined to the points thus illustrated; it contains a full recognition of freedom of deliberation.

Money grants to be declared by the speaker.

Right of the commons to debate all matters of public interest.

The right of the commons to consider and debate on every matter of public interest was secured to them by the recognition of their freedom of deliberation; for although in words the king acknowledged only their right to 'commune on the state of the realm and the necessary remedies,' there was no question of foreign policy or domestic administration that might not be brought under that head. The kings moreover, in the old idea of involving the third estate in a common responsibility with themselves for all national designs, did not hesitate to lay all sorts of business before them; and the commons, as before, were inclined to hang back rather than rashly to approach matters in which they saw they might have little influence and incur much blame. The care taken by Henry V in preparing for his French war is an abundant illustration of this[3]; but many other examples may be found. The petitions on Lollardy show that even the clergy were not jealous of the commons when they were

[1] Rot. Parl. iii. 455, 456.
[2] Ib. iii. 609; see above, p. 61.
[3] Above, pp. 82–85.

ranged on the side of orthodoxy; the closing of the great schism was a matter on which the chancellor dilated in his opening speech and on which the commons of their own accord urged the king to labour[1]. The treaty between Henry V and Sigismund in 1416 was read before the commons as well as the lords, and by their common advice and assent, in the parliament and by authority of the same, ratified, approved, and confirmed[2]. The treaty of Troyes contained a provision that without the consent of the three estates of the two kingdoms peace should not be made with the dauphin; in 1446 the commons joined in the act by which the king was released from that obligation[3]. Nor was any great reluctance felt to allow the commons to touch the most delicate questions that came before the council: in 1426 the speaker of the commons was bold enough to express to the duke of Bedford their sorrow for the quarrels which had taken place between the great lords, referring unquestionably to Beaufort and Gloucester[4]; in 1427 they petitioned the king to intercede with the pope in favour of archbishop Chichele[5]; in 1433 they joined in taking the oath of concord by which Bedford attempted to secure union in the government and national support for it before he left England, and in the same parliament they petitioned the king that Bedford might remain in the country[6]. It is, however, unnecessary to multiply examples of a truth which is apparent in every article of the parliamentary rolls. With the single exception of the cases in which the parliament attempted to tax the spiritualities or otherwise interfere with the administration of the clergy, there is really no exception to the accepted rule, that every question of home administration or foreign policy might be canvassed in the assembly of the commons.

Discussion on foreign politics.

On the treaty of Troyes.

On the quarrels of the lords.

The share of the commons in legislation, whether expressed by the mention of their petition in the preamble of the statutes, or by their assent to measures which had been previously discussed by the lords, may be regarded as theoretically complete

Share of the commons in legislation.

[1] Rot. Parl. iii. 465, 492; iv. 70 sq.
[2] Ib. iv. 96, 97; Rymer, ix. 403.
[3] See above, p. 134.
[4] Rot. Par. iv. 296.
[5] Ib. iv. 322.
[6] Ib. iv. 422 sq.; above, p. 118.

Pains taken by the commons to secure the exact enrollment of their petitions when granted.

before Henry IV began to reign. But for several years there continues to be seen some mistrust of the honesty of the officials in the process of turning petitions into acts, or engrossing the acts themselves. In 1401, as we have seen, the speaker had to petition that the commons might not be hurried through public business; and that the petitions which were granted might be enrolled before the justices left the parliament[1]. In the same parliament they informed the king that they had been told that the permission given him in the last session to dispense with the statute of provisors had been enacted and entered in the roll in a form different from that in which it was granted. The king under protest allowed the rolls to be searched, and it was found that they were mistaken[2]. In 1406 the commons asked that certain elected members might be appointed to view the enrolment and engrossing of the acts of parliament; and this was granted[3]. But the prejudice no doubt continued to be strongly felt, and it was not until the second year of Henry V that the full security was obtained, and the king undertook that the acts when finally drawn up should correspond exactly with the petitions[4]. The plan subsequently adopted of initiating legislation by bill rather than by petition completed, so far as rules could ensure it, the remedy of the evil. A good instance of the careful superintendence which the commons kept up over the wording of public documents is found in the parliament of 1404, when the king submitted to them the form of the commissions of array about to be issued; the commons cancelled certain clauses and words and requested that for the future such commissions should be issued only in the corrected form. The king consulted the lords and judges, and very graciously agreed[5].

Henry V secures them in the right.

Attempt to make supply depend on redress.

The attempt to bind together remedial legislation and grants of money, to make supply depend upon the redress of grievances, was directly and boldly made by the commons in 1401; the commons prayed that before they made any grant they might be informed of the answers to their petitions[6]. The

[1] Rot. Parl. iii. 455, 456. [2] Ib. iii. 465. [3] Ib. iii. 585.
[4] See above, p. 81. [5] Rot. Parl. iv. 526, 527. [6] Ib. iii. 458.

king's answer, given on the last day of the session, amounted to a peremptory refusal; he said 'that this mode of proceeding had not been seen or used in the time of his progenitors or predecessors, that they should have any answer to their petitions before they had shown and done all their other business of parliament, whether it were matter of a grant or otherwise; the king would not in any way change the good customs and usages made and used of ancient times.' It is probable, however, that the point was really secured by the practice, almost immediately adopted, of delaying the grant to the last day of the session, by which time no doubt the really important petitions had received their answer, and at which time they were enrolled[1]. Speedy execution, however, was a different thing, and the petition of the commons for it proves that delay was a weapon by no means idle or harmless in the hands of the servants of the law.

The king's refusal.

The object informally gained.

693. That the commons should have a decisive share in the bestowal of money grants had become since the reign of Edward III an admitted principle; and the observance of the rule is illustrated by the history of every parliament. In the foregoing pages the regular votes of taxation have been noticed as they occurred; and the decision of Henry IV in 1407 has been referred to as recognising the right of the commons to originate and, after it has received the assent of the lords, to announce the grant, generally on the last day of the session. The ordinary form of the grant expressed this; it was made by the commons with the assent of the lords spiritual and temporal. This particular form curiously enough occurs first in the grants made to Richard II in 1395, the previous votes of money having been made by the lords and commons conjointly[2]. It was observed in 1401 and 1402, and henceforth[3] became the constitutional

Share of the commons in taxation

expressed in the words of the grant.

[1] Sir H. Nicolas (Ordin. i. p. lxiv) mentions a case in which it was ordered that an error in the Roll should be corrected, and no such correction appears to have been made: from which he argues that the Rolls may not have been ingrossed for two or three years after the session. But this could only be exceptional.

[2] Rot. Parl. iii. 331.

[3] Not however without exceptions. In 1404 the lords for themselves and the ladies temporal and all other persons temporal granted a tax of 20s. on the £20 of land; Rot. Parl. iii. 546.

Departure from the ordinary usage.

form. It may however be questioned whether Henry's dictum in 1407 was at the time understood to recognise the exclusive right of the commons to originate the grant. On one occasion in the reign of Edward IV there was a marked departure from the form established by long usage. This was in 1472, when on the occasion of an act for raising a force of 13,000 archers, the commons, with the advice and assent of the lords, granted a tenth of the revenue and income not belonging to the lords of parliament; and the lords, without any reference to the advice of the commons, followed it up with a similar grant from their own property[1]. It is questionable whether this was not a breach of the accepted understanding, but no objection was taken to it at the time; the grant, as a means of raising additional funds, failed of its object, and it did not become a

Attempt of the commons to tax the stipendiary clergy.

precedent. The attempt of the commons in 1449 to tax the stipendiary clergy, an attempt perhaps made by oversight, was defeated by the king, who referred the petition which contained their proposal to the lords spiritual to be transmitted to the convocation[2]. As however throughout this period the convocations followed, with but slight variations, the example set by the commons, the practical as well as the formal determination of the money grants may be safely regarded as having now become one of the recognised functions of the third estate.

694. The power which the exercise of this function gave them was freely exercised in more critical matters than those of political deliberation and legislation; and perhaps the hold which it gave them on the royal administration, both in state and household, is the point in which the growth of constitutional ideas is most signally illustrated by the history of this century.

Appropriation of grants to special purposes.

The practice of appropriating particular grants to particular purposes had been claimed under Richard II[3]; it was observed under Henry IV and his successors; the greater grants were almost invariably assigned to the defence of the realm; tunnage and poundage became the recognised provision for the safeguard of the sea[4]; the remnants of the ancient crown lands

[1] Rot. Parl. vi. 4–8.
[2] Ib. v. 152, 153.
[3] Vol. ii. p. 563 sq.
[4] See above, p. 243.

were set apart for the expenses of the household, for which they were obviously insufficient, and supplementary grants were made from the other sources of national income to enable the king to pay his expenses; and even before Calais had become the only foreign possession of the crown, a certain portion or poundage of the subsidy on wool was regularly assigned to it[1]. But it was the exigencies of the household which gave the commons their greatest hold on the crown, and it was a hold which the kings rarely attempted to elude or to resist. One result of their interference in this respect was the separation of the household or ordinary charges, the civil list or king's list, as Fortescue calls it, from the extraordinary charges of the crown; a point which the commons attempted to secure in 1404 by apportioning revenue to the amount of £12,100; in 1406 it was proposed to vote £10,000 for the purpose, and in 1413 that sum was assigned to the king as a payment to take precedence of all others, in consideration of the great charges of his hostel, chamber, and wardrobe. The attempts made to regulate the lavish expenditure and to relieve the poverty of Henry VI have been enumerated in our survey of the history of his reign. They show, by the diminution of the sums apportioned to him, either that the royal demesnes were alarmingly reduced and the royal estate abridged, or else that the distinction between royal and national expenditure was more clearly seen, and the different departments more independently administered. The acts of resumption which had been urged by the commons from the very beginning of the century were first in 1450 adopted by Henry VI as a means of recruiting his treasury, but they contained invariably such a list of exceptions as must have nearly neutralised the intended effect of the acts. The crown continued very poor until Edward IV and Henry VII devised new modes of enriching themselves, and in its poverty the commons saw their great opportunity of interference.

Assignments to the king, to Calais, to the household.

Separation of the household charges from those of the kingdom.

Increasing poverty of the crown.

Acts of resumption.

[1] For example, in 1449, the commons petition that 20*s*. from each sack of wool taxed for the subsidy may be assigned to Calais, 10*s*. for wages, 5*s*. for victualling, 5*s*. for repairs. The king alters this, and assigns 13*s*. 4*d*. for wages and victuals, and 6*s*. 8*d*. for repairs; Rot. Parl. v. 146, 147. A similar arrangement had been made in 1423 by the Council; Ord. iii. 19, 95.

Interference of the commons with the action of the king.

Very signal examples of such interference force themselves on our notice both early and late. The request made in 1404 that Henry IV would dismiss his confessor, was followed up with a petition for the removal of aliens from the household[1]. In 1450 Henry VI was asked to send away almost all his faithful friends[2]. He was told that his gifts were too lavish and must be resumed[3]. In every case he had to yield, and it was his unwillingness as well as his inability to resist that caused the nation to conceive for him a dislike and contempt, from which the goodness of his intentions might have saved him. Where the private affairs of the household were thus scrutinised, it could not be expected that the conduct of public officers could escape. The practice of impeachment directed against Michael de la Pole in 1386 was revived in 1450 for the destruction of his grandson. But the process of events during the wars of the Roses was too rapid, and the parliaments were too imperfect and one-sided to be regarded as fair tribunals. The constitution receives from such proceedings more lessons of warning than of edification. The impeached minister, like the king who is put on his trial, when he has become weak enough to be impeached, may remain too strong to be acquitted; and the majority which is strong enough to impeach is strong enough to condemn. In Suffolk's case, as we have seen, neither king nor lords had strength enough to ensure a just trial; Henry's decision was an evasion of a hostile attack rather than the breach of a recognised rule. The bills of attainder which on both sides followed the alternations of fortune in the field, illustrate political and personal vindictiveness, but contribute only a miserable series of constitutional precedents. The prohibition of appeals of treason made in parliament, which was enacted by Henry IV in 1399[4], was a salutary act, although it did not preclude the use of the still more fatal weapons. The rejected petition of 1432[5], in which the commons prayed that, neither in parliament nor council, should any one be put on trial for articles touching

Practice of impeachment.

Bills of attainder.

[1] Rot. Parl. iii. 524, 527.
[2] Ib. v. 216.
[3] Ib. v. 217.
[4] Above, p. 23.
[5] Rot. Parl. iv. 403.

fitness of a legislative assembly for entertaining such impeachments. But the practice was too strong to be met by weak legislation, and had, with all its cruelty and unfairness, some vindication in the lesson which it could not fail to impress on unworthy ministers.

Audit of accounts insisted on.

The rule of insisting on a proper audit of account was a corollary from the practice of appropriating the supplies to particular purposes. It was one which was scarcely worth contesting. In 1406 the commons, who objected to making a grant until the accounts of the last grant were audited, were told by Henry that 'kings do not render accounts'; but the boast was a vain one; the accounts were in 1407 laid before the commons without being asked for; and the victory so secured was never again formally contested. The statement laid by Lord Cromwell before the parliament of 1433 shows that the time was past for any reticence on the king's part with regard to money matters[1].

Secured.

General conclusion from these facts.

In this attempt to enumerate and generalise upon the chief constitutional incidents of a long period, it is not worth while at every point to pronounce a judgment on the good faith of the crown or the honesty of the commons; or to discuss the question whether it was by compulsion or by respect to the terms of their coronation engagements that the Lancastrian kings were actuated in their overt acceptance and maintenance of constitutional rules. It is upon the fact that those rules were observed and strengthened by observance, that they were not broken when the king was strong, or disingenuously evaded when he was weak, that the practical vindication of the dynasty must turn. Henry IV, as has been said more than once, was a constitutional politician before he became king, and cannot be charged with hypocrisy because when he became king he acted on the principles which he had professed as a subject. Henry V in all that he did carried with him the heart of his people. Henry VI was honest; he had been brought up to honour and abide by the decisions of his parliament; the charge of falseness, by which the strong so often attempt to destroy the

The rule of the house of Lancaster was constitutional.

[1] Above, pp. 54, 117.

Best side of the Lancaster rule.

last refuge which the weak find in the pity and sympathy of mankind, is nowhere proved, and very rarely even asserted, against him. But the case in favour of these kings does not depend on technicalities. By their devotion to the work of the country, by the thorough nationality of their aims, their careful protection of the interests of trade and commerce, their maintenance of the universities, the policy of their alliances, their attention to the fleet as the strongest national arm, the first two Henries, Bedford, Beaufort, and in a less degree Henry VI and Gloucester[1], vindicated the position they claimed as national ministers, sovereign or subject.

Misfortunes of the Lancaster reigns.

695. There is another side to the question. The Lancastrian reigns were to a great extent a period of calamity. There were pestilences, famines, and wars: the incessant border warfare of the reign of Henry IV tells not only of royal poverty and weakness, but of impolicy and of disregard for human suffering.

Mischief wrought by the long war.

The war of Henry V in France must be condemned by the judgment of modern opinion; it was a bold, a desperate undertaking, fraught with suffering to all concerned in it; but it is as a great national enterprise, too great for the nation which undertook it to maintain, that it chiefly presents itself among the prominent features of the time. It is common and easy to exaggerate the miseries of this war; its cost to England in treasure and blood was by no means so great as the length of its duration and the extent of its operations would suggest. The French administration of Bedford was maintained in great measure by taxing the French[2], rather than by raising supplies from England, and the great occasions of bloodshed were few and far between. But it did produce anarchy and exhaustion in France, and

[1] The Libel of English policy, whether addressed to Cardinal Beaufort or Lord Hungerford the treasurer, in or about 1436, in a very remarkable way presses the safeguard of the sea and the development of commerce upon the ministers; it shows however that some such pressure was needed; quoting the saying of Sigismund, that Dover and Calais were the two eyes of England, and looking back with regret on the more efficient administration of Henry V. It is printed in the Political Poems, vol. ii. pp. 157–205; and there is a tract of Sir John Fortescue to the same purpose, Opp. i. p. 549. See too Capgrave, Ill. Henr. p. 134.

[2] £20,000 a year however was paid by Henry VI to the Duke of York as lieutenant of France, Ord. v. 171.

over-exertion and consequent exhaustion in England; and from these combined causes arose the most prominent of the impulses that drove Henry VI from the throne. Still the war was to a certain extent felt to be a national glory, and the peace that ended it a national disgrace, which added a sense of loss and defeat over and above the consciousness that so much had been spent in vain.

Exhaustion produced by the war.

But neither national exhaustion, resulting from this and other causes, nor the factious designs of the house of York, nor the misguided feeling of the nation with respect to the peace, nor the unhappy partisanship and still more unhappy leadership of Margaret of Anjou, would have sufficed to unseat the Lancastrian house, if there had not been a deeper and more penetrating source of weakness; a source of weakness that accounts for the alienation of the heart of the people, and might under other circumstances have justified even such a revolution. When the commons urged upon Henry IV the need of better and stronger governance, they touched the real, deep, and fatal evil which in the end was to wear out the patience of England. Although sound and faithful in constitutional matters, the Lancastrian kings were weak administrators at the moment when the nation required a strong government. It was so from the very beginning[1]. Constitutional progress had outrun administrative order. Perhaps the very steps of constitutional progress were gained by reason of that weakness of the central power which made perfect order and thorough administration of the law impossible; perhaps the sources of mischief were inherent in the social state of the country rather than in its institutions or the administration of them; but the result is the same on either supposition; following events proved it. The Tudor government, without half the constitutional liberties of the Lancastrian reigns, possessed a force and cogency, an energy and a decision which was even more necessary than law itself. A parallel not altogether false might be drawn between the eleventh, or even the twelfth

These causes insufficient to account for the fall of the house of Lancaster.

The weakness of that house betrayed from the first.

[1] See the letter addressed to Henry IV by Philip Repingdon in 1401; Beckington, i. 151; Ad. Usk, pp. 65, 66; letter of Chandler to Beckington in 1452, ib. p. 268.

Parallel with earlier history.

century, and the fifteenth. Henry VI resembled the Confessor in many ways. Henry VII brought to his task the strength of the Conqueror and the craft of his son: England under Warwick was not unlike England under Stephen, and Henry of Richmond had much in common with Henry of Anjou.

Want of governance.

The want of 'governance' constituted the weakness of Henry IV; he inherited the disorders of the preceding reign, and the circumstances of his accession contributed additional causes of disorder. The crown was impoverished, and with impoverishment came inefficiency. The treasury was always low, the peace was never well kept, the law was never well executed; individual life and property were insecure; whole districts were in a permanent alarm of robbery and riot; the local administration was either paralysed by party faction or lodged in the hand of some great lord or some clique of courtiers. The evil of local faction struck upwards and placed the elections to parliament at the command of the leaders. The social mischief thus directly contributed to weaken the constitution. The remedy for insufficient 'governance' was sought, not in a legal dictatorship such as Edward I had attempted to assume, nor in stringent reforms which indeed without some such dictatorship must have almost certainly failed, but in admitting the houses of parliament to a greater share of influence in executive matters, in the 'afforcing' or amending of the council, and in the passing of reforming statutes.

Administrative weakness.

Recognition of the evil.

It is curious to mark how from the very beginning of the century men saw the evils and failed to grasp the remedy. Not to multiply examples; in 1399 the commons petitioned against illegal usurpations of private property[1]; the Paston Letters furnish abundant proof that this evil had not been put down at the accession of Henry VII. The same year the county of Salop was ravaged by armed bands from Cheshire[2]. The country was infested with malefactors banded together to avoid punishment[3]. In 1402 there is a petition against forcible entries by the magnates[4]. In 1404 the war between the earls of

[1] Rot. Parl. iii. 434.
[2] Ib. iii. p. 441.
[3] Ib. iii. 445.
[4] Ib. iii. 487.

Northumberland and Westmoreland was regarded by the parliament as a private war; and Northumberland's treason was condoned as a trespass only[1]. In 1406 the king had to remodel his council in order to ensure better governance; but the petition for 'good and abundant governance' was immediately followed by a request for the better remuneration of the lords of the council, and the speaker had to insist on more co-operation from the lords in the work of reform[2]. In 1407 the king was told that the better and more abundant governance had not been provided, the sea had been badly watched, and the marches badly kept[3]. In 1411 a statute against rioters was passed[4]. On the accession of Henry V the cry was repeated; the late king's promises of governance have been badly kept; the marches were still in danger; the Lollards were still disturbing the peace; there were riots day by day in diverse parts of the realm[5]. The parliament of 1414 reissued the statute against rioters[6]; in 1417, according to the petitions, large bands of associated malefactors were ravaging the country, plundering the people, holding the forests, spreading Lollardy, treason, and rebellion, robbing the collectors of the revenue[7]. Matters were still worse in 1420; whole counties were infested by bandits; the scholars of Oxford were waging war on the county; the inhabitants of Tynedale, Redesdale, and Hexhamshire had become brigands; all the evils of the old feudal immunities were in full force[8]. Similar complaints accumulate during the early years of Henry VI, and seem to reach the highest regions of public life in the armed strife of Gloucester and Beaufort. But the general spirit of misrule was quite independent of party and faction. The quarrels of the heir male and heirs general of the house of Berkeley, carried on both by law and by arms, lasted from 1421 to 1475, through three generations[9]. In 1437 lords Grey and Fanhope were at war in

Private war.

Frequent remonstrances.

Statutes against rioters.

Bands of robbers.

Complaints under Henry VI.

[1] Above, p. 43.
[2] Rot. Parl. iii. 571 sq., 576 sq., 585.
[3] Ib. iii. 609, 610.
[4] 13 Hen. IV, c. 7; Statutes ii. 169.
[5] Rot. Parl. iv. 4.
[6] 2 Hen. V, c. st. i. c. 9; Statutes ii. 186.
[7] Rot. Parl. iv. 113.
[8] Ib. iv. 124, 125.
[9] Dugdale, Baronage, i. 362–365.

Instances of public disorder.

Bedfordshire[1], and in 1438 the two branches of the house of Westmoreland, one under the earl, the other under his stepmother, the sister of Cardinal Beaufort, were at open war[2]. In 1441 the earl of Devon and lord Bonneville contested in arms the stewardship of Cornwall[3]. The struggles of Egremont and Neville, of the duke of Exeter and lord Cromwell, were private wars. In 1441 when archbishop Kemp[4] was one of the king's most trusted councillors, there was war between the tenants of his liberty of Ripon and the king's tenants of Knaresborough forest; and the Ripon men brought down the half-outlawed bandits from the archbishop's liberty of Tynedale to help them. By the light of these illustrations the struggle between York and Lancaster seems scarcely more than a grand and critical instance of the working of causes everywhere potent for harm.

Imperfect enforcement of law.

The enforcement of law under such circumstances was scarcely attempted: although it was an age of great judges[5] the administration of the law was full of abuses; the varieties of conflicting jurisdictions, the facilities for obtaining, and cheaply obtaining, writs of all kinds, gave to the strong aggressor a legal standing-ground which they could not secure for the victim[6]; the multiplication of legal forms and functionaries was inefficient it would seem for any good purpose; these evils, and the absence of any determined attempt to remedy them, brought about a strong and permanent disaffection.

False charges against the government.

As is ever the case, the social miseries called down upon the government an accumulation of false charges. The nation complained of the foreign policy of Suffolk; and urged on the king the expulsion of Somerset from

[1] Ordinances, v. 35.

[2] Excerpta Historica, pp. 2, 3; Ordinances, v. 35–40; 173–180.

[3] See above, p. 169.

[4] Rymer, xi. 27; Plumpton Papers, ed. Stapleton, pp. liv. sq.

[5] Reeves, Hist. of English Law, vol. iii. pp. 108, 109, speaks with high praise of the administration of justice during the troublous years of Henry VI. No doubt the law was ably discussed and the judges were great judges, but justice was not enforced; there was no governance.

[6] Abundant illustration of this will be found in the Paston Letters. Even royal letters interfering with the course of justice could be easily purchased; e.g. Henry VI issues letters to the sheriff of Norfolk directing him to impannel a jury to acquit Lord Molines; Paston Letters, i. 208: such a letter might be bought for a noble, ibid. p. 215.

the council. The rebels, under Cade, almost justified on the ground of misgovernment, sought their object by charges of treason against men who, however selfish or incapable, were at all events faithful. The duke of York, who might have ruled England in strength and peace as he had governed Normandy, and might have won the wild English as he had won the wild Irish, could not push the claims of the nation for efficient justice without urging his own claim first to the foremost place in council and then to the crown itself. It was the lack of the strong hand in reform, in justice, and in police, the want of governance at home, that definitely proved the incapacity of the house of Lancaster, and that made their removal possible. It was the fatal cause of their weakness, the moral justification of their fall. And it was in the physical and moral weakness and irresolution of Henry VI, and in his divided councils, that this fatal deficiency was most fatally exemplified. Yet he was set aside and his dynasty with him on an altogether different occasion, and a widely discordant plea.

Charges of treason, a proof of disaffection and weak governance.

696. The house of Lancaster had reigned constitutionally, but had fallen by lack of governance. The house of York succeeded, and, although they ruled with a stronger will, failed altogether to remedy the evils to which they succeeded, and contributed in no small degree to destroy all that was destructible in the construction. The record of the public history of the reigns of Edward IV and Richard III shows how ill they succeeded in securing internal peace or inspiring national confidence. England found no sounder governance under Edward IV than under Henry VI; the court was led by favourites, justice was perverted, strength was pitted against weakness, riots, robberies, forcible entries were prevalent as before. The house of York failed, as the house of Lancaster had failed, to justify its existence by wise administration. As to the constitutional side of the question, the case is somewhat different. One good result had followed the constitutional formalism of the three reigns; the forms of government could not be altered. But they might be overborne and perverted; and the charge of thus wresting and warping them is shared by the house of

The government of the house of York, stronger but not sounder than that of Lancaster.

The house of York anticipated the policy of the Tudors.

York with the house of Tudor. Henry VII, combining the interests of the rival roses, combines the leading characteristics of their respective policies; with Lancaster he observes the forms of the constitution, with York he manipulates them to his own ends. The case against the house of York may be briefly stated; it rests, as may be imagined, primarily on legal and moral grounds, but under these there lurks a spirit defying and ignoring constitutional restraints. Edward IV claimed the throne, not as an elected king, but as the heir of Richard II; the house of Lancaster had given three kings 'de facto non de jure' to England. Their acts were only legal so far as he and his parliaments chose to ratify them. He did not then owe, on his own theory, so much regard to the constitution as they had willingly rendered. Nor did he pay it. He did not indeed rule altogether without a parliament, but he held sessions at long intervals, and brought, or allowed others to bring, before them only the most insignificant matters of business. His statute-roll contains no acts for securing or increasing public liberties; his legislation on behalf of trade and commerce contains no principles of an expanding or liberating policy. To register grants of money, resumptions of gifts, decrees and reversals of attainders, exchanges of property, private matters of business, has become the sole employment of the assembly of the estates; there is no question of difficulty between liberty and prerogative; no voice is raised for Clarence; no tax is refused or begrudged. Outside parliament misrule is more obviously apparent. The collection of benevolences, regarded even at the time as an innovation, was perhaps a resuscitated form of some of the worst measures of Edward II and Richard II, but the attention which it aroused under Edward IV shows how strange it had become under the intervening kings. The levies for the war with Scotland were raised under the old system of commissions of array which had been disused since the early years of Henry IV. The numerous executions which marked the earlier years of Edward's reign show that he considered the country to be in a condition to which the usages of martial law were fairly applicable. Edward himself took personal part in the

Manipulation of parliamentary institutions.

Benevolences.

Commissions of array.

trials of men who had offended him. The courts of the constable and the marshal sent their victims to death on frivolous charges and with scant regard for the privilege of Englishmen. The same reign furnishes the first authoritative proofs of the use of torture in the attempt to force the accused to confession or to betray their accomplices.

Legal severities

A few instances of each of these abuses will suffice.

Suspension of parliamentary action.

During the twenty-five years of the York dynasty the country was only seven times called upon to elect a new parliament; the sessions of those parliaments which really met extended over a very few months; their meetings being frequently held only for the purpose of prorogation. No parliament sat between January 1465 and June 1467, or between May 1468 and October 1472; and between January 1475 and January 1483 the assembly was only called together for forty-two days in 1478 to pass the attainder of the duke of Clarence. The early parliaments had given the king an income for life. The long intermissions were acquiesced in by the nation, because they feared additional demands; but it was well known and recorded that the king avoided the summoning of parliament because he anticipated severe criticism on his impolicy and extravagance. Servile as his parliaments were, he would rather rule without any such check. The practice of the later years of Henry VI, during which elections had been as much as possible avoided, furnished him with precedents for long prorogations; Edward suspended parliamentary action for years together; and England, which had been used to speak its mind once a year at least, was thus reduced to silence.

Legislative poverty of the sessions of parliament.

The records of the sessions are so barren as to silence any regrets at their infrequency. The reign of Edward IV, as has been well said[1], is the first reign in our annals in which not a single enactment is made for increasing the liberty or security of the subject. Nor can it be alleged that such enactments were unnecessary, when frequent executions, outrageous usurpations, and local riots form the chief subject of the annals of the time. Commerce increased; and the increase of commerce

[1] Hallam, Middle Ages, iii. 198.

Commercial legislation.

attests the increase of public confidence, but by no means justifies the policy which arrests rather than invites that confidence; and commercial activity, especially in such states of society as that through which England was now passing, was to some extent a refuge for exhausted families, and a safety valve for energies shut out of their proper sphere.

Taxation by benevolences.

The collection of benevolences, in which the age itself recognised a new method of unlawful taxation, is an obscure point. If it were not that both the chroniclers and the statute book assert the novel character of the abuse, we might in the paucity of records[1] be tempted to doubt whether the charge of inno-

[1] There is among the Ordinances of the Privy Council, vol. v. pp. 418 sq., a set of instructions to commissioners for raising money which is without date, but which is referred by Sir. R. Cotton to the 20th, by Sir H. Nicolas to the 21st, and by another modern note to the 15th of Henry VI. They are directed to assemble the inhabitants of certain towns above the age of sixteen, and to meet an assembly of the body of the counties to which two men from each parish are to be summoned by the sheriff: the names of those present are to be entered in two books, and the commissioners are then to explain that by the law the king can call on his subjects to attend him at their own charges in any part of the land for the defence of the same against outward enemies; that he is unwilling to put them to such expense and asks them of their own free will to give him what they can afford; at least as much as would be required for two days personal service. No inconvenient language or compulsion is to be used. Another undated series of instructions for the collection of men and money for the relief of Calais, is printed from the same MS. in Ordin. iv. 352. These instructions, if the date be rightly assigned, would seem to show that the idea of a benevolence was at all events not strange under Henry VI; but there is no authority for the date, the instructions do not appear ever to have been issued, and if any such taxation had taken place it must have appeared among the sins laid to the charge of Henry's government. Until better information is forthcoming, it would be more reasonable to refer it to the reign of Edward IV or Henry VII. Other instances in which such a charge has been made against the Lancaster kings are these: in 1402 Henry IV wrote to a large number of lords and others accrediting Sir William Esturmyn 'pur vous declarer le busoing que nous en (monoye) avons, li quel en ce veuillez croire et faire a notre priere ce qu'il vous requerera de notre part en celle partie;' Ord. ii. 73: in 1421 seven persons were summoned before the council in default of payment of sums which they had promised to lend the king; ib. ii. 280: and in or about 1442 Henry VI wrote to the abbot of S. Edmund's, asking that ye so tendryng thees our necessitees wol lene us . . . such a notable summe of mony to be paied in hande as our servant bearer of thees shall desire of you.' In another letter he asks for a loan of 100 marks to be secured by Exchequer tallies; Ellis, Orig. Lett. 3rd series, i. 76–81. Sets of instructions to the same effect will be found in the Ordinances, v. 187; cf. pp. 201, 414; vi. 46–49; 236 sq.; 322 sq. But these cases, most severely interpreted, involve only the sort of loans that were sanctioned by parliament.

vation brought against Edward IV were true, or to suspect that, among the many financial expedients adopted during the Lancastrian troubles, he might have found something like a precedent. Of this however there is no sufficient example forthcoming, and, although a treasurer like the earl of Wiltshire may not unreasonably be supposed to have now and then extorted money by violence, the popularity of Henry VI and Margaret was never so great as to enable them to become successful beggars. Such evidence as exists shows us Edward IV canvassing by word of mouth or by letter for direct gifts of money from his subjects[1]. Henry III had thus begged for new year's gifts. Edward IV requested and extorted 'freewill offerings' from every one who could not say no to the pleadings of such a king. He had a wonderful memory too, and knew the name and the particular property of every man in the country who was worth taxing in this way. He had no excuse for such meanness; for the estates had shown themselves liberal, he was rich in forfeitures, and an act of resumption, passed whenever the parliament met, was enough to adjust the balance between income and necessary expenditure. He grew richer still by private enterprise. Against Richard III the case is equally strong, for although his exigencies were greater he acted, in collecting benevolences, in the teeth of a law which had been passed in his own parliament; and, although in this respect he had probably to bear much of the odium which ought to have fallen upon Edward, he had

Novelty of the expedient.

Edward's financial ability.

Richard's benevolences.

[1] See above, p. 213. In the York Records (Davies, p. 130) of 1482 the name of Benevolence is applied to the contingent of armed men furnished for the Scottish expedition: 'the benivelence graunted to the kynges highnes in the last viage his highnes purposed in his most roiall person to go ayanest his auncient enemyes the Scottes, that is to say a capitan and six score archers;' see also p. 279 note 3 below. The common form in which a benevolence was demanded from the country in general, may be seen in the letters patent of Henry VII, July 7, 1491; Rymer, xii. 446, 447. The commissioners were directed to communicate 'cum talibus nostrorum subditorum ... prout vobis melius videbitur, eis nostrum propositum et mentem plenariam de et in praemissis et eorum singulis intimantes, eos movendo exhortando et requirendo ut nobis in hoc tam magno arduoque negotio, non solum nostrum statum verum etiam et eorum salutem concernente, juxta eorum facultates assistant et opem in personis et aliis mediis et modis, prout vobis et eis melius visum fuerit, conferant.' The promises so obtained were, by the Act 11 Hen. VII. c. 10, enforced by imprisonment; Statutes, ii. 576.

A sign of absolute power.

been the strongest man in Edward's councils. That the benevolences were any great or widely felt hardship is improbable; Edward could not have maintained his popularity if they had been. But they were unconstitutional; they were adopted with the view of enabling the sovereign to rule without that reference to parliamentary supply and audit which had become the safeguard of national liberty. A king with a life revenue and an unchecked power of exacting money from the rich is substantially an absolute sovereign: the nation, whether poor and exhausted as in the earlier days, or devoting itself to trade instead of politics, as in the last years of the dynasty, parts too readily with its birthright and awakes too late to its loss.

Maintenance of armed forces.

The loss of records and the anarchy of the last years of the reign of Henry VI leave us in great doubt as to the means by which forces were raised to maintain order in the king's name throughout England, although we know that the king's name was freely used by both sides in the actual conflict. Royal letters, however analogous to, if not identical with, the commissions of array which received their final form in 1404, were no doubt the most convenient expedient for reinforcing the royal army[1]; whilst the rebel force, which the duke of York and the Nevilles until they got the upper hand were able to bring into the field, was largely composed of their own tenants and the inhabitants of disaffected districts[2] serving for pay, and probably organised in much the same way as they would have been if marshalled under royal authority. This regularity was, it may be supposed, still further exemplified when, in the later stages of the struggle, the northern counties were pitted against the southern, and the York party, as well as queen Margaret, claimed to be acting in the king's name. In a time of civil war

[1] See examples in Rymer, xii: a writ to collect the posse comitatus against rebels, in 1457, p. 401; commission to the earl of Pembroke to take levies in 1460, p. 445, &c.

[2] The letter of the duke of York to the men of Shrewsbury in 1452 will serve as an illustration: 'I . . . am fully concluded to proceed in all haste against him with the help of my kindred and friends . . . praying and exhorting you to fortify, enforce, and assist me, and to come to me with all diligence wheresoever I shall be or draw, with as many goodly and likely men as ye may make to execute the entent aforesaid;' White Rose, pp. xli, xlii.

however it is useless to look for constitutional precedent; the prevalence of disorder is only adduced as furnishing a clue to the origin of abuses which emerge when the occasion or excuse for them is over. The commissions of array by which Edward IV and Richard III collected forces for the war with Scotland do not form a prominent article in the indictment against them; for the country had become used to fighting, and the obligation to supply men and money for their maintenance in case of invasion was a common-law obligation however jealously watched and however grudgingly fulfilled[1]. These armies were not raised by authority of the parliament, nor paid by the government for the services performed beyond the limits of their native counties, nor were they required against sudden invasion[2]. They were not a part of the host of archers

Commissions of array under Edward IV and Richard III.

[1] The law as settled by 4 Hen. IV. c. 13 in 1402, and exemplified in Commissions of Array from 1404 onward was that except in case of invasion none shall be constrained to go out of their own counties; and that men chosen to go on the king's service out of England shall be at the king's wages from the day they leave their own counties. As the Welsh and Scottish wars of Henry IV were defensive against invasion, commissions of array in which the counties must have borne the expense of the force furnished were frequently issued; Rymer, viii. 123, 273, 374, &c.; and the clergy were arrayed under the same circumstances; ib. 123; ix. 253, 601, &c. The armies collected by Henry V for his war in France consisted partly of a feudal levy, i. e. of a certain force furnished by those who had received estates from Edward III with an obligation to serve at Calais, &c. (Rymer, viii. 456, 466); but chiefly of (1) lords and leaders of forces raised by themselves, who served the king by indenture; and (2) of volunteers raised by the king's officers at his wages, 'omnes qui vadia nostra... percipere voluerint'; ib. ix. 370. In 1443 Henry VI issued letters of privy seal for an aid of men, victuals, and ships; Ord. v. 265. In 1464 by letters close Edward IV orders the sheriffs to proclaim that every man from sixteen to sixty be well and defensibly arrayed, and that he so arrayed be ready to attend on his highness upon a day's warning in resistance of his enemies and rebels and the defence of this his realm; Rymer, xi. 524; cf. 624, 652, 655, 677. This was peremptory but not illegal.

[2] In the Commission for Array against the Scots in 1480 the Scots are regarded as invaders; Rymer, xii. 117. But the abuse of the plea is clear from the language of the York Records, in which the force furnished is termed a benevolence: the letters under which it was levied were from the duke of Gloucester (p. 107), the number of soldiers was discussed in the city council and the captain appointed there (p. 112); it was agreed by the king's high commandment by his gracious letters that the city and liberties should furnish a captain and 120 archers, 40 of them to be furnished by the Ainsty; and that the constables in every parish should collect the money affered (assessed) in each parish, to be delivered to the captain, who was bound to return any overplus unexpended; pp. 115, 116. See also Plumpton Papers, pp. 40-42. The instructions given by Richard III to the Commissioners of Array in 1484 (Letters, i. 85) fully bear out this.

Abuse of commissions of array.

which the parliament of 1453 granted 'to be maintained by those on whom the burden should fall,' nor of the like force voted in 1472, for the payment of which the lords and commons voted a separate tenth. They were levied by privy seal letters from the king, and were paid by the districts which supplied them irrespective of the nature of their service. The obligation was based no doubt on the ancient law and statute of Winchester; the abuse had, no doubt, abundant precedent during the reign of Edward III, but it was an abuse notwithstanding, and must be viewed as part of a general policy of irresponsible government[1].

Judicial iniquities of the period.

Under such a government, whether in times of civil war or during the periods of peace that are possible in a reign of terror, judicial iniquities are quite compatible with the maintenance of the forms of law. During the troubled days of Henry VI the courts sat with regularity and the judges elaborated their decisions, when it depended altogether on the local influence of the contending parties whether the decisions should he enforced at all. In criminal trials the most infamous tyrannies may coexist with the most perfect formality, and after a regular trial and legal condemnation the guilty and the innocent alike, at least among the minor actors, may be avenged but cannot be rehabilitated. The York kings have left an evil reputation for judicial cruelties; the charge is true, although it must be shared with the men who lent themselves to such base transactions and with the age which was sufficiently demoralised to tolerate them. The wanton bloodshed of the civil war, the earlier political executions, the long series of blood-feuds dating from the beginning of the fourteenth century, the generally inhuman savageness of the criminal judicature, all tended the same way. Edward IV and Richard III are not condemned because they shared the character of their times, but because under their influence that character, already sanguinary, took new forms of vindictive and aggressive energy. The cruel executions of persons taken in armed resistance, of which men like Tiptoft and

Gross cruelties.

[1] Grose, Military Antiquities, i. 71, has printed a paper presented by Sir Robert Cotton to the king, MS. Cotton Julius F. 6, on the provision of forces at the charge of the counties. The question is one of some prospective importance; Hallam, Const. History, ii. 133.

Montague bear the immediate responsibility, may be extenuated as exceptional, as the necessary results of civil strife, or as the ordinary action of wild martial law; yet Tiptoft, the cultivated disciple of the Renaissance, has an evil pre-eminence as the man who impaled the dead bodies of his victims, and thus exceeded even the recognised legal barbarities; and Montague went beyond precedent in murdering his prisoners. The practice of torture for the purpose of obtaining evidence from unwilling witnesses is another mark of the time. Sir John Fortescue alleges the use of torture as a proof of the inferiority of French to English law[1]; meaning thereby, as it is argued, not that the practice was unknown altogether, but that it was employed only under the prerogative authority of the crown, and not under the common law. It is under Edward IV however that we find the first recorded instances in medieval history of its use in England. In 1468 a man named Cornelius, who carried letters of Queen Margaret, was burned in the feet[2] to make him betray his accomplices; John Hawkins, one of the persons whom he mentioned, was racked, and accused Sir Thomas Cook, an alderman of London. Cook was tried by jury before a special commission of judges, one of whom, Sir John Markham, directed the jury to find him guilty of misprision, not of treason. The jury complied and Markham was deprived of his judgeship[3]. The tradition of the Tower, that the rack which bore the name of the duke of Exeter's daughter was introduced by John

Practice of torture.

Instances of its employment.

[1] Fortescue, de Laudibus, c. 22. That torture was not altogether unknown in England is certain. Mr. Pike, History of Crime, i. 427, adduces from the Pipe Roll, 34 Hen. II, the case of a man who was fined 'quia cepit quandam mulierem et eam tormentavit sine licentia regis;'—Edward II gave leave for the application of 'quaestiones' in the trial of the Templars; Wilk. Conc. ii. 314; Foedera, ii. 118, 119. In the 22 Edw. III a commission was issued to inquire into the practice of torturing men by gaolers to compel them to become approvers; Pike, Hist. Cr. i. 481. Jardine, in his 'Reading on Torture,' concludes that the practice was allowed by royal licence, and was known to the prerogative although not to the common law. His argument that the silence of the Records proves the commonness of the usage is not conclusive.

[2] W. Worcester, p. 789.

[3] Foss, Biogr. Jur. p. 435; Stow, p. 420, says that Hawkins was racked on the brake called the duke of Exeter's daughter. The factitious speech of the duke of Buckingham in 1483 (above, p. 224) implies that Cook himself was tortured.

The rack in the Tower.

Holland, duke of Exeter and constable of the Tower under Henry VI[1], may not be entirely unfounded: the Hollands were a cruel race, and the duke of Exeter, who was one of the bitter enemies of the Beauforts, was an unscrupulous man who may have tortured his prisoners. Here however is the first of a chain of horrors that run on for two centuries. Another abuse which had the result of condemning its agents to perpetual infamy was the extension of the jurisdiction of the High Constable of England to cases of high treason, thus depriving the accused of the benefit of trial by jury and placing their acquittal or condemnation in the hands of a political official. When Edward IV, early in his reign, gave the office of constable to Tiptoft he invested him with unparalleled powers; he was to take cognisance of and to proceed in all cases of high treason by whomsoever they might be initiated; to hear, examine, and conclude them, 'even summarily and plainly, without noise and show of judgment, on simple inspection of fact'; he was to act as king's vicegerent, without appeal and with power to inflict punishment, fine, and other lawful coercion, notwithstanding any statutes, acts, ordinances, or restrictions made to the contrary[2]. Similar powers were conferred on the earl Rivers in

Jurisdiction of the constable.

Powers confided to him.

[1] Stow, p. 420; Coke, 3 Inst. p. 34, represents the introduction of the rack as a part of a scheme which John Holland, duke of Exeter, and the unfortunate duke of Suffolk contrived for introducing the civil law into England. Exeter and Suffolk however were personal enemies and rivals, Exeter being a close ally of duke Humfrey.

[2] Edward, in the patent of Aug. 24, 1467, by which he appointed lord Rivers, rehearses that of Feb. 7, 1462, by which Tiptoft was appointed, and in which he vests in him all powers which the constable enjoyed in and since the reign of William the Conqueror: 'ad cognoscendum et procedendum in omnibus et singulis causis et negotiis de et super crimine laesae Majestatis seu ipsius occasione, caeterisque causis quibuscunque, per praefatum comitem ut Constabularium Angliae, seu coram eo, ex officio, seu ad instantiam partis qualitercunque motis, movendis, seu pendentibus . . . causasque et negotia praedicta, cum omnibus et singulis suis emergentibus incidentibus et connexis, audiendum, examinandum et fine debito terminandum, etiam summarie et de plano sine strepitu et figura judicii, sola facti veritate inspecta, ac etiam manu regia si oportunum visum foret eidem Johanni, consanguineo nostro, vices nostras, appellatione remota, ex mero motu et certa scientia nostra praedicta, similiter commiserimus plenariam potestatem, cum cujuslibet poenae, mulctae et alterius cohertionis legitimae, executionisque rerum quas in ea parte decerneret, facultate, &c. . . . Statutis, ordinationibus, actibus et restrictionibus in contrarium editis,

1467, and on his death Tiptoft was again invested with them. It was by this supreme and irresponsible judicature that so many of the Lancastrians were doomed. The earl of Oxford and his son and four others were tried by the law of Padua[1], of which Tiptoft was a graduate, and beheaded in 1462. Twelve of the prisoners taken at Hexham were condemned and executed in the same summary fashion at York[2]. Sir Ralph Grey, the defender of Alnwick, was the same year tried by Tiptoft and beheaded in the king's presence[3]. Lord Rivers, from whom better things might have been hoped, disposed of two of the defenders of Harlech by the same process[4]. It was the application of martial law to ordinary cases of high treason. The military executions on both sides, the massacre of prisoners, the illegal reprisals of Warwick and Clarence in 1469 and 1470, were alike unjustifiable, but in the commission and jurisdiction of these two constables England saw a new and unconstitutional tribunal avowedly erected in contempt of statute and usage. But even where the forms of the common law were followed, the crushing policy of the government made itself felt. The doctrine of constructive treason[5] was terribly exemplified in the cases of Burdett, Stacy, and Walker. Yet these men were tried with all the ceremonies of law, and by special commissions consisting of the judges and chief men of the land[6]. Clarence, when he wished to punish the suspected poisoner of his wife, had the prisoner tried before an unimpeachable tribunal, yet the act was recognised as violent and illegal[7]. But the trial and execution of Clarence himself and the conduct of Edward in that trial were not more repugnant to English constitutional beliefs than was the treatment of the men who had fallen victims to their

Instances of its exercise.

Constructive treasons.

Legal severities.

caeterisque contrariis non obstantibus quibuscunque.' Rymer, xii. 581, 654. Well may Coke say that this is directly against the common law; 4 Inst. p. 127.

[1] 'By lawe Padowe'; Warkworth, p. 5.

[2] W. Worc. p. 782.

[3] Ib. p. 783; Chron. White Rose, p. lxxxix.

[4] W. Worc. p. 791.

[5] Blackstone, Comm. iv. 79; Hale, Placita Coronae, i. 115; Reeves, Hist. Engl. Law, iv. 109; Stow, Chr. p. 430.

[6] Baga de Secretis, 3rd rep. Dep. Keeper, App. ii. p. 213. Stacy is said to have been tortured and made to betray Burdett; Cont. Croyl. p. 561; but of course before the trial.

[7] Baga de Secretis, p. 214; Rot. Parl. vi. 173.

common and rival ambitions. The execution of lord Welles and Sir Thomas Dymock in 1470 was an extra-judicial murder[1]. That of Buckingham in 1483 was strictly legal. Henry IV in the beheading of Scrope and Mowbray, and Henry V in the execution of Cambridge, Scrope, and Grey, had set a fruitful example; but if they sowed the wind their posterity reaped the whirlwind.

No sound peace under the house of York.

Notwithstanding the energy which marked the earlier years of Edward's reign, and the sincere endeavour, with which in any view of his character he must be credited, to restore domestic peace and enforce the law, the country enjoyed under him scarcely more security than it had under his predecessor. The statutes of liveries and maintenance, of labourers and artificers, the enactments against rioters and breakers of truce, were very insufficiently enforced; the abuses which had sprung up in the more disturbed districts of the north were not put down by mere legislation, nor did they disappear even under the strong and crushing policy of repression; more perhaps was done by the personal influence of Richard in Yorkshire than by any administrative reforms; yet the evil remained. The surviving baronage had not learned wisdom from the extinction of its lost members, and the revived feudalism, typified by the practices of livery and maintenance, was, in all districts where the Yorkist party was supreme, allowed its full play. Thus notwithstanding Edward's attempts to maintain the law and to crush the nobles, scarcely a month after his death the opposing factions of the court had rallied to themselves, under new designations but in real identity, the very same elements, forces and rival influences that had been arrayed against each other in the earlier struggle of the Roses. The private warfare of the great houses continues throughout with scarcely abated vigour. The very policy of Edward with regard to those houses was novel and hazardous; for he departed from the immemorial practice of his predecessors in order to crush the offender of the moment. Since the accession of the house of Plantagenet the kings had avoided enforcing perpetual forfeitures, except in extreme cases. The Mortimers, the

Edward's policy with regard to the baronage.

Measures of extirpation.

[1] Above, p. 207.

Despensers, the Percies, the Montacutes, had all, after long or short terms of eclipse, been restored to their estates and dignities. Edward, whose own family owed its existence to this rule, was the first king who ostentatiously disregarded it. By bestowing the Percy earldom on John Neville, that of Pembroke on William Herbert, and that of Devon on Humfrey Stafford of Southwick, he laid down a principle of extermination against political foes which was foreign to English practice, and arrayed against himself the strongest and best elements of feudal life, the attachment of the local populations to their ancient lords.

Summary of the position of the house of York.

That these particular features of the policy of the York kings warrant us in believing that they had a definite design of assuming absolute power, it would be hazardous to affirm. They more probably imply merely that there was no price which they were not prepared to pay for power, and that they were restrained by no political principles or moral scruples from increasing their hold upon it. Edward IV in more than one point resembled Edward III, and cared more for the substance of power than for the open and ostentatious pretence of absolutism which had cost Richard II his throne and life. Of Richard III we know little more than that he was both abler and more unscrupulous than his brother: for both it may be pleaded that we have to read their history through a somewhat distorted medium. It may seem but a halting conclusion to assert that their attitude towards the constitution was opposed to that of the Lancaster kings rather as a contrary than as a contradictory. The Lancaster dynasty was not strong enough to maintain and develop the constitution; the York dynasty was strong enough to dispense with it but not to destroy it. The former acted on the hereditary traditions of the baronage, the latter on the hereditary traditions of the crown. The former conserved, without being able to reinvigorate it, all that survived of the early ennobling idea according to which the national life had thus far advanced. The latter anticipated, without definitely formulating it, much of the policy which was to mark the coming era, to grow stronger, and then to decay and vanish before the renewed force of

Contrast of York and Lancaster.

national life; a force which had recovered strength during the compulsory rest and peace enjoyed under the Tudors, and awoke under the Stewarts to a consciousness of its identity with the earlier force which had guided the earlier development. So, to speak loosely and generally, the Lancastrian rule was a direct continuity, and the Yorkist rule was a break in the continuity, of constitutional development; both alike were stages in the discipline of national life. Neither of the two tried its experiment in good days. The better element had to work in times of decay and exhaustion; the worse element had the advantage of the new dayspring; for the revival of life which is the great mark of the Tudor period had begun under Edward IV. There was a disparity in both periods between national health and constitutional growth.

General conclusion. Thus then the acquittal of the house of Lancaster does not imply the condemnation of the house of York; nor do those circumstances which might mitigate our condemnation of the latter, at all affect our estimate of the general character of the former. In tracing the history of both, the personal qualifications of the rulers form a conspicuous element; and it might be an interesting question for imaginative historians to determine what would have been the result if Henry VI and Edward IV had changed places; if it had fallen to the strong unscrupulous masculine Yorkist to work the machinery of a waning constitutional life, and to the weak incompetent Lancastrian to maintain the doctrine, or to anticipate the first impulses, of personal absolutism. We need trouble ourselves with no such problem: the constitution had in its growth outrun the capacity of the nation; the nation needed rest and renewal, discipline and reformation, before it could enter into the enjoyment of its birthright. The present days were evil; we cannot look without pity and sorrow on that generation of our fathers whose virtues were exemplified in Henry of Lancaster and its strength in Edward of York.

CHAPTER XIX.

THE CLERGY, THE KING, AND THE POPE.

697. Problem of Church and State.—698. Plan of the chapter.—699. The clerical estate or spiritualty.—700. Relations between the Pope and the Crown.—701. Appointment of Bishops.—702. The pall.—703. Legations.—704. Papal interference in election of bishops.—705. Elections in the thirteenth century.—706. The pope's claim to confer the temporalities.—707. Papal provisions.—708. Legislation on provisions.—709. The compromise on elections.—710. Elections to abbacies.—711. The ecclesiastical assemblies.—712. Ecclesiastical Legislation; for the clergy by the clergy.—713. By the clergy for the laity.—714. By parliament for the clergy.—715. Statute of provisors.—716. Statute of praemunire.—717. Legislation in parliament for the national church.—718. Ecclesiastical Taxation; by the pope.—719. Taxation by convocation.—720. Attempt in parliament to tax the clergy.—721. Of the clergy to tax the laity.—722. Ecclesiastical Judicature; of the king's courts over the clergy. —723. Of the court Christian; in temporal matters.—724. In disciplinary cases.—725. Over ecclesiastics.—726. Appeals to Rome. —727. Legislation against heresy.—728. Social importance of the clergy.—729. Intellectual and moral influence of the clergy.

Importance of the relations of the Church to the State.

697. The position of the clerical estate, and the importance of ecclesiastical influence in the development of the Constitution, have in the foregoing chapters presented themselves so prominently, that a reader who approaches medieval history from an exclusively modern starting-point may well suppose that these subjects have already received more than a due share of attention. But there still remain many points of ecclesiastical interest, which have a close bearing on national growth; and without some comprehension of these it is vain to attempt to understand the transitional period which we have now reached, or to estimate the true value of the influences which

the coming age of change was to contribute to the world's history. And some of these points require rather minute treatment.

Intrinsic difficulties of the subject.

The careful study of history suggests many problems for which it supplies no solution. None of these is more easy to state, or more difficult to handle, than the great question of the proper relation between Church and State. It may be taken for granted that, between the extreme claims made by the advocates of the two, there can never be even an approximate reconciliation. The claims of both are very deeply rooted, and the roots of both lie in the best parts of human nature; neither can do violence to, or claim complete supremacy over, the other, without crushing something which is precious. Nor will any universal formula be possible so long as different nations and churches are in different stages of development, even if for the highest forms of Church and State such a formal concordat be practicable. A perfect solution of the problem involves the old question of the identity between the good man and the good citizen as well as the modern ideal of a free church within a free state. Religion, morality, and law, overlap one another in almost every region of human action; they approach their common subject-matter from different points and legislate for it with different sanctions. The idea of perfect harmony between them seems to imply an amount of subordination which is scarcely compatible with freedom; the idea of complete disjunction implies either the certainty of conflict on some if not all parts of the common field of work, or the abdication, on the one part or on the other, of some duty which according to its own ideal it is bound to fulfil. The church, for instance, cannot engross the work of education without some danger to liberty; the state cannot engross it without some danger to religion; the work of the church without liberty loses half its value; the state without religion does only half its work. And this is only an illustration of what is true throughout. The individual conscience, the spiritual aspiration, the moral system, the legal enactment, will never, in a world of mixed character, work consistently or harmoniously in all points.

Perfect adjustment of relations between Church and State, not to be realised.

For the historian, who is content to view men as they are and appear to be, not as they ought to be or are capable of becoming, it is no dereliction of duty if he declines to lay down any definition of the ideal relations between Church and State. He may honestly and perhaps wisely confess that he regards the indeterminateness and the indeterminability of those relations as one of the points in which religion teaches him to see a trial of his faith incident to a state of probation. The practical statesman too may content himself with assuming the existence of an ideal towards which he may approximate, without the hope of realising it; trying to deal equitably, but conscious all the time that theoretical considerations will not solve the practical problem. Even the philosopher may admit that there are departments of life and action in which the working of two different laws may be traced, and yet any exact harmonising of their respective courses must be left for a distant future and altered conditions of existence.

Relations with foreign churches add another element of difficulty.

Nor does our perplexity end here. Even if it were possible that in a single state, of homogeneous population and a fair level of property and education, the relations of religion, morality and law could be adjusted, so that a perfectly national church could be organised and a system of cooperation work smoothly and harmoniously, the fact remains that religion and morality are not matters of nationality. The Christian religion is a historical and Catholic religion; and a perfect adjustment of relations with foreign churches would seem to be a necessary adjunct to the perfect constitution of the single communion at home. In the middle ages of European history, the influence of the Roman church was directed to some such end. The claim of supremacy made for the see of Rome, a claim which its modern advocates urge as vehemently as if it were part of the Christian Creed, was a practical assertion that such an adjustment was possible. But whether it be possible or no in a changed state of society, the sober judgment of history determines that, as the world is at present moved and governed, perfect ecclesiastical unity is, like a perfect adjustment between Church and State, an ideal to be aimed at rather than to be hoped for.

Practical limitation of the subject as treated in this chapter.

698. The historian who has arrived at such a conviction cannot fairly be expected to indulge in much theorising; and he ought not to be tempted to exalt his own generalisations into the rank of laws. The scope of the present work does not admit of any disquisition upon the whole of this great subject; nor need it be attempted. This being granted, our investigation becomes limited to the practical points in which during the middle ages the national church of England, by its dealings with the crown and parliament, or by its dealings with the papacy, or by its own proper work unaffected by those influences, connected itself with the growth of national life, character, and institutions. And the arrangement of the present chapter is accordingly a simple arrangement for convenience. There are four or perhaps five regions of constitutional life in which the work of the National Church comes into contact with the work of the State, or with that of the Roman See, or with both: these are the departments of constitutional machinery or administration, of social relations, morality, spiritual liberty, and possibly also of political action. Within the first of these departments come all questions of organisation, legislation, taxation and judicature, with the subordinate points of property and patronage. The second, third and fourth will call for a brief and more speculative examination, as they affect national character and opinion, especially in relation to the period of transition and the approaching Reformation. The last department, that of political action, may be considered to have been treated in the preceding pages, not indeed completely, but in proportion to the general scale of our discussion.

The English spiritualty in the middle ages.

699. An attempt has been made in preceding chapters of this book to illustrate, as they have come into the foreground, the most important points of our early Church History. These points it is unnecessary to recapitulate; it will be sufficient to assume that, in approaching the history of the medieval church, we may regard the spiritualty of England, the clergy or clerical estate, as a body completely organised, with a minutely constituted and regulated hierarchy, possessing the right of legislating for itself and taxing itself, having its recognised assemblies, judi-

cature and executive, and, although not as a legal corporation holding common property, yet composed of a great number of persons each of whom possesses corporate property by a title which is either conferred by ecclesiastical authority, or is not to be acquired without ecclesiastical assent. Such an organisation entitles the clergy to the name of a 'communitas,' although it does not complete the legal idea of a corporation proper. The spiritualty is by itself an estate of the realm; its leading members, the bishops and certain abbots, are likewise members of the estate of baronage; the inferior clergy, if they possess lay property or temporal endowments, are likewise members of the estate of the commons. The property which is held by individuals as officers and ministers of the spiritualty is either temporal property, that is, lands held by ordinary legal services, or spiritual property, that is, tithes and oblations. As an estate of the realm the spiritualty recognises the headship of the king, as a member of the Church Catholic it recognises, according to the medieval idea, the headship of the pope. Its own chief ministers, the bishops under their two metropolitans and under the primacy of the church of Canterbury, stand in an immediate relation to both these powers, and the inferior clergy have through the bishops a mediate relation, while as subjects and as Catholic Christians they have also an immediate relation, to both king and pope. They recognise the king as supreme in matters temporal, and the pope as supreme in matters spiritual; but there are questions as to the exact limits between the spiritual and the temporal, and most important questions touching the precise relations between the crown and the papacy. On medieval theory the king is a spiritual son of the pope; and the pope may be the king's superior in things spiritual only, or in things temporal and spiritual alike.

Its corporate character.

An estate of the realm.

Its property.

Headship in things temporal and spiritual.

700. The temporal superiority of the papacy may be held to depend upon two principles: the first is embodied in the general proposition asserted by Gregory VII and his successors that the pope is supreme over temporal sovereigns: the spiritual power is by its very nature superior to the temporal, and of that spiritual power the pope is on earth the supreme depositary. This

Relations between the crown and the papacy.

proposition may be accepted or denied, but it implies a rule equally applicable to all kingdoms. The second principle involves the claim to special superiority over a particular kingdom, such as was at different times made by the popes in reference to England, Scotland, Ireland, Naples, and the empire itself, and turns upon the special circumstances of the countries so claimed. These two principles are in English history of unequal importance: the first, resting upon a dogmatic foundation, has, so far as it is recognised at all, a perpetual and semi-religious force; the latter, resting upon legal assumptions and historical acts, has more momentary prominence, but less real significance. The claim of the pope to receive homage from William the Conqueror, on whatever it was based, was rejected by the king, and both he and William Rufus maintained their right to determine which of the two contending popes was entitled to the obedience of the English church[1]. Henry II, when he received Ireland as a gift from Adrian IV, never intended to admit that the papal power over all islands, inferred from the Donation of Constantine, could be understood so as to bring England under the direct authority of Rome; nor when, after Becket's murder, he declared his adhesion to the pope, did he contemplate more than a spiritual or religious relation[2]. John's surrender and subsequent

Questions of the special dependence of the kingdom on the pope.

[1] On the answer of the Conqueror to Gregory's demand of fealty see vol. i. p. 285; 'fidelitatem facere nolui nec volo, quia nec ego promisi nec antecessores meos antecessoribus tuis id fecisse comperio.'

Henry I writes to Paschal II; 'beneficium quod ab antecessoribus meis beatus Petrus habuit, vobis mitto; eosque honores et eam obedientiam quam tempore patris mei antecessores vestri in regno Angliae habuerunt tempore meo ut habeatis volo, eo videlicet tenore ut dignitates usus et consuetudines quas pater meus tempore antecessorum vestrorum in regno Angliae habuit, ego tempore vestro in eodem regno meo integre obtineam. Notumque habeat Sanctitas vestra quod me vivente, Deo auxiliante, dignitates et usus regni Angliae non minuentur. Et si ego quod absit in tanta me dejectione ponerem, optimates mei, immo totius Angliae populus, id nullo modo pateretur. Habita igitur, carissime pater, utiliori deliberatione, ita se erga nos moderetur benignitas vestra, ne, quod invitus faciam, a vestra me cogatis recedere obedientia;' Foed. i. 8; Bromton, c. 999; Foxe, Acts &c., ii. 163.

[2] The curious expression found in a letter addressed in Henry's name to Alexander III, among the letters of Peter of Blois, has been understood to imply that the king on the occasion of his absolution placed the kingdom in that feudal relation which was afterwards created by John's submission: 'Vestrae jurisdictionis est regnum Angliae et quantum ad feudatarii juris obligationem vobis duntaxat obnoxius teneor et astringor;' Opp. ed. Busaeus,

homage first created the shadow of a feudal relation, which was respected by Henry III, but repudiated by the parliaments of Edward I and Edward III[1], and passed away leaving scarcely a trace under the later kings. The great assumption of universal supremacy, with the resistance which it provoked, and the evasions at which it connived, gives surpassing interest to another side of medieval history. This claim however in its direct form, that is, in the region of secular jurisdiction, the assertion that the pope is supreme, so that he can depose the king or release the subject from his oath and duty of allegiance, does not enter into this portion of our subject. The discussions which took place on the great struggle between John XXII and Lewis of Bavaria had their bearings on later history, but only affect England, in common with the Avignon papacy and the great schism, as tending to shake all belief in the dogmatic assumptions of Rome. The parliament of 1399 declared that the crown and realm of England had been in all time past so free that neither pope nor any other outside the realm had a right to meddle therewith[2].

The general claims of spiritual supremacy for the popedom.

The claim of spiritual supremacy, within the region of spiritual jurisdiction and property, will meet us at every turn, but the history of its origin and growth belongs to an earlier stage of ecclesiastical history.

Theory of uniting temporal and spiritual sovereignty.

The idea of placing in one and the same hand the direct control of all causes temporal and spiritual was not unknown in the middle ages. The pope's spiritual supremacy being granted, complete harmony might be attained not only by making the pope supreme in matters temporal, but by delegating to the king supremacy in matters spiritual. Before the struggle about investiture arose, Sylvester II had empowered

p. 245. It is possible that the papal legates were instructed to obtain such a concession from Henry, as in the Life of Alexander the king is said to swear 'quod a domino Alexandro papa et ejus catholicis successoribus recipiemus et tenebimus regnum Angliae.' But no such concession is mentioned in any contemporary account of the purgation, nor could it have been unknown to English historians if it had really taken place. The letter of Peter has of course no claim to be authoritative and may be only a scholastic exercise. The matter is however confessedly obscure. See Robertson, Life of Becket, p. 303, and the authorities there quoted.

[1] Vol. i. p. 522; vol. ii. pp. 152, 415. [2] Vol. ii. pp. 504, 505.

Royal legations.

the newly-made king Stephen of Hungary to act as the papal representative in regulating the churches of his kingdom[1]; and after that great controversy had begun, Roger Wiscard, as duke of Sicily, received from Urban II[2] a grant of hereditary ecclesiastical jurisdiction, which, under the name of the 'Sicilian monarchy,' became, in the hands of his successors, a unique feature of the constitution of the kingdom. It is not improbable that early in the Becket controversy such a solution of the difficulties under which Alexander III was labouring might have been attempted in England: certainly the contemporary chroniclers believed that Henry II, when he was demanding the legatine office for Roger of York, received from the pope an offer of the legation for himself[3]. But there were not wanting men who would try to persuade him that even without any such commission he was supreme in spiritual as well as in temporal matters. Reginald Fitz Urse, when he was disputing with Becket just before the murder, asked him from whom he had the archbishopric? Thomas replied, 'The spirituals I have from God and my lord the pope, the temporals and possessions from my lord the king.' 'Do you not,' asked Reginald, 'acknowledge that you hold the whole from the king?' 'No,' was the prelate's answer; 'we have to render to the king the things that are the king's, and to God the things that are God's[4].' The words of the archbishop embody the commonly received idea; the words of Reginald, although they do not represent the theory of Henry II, contain the germ of the doctrine which was formulated under Henry VIII[5].

Story of the legation offered to Henry II.

Supremacy in spirituals claimed for him.

[1] 'Ecclesias Dei, una cum populis *nostra vice* ei ordinandas relinquimus.' See the Bull dated March 27, 1000; in Cocquelines, Bullar. i. 399; Gieseler, ii. 463.

[2] July 5, 1098; on the great question of the 'Sicilian Monarchy' see Giannone, Hist. Naples, l. x. c. 8; Mosheim, Church Hist. ii. p. 5; Gieseler, vol. iii. p. 33. The words are 'quae per legatum acturi sumus per vestram industriam *legati vice* exhiberi volumus, quando ad vos ex latere nostro miserimus.'

[3] Hoveden, i. 223: 'ad petitionem clericorum regis concessit dominus papa ut rex ipse legatus esset totius Angliae.' Cf. Gervase, c. 1388. As a matter of fact it was the legation of the archbishop of York that was in question; see Robertson, Becket, pp. 105, 106.

[4] W. Fitz Stephen, S. T. C. i. 296.

[5] On the meaning of the word spiritual especially in connexion with the

701. Whatever was the precise nature of the papal supremacy, the highest dignity in the hierarchy of the national church was understood to belong to the church of Canterbury, of which the archbishop was the head and minister; he was 'alterius orbis papa;' he was likewise, and in consequence, the first constitutional adviser of the crown. The archbishop of York and the bishops shared, in a somewhat lower degree, both his spiritual and his temporal authority; like him they had large estates which they held of the king, seats in the national council, preeminence in the national synod, and places in the general councils of the church. The right of appointing the bishops and of regulating their powers was thus one of the first points upon which the national church, the crown, and the papacy were likely to come in collision.

Dignity of archbishops and bishops.

Right of appointment to sees.

The cooperation of clergy and laity in the election of bishops before the Conquest has been already illustrated [1]. The struggle between Henry I and Anselm on the question of investiture terminated in a compromise which placed the election in the hands of the chapters of the cathedrals, the consecration in that of the metropolitan and comprovincial bishops, and the bestowal of temporal estates and authority in the hands of the king [2]. Stephen at his accession confirmed to the churches the right of canonical election [3]; Henry II and Richard observed the form; and John, shortly before he granted the great Charter, issued as a bribe to the bishops a shorter charter confirming

Canonical right confirmed by Stephen and John.

oath taken by the bishops to the crown see an essay by Mr. J. W. Lea, published in 1875; 'The bishops' oath of homage.' Under *spiritualia* are really included three distinct things, which may be described as (1) spiritualia characteris vel ordinis—the powers bestowed at consecration; (2) spiritualia ministerii vel jurisdictionis, the powers which a bishop receives at his confirmation and in virtue of which he is supposed to act as the servant or representative of his church, which guards these spiritualities during the vacancy; (3) spiritualia beneficii, the ecclesiastical revenue arising from other sources than land; which 'spiritualia' he acquires together with the temporalities on doing homage. These last are the only spiritualia which he holds of the crown, the first and second never being in the royal hands to bestow. And these are often both in legal and common language included under the term temporalities.

[1] Vol. i. pp. 134, 135.

[2] Flor. Wig. A.D. 1107; Eadmer, lib. iv. p. 91; see above, vol. i. pp. 316, 317.

[3] Select Charters, p. 115; Statutes, i. 3; above, vol. i. p. 321.

the right of free election, subject to the royal licence and approval, neither of which was to be withheld without just cause[1]. This charter of John may be regarded as the fullest and final recognition of the canonical right which had been maintained as the common law of the church ever since the Conquest; which had been ostensibly respected since the reign of Henry I[2]; and which the crown, however often it evaded it, did not henceforth attempt to override. The earlier practice, recorded in the Constitutions of Clarendon[3], according to which the election was made in the Curia Regis, in a national council, or in the royal chapel before the justiciar, a relic perhaps of the custom of nominating the prelates in the Witenagemot, was superseded by this enactment: the election took place in the chapter-house of the cathedral, and the king's wishes were signified by letter or message, not as before by direct dictation. When the elected prelate had obtained the royal assent to his promotion, the election was examined and confirmed by the metropolitan; and the ceremony of consecration completed the spiritual character of the bishop. On his confirmation the elected prelate received the spiritualities of his see, the right of ecclesiastical jurisdiction in his diocese, which during the vacancy had been in the hands of the archbishop or of the chapter[4]; and at his consecration he made a profession of obedience to the archbishop and the metropolitan church. From the crown, before or after consecration, he received the temporalities of his see, and thereupon made to the king a promise of fealty answering to the homage and fealty of a temporal lord[5].

Method of elections.

Restitution of spiritualities and temporalities.

Profession and Fealty.

702. It was not until the thirteenth century that the popes

[1] Select Charters, p. 280; Statutes, i. 5; Foed. i. 126, 127: this charter was confirmed by Innocent III and also by Gregory IX.

[2] Bishop Roger of Salisbury is said to have been the first prelate canonically elected.

[3] Select Charters, p. 133.

[4] The question to whom the custody of the spiritualities belonged during the vacancy of the see was disputed between the archbishop and the chapters, and was settled in the course of the thirteenth century by separate agreement with the several cathedral bodies. The archbishops moreover regarded the restitution of spiritualities before consecration as an act of grace; see Gibson, Codex, p. 133.

[5] See above, vol. i. p. 357, and the forms of oath given by Mr. Lea in his essay mentioned above, p. 294.

began to interfere directly in the appointment to the suffragan sees. Over the metropolitans they had long before attempted to exercise a controlling influence, in two ways: by the gift of the pall, and by the institution of legations. The pall was a sort of collar of white wool, with pendent strips before and behind, embroidered with four purple crosses[1]. The lambs from whose wool it was made were annually presented by the nuns of S. Agnes, blessed by the pope, and kept under the care of the apostolic subdeacons; and the pall, when it was ready for use, was again blessed at the tomb of S. Peter and left there all night. It was presented to the newly-appointed metropolitans at first as a compliment, but it soon began to be regarded as an emblem of metropolitan power, and by and by to be accepted as the vehicle by which metropolitan power was conveyed. The bestowal of the pall was in its origin Byzantine, the right to wear some such portion of the imperial dress having been bestowed by the emperor on his patriarchs: in the newer form it had become a regular institution before the foundation of the English church; S. Gregory sent a pall to Augustine, and so important was the matter that, even after the breach with Rome, archbishop Holdegate of York went through the form of receiving one from Cranmer[2]. Until he received the pall the archbishop did not, except under very peculiar circumstances, venture to consecrate bishops[3]. On the occasion of its reception he had to swear obedience to the pope in a form which gradually became more stringent[4]; in early times he undertook a journey to Rome for

Papal interference with the appointment of metropolitans.

The Pall.

Origin of the pall.

Its importance.

[1] See Maskell, Monumenta Ritualia, iii. p. cxxxv; Alban Butler, Lives of the Saints, Jan. 21, and June 8; Decr. p. i. dist. 100; Greg. IX, lib. ii. tit. 6. c. 4.

[2] The ceremony used on the occasion is printed from Cranmer's Register in the Gentleman's Magazine for November 1860, p. 523. The oath taken by Holdegate on the occasion is printed in the Concilia. The oath taken by Cranmer and his protest at the same time are given in Strype's Memorials of Cranmer, Appendix, nos. v and vi.

[3] Thus in 1382 archbishop Courtenay was present at the consecration of the bishops of London and Durham, but did not lay on his hands, because he had not received the pall; Ang. Sac. i. 121. This was not however required by the canon law; Greg. IX, lib. i. tit. 6. c. 11. The occasions on which the archbishops received the pall will be found in my Registrum Sacrum Anglicanum, pp. 140, 141.

[4] The custom is said by Gieseler to appear first in 1073; see Eccl. Hist. (ed. Hull), vol. iii. p. 168, where several forms are given. The oath taken

the purpose; but after the time of Lanfranc it was generally brought by special envoys from the apostolic see, and a great ceremony took place on the occasion of the investiture. This transaction formed a very close link between the archbishop and the pope, and, although the pall was never refused to a duly qualified candidate, the claim of a discretion to give or refuse in fact attributed to the pope a power of veto on the elections made by national churches and sovereigns.

The legation.

703. The bestowal of legatine authority on the archbishops came into use much later. England before the Conquest had been singularly exempt from direct interference. The visits of the archbishops to Rome, to receive the pall in person, seem to have been regarded as a sufficient recognition of the dignity of the apostolic see; there were no heresies to require castigation from the central court, and the local and political quarrels of the kingdom were too remote from papal interests to be worth the trouble of a legation. In the earlier days an occasional envoy appeared, either to strengthen the missionary efforts of the native church, or to obtain the assent of the English prelates to the enactments of Roman councils; and in the reign of the Confessor a legation had been sent by Alexander II probably with a view of remedying the evils caused by the adhesion of Stigand to the antipope Benedict X. The visitatorial jurisdiction which Gregory VII attempted to exercise had been resisted by the Conqueror, who, although in 1070 he availed himself of the presence of the legates to displace the hostile bishops, had formally laid down the rule that no legate should be allowed to land in England unless he had been appointed at the request of the king and the church[1]. Nor was the arrival

Rarity of legations to England before the Norman Conquest.

Resistance to legatine authority.

by archbishop Neville of York in 1374 is printed in the Registrum Palatinum, iii. 524-528. See also Foxe, Acts and Monuments, ii. 261.

[1] See Eadmer, lib. v. p. 118; where the legation of abbot Anselm is rejected by the clergy and magnates; and lib. vi. p. 138, where Henry I declares that he will not part with the privileges which his father had obtained from the holy see, 'in quibus haec, et de maximis una, erat quae regnum Angliae liberum ab omni legati ditione constituerat.' Cf. Flor. Wig. ii. 70. Lanfranc received authority from Alexander II to settle two causes left undetermined by the legates in 1070; 'nostrae et apostolicae auctoritatis vicem;' Wilk. Conc. i. 326; Foed. i. 1. See Gieseler, Eccl. Hist. (ed. Hull), iii. 184.

of such an officer more welcome to the clergy. Anselm had to remonstrate with Paschal II for giving to the archbishop of Vienne legatine power over England, and in doing so to assert that such authority belonged by prescriptive right to the see of Canterbury[1]. The visit of John of Crema, who held a legatine council at London in 1125, was regarded as an insult to the church of Canterbury, and as soon as he had departed the archbishop, William of Corbeuil, went to Rome, where he obtained for himself a commission as legate with jurisdiction over the whole island of Britain[2]. The precedent thus set was an important one: the placing of the legatine power, that is, the visitatorial jurisdiction of the Roman see as then defined, in the hand of the metropolitan of Canterbury, at once forced the kings, who had refused to receive the legate *a latere*, to admit the supreme jurisdiction of the pope when vested in one of their own counsellors; it also had the effect of giving to the ordinary metropolitan jurisdiction the appearance of a delegated authority from Rome[3]. On the death of William of Corbeuil, bishop Alberic of Ostia was sent on a mission of reform, and on his departure Henry of Blois, bishop of Winchester, obtained the office of legate in preference to the newly-elected archbishop Theobald[4]. The death of pope Innocent II brought bishop Henry's legation to an end, and the influence of Theobald prevented the succeeding popes from renewing it. In 1150 Eugenius III ventured to bestow the office on Theobald, who retained it as long as he lived. Thomas Becket, who succeeded him, had not obtained the commission before he quarreled with

The legation committed to the archbishop of Canterbury.

Henry of Blois, Theobald, and Thomas Becket.

[1] See Eadmer, lib. iii. p. 58; Anselm Epistt. iv. 2. Anselm says, 'Quando Romae fui ostendi praefato domino papae de legatione Romana super regnum Angliae, quam ipsius regni homines asseverant ab antiquis temporibus usque ad nostrum tempus ecclesiam Cantuariensem habuisse . . . Legationem vero quam usque ad nostrum tempus, secundum praedictum testimonium Ecclesia tenuerat, mihi dominus papa non abstulit.'

[2] See the Bull of Honorius II, dated Jan. 25, 1126; Ang. Sac. i. 792; cf. Cont. Fl. Wig. ii. 84.

[3] In 1439 the clergy had to petition that the acts of the spiritual courts might not be so construed as to bring them under the statute of praemunire; Wilk. Conc. iii. 534.

[4] March 1, 1139; W. Malmesb. Hist. Nov. ii. § 22; John Salisb. ep. 89.

the king; and Henry, in consequence of that quarrel, exerted himself to such purpose that the pope nominated as legate archbishop Roger of York[1]. But two years later, when the pope was stronger and Henry had put himself in the wrong, Thomas received the commission[2], under which he proceeded to anathematise his opponents. The next two archbishops, Richard and Baldwin, were made legates as matter of course. When Baldwin went to the Crusade, William Longchamp obtained the office, which he retained until the death of the pontiff who appointed him[3]. Hubert Walter, two years after his appointment as archbishop, was made legate[4], and had to drop the title on the death of Celestine III. Langton was formally appointed by Innocent III, but was hampered in the exercise of his duty by Gualo and Pandulf, until in 1221 he obtained a promise from Honorius III that as long as he lived no other legate should be sent. From that date the archbishops seem to have received the ordinary legatine commission as soon as their election was recognised at Rome; they were 'legati nati'[5]; and the title of legate of the apostolic see was regularly given to them in all formal documents. But this was not understood as precluding the mission of special legates, or legates *a latere*, who represented the pope himself and superseded the authority of the resident legates. Such were, in the thirteenth century, Otho and Othobon and that cardinal Guy Foulquois who assisted Henry III against Simon de Montfort[6]. Their visits were either prompted by the king when he wanted support against the nation, or were forced on king and nation alike by the necessities of foreign politics.

Legation of William Longchamp.

Legation of Langton.

Regular legation of the archbishops.

Occasional legates.

The history of the fifteenth century gave a renewed prominence to the office. Martin V had revived the policy of Gregory VII, and, relying on the doctrine that all bishops are but servants of the see of Rome, had insisted that

[1] Feb. 27, 1164. [2] Apr. 24, 1166. [3] Vol. i. p. 498.
[4] Mar. 18, 1195; Hoveden, iii. 290. [5] See Wilk. Conc. iii. 484.
[6] The full list of papal legations sent to England during the middle ages would be a very long one. It is necessary to distinguish carefully between the mission of mere occasional envoys such as troubled England in the reign of Henry III and the regular plenipotentiary legates such as Otho and Othobon.

Chichele should procure the repeal of the Statutes of Provisors[1]. Chichele had not the power to effect this, and the pope, notwithstanding his professions of obedience, believed that he had not the will. He issued letters therefore in which he suspended the archbishop from his legatine office, but Chichele protested, and the bulls were seized by royal order[2]. Henry Beaufort, bishop of Winchester, was made legate for the Bohemian war, and his presence in England during the continuance of the commission was resented by Chichele as an assumption of dangerous power. Gloucester protested in the king's name against his reception as legate[3]. But his legation did not supersede the ordinary jurisdiction. After the death of Chichele the old rule was observed, and the archbishop of Canterbury, being generally a cardinal, fulfilled in some measure the functions of a legate *a latere* as well. Stafford, Dene, and Warham were not cardinals, but ordinary legates. It was the legatine commission of Wolsey, unexampled in its fulness and importance, which, under the disingenuous dealing of Henry VIII, who had applied for the commission and granted licence to accept it, was made the pretext of his downfall, and which, after involving the whole English church in the penalties of praemunire, resulted in the great act of submission which made the king, 'so far as is allowed by the law of Christ,' supreme head on earth of the Church of England. The combination of the ordinary metropolitan authority with the extraordinary

Chichele threatened with suspension from his legation

The legatine office the fifteent century.

Its importance in the case of Wolsey.

[1] The long correspondence on this point and other questions in dispute is printed by Wilkins in the Concilia, iii. 471–486. There was some underhand work going on at the time, probably connected with the Beaufort and Gloucester quarrel.

[2] Wilk. Conc. iii. 484, 485. The archbishop appealed against the papal suspension to the decision of a general council, March 22, 1427; and royal orders for seizing the bulls were issued March 1; ib. p. 486. The suspension does not seem to have taken effect.

[3] The protest of Richard Caudray, the king's proctor, against Beaufort's visit to England as legate in 1428 is printed in Foxe, Acts and Monuments, iii. 717. He asserts that the kings of England 'tam speciali privilegio quam consuetudine laudabili legitimeque praescripta, necnon a tempore et per tempus cujus contrarii memoria hominum non existit pacifice et inconcusse observata, sufficienter dotati legitimeque muniti, quod nullus apostolicae sedis legatus venire debeat in regnum suum Angliae aut alias suas terras et dominia nisi ad regis Angliae pro tempore existentis vocationem, requisitionem, invitationem, seu rogatum.'

legatine authority, having thus for ages answered its purpose of giving supreme power to the pope, and substituting an adventitious source of strength for the spontaneous action of the national church, brought about a crisis which overthrew the papal power in England, and altered for all time to come the relations of Church and State.

Legation of the archbishops of York.

The dignity of the pall and the ordinary commission of legate were of course only given to the primates; the archbishops of York, from the time of Thoresby, who was made legate in the year 1352, down to the reformation, received the legatine commission as well as the pall[1].

704. The attempts of the pope, parallel with the attempts of the king, to obtain a decisive voice in the appointment of suffragan bishops, have a history which brings out other points of interest, some of which are common to the archiepiscopal sees also. The papal interference in these appointments might be justified either by supposing the confirmation of an undisputed election to be needed, or by the judicial character of the apostolic see in cases of dispute or appeal. If we set aside the instances of papal interference which belong to the missionary stage of Anglo-Saxon church history, the first cases in which direct recourse to Rome was adopted for the appointment of bishops were those of Giso of Wells and Walter of Hereford. These two prelates, having doubts about the canonical competency of archbishop Stigand, went to Nicolas II in 1061, and received consecration at his hands[2]. In this case the actual nomination had been made at home, and the question at issue was one which might fairly be referred to the arbitration of the apostolic see. In 1119 Calixtus II, taking advantage of the dispute between archbishop Ralph and the king on one side, and Thurstan the archbishop elect of York on the other, relative to the obedience due by York to Canterbury, consecrated Thurstan in opposition to both king and primate[3]; but here the pope believed himself

Interference of the popes in episcopal appointments.

Origin in disputed cases.

[1] The legatine commission of the archbishop of York was perhaps a result of the settlement of the great dispute between the two primates as to the right to bear their crosses erect in each other's province; see Raine, Lives of the Archbishops of York, i. 456, 457.

[2] Chr. Sax. A.D. 1061.

[3] Ord. Vit. lib. xii. c. 21.

to be asserting the cause of justice, and, after some delay, the opposing parties acquiesced in the decision: there was no question as to the appointment, only as to the conditions of consecration. As soon however as the clergy under Stephen had obtained a real voice in the election of the bishops, questions were raised which had the effect of referring numberless cases to the determination of the pope as supreme judge. The king's right of licencing, and of assenting or withholding assent to, the election, was backed up by his power of influencing the opinion of the electors. In every chapter he had a party who would vote for his nominee, if he cared to press one upon them; the shadowy freedom of election left room for other competition besides; the overt exercise of such royal influence, the frequent suspicion of simony, and the various methods of election by inspiration, by compromise, or by scrutiny[1], were fruitful in occasions for appeal. The metropolitan could quash a disputed election, but his power of confirming such a one was limited by this right of appeal[2]. Under Stephen, who was seldom strong enough to force his candidate on the chapters[3], the royal influence was sometimes set aside in favour of the papal, and was more than once a matter of barter. The election of archbishop Theobald was transacted under the eye of the legate Alberic, who consecrated him[4]; the election of Anselm, abbot of S. Edmund's, to the see of London, was opposed by the dean of S. Paul's and his kinsmen, and, after being discussed at Rome, was quashed by the same legate[5]; archbishop William of York, the king's nephew, was after consecration deposed by Eugenius III, and Henry Murdac, abbot of Fountains, appointed in his stead[6]; Gilbert Foliot, bishop of Hereford, was consecrated by the archbishop when in exile, on the nomination of the Angevin

Multiplication of disputes.

Causes of dispute.

Disputed cases carried to Rome.

[1] See vol. i. p. 635.

[2] This was ruled by Alexander IV in 1256; Ang. Sac. i. 637.

[3] In 1136 Stephen restored the possessions of the see of Bath to the bishop elect, 'canonica prius electione praecedente;' Foed. i. 16.

[4] R. Diceto, i. 252.

[5] Ib. i. 250, 251.

[6] John of Hexham (ed. Raine), p. 154. William was deposed because he had been elected 'ex ore regis' and had been consecrated in defiance of an appeal; ib. p. 142.

party opposed to Stephen[1]; Richard de Belmeis was confirmed in the see of London by the pope, but, in order to obtain royal recognition, hampered himself with debt which hurried him to his grave[2]; Hugh de Puiset, whose election to Durham was quashed by his metropolitan, sought and found consecration at Rome[3]. Matters were different under Henry II, who failed however in his attempts to prevent appeals to Rome on this point; the election of Thomas Becket to Canterbury was effected without opposition, the papal confirmation and gift of the pall being apparently a matter of course quite as much as the consent of the monks and the bishops; but after Becket's death and the confusion which his long struggle had caused, Henry found himself obliged to seek at Rome a decision of the critical questions which arose as to the episcopate. To the consecration of the prelates chosen in 1173 objections were raised in every quarter; the canonical competency and the formal completeness of the election were denied on the clerical side; the young king Henry opposed his father's acts of licence and assent[4]; and although Alexander III confirmed the elections, neither king nor chapters gained strength by the decision. At the end however of the twelfth century the relations of the three parties were sufficiently well ascertained. The royal licence and assent were indispensable; the elective right of the chapters and the archiepiscopal confirmation were formally admitted; and the power of the pope to determine all causes which arose upon disputed questions was too strongly founded in practice to be controverted by the crown. This power was however, in the case of the suffragans, an appellate jurisdiction only. It was the archbishops alone who required papal confirmation and recognition by the gift of the pall; nor, although Paschal II had claimed a right to take cognisance of and to confirm all elections, was the metropolitan authority of Canterbury and York as yet overruled. The claim of the bishops to take part in the election of the archbishops, which was occasionally enforced during the

Case of the election of Becket.

Appeals carried to Rome.

Position of affairs at the close of the twelfth century.

[1] Gervase, c. 1364.
[2] See R. Diceto, vol. i. pref. pp. xxiv, xxv.
[3] Gervase, c. 1375.
[4] R. Diceto, i. 368, 369; Gervase, cc. 1425 sq.

twelfth century, was rejected by Innocent III, and was never raised afterwards[1].

705. The history of the thirteenth century is a long record of disputes, beginning with the critical struggle for Canterbury after the death of Hubert Walter. But even before this Innocent III had asserted, in the case of a suffragan see, a new principle of justice[2]. In 1204, when the see of Winchester was vacant, the chapter was divided between the dean of Salisbury and the precentor of Lincoln; the pope at the king's request consecrated Peter des Roches, and laid down the rule that where the electors have knowingly elected an unworthy person they lose the right of making the next election. The appointment of Langton to Canterbury was not brought under this rule, but had its special importance in this: hitherto the pope had done no more than reject unfit candidates or determine the validity of elections; now he himself proposed a candidate, pushed him through the process of election, and confirmed the promotion although the royal assent was withheld. It was seen to be an extreme measure, but it served as a precedent. On Langton's death the king, by promising a large grant of money to the pope, prevailed on him to quash the election made by the monks, to keep the appointment to himself, and to nominate the person whom the king

Proceedings of Innocent II.

Important point in the case of Langton;

in the case of Richard.

[1] Of the early archbishops after the Conquest, Lanfranc and Anselm were nominated by the kings with some show of acceptance in the national council; Ralph was chosen by the prior and monks and accepted by the king and bishops; William of Corbeuil was chosen by the monks out of four proposed by the bishops to the king against the wish of the monks; Theobald was chosen by the bishops and the monks in national council; Becket by the bishops, monks, and clergy of the province, in the presence of the Justiciar. After Becket's death, Roger abbot of Bec was chosen by the bishops, but declined the election; after some delay the monks chose two candidates, Odo their prior and Richard prior of Dover; the bishops selected the latter, and he was confirmed by the pope. Baldwin, his successor, was chosen first by the bishops, Dec. 2, 1184, and then by the monks, Dec. 16, in separate elections, both under royal pressure. Reginald Fitz Jocelin was chosen by the monks in opposition to the bishops and to the king's nomination; Hubert Walter by the monks on Saturday May 29, 1193, and by the bishops on the following Sunday, each party claiming the right and shutting their eyes to the act of the other. On Hubert's death the bishops acting with the king chose John de Gray, the monks their subprior. At Langton's appointment the strife ended; see vol. i. p. 520.

[2] Decr. Greg. IX, lib. i. tit. 6. c. 25.

recommended[1]. This Gregory IX did 'ex plenitudine potestatis,' and thus by Henry's connivance re-asserted the principle laid down by Innocent in 1204, that, in case of an election quashed upon appeal, the judge has an absolute right of appointment. Archbishop Edmund was appointed in 1234 in the same summary way in which Langton had been chosen in 1207[2]; Boniface was elected by the chapter at the earnest petition of the king[3]; Kilwardby and Peckham[4] were nominated by the pope 'ex plenitudine potestatis,' the king exacting, in the former case at least, an acknowledgment, on the restitution of the temporalities, that the recognition was a matter of special favour and not to be construed as a precedent[5]. In the case of Peckham he introduced into the writ of restitution a clause saving his own rights[6]. Robert Winchelsey was appointed with the unanimous consent of all parties[7].

Case of Edmund.

Cases of Kilwardby and Peckham.

Case of Winchelsey.

Whilst the primacy was thus made the prize of the stronger and more pertinacious claimant, the appointments to the bishop-

[1] Vol. ii. p. 42; M. Paris, pp. 255, 256.

[2] The pope quashed three elections made by the monks and then empowered them to elect Edmund; M. Paris, pp. 385, 386.

[3] M. Paris, pp. 555, 556.

[4] On the death of Boniface, William Chillenden, prior of Canterbury, was elected, and renounced the election, whereupon the pope nominated Kilwardby by provision; Ann. Winton. p. 112; Waverl. p. 379. Kilwardby was made a cardinal in 1278; the monks thereupon elected bishop Burnell the chancellor. The pope provided Peckham, and Burnell, whose election was quashed, did not further contest the point. See Prynne, Records, iii. 214.

[5] The words are very important: 'Cum, ecclesiis cathedralibus in regno Angliae viduatis, et de jure debeat et solet de consuetudine provideri per electionem canonicam ab hiis potissime celebrandam collegiis, capitulis et personis ad quas jus pertinet eligendi, petita tamen prius ab illustri rege Angliae super hoc licentia et optenta; et demum celebrata electione persona electi eidem regi debeat praesentari, ut idem rex contra personam ipsam possit proponere si quid rationabile habeat contra eam, videtur eidem domino regi et suo consilio quod sibi et ecclesiae, cujus ipse patronus est pariter et defensor, fiat praejudicium in hac parte, praecipue si res trahitur in aliis ecclesiis Angliae in exemplum, quod summus pontifex hiis omissis in hoc casu, ubi nec in materia nec in forma electionis inventum est fuisse peccatum, nec in ipsius litteris expressum, potestatem sibi assumpserit ipsi ecclesiae providendi,' &c; Prynne, Records, iii. 122*.

[6] Prynne, Records, iii. 223.

[7] The election of Winchelsey, one of the very few which the popes allowed to be canonical, is described at length in the bull of confirmation issued by Celestine V; Wilkins, Conc. ii. 197, 198.

rics were a constant matter of dispute. The freedom of election promised by John had resulted in a freedom of litigation and little more. The attempts of Henry III to influence the chapters were undignified and unsuccessful; his candidates were seldom chosen; the pope had a plentiful harvest of appeals. Between 1215 and 1264 there were not fewer than thirty disputed elections carried to Rome for decision[1]. On the last of these occasions, a contested election to Winchester in 1262, the pope, wearied with discussion, adopted the plan which Innocent III and Gregory IX had followed, rejected both candidates, declared the elective power to be forfeited, and put in his own nominee[2]. This bold measure had the effect of stopping appeals for a time; only one case more occurred during the reign of Henry III. In 1264 the canons of York elected William Langton; the pope appointed S. Bonaventura, who, knowing the disturbed state of the kingdom, declined the appointment. The chapter was then allowed to postulate the bishop of Bath[3].

Numerous disputed elections to suffragan sees under Henry III.

706. Under Edward I there were only twelve cases of the kind; yet, although the rarity of the appeals shows the king to have become stronger, they were so managed by the popes as to increase their own influence, and the result was the extinction, for more than a century, of the elective right of the chapters[4]. The practice of translating bishops from one see to another, a practice which had been very rare until now, gave an opportunity for a new claim. Only papal authority could loose the tie that bound the bishop to the church of his consecration[5];

Gradual suspension or extinction of the elective rights of chapters.

[1] The details of most of these disputes may be found in the second volume of Prynne's Records.

[2] The monks were divided; fifty-four chose Oliver de Tracy, seven chose Andrew of London; the pope provided John of Exeter; Ann. Winton. p. 99.

[3] See Raine, Fasti Eboracenses, i. 302.

[4] The most famous case in the first half of Edward's reign was the papal provision of John of Pontoise to the see of Winchester, which the pope made after quashing an election; he had great difficulty in obtaining his temporalities; Prynne, Records, iii. 292, 1255, 1261. In 1280 the chapter of Carlisle elected without royal licence, damaging the interest of the crown, as it was alleged, to the amount of £60,000; ib. p. 1230.

[5] Anselm, Epp. iii. 126; Decr. Greg. IX, lib. i. tit. 7. Nicolas IV ordered that all postulations, that is, elections of persons disqualified, including translations, should be personally sued out at Rome. In 1287 Honorius IV, on a case of the kind arising, reserved the provision to the see of Emly; Theiner, Vet. Mon. p. 138.

Papal rights on translation.

it was the pope's duty and privilege that the divorced church should not remain unconsoled, and when, on the petition of the king or the chapter, he had authorised the translation, he filled up the vacancy so caused[1]. Thus in 1299, when, on a double election at Ely, both candidates had surrendered their rights to the pope, Boniface VIII nominated the bishop of Norwich to Ely, and filled up Norwich with one of the two complaisant disputants from Ely[2]. On the next vacancy at Ely, in 1302, he appointed a candidate, Robert Orford, whose election archbishop Winchelsey had refused to confirm, but who had renounced the election by the chapter before he accepted the nomination by the pope[3]. Nearly at the same time the see of Worcester was vacant, and a monk of the house, named John of S. German, was elected to fill it. He was accepted by the king, but made such a show of reluctance that Winchelsey delayed his confirmation, and the matter was carried to Rome. There Boniface VIII obtained from John the renunciation of his claim, and immediately consecrated to the see a Franciscan named William Gainsborough.

Boniface VIII provides to sees.

He attempts to confer the temporalities as well as the spiritualities.

Boniface was not content with the substance of supreme power; he took in both these cases a further step in which he directly attacked the king's constitutional relation to the episcopate. In the preceding century a custom had been

[1] The only translations, except to the archiepiscopal sees, which took place from the Conquest to the reign of Edward I, were the following; Hervey from Bangor to Ely in 1109 (Anselm, Epp. iii. 126); Gilbert Foliot from Hereford to London in 1163 (see the pope's letter in R. Diceto, i. 309); Richard le Poor from Chichester to Salisbury in 1217, and thence to Durham in 1228 (Ang. Sac. i. 731); William of Raleigh from Norwich to Winchester in 1244, having been elected to Winchester before he was bishop of Norwich (Ang. Sac. i. 307); Nicolas of Ely from Worcester to Winchester 'per ordinationem domini papae Clementis,' in 1268 (ibid. p. 312). In all these cases the pope was consulted; but he did not in all of them fill up the see vacated by translation. In the last case the king exacted an acknowledgment of the same kind as that obtained from archbishop Kilwardby; Prynne, Records, iii. 122.

[2] The monks of Ely were divided, the majority chose their prior John, the minority John Langton, the king's treasurer; the prior appealed to the pope, who, having failed to make them unanimous, translated the bishop of Norwich and appointed the prior to Norwich; Ang. Sac. i. 639; Prynne, Records, iii. 799.

[3] Winchelsey rejected Orford on account of his literary insufficiency; Ang. Sac. i. 640; Prynne, Records, iii. 919.

gradually introduced into the Irish church, according to which the pope conferred on the bishops at their confirmation both the spiritual and the temporal administration of their churches[1]. Boniface had in 1300 attempted to extend this practice to the see of York: and when Thomas Corbridge, archbishop elect, had gone to Rome for confirmation, the pope had prevailed on him to resign the right conferred by election and then re-appointed him[2], solemnly committing to him both the spiritual and the temporal administration of his see. Edward I restored the temporalities, apparently without noticing the innovation; but when, a few months after, the usurpation was repeated on the appointment of an archbishop of Dublin, Edward compelled the new-made prelate to renounce all words in the Bull that were prejudicial to the royal authority[3]. The experiment was again tried in the cases of Orford and Gainsborough, and on the latter, who had obtained his appointment without any reference to the king, his indignation fell heavily; and the bishop only recovered his temporalities by a payment of 1000 marks[4]. The renunciation of the offensive words in the Bulls of provision afterwards became a regular ceremony on

The bishops obliged to renounce the words, in the papal bulls, prejudicial to royal authority.

[1] Prynne, Records, iii. 992, 1149; Wilk. Conc. ii. 266. The words are 'curam sibi et administrationem ipsius ecclesiae in spiritualibus et temporalibus committendo.' In the letters confirming the election of a bishop of Killaloe in 1253, Innocent IV had used the form 'plena tibi ejusdem ecclesiae tam in spiritualibus quam in temporalibus administratione concessa;' Theiner, Vet. Mon. p. 58. In the bulls for the Scottish sees at the same time the claim is insinuated but not definitely expressed; ibid. pp. 60, 61. In an appointment to Cashel the pope exhorts the archbishop 'quatenus ecclesiam tibi commissam in spiritualibus et temporalibus ita studeas gubernare quod &c.;' ibid. p. 62. Alexander IV uses the form without hesitation in some cases; Nicolas III in 1277 commits both temporals and spirituals to John of Darlington, archbishop elect of Dublin; ibid. p. 119; but avoids the form in the appointment to S. Andrew's in 1280; ibid. p. 124. Honorius IV does not use the form in confirming the election to Dublin in 1280; and a wish for the prosperity of the church in both departments is all that is expressed until the reign of Boniface VIII, who in 1292 uses the direct form in the provision of the bishops of Ross, ibid. p. 157; of Caithness, of Brechin, pp. 161, 164, of S. Andrew's, p. 165, and Moray, p. 166. The next case is that of the archbishop of Dublin referred to in the text. In the case of John of Darlington no remonstrance was made; Prynne, Rec. iii. 226. The words occur in the confirmation of an abbot of Evesham in 1284; Prynne, Rec. iii. 1269.

[2] Prynne, Records, iii. 859, 860.

[3] Ib. iii. 865.

[4] Thomas, Survey of Worcester, App. p. 85. See similar protests, under Edward I, in Prynne, Rec. iii. 1132.

the restitution of the temporalities. These offensive words had long been inserted in the letters by which the popes appointed the Irish bishops. In the case of the English church, either Corbridge's case was the first in which the usurpation was attempted, or else Edward's suspicions as to the real bent of Boniface's policy had been aroused by his recent proceedings in the matters of clerical taxation and his claim to the superiority of Scotland.

The popes now assume the direct patronage to vacant sees.

707. In all the cases hitherto cited the pope either had acted as a judge, or had skilfully availed himself of opportunities which were brought before him in his capacity as judge. But from the beginning of the fourteenth century his interference in the appointment of bishops takes a new form, and he assumes the patronage as well as the appellate jurisdiction. This was done by the application to the episcopate of the rights of provision and reservation which had been exercised long before in the case of lower preferments. The first direct attack on patronage had been made in 1226, when the papal envoy Otho was sent to England to demand two prebends in each cathedral church for the use of the pope[1]. Some few Italians were already beneficed in England, but these, probably in all cases, owed their promotion either to the king or to the bishops, who thus repaid the services of their agents at Rome, or gratified the popes by liberality to their relations. Otho's request was refused by the church, but in 1231 Gregory IX issued orders to the English bishops to abstain from presenting to livings until provision had been made for five Romans unnamed[2]. The barons forbade the bishops to comply, and prohibited the farmers of livings in the hands of foreigners from sending the revenue out of the country. Notwithstanding their attitude of defiance, Gregory in 1239 attempted to extend the usurpation to livings in private patronage[3], and, when this was defeated, he directed in 1240 the bishops of Lincoln and Salisbury to provide for not

Growth of the system of provisions.

[1] Above, vol. ii. p. 38.

[2] M. Paris, p. 371. On the growth of this form of usurpation in the Western Church generally see Gieseler, Eccl. Hist. (ed. Hull), vol. iii. p. 173; vol. iv. p. 79. England seems to have been the great harvest-field of imposition.

[3] M. Paris, p. 513.

less than three hundred foreign ecclesiastics[1]. This claim was one of the burdens that broke down the spirit of archbishop Edmund and drove him into exile. Innocent IV continued the practice which Gregory had begun, notwithstanding annual remonstrances from the bishops and an appeal to a general council. From time to time he promised to abstain, but, by the use of the infamous *non obstante* clause, managed to evade the performance of his word. In 1253, however, he recognised in the fullest way the rights of patrons, and undertook to abstain from all usurped provisions[2]. The same year Henry III made a similar promise on his part to abstain from interference in elections[3]; a promise which in 1256 was enforced by the parliament which rehearsed and confirmed the Charter of John[4]. In 1258 freedom of election was one of the articles demanded by the barons in the Mad Parliament. Notwithstanding this legislation, however, the claim of the pope was enforced during the whole reign of Edward I[5]; and it was not until his last year, 1307, that the laity, in the parliament of Carlisle, forced the question upon the king's attention. Edward had perhaps connived at some amount of usurpation in this particular point, in order to secure objects which were for the time of more importance; the appointment to benefices was but one of many ways of papal exaction; the king was in 1307 on friendly terms with the pope, and wished to avoid another rupture such as had happened in 1297. Nothing more was done at the time[6]. The weakness of Edward II[7] and the exigencies of the papacy

Interference with elections renounced in 1253; but continued notwithstanding.

The power strengthened by compromise.

Provision extended to bishoprics.

[1] M. Paris, p. 532.

[2] M. Paris, Additam. pp. 184–186; Foed. i. 175; Ann. Burton, pp. 284, 314–317.

[3] M. Paris, pp. 865, 866.

[4] Ib. p. 920.

[5] The countless instances given by Prynne, in the third volume of his Records, defy even an attempt at classification here.

[6] Rot. Parl. i. 222; Prynne, Records, iii. 1168 sq.; above, vol. ii. p. 156.

[7] In 1307 the pope committed the temporalities as well as the spiritualities of Armagh to Walter Jorz; Foed. ii. 3. Edward compelled him to renounce the obnoxious words; ib. p. 7. Several similar attempts to repel aggression were made in the following years; ib. 77, 96: John de Leek, archbishop of Dublin in 1311, has to renounce the words; ib. p. 140: the pope repeats them the same year in the provision to Armagh; p. 149: similar cases are found; ib. pp. 185, 197. In 1307, when Worcester was

emboldened Clement V and his successors to apply to the episcopal sees the system of provision and reservation[1].

Clement V reserves the appointment to Canterbury.

In 1313, on the death of archbishop Winchelsey, the monks of Canterbury elected the learned Thomas Cobham as his successor, although Edward had begged them to choose his tutor, Walter Reynolds, bishop of Worcester. Winchelsey had died on the 11th of May; on the 23rd of June the prior heard a rumour that the pope had reserved the appointment for his own nomination, and on the 7th of July letters were produced, bearing date April 27, in which Clement expressed this intention. The prior thinking, as he said, that nothing was impossible with God, entreated the pope to nominate Cobham; but on the 1st of October he appointed Reynolds by virtue of the reservation[2], and immediately filled up the see of Worcester which Reynolds vacated. Clement died in 1314, and the papacy was vacant for two years, during which the English bishops were appointed by compromise between the crown and the chapters. But John XXII, who was elected in 1316, immediately followed in the steps of Clement. In 1317 he reserved the appointments to Worcester, Hereford, Durham, and Rochester[3]; in 1320 to Lincoln and Winchester[4]; in 1322 to Lich-

Papal appointments by reservation and provision, under Edward II and Edward III.

vacant and archbishop Winchelsey was abroad, Edward, who had obtained the election of Reynolds to that see, wrote to the pope to pray him to confirm it, because he did not wish the matter to come before the papal administrator of the spiritualities of Canterbury; Foed. ii. 15: and the same year he asked the same favour for bishop Stapledon of Exeter against whose election an appeal was made; ib. p. 19. Early in 1308 he heard that the pope had reserved the provision to Worcester and protested against it; p. 29. The pope appointed Reynolds, using the words prejudicial to royal authority; Thomas, Worcester, App. p. 99.

[1] The form of a provision after reservation declared that during the life of the last incumbent the pope had reserved the appointment for his own bestowal, thereby making void any attempt to fill it up; but that on the occurrence of the vacancy, being anxious that there should be no delay, he had specially applied himself to find a fit person; he therefore preferred the person named, who in many cases was the elect of the chapter or the royal nominee. There are a great many such bulls in the Foedera.

[2] Foed. ii. 228. The Bull contained the offensive words which the new archbishop had formally to renounce; ib. p. 237; see also the case of Durham, p. 328.

[3] Foed. ii. 313, 319, 328; Ang. Sac. i. 357, 533.

[4] Foed. iii. 422, 425. The provision to Lincoln does not mention the temporalities; but the bishop was kept out of them by Hugh le Despenser; ib. p. 697.

field[1]; in 1323 to Winchester[2]; in 1325 to Carlisle and Norwich[3]; in 1327 to Worcester, Exeter, and Hereford[4]; in 1329 to Bath[5]; in 1333 to Durham[6]; in 1334 to Canterbury, Winchester, and Worcester[7]. In many of these cases the king played into the pope's hands, or the pope appointed the person recommended by the king. Haymo Heath, who was elected to Rochester in 1317, found arrayed against him as competitor the queen's confessor, who produced letters of recommendation from the queen and the king and three queens of France; he also had a papal reservation, but his death in 1319 left Haymo in quiet possession of his see[8]. In 1327 bishop Berkeley of Exeter[9], and 1329 Ralph de Salopia[10], bishop of Bath, obtained their sees in spite of reservations. But cases were very rare in which any voice in the appointment was allowed to the chapters. In 1328 the pope, in a letter to archbishop Mepeham, expressed his general intention of reserving all appointments caused by translation[11]. All sees vacated by bishops who died at the papal court were also regarded as perquisites[12]. Mepeham himself fell a victim to the pope's policy, for he died of mortification at being repelled in his metropolitical visitation by Grandison, bishop of Exeter, who announced that the pope had exempted him from any such jurisdiction.

Occasional defeat of the papal candidate.

[1] Foed. iii. 495; Ang. Sac. i. 443.

[2] Foed. iii. 525: the temporalities are mentioned in the Bull; bishop Stratford had to give security for 10,000 marks before he recovered them; ib. p. 687.

[3] Ann. Lanerc. A.D. 1325; Ang. Sac. i. 413. Bishop Ayermin of Norwich was kept out of his temporalities by Hugh le Despenser in consequence.

[4] Foed. iii. 715, 723, 726. The provision to Exeter was justified by the death of the last bishop at the papal court; Oliver, Bishops of Exeter, p. 76; that to Hereford by the translation of Orlton.

[5] This provision was defeated, and the person elected obtained the see; Ang. Sac. i. 568.

[6] See below, p. 314.

[7] Stratford of Winchester was promoted to Canterbury; Orlton from Worcester to Winchester, and Simon Montacute to Worcester; the provision to Canterbury was done thus; the monks elected Stratford and the king approved; the pope 'dissembled,' or pretended that he had not heard of the election and appointed the same person. See Thomas, Worc., App. p. 109.

[8] Ang. Sac. i. 357, sq.

[9] Oliver, Bishops of Exeter, p. 73.

[10] Ang. Sac. i. 568.

[11] Wilk. Conc. ii. 546.

[12] Extrav. Comm. lib. i. tit. 3. c. 4; lib. iii. tit. 2. cc. 1, 13.

Collusion of the king with the pope.

708. Edward III, during the early years of his reign, contentedly acquiesced in the pope's assumptions, and up to the year 1350 the right of provision was exercised without check. The king occasionally remonstrated[1], but the effect of the remonstrance was weakened by his constant petitions for the promotion of some friend of his own. It was on an occasion of this kind, the petition made for Thomas Hatfield of Durham, in 1345, following a strong remonstrance presented in 1343, that Clement VI made the famous remark—'If the king of England were to petition for an ass to be made bishop, we must not say him nay[2].' Archbishop Stratford was a papal nominee, and his first act was to set aside Robert Graystanes the elect of Durham, who had not only been regularly chosen and confirmed, but consecrated also: the king had petitioned and the pope had reserved in favour of the more famous Richard de Bury[3].

Cases of Hatfield and Bury.

Statute of Provisors.

By the Statute of Provisors, in 1351[4], it was enacted that all persons receiving papal provisions should be liable to imprisonment, and that all the preferments to which the pope nominated should be forfeit for that turn to the king. But even this bold measure, in which the good sense of the parliament condemned the proceedings of the pope, was turned by royal manipulation to the advantage of the crown alone. A system was devised which saved the dignity of all parties. When a see became vacant, the king sent to the chapter his licence to elect, accompanied or followed by a letter nominating the person whom he would accept if elected. He also, by letter to the pope, requested that the same person might be appointed by papal provision. With equal complaisance the chapters elected and the popes provided. The pope retained, however, the nomination to sees vacant by translation, which vacancies he took care to multiply. This arrangement was very displeasing to the country, for the question of patronage, in other cases besides bishoprics, was becoming complicated to an extreme degree:

Practical compromise, evading the rights of the chapters.

[1] For example in 1343; Wals. i. 254–258.
[2] Walsingham, i. 255 sq.; Ypod. Neust. p. 284.
[3] Hist. Dunelm. Scriptores, pp. 120, 121.
[4] 25 Edw. III. Stat. iv; Statutes, i. 316.

the king presented to livings which were not vacant, and displaced incumbents by his writ of '*quare impedit*[1]; the pope's right of reservation affected the tenure of every benefice in the country. At length, after long debates by way of letter, in 1374 a congress was held at Bruges for determining the general question; in 1375 Gregory X annulled the appointments which he and his predecessor had made in opposition to the king[2], and in 1377 Edward was able to announce that, whilst he himself gave up certain pieces of patronage, the pope had by word of mouth undertaken to abstain from reservations and to allow free elections to bishoprics[3]. But this promise was as illusory as all that had gone before. The troubles of the next reign prevented England from taking advantage, as might have been expected, of the weakness of the papacy, now in a state of schism. Richard and his opponents were alike intent rather on using the papal influence for their own ends, than on securing the freedom of the church. In 1388 Urban VI, at the instance of the lords, translated Alexander Neville from York to S. Andrews, and Thomas Arundel from Ely to York. Such a breach of the law would in ordinary times have called forth a loud protest, but party spirit was rampant, and none was heard. In 1390 the Statute of Provisors was re-enacted and confirmed, and in 1393 the great Statute of Praemunire secured, for the time, the observance of the Statute of Provisors[4]. In 1395 the election to Exeter was made without papal interference; but in 1396 the bishops of Worcester and Asaph were appointed by provision[5]; and in 1397 Richard procured the pope's assistance in translating Arundel to S. Andrews, and in appointing Walden to Canterbury[6]; Boniface IX, the same year,

Congress at Bruges.

Promise of free elections made in 1377.

Translations of political importance under Richard II.

[1] The form of this writ is thus given by Fitz Herbert, Nat. Brev. f. 32: 'Rex Vicecomiti Lincoln. salutem. Praecipe W. archiepiscopo et R. quod permittant nos praesentare idoneam personam ad ecclesiam de W. quae vacat et ad nostram spectat donationem, et unde praedictus W. archiepiscopus et R. nos injuste impediunt ut dicitur et nisi &c., summone &c. praedictum archiepiscopum et R. quod sint coram nobis &c. vel coram justitiariis nostris de Banco, &c.' On the legal questions connected with it, see Gibson, Codex, pp. 824, 827–830.

[2] See above, vol. ii. p. 427.

[3] See above, vol. ii. p. 427.

[4] 16 Rich. II. Stat. 5; Statutes, ii. 84, 85.

[5] Rymer, vii. 793, 797.

[6] See above, vol. ii. 497.

translated bishop Bockingham from Lincoln to Lichfield against his own will, and appointed Henry Beaufort in his place[1].

Right of election revived under Henry V, for a short time.

709. Archbishop Arundel and Henry IV managed the episcopal appointments during the later years of the great schism; and Henry V, among the other pious acts by which he earned the support of the clergy, restored the right of election to the chapters, the parliament also agreeing that the confirmation of the election should be performed as it had been of old by the metropolitans[2]. For two or three years the whole of the long disused process was revived and the church was free. But Martin V, when he found himself seated firmly on his throne, was not content to wield less power than his predecessors had claimed. He provided thirteen bishops in two years, and threatened to suspend Chichele's legation because he was unable to procure the repeal of the restraining statutes. An attempt of the pope however to force bishop Fleming into the see of York was signally defeated[3]. The weakness and devotion of Henry VI laid him open to much aggression; during the whole of Stafford's primacy the pope filled up the sees by provision; the council nominated their candidates; at Rome the proctors of the parties contrived a compromise; whoever otherwise lost or gained, the apostolic see obtained a recognition of its claims[4]. During the later years of our period the deficiency of records makes it impossible to determine whether the exercise of that claim were

Plan followed under Henry VI.

[1] Wals. ii. 228.

[2] Rot. Parl. iv. 71. A good example of an election under this arrangement will be found in the case of Philip Morgan, in 1419, of Worcester; Thomas, App. pp. 130 sq.: another is that of bishop Bourchier; ib. 141 sq.

[3] On the death of archbishop Bowet in 1423, the pope translated bishop Fleming of Lincoln to the vacant see; the chapter who, with the royal licence and assent had chosen bishop Morgan of Worcester, refused to receive Fleming; and after some discussion the dispute was compromised by the translation of bishop Kemp from London to York. This was agreed on by the council Jan. 14, 1426; on the 8th of April Kemp was elected to York, on the 22nd he received the temporalities, and on the 20th of July the pope consented to 'provide' him. See Ord. iii. 180; Godwin, de Praes. p. 692.

[4] Abundant illustrations of this diplomacy will be found in the Proceedings of the Privy Council and among Beckington's Letters. In 1434 the king at the instance of the commons appointed Bourchier to Worcester, the pope provided Thomas Brouns to the same see; Rochester, which was in the archbishop's patronage, was vacant at the time; the quarrel was settled by the appointment of Brouns to Rochester; Ord. iv. 278, 281, 285.

real or nominal; certainly the kings had no difficulty in obtaining the promotion of their creatures; a few Italian absentees were, on the other hand, allowed to hold sees in England and act as royal agents at Rome. Under Henry VII and Henry VIII the royal nominees were invariably chosen; the popes had other objects in view than the influencing of the national churches, and the end of their spiritual domination was at hand. The clergy too were unable to stand alone against royal and papal pressure, and placed themselves at the disposal of the government; the government was ready to use them, and paid for their service by promotion.

The crown is the ultimate winner.

Cases of deprivation.

English church history during the middle ages furnishes happily only very few instances in which a bishop was for any penal reason removed from his see. In these few cases, for the sake of security no doubt, the papal assistance was generally invoked. William the Conqueror got rid of the native prelates, with the aid of a legation from Rome, by the act of a national council. Bishop Everhard of Norwich was deposed in 1145 for cruelty; but history has not recorded the exact process[1]. Geoffrey of S. Asaph was compelled in 1175 to resign as unwilling to reside on his see; and some of the later cases of resignation may have been the results of legal or moral pressure. The threat of deprivation, although often held out by the popes as an ultimate resource against contumacious prelates, was never carried into effect. The political troubles of the reign of Richard II involved certain changes which the popes, who were too weak to resist much pressure, brought about, as we have seen, by fictitious translations. The removal of bishop Pecock of Chichester in 1457 was not a case of formal and legal deprivation; he was declared to be, in consequence of heresy, illegally possessed of his see, and the pope was requested to deprive him, but nothing more definite was done. The removal therefore of a spiritual lord is not in constitutional history a point so important as the right of appointment.

Additional sees.

Permanent additions to the episcopal body by the institution of new bishoprics were probably sanctioned by papal as well as national recognition, but on this point there is little evidence.

[1] H. Hunt.; Ang. Sac. ii. 700.

The foundation of the see of Ely in 1109 was confirmed by the pope, if the extant documents are genuine; the institution of the sees of Carlisle and Whithern in 1133 took place when a brisk communication was open with Rome, and can hardly have lacked the papal sanction.

Importance of this discussion.

The great importance of this discussion must justify its length. The point at issue was not merely whether the king or the pope should rule the church through the bishop, but whether the king and nation should accept, at the pope's dictation, the nomination of so large a portion of the House of Lords as the bishops really formed. When the average number of lay lords was under forty, the presence of twenty bishops nominated by the pope, and twenty-six abbots elected under Roman influence, would have placed the decision of national policy in foreign hands. The kings had no easy part to play, to avoid quarrelling with the clergy and yet to maintain a hold upon them. Nor had they to struggle with the pope alone, but with a great body of European opinion which he could bring to bear upon them. The English reformation, by itself, would have been impossible unless the unity of that European consensus had been already broken.

The appointment of abbots less contested than that of bishops.

710. It might have been expected that the right of appointment to the twenty-six parliamentary abbacies would have been to the pope and to the king an object of not less importance than the nomination to bishoprics; and, as the process of election was much the same in the two cases, it offered the same opportunities for interference. The forms of licence to elect, the modes of election, assent, and restitution to temporalities were exactly parallel in all monasteries of royal foundation, although in such of them as were, like S. Albans, exempt from all spiritual jurisdiction but that of the pope, the action of the archbishops was excluded, and the abbots elect sought confirmation, if not benediction also, at Rome. Neither the king however nor the pope attempted much interference in this quarter[1]. The monasteries were the stronghold of papal in-

[1] There are some few instances; for example, Edmund Bromfield obtained a provision to the abbey of S. Edmund's in 1379 contrary to the Statute of

fluence, which they supported as a counterpoise to that of the diocesan bishops; the pontiffs were too wise to overstrain an authority which was so heartily supported, and they trusted the monks. The kings let them alone for other reasons: the abbots were not so influential as the bishops in public affairs, nor was the post equally desirable as the reward for public service; with a very few exceptions the abbacies were much poorer than the bishoprics, and involved a much more steady attention to local duties, which would prevent attendance at court. But probably the chief cause of their immunity from royal usurpation was the certainty that any attempt to infringe their liberties would have armed against the aggressors the whole of the monastic orders, with their widespread foreign organisation and overwhelming influence at Rome. One result of this immunity was that scarcely any abbot during the later middle ages takes any conspicuous part in English politics; the registers of the abbeys are no longer records of national history, but of petty law-suits; the monastic life separates itself more widely than ever from the growing life of the nation; the temporalities of the monasteries are offered to the king by the religious reformers as a ready source of revenue, by the confiscation of which no one can lose; when the great shock of the Reformation comes at last, the whole system falls at one blow, and vast as the ruin is at the time, it is forgotten before the generation that witnessed it had passed away.

Danger of touching the privileges of the convents.

711. The convocations of the two provinces, as the recognised constitutional assemblies of the English clergy, have undergone, except in the removal of the monastic members at the dissolution, no change of organisation from the reign of Edward I down to the present day. The clergy moreover are still summoned in the parliamentary writ of the bishops, to attend by their proctors at the session of parliament. On both these points enough has been said in former chapters[1]; and here it is necessary only to mention the particulars in which external action was applied to

The constitution of convocation little changed in the middle ages.

Provisors; Cont. Murim. p. 235. And in 1347 the commons petitioned against papal provisions to abbeys and priories; Rot. Parl. ii. 171.

[1] Vol. ii. pp. 194–200.

multiply meetings or accelerate proceedings. The clergy from the very first showed great reluctance to obey the royal summons under the *praemunientes* clause, and accordingly during a great part of the reigns of Edward II and Edward III, from the year 1314 to the year 1340[1], a separate letter was addressed to the two archbishops at the calling of each parliament, urging them to compel the attendance of the clerical estate. This was ineffectual; and after the latter year the crown, having acquiesced in the rule that the clerical tenths should be granted in the provincial convocations, seems to have cared less about the attendance of representative proctors in parliament. On two or three critical occasions the clerical proctors were called on to share the responsibilities of parliament[2], but their attendance ceased to be more than formal, and probably from the beginning of the fifteenth century ceased altogether.

Failure of attempts to compel the attendance of the clergy in parliament.

Question of the relation of convocation to parliament.

With regard to the constitution of the Convocations the only question which has taken its place in political history is that of their relation to parliament: and this question affects only those sessions of convocation which were held in consequence of a request or a command issued by the king with a view to a grant

[1] In June 1311 the clergy were summoned, to the parliament in which the Ordinances were published, by the usual *praemunientes* clause. Under the guidance, probably, of Winchelsey, who was anxious to extend their immunities, they demurred to electing proctors, and, when in October the king called another meeting of parliament for November 18, he wrote to the two metropolitans urging them to compel the attendance of the proctors. Winchelsey took offence at the wording of this writ, and on October 24, the king issued another in which he said that nothing offensive was intended, and that the writ should be amended in parliament; Parl. Writs II. i. 58; Wake, State of the Church, pp. 260, 261. In 1314, March 27, the king summoned the archbishops to meet the royal commissioners in their respective convocations to discuss an aid. The clergy immediately protested against the royal citation, and having met, recorded their protest and broke up; Parl. Writs, II. i. 123. When then on July 29 the king summoned a new parliament, he wrote special letters to the archbishops urging them to enforce attendance under the praemunientes clause; ib. p. 128. This practice was followed down to 1340. On the 1st of December 1314 the prior and convent of Canterbury protested against the archbishop's citation under the premunition, first, 'in eo quod ad curiam secularem, puta Domini regis parliamentum quod in camera ejusdem domini regis fuit inchoatum et per dies aliquos continuatum;' secondly, because the abbots and priors were not summoned; ib. p. 139; they complied however with the summons. See above, vol. ii. pp. 328, 331.

[2] See above, vol. ii. 347, 494, 495.

of money. The organisation of the two provincial assemblies was applicable to all sorts of public business, and the archbishops seem to have encountered no opposition from the king on any occasion on which they thought it necessary to call their clergy together. The means to be taken for the extirpation of heresy, for the reform of manners, for the dealings with foreign churches and general councils, might be, and no doubt were, generally concerted in such assemblies. Archbishop Arundel and his successors held many of these councils, which are not to be distinguished from the convocations called at the king's request in any point except that they were called without any such request. As however parliaments and convocations had this much in common, that the need of pecuniary aid was the king's chief reason for summoning them; it might naturally be expected that, when a parliament was called, the convocations would at no great distance of time be summoned to supplement its liberality with a clerical gift. We have seen how regularly this function was discharged during the fifteenth century, and how the clerical grant followed in due proportion the grant of the laity. But although nearly in every case there is a session of convocation to match the session of parliament, the session of convocation cannot be regarded as an adjunct of parliament. Archbishop Wake, in his great controversy with Atterbury, showed from an exhaustive enumeration of instances that, even where the purpose of the two assemblies was the same, there was no such close dependence of the convocation upon the parliament as was usual after the changes introduced by Henry VIII. The king very seldom even suggests the day for the meeting of convocation; its sessions and adjournments take place quite irrespective of those of the parliament; very rare attempts are made to interfere with its proceedings even when they are unauthorised by the royal writ of request; and after the accession of the house of Lancaster, they are not interfered with at all. On the side of the papacy interference could scarcely be looked for. As a legate could exercise no jurisdiction at all without royal licence, a legatine council could not be held in opposition to the king's will; but the days of legatine councils

The provincial councils or convocations.

Meetings of convocation correspond with but do not regularly accompany parliaments.

The meetings of convocations or provincial councils little interfered with.

of the whole national church seemed at all events to be over; there is no trace of any important meeting of such assembly between the days of Arundel and those of Wolsey[1]; although, from the date at which both archbishops acquired the legatine character, the provincial convocations might both be regarded as legatine councils.

Varieties of ecclesiastical legislation. 712. The history of ecclesiastical legislation, so far as it enters into our present consideration, comprises three distinct topics; the legislation of the clergy for the clergy, of the clergy for the laity, and of the laity for the clergy; and under each of these the several attempts at interference with, and resistance to, such legislation. Under each head moreover we have to distinguish in the case of the clergy between the pope and the national church, as regards both attempts at legislation and attempts at restriction; whilst in the case of the laity we must not less carefully discriminate between the action of the crown, of the parliament, and of the common law. An exhaustive discussion of the subject, even thus limited, would be out of all proportion to the general plan of this work, even if controversial points could be treated in it. It is however necessary to attempt to classify, under some such arrangement, the particular points of the subject which have an important bearing on our national history; and as most of these have been noted in their chronological order in our narrative chapters, the recapitulation need not occupy much space.

Laws made by ecclesiastical authority for the clergy. The laws made by spiritual authority for the spiritualty, by the clergy for the clergy, include, so far as medieval history is concerned, the body of the Canon Law, published in the Decretum of Gratian and its successive supplements, such particular edicts of the popes as had a general operation, the canons of general councils, the constitutions of the legates and legatine councils which in the fifteenth century were codified by Lyndwood in the Provinciale, the constitutions published by the archbishops and the convocations of their provinces, and those

[1] In 1408 the archbishop of Bourdeaux is said to have held a legatine council at London to discuss the state of the papacy; Cont. Eulog. iii. 413; but he seems to have merely been the envoy of the cardinals sent to debate the matter with the English clergy; see Wilkins, Conc. iii. 308, 311, 312.

of individual bishops made in their diocesan synods. All these may be included under the general name of Canon Law; all were regarded as binding on the faithful within their sphere of operation, and, except where they came into collision with the rights of the crown, common law or statute, they were recognised as authoritative in ecclesiastical procedure.

Canon Law.

In the general legislation of the church, the English church and nation had alike but a small share; the promulgation of the successive portions of the Decretals was a papal act, to which Christendom at large gave a silent acquiescence[1]: the crown asserted and maintained the right to forbid the introduction of papal bulls without royal licence, both in general and in particular cases; and the English prelates had their places, and the ambassadors accredited by the king and the estates had their right to be heard in the general councils of the church. But except in the rare case of collision with national law, the general legislation of Christendom, whether by pope or council, was accepted as a matter of course.

General legislation of the Church.

Restraint on the admission of papal Bulls.

In the acts of the national church, whether legatine, provincial, or diocesan, the legislative power was exercised by the presiding prelate in his own name and in that of his brethren; the legate Otho made constitutions, 'supported by divine help and by the suffrage and consent of the present council[2];' and Othobon legislated 'with the approbation of the present council[3].' The archbishops, who issued constitutions after the organisation of the provincial convocations was perfected, acted with the advice and consent of their brethren the bishops and the clergy of their provinces. The province of York by its convocation accepted the provincial code of the province of Canterbury[4]. The diocesan regulations made by particular bishops were either

National church legislation in council.

[1] See Blackstone, Comm. i. 79, 80: 'All the strength that either the papal or imperial laws have obtained in this realm or indeed in any other kingdom in Europe, is only because they have been admitted and received by immemorial usage and custom in some particular cases and some particular courts, . . . or else because they are in some other cases introduced by consent of parliament.' In the statute de Bigamis (Statutes, i. 44) Edward I recognises and extends the application of a constitution of the general council of Lyons.

[2] Johnson, Canons, ii. 157.

[3] Ib. ii. 213.

[4] Blackstone, Comm. i. 83; Wilkins, Conc. iii. 663; Johnson, Canons, ii. 513.

Diocesan enactments.

mere repetitions of general enactments, or rules of the nature of local ordinances, and require no notice here.

Royal right of restraining legislation.

The calling of the assemblies in which such legislation could be transacted was, as a matter of fact, subject to royal permission or approval, and the right of the king to forbid such a council or to limit its legislative powers was during the Norman reigns both claimed and admitted. William the Conqueror did not allow the archbishop in a general council of the bishops to 'ordain or forbid anything that was not agreeable to his royal will, or had not been previously ordained by him[1].' William Rufus prevented the holding of such an assembly for thirteen years[2]. Henry I acted on his father's principle, and added his royal confirmation to the ecclesiastical legislation which he approved[3]. Stephen struggled in vain against the claims of the clergy to independent power of legislation, and retorted by measures of oppression; but Henry II contented himself with aiding the conciliar legislation, which he knew himself to be strong enough by fair means to control. Hubert Walter held a 'general' council in spite of a prohibition of Geoffrey FitzPeter[4]; but he was himself chancellor at the time, and the protest of the justiciar may have been only formal. As a rule the later sovereigns, instead of restricting the liberty of meeting, contented themselves with warning the clergy not to infringe the royal rights. In 1207 for instance John warned the council of S. Alban's not to do anything contrary to the customs of the realm, and to defer their deliberations until they had conferred with him[5]. In 1281 again Edward I in the strongest language forbade the archbishop and bishops, as they loved their baronies, to discuss any questions touching the crown, the king's person or council,

Royal confirmation.

Prohibition by the justiciar.

Warnings addressed by the king to councils.

[1] Above, vol. i. p. 286.

[2] Anselm, Epp. iii. 40.

[3] 'Sciatis quod auctoritate regia et potestate concedo et confirmo statuta concilii, a Willelmo Cantuariensi archiepiscopo et sanctae Romanae ecclesiae legato apud Westmonasterium celebrati, et interdicta interdico. Si quis vero horum decretorum violator vel contemptor exstiterit, si ecclesiasticae disciplinae humiliter non satisfecerit, noverit se regia potestate graviter coercendum, quia divinae dispositioni resistere praesumpsit;' Foed. i. 8.

[4] Hoveden, iv. 128; R. Diceto, ii. 169. This was an attempt made by Hubert as primate to convene the whole of the English clergy.

[5] Rot. Pat. i. 72; Foed. i. 94; a similar warning of 18 Hen. III is cited by Coke upon Littleton, s. 137; and other instances 4 Inst. pp. 322, 323.

or to make any constitution against his crown and dignity [1]. But these and similar prohibitions were simply cautionary; so long as the councils confined their deliberations to matters of spiritual or ecclesiastical interest the kings either actively assisted or quietly acquiesced in the freedom of deliberation and legislation; nor in later times were the parliaments more than duly jealous or watchful in this respect, so long as the legislation was such as would bind the clergy alone, or the laity only *in foro conscientiae.*

713. Any attempts made by the spiritualty in council and convocation, or by the pope and his legates, to bind the laity by legislative enactment, must be looked for in those regions of ecclesiastical jurisprudence where the state had placed in the hands of the church, or the church had acquired by prescription, an ill-defined amount of judicial authority; or in other words, in those departments of judicature in which, according to the charter of William the Conqueror, the ministers of the common law undertook to compel the execution of ecclesiastical sentences. The most important of these departments during the early middle ages were the jurisdiction by which matrimonial suits were regulated, by which testamentary causes were decided, and by which the payment of tithes and ecclesiastical fees was enforced; from the beginning of the fifteenth century the jurisdiction in cases of heresy was another field for co-operation between the two powers, and there were besides such cases of slander, usury, and other minor offences, as could be tried in the spiritual courts. In each of these points, the baronage first, and the parliament afterwards, showed some jealousy of ecclesiastical legislation; the barons at the council of Merton, in 1236, rejected the proposition, to which the prelates had agreed, that illegitimate children are made legitimate by the subsequent marriage of their parents; the excessive charges made on the probate of wills are a frequent subject of complaint in parliament; and the constitution framed by archbishop Stratford in 1343 against those who refused to pay tithe of underwood called forth a petition from the commons, in 1344, that no petition

Instances of legislation by the clergy for the laity.

In matrimonial, testamentary and tithe questions.

Illustrations.

[1] Wilkins, Conc. ii. 50; see above, vol. ii. pp. 113, 114.

made by the clergy to the injury of the laity might be granted without examination before the king and the lords[1]. Almost all the examples however, in which the clergy went beyond their recognised rights in regulating the conduct of the laity, come under the head of judicial rather than of legislative action; in that department the common law had its own safeguards, and could ignore and quash proceedings founded on any canonical enactment that ran counter to it. Petitions in parliament against the encroachments of the spiritual courts are frequent, any direct conflict between the two legislatures is extremely rare. In the normal state of English politics the prelates, who were the real legislators in convocation and also formed the majority in the house of lords, acted in close alliance with the crown, and, under any circumstances, would be strong enough to prevent any awkward collision; if their class-sympathies were with the clergy, their great temporal estates and offices gave them many points of interest in common with the laity. Thus, although, as the judicial history shows, the lines between spiritual and temporal judicature were very indistinctly drawn, England was spared during the greatest part of the middle ages any war of theories on the relations of the church to the state. Even when the great question of heresy arose, few disputes of importance found a hearing in parliament; and if contemporary history testifies to some amount of popular disaffection caused by ecclesiastical laws, the records of parliament show that such disaffection found little sympathy in the great council of the nation. All attempts of the pope or general councils to legislate in matters affecting the laity were limited in their application, on the one hand by the common law, and on the other hand by the statute of praemunire. The subject of heresy may be reserved for a separate section.

Judicial interference more common than legislative assumption.

The position of the bishops prevented any difficulty between ecclesiastical and civil legislation.

Legislation in parliament touching the clergy.

714. The enactments made by the king in parliament to regulate, restrict, or promote the action of the spiritualty are very numerous, as might indeed be expected from the general tenour of a history in which the clerical estate played so great a part. Under this head it would be possible to range nearly everything

[1] See above, vol. ii. pp. 396, 596.

that has here been classified under all the other departments of administration. Most points of importance, however, occur in the history of taxation and judicature, and these will be noticed separately; as so much has been said on the topic in the earlier chapters of this work, a very brief recapitulation will be sufficient. The claim of William the Conqueror and his sons to determine, by their recognition, to which of the competitors for the papacy the obedience of the English Church was due may stand first in the series of these acts. In 1378 the English parliament following the same idea declared Urban VI to be the true pope, in opposition to the antipope supported by France and Scotland. But such measures are in fact political rather than legislative, and in their very nature exceptional. The most prominent place belongs to the statutes by which the papal usurpations or aggressions were met under the successors of Henry III, especially the legislation exemplified in the statutes of provisors and praemunire.

The king's claim to recognise the lawful pope.

Restriction of papal assumptions.

715. The great statute of provisors, passed in 1351, was a very solemn expression of the national determination not to give way to the pope's usurpation of patronage. It was the result of a series of efforts to throw off the yoke imposed in the thirteenth century by the successive encroachments on the free election to bishoprics, the history of which has been already traced. These efforts had begun under the influence of the school of Grosseteste, who, however much he may have been inclined to aid the pope in other ways, was determinedly opposed to the appointment of foreigners, ignorant of the English language or non-resident altogether, to the care of English churches. The papal provisions were not only usurpations of patronage, and infringements of canonical liberty, but the occasion of the loss of Christian souls. Yet in spite of the dislike with which they were viewed, petition, remonstrance, and even legislation seemed powerless against them. The clergy were afraid of the pope, the king found it convenient to use the power which connivance with the pope gave him in the promotion of his servants; and, to the baronage and the commons alike, the withdrawal of money from the realm by the aliens whom

Legislation on Provisors.

Growth of opposition to the system.

the pope provided was a point of at least as much importance as the spiritual loss of the church. Not to recur to the constant presentments of gravamina which furnished employment to the councils and parliaments of the thirteenth century, it will be enough to point to the legislation attempted in the parliament of Carlisle in 1307. The petition of the earls, barons, and commonalty of the land presented to the king in that parliament, the words of which were afterwards rehearsed in the statute of provisors, state that the church in this realm was founded by the king and his ancestors, and by the earls and barons and their ancestors, that they and their people might learn the faith, and provision might be made for prayer, alms, and hospitality; the recent action of the pope had tended to throw the great estates devoted to these purposes into the hands of aliens. The articles enumerated in the petition touch several other points of aggression, a claim recently made to the goods of intestates and to property not distinctly bequeathed by testators, the attempt to tax the temporalities of the clergy, the demand of first-fruits and of an increased contribution of Peter's pence[1]. The immediate result of the petition was a statute forbidding the religious houses to send money abroad, a prohibition addressed to William de Testa, the papal agent, forbidding him to proceed under the instructions committed to him, a letter of remonstrance to the pope, and orders, which were afterwards suspended, that the sheriffs should arrest the officers employed as papal collectors. Edward, whose death was known to be very near, was in no condition to dispute with the legate, Peter of Spain, and before a concordat could be arranged he died[2]. The struggle continued languidly under Edward II; he himself and the representatives of his father's policy were still inclined to resistance; but the opposition, headed by the earl of Lancaster, and supported to some extent by French and clerical influence, avoided offending the pope; and, although aggressions were multiplied and preventive measures and remonstrances were now and then tried[3], no

Attempted legislation of 1307.

Petition of the parliament of Carlisle.

Failure of the attempt at legislation.

State of affairs under Edward II.

[1] Rot. Parl. i. 219–223; Statutes, i. 150. [2] See above, vol. ii. p. 156.

[3] Letters forbidding the introduction of papal bulls without licence were

legislation was attempted until Edward III had been for some years on the throne. In 1343 the king was desired to write to the pope against the promotion of aliens, and to attempt some such legislation as had been contemplated in the parliament of Carlisle. After a search for the records of that parliament, an ordinance was prepared and passed with the assent of the baronage and commons, which forbade the introduction, reception, and execution of papal bulls, reservations, and other letters into the realm, and ordered the arrest of all persons contravening the order [1]. This ordinance was not however enrolled as a statute; and although in the next parliament a petition of the commons for the perpetual affirmation of the act received the assent of the king and baronage [2], three years later the law was unexecuted; the king had written to the pope, but no remedy had been devised. The remonstrance was repeated with no better result [3]. At last, in the parliament of 1351, the enactment was elaborately amended and framed into a perpetual statute [4]. By this act it was ordered that elections to elective benefices and dignities should be free, and that patrons should have their rights; that if the pope should reserve an elective promotion the king should have the collation, and if he should usurp a presentation on advowson the king should present for that turn: all persons procuring or accepting papal promotions were to be arrested, and on conviction fined and bound over to satisfy the party whose rights had been infringed. The assent of the lords spiritual was not formally given to this statute, and, important as it is, it seems to have been from the first evaded. In 1352 the purchasers of Provisions were declared outlaws; in 1365 another act repeated the prohibitions and penalties [5]; and in 1390 the parliament of

Remonstrances by Edward III.

Ordinances of 1343.

Statute of 1351.

The lords spiritual withhold consent.

issued by Edward II in 1307; Foed. ii. 13; by Edward III in 1327, ib. p. 726; and in 1376; Wilk. Conc. iii. 107. In 1376 William Courtenay, then bishop of London, published a papal bull against the Florentines, for which he was brought before both the king and chancellor and forced to retract the publication, which he did by proxy at S. Paul's Cross; Cont. Eulog. iii. 335.

[1] Rot. Parl. ii. 144, 145. [2] Ib. ii. 153, 154. [3] Ib. ii. 172, 173.

[4] Rot. Parl. ii. 232, 233; st. 25 Edw. III, st. 4; Statutes, i. 316 sq., 323.

[5] 38 Edw. III, stat. 2; Statutes, i. 385; Rot. Parl. ii 284, 285; see above, vol. ii. p. 598.

Parliamentary confirmations. Richard II rehearsed and confirmed the statute[1]. By this act forfeiture and banishment were decreed against future transgressors. The two archbishops entered a formal protest against it as tending to the restriction of apostolic power and the subversion of ecclesiastical liberty[2]. Recognition of the validity of the act. The parliaments however of Henry IV and Henry V recognised the validity of the legislation, and Chichele, as we have seen, incurred the displeasure of Martin V because he could not obtain a repeal[3]. How ill the statutes were kept we have already noted.

History of the Statute of Praemunire. 716. The history of the statute of praemunire starts from a somewhat different point but runs parallel for the most part with the legislation on the subject of provisions. It was intended to prevent encroachments on and usurpations of jurisdiction, as the other was framed for the defence of patronage. Ordinance against suing in foreign courts in 1353. The ordinance of 1353, which was enrolled as 'a statute against annullers of judgments in the king's courts,' condemns to outlawry, forfeiture, and imprisonment, all persons who, having prosecuted in foreign courts suits cognisable by the law of England, should not appear in obedience to summons, and answer for their contempt[4]. The name 'praemunire,' which marks this form of legislation, is taken from the opening word of the writ by which the sheriff is charged to summon the delinquent[5]. It is somewhat curious that the court of Rome is not mentioned in this first act of praemunire; as the assembly by which it was framed was not a proper parliament, it may not have been referred to the lords spiritual; their assent is not mentioned. Legislation of 1365. The act however of 1365, which confirms the statute of provisors, distinctly brings the suitors in the papal courts under the provisions of the ordinance of 1353, and against this the prelates protested[6]. Statute of Praemunire of 1393. In spite of the similar protest in 1393, the parliament passed a still more important statute, in which the word praemunire is used to denote the process by which the law is enforced. This act, which is one of the strongest defensive measures taken during the middle ages against Rome, was called

[1] 13 Ric. II, st. 2. c. 2; above, vol. ii. p. 598.
[2] Rot. Parl. iii. 264.
[3] Above, p. 301.
[4] 27 Edw. III, st. 1; Statutes, i. 329; vol. ii. p. 410.
[5] Gibson, Codex, p. 80.
[6] Above, vol. ii. p. 598.

for in consequence of the conduct of the pope, who had forbidden the bishops to execute the sentences of the royal courts in suits connected with patronage. The political translations of the year 1388 were adroitly turned into an argument: the pope had translated bishops against their own will to foreign sees, and had endangered the freedom of the English crown, 'which hath been so free at all times that it hath been in subjection to no earthly sovereign, but immediately subject to God and no other, in all things touching the regalie of the said crown.' The lords spiritual had admitted that such encroachments were contrary to the right of the crown, and promised to stand by the king. It was accordingly enacted that all persons procuring in the court of Rome or elsewhere such translations, processes, sentences of excommunication, bulls, instruments, or other things which touch the king, his crown, regality, or realm, should suffer the penalties of praemunire. Archbishop Courtenay's protest already referred to, whilst it admits the facts stated in the preamble, simply guards against limiting the canonical authority of the pope: the words of the protest are incorporated in the statute itself[1]. Nor was the legislation exemplified in the statutes of praemunire and provisors a mere 'brutum fulmen;' although evaded by the kings,—notably by Richard himself in the translation of Arundel to S. Andrews, in 1397,—and, so far at least as the statute of provisors was concerned, suspended from time to time by consent of the parliament, it was felt by the popes to be a great check on their freedom of action; it was used by Gloucester as a weapon against Beaufort; the clergy, both under papal influence and independently, petitioned from time to time for its repeal[2]; and in the hands of Henry VIII it became a lever for the overthrow of papal supremacy. It furnishes in ecclesiastical history the clue of the events that connect

Statute of Praemunire.

Courtenay's protest.

Disquietude of the pope and clergy under the restraint.

[1] 16 Ric. II, c. 5; Statutes, ii. 84.

[2] In the convocation of 1439 especially; see Wilkins, Conc. iii. 533; and again in 1447; ib. p. 555. It is fair to say that these clerical remonstrances were called forth rather by the chicanery of the lawyers than by any affection for the papal jurisdiction; the lawyers now and then chose to treat the ordinary ecclesiastical jurisdiction as foreign, and so to bring all the courts Christian under the operation of the statute of praemunire.

the Constitutions of Clarendon with the Reformation; and if in a narrative of the internal history of the constitution itself it seems to take a secondary place, it is only because the influences which it was devised to check were everywhere at work, and constant recurrence to their potent action would involve two separate readings of the history of every great crisis and every stage of growth.

Legislative interference by the state with the national church.

717. The several legislative measures by which at various times the crown or the parliament endeavoured to regulate the proceedings of the national church may be best arranged by reference to the particular subject-matter of the acts. They are important constitutional muniments, but are not very numerous or diversified. First among them come the ordinances or statutes by which the tenure of church property was defined and its extension limited. The establishment of the obligation of homage and fealty due for the temporalities or lands of the clergy was the result of a compromise between Henry I and Anselm, and it was accordingly not so much an enactment made by the secular power against the ecclesiastical, as a concordat betwixt the two. It was not so with the mortmain act, or with the series of provisions in which the statute 'de religiosis' was prefigured, from the great charter downwards. To forbid the acquisition of lands by the clergy without the consent of the overlord of whom the lands were held was a necessary measure, and one to which a patriotic ecclesiastic like Langton would have had no objection to urge. But the spirit of the clergy had very much changed between 1215 and 1279, and the statute 'de religiosis,' which was not so much an act of parliament as a royal ordinance, was issued at a moment when there was much irritation of feeling between the king and the archbishop[1]. It was an efficient limitation on the greed of acquisition, and although very temperately administered by the kings, who never withheld their licence for the endowment of any valuable new foundation, it was viewed with great dislike by the popes, who constantly urged its repeal, and by the monks, whose attempts to frustrate the intention of the law, by the

Concordat of Henry and Anselm.

Restriction on the acquisition of lands.

Statute 'de religiosis.'

Clerical disquietude under the restraint.

[1] Vol. ii. pp. 112, 113.

invention of trusts and uses, are regarded by the lawyers as an important contribution to the land-law of the middle ages. Other instances of legislation less directly affecting the lands of the church were the acts by which the estates of the Templars were transferred to the Hospitallers[1], and the many enactments from the reign of Edward III downwards, by which the estates of the alien priories were vested in the king. Beyond these, however, which are mere instances of the use of a constitutional power, it is certain that not only the parliaments but the crown and the courts of law exercised over the lands of the clergy the same power that they exercised over all other lands; they were liable to temporary confiscation in case of the misbehaviour of their owners, to taxation, and the constrained performance of the due services; and although they were not liable to legal forfeiture, as their possessors could be deprived of no greater right in them than was involved in their official tenure, they might be detained in the royal hands on one pretext or another for long periods without legal remedy. The patronage of parish churches was likewise a temporal right, and although the ecclesiastical courts made now and then a vain claim to determine suits concerning it, it was always regarded as within the province of state legislation. The spiritual revenues of the clergy, the tithes and offerings which were the endowment of the parochial churches, were subject to a divided jurisdiction; the title to ownership was determined by the common law, the enforcement of payment was left to the ecclesiastical courts[2]. The attempts of the parliament to tax the spiritualities were very jealously watched, and generally, if not always, defeated. The parliament, however, practically vindicated its right to determine the nature of the rights of the clergy to tithe of underwood, minerals, and other newly asserted or revived claims. In 1362 a statute fixed the wages of stipendiary chaplains[3].

Church lands subject to the Common Law.

Legal treatment of church lands.

Patronage a temporal right.

Tithes, a divided jurisdiction.

Minor points.

A second department in which the spiritualty was subjected to the legislative interference of the state was that of judicature. In this region a continual rivalry was carried on from the Con-

Restriction of ecclesiastical judicature by state legislation.

[1] 17 Edw. II, st. 2; Statutes, i. 194.

[2] See below, p. 342.

[3] Statutes, i. 374.

quest to the Reformation, the courts of the two powers, like all courts of law, being prone to make attempts at usurpation, and the interference of the crown as the fountain of justice, or of the parliament as representing the nation at large, being constantly invoked to remedy the evils caused by mutual aggression. Of the defining results of this legislation the 'articuli cleri' of 1316, and the writ of 'circumspecte agatis,' neither of them exactly or normally statutes, are the chief landmarks. In order to avoid repetition, we may defer noticing these disputes until we come to the general question of judicature.

Miscellaneous legislation for the clergy.

Outside these two regions of administration there are some few acts of the national legislature in which the interests or acts of the clergy are contemplated in a friendly and statesmanlike spirit, which rises above the quarrels of the day or of the class. Such probably were the statutes passed in 1340, 1344, and 1352[1], at the request of the clergy; most of their provisions, however, concern property or jurisdiction.

Cognisance of the great schism.

The ordinance of 1416, by which it was enacted that during the continuance of the schism in the church the bishops elect should be confirmed by their metropolitans[2], seems a singular instance of the parliament legislating for the clergy where they might have legislated for themselves. The petitions of the parliament for measures which might tend to close the schism are not indeed legislative acts, but may be adduced as proof that the attitude of the commons towards the church, even at moments when there was much reason for watchfulness, was neither unfriendly nor unwise.

Discussions on heresy.

In the struggle against heresy the policy of the parliaments was not uniform, but if the petitions against the clergy, which were ineffectually brought forward, are to be set off against the statutes against the Lollards, the result shows that in the long run the sympathies of the three estates were at one. In coming to such a conclusion, it must not be forgotten that the clergy, during nearly the whole period of the Lollard movement, had great influence with the king, were in possession of the greatest offices of state, possessed a majority of votes in the house of lords, and had an additional source of strength in the support of

[1] Statutes, i. 292, 302, 324.

[2] Above, p. 316.

the pope and foreign churches. But even if all these influences are taken into account, a united and resolute determination of the commons, such as in 1406 was brought to bear upon the king, must have made itself felt in legislation, and could not have contented itself with protest and petition.

718. In the department of finance and taxation, one of the great factors of the social problem may be briefly treated and dismissed; the pecuniary assumptions and exactions of the papacy are more important in political history than as illustrations of constitutional action. From the nation at large no imperative claim for money was made by the popes after the reign of Henry III, except in 1306, when William de Testa was empowered by Clement V to exact a penny from every household as Peter's pence, instead of accepting the prescriptive traditional composition of £201 9s. for the whole kingdom[1]: the tribute promised by John was stopped in the year 1366 by the resolution of parliament[2]. Voluntary payments for bulls and dispensations do not come within the scope of our present inquiries. The burden of papal exaction had, even in the thirteenth century, fallen chiefly on the clergy, and from the beginning of the fourteenth it fell wholly upon them. Contributions from the nation at large for papal purposes, such as crusades and the defence against the Turks, were collected by the pope's agents in the form of voluntary gifts. The pope had a regular official collector who gathered the offerings of the laity as well as the sums imperatively demanded from the clergy, and who was jealously watched by both[3]. A series of petitions against the proceedings of this most unpopular official was presented in the parliament of 1376. In 1390 the king had to reject a petition that the collector might be banished as a public

Ecclesiastical taxation by the popes.

Papal exactions.

The papal collector.

Petitions against him.

[1] Rot. Parl. i. 220. Innocent III in 1213 complained that the English bishops paid only 300 marks for Peter's pence, retaining 1000 for themselves; Foed. i. 118.

[2] Vol. ii. p. 415.

[3] He was regarded as a mere spy, sent to live in London and to hunt up vacancies and other opportunities for papal claims; he kept up the state of a duke; and he had begun to take first-fruits and sent out of the country annually 20,000 marks. It was no doubt in consequence of these representations that the collector's oath was framed; Rot. Parl. ii. 338–340. In 1377 the commons petitioned that the collector might be an Englishman; ib. p. 373.

Oath administered to him.

enemy. The oath which he was made to take was stringent enough; he swore fealty to the king; that he would not do or procure anything prejudicial to the king, the realm, or the laws; would give the king good advice, and would not betray his secrets; would suffer the execution of no papal mandates hurtful to the kingdom; would receive no such mandates without laying them before the council; would export no money or plate without leave from the king, nor send any letters out of the kingdom contrary to the king's interests; that he would maintain the king's estate and honour; that he would not collect first-fruits from benefices in the king's gift, nor from those given by the popes by way of expectative; that he would attempt no novelties, and would not leave the kingdom without permission[1]. In 1427 the pope's collector having introduced bulls of provision contrary to the statute, was imprisoned, and only released on bail after a brisk discussion in the privy council[2]; and there are many indications that the fulfilment of the oath was generally enforced.

Enforcement of the oath.

Papal exactions from the clergy.

On the clergy the hand of the papacy was very heavily laid. The exactions of tenths of ecclesiastical revenue, which were so common under Henry III, were not indeed collected without the consent of the payers, given in provincial synod, but the consent was almost compulsory[3]; the king was in alliance with the pope, and even Grosseteste admitted that the papal needs were great and must be satisfied. Edward I and Edward II had been obliged alike to allow these heavy exactions[4], and had in some instances shared with the popes the profits of transactions which they did not venture to contravene. But after the settlement of the papacy at Avignon the pressure was very much lessened; other modes of raising money were devised. Richard II, in 1389, ventured to forbid the collection of a papal subsidy[5]; when in 1427 the

Restrictions and evasions.

[1] Rymer, vii. 603; Prynne, on the Fourth Institute, p. 146.

[2] Ordinances, iii. 268.

[3] See Ann. Burton, pp. 356, 360; and a list of papal exactions, ib. pp. 364 sq.

[4] See the instances recorded above; vol. ii. pp. 104, 113, 119, 124, 325, 353, 376.

[5] Wilk. Conc. iii. 20; Rymer, vii. 645; Rot. Parl. iii. 405; instances of papal petitions for subsidy are not unfrequent; see Wilk. Conc. iii. 13, 48.

pope demanded a tenth for the crusade against the Hussites, the council and convocation contrived to pass the proposition by without direct refusal[1]; a similar course was followed in 1446, when the pope demanded a like subsidy[2]. But the other forms of exactions were endured at least with resignation. The claim to the first-fruits of bishoprics and other promotions was apparently first made in England by Alexander IV in 1256, for five years[3]; it was renewed by Clement V in 1306, to last for two years[4]; and it was in a measure successful. By John XXII it was claimed throughout Christendom for three years, and met with universal resistance[5]. The general and perpetual claim seems to have followed upon the general admission of the pope's right of provision and the multiplication of translations, the gift being at first a voluntary offering of the newly-promoted prelates. Stoutly contested as it was in the council of Constance[6], and frequently made the subject of debate in parliament and council[7], the demand must have been regularly complied with; in the petition of convocation in 1531 on the abolition of annates, it is stated that the first-fruits of the temporalities of bishoprics as well as of the spiritualities were paid, and the act which bestowed these annates on the king mentions the sum of £160,000 as having been paid on this account to the pope between 1486 and 1531[8].

Firstfruits of promotions.

719. The history of the steps by which ecclesiastical property was made to contribute its share towards the national income, and of the methods by which the process of taxation was conducted, has been traced in our earlier chapters up to the time

Taxation of the clergy for national purposes.

[1] Wilk. Conc. iii. 514.

[2] Ib. iii. 541–552.

[3] Ann. Burton, p. 390.

[4] Rot. Parl. i. 221; the claim is there spoken of as unheard of. Edward allowed it to be enforced; p. 222. In the parliament of 1376 it is said to be a new usurpation; ib. ii. 339. On the general history of Annates see Gieseler (Engl. ed.), vol. iv. pp. 86, 102–108.

[5] Gieseler, Eccl. Hist. vol. ii. p. 86; see also Extrav. Comm. lib. iii. tit. 2. c. 11.

[6] Gieseler, Eccl. Hist. vol. iii. p. 102.

[7] The act 6 Hen. IV, c. 1, declares that double and treble the amount formerly paid under this name was then exacted, and restricts it to the ancient customary sums.

[8] 23 Hen. VIII, c. 20; Statutes, iii. 386.

at which right of the provincial convocations to self-taxation became so strongly established that the king saw no use in contesting it. This right was a survival of the more ancient methods by which the contributions of individuals, communities and orders or estates, were requested by separate commissions or in separate assemblies. It was in full exercise from the early years of Edward I, and accordingly was strong enough in prescriptive force to resist his attempts to incorporate the clergy as an estate of parliament by the praemunientes clause. Although in some of the parliaments of the earlier half of the fourteenth century the report of the clerical vote was brought up in parliament by the clerical proctors, and the grants may have been in some cases made by the parliamentary assembly of the clergy[1], the regular and permanent practice was, that they should be made by the two convocations. In 1318 the parliamentary estate of the clergy refused the king money without a grant of the convocations; in 1322 the parliamentary proctors made a grant, but the archbishops had to call together the convocations to legalise it. In 1336 the representatives of the spiritualty granted a tenth in parliament, but this seems to have been an exception to the rule[2], for in 1344 they merely announced the grant which the provincial convocations had made. In fact, from the period at which the records of the convocations begin the grants were so made. With the convocations the kings very prudently abstained from direct interference. When money was wanted the king requested the archbishops to collect their clergy and ask for a grant; the archbishops, through their provincial deans, summoned their provincial synods, as they might do for any other purpose, and the clergy assembled without the pressure of a royal writ or such direct summons as would derogate from their spiritual independence. When they met, the king, either through the archbishop or through special commissioners, acquainted them with his necessities, and the votes were made either conditionally on the

Self-taxation of the clergy.

Process of taxing the clergy.

[1] See vol. ii. pp. 339, 344, 353, 380, and especially p. 395; the clerical grants are generally mentioned in the notes.

[2] See vol. ii. pp. 378, 379.

granting of petitions, or unconditionally, in much the same way as they were made in parliament. The clerical vote usually took the form of a tenth or a portion of a tenth, or a number of tenths, of spiritual property, assessed on the valuation of pope Nicolas in 1291; the parochial clergy shared with the towns the burden of a heavier rate of taxation than the counties and the baronial lands, which paid a fifteenth; the latter were of course subject to feudal services from which the former were exempt. The produce of an ecclesiastical tenth seems to have been a diminishing quantity, owing probably to the multiplication of exemptions, especially the exemption of livings under ten marks value; under the full valuation of 1291 it ought to have amounted to £20,000[1]; we learn, however, from a letter addressed by Henry VII to the bishop of Chichester, that in his reign it was estimated at no more than £10,000. The lay tenth and fifteenth had at the same time sunk to £30,000[2]. The history of the two forms of grant is the same; as the spiritual tenth was levied on the assessment of 1291, the lay tenth and fifteenth was paid according to an assessment of 1334[3], the counties and their subdivisions being expected to account for the sums which they had furnished in that year, and the particular incidence being regulated by local assessments. Both were unelastic, and required to be supplemented as time went on. Accordingly, just when the parliaments are found introducing new forms of subsidy, income tax, poll tax, or alien tax, the clergy have to provide some corresponding methods of increasing their grants. The stipendiary clergy were brought under contribution by archbishop Arundel, who, as we have seen, had some difficulty in reconciling with justice the collection of the priests' noble, by a vote of convocation, from a class of clergy which was not

Clerical tenths.

Amount of a clerical tenth.

The old valuations.

New forms of ecclesiastical impost.

[1] See above, vol. ii. p. 549.

[2] In 1497 the convocation of Canterbury granted £40,000 to the king, payable in two moieties. Henry excuses the payment of £10,000, 'which is as we understand to the value of one hole disme.' The laity had granted a tenth and fifteenth amounting to £30,000. The king's debts were £58,000; W. Stephens, Memorials of Chichester, pp. 178, 179.

[3] Coke, 4 Inst. p. 34; Brady, Boroughs, p. 39; Blackstone, Comm. i. 308; Madox, Firma Burgi, pp. 119 sq.

represented in convocation[1]. The difficulty was probably overcome by a diocesan visitation or some other proceeding of the individual bishops.

Forbearance of the laity in dealing with spiritualities.

720. Of this liberty of convocation the kings were carefully observant; and the parliaments not less so. Frequently as the knights of the shire proposed to seize the temporalities of the clergy, they never threatened the spiritualities; they attacked the position of the bishops and religious orders, but not that of the parochial clergy. And the clergy were generally willing to make a virtue of the necessity which lay upon them; they never, or only in the rarest cases, refused their tenth when the parliament had voted its proper share. On one occasion, indeed, we have seen the commons taking the clerical grant into account and presuming upon the gift of the priests' noble in a way that called for the king's interposition[2]. He reminded them that it was not for them but for the convocations to decide that that tax should be voted. But although the clergy had thus retained the power to consent or to refuse, they had no direct voice in the disposal of the grants they bestowed; the sums collected went to the general fund of the revenue, and were appropriated to special purposes by the commons or by the council. In all these points the period on which we have been last employed witnessed no important change; but the disuse of the attendance of the clergy in parliament, their constant complaisance in supplementing the parliamentary grants, and the increasing tendency to regard convocation as a constitutional supplement of parliament, are all signs of a progress towards the state of things in which it became possible for Henry VIII to effect the great constitutional change that marks his reign.

The king forbids the commons to tax the stipendiary clergy.

General acquiescence.

Clerical taxation of the laity not attempted or unsuccessful.

721. Of attempts by the clergy, except under papal authority, to tax the laity, or to enforce any general payments from them, English history has no trace. The cases in which tithes were claimed for underwood, in which the nearest approach seems to be made to such a proceeding, have been already noticed. Other attempts made in provincial synods to extend the area

[1] See above, pp. 45, 47.

[2] Above, p. 143.

of titheable property seem to have failed[1]. Indirect exactions, in the form of fees or fines in the spiritual courts, mortuaries and customary payments, scarcely come within the scope of our consideration, except as part of a very general estimate of the causes which alienated the laity from the clergy.

Jurisdiction in ecclesiastical matters.

722. We thus come to the last of our constitutional inquiries, that of judicature; the subject of jurisdiction of, by, and for the clergy, which has been through the whole period of English history one of the most important influences on the social condition of the nation, the occasion of some of its most critical experiences, and one of its greatest administrative difficulties. In the very brief notice which can be here given to it, it will be necessary to arrange the points which come before us under the following heads: first, the jurisdiction exercised by the secular courts over ecclesiastical persons and causes; secondly, the jurisdiction exercised by the spiritual courts over laymen and temporal causes; thirdly, the jurisdiction of the spiritual courts over the clergy; and fourthly, the judicial claims and recognised authority on judicial matters of the pope of Rome.

Division of the subject.

Royal jurisdiction over the temporalities of the clergy.

All suits touching the temporalities of the clergy were subject to the jurisdiction of the king's courts, and against so reasonable a rule scarcely any traces of resistance on the part of the clergy are found. Yet it is not improbable that during the quarrels of the twelfth century some question on the right of the bishops to try such suits may have arisen. Glanvill gives certain forms of prohibition in which the ecclesiastical judges are forbidden to entertain suits in which a lay fee is concerned[2]; and Alexander III, in a letter addressed to the bishops in 1178, directed them to abstain from hearing such causes, the exclusive jurisdiction of which belonged to the king[3]. In reference to lands held in frankalmoign, disputes between

Lands held in frankalmoign.

[1] Especially the demand of a tithe of personalty; see on this subject Gibson, Codex, pp. 690 sq.; Prynne, Records, iii. 332 sq. In 1237 the clergy petitioned that secular judges may not be allowed to determine 'utrum dandae sint decimae de lapidicinis vel silvicaediis, vel herbagiis vel pasturis vel de aliis decimis non consuetis;' Ann. Burton, p. 254. In archbishop Gray's Constitutions, cir. A.D. 1250, the obligation to pay tithe of personalty is strongly urged; Johnson, Canons, ii. 179.

[2] Glanvill, lib. xii. cc. 21, 22, 25.

[3] R. Diceto, i. 427.

clergymen belonged to the ecclesiastical courts; but the question whether the land in dispute was held by this tenure or as a lay fee, was decided by a recognition under the king's writ[1]. The jurisdiction as to tithes was similarly a debateable land between the two jurisdictions; the title to the ownership, as in questions of advowson and presentation[2], belonging to the secular courts, and the process of recovery belonging to the court Christian[3]. The right of defining matters titheable was claimed by the archbishops in their constitutions, but without much success, the local custom and prescription being generally received as decisive in the matter. The right of patronage was determined in the king's courts. In each of these departments, however, some concert with the ecclesiastical courts was indispensable; many issues of fact were referred by the royal tribunals to the court Christian to be decided there, and the interlacing, so to speak, of the two jurisdictions was the occasion of many disputes both on general principle and in particular causes. These disputes, notwithstanding the legislative activity of the kings and the general good understanding which subsisted between them and the prelates, were not during the middle ages authoritatively and finally decided. It is enough for our present purpose to state generally the tendency to draw all causes which in any way concerned landed property into the royal courts, and to prevent all attempts at a rival jurisdiction.

Questions of right to tithe.

Questions of patronage.

Cooperation of the two judicatures.

General harmonious working.

Personal actions between clerk and lay.

The same interlacing of judicatures, similar disputes, and a like tendency, are found in the treatment of personal actions between laymen and clergymen; the fifteenth Constitution of Clarendon[4], which insists that the cognisance of debts, in which the faith of the debtor has been pledged, belongs to the king's jurisdiction, was contravened by the canon of archbishop

[1] Const. Clar. no. 9; Glanvill, lib. 12. c. 15; against this the clergy petitioned in 1237; Ann. Burton, p. 254.

[2] Glanvill, lib. 4.

[3] The processes for recovery of tithe, and the jurisdiction in subtraction of tithe, have a long history of their own which does not concern us much. The statement in the text is Blackstone's conclusion, Comm. vol. iii. p. 88; but the details may be found in Reeves's History of English Law, iv. 85 sq.; cf. Prynne, Records, iii. 332; Gibson, Codex, pp. 690 sq.; and Ann. Burton, p. 255.

[4] Select Charters, p. 134.

Boniface, who, in 1261, attempted to draw all such pleas into the ecclesiastical courts[1]; but there is no reason to suppose that such a canon was observed, still less that it was incorporated into the received jurisprudence of the realm. A still larger claim was made in 1237, when the clergy demanded that a clerk should never be summoned before the secular judge in a personal action in which real property is untouched[2]; but this, with many other gravamina presented on the same occasion, could never find a favourable hearing notwithstanding the high authority of Grosseteste, who maintained them; and after the reign of Edward I they are heard of no more except as theoretical grievances.

Claims of the clergy not allowed.

In criminal suits the position of the clergy was more defensible. The secular courts were bound to assist the spiritual courts in obtaining redress and vindication for clergymen who were injured by laymen; in cases in which the clerk himself was accused, the clerical immunity from trial by the secular judge was freely recognised. If the ordinary claimed the incriminated clerk, the secular court surrendered him for ecclesiastical trial: the accused might claim the benefit of clergy either before trial or after conviction in the lay court; and it was not until the fifteenth century that any very definite regulation of this dangerous immunity was arrived at[3]. We have seen the importance which the jurisdiction over criminous clerks assumed in the first quarrel between Becket and Henry II. It was with the utmost reluctance that the clergy admitted the decision of the legate Hugo Pierleoni, that the king might arrest and punish clerical offenders against the forest law[4].

Criminal suits.

Benefit of clergy.

Jurisdiction over criminous clerks.

[1] Johnson, Canons, ii. 196.

[2] Ann. Burton, p. 254: 'item petunt quod clerici non conveniantur in actione personali quae non sit super re immobili coram judice saeculari, sed coram judice ecclesiastico, et quod prohibitio regis non currat quo minus hoc fieri non possit.'

[3] Blackstone, Comm. iv. 365 sq.

[4] R. Diceto, i. 410. In a letter addressed to the pope Henry states the concessions which he has made to the legate; 'videlicet quod clericus de cetero non trahatur ante judicem saecularem in persona sua de aliquo criminali neque de aliquo foris facto excepto foris facto forestae meae, et excepto laico feodo unde mihi vel alii domino saeculari debetur servitium;' he will not retain vacant sees or abbeys in hand for more than a year;

The ordinary, moved by a sense of justice, or by a natural dislike to acknowledge the clerical character of a criminal, would not probably, except in times of political excitement, interfere to save the convicted clerk; and in many cases the process of retributive justice was too rapid to allow of his interposition.

Prelates threatened with the punishment of treason. It is not a little curious, however, to find that Henry IV, at the time of his closest alliance with Arundel, did not hesitate to threaten archbishops and bishops with condign punishment for treason[1]; that on one famous occasion he carried the threat into execution[2], and that the hanging of the mendicant friars, who spread treason in the earlier years of his reign, was a summary proceeding which would have endangered the throne of a weak king even in less tumultuous times. Into the legal minutiae of these points we are not called on to enter: as to their social and constitutional bearing it is enough to remark

Influence of class immunities. that, although in times when class jealousies are strong, clerical immunities are in theory, but in theory only, a safeguard of society, their uniform tendency is to keep alive the class jealousies; they are among the remedies which perpetuate the evils which they imperfectly counteract. In quiet times such immunities are unnecessary; in unquiet times they are disregarded.

Ecclesiastical jurisdiction in matters temporal, matrimonial, and testamentary. 723. Of the temporal causes which were subject to the cognisance of the ecclesiastical court the chief were matrimonial and testamentary suits, and actions for the recovery of ecclesiastical payments, tithes and customary fees. The whole jurisdiction in questions of marriage was, owing to the sacramental character ascribed to the ordinance of matrimony, throughout Christendom a spiritual jurisdiction. The ecclesiastical jurisdiction in testamentary matters and the administration of the goods of persons dying intestate was peculiar to England and the sister kingdoms, and had its origin, it would appear, in times soon after the Conquest. In Anglo-Saxon times there

the murderers of clerks are subjected to perpetual forfeiture besides the customary lay punishment; and clerks are exempted from trial by battle. On the later phases of this dispute see Ann. Burton, pp. 425 sq., where is a tract by Robert de Marisco on the privileges of the clergy.

[1] Rymer, viii. 123.

[2] Above, pp. 50, 51.

seems to have been no distinct recognition of the ecclesiastical character of these causes, and even if there had been they would have been tried in the county court. Probate of wills is also in many cases a privilege of manorial courts which have nothing ecclesiastical in their composition, and represent the more ancient moots in which no doubt the wills of the Anglo-Saxons were published. As however the testamentary jurisdiction was regarded by Glanvill [1] as an undisputed right of the church courts, the date of its commencement cannot be put later than the reign of Henry I, and it may possibly be as old as the division of lay and spiritual courts. The 'subtraction of tithe' and refusal to pay ecclesiastical fees and perquisites was likewise punished by spiritual censures which the secular power undertook to enforce.

Growth of the testamentary jurisdiction.

Subtraction of tithe.

As all these departments closely bordered upon the domain of the temporal courts, some concert between the two was indispensable; and there were many points on which the certificate of the spiritual court was the only evidence on which the temporal court could act: in questions of legitimacy, regularity of marriage, the full possession of holy orders and the fact of institution to livings, the assistance of the spiritual court enabled the temporal courts to complete their proceedings in questions of title to property, dower and patronage [2]; and the more ambitious prelates of the thirteenth century claimed the last two departments for the spiritual courts [3]. In this however they did not obtain any support from Rome, and at home the claim was disregarded. Besides these chief points, there were other minor suits for wrongs for which the temporal courts afforded no remedy, such as slander in cases where the evil report did not cause material loss to the person slandered: these belonged to the spiritual courts and were punished by spiritual penalties [4].

Certificate of the ecclesiastical court, necessary for temporal justice.

Minor causes in courts Christian.

[1] Glanvill, lib. vii. c. 8; Blackstone, Comm. iii. 96 sq.; Prynne, Records, iii. 140; Gibson, Codex, pp. 551 sq.

[2] Blackstone, Comm. iii. 335 sq. [3] See Johnson, Canons, ii. 331.

[4] Blackstone, Comm. iii. 123, 124. In 1237 the clergy complain that such suits are withdrawn from them; 'ne quis tractet causam in foro ecclesiae sive de perjurio, sive de fide laesa, de usura vel simonia vel

Suits 'pro correctione animae.'

724. Besides the jurisdiction in these matters of temporal concern, there was a large field of work for the church courts in disciplinary cases; the cognisance of immorality of different kinds, the correction of which had as its avowed purpose the benefit of the soul of the delinquent. In these trials the courts had their own methods of process derived in great measure from the Roman law, with a whole apparatus of citations, libels, and witnesses; the process of purgation, penance, and in default of proper satisfaction, excommunication and its resulting penalties enforced by the temporal law. The sentence of excommunication was the ultimate resource of the spiritual courts. If the delinquent held out for forty days after the denunciation of this sentence, the king's court, by writ of significavit[1] or some similar injunction, ordered the sheriff to imprison him until he satisfied the claims of the church.

Process on excommunication.

Number of ecclesiastical courts.

These proceedings furnished employment for a great machinery of judicature; the archbishops in their prerogative courts, the bishops in their consistories, the archdeacons in some cases, and even the spiritual judges of still smaller districts, exercised jurisdiction in all these matters; in some points, as in probate and administration, co-ordinately, in others by way of delegation or of review and appeal.

Prohibitions issued by the king's court.

With the constitution of these courts the secular power meddled little. With their proceedings, whenever due cause was shown, it might interfere by prohibitions issued by the king's courts of law or equity[2]; and the claim of the kings that none of their vassals or servants should be excommunicated without their leave exempted a large number of persons from the jurisdiction of the church courts. The prohibitions were a standing grievance with the clergy, and were probably granted in many cases without due consideration. They were indeed frequently a sort of protest made by the temporal courts against the assumptions and encroachments of the courts Christian. The councils of the thirteenth century constantly complained of

Complaints of the clergy against prohibitions.

defamatione, nisi tantum super testamento vel matrimonio.' Ann. Burton, p. 256. See too above, vol. ii. pp. 57, 65.

[1] Blackstone, Comm. iii. 102; see below, p. 357.

[2] Blackstone, Comm. iii. 112; Gibson, Codex, pp. xix, 1064, sq.

these vexatious proceedings[1], although by their own attempts to extend their jurisdiction they constantly provoked retaliation. In 1247 Henry III attempted to restrict this branch of ecclesiastical jurisdiction to matrimonial and testamentary causes, and Edward I acted upon that rule[2]. The writ of circumspecte agatis, by defining the exercise of the royal power of prohibition, succeeded in limiting the functions of the church courts. This writ, which was regarded as a statute, directed that prohibitions should not be issued in cases of spiritual correction, neglect of churchyards, subtraction of tithes, oblations, mortuaries, pensions due to prelates, assault of clergymen, defamation, and breach of oath. In cases which concerned the right of patronage, tithe suits between parsons for more than a fourth part of the tithe of a parish, and pecuniary penances, prohibitions were to be enforced. In cases of assault on a clerk the injured person might appeal to the king's courts on account of the breach of the peace, and likewise to the bishop's court for sentence of excommunication; and in cases of defamation the spiritual court might commute penance for pecuniary payment in spite of prohibition[3]. The later statutes of 1316, 1340, and 1344, are amendments and expansions of the principles here laid down.

Restriction of ecclesiastical jurisdiction.

The writ 'circumspecte agatis.'

725. The jurisdiction of the spiritual courts over spiritual men embraced all matters concerning the canonical and moral conduct of the clergy, faith, practice, fulfilment of ecclesiastical obligations, and obedience to ecclesiastical superiors. For these questions the courts possessed a complete jurisprudence of their own, regular processes of trial, and prisons in which the convicted offender was kept until he had satisfied the justice of the church. In these prisons the clerk convicted of a crime, for which if he had been a layman he would have suffered death, endured lifelong captivity[4]; here the clerk convicted of treason or felony in the secular court, and subsequently handed over

Jurisdiction over the clergy.

The bishops' prisons.

[1] Ann. Burton, pp. 254 sq.; 403 sq.; 413 sq.; 422 sq.
[2] See M. Paris, p. 727; vol. ii. p. 65; and the forms of prohibition in Prynne's Records, iii. 780; Britton, i. 90, ii. 284.
[3] Statutes, i. 101, 102; above, vol. ii. p. 119.
[4] See Boniface's Constitution of 1261; Johnson, Canons, ii. 208.

Tendency to abuse.

to the ordinary, was kept in safe custody. In 1402, when Henry IV confirmed the liberties of the clergy, the archbishop undertook that no clerk convicted of treason, or being a common thief, should be admitted to purgation, and that this should be secured by a constitution to be made by the bishops[1]. These prisons, especially after the alarms consequent on the Lollard movements, were a grievance in the eyes of the laity, who do not seem to have trusted the good faith of the prelates in their treatment of delinquent clergy[2]. The promise of archbishop Arundel was not fulfilled.

Into the peculiar questions of ecclesiastical jurisdiction we are not called to inquire, for in so far as it worked within its own proper sphere, its proceedings had no bearing on the subject before us. One further point, and that a most important one, the question of appeals to Rome, must be likewise briefly noticed and dismissed.

Rarity of early appeals from England to Rome.

726. Except in the earliest days of Anglo-Saxon Christianity, when Wilfrid carried his suit to Rome, contrary to the decisions of the kings and witan of Northumbria, there are no traces of appeals to the pope earlier than the Norman Conquest. Recourse was indeed from time to time had to the holy see for the determination of points touching the bishops for which insular history and custom furnished no rules; in the ninth century a pope interceded to obtain the restoration of a dethroned king of Northumbria[3], and king Kenulf of Mercia, who had obtained papal confirmation of the restored dignity of Canterbury, is said to have declared that neither for pope nor for Caesar would he consent to the restoration of archbishop Wulfred[4]; but on these three occasions the points at issue were political rather than legal, and the action of the papal envoy that of a mediator rather than a judge. Even in the later days of the West-Saxon dynasty, when intercourse with the continental powers was much more frequent than before, the case of an application to Rome for leave to marry within

In Anglo-Saxon times.

[1] See Wilkins, Conc. iii. 271, 272.

[2] See the petition of 1410, above, p. 63; and below, p. 360.

[3] Councils, &c., iii. 561.

[4] Councils, &c., iii. 587, 588, 602.

the prohibited degrees seems to be the only recorded instance of a judicial resort thither; and in that case Dunstan is found resisting the papal mandate[1]. There can be no doubt that the Norman kings, influenced by continental usage, and not in the first instance unwilling to extend the authority of the papacy to which they knew themselves to be indebted, allowed the introduction of the practice of referring cases to the successor of S. Peter as supreme judge, although they did, as much as they could, restrain the practice by making their own licence an absolutely necessary preliminary. Anyhow, even in the reign of the Conqueror, disputed questions were carried to Rome for decision. William had before the Conquest been a suitor there in the matter of his marriage. The questions at issue between the sees of York and Canterbury were debated there. The bishop of Durham in his quarrel with William Rufus[2] threatened to appeal to the pope in a tone that shows the idea of such an appeal to be familiar to the persons to whom he spoke: and one of Anselm's charges against that king was that he hindered the prosecution of appeals[3]. It would seem certain from these facts that thus early, in matters which the royal tribunal was incompetent to decide, a right of appeal, under royal licence, was recognised. That Henry of Blois, whilst he filled the office of legate, from 1139 to 1144, introduced the practice, is an unwarranted conclusion from the words of the contemporary writer, which seem to refer rather to appeals to his own legatine jurisdiction than to that of the court of Rome[4]. But although the custom was older, the frequency of appeal much increased under Stephen. In a legatine council held by archbishop Theobald in the king's presence, in 1151, three appeals were made to the pope[5]. We have noted the cases of disputed elections that occurred in his reign. Early in the next reign we find a matrimonial cause, that of Richard Anesty, referred to Rome, and the correspondence of John of Salisbury shows that in almost every department of ecclesiastical jurisdiction the system was in full working before the election of

Introduction of papal appeals.

Legation of Henry of Blois.

Multiplication of appeals.

[1] Memorials of S. Dunstan, p. 67. [2] See above, vol. i. p. 440.
[3] See above, p. 323. [4] H. Hunt. f. 226. [5] Ibid.

Becket to the primacy[1]. By the Constitutions of Clarendon Henry attempted to stop or at least to control it. He forbade beneficed ecclesiastics to quit the realm without licence, and, having provided a regular succession of appellate courts from that of the archdeacon to that of the archbishop, ordered that without royal assent controversy should proceed no further[2]. This restriction of the liberty of appeal was one of the great points of the struggle with Becket, and, when the king was forced to abandon the Constitutions, he was made to swear in a special clause that he would not impede nor allow others to impede the free exercise of the right of appeals in ecclesiastical causes, provided that the appellants might, if they were suspected, be called upon to give security that they would not seek to harm the king or the kingdom[3]. But although the king was thus obliged to surrender one of the most important of the points for which he had contended, and to allow, as the later records of his reign show, constant reference to the pope in cases which the national church was competent to decide, he was able to limit the appeals to strictly ecclesiastical questions, in some cases to defeat the purpose of the appellants, and in others to avoid giving formal recognition to the decisions of the foreign court. In the two famous causes of the next reign, that of the monks of Canterbury against archbishop Hubert, and that of the election to S. David's, the king relied rather on the means which he took to persuade or force the appellants to withdraw the appeal, than on any constitutional right to prohibit it; and in the Canterbury case Richard I showed no small skill in prevailing on the parties to accept an arbitration even when the Roman legate was waiting to determine the appeal[4]. The church history of the thirteenth century, after the collapse of John's attempt to resist Innocent III, is full of appeals. Falkes de Breauté appealed against his outlawry and banishment, archbishops Richard and Edmund appealed against their monks; almost every new bishop had to

Forbidden by Henry II in the Constitutions of Clarendon.

Prohibition withdrawn.

Appeals eluded and evaded.

Appeals under Henry III.

[1] Foed, i. 20.
[2] Select Charters, p. 133.
[3] Hoveden, ii. 35; Bened. i. 32.
[4] Epistolæ Cantuarienses, pp. 322, 323.

fight a battle at Rome before he could obtain his see; Henry III himself sought in a papal sentence of absolution a release from the solemn obligations by which he had bound himself to his people. With the reign of law which was restored under his son, the practice was discouraged and restricted but not forbidden; its exercise was limited by the certainty that in most cases safer and cheaper justice could be found at home. Yet appeals did not cease, and the custom of seeking dispensations, faculties, and privileges in matrimonial and clerical causes increased. Archbishop Winchelsey had a suit with the monks of S. Augustine's which lasted for eight years[1]. Even the statutes of praemunire did not prevent the suing for justice in the papal court, in causes for which the English common law provided no remedy. But from the date of this legislation this particular practice became less historically important: the collusion, so to call it, between the crown and the papacy, as to the observance of the statute of provisors, extended also to the other dealings with the Curia. No attempt was made to prevent the sale of dispensations, and when an appeal was carried to Rome, and the pope had on the usual plan appointed judges-delegate to hear the parties in England, the royal veto was rarely if ever interposed. Probably however such appeals were not numerous, and in comparison with the sums raised by dispensations, the pecuniary results were inconsiderable. Still so great was the influence which the Roman court possessed in all political and social matters, that every bishop had his accredited agent at Rome, and by presents and pensions had to secure the good offices of the several cardinals and other prelates. It is a pitiful thing to read the letters of archbishop Chichele to the great ecclesiastics of the pontifical court, or to trace in those of bishop Beckington the paltry intrigues which determined the action of the supreme tribunal of Christendom. In the fifteenth century, notwithstanding the bold policy of Martin V and the somewhat sub-

Improvement under Edward I.

Operation of the statute of praemunire.

Diminution in the number and importance of causes referred to Rome.

Network of papal litigation.

[1] Prynne, Records, iii. 836. See also a form of appeal by Godfrey bishop of Worcester against archbishop Peckham, Thomas, Worcester, App. p. 38; and cases of appeal mentioned in the Rolls of Parliament, i. 50, 208; ii. 82.

missive attitude of the Lancaster kings, the direct influence exerted by the papacy in legal proceedings in England had become very small: questions which had once been bitterly contested had become matters of compromise; the papal jurisdiction in minor matters had become a thing of course, and in greater matters it was seldom heard of. The kings, who freely availed themselves of the powers which they obtained by good understanding with Rome, were tolerant of pretensions which, except in one point, were little more than pretensions. That one point, the drawing of revenue from England, was indeed contested, and now and then was the subject of some sharp recriminations in which the parliament as well as the king had to speak the mind of the nation. But most of the mischiefs caused by the old system of appeal, a system which at once crushed the power of the diocesan and defied the threats of metropolitan and king, were extinguished by the growth of sound principles in the courts of law, by the determined policy of the statute of praemunire, and by the general conviction that the decisions purchased at Rome could not be executed or enforced except with the leave of the courts at home. The papal policy had become obstructive rather than aggressive; its legal machinery was becoming subservient to royal authority, not a court of refuge or of remedy: and had not the doctrinal reformation given to the remodelled Curia a new standing ground, which on any theory was higher than the old position of territorial and pecuniary adventure into which it was rapidly sinking, the action of the papacy in England might have altogether ceased. It was a curious coincidence that the great breach between England and Rome should be the result of a litigation in a matrimonial suit, one of the few points in which the Curia had continued to exercise any real jurisdiction.

Gradual diminution of importance.

The question of heresy and its treatment.

In the foregoing outline of the legislative and judicial relations of church and state, the subject of heresy has been set aside for more particular treatment. It is a subject which comes into prominence as the older constitutional questions between the two powers become less important; and its interest is, from the point at which we have arrived, mainly prospective. It has however great importance both legally and socially, and the history of the legislation concerning it, so far as we can now follow it, furnishes most valuable illustrations of the curious interlacing of the spiritual and temporal polities on which we have had again and again to remark.

Immunity of England from heretical error.

727. The English church had up to the close of the fourteenth century been singularly free from heresy[1]: it had escaped all such horrors as those of the Albigensian crusade, and had witnessed with but slight interest the disputes which followed the preaching of the spiritual Franciscans. Misbelief and apostasy were indeed subjects of inquest at the sheriff's tourn, and the punishment of 'mescreauntz apertement atteyntz' was burning[2]. If however there was any persecution of heresy in England before the year 1382, it must have taken the ordinary form of prosecution in the spiritual court; the heretic when found guilty would after his forty days of grace be committed to prison by the writ 'de excommunicato capiendo,' or 'significavit,' until he should satisfy the demands of the church[3]. But it is highly improbable that if any such cases occurred the scrutiny of controversial historians and of legal antiquaries should have alike failed to discover them.

Recognised process of ecclesiastical law.

Wycliffe the first important person prosecuted for heresy.

The first person against whom any severe measures were taken was John Wycliffe himself. He had risen to eminence as a philosophic teacher at Oxford. Although he was in the main a Realist, he had adopted some of the political tenets of the Franciscan Nominalists, and, hating the whole policy of the mendicant orders, had formed views on the temporal power of

[1] The early cases of medieval heresy in England are these; (1) the appearance of certain 'pravi dogmatis disseminatores' in 1165 or 1166; they were 'Publicani,' and spoke German, and were condemned in a council held at Oxford to be branded, flogged and excommunicated, and proscribed by the Assize of Clarendon. They quitted England after making one convert; R. Diceto, i. 318; Will. Newb. lib. ii. c. 13. (2) In 1222 a deacon who had apostatised to Judaism was condemned in a council at Oxford and burned; Ann Wykes, p. 63; or hanged, M. Paris, p. 315. (3) In the troubles of the Franciscans, some of the unfortunate friars are said to have perished in England; Ann. Mels. ii. 323; but the authority for the statement is insufficient. See above, vol. ii. p. 470.

[2] Britton, i. 42, 179; cf. Fleta, p. 113.

[3] Gibson, Codex, p. 1102; Rot. Claus. (ed. Hardy), ii. 166; Rot. Parl. iii. 128.

the papacy akin to those of Marsilius and Ockham, blending with them the ideal of apostolic poverty as the model of clerical life. As his opinions in the later years of his life developed rapidly, it is not surprising that he came to look on the sacramental system of the medieval church with suspicion and dislike, as the real basis on which papal and clerical authority rested. Speculations on philosophical dogmas, and a certain amount of loose thought on doctrinal matters, the age of Edward III easily tolerated; archbishop Sudbury, if he were not afraid of Wycliffe, was not actively hostile to him; he had friends at court, and his reputation was so high that he was employed by the king in the negotiations with the pope which were held at Bruges in 1374. It was his share in the anti-clerical policy broached by the earl of Pembroke in 1371, and by John of Gaunt in 1376, which drew down upon him the hostility of the bishops[1]. The convocation which met Feb. 3, 1377, insisted on the restoration of bishop Wykeham, on whom John of Gaunt had avenged the humiliation which he had received in the Good Parliament, and urged the prelates to attack Wycliffe, whom they regarded as the chief counsellor of their great enemy. He was accordingly on the 29th brought before the bishops at S. Paul's; but the affray between his noble protectors and the citizens of London, provoked by the insult offered to bishop Courtenay, prevented the trial from proceeding, and the precise charges then laid against him are unknown[2]. A few months after the pope, under the influence of the friars, urged the bishops to attack him again, and in his letters distinctly alleged Wycliffe's following of Marsilius of Padua and John de Janduno as proving him to be a heretic[3]. Again a prosecution was attempted; Wycliffe was brought before a body of bishops at Lambeth, but again a popular tumult, encouraged by the attitude of the court, put

Development of his views.

First attempt to try him.

Second attempt.

[1] See above, vol. ii. pp. 420, 436, 438.

[2] The annalists give a sketch of the heresies generally imputed to Wycliffe, but not the precise points on which the investigation was attempted in 1377. Cont. Murimuth, pp. 222–224; Wals. i. 325. Cf. Shirley, Fasc. Zizan. pref. p. xxvii.

[3] By letters dated May 22, 1377; Wals. i. 345; Chr. Angl. p. 174.

His opinions condemned.

an end to the trial. Although he lived six years longer, and by his attacks on the sacramental system exposed himself, far more than before, to charges of doctrinal heresy, and although his opinions were formally condemned, no further attempt was made to molest him personally. Thus his opinions regarding the wealth and power of the clergy were the occasion of the first attack upon him; the pretext of the second was his theory on the papacy; and he was not brought to trial for his views on the sacraments. Of the spiritual, the philosophical, and the political elements in Wycliffe's teaching, the last was far the most offensive to the clergy and the most attractive to the discontented laity. In Wycliffe himself there is no reason to doubt that all the three were matters of conviction; but neither is there any reason to doubt that the popular favour which attended on his teaching was caused mainly by the desire for social change. Both he and his adversaries recognised the fact that on the sacramental system the practical controversy must ultimately turn; the mob was attracted by the idea of confiscation.

Legislation against heresy in 1382.

As soon as the alarm of Wat Tyler's rising had subsided, Courtenay, who had succeeded the murdered Sudbury as archbishop of Canterbury, undertook the task of repressing the new heresy which Wycliffe's emissaries were spreading at Oxford and in the country at large. In the first parliament of 1382 he procured the passing of an act against heretic preachers. That parliament sat from May 7 to May 22, and its acts were promulgated on the 26th; the statute touching heresy stated that unlicensed preachers of heresy, when cited before the ordinaries, refused to obey and drew people to hear them and to maintain them in their errors by great 'routs;' it enacted that commissions should be directed out of chancery to the sheriffs and others, to arrest the particular persons certified by the bishops to be heretics or favourers of heresy, that the sheriffs should arrest them, and they should be held in strong prison until they satisfied the church; in other words, instead of waiting until the heretic had been tried, found guilty, and excommunicated, the sheriff was to arrest under a commission from the chancellor issued on the bishop's certificate[1]. This was not all: on the 17th of May the archbishop had assembled a body of bishops, jurists, and divines, who drew up a series of propositions which were ascribed to the heterodox preachers and which they pronounced to be heretical[2]. During the consultations of this body, which lasted until May 21, an earthquake was felt in London, which caused no small consternation, and the heretics regarded it as a divine interposition in their favour[3]. On the 12th of July the archbishop obtained from the king letters empowering the bishops to arrest all persons who maintained the condemned propositions, to commit them to their own prisons, or to those of other authorities, and to keep them there until the council should determine what was to be done with them[4]. A brisk series of prosecutions followed during the summer; trials were held and excommunications issued; but the delinquents submitted; and when in the October parliament the knights of the shire insisted that the statute of May, not having duly passed the commons, should be repealed, all attempts at further persecution ended for the time[5]. The clergy had to content themselves with the old process of the spiritual courts[6]; the Lollard party were emboldened to bring before parliament the extravagant propositions of their rashest leaders[7].

Council of 'The earthquake.'

Royal letters.

Repeal of the statute.

Wycliffe died in 1384; soon after the political troubles of Richard's reign threw the religious difficulty altogether into the shade; the condition of the papacy was not such as to invite critical examination. After the victory of the appellants in 1388 royal letters were issued for the seizure of heretical books and the imprisonment of heretical teachers[8], and in 1389 an attack made by Courtenay on the Leicestershire Lollards, under the royal

Prosecutions and recantations.

[1] Rot. Parl. iii. 125; Stat. 5 Ric. II, p. 2. c. 5; Statutes, ii. 25.

[2] Wilkins, Conc. iii. 157 sq.; Fasc. Ziz. pp. 272 sq.

[3] Wycliffe, Trialogus, iv. 27, 36, 37; Fasc. Ziz. p. 283.

[4] Wilkins, Conc. iii. 156. Letters in the same sense were directed to the chancellor of Oxford; ib. p. 167; Fasc. Ziz. pp. 312 sq.

[5] Rot. Parl. iii. 141; see above, vol. ii. pp. 470, 471.

[6] See for example the injunctions issued by bishop Wakefield of Worcester in 1387; Wilk. Conc. iii. 202; Thomas, Worc. App. p. 123.

[7] Fasc. Ziz. pp. 360–369; above, vol. ii. p. 488.

[8] Wilk. Conc. iii. 191; above, vol. ii. p. 488; Prynne, 4th Inst. pp. 396–398.

letters of 1382, ended in the submission of the accused[1]. In 1391 the prosecution of Swynderby showed that the prelates had no other legal weapon against the heretics than the old spiritual process, whilst the heretics took care not to provoke extreme measures by their obstinacy[2].

A long manifesto of the party, presented in parliament in 1395, roused Richard himself to take measures of precaution, and suggested further proceedings[3].

The statute 'de haeretico,' passed in 1401.

In 1396 Thomas Arundel succeeded to the primacy; he immediately held a council which condemned the heretical propositions[4]; but political affairs prevented any new legislation until, in 1401, having obtained the promise of aid from the king and the help of a sympathetic parliament, he procured the passing of the statute 'de haeretico[5].' This act went far beyond that of 1382, both in its description of the evil and in the nature of the remedy prescribed. A certain new sect had arisen which usurped the office of preaching, and which, by holding unlawful conventicles, teaching in schools, circulating books and promoting insurrection, defied all authority; the diocesan jurisdiction was helpless without the king's assistance, for the preachers migrated from diocese to diocese, and contemned the citations of the courts; the prelates and clergy, and the commons also, had prayed for a remedy, the former in a long, and the latter in a brief petition; in conformity with their request the king in the usual form granted, established, and ordained that none should presume to preach openly or privately without the licence of the diocesan except curates in their own churches, and that none should teach heresy, hold conventicles, or favour the new doctrines: if any should offend, the diocesan of the place should

Tenour of the act.

[1] Wilk. Conc. iii. 208 sq.

[2] Swynderby's appeal (Foxe, Acts and Monuments, iii. 127) states distinctly that after excommunication the bishop must seek the succour of the king's law and 'by a writ of significavit put a man in prison.' Death is the punishment of heresy, but the sentence cannot 'be given without the king's justices;' ib.

[3] See above, vol. ii. pp. 488, 489. Royal letters of the year 1394, against a heretic in Hereford, are in Prynne, 4th Institute, pp. 227, 228, and proceedings against Wycliffe's books were constantly going on at Oxford during these years.

[4] Wilk. Conc. iii. 227 sq.

[5] See above, p. 32.

Statute 'de haeretico.'

cause him to be arrested and detained in his prisons till canonical purgation or abjuration, proceedings for which should take place within three months of the arrest: if he were convicted he should be imprisoned by the diocesan according to the measure of his default, and fined proportionably; but if he should refuse to abjure, or relapse after abjuration, so that according to the canons he ought to be left to the secular court, he should be given up to the sheriff or other local magistrate and be publicly burned[1]. By this act then the bishop had authority to arrest, imprison, and try the criminal within three months, to detain him in his own court, and to call in the sheriff to burn him. The parliament which passed the statute broke up on the 10th of March.

Trial and execution of Sawtre.

The archbishop however had not waited for this to make an example. The heretic clerk Sawtre during the session of parliament had been brought before the bishops in convocation, tried and condemned[2]. On the 26th of February the king's writ was issued for his execution. The coincidence of the two events is somewhat puzzling: the execution of Sawtre under the royal writ has led the legal historians to believe that prior to the passing of the act of 1401, it was possible, in the case of a condemned heretic, for the king to issue a writ

Question of the writ 'de haeretico comburendo.'

'de haeretico comburendo' analogous to the writ 'de excommunicato capiendo[3].' But no other instance of the kind can be found[4]; and most probably no such process had ever been followed. Why Arundel should have hurried on Sawtre's execution by royal writ instead of waiting until by his own order to the sheriff the sentence could have been enforced under the act, is not clear; unless, as there is some authority for supposing, he anticipated a popular attempt at rescue[5]. It was

[1] 2 Hen. IV, c. 15; Statutes, ii. 125.

[2] Wilk. Conc. iii. 254.

[3] Blackstone, Comm. iv. 46.

[4] Although Blackstone declares that a writ of the kind is found among our ancient precedents, and refers to Fitz Herbert, Natura Brevium, 269, the only example of the writ given there is the writ in Sawtre's case; and Fitz Herbert's argument, that such a writ could only issue on the certificate of a provincial synod and was not a writ of course but specially directed by the king in council, is based on that single example.

[5] Adam Usk (p. 4) mentions an alarm of a Lollard rising in London during this session of parliament.

under these circumstances that the first execution for Lollard heresy took place in England. By the laws and customs of foreign states burning was the regular form of execution for such an offence; in England it was the recognised punishment due for heresy in common with arson and other heinous crimes[1]; and there was nothing apparently in its enforcement here that shocked the feelings of the age.

First execution for Lollardy.

The act of 1401 neither stopped the growth of heresy nor satisfied the desires of the persecutors. The social doctrines with which Wycliffe's rash followers had supplemented the teaching of their leader, had probably engaged the sympathies of the discontented in the project of unseating the new king. In the parliament of 1406 a petition was laid before Henry, supported by the prince of Wales and the lords, and presented by the speaker of the commons[2]. In this document the action of the Lollards is described as threatening the whole fabric of society; the attacks on property endangered the position of the temporal and spiritual lords alike; to them were owing the reports that king Richard was alive and the pretended prophecies of his restoration: the king was asked to enact that any persons promulgating such notions should be arrested and imprisoned, without bail except by undertaking before the chancellor, and should be brought before the next parliament, there to abide by such judgment as should be rendered by the king and the lords; that all lords of franchises, justices, sheriffs, and other magistrates should be empowered and bound to take inquest of such doings by virtue of this statute without any special commission, and that all subjects should be bound to assist. Henry agreed to the petition, and the statute founded upon it was ordered to take effect from the approaching Epiphany and to hold good until the next parliament. Strange to say, nothing more was heard of it; whether it was merely intended as a temporary expedient, whether the Lollard knights procured its suppression, or the archbishop had seen the impolicy of confusing the spiritual and temporal jurisdictions, or whether it was not a premature attempt of the

Insufficiency of the statute.

Great petition of 1406.

Act found upon it.

No result follows.

[1] Above, p. 353; Britton, i. 42.

[2] Rot. Parl. iii. 583, 584.

prince to legislate on the principle which he adopted after the death of Arundel and when he was king himself, it is not possible to decide. Opinions have been divided as to the purport of the petition, and it has even been maintained that it was intended to substitute for the ecclesiastical persecution a milder form of repression over which the parliament could exert more direct authority[1]. But the language of the petition carefully considered seems to preclude any such conclusion; and it seems best to refer the disappearance of the statute either to a jealousy between the prince and the archbishop, of which there are other traces at a later time, or to a feeling of distrust existing between the spiritual and secular courts. The patent rolls of the ninth year of the reign contain several commissions issued by the king's authority for the suppression of heresy and the arrest of Lollard preachers after royal inhibition[2]; it is possible that these measures may have been taken under this statute.

Different views of this proposed measure.

Arundel's constitutions.

The next parliament was that of Gloucester, in October 1407; nothing however was done respecting the Lollards in that session. Although Arundel found time to issue a series of constitutions against them in 1409, the condition of the papacy itself occupied the minds of the bishops too much during the following years to allow time for the repression of heresy. In 1410 a parliamentary struggle took place, of which some account has been already given[3]. The knights of the shire petitioned, according to Walsingham, that convicted clerks might not be handed over to the bishops' prisons, and that the recent statute according to which the Lollards whenever and wherever arrested might without royal writ be imprisoned in the nearest royal prison, might be modified[4]. A petition of similar character appears on the rolls; the purport of which is that persons arrested under the provisions of the act of 1401 may be admitted to bail and make their purgation in the county in which they are arrested, such arrests to be henceforward made

Petition of 1410.

[1] Hallam (Middle Ages, iii. 90) supposes that the clergy prevented it from appearing on the Statute Roll.

[2] Rot. Pat. Calend. pp. 254, 256.

[3] Above, pp. 63, 64.

[4] Wals. ii. 283.

by the king's officers without violent affray[1]. To this prayer the king returned an unfavourable answer, and it is probable that this was the petition which the commons asked to have back, so that nothing might be enacted thereupon[2]. In this parliament also was first broached the elaborate scheme of confiscation which became a part of the political programme of the Lollards[3]. During this session a frightful execution took place under the act of 1401, and on this occasion the victim was a layman: John Badby, a tailor of the diocese of Worcester, had been excommunicated for heresy by the bishop and had refused to abjure; he was brought before the archbishop and clergy in convocation and, persisting in his refusal, was handed over to the secular arm with a petition, addressed by archbishop Arundel to the lords, that he might not be put to death[4]. Whether the petition were a piece of mockery or not, the unfortunate man was burned, the prince of Wales being present at the execution and making a vain attempt to procure a recantation. This event took place on the 10th of March; it seems to have been the first execution under the act, and accordingly in the record of the convocation the whole statute is recorded apparently in justification[5]. In the following month Sir John Oldcastle's church at Cowling was placed under interdict in consequence of the contumacy of his chaplain, but the sentence was remitted within a few days[6], and Oldcastle as well as his followers had peace until the death of the king.

Proposal of confiscation.

Execution of Badby.

Beginning of Oldcastle's troubles.

On the accession of Henry V Arundel as we have seen renewed his attack on the Lollards: Oldcastle was tried, condemned and allowed to escape from prison. The abortive attempt at revolution followed[7]; and Henry V in the parliament of 1414 proceeded to legislate finally and more fiercely against the remnant of the heretic party. Arundel was dead, and whatever had been his influence in forwarding or in preventing the measures proposed in 1406, the

Legislation of Henry V against heresy.

[1] Rot. Parl. iii. 626.
[2] Rot. Parl. iii. 623; above, p. 63.
[3] Above, pp. 63 sq.
[4] Wilk. Conc. iii. 324–329; Foxe, iii. 235–238; Wals. ii. 282.
[5] Wilk. Conc. iii. 328.
[6] Ib. iii 330, 331.
[7] See above, pp. 78-80.

Development of policy.

king proceeded to legislate on the principle which was then propounded. That principle was to make heresy an offence against the common law as against the canon law, and not merely to use the secular arm in support of the spiritual arm, but to give the temporal courts a co-ordinate power of proceeding directly against the offenders. If we suppose that Henry V was now acting under the advice of the Beauforts, as may be generally assumed when he acted in opposition to the advice of Arundel, this policy may be described as the policy of the Beauforts; and the cardinal's expedition to Bohemia may be regarded as a later example of the same idea of intolerance. But it is not necessary to look for the suggestion further than to the king himself, who, in the full belief of his duty as maintainer of orthodoxy, no doubt thought it incumbent upon him to place himself in the van of the army of the church. The purport of the act is as follows: in the view of the recent troubles caused by the Lollards and their supporters the king, with the advice of the lords and at the prayer of the commons, enacts that the chancellor, treasurer, judges, and all officers of justice shall on their appointment swear to do their utmost to extirpate heresy, to assist the ordinaries and their commissaries; all persons convicted before the ordinaries and delivered over to the secular arm, are to forfeit their lands as in case of felony, the lands which they hold to the use of others being however excepted; they are also to forfeit their chattels to the king. So far the act is only an expansion of the law of 1401; the following clauses go further: the justices of the bench, of the peace, and of assize are now empowered to inquire after heretics, and a clause to that effect is to be introduced into their commissions: if any be so indicted the justices may award against them a writ of capias which the sheriffs shall be bound to execute. The persons arrested are to be delivered to the ordinaries by indenture to be made within ten days of the arrest, and are to be tried by the spiritual court: if any other charges are laid against them in the king's court they are to be tried upon them before being delivered to the ordinary, and the proceedings so taken are not to be taken in evidence in the spiritual court; the person

Tenour of the act of 1414.

indicted may be bailed within ten days; the jurors by whom the inquest is to be taken are to be men who have at least five pounds a year in land in England or forty shillings in Wales; if the person arrested break prison before acquittal the king shall have his chattels, and also the profits of his lands until he be forthcoming again, but if he dies before conviction, the lands go to his heirs[1].

Later attempts to legislate.

This is the last statute against the Lollards, and under it most of the cruel executions of the fifteenth and sixteenth centuries were perpetrated. It was not however the last occasion upon which parliamentary action was attempted. In 1422 the Lollards were again formidable in London, and the parliament, on the petition of the commons, ordered that those who were in prison should be at once delivered to the ordinary according to the statute of 1414; a similar order was given in 1425[2]. In 1468 Edward IV, with exceptional tenderness, rejected a petition that persons who had committed the acts of sacrilege which were attributed to the Lollards should be regarded as guilty of high treason[3].

Change of political feeling with regard to the Lollards.

Outside the parliament the still unextinguished embers of political Lollardy continued to burn; in the attempted rising of Jack Sharpe in 1431 the Lollard petition of 1410 was republished and circulated[4], and it is not improbable that some Lollard discontent was mingled with the popular complaints in 1450. But the influences which had supported the early Wycliffites were extinct. The knights of the shire no longer urged the spoliation of the clergy; the class from which they were drawn found plunder enough elsewhere; the universities produced no new schoolmen; the friars experienced no revival or reform; and, although learning was liberally nurtured by the court, freedom of opinion found little latitude. Bishop Pecock of Chichester, who had endeavoured to use against the erroneous teaching of the Lollards some controversial weapons which implied more independent thought than

Case of bishop Pecock.

[1] 2 Hen. V, stat. 1. c. 7; Statutes, ii. 181 sq.
[2] Rot. Parl. iv. 174, 292.
[3] Ib. v. 632.
[4] Above, p. 112.

his brethren could tolerate, was driven out of the royal council with one accord by the lords, was tried for heretical opinions before the archbishop and bishops of his province, and condemned[1]. Like so many of the earlier Lollards he chose submission rather than martyrdom, abjured and recanted; in spite of papal mediation he was not restored to his see, but kept in confinement, and remained a pensioned prisoner as long as he lived. He is almost a solitary instance of anything like spiritual or intellectual enlightenment combining with heretical leanings to provoke the enmity or jealousy of the clergy.

Bishop Pecock.

Local influence of Lollardy.

The political views of the Lollards too were a very subordinate element in the dynastic struggle of the century. It is certainly curious that the early Lollard knights came chiefly from those districts which were regarded as favourable to Richard II, to the Mortimers, and afterwards to the house of York. Herefordshire, Gloucestershire, Bristol, and now and then Kent, are the favourite refuge of the persecuted or the seed-plots of sedition; Jack Sharpe of Wigmoreland led the rising of 1431, as the so-called John Mortimer led that of 1450. But the common idea of resistance to the house of Lancaster was probably the only link which bound the Lollards to the Mortimers, at least after the old court influences of Richard's reign were extinguished. There were Lollards in Kent and London as well as Yorkists, but the house of York when it came to the throne showed no more favour to the heretics than the house of Lancaster had done.

Possible connexion with dynastic faction.

Question of the number of executions.

It is difficult to form any distinct notion of the way in which the statutes against the Lollards operated on the general mass of the people; they were irregularly enforced, and the number of executions which took place under them has been very variously estimated[2]. Although the party had declined politically,

[1] Wilkins, Conc. iii. 576; Babington, Pecock's Repressor, vol. i. pref. pp. xxxvi–lvii.

[2] Adam of Usk (p. 3), in drawing a parallel between the Israelites who worshipped the golden calf, and the Lollards, has some words which might lead to misapprehension; they must be read as follows, 'Unde in pluribus regni partibus et praecipue-Londonia et Bristolia, velut Judaei ad montem Oreb propter vitulum conflatilem mutuo in se revertentes, xxiii milium de suis miserabilem patientes casum merito doluerunt, Anglici inter se de

so far as not to be really dangerous at any time after Oldcastle's death, considerable liberty of teaching must have been allowed, or otherwise bishop Pecock's historical position is absolutely unintelligible. If he were, as he thought, a defender of the faith, the enemies against whom he used his controversial weapons must have existed by toleration; if he were himself heretical, the avenues to high promotion must have been but negligently guarded. But the whole of the age in which the Lollard movement was working was in England as elsewhere a period of much trouble and misgovernance; men, parties, and classes were jealous and cruel, and although there was an amount of intellectual enlightenment and culture which is in contrast with the preceding century, it had not yet the effect of making men tolerant, merciful, or just. Tiptoft's literary accomplishments left him the most cruel man of his cruel time. In the church the gentle and munificent wisdom of men like Chichele and Waynflete had to yield the first place in power to the politic skill and the unscrupulous partizanship of men like Bourchier, who persecuted the assailants of truths which had little or no moral influence upon the persecutor.

Some liberty of teaching allowed.

Inconsistencies of the age.

728. The social importance of the clergy in England during the middle ages rested on a wider basis than was afforded by their constitutional position. The clergy, as a body, were very rich; the proportion of direct taxation borne by them amounted to nearly a third of the whole direct taxation of the nation;

Political and social weight of the clergy.

fide antiqua et nova altercantes omni die sunt in puncto quasi mutuo ruinam et seditionem inferendi.' There is no statement of 23,000 executions, but of the danger of internal schism. The London chroniclers furnish a considerable number of executions under Henry V and Henry VI; thirty-eight persons were hanged and burned after Oldcastle's rising in 1414; in 1415 were burned John Claydon and Richard Turmyn; Gregory, p. 108; in 1417 Oldcastle; in 1422 William Taylor, priest, p. 149; in 1430 Richard Hunden, p. 171; in 1431 Thomas Bagley, p. 171; Jack Sharpe and five others were hanged, p. 172; in 1438 John Gardiner was burned, p. 181; in 1440 Richard Wych and his servant, p. 183; in 1466 William Balowe was burned, p. 233; in 1467 four persons were hanged for sacrilege, p. 235. Foxe adds a few more names; Abraham, White, and Waddon, 1428–1431 (vol. iii. p. 587); John Goose in 1473, p. 755. There were many prosecutions, as may be seen in the Concilia as well as in Foxe, but in the vast majority of cases they ended in penance and recantation.

they possessed in the constitution of parliament and convocation a great amount of political power, a majority in the house of lords, a recognised organisation as an estate of parliament, two taxing and legislating assemblies in the provincial convocations; they had on their great estates jurisdictions and franchises equal to those of the great nobles, and in the spiritual courts a whole system of judicature parallel to the temporal judicature —but more inquisitorial, more deeply penetrating and taking cognisance of every act and every relation of men's lives. They had great immunities also, and a corporate cohesion which gave strength and dignity to the meanest member of the class.

Their social power.

Great numbers of persons ordained.

One result of these advantages was the existence of an exceedingly large number of clergymen, or men in holy orders. The lists of persons ordained during the fourteenth and fifteenth centuries are still extant in the registers of the bishops; the ordinations were held at least four times a year, and the number admitted on each occasion was rarely below a hundred. In 1370, bishop Courtenay, acting for the bishop of Exeter, ordained at Tiverton 374 persons; 163 had the first tonsure, 120 were ordained acolytes, thirty subdeacons, thirty-one deacons, and thirty priests[1]. The ordination lists of the bishops of Durham[2] furnish numbers smaller than these, but still so large as to make it a difficult question how so large a body of candidates for preferment could be provided for. To these lists the mendicant orders contribute but a small per-centage, the

[1] Maskell, Mon. Rit. iii. Thomas, in the Survey of Worcester, gives the following numbers:—

	Acolytes.	Subdeacons.	Deacons.	Priests.	Total.
At Cirencester, June 1, 1314	105	140	133	85	463
Worcester, Dec. 21, 1314	50	115	136	109	310
Worcester, Dec. 22, 1319		43	96	91	230
Ambersley, Dec. 18, 1322	120	102	50	60	332
Tewkesbury, Trinity, 1329	218	47	79	62	406
Campden, Trinity, 1331	221	100	47	51	419
Ambresley, June 2, 1335	251	115	133	22	521
Worcester, April 9, 1337	391	180	154	124	849
Tewkesbury, June 6, 1338	204	141	117	149	613.

[2] In the Registrum Palatinum, vol. iii. One year's ordinations taken at random may suffice:

	Acolytes.	Subdeacons.	Deacons.	Priests.	Total.
In 1341 at Pentecost	86	26	31	16	159
in September	16	10	18	19	63
in December	11	14	5	8	38.

persons who supplied the place of non-resident pluralists, or who acted under the incumbents as parish priests, were not numerous, the whole number of parish churches being not much over 8000; a large proportion of candidates were ordained on the title of chaplaincies, or rather on the proof that they were entitled to small pensions from private persons who thus qualified them for a position in which, by saying masses for the dead, they could eke out a subsistence[1]. The persons so ordained were the stipendiary priests, who in the reign of Henry IV were so numerous that a poll tax of six and eightpence upon them formed an important branch of the revenue[2]. They were not represented in convocation, but they had every clerical immunity, and they brought a clerical interest into every family. A slight acquaintance with medieval wills is enough to prove that almost every man who was in such circumstances as made it necessary for him to make a will, had sons or near kinsmen in orders. Sometimes they were friars; more generally, in the yeoman class, chantry priests; the country knights had kinsmen in their livings and among the monks of the great monasteries; the great nobles and the king's ministers looked on the bishoprics as the provision for their clerical sons. The villein class, notwithstanding legal and canonical hindrances, aspired to holy orders as one of the avenues to liberty[3]. And this great diffusion of interest must be set against all general statements of the unpopularity of the clergy in the later middle ages. There were just complaints of unfair distribution of patronage, and of concentration of great endowments in few

Large privileged class;

drawn from all ranks of society.

[1] Thus 'Willelmus de Blenkow, ad titulum V. Marcarum de Johanne Forestario, de quo reputat se contentum;' Reg. Pal. iii. 137. The mischiefs arising from this system are forcibly stated by archbishop Islip; 'curas animarum gerere negligunt, et onera curatorum caritate mutua supportare; quin immo eis penitus derelictis ad celebranda annualia et ad alia peculiaria se conferunt obsequia,' &c. Wilkins, Conc. iii. 1; cf. pp. 50, 51, 213. The same archbishop fixed a maximum amount of stipend; ib. p. 135.

[2] See above, p. 47.

[3] The restriction on the liberty of unfree persons to be ordained dates from very early times, and was intended no doubt to prevent persons seeking ordination from a worldly motive as well as to save the rights of the master over his dependents. In the Apostolic Canons it is based on the latter reason. See Maskell, Mon. Rit. iii. pp. xcvii, xcviii; and above, vol. ii. p. 463, vol. i. p. 431; Decr. p. i. dist. 54; Greg. ix. lib. i, tit. 18.

hands; but against class jealousy there was this strong safeguard: every tradesman or yeoman might live to see his son promoted to a position of wealth and power.

Classes from which the bishops were taken.

Some important generalisations may be drawn from a study of the episcopal lists from the time of the Conquest downwards: under the Norman kings the sees were generally occupied by men of Norman birth, either such as were advanced by Lanfranc on the ground of learning and piety, or such as combined with distinguished birth that gift of organisation which belonged to the Norman feudalist; to one class belonged Lanfranc himself and Anselm, to the other Osmund of Salisbury, who was a Norman baron, but also the reformer of the medieval liturgy, and William Giffard the minister of Henry I. As the ministerial system advanced, the high places of the church were made the rewards of official service, and official servants, having no great patrimonies, cultivated the cathedral foundations as a provision for their families; hence arose the clerical caste which was so strong under Henry I and Stephen. Here and there we find a scholar like Robert of Melun, or Gilbert the Universal. Already the great nobles showed their appreciation of the wealth of the church; Everard bishop of Norwich was of the house of Montgomery, Henry of Winchester was a grandson of the Conqueror, and the pious Roger of Worcester, the friend of Becket, was a son of Earl Robert of Gloucester. Hugh de Puiset, bishop of Durham. and S. William, archbishop of York, were nephews of Stephen. Nor was the example lost upon the later kings or barons: Henry II gave the archbishopric of York to his son; Henry III obtained Canterbury for his wife's uncle, and Winchester for his own half-brother; Fulk Basset, bishop of London, was a baron both temporal and spiritual. The noble Cantilupes served their generation as bishops of Hereford and Worcester. The next age saw the culmination of the power of the mendicant orders; Kilwardby, Peckham, and Bradwardine sat at Canterbury; another avenue to power was thus open to men of humble birth, and when the short-lived popularity of the friars was over, the avenue was not closed. Wykeham, Chichele, and

Officials promoted.

Scholars promoted.

Royal and noble prelates.

Prelates from the mendicant orders.

Waynflete rose by other means, services done in subordinate office, but they amply justified the system by which they rose in the great collegiate foundations by which they hoped to raise the class from which they sprang. Side by side with them are found more and more men of noble names, Beaumont, Berkeley, Grandison, Charlton, Despenser, Courtenay, Stafford, Beaufort, Neville, Beauchamp, and Bourchier, taking a large share, but not the whole, of the great dignities. Last, a Wydville rises under Edward IV; and then under Henry VII a change takes place; new men are advanced more frequently, and meritorious service again becomes the chief title to promotion; the humiliation of the baronage has perhaps left few noble men capable of such advancement. In this, as in some other points, medieval life was a race for wealth; the poor bishoprics were left to the friars; scarcely any great man took a Welsh see except as a stepping-stone to something better. Still it may fairly be said that during the latter centuries a poor and humble origin was no bar to great preferment; and the meanest stipendiary priest was not only a spiritual person, but a member of an order to which the greatest families of the land, and even the royal house itself, thought it no humiliation to contribute sons and brothers.

Preponderance of noble names.

Meritorious service a title to promotion.

General diffusion of clerical interest.

Against this diffusion of influence and interest has to be set the fact, that it was only on points of the most general and universal application that a body so widely spread, and so variously composed, could be brought to act together. Against any direct interference from the temporal power, unauthorised taxation or restrictive legislation, the clergy might act as a body; but within the sphere of ecclesiastical politics, and within the sphere of temporal politics, they were as much liable to division as were the baronage or the commons. The seculars hated the regulars; the monks detested the friars; the Dominicans and Franciscans regarded one another as heretics; the Cistercians and the Cluniacs were jealous rivals: matters of ritual, of doctrine, of church policy—the claims of poverty and chastity, the rights and wrongs of endowments—the merits of rival popes, or of pope and council—licenced and unlicenced

Internal divisions of the clerical body.

preaching, licenced and unlicenced confession and direction—were fought out under the several standards of order and profession. And not less in the politics of the kingdom. As in early days the regulars sustained Becket and the seculars supported Henry II, under John the clergy were divided between the king and the bishops; the Franciscans of the thirteenth century were allied with Grosseteste and Simon de Montfort; under Edward III they followed Ockham and Marsilius, and linked Grosseteste with Wycliffe; under Henry IV they furnished martyrs in the cause of restoration. In the great social rising of 1381, clergy as well as laymen were implicated; secular priests as well as friars died for Richard II; and later on the whole body of the clergy was arrayed for or against one of the rival houses. It was well that it was so, and that the welfare of the whole English church was not staked on the victory of a faction or a policy, even though the faction may have been legally or the policy morally the best. The clergy could no longer, as one united estate, mediate with authority between parties, but they might, and probably did, help on reconciliation where reconciliation was possible, and somewhat humanise the struggle when the struggle must be fought out.

Political partisanship among the clergy.

Diffusion of elementary education resulting from the widespread clerical body.

729. The existence of a clerical element in every class of society, and in so large proportion, must in some respects have been a great social benefit. Every one admitted even to minor orders must have been able to read and write; and for the subdeaconate and higher grades a knowledge of the New Testament, or, at the very least, of the Gospels and Epistles in the Missal was requisite[1]. This was tested by careful examination in grammar and ritual, at every step; even a bishop elect might be rejected by the archbishop for literary deficiency[2]; and the

[1] The rules on the subject of examination were very strict; see Maskell, Mon. Rit. iii. xcv sq.

[2] Thus in 1229 Walter elect of Canterbury was rejected by the pope for failing in his examination; M. Paris, p. 356. There are some instances in which this was overruled. Lewis Beaumont of Durham could scarcely read the hard words in his profession of obedience; see vol. ii. p. 318; Robert Stretton elect of Coventry was rejected by archbishop Islip but forced by the king and the pope into his see; he could not read his profession, and it was read for him; Islip in disgust declined to take part

bishop who wittingly ordained an ignorant person was deemed guilty of deadly sin. The great obscurity which hangs over the early history of the universities makes it impossible to guess how large a portion of the clergy had received their education there; but towards the close of the period the foundation of colleges connected with particular counties and monasteries must have carried some elements of higher education into the remotest districts; the monastic and other schools placed some modicum of learning within reach of all. The rapid diffusion of Lollard tracts is itself a proof that many men could be found to read them; in every manor was found some one who could write and keep accounts in Latin; and it was rather the scarcity and cost of books, than the inability to read, that caused the prevalent ignorance of the later middle ages. Some germs of intellectual culture were spread everywhere, and although perhaps it would still be as easy to find a clerk who could not write as a layman who could, it is a mistake to regard even so dark a period as the fifteenth century as an age of dense ignorance. In all classes above the lowest, and especially in the clerical class, men travelled both in England and abroad more than they did after the Reformation had suspended religious intercommunion and destroyed the usefulness of ecclesiastical Latin as a means of communication. For clerks, if not for laymen also, every monastery was a hostelry, and the frequent intercourse with the papal court had the effect of opening the clerical mind to wider interests.

Colleges and schools.

Knowledge of Latin common.

Active intercourse with foreign nations.

It would have been well if the moral and spiritual influence of the clerical order had been equally good; but, whilst it is necessary to guard against exaggerated and one-sided statements upon these points, it cannot be denied that the proved abuses of the class go far to counterbalance any hypothetical advantages ascribed to its influence. The majority of the persons

Moral influence questionable.

in the consecration; Ang. Sac. i. 44, 449. Robert Orford elect of Ely was rejected by Winchelsey 'ob minus sufficientem literaturam'; on application to the pope he convinced him that he had not failed in his examination but had answered logically not theologically; ib. p. 641. Giraldus Cambrensis has some amusing stories about the bad Latin of the bishops of his time; but on the whole the cases of proved incompetence are very few.

Mischief arising from the number of half employed clergy.

ordained had neither cure of souls nor duty of preaching; their spiritual work was simply to say masses for the dead; they were not drawn on by the necessities of self-culture either to deeper study of divine truth or to the lessons which are derived from the obligation to instruct others; and they lay under no responsibility as bound to sympathise with and guide the weak. The moral drawback on their usefulness was even more important, because it affected the whole class and not a mere majority. By the necessity of celibacy they were cut off from the interests of domestic life, relieved from the obligations to labour for wives and families of their own, and thus left at leisure for mischief of many sorts. Every town contained thus a number of idle men, whose religious duties filled but a small portion of their time, who had no secular responsibilities, and whose standard of moral conduct was formed upon a very low ideal. The history of clerical celibacy, in England as elsewhere, is indeed tender ground; the benefits which it is supposed to secure are the personal purity of the individual, his separation from secular ways and interests, and his entire devotion to the work of God and the church. But the results, as legal and historical records show us, were very different. Instead of personal purity, there is a long story of licenced and unlicenced concubinage, and, appendant to it, much miscellaneous profligacy and a general low tone of morality in the very point that is supposed to be secured. Instead of separation from secular work is found in the higher class of the clergy entire devotion to the legal and political service of the country, and in the lower class idleness and poverty as the alternative. Instead of greater spirituality, there is greater frivolity. The abuses of monastic life, great as they may occasionally have been, sink into insignificance by the side of this evil, as an occasional crime tells against the moral condition of a nation far less fatally than the prevalence of a low morality. The records of the spiritual courts of the middle ages remain in such quantity and in such concord of testimony as to leave no doubt of the facts; among the laity as well as among the clergy, of the towns and clerical centres, there existed an amount

Evils resulting from clerical celibacy.

of coarse vice which had no secrecy to screen it or prevent it from spreading. The higher class of the clergy were free from any general faults of the kind; after the twelfth century, when many of the bishops were, if not married, at least the fathers of semi-legitimate families, the episcopal character for morality stands deservedly high; bishop Burnell, the great minister of Edward I, is perhaps an exception[1]; but there is scarcely a case of avowed or proved immorality on record until we reach the very close of the middle ages, and there is no case of the deprivation of a bishop for any such cause. The great abbots were, with equally rare exceptions, men of high character. It is in the obscurity of the smaller monasteries and in the self-indulgent, unambitious, and ignorant ranks of the lowest clergy, that we find the vices which called in the former class for summary visitation and suppression, and in the latter for the exercise of that disciplinary jurisdiction which did so much to spread and perpetuate the evils which it was created to cure. For the spiritual courts, whilst they imposed spiritual penalties, recognised perfunctory purgations, and accepted pecuniary fines, really secured the peccant clerk and the immoral layman alike from the due consequences of vice, such as either stricter discipline or a healthier public opinion would have been likely to impose. And in this, as in other particulars, the medieval church incurred a fearful responsibility. The evils against which she had to contend were beyond her power to overcome, yet she resisted interference from any other hand. The treatment of such moral evils as did not come within the contemplation of the common law were left to the church courts; the church courts became centres of corruption which archbishops, legates, and councils tried to reform and failed, acquiescing in the failure rather than allow the intrusion of the secular power. The spiritual jurisdiction over the clergy was an engine which

Good character of the higher clergy.

Abuses of the spiritual courts.

Their incapacity of reform.

[1] Burnell is probably the bishop who had five sons, and against whom archbishop Peckham attempted a prosecution in 1279; Wilk. Conc. ii. 40. He was Peckham's personal rival, and one annalist who mentions his death in 1292 speaks of his 'consanguineas, ne dicam filias' and 'nepotibus suis seu filiis'; Ann. Dunstable, p. 373.

Unwillingness to give up clerical privilege.

the courts altogether failed to manage, or so far failed as to render reformation of manners by such means absolutely hopeless: yet any interference of the temporal courts was resented and warded off until the evil was irremediable, because a clerk stripped of the reality of his immunities, but retaining all the odium with which they had invested him, would have no chance of justice in a lay court. Thus on a small stage was reproduced the result which the policy of the papacy brought about in the greater theatre of ecclesiastical politics. The practical assertion that, except by the court of Rome, there should be no reformation, was supplemented by an acknowledgment of the evils that were to be reformed, and of the incapacity of the court of Rome to cure them: there popes and councils toiled in vain; they could bear neither the evils of the age nor their remedies. Strange to say, some part of the mischief of the spiritual jurisdiction survived the Reformation itself, and enlarged its scope as well as strengthened its operation by the close temporary alliance between the church and the crown. To this the English church owes the vexatious procedure of the ecclesiastical tribunals and the consequent reaction which gave so much strength to Puritanism: nay, Puritanism was itself leavened with the same influences, and instead of struggling with the evils of the system which it attacked, availed itself of the same weapons, met a like failure, and yielded to a like reaction. But on this point, as has been said before, it is useless to dogmatise; and no mere theory, however consistent and perfect in itself, can either insure its own realisation or prove itself applicable to different ages and stages of growth.

Vitality of these abuses.

CHAPTER XX.

PARLIAMENTARY ANTIQUITIES.

730. Parliamentary usages, definite or obscure.—731. Plan of the chapter.—732. Choice of the day for parliament.—733. Annual parliaments.—734. Length of notice before holding parliament.—735. Choice of the place of session.—736. The Palace of Westminster.—737. Parliaments out of London.—738. Share of the council in calling a parliament.—739. Issue and form of writs.—740. Writs of summons to the lords.—741. Writs of the justices.—742. Writs to the Sheriffs for elections.—743. County elections.—744. Return on indenture.—745. Borough elections.—746. Contested and disputed elections.—747. Manucaption and expenses.—748. Meeting of parliament and opening of the session.—749. Separation of the houses.—750. House of Lords.—751. Ranks of the peerage.—752. Number of lords temporal.—753. Number of lords spiritual.—754. Justices in the House of Lords.—755. Clerical proctors.—756. Numbers and distribution of seats in the House of Commons.—757. Clerks.—758. The Speaker of the Commons.—759. Business laid before the houses by the king.—760. Supply and account.—761. Form of the grant.—762. Proceeding in legislation.—763. The Common petitions.—764. Form of statutes.—765. Details of procedure.—766. Sir Thomas Smith's description of a session.—767. Judicial power of the Lords.—768. Prorogation.—769. Dissolution.—770. Writ of expenses.—771. Distinctions of right and privilege.—772. Proxies of the Lords.—773. Right of protest.—774. Freedom of debate.—775. Freedom from arrest.—776. Privileges of peerage.

730. The rules and forms of parliamentary procedure had, before the close of the middle ages, begun to acquire that permanence and fixedness of character which in the eyes of later generations has risen into the sanctity of law. Of these rules and forms some are very ancient, and have preserved to the present day the exact shape in which they appear in our earliest parliamentary records; others are less easily discovered in the

Antiquity of parliamentary customs.

Difference in their history.

medieval chronicles and rolls, and owe their reputation for antiquity to the fact that, when they make their appearance in later records, they have already assumed the prescriptive dignity of immemorial custom. To the former class for instance belong the formulae of the legislative machinery, the writs for assembling parliament, the methods of assent and dissent, the enacting words of statutes, the brief sentence of royal acceptance or rejection; to the latter class belong the methods of proceeding which are less capable of being reduced to written record; the machinery of initiation and discussion, of committees and reports; the process by which a Bill passes through successive stages before it becomes an Act, the more minute rules of debate, and the more definite elaboration of points of privilege. Both classes of forms are subject to a certain sort of expansion; but the former seems to have reached its full growth before any great development of the latter can be distinctly traced. And this difference is not to be explained on the theory that, as time went on, freedom of debate and activity of discussion compelled the use of new rules and the formation of a customary code, while the more mechanical part of the old system was found to answer all purposes as well as ever. There can be little question that debates were as fierce and as tedious in the minority of Henry VI as in the troublous days of Charles I. No doubt the public interest in politics, fostered by improved education and stimulated by religious partisanship, gave to the latter a wider influence and made a more distinct impression on national memory. As early as the seventeenth century the speeches of parliamentary orators were addressed to the nation at large; although the publication of the debates was still in the distant future. But the fact that the rule and method of debate does, when it first appears, wear the habit of custom, the constant appeal to precedent and prescription, the whole history and theory of privilege, seem to show that the silence of earlier record is not to be interpreted as negation. A very faint idea of parliamentary activity would be formed from the isolated study of the journals of either house. The rolls of parliament, in like manner, furnish scarcely a skeleton of the proceedings of the earlier sessions.

Records clear.

Usages obscure.

Reason for this obscurity.

Published speeches, the diaries of clerks and members, unauthorised and authorised reports of debate, enable us to realise, in the case of the later parliaments, almost all that is historically important. For the medieval period we have no such helps; and for some particular parts of it we have no light at all, or what is more puzzling still, cross lights and discordant and contradictory authorities.

Want of records as to the details of usage.

731. In the present chapter our design is to collect such particulars as may help to complete our idea of the medieval parliament in its formal aspect, to describe the method of summoning, choosing and assembling the members; to trace, as far as we can, the process of initiation, discussion, and enactment, and to mark the points up to which the theory of privilege had grown at the close of our period. It will be no part of our plan to venture into the more dangerous regions of modern procedure; but where in the earlier forms the germs of such later developments are discoverable it will be sufficient to indicate them. In pursuance of this plan our first step is to recapitulate the points of interest involved in the determination of the time, place, and forms of summons, for parliament; the next step is to describe the process of election of the elected members; we can then proceed to the consideration of the session itself, the arrangement of the houses, their transaction of business, intercourse, prorogation and dissolution; and close the survey with a brief notice of the history of privilege.

Plan of this chapter.

732. The determination of the time at which the parliament was to be held rested primarily with the king; but the choice of the particular day or season of the year, as well as the frequency or infrequency of sessions, and the use of adjournment or prorogation, was variously decided according to the character which the assembly possessed at the several stages of its growth. The witenagemotes of the Anglo-Saxon kings, if we may draw a general conclusion from the scanty indications of particular charters, were mostly held on the great festivals of the church or at the end of harvest[1]; the great councils of the Norman kings generally, although not invariably, coincided with the

Choice of the day for the meeting of parliament.

[1] Vol. i. pp. 123, 124; notes 1, 2, 3.

Coincidence of legal and parliamentary terms.

crown-wearing days at Christmas, Easter, and Whitsuntide[1]; and, as long as the national council retained as its most prominent feature the character of a court of justice, so long it must have been almost necessary that it should meet on fixed days of the year. That character it retained until the representation of the commons came to be recognised as an indispensable requisite for a legal parliament, and the name of parliament came to be finally restricted to the assembly of the three estates. This date can scarcely be placed earlier than the beginning of the reign of Edward III, when the distinction was completely drawn between a Great Council, however summoned and however constituted, and the regular parliament. But even after this date, although the administration of justice had ceased to form the most important part of the public business, and the granting of supplies, presentation of petitions, and discussions of national policy, were matters which required punctuality and certainty much less than the administration of justice, the influence of custom, and the same reasons of convenience which had originally assigned days and seasons for legal proceedings, continued to affect the choice of a day for parliament. Under Henry II and his successors down to Henry III, the national councils met as well on the great festivals as on the terminal days of the law courts; but irregularly and not exclusively on those days. The provisionary government of 1258 fixed three days in the year, which have a less distinct reference to these points of time, the octave of Michaelmas, October 6, the morrow of Candlemas, February 3, and the 1st of June, three weeks before the feast of S. John the Baptist at Midsummer[2]: by this expedient the awkwardness of depending on the moveable feasts was avoided. That arrangement however was short-lived. Edward I, during the early part of his reign, seems to have followed the terminal days of the courts of law.

Legal terms.

These terminal days had their historical origin in the distinction made by the Roman lawyers between *dies fasti* and *dies nefasti*, the former being the days on which the courts and comitia might

[1] Vol. i. pp. 369, 370.
[2] See above, vol. ii. p. 76.

be held, the *dies nefasti* those on which they were forbidden. After the adoption of Christianity the more solemn seasons of the church took the place of the old *dies nefasti*, and were set apart from legal work by the civil and canon law[1]. The distinction is noted in the compilation called the laws of Edward the Confessor, which describes the custom of England as it existed under the justiciar Glanvill; according to this rule the peace of God and the church was to be observed from the beginning of Advent to the octave of the Epiphany, from Septuagesima to the octave of Easter, and from the Ascension to the octave of Pentecost, besides Sundays and holy days[2]. Under these designations the later term days are denoted; the octave of Epiphany is the feast of S. Hilary, from which the Hilary or Lent term begins; and the octaves of Easter and Whitsuntide have the same relation to the Easter and Trinity terms. The ending of the third and the beginning of the fourth term depended on the harvest; an operation so important that not only the schools and the law courts were closed during its continuance, but even civil war was suspended by common consent of the parties, and the parliament itself was prorogued or adjourned during the vacation. The exact days for beginning and ending business varied in the courts and universities, and were from time to time altered by legislation. For parliamentary business the fourth or Michaelmas term may be considered to have begun on the quindene of S. Michael, October 13th, the feast of the translation of S. Edward the Confessor, a memorable and critical day on more than one occasion of English history.

The law terms and vacations.

Custom or convenience seems in quiet times to have prescribed these days as fitting days for parliaments; and no doubt the lawyers, who formed an important element in the house of commons, found the coincidence of the parliamentary and legal days of business very opportune for their own interests; the barons and bishops who had attended the court on the great festivals may also have found it convenient to remain in town after

Convenience of observing the term days.

[1] See Reliquiae Spelmannianae, pp. 69 sq; Nicolas, Chronology of History, p. 383.

[2] Ll. Edw. Conf. § 2; cf. Canute, Eccl. § 17; Ethelred, v. § 19, vi. § 25.

Coincidence of the parliamentary and law terms.

the conclusion of the festivities, instead of making an additional journey. Anyhow, in the great majority of cases throughout the middle ages, the day of parliamentary summons is fixed with reference to the beginning of the Law Terms. In less quiet times it was impossible to observe such a rule; and, after long prorogations and less frequent elections had become usual, the old days were less regarded. But the importance of the autumnal vacation always made itself felt; Edward III in 1352 summoned only half the house of commons, that harvest might not be neglected[1]; and the same cause, which in 1215 stayed the outbreak of war until the harvest was housed, led to the prorogation of parliaments under Henry VI and Edward IV from July to November, the harvest apparently falling later in the year as time went on and tillage increased.

Annual parliaments.

733. As the political functions of the national parliament became more prominently important than the judicial work of the king in his full council, it became a point of public security that regular and fairly frequent parliaments should be held; and the demand for annual parliaments accordingly emerges very soon after the final admission of representatives of the commons. We have in a former chapter noted the political bearing and history of this demand[2]. The ordinances of 1311 and acts of parliament in 1330 and 1362 established the rule that parliaments should be held annually and oftener if it were found necessary. The greatest number of sessions held in one year was four, in the year 1328[3]. As each session involved a fresh election, and as the wages of the members formed a heavy item in local taxation, it is no wonder that, except in times of political excitement, even the annual parliaments became somewhat burdensome. Before the close of the fourteenth century the law was frequently transgressed, and two or three years passed without a session. There was no parliament held in 1364, 1367, 1370, or between 1373 and 1376: under Richard II, the years 1387, 1389, 1392 and 1396, are marked by a suspension of the national action; under Henry IV there was no

Ordered by law.

Neglect of the rule.

[1] See above, vol. ii. p. 408; Lords' Report, iv. 593.
[2] See above, vol. ii. p. 612.
[3] Vol. ii. p. 371.

parliament between 1407 and 1410; under Henry V there was at least one session each year. Under the Lancastrian kings the sessions had become so much longer than in earlier times that an intermission of a year was often more or less welcome; but the longer intervals begin contemporaneously with the family troubles; no parliament was held in 1440 or 1441, in 1443 or 1444; the parliament called in February 1445 sat by adjournment until April 1446; there was no session in 1448, 1452, 1457 or 1458. Edward IV held only six parliaments, or appealed to the country only six times during a reign of two and twenty years.

Long sessions and prorogations.

734. The great charter had prescribed for the holding of the commune consilium a summons, to be issued at least forty days before the day of meeting. This rule was regarded as binding in the reign of Elizabeth[1], and was observed until the union with Scotland; but not without occasional exceptions. The famous parliament of Simon de Montfort was called at twenty-seven days' notice[2]; the almost equally famous parliament of 1294 at thirty-five[3], which is the modern rule; in most other cases under Edward I and Edward II the notices are much longer. The summons for the parliament of 1327, in which Edward II was deposed, was issued thirty-five days before the meeting[4]; in 1330 Edward III apologised for abridging the notice to thirty-one days; business was pressing and he had taken the advice of the lords[5]; in 1352 the council, to which only one knight of each shire was summoned, was called only twenty-eight days beforehand[6]. Richard II invariably gave long notices; the parliament in which he was deposed was summoned exactly forty days before his resignation, and the first parliament of his successor, for which only seven days' warning was given, consisted of the same members that were summoned for the week before. These seem to be the only important

Forty days' notice of the meeting of parliament.

Few exceptions to the rule.

[1] Sir T. Smith, Commonwealth; see below, p. 468.

[2] Dec. 24 for Jan. 20; Select Charters, p. 406; Lords' Report, iv. 34.

[3] Oct. 8 for Nov. 12; ibid. p. 60.

[4] Above, vol. ii. p. 360.

[5] Lords' Report, i. 492; the king apologised for the short notice in the writ, stating that he acted with the assent of the prelates and magnates, and that the act should not be a precedent to the damage of any.

[6] Lords' Report, iv. 593.

variations from the rule of Magna Carta; the notices vary generally rather in excess than defect, but in many cases it is exactly observed[1].

Place of parliaments.

735. A more ancient and uniform prescription than that which affected the time for holding parliament regulated the choice of the place of session. Westminster was from the days of Edward the Confessor the recognised home of the great council of the nation as well as of the king. How this came about, history does not record; it is possible that the mere accident of the existence of the royal palace on the bank of the Thames led to the foundation of the abbey, or that the propinquity of the abbey led to the choice of the place for a palace; equal obscurity covers the origin of both. It is possible that under the new name of Westminster were hidden some of the traditions of the old English places of councils, of Chelsea or even of the lost Clovesho. But when the palace and the abbey had grown up together, when Canute had lived in the palace and Hardicanute had been buried in the abbey, and when the life and death of the Confessor had invested the two with almost equal sanctity, the abbey church became the scene of the royal coronation, and the palace the centre of all the work of government. The crown, the grave, the palace, the festival, the laws of king Edward, all illustrate the perpetuity of a national sentiment typifying the continuity of the national life. There the conqueror kept his summer courts, and William Rufus contemplated the building of a house of which the great hall which now survives should be only one of the bed-chambers[2]. At Westminster Henry I held his councils[3], and Stephen is said to have founded the chapel of his patron saint[4] within the palace. Although the courts continued to attend on the king, they like him rested, when they did rest, at Westminster; there was the certain place where, according to the great charter, the common pleas were to be held when they

The palace of Westminster.

Memories of Edward the Confessor.

Under the Norman kings.

[1] After the union with Scotland the notice was given fifty days beforehand; by the 15 Vict. c. 23, this period has been reduced to thirty-five days after the proclamation, appointing a time for the first meeting of parliament; May, Treatise on the Law, Proceedings and Usage of Parliament, p. 44.

[2] Stow's London, ed. Strype, bk. vi. p. 47.

[3] Flor. Wig. A.D. 1102.

[4] Mon. Angl. vi. 1348.

ceased to follow the king[1]; there the annual audits of the exchequer were already settled. Although Henry II held his more solemn councils in a more central place, and where there was more room for the camps of the barons to be collected round him, he frequently met both clergy and baronage there; the clergy in the abbey, the barons in the hall, found their proper council chamber. From the beginning of the reign of Henry III the custom seems to have acquired the sanctity of law; he rebuilt the abbey and added largely to the palace, and by his devotion to the memory of the Confessor professed himself, if he did not prove himself, the heir of the national tradition. So well established was the rule, that in the troubled times which followed the legislation of Oxford, the king avoided Westminster, thinking himself safer at S. Paul's or in the Tower, and the barons refused to attend the king at the Tower according to his summons, insisting that they should meet at the customary place at Westminster and not elsewhere[2]. The next reign saw the whole of the administrative machinery of the government permanently settled in and around the palace; and thus from the very first introduction of representative members the national council had its regular home at Westminster. There, with a few casual exceptions, to be noticed hereafter, all the properly constituted parliaments of England have been held.

Westminster becomes the usual place for parliaments.

Westminster the seat of government.

736. The ancient palace of Westminster, of which the most important parts, having survived until the fire of 1834 and the construction of the New Houses of Parliament, were destroyed in 1852, must have presented a very apt illustration of the history of the Constitution which had grown up from its early simplicity to its full strength within those venerable walls[3]. It was a curious congeries of towers, halls, churches, and chambers. As the administrative system of the country had been developed largely from the household economy of the king, the national palace had for its kernel the king's court, hall, chapel, and chamber. It had gathered in and incorporated other buildings

Interest of the old parliament houses.

[1] Art. 17.

[2] Ann. Dunst. p. 217.

[3] See Brayley and Britton, History of the Ancient Palace of Westminster, and Smith's Antiquities of Westminster.

Historical interest of Westminster.

that stood around it; successive generations had added new wings, built towers, and dug storehouses. As time went on, every apartment changed its destination: the chamber became a council room, the banquet hall a court of justice, the chapel a hall of deliberation; but the continuity of the historical building was complete, the changes were but signs of growth and of the strength that could outlive change. Almost every part of the palace had its historical hold on the great kings of the past. In the Painted Chamber Edward the Confessor had died; the little hall or White Hall was believed to be the newly fashioned hall of his palace; the Great Hall, the grandest work of sovereign power, was begun by William Rufus and completed by Richard II. The chapel of S. Stephen was begun by Stephen, rebuilt by Edward I, and made by Edward III the most perfect example of the architecture of his time.

Plan of the buildings.

The ancient Exchequer buildings stood east and west of the entrance of the Great Hall; the Star Chamber in the south-eastern corner of the court that extended in front of the Hall. The King's Bench was held at the south end of the Hall itself. The more important of the parliamentary buildings lay south and east of the Hall. To the south-east, and at right angles with the Hall, the church of S. Stephen ran down to the river: at right angles to the church, separated from the Great Hall by a vestibule, was the lesser or White Hall; south and east of the White Hall and parallel with S. Stephen's chapel, was the Painted Chamber, or Chamber of S. Edward; and at right angles to it again was the king's Great Chamber, the White Chamber, or Chamber of the Parliament. Beyond this was the Prince's Chamber [1], which reached to the limit of the palace buildings southwards, and looked on the river. Of these buildings the King's Chamber, or Parliament Chamber [2], was the House of Lords from very early times until

[1] Probably the small chamber south of the White Chamber (Foedera, ii. 1122), where Stratford in 1340 received the Great Seal. The 'Prince' must have been Edward the Black Prince, who after the parliament of 1371 called the burghers into his own chamber, and obtained a grant of tunnage and poundage from them. It was afterwards the 'Robing Room.'

[2] Brayley and Britton, p. 401; the old house of lords or chamber of parliament, and the prince's chamber, were pulled down in 1823; ibid. p. 421.

the union with Ireland, when the peers removed into the lesser or White Hall, where they continued until the fire. The house of commons met occasionally in the Painted Chamber, but generally sat in the Chapter House or in the Refectory of the abbey, until the reign of Edward VI, when it was fixed in S. Stephen's chapel[1]. The Painted Chamber, until the accession of Henry VII, was used for the meeting of full parliament, and for the opening speech of the Chancellor; it was also the place of conference between the two houses. After the fire of 1834, during the building of the new houses, the house of lords sat in the Painted Chamber, and the house of commons in the White Hall or Court of Requests. It was a curious coincidence certainly that the destruction of the ancient fabric should follow so immediately upon the great constitutional change wrought by the reform act, and scarcely less curious that the fire should have originated in the burning of the ancient Exchequer tallies, one of the most permanent relics of the primitive simplicity of administration[2].

The old houses of parliament.

The work of parliament was not always carried on within the walls of the palace. The neighbouring abbey furnished occasionally both lodging and meeting rooms for the estates. Of the monastic buildings the refectory, the infirmary, and the chapter house, were, after the church itself, most signally marked by historical usage. The refectory was a frequent place of meeting for the barons under Henry III; there in 1244 they bearded the king and the pope[3]; and at a later period the commons frequently sat there. The infirmary or chapel of S. Katharine, was at one time the regular place of session for the bishops[4]. In the chapter house, in 1257, Henry III confessed his debt to the pope[5]; the parliament of Simon de Montfort assembled there[6], and it afterwards came to be regarded as the

The abbey also used in time of parliament.

[1] In 1548; Brayley and Britton, p. 361.
[2] The tallies had been in use until 1826; Brayley, &c. p. 425.
[3] M. Paris, p. 639.
[4] M. Paris, p. 640. They met in the chapel of S. John the Evangelist; but the chapel of S. Katharine was the place were consecrations were most frequently performed.
[5] See above, vol. ii. p. 70.
[6] Liber de Antiquis Legibus, p. 71.

Occasional sessions at Blackfriars.

'ancient and accustomed house' of the commons. The proper home of convocation was in the lady chapel of S. Paul's. On one or two occasions, when the condition of the palace or other reasons compelled it, the parliament was held at Blackfriars. This was the case in 1311[1], when the Ordinances were published, and likewise for a few days in 1449[2]. Richard II held his revolutionary parliament of 1397 in a great wooden building erected in the court before Westminster Hall[3]. Almost every exception to the rule has some historical significance.

Occasions on which parliaments were held at a distance from London.

737. Most of these exceptions were owing to circumstances, sanitary or political, which made it necessary or advisable to summon the estates to some place distant from London. Not to multiply instances, it may suffice to mention the cases, occurring after the incorporation of the commons, in which the parliaments met away from Westminster, and such only as concern true and full parliaments from 1295 onwards. Far the largest number of these exceptional sessions were held at York during the long struggle with the Scots, when the presence of the king and barons was imperatively required in the north. Edward I in 1298; Edward II in 1314, 1318, 1319, and 1322; Edward III twice in 1328, in 1332, 1333, 1334 and 1335, held sessions at York[4]. In 1464 Edward IV summoned the estates to the same place: the great hall of the archbishop's palace was the scene of the short session[5]. Next in point of distinction to York come Northampton and Lincoln, at each of which four parliaments have sat. The central position of Northampton had made it a favourite council ground with Henry II; Edward II held his first parliament there in 1307; Edward III followed the example in 1328 and 1338; and in 1380 the parliament which voted the famous poll tax met at the same place[6]; the lords sat in a great chamber, the commons in the new dormitory of the priory of S. Andrew[7]. The four parliaments of Lincoln belong to the years 1301, 1316, and

At York, North-ampton, and Lincoln.

[1] See vol. ii. p. 328.
[2] Rot. Parl. v. 171.
[3] Annales Ricardi, p. 209; Brayley, p. 283.
[4] Vol. ii. pp. 148, 338, 343, 344, 351.
[5] Rot. Parl. v. 499.
[6] See above, vol. ii. pp. 315, 371, 378, 448.
[7] Rot. Parl. iii. 88.

1327[1]; the first session of 1316 was opened in the hall of the deanery, and the lords sat in the chapter house of the cathedral and at the convent of the Carmelites[2]. Three parliaments were held at Winchester, one in 1330, when Edmund of Woodstock was beheaded, one in 1393, and a third in 1449 when the plague was at Westminster. Besides these a supplementary great council was held at Winchester in 1371[3]. Bury S. Edmund's witnessed two famous sessions, one in 1296, when archbishop Winchelsey produced the bull *clericis laicos*; the other in 1447 marked by the death of duke Humfrey; the parliament was opened in the refectory of the abbey[4]. Leicester saw three parliaments, one under Henry V in 1414, when the lords sat in the great hall of the Grey Friars, and the commons in the infirmary of the same convent: another session was held there in 1426, 'the parliament of bats,' when the lords sat in the great hall of the castle, and the commons in a lower chamber; a third session was held by prorogation in 1450[5]. At Coventry in 1404 the unlearned parliament sat in the great chamber of the prior's house; and in 1459, in the chapter house, the Lancastrian party attainted the duke of York[6]. Reading had two sessions, one in 1453, when Henry VI was insane, the other in 1467, when the plague was raging: on the first occasion the refectory was used, on the second a great chamber in the abbey[7]. There were two parliaments at Salisbury, one in 1328 and one in 1384; the latter in the great hall of the bishop's palace[8]. Gloucester also was the seat of parliament in 1378, when John of Gaunt feared to meet the Londoners, and in 1407; in 1378 the lords sat in the great hall of the abbey, the commons in the chapter house; in 1407 the commons occupied the refectory[9]. Carlisle, Nottingham, Cambridge, and Shrewsbury, each saw one session; Carlisle witnessed the famous parliament of 1307; at Nottingham in

Parliaments at Winchester, St. Edmund's, Leicester, Coventry, Reading, Salisbury, Gloucester and elsewhere.

[1] See above, vol. ii. pp. 150, 339, 340, 370. [2] Rot. Parl. i. 350.
[3] See above, vol. ii. pp. 372, 422, 484.
[4] See above, vol. ii. p. 130; iii. p. 135; Rot. Parl. v. 128.
[5] See above, pp. 81, 103, 150; Rot. Parl. iv. 15, 16, 295; v. 192.
[6] See above, pp. 46, 180; Rot. Parl. iii. 545; v. 345.
[7] See above, p. 163, Rot. Parl. v. 227, 619.
[8] See above, vol. ii. pp. 371, 467; Rot. Parl. iii. 166.
[9] See above, vol. ii. p. 446; iii. 60; Rot. Parl. iii. 32, 608.

Parliaments not at Westminster. 1336 Edward III obtained supplies for beginning the French war; the commission of government in 1388 held a legislative session at Cambridge[1], and at Shrewsbury in 1398 Richard II carried into execution his scheme of absolute government. The inference from this long list is that the liberties of England were safest at Westminster.

The choice of the day of meeting determined by the king in council.

738. Within the prescriptive or customary limits the determination of the time and place for holding parliaments was left to the king himself; the constitutional law being amply satisfied by an annual session. As the greater development of the executive functions of the royal council agrees in point of time with the recognised development of the representative system, the choice of time and place as well as the preparation of financial and legal agenda was almost from the first a part of the business of the council. The order for the affixing of the great seal was given by sign manual or writ of privy seal to the clerk of the crown in chancery who issued the writs. The advice of the council is specified in the writ of summons from the forty-sixth year of Edward III[2]. Until the presence of the commons had come to be recognised as an integral part of parliament, the baronial council was often summoned alone, and when the demand for money arose, the commons were called in and a parliament summoned by the regular writs. Accordingly, during the reign of Edward II, we may, in many cases, by comparing the date of the baronial summons to council with the date of

[1] The Cambridge parliament is said to have been held at Barnwell, where the king lodged; Cooper, Annals of Cambridge, i. 135. The parliament of 1447 which met at S. Edmund's was in the first instance summoned to Cambridge.

[2] 'Quia de avisamento consilii nostri, &c.'; Coke, 4 Inst. p. 4; Lords' Report, iv. 653. The earlier writs begin generally 'Quia super diversis et arduis negotiis, &c.'; ib. p. 318, &c. The notes 'per breve de privato sigillo'; ib. pp. 64, 205, &c.; or 'per ipsum regem et consilium,' pp. 397, 416, &c., often appear in the margin of the writ. 'Per ipsum regem' means that the writ is sealed by the king's sign manual or order under the privy signet; 'Per breve de privato sigillo,' that the sign manual was warrant to the privy seal under which the order was given for affixing the great seal; 'Per ipsum regem et consilium,' that the writ had been issued under the joint supervision of king and council. See on the whole history of the seals, Sir H. Nicolas, Ordinances, &c. vi. pp. cxl. sq. clxxxiv. &c.; Elsynge, Ancient Method of holding Parliaments, pp. 27, 29.

the subsequent summons to parliament, infer that the day of parliament was fixed in the meeting of the barons[1]. And this practice no doubt prevailed down to the days of the Lancastrian kings; for the French war of Henry V was considered in a great council of notables, lords and others, before it was discussed in parliament[2]. In 1386 a great council of 'seigneurs et autres sages' held at Oxford deliberated on the expediency of the king going to war, and by advice of that council Richard summoned the parliament[3]. As a rule however this duty belonged to the privy council or continual ordinary council of ministers. It was no doubt a matter of some delicacy, in troubled times, to arrange the course of business so as to avoid bringing the personal disputes of the great lords before the assembled commons: a good example of this will be found in the case of the council held at Northampton in which the business was prepared for the parliament of 1426, when Gloucester had refused to meet Beaufort as chancellor[4]. The most important exception to this rule is the very rare case in which the parliament itself attempted to fix the day for the next session. The most important recorded instance of such an event belongs to the merciless parliament of 1388, when the king was in the hands of the appellant lords and the house of commons was entirely at their beck. Although the proposal was couched in the form of a petition, it was rejected by the king, and the next session was held a full month before the day proposed[5]. In 1328 and 1339, however, the day for the next session was fixed before the dissolution of the parliament[6].

Preliminary great councils.

Preliminary privy councils.

The day fixed in a preceding parliament.

739. As soon as the day and place of session were fixed, the writs of summons were prepared in the royal chancery and

Issue of writs.

[1] This is sometimes stated in the writ itself circumstantially; as in 1330, Lords' Report, iv. 397; and 1331, ib. p. 403: 'de consilio praelatorum et magnatum nobis assistentium.'

[2] See above, p. 84.

[3] Rot. Parl. iii. 215.

[4] See above, p. 103.

[5] Rot. Parl. iii. 246.

[6] In 1328 the day for the parliament to be held at York on July 31 was fixed by the king with assent of the lords, at the previous parliament of Northampton; Lords' Report, iv. 381. In 1339, 'Item fait a remembrer de somoundre le parlement as oytaves de Seint Hiller suadit'; Rot. Parl. ii. 106; cf. p. 105: see also in connexion with this parliament, vol. ii. p. 381, and below, p. 398.

Interest attaching to the writs.

issued under the great seal. As these writs were returned to the parliament itself, or later into chancery, and as copies of them were enrolled on the close rolls at the time of issue, the great numbers of extant copies form an important branch of the national treasure of record. The ingenuity of legal antiquaries has found in them much material for interesting discussion[1], which cannot be here reproduced. The essential portion of the writs has continued to be the same throughout the existence of parliamentary institutions, but the forms have undergone great variation at different times, and quite as much historical interest belongs to the variations as to the permanent identity of the essential parts. These variations were unquestionably the work of the king and council[2], the form of writ having been originally settled by no constitutional act except in the very general terms of the great charter[3]; but certain additions were made by acts of parliament, the omission of which would have the effect of invalidating the summons; such in particular were the clauses inserted in consequence of the amendments of election law under Henry IV, Henry V, and Henry VI. Yet, like the times and places of session, the form of writ had in the fourteenth century attained a sort of sanctity which it was exceedingly dangerous to violate; Richard II was compelled to withdraw the clause by which he ordered the sheriffs to return impartial persons; and the order, given in 1404, that lawyers should not be

Writs altered by act of parliament.

[1] 'Manifold rare, delightful varieties, forms, diversities, and distinct kinds of writs of summons'; Prynne, Register, i. p. 395.

[2] Prynne argues against Coke's statement that the form of writ could not be altered but by act of parliament; Register, i. 396; ii. 161; and has also some important remarks on the right to demand a writ; Coke argues that the writ is issued 'ex debito justitiae,' Prynne that it is altogether in the royal power, and of the class of 'magistralia,' not 'brevia formata sub suis casibus.' But the question is one of a very technical character, although it has a bearing on rights of peerage. Bracton, lib. 5. f. 413, divides 'Brevia originalia' into several classes; first, 'quaedam sunt formata sub suis casibus et de cursu et de communi concilio totius regni concessa et approbata, quae quidem nullatenus mutari poterint absque consensu et voluntate eorum'; others are 'judicialia,' which vary according to the suits in which they are used; a third class, 'magistralia,' which often vary 'secundum varietatem casuum et querelarum'; a fourth are 'personalia,' and a fifth 'mixta.'

[3] 'Ad certum diem scilicet ad terminum quadraginta dierum ad minus, et ad certum locum; et in omnibus litteris illius summonitionis causam summonitionis exprimemus'; Mag. Cart. Art. 14.

elected, was made the ground of a charge of unconstitutional conduct brought against Henry IV.

Special writs to the lords and judges.

740. Special writs of summons were addressed to the lords, spiritual and temporal, and to the judges or occasional counsellors who were called to advise the king in the upper house of parliament. The summons of the parliamentary assembly of the clergy was inserted in the writs to the archbishops and bishops, and all the summonses of representatives of the commons were addressed to the sheriffs of the counties. The variations in the writs addressed to the lords are of minor importance, as they are chiefly found in the clauses in which the king gives an account of the cause which has moved him to call the parliament; but some peculiarities marking the various writs of the barons, bishops, abbots, and judges, deserve special notice[1]. On the other hand the changes which were from time to time introduced or attempted in the writs for the elections to the house of commons, point in some cases to important, in some to very obscure causes in contemporary history.

Variations in the forms.

The writs enrolled and issued first were those addressed to the lords spiritual; the archbishop of Canterbury being by his

[1] These points will be seen best by giving a specimen of the writs: 'Rex venerabili in Christo patri H. eadem gratia archiepiscopo Cantuariensi, totius Angliae primati, salutem. (i) Quia de avisamento consilii nostri pro quibusdam arduis et urgentibus negotiis, nos statum et defensionem regni nostri Angliae ac ecclesiae Anglicanae contingentibus, quoddam parliamentum nostrum apud Westmonasterium die lunae proxime post festum Sancti Lucae Evangelistae proxime futurum teneri ordinavimus, et ibidem (ii) vobiscum ac cum ceteris praelatis, magnatibus et proceribus dicti regni nostri colloquium habere et tractatum; vobis (iii) in fide et dilectione (to the lords temporal 'in fide et ligeancia') quibus nobis tenemini firmiter injungendo mandamus quod, consideratis dictorum negotiorum arduitate et periculis imminentibus, cessante quacunque excusatione, dictis die et loco personaliter intersitis nobiscum ac cum praelatis magnatibus et proceribus praedictis super praedictis negotiis (iv) tractaturi vestrumque consilium impensuri. Et hoc, sicut nos et honorem nostrum ac salvationem et defensionem regni et ecclesiae praedictorum expeditionemque dictorum negotiorum diligitis, nullatenus omittatis. (v) Praemunientes priorem et capitulum ecclesiae vestrae Cantuariensis ac archidiaconos totumque clerum vestrae diocesis quod iidem prior et archidiaconi in propriis personis suis, ac dictum capitulum per unum, idemque clerus per duos procuratores idoneos plenam et sufficientem potestatem ab ipsis capitulo et clero divisim habentes, dictis die et loco personaliter intersint ad consentiendum hiis quaè tunc ibidem de communi consilio dicti regni nostri divina favente clementia contigerit ordinari. Teste &c.;' Lords' Reports, iv. 827.

Writs to the bishops.

ancient privilege entitled to the first summons; then followed the writ to the archbishop of York and the suffragan bishops. The normal form of the writ contained, first, a clause declaring the cause on account of which the king has ordered the parliament to be summoned, with the time and place of meeting; a description of the body whose deliberations the recipient is to share, 'cum ceteris praelatis magnatibus et proceribus regni nostri'; this is followed by an injunction on the recipient to attend, 'vobis mandamus in fide et dilectione quibus nobis tenemini,' and a description of the function which he is to discharge 'tractaturi vestrumque consilium impensuri.' Finally the praemunientes clause directs the bishop to warn the clergy of his diocese to appear, the deans and archdeacons in person and the minor clergy by their proctors, on the same occasion, to do or consent to the things which may then and there be determined.

The cause of summons stated in the writ.

It is on the varying of these few expressions that all the distinctive interest of the writs of the prelates depends. The first clause admits of infinite but non-essential variation; and is continually changed. The highest note is struck when Edward I reminds the bishops that what touches all should be approved by all[1]; or when that great king and his successors from time to time explain that the enemy is bent on destroying the English tongue from off the face of the earth[2]. The barest matter of fact is touched when the form becomes 'quia de advisamento consilii nostri pro quibusdam arduis et urgentibus negotiis, nos statum et defensionem regni nostri Angliae et ecclesiae Anglicanae contingentibus, quoddam parliamentum nostrum tenere ordinavimus.' The changes however are not essential and touch no constitutional point.

The position of the word *ceteris*.

The second point is important; the king's intention is to deliberate with the other prelates and magnates of the kingdom, 'cum caeteris praelatis, magnatibus et proceribus'; the writ of the temporal lords runs 'cum praelatis, et ceteris magnatibus et proceribus,' and that of the judges or additional

[1] See vol. ii. p. 128; Select Charters, p. 474.

[2] See the writs of 23 Edw. I, 7 Rich. II; Lords' Report, iv. 67, 706; cf. Rot. Parl. ii. 150.

counsellors omits the word 'ceteris' and frequently inserts the clause 'cum ceteris de consilio nostro.' The omission of the word 'ceteris' has the great legal force of excluding the judges from claiming the position of peers of parliament. The difference of its position in the writs of the lords spiritual may be construed as placing their right as members of the lords' house upon a different footing from that of the temporal lords, but this is not a necessary or probable inference.

Judges not lords of parliament.

The third point of importance is the regular use of the words 'fide et dilectione' in the writs of the prelates [1]; the corresponding form in the writ of the lords temporal is 'fide et homagio,' or 'homagio et ligeantia.' The former expression is sometimes used in the lay writs, but the latter is never used to ecclesiastics: the force of the distinction lying in the fact that the bishops as bishops did not do homage, and the abbots shared the benefit of the immunity [2]. This point has some further importance in relation to the writs of the lords temporal.

The words 'fide et dilectione' distinctive of the writs of the prelates.

The fourth point, the use of the words 'tractaturi et consilium vestrum impensuri' marks the theoretical position of the upper house and its attendant judges: they are counsellors preeminently; no such words occur in the writs under which the representative members are elected.

The function expressed in *tractaturi*, &c.

Lastly the praemunientes clause, which of course occurs only

[1] On the importance of the expression 'fide et dilectione' see Prynne, Reg. i. 194, 195, 206–208. It is difficult to draw any distinct inference from the use of the words 'dilectione' and 'homagio' under Edward I; for occasionally both terms are used in writs of the same character; it seems, however, clear that after the great quarrel with the earls in 1297 the king never summoned the temporal lords to *parliament* 'in fide et dilectione,' but always 'in fide et homagio': in 1295, 1296, and 1297, he uses the former expression; in 1298 he omits the adjuration altogether, and in 1299 and onwards uses the sterner form. See the writs of those years in the Lords' Report and the Parliamentary Writs. 'Fide et homagio,' thus became the regular form; and in 1317 the difference is specially noted in the Close Rolls, where the two sets of writs are described as identical so far; 'excepto hoc quod ubi dicitur in fide et dilectione, ibi dicetur in fide et homagio'; Parl. Writs, II. i. 171. It is just possible to draw from the *military* writs a further inference; in 1294 John Balliol is cited 'in fide et homagio,' to send his service of armed men to Portsmouth, June 25; on June 29 he is desired 'in fide et dilectione' to send some of them with the king to France; here the former expression may imply the feudal duty, and the latter the general bond of fealty: but this will not apply in all cases; Parl. Writs, i. 261.

[2] See above, vol. i. p. 387; and iii. p. 296.

The praemunientes clause. in the writs of the bishops, directs the attendance of the beneficed clergy, and defines their function: from the twenty-eighth year of Edward I to the year 1340, they are generally, but not invariably, summoned like the commons 'ad faciendum et consentiendum'; from 1340 generally, and from the first year of Richard II invariably, 'ad consentiendum' only[1]; the meaning of the word 'faciendum' here must be ruled by its interpretation in the writs to the sheriffs for the election of knights of the shire. It would seem that the summons 'ad faciendum' was withdrawn from the moment that the king despaired of prevailing on the clergy to vote money in parliament instead of convocation. *Writs to the guardians of spirituals, and bishops elect.* When a bishopric was vacant the writ which would ordinarily be directed to the bishop was frequently addressed to the guardian of the spiritualities of the see, or if a bishop had been elected and not completely invested or consecrated, to him as bishop elect; when the bishop was abroad the writ was directed to his vicar-general[2]. The writs of the abbots and priors correspond with those of the bishops in all other points, but omit the praemunientes clause.

Writs of the lords temporal. The writs of the lords temporal differ from those of the bishops, in the change of the position of the word 'ceteris,' in the omission of anything corresponding with the praemunientes clause, and in the use of the form 'fide et homagio,' 'fide et ligeantia,' or 'homagio et ligeantia.' *The form fide et homagio.* The difference between these expressions has been understood to indicate some difference between the barony by tenure, of which the homage would be a more distinct feature, and the barony by writ, where the oath of allegiance would take the place of the form of homage. But the words are used with so little discrimination that no such conclusion can be with any probability drawn from them; and the

[1] In 1371 they are summoned 'ad consulendum et consentiendum'; Lords' Reports, iv. 647. It is certainly a significant coincidence that the word 'faciendum' should be withdrawn just when the king ceased to send his second letter to the archbishops ordering the enforcement of the summons. See above, p. 320.

[2] Specimens of the writ to the guardians of the spiritualities may be seen in Parl. Writs, I. 25, 47, 137; II. i. 155; Prynne, Register, i. 152, 153; and to bishops elect, Parl. Writs, I. 26, 47; to the vicars general, Lords' Reports, iv. 500, 501.

words homage and allegiance are in this collocation synonymous or redundant[1].

741. The writs of the judges and counsellors[2] correspond so very closely with those of the barons that it would seem almost an afterthought to exclude them from equality in debate. The variations already noticed, the omission of the word 'ceteris,' the introduction of 'ceterisque de consilio nostro,' and the absence of the injunction 'fide et homagio' are interpreted as having that effect. Summons of the judges.

All these writs are tested by the king himself, and issued under the great seal. The note 'per breve de privato sigillo' is frequently attached to the copy on the close roll, signifying that the great seal had been attached in compliance with a writ of privy seal ordering it to be done. The form 'per ipsum regem' denotes that the warrant has been issued under the sign manual and the royal signet. The later note 'per ipsum regem et consilium,' which appears occasionally in the writs of Edward II and very frequently after the accession of Edward III, has the Attestation of the writs.

[1] See Prynne, Reg. i. p. 206; Coke, 4th Inst. p. 5. An examination of the writs shows that Edward I occasionally used the form 'en la foi et en la ligeaunce,' Parl. Writs, I. 317; but that Edward III introduced it into common use in writs of summons to both councils and parliaments: sometimes he uses both words, 'fide, homagio et ligeantia'; Lords' Report, pp. 594, 599: but no conclusion can be drawn as to the purpose of the change: from 1354 onwards the two words are used indiscriminately, and from the accession of Richard II 'ligeantia' is the regular word.

[2] See Parl Writs, II. i. 42; Prynne, Reg. i. pp. 341 sq., 361 sq., 365. In several cases, if the Close Rolls are to be trusted, the writs to the justices are identical with those to the lords; but these may be accidental errors. Occasionally, when the counsellor cited is a clergyman, 'in fide et dilectione' is used, as in 1311, to Robert Pickering; but generally the clause is omitted. A specimen of the form is subjoined; it is the writ corresponding with that to the archbishop, given above, p. 391: 'Rex dilecto et fideli suo Willelmo Hankeforde capitali justitiario suo salutem. Quia &c. *ut supra usque ibi* tractatum, *et tunc sic:* vobis mandamus firmiter injungentes quod omnibus aliis praetermissis dictis die et loco personaliter intersitis nobiscum ac cum ceteris de consilio nostro super dictis negotiis tractaturi vestrumque consilium impensuri: et hoc nullatenus omittatis'; Lords' Report, iv. 829. Here the omission of the word 'ceteris' is not noted. But the writ to William de Shareshull in 1357 contains the words 'vobiscum et cum prelatis, magnatibus, et proceribus dicti regni nostri Angliae ac aliis de consilio nostro'; ib. p. 615. It should be said that the writs to *councils* vary more than those to parliament; the judges being occasionally summoned 'in fide et ligeantia,' and in other points being placed on a level with the lords.

same force, denoting that the privy seal writ had issued after deliberation in the privy council[1]. This feature belongs to all the parliamentary writs alike. The writs addressed to the prelates, barons, and counsellors ordering them to attend in a great council are worded in language very similar to that of the writs of parliament; but they express the king's intention of holding a council, 'consilium' or 'tractatum,' not a parliament; the writs to the bishops omit the praemunientes clause, and there are no writs to the sheriffs. Some doubt may occasionally arise so long as the word 'colloquium' is used for both parliament and council, although that word is properly equivalent to 'parliamentum': the word 'parliamentum' is however used most frequently from the latter years of Edward I, and exclusively after the first year of Edward III.

Writs of summons to a great council.

742. The writs to the sheriffs, ordering the election of representatives of the commons, correspond with the writs of the lords only so far as concerns the recital of the cause of summons, and in earlier writs this is frequently abbreviated. After declaring the occasion of meeting and the king's intention of treating with the prelates, magnates, and 'proceres,' no share in the deliberative function being assigned to any other persons, the writ proceeds to order the election of knights, citizens, and burgesses, who are to have full and sufficient power, on behalf of their constituencies, to consent to and to do what by God's favour may be determined by the common counsel of the kingdom, on the matter premised[2]. The sheriff is himself to bring up the

Writs addressed to the sheriffs.

[1] See above, p. 388, note 2. In the parliament of Coventry held in 1459, a petition was presented on behalf of the sheriffs who had returned members under privy seal writs; the king was asked to declare the elections valid, and discharge the sheriffs from blame; and this was done. See Prynne, Reg. ii. 141; Rot. Parl. v. 367. The writs are indeed given in the regular form in the Lords' Report, iv. 940, 945; but in the act of 1460, which repealed the acts of the parliament of Coventry, it is alleged, as one of the reasons of the invalidity of those acts, that the members were returned, some of them without any due or free election, others without any election at all, against the course of the king's laws and the liberties of the commons of this realm, by virtue of the king's letters of privy seal without any due election; Rot. Parl. v. 374; Prynne, Reg. i. 142.

[2] 'Ita quod iidem milites plenam et sufficientem potestatem pro se et communitate comitatus praedicti, et dicti cives et burgenses pro se et communitatibus civitatum et burgorum praedictorum, divisim ab ipsis habeant

names of the persons chosen and the writ, until by the statute of Henry IV in 1406 the indenture tacked to the writ is declared to be the sheriff's return, and is ordered to be sent into chancery. Such is the essential form of the writ; the many important variations in detail, touching the status of the persons to be chosen and the process of election, are valuable indications of political and social history. They must be taken in chronological order.

How the return was to be made.

The changes in the clauses which describe the character of the persons eligible as knights of the shire begin very early. The first form, that of 1290, 1294, and 1295[1], prescribes the election to be made 'de discretioribus et ad laborandum potentioribus[2];' the form is varied in 1302, the words being 'de discretioribus ipsius comitatus[3],' and in 1306 the clause directing the election of burgesses runs 'et de quolibet burgo duos burgenses vel unum secundum quod burgus fuerit major vel minor[4].' Both these variations were temporary; the older form is resumed and observed down to 1324, when Edward II, apparently despairing of getting a parliament together, and having in 1322 been obliged to receive valetti or esquires instead of knights of the shire for several counties, dispensed with the demand for discreet and able knights by adding 'seu aliis, de comitatu tuo assensu et arbitrio hominum ejusdem comitatus nominandos[5].' As however he omitted the summons for the

Variations in the form describing the persons to be elected as knights of the shire.

ad faciendum et consentiendum hiis quae tunc ibidem de communi consilio regni nostri favente Domino ordinari contigerit super negotiis antedictis'; Lords' Report, iv. 786.

[1] Parl. Writs, i. 21, 25, 29, 48, &c.

[2] In 1297 the description is 'de probioribus et legalioribus'; this meeting however was not, strictly speaking, a parliament, but the council to which the knights were called to receive the copies of the confirmed charters. Parl. Writs, i. 56.

[3] Parl. Writs, i. 115: in 1305, 'de discretioribus et ad laborandum potentioribus'; ib. p. 138.

[4] Parl. Writs, i. 182, 183.

[5] In 1311 the sheriff of Rutland sends two 'homines,' having no knights; Parl. Writs, ii. 1, 51. In 1322 Worcestershire returned a valettus or yeoman, who received only 2*s.* for his expenses; ib. ii. 1, 277: Devon returned one, Middlesex, Hereford and Leicester two; ib. 278. In 1324 all are called milites; ib. 313. In 1324 the summons to the barons is 'in fide et dilectione,' and 'seu aliis' is in the Sheriffs' Writs, II. i. 317; in the returns for Herefordshire it is specified that the persons elected are not knights; Lincolnshire returns a 'serjaunt'; the number of belted knights made out by Prynne belongs to the parliament of 1325; ib. pp. 346, 347; when the persons not knighted have only 3*s.* a day.

Attempts to secure the election of real knights.

clergy and borough members altogether, this writ cannot be regarded as a writ of parliament. In the next parliament, that of 1325, only twenty-seven of the knights of the shire were belted knights. The writs for the parliament of Northampton in 1328 forbid the attendance of members with a multitude of armed retainers[1]; and an additional writ in 1330 enjoined on the sheriff to obtain the election of persons not suspected of legal malpractices: 'deux des plus leaux et plus suffisauns chivalers ou serjauntz de meisme le countee qui soient mie suspicionous de male coveigne, ne communes meintenours des parties[2].' This was with a view to the next parliament, in which Mortimer was condemned. Although the result was satisfactory for the moment, and no change in the writ was required for some years, abuses had already begun to creep in, and in 1339 the commons, declaring that they could not assent to the proposed grant without having recourse to their constituencies, asked for a new election in which the sheriff should be told 'que deux de mielx vanez chivalers des contez[3]' should be chosen, and the sheriffs and other servants of the crown should be excluded. This proposition was accepted; and in the writs for the next parliament the king, after remarking that the perfunctory transactions of the elections has been a serious hindrance to business, enjoins the election of two knights girt with swords, for the county, and two burgesses for each borough, 'de discretioribus et probioribus militibus, civibus et burgensibus comitatus civitatum et burgorum et ad laborandum potentioribus[4].' The sheriffs are not however yet excluded.

An order for belted knights to be chosen.

The enforcement of knighthood as a qualification for election seems to have caused a difficulty; the words 'gladiis cinctos[5]' occur in the writs for March 1340, but are omitted after that parliament, although the rest of the formula is retained. In 1342 the qualifications of the candidates are indicated by the words 'de discretioribus et legalioribus[6]'; in 1343 'probioribus'

[1] Lords' Report, iv. 383; Prynne, Reg. ii. 79, 80.
[2] Prynne, Reg. ii. 85, 86; see above, vol. ii. p.619. Rot. Parl. ii. 443.
[3] Rot. Parl. ii. 104.
[4] Lords' Report, iv. 509; Prynne, Reg. ii. 88, 89.
[5] Lords' Report, iv. 517; Prynne, Reg. ii. 90.
[6] Lords' Report, iv. 543.

recurs[1]. In 1347 occurs the curious and important notice that the king does not call the parliament with the intention of imposing aids or tallages, but that justice may be done to the people; a very necessary undertaking at a moment when the king's recent proceedings had shaken public confidence. The assurance does not seem to have been satisfactory[2]; at all events the parliament which met was not sufficiently pliable; and the writ for the next year orders the election to be made 'de aptioribus discretioribus et magis fide dignis'; the knights are again to be belted knights, 'gladio cinctos et ordinem militarem habentes et non alios'; and the sheriff is warned that he is so to conduct the election as not to risk being regarded as a hinderer of the king's business[3]. In 1350 the writ issued for the parliament of 1351 reveals a new difficulty: it was impossible to secure the election of belted knights, but honest and peaceful country gentlemen might be hoped for; the king accordingly directs that such persons shall be chosen as are not pleaders or maintainers of quarrels, or men who live by such gains, but men of worth and good faith, and lovers of the public good. This form is observed until the year 1355[4]. In the meantime two great councils were held, the writs for which are exceptionally worded; in 1352 the sheriff is to return one knight 'de provectioribus discretioribus et magis expertis[5],' the number being reduced that the work of harvest may not be impeded; in 1353[6] one belted knight of the same qualifications is to be returned. The regular order of parliaments, which had been interrupted by the plague, was resumed in 1355, and the writs omit the caution against maintainers and restore the clause ordering the return of belted knights; in 1356 both these are omitted, but the counties are warned that no one legally elected will be excused[7]; in 1357 the belted knights are again asked for, and both knights and

Variations in the writs of the sheriffs.

Maintainers of quarrels are not to be chosen.

[1] Lords' Report, iv. 547.
[2] Lords' Report, iv. 573, 575; Prynne, Reg. ii. 90.
[3] Lords' Report, iv. 580, 583; Prynne, Reg. ii. 91.
[4] Lords' Report, iv. 590, 593, 603, 605; Prynne, Reg. ii. 92.
[5] Lords' Report, iv. 595; Prynne, Reg. ii. 92, 93.
[6] Lords' Report, iv. 600.
[7] Lords' Report, iv. 608.

Qualifications of the knights insisted on.

burgesses are to be chosen 'de elegantioribus personis[1].' Between 1356 and 1371 the variations are unimportant; one writ for 1360 retains the warning against improvident elections, and another directs that the knights shall be chosen in full county court[2]; in 1362 the demand is for the choice of men 'de melioribus validioribus et discretioribus[3],' varied in 1364 to 'valentioribus[4].' This qualification is in 1370 expanded still further; the knights are to be belted knights and more approved by feats of arms, circumspect and discreet[5]. In 1372 was issued the parliamentary ordinance[6] forbidding the election of lawyers and excluding the sheriffs from candidature. In conformity with this rule the writs of 1373 are very explicit, but the lawyers are not specifically excluded: the knights of the shire are to be belted knights or squires, worthier and more honest and more expert in feats of arms, and discreet, and of no other condition; the citizens and burgesses are to be chosen from the more discreet and more sufficient of the class who have practical acquaintance with seamanship and the following of merchandise; no sheriff or person of any other condition than that specified may be chosen[7]. The form does not seem to have been approved. Two years later the simpler rule[8] prescribing 'duos milites gladiis cinctos magis idoneos et discretos' appears; the prohibition of the sheriff continues to be a part of the writ. Yet in the Good Parliament half the county members were squires unknighted. The petition of 1376 that the knights may be chosen by common election of the better folk of the shire, and not merely nominated by the sheriff without due election, was set aside by the king; but the request seems to have been regarded as a warning to the crown not to tamper with the elections. Under Richard II the direction to elect in

Lawyers and sheriffs not to be chosen.

Petition of 1376.

[1] Lords' Report, iv. 616; Prynne, Reg. ii. 99: this writ also directed the members to be present personally on the first day of the parliament.
[2] Lords' Report, iv. 623, 626; Prynne, Reg. ii. 100.
[3] Lords' Report, iv. 632; Prynne, Reg. ii. 101.
[4] Lords' Report, iv. 638, 441, 643, 646; Prynne, Reg. ii. 102.
[5] Lords' Report, iv. 648; Prynne, Reg. ii. 106.
[6] See above, vol. ii. 425.
[7] Lords' Report, iv. 661; Prynne, Reg. ii. 114, 115.
[8] Lords' Report, iv. 664, 667; Prynne, Reg. ii. 116.

full county court and by assent of the same was always inserted. Although John of Gaunt was able the next year to pack the parliament with his own adherents, it is a long time before any new variation occurs in the writs. From the year 1376 onwards the sheriffs are directed to cause to be elected 'duos milites gladiis cinctos magis idoneos et discretos' and for the towns two members 'de discretioribus et magis sufficientibus.' In one writ of 1381 the old form is reverted to[1]; in 1382 the knights to be returned are to be either the same as attended the last parliament, or others; a hint perhaps to return the same[2]; in 1387 Richard's unlucky attempt to secure men 'in modernis debatis in magis indifferentes[3]' was summarily defeated; and the following year the clause inserted in 1373, forbidding the election of persons of any other condition than that specified, was permanently omitted[4], the sheriffs alone being disqualified. With these exceptions the writs remain uniform until the year 1404, when Henry IV stirred up strife by excluding lawyers from his 'unlearned parliament[5].'

Variations become less frequent.

From this date all the changes in the writs are made in consequence of the statutes by which from time to time the elections were regulated, and they generally reproduce the exact language of the acts. The clause of the statute of 1406 ordering that the election be made by the whole county in the next county court[6], and the names chosen be returned in an indenture, appears as part of the writ: this example is followed down to the year 1429. In 1430, after the passing of the statute which fixes the forty shillings franchise, the same rule is followed, the clause of the act being inserted in the writ[7]. Again in 1445 the commons petitioned that the statutes touching elections should be better enforced: the king agreed, and added that the persons chosen

Changes made in consequence of alterations in the law.

[1] Lords' Report, iv. 693: 'discretioribus, probioribus et ad laborandum potentioribus.'

[2] Lords' Report, iv. 696.

[3] Ib. iv. 725, 726.

[4] Ib. iv. 731; Prynne, Reg. ii. 117.

[5] Lords' Report, iv. 792; Prynne, Reg. ii. 123.

[6] 'Quod facta proclamatione in proximo comitatu tuo ..... libere et indifferenter per illos qui proclamationi interfuerunt'; Lords' Report, iv. 802; Prynne, Reg. ii. 126.

[7] Lords' Report, iv. 877; Prynne, Reg. ii. 132.

should be notable knights of the shire which elected them, or else notable squires, gentlemen of birth capable of becoming knights, and that no man of the degree of yeoman or below it should be eligible [1]. The result of the petition and its answer was a long statute, all the essential clauses of which were inserted in the writs from the year 1446 to the end of the reign. Edward IV altered the form in his first year [2], omitting specific references to the two statutes of Henry VI and the restrictions inserted in 1446, but retaining the more essential parts of the prescribed procedure. This form is observed to the end of the period before us.

Final changes in the form.

General inferences from these variations.

It is difficult to draw any definite conclusions from the variations which occur in the writs of Edward III; they seem, however, to imply a mistrust of the influences supposed to be at work in the county courts; and to have a general intention of urging the election of men of knightly rank and education, to the exclusion of professional lawyers and the maintainers of private suits. The mischief of faction and the danger of sacrificing public interest to private emolument were sufficient reasons for the restrictions inserted. The fact, that the king could insert them without remonstrance, does not prove that by dealing with the sheriffs he could procure their enforcement: the number of variations implies some power of resistance; the lawyers were not excluded and belted knights were not always chosen. Yet the king no doubt felt that his power, even thus liable to be thwarted, was safer as it was than it would be if it were hampered with any constitutional change in the body of electors. He maintained accordingly the customary right of the county courts. The changes introduced under the Lancaster kings have already been noticed: they possibly imply a more important change in the constitution of country society, and claim a more distinct place in social history. We cannot question that the act of 1430 was demanded by the disorderly condition of the county courts, or that that of 1445 was the result of the choice of unfit and incompetent members. The lack of

The king's power to alter the writs.

His wish to maintain custom;

and to enforce order.

[1] Lords' Report, iv. 913, 920, 924, &c.; Prynne, Reg. ii. p. 135.
[2] Lords' Report, iv. 951 sq.

governance common to the whole Lancaster period is exemplified in both the complaints. The tenour of the history is enough, without a statutory rehearsal, to prove that there were riots even in the most solemn shiremoots, and that unworthy members sat in the fickle and subservient parliaments.

Writs to the sheriffs of cities.

The writs to the sheriffs did not quite complete the composition of the lower house. Those cities and towns which were made counties by themselves, or had sheriffs of their own, London, Bristol, York, Norwich, Lincoln, Newcastle-on-Tyne, Hull, Southampton, Nottingham, Coventry, Canterbury, had writs addressed to their sheriffs; the constable of Dover and warden of the Cinque Ports had the writ for the election of the barons of the Cinque Ports; the duke of Lancaster, or more generally the chancellor of the duchy or county palatine of Lancaster, had the writ for Lancashire and its towns. None of these writs exhibit any important differences.

to the Cinque Ports and Lancashire.

Proceedings on the receipt of the writs.

743. The abbots, barons, and judges, on the receipt of their writs, had little to do except to obey: the bishops had besides this to order the election of the clerical proctors, which they did by forwarding the writ with a precept of their own to the archdeacons to enforce it[1]; and, where the process was transacted at all, it was transacted in much the same way as the elections to convocation, by summoning the whole body of the beneficed clergy in the several archdeaconries. The work of the sheriffs was much more critical and complicated. The method of election to the house of commons, the questions of qualification and suffrage, and the theory as compared with the practice of the county court, open a wide field for discordant conjectures.

County elections.

The writ was returnable, as we have seen, in about forty days, and the election was to be made in the county court: and this is nearly all that can be certainly affirmed of the

[1] Forms of electing clerical proctors under the 'praemunientes' clause will be found, in the case of cathedrals, Parl. Writs, I. 31, 34, 140, II. i. 293–296; and in the case of the diocesan clergy, one of A.D. 1304, Wake, State of the Church, app. p. 31. A list of the clerical proctors in the parliament of Carlisle is given, Parl. Writs, I. 184–186. Atterbury gives a long series of instances in which proctors were elected under this clause, coming down to the year 1678; Rights, Powers, and Privileges of Convocation, Additions to the first edition, addenda, pp. 81–93.

early elections. It would be a waste of ingenuity to speculate on the different courses that a sheriff, unguided by custom, may have adopted; and, for the sake of a definite view, we must advance at once to the period which was affected by the statute of 1406. This statute orders that proceedings shall begin in the first county court holden after the receipt of the writ, and that the election shall be made in full county court by the persons present, specifying further the form of the return[1].

Proceedings under the statute of 1406.

Unfortunately we have but few such data as would enable us to determine the nature of the 'plenus comitatus' thus recognised as the elective body. As the proceedings are to begin in the first county court held within the forty days that elapse before the return of the writ, it is obvious that the court in question must be the court held every month or every three weeks by the sheriff, and not the sheriff's tourn which was held but twice a year. That this was the practice appears from the cases in which the sheriff, having to account for not returning knights of the shire in time for the opening of the session, pleads that no county court occurred before that date, and is excused[2].

Election in the first county court.

[1] The following is the clause of the statute: 'Item nostre seigneur le roy al grevouse compleint de sa commune del non dewe eleccion des chivalers des countees pur le parlement, queux aucune foitz sont faitz de affeccion des viscountz et autrement encountre la forme des briefs as ditz viscountz directe, a grand esclaundre des countees et retardacion des busoignes del communalte du dit countee, nostre soverein seigneur le roy vuillant a ces purveier de remedie, de l'assent des seigneurs espirituelx et temporelx et de tout la commune en cest present parlement, ad ordeignez et establiz que desore enavant les eleccions des tielx chivalers soient faitz en la forme quenseute; cest a saver que al proschein countee a tenir apres la livere du brief du parlement, proclamacion soit fait en plein countee de le jour et lieu de parlement, et que toutz ceux qui illoeques sont presentz sibien suturez duement somoines pur cele cause come autres, attendent la eleccion de lours chivalers pur le parlement; et adonques en plein counte aillent al eleccion liberalment et endifferentement non obstant aucune prier ou commaundement au contrarie; et apres quils soient esluz, soient les persones esluz presentz ou absentz, soient lour nouns escriptz en endenture dessoutz les sealx de toutz ceux qui eux eslisent, et tacchez au dit brieve du parlement; quele endenture issint ensealez et tacchez soit tenuz pur retourne au dit brief quant as chivalers des countees, et que en briefs de parlement affairs en temps advenir soit mys cest clause; et electionem tuam in pleno comitatu tuo factam distincte et aperte sub sigillo tuo et sigillis eorum qui electioni illi interfuerint nos in cancellaria nostra ad diem et locum in brevi contentum certifices indilate'; 7 Hen. IV, c. 15, Statutes, ii. p. 156: cf. Rot. Parl. iii. 601.

[2] This was the custom before the act was passed; in 1327 the sheriff of

This monthly or three weeks county court had however very much diminished in importance since the thirteenth century; almost all the great people of the county were relieved by the statute of Marlborough from attendance upon it; many of its earlier functions had been handed over to the justices of the peace, and its ordinary judicial work was the decision of pleas of debt, which required the attendance of the parties to suits and the rota of qualified jurors, and of none others. As this would obviously be no true representation of the county, we expect to find that for the occasion of an election other persons were specially cited, and it is clear from the act of 1406 that this was the case; 'all that be there present as well suitors duly summoned for the same cause, as others, shall attend to the election.' From this it appears that although the court was the ordinary court, the persons composing it, or forming the most important part in it, were summoned for the purpose of the election. On the rolls of the parliament by which the statute was passed there is an article, enjoined under oath on the members of the council, ordering that in the writs to the sheriffs they should be directed to have proclamation made in all the market towns of their counties, of the day and place of election, fifteen days before the day fixed for the election. But although enacted by the king and sworn by the council the clause was never enforced[1]. Some such warning was, however, absolutely

Election in the ordinary county court.

Persons summoned to the election.

Order for fifteen days notice not incorporated in the statute.

Surrey and Sussex reports that between the day on which he received the writ and the day fixed for the parliament no county court was held, and therefore no election was made. In 1314 the sheriff of Wilts says that he received the writ only three days before the day of parliament, and that on that day, notwithstanding the brevity of notice, the members were 'celeriter electi'; Prynne, Reg. iii. 172; Parl. Writs, II. i. 149. A similar case occurred in Devon in 1449; Prynne, Reg. iii. 151: there no county court was held until two days before the parliament met. In Leicestershire in 1450 the election took place after the parliament met, for the same reason; ib. p. 163.

[1] 'Item pur ce que les viscountz retornent chivalers du countee pur venir au parlement noun duement esluz, que ordeine soit, que en toutes tielx briefs qui isseront desore hors de la chauncelrie direct as viscountz pur tielx chivalers eslire pur venir au parlement, soit contenuz, que proclamacion soit fait en toutes les villes marches du countee du jour et lieu ou les ditz chivalers serront esluz xv jours devaunt le jour d'election, aufin que les suffisauntz persones enhabitantz en le dit countee y puissent estre pur faire election suis dit en due manere; et que les ditz viscontz qu'ore sont, et qui pur le temps serront, soient seremente a ce tenir et executer, sanz fraude ou affection de nulluy'; Rot. Parl. iii. 588.

Power of the sheriff to cite electors.

necessary, and even if the sheriff could, on the spur of the moment, get together a county court, the election of borough members could not possibly be left to the chance of some of the authorities of each town being present at the county court. Strictly speaking then, the proceedings must have begun not in the county court itself but in the citation of the electors by the sheriff which preceded the holding of the court, whether according to the article just mentioned or in conformity with established custom.

Possible misuse.

And the discharge of this function lodged great power in the hands of the sheriff; he might issue a general notice, or might summon the suitors who were bound by their tenure to attend[1], or might cite his especial friends, or might cite no one at all, and so transact the election in the presence of the casual suitors as to deprive the county of its right for the time.

The *plenus comitatus.*

But that the county court, however composed, was the 'plenus comitatus,' and that all persons present had the right of joining in the proceedings, seems certain from the wording of the statute, and the statute does not appear in these points to have made any change in law or usage. The petition of 1376

[1] On this point the Lords' Report (i. 149) expresses the opinion that the county court in which elections were held was the court baron of the county, and the proper suitors were only those who held land in the county, as distinguished from the sheriff's tourn which was to be attended by all residents. The three weeks or six weeks or monthly court is certainly the one meant by the next county court; but it could hardly be regarded as a full county court if it contained only the persons legally liable to attendance, who were allowed moreover under the statute of Merton to appear by their attorneys. The reasons for holding that originally the fullest assembly of the shire was intended are given above, vol. ii. pp. 225 sq. If the theory of the Lords' Report went no further, it might be accepted as stating one at least of the intelligible ways in which the franchise was lodged in the hands of the freeholders; but the report inclines to the belief that the freeholders electing were freeholders holding directly under the king (p. 151), and that accordingly the article of Magna Carta ordering the general summons of the minor tenants was carried into effect. It is evident however that the elections were attended by many who were not freeholders, or even proper suitors. The subject is obscure, and the customs were probably various. On the theory maintained in vol. ii, the original electors under Edward I were the persons legally constituting the county court, all landowners, and from every township the reeve and four men; before the close of the reign of Edward III the whole body of persons assembled made the election whether they were legal suitors or not; the act of 1406 does not venture to alter this, but that of 1430 reestablishes the right of the freeholders, although only in the persons of the 40s. freeholders.

shows that the election was often carried through in the absence of the better people of the county[1]; the act of 1430 declares that it was often dispatched by the rabble[2]; the variations of the writs show that the persons whose influence was most dreaded were lawyers and promoters of litigation. The petition of 1376 again shows that the sheriffs exercised an influence which threw the electoral right of the suitors into the shade; the act of 1382[3], which forbids the sheriffs to omit the regular cities or boroughs from his returns[4], proves that his influence was used even to extinguish the right of certain boroughs to return representatives; a petition of Rutland in 1406 shows that he was able occasionally to return members who had not been duly elected[5]. On any theory the conclusion is inevitable that the right of electing was not duly valued, that the duty of representation was in ordinary times viewed as a burden and not as a privilege; that there was much difficulty in finding duly qualified members, and that the only people who coveted the office were the lawyers who saw the advantage of combining the transaction of their clients' business in London with the right of receiving wages as knights of the shire at the same time. Thus, whilst in theory the right of election was so free that every person who attended the county court might vote, in practice the privilege was not valued, the power of the sheriff, and of the crown exercised through him, was almost uncontrolled in peaceful times, and in disturbed times the whole proceeding was at the mercy of faction[6]. This is of course a view of the worst phase of the business: no doubt in many cases the sheriffs were honest and faithful men, and the elections were duly held, but custom and not law prescribed the process, and until the act of 1406 neither law nor custom remedied the abuse.

Disorders of the county court.

Influence of the sheriff in making the returns.

The privilege of representation not sufficiently valued.

744. This consideration enables us to see the importance of the one change introduced by the act of Henry IV. It directs that after the election the names of the persons chosen 'shall be

Change under Henry IV.

[1] Rot. Parl. ii. 355; above, vol. ii. p. 433.
[2] Above, p. 258.
[3] Above, vol. ii. p. 433.
[4] St. 5 Rich. II. stat. 2. c. 4.
[5] See below, p. 422.
[6] See below, p. 415.

Law for the return to be made on an indenture between the sheriff and the electors.

written in an indenture under the seals of them that did choose them'; this indenture is to be tacked to the writ and is to be holden as the sheriff's return. By this rule the arbitrary power of the sheriff is directly abolished; the return is made essentially by the voters, and the crown is enabled by examining the indenture to see at once the character of the persons who have taken part in the election. The indenture itself was not new; under that name or under the name of 'pannel' the sheriff's return had from the first been endorsed on or sewed to the writ; the novelty was in the security which the form of the indenture gave to the authenticity of the return.

Importance of the indentures.

A great number of these indentures are preserved[1], and from these some inferences more or less conclusive may be drawn. We must take it for granted that the persons who sealed the indenture were those who were specially cited by the sheriff, or drawn from the same class of society; and that the ordinary suitors or the persons who attended in consequence of any general proclamation must be regarded as included in the term 'plures alios' or 'cum multis aliis,' or 'in pleno comitatu,' in which the indenture embraces the residue of the electors[2].

Number of the persons sealing the indentures.

The number of persons who seal the indenture, is in every case comparatively small: in 1407 the indenture for Cambridge was sealed by twelve persons, for Huntingdon by eight; in 1411 twelve join in the return for Kent, six 'cum multis aliis de communitate' for Derbyshire; in 1413 twenty-six persons elect for Wiltshire; in 1414 fourteen elect for Cumberland, sixteen 'ex assensu totius communitatis' for Somersetshire, twelve for Kent, nineteen for Surrey, twenty-four for Sussex, the same number for Dorset and Somerset, eleven and many others for Warwickshire; in 1424 eighteen for Lancashire; in 1447 thirty-one for Gloucestershire, thirty for Surrey; the number of names rarely if ever exceeds forty.

The quality of the persons who seal the indentures is less

[1] See Prynne, Reg. ii. 128–132; iii. 173–177, 252–312.

[2] 'Plures alios'; see the indenture for Cornwall, Prynne, Reg. ii. p. 128; 'per assensum et consensum .... et omnium aliorum fidelium ibidem existentium'; ibid, pp. 129, 130.

easily tested. A comparison however of the names given in the indentures with the lists of sheriffs and knights of the shire for the respective counties, seems to show that whilst a fair proportion of the electors belonged to the families that furnished sheriffs and knights, the majority of the names are of a less distinguished class: either ordinary squires who would not aspire to the office of sheriff, or, as possibly may be inferred from the character of the surnames, simple yeomen. Unfortunately the smallness of the number of indentures copied by Prynne makes it impossible to argue very confidently on this point.

Quality of the sealers.

As for the character in which the persons who thus represent themselves as electors acted, opinions may differ. It is most probable that they acted primarily as certifying the return, and making themselves responsible for its correctness, and not as the only electors or as a body deputed by the county court to make the election for the whole constituency. Notwithstanding the terms of the act, directing that the indenture shall be sealed by all who have taken part in the election, it is certain that others who did not seal, and who probably had no seals, joined in it. One remarkable instance proves that such was occasionally the case, and suggests that it was also the rule. In 1450 the electors for Huntingdonshire suspected that the sheriff was going to make a false return, and accordingly sent in a letter to the king which is found in company with the return. The indenture contains the names of three squires and two other persons who with 'alii notabiles armigeri, generosi et homines libere tenentes qui expendere possunt quadraginta solidos per annum' had made the election. The letter to the king is sealed by 124 who declare that they, with 300 more good commoners of the same shire, had elected two knights; 70 others had voted for a person whom they regarded as disqualified by his birth[1]. Besides the interest of this document, which is an important illustration of a contested election, it proves that whilst five names were sufficient for the indenture, 121 more were included in the general clause

Questions as to the character in which they acted.

Election for Huntingdonshire in 1450.

[1] Prynne, Reg. iii. pp. 156–159.

Election for Huntingdonshire.

'alii notabiles,' and that 300 more freeholders had voted in the majority against 70 in the minority. In the election then for this small county, which had in 1741 about 1600 voters, and in 1852 contained only 2,892 registered electors, in 1450, 494 freeholders voted.

In some cases the sealers may have been a committee for election.

But although this case conclusively proves that the right of election was not exercised by those only who sealed the indenture, it is quite possible that in some instances they were delegated representatives of the whole body of suitors. In 1414 the indenture for Somersetshire states that the sealers made the election 'ex assensu totius communitatis[1],' a form borrowed no doubt from the ancient return by the sheriff; but possibly implying that the election, like the ecclesiastical election 'per compromissionem' passed through two stages. And although there are no words in the returns that imply such to have been the case, at the same time it must not be forgotten that the custom of electing committees for various purposes had long existed in the county courts, and that the analogy of the borough elections, which went through two or three stages of the kind, may have affected the county elections also. Here again no evidence is at present forthcoming. But there can be little doubt that the indenture was intended rather as a check on the sheriff than as a restriction on the body of electors: like the manucaption, it served to secure due compliance with the writ. Occasionally the sealers may have quietly 'cooked' the return. The same inference may be drawn from the fact that the borough members were often returned by the same sealers as the knights of the shire: not that they were chosen by them, but that the return was certified by their authority. Unquestionably the power of the magnates whenever it was exerted, the influence of the crown exercised through the sheriff, the risk of popular tumult, and the persistence of local usage, as well as the freedom of the county courts, must be allowed to balance one another, and to affect the result.

General object served by the indenture.

The strangest instance of local usage is found in the inden-

[1] Prynne, Reg. iii. p. 171.

tures of return for Yorkshire, which are quite unlike those of the other counties, but so consistent with one another for a series of years as to prove continuity of usage[1]. The indentures of the reigns of Henry IV and Henry V, and of Henry VI down to his twenty-third year, show that the electors who sealed the return were the attorneys of the great lords of the franchises. The indentures for 1411 and 1414[2] may serve as specimens of the series: in 1411 the electors are the attorneys of Ralph earl of Westmoreland, Lucia countess of Kent, Peter baron de Mauley, William baron de Roos, Ralph baron of Greystoke, Sir Alexander de Metham, and Sir Henry Percy; they represent their masters as common suitors to the county court of Yorkshire from six weeks to six weeks; in 1414 the indentures are sealed by the attorneys of the archbishop of York, the earl of Westmoreland, the earl Marshall, the lord le Scrope of Masham, Peter de Mauley, Sir William Metham, the lord de Roos, Margaret lady Vavasour, and Henry Percy. These indentures differ from the others not only in the character of the electors but in the nature of the interest they represent; for in the other counties it is rarely that any one above the rank of esquire appears as a party to the election. One conclusion that can be safely drawn is that the sheriff of Yorkshire in 1411 understood the writ differently from the other sheriffs, and that his successors followed slavishly in his steps. Of course it is possible that the Yorkshire county court jurisdiction may have been long broken up among the courts

Indentures for the Yorkshire elections from 1407, to 1445.

Curious features of these returns.

[1] Prynne, Reg. iii. pp. 152–154, 155.

[2] The form in 1411 is this: The indenture made between the sheriff of the one part and the attorneys of the lords 'sectatorum communium [i.e. the lords] annuatim ad comitatum Ebor. de sex septimanis in sex septimanas, ex parte altera, testatur quod facta proclamatione per dictum vicecomitem in comitatu praedicto, virtute cujusdam brevis &c. &c. praedicti attornati unanimi assensu et voluntate in praedicto comitetu existentes et plenariam potestatem de sectatoribus praedictis separatim habentes, libere et indifferenter elegerunt duos milites etc.' After the act of 1445 the form is changed: it then becomes an indenture between the sheriff and forty-three squires and others 'electores militum ad parliamentum,' &c.; but these persons still make the election 'unanimi assensu et consensu,' without any reference to the remainder of the county court. Prynne seems to imply that the first form was followed down to 1445, but he gives no instances between 1429 and 1447.

Yorkshire elections.

of the wapentakes and great franchises; so that recourse in petty causes was seldom had to it; and it will be remembered that in 1220[1] the stewards of the lords were the leading members of it. But although the great size of the county, and of the private jurisdictions embraced in it, may have led to such an attenuation of the six weeks' court, the assizes of the justices were always largely attended, and there could have been no difficulty in assembling a very large body of yeomen freeholders. The simplest solution is to view the return simply as a certificate of an uncontested election. The anomaly, whatever its cause, was remedied by the act of the 23rd Henry VI; after which date the returns were made in the common form.

Legislation under the House of Lancaster on elections.

The changes in the forms of the county elections made by the later Lancastrian legislation may be briefly stated: the act of 1410 placed the conduct of the elections under the cognisance of the justices of assize and established the penalty of £100 on the sheriff, and forfeiture of wages as the punishment of the members unduly returned[2]: the act of 1413[3] enforced residence as a qualification of both electors and elected; and that of 1427 gave the accused sheriff and knight the right to traverse the decision of the justices[4]. The act of 1430[5] besides establishing the forty shillings' freehold as a qualification for electors, gave the sheriff power to examine on oath the persons who tendered their votes, as to the extent of their property; and that of 1432 ordered that the freehold qualifying the elector

[1] Vol. ii. p. 214.
[2] See above, p. 257; St. 11 Hen. IV. c. 1; Statutes, ii. 162.
[3] St. 1 Hen. V, c. 1; Statutes, ii. 170.
[4] St. 6 Hen. VI, c. 4; Statutes, ii. 235.
[5] St. 8 Hen. VI, c. 7: 'que les chivalers des countes deins le roialme D'engleterre a esliers a venir a les parlementz en apres a tenirs, soient esluz en chescun counte par gentz demeurantz et receantz en icelles dount chescun ait frank tenement a le valu de xls. par an al meins outre les reprises; et que ceux qui serront ensy esluz soient demeurantz et receantz deins mesmes les countes; et ceux qui ount le greindre nombre de yceulx que poient expendre par an xls. et outre, come desuis est dit, soient retournez par les visco ntz de chescun countee chivalers pur le parlement par endenturs ensealles parentre les ditz viscontz et les ditz elisors ent affaires; et eit chescun vicont D'Engleterre poair par auctorite suisdite examiner sur les seintz Evangelies chescun tiel elisour come bien il poet expendre par an'; Statutes, ii. 243.

should be situated within the county[1]. By the act of 1445 it is further ordered that the sheriffs shall send to the magistrates of the several cities and boroughs within their counties a precept for the election to be made by the citizens and burgesses and returned by indenture between them and the sheriff[2]; the penalty on the negligent sheriff is £100 to the king and £100 to the offended party, on the negligent mayor or bailiff £40 to each; the hours of the elections are fixed between eight and eleven in the morning; the persons to be elected are not to be of or below the degree of yeoman[3]; and these directions are to be inserted in the writs. If we may argue from the later indentures none of these regulations made much change in the form of the proceedings: the same class of men seal the returns before and after the act of 1430, and the same class of men are returned before and after the legislation of 1445.

Precepts for borough elections.

Penalties for non-observance.

Exclusion of yeomen from being returned.

745. The variations of the process of city and borough elections are, if not more extensive, at least more intelligible than those of the county elections; the electoral bodies were more definitely constituted and the factors more permanent. Yet the historical difficulties of the subject are very great, and the materials for a trustworthy conclusion very scanty.

City and borough elections

As the formal election of the borough members took place, throughout the whole of this period, in the county court, and the returns were made in the same document as those of the knights of the shire, the causes which disturbed the regular and orderly elections of the latter, influence, custom and faction, would also affect those of the former; and to these was added the fact that many towns felt a great reluctance to send members at

Formally transacted in the county court.

[1] St. 10 Hen. VI, c. 2; Statutes, ii. 273.

[2] The statute of 1445 states that of late divers sheriffs have not made due election, or returned good and true men; sometimes no return has been made of the persons really chosen, but persons have been returned who have not been chosen; and the returns of the boroughs have been altered by the sheriffs; the sheriffs have made no returns, or the writs have been embezzled; they have sent no precept to the boroughs, and the penalties were not sufficient to ensure obedience. See St. 23 Hen. VI, c. 14; Statutes, ii. 340. Compare the petition of 1436, below, p. 415.

[3] In 1447 the indenture for Surrey is in English, and the sealers say that they 'as notable squires and gentlemen,' have elected: Sussex makes a like return in Latin; Prynne, Reg. iii. 173, 174.

all, and so to put themselves to the cost of their wages and acknowledge themselves liable to the higher rate of taxation. Accordingly in some of the earlier returns it is possible that the sheriff, or the persons who joined with him in electing the knights of the shire, elected the borough members also[1]; that both were elected 'in pleno comitatu' in a very perfunctory way; and that the sheriff omitted towns that he wished to favour and exercised that irresponsible authority which the statute of 1382 was intended to abolish[2]. But as a rule it is more probable that a delegation of burghers from each town attended the county court and either announced to the sheriff their own choice made on the spot, or declared the names of those whom their townsmen had chosen in their own town-meeting. From the returns of the reign of Edward II it is clear that the sheriff communicated the royal writ to the towns of his county and awaited their answer, before recording the names of their members; if they neglected to answer he noted the fact on the writ[3]. And this may be regarded as the legal method of proceeding; the town authorities received notice to prepare for the formal election at the time when they were cited to the county court. This notice or mandate of the sheriff to the towns was known as the sheriff's precept, and we learn from the act of 1445 that although at that date many of the sheriffs neglected

Power of the sheriff to omit boroughs.

Borough elections reported in the county court.

The writ notified to the borough officers.

The sheriff's precept.

[1] Returns made by the bailiffs of places where the bailiffs had the returns, are in Parl. Writs. i. 67, and others made by the sheriff where no such intermediate transaction took place, ib. i. 70, 75. Instances in which the return for the boroughs was made not only in the county court but by the sealers of the indenture of the knights are given by Prynne, Reg. iii. pp. 175 sq. Possibly these were the sole electors and the boroughs had neglected their duty, but far more probably the return is to be regarded as a mere certificate of election.

[2] See above, vol. ii. p. 616.

[3] A very good instance of this practice occurs in 1322; the sheriff of Suffolk gives on a schedule annexed to the writ not only the names of the elected members and their manucaptors, but the names of the bailiffs of the boroughs who sent in the returns. The next year the same plan is adopted, and, one of the elected knights not having a manucaptor, the sheriff issued a 'precept' to the steward of the liberty of S. Edmund's who replied that the knight in question was away on duty in the north; Prynne, Reg. iii. 181-184. The 'precept' is the document by which the sheriff directs the execution of the writ. The common return by the sheriffs 'Ballivi nullum mihi dederunt responsum' proves that this was the rule.

to send the precept to their boroughs, the rule that it should be done was held binding, and by that act it was enforced[1]. However negligently or perfunctorily then the sheriff might conduct the business, the legal plan varied little; it was his duty to transmit a copy of the writ with his precept to the town magistrates; they superintended the real election; and by their messengers or deputies the formal announcement, or formal election, was made in the county court; and the same messengers or deputies, after the act of 1406, were parties to the indenture of return. Of the part of the work done in the county court the indenture for Dorsetshire in 1414 may be taken as an illustration; in that year in the shire moot the members for Dorchester were elected by the assent of the whole community of the borough of Dorchester by burghers of the town; those for Bridport by four burghers of Bridport; and those of the rest of the towns in exactly the same way; all are returned on one indenture, but the process takes place in each case uniformly[2]; four representative burghers attend, like the four men and the reeve in the ancient folkmoots, and on behalf of their neighbours transact the business of the day. That business may have been the primary election; but in many cases and perhaps in all it was only the report of the election made at home. It is probable that in the large and better organised towns this formality was always observed, whilst in those which had no chartered government the sheriff would be left to manage the election as he pleased. It certainly appears from a petition presented in 1436, that the interference of the sheriffs in the town elections was both arbitrary and vexatious; they returned members who had not been duly elected; the commons prayed that they might be compelled to do right, or be fined[3].

Sheriff's precept ordered by law.

Instance of the borough elections returned on the indenture.

When the time comes for the ancient towns of England to reveal the treasures of their municipal records, much light must be thrown upon the election proceedings of the middle ages. At present what little is known of them is to be gathered from a few scattered sources; but it would appear certain that the

Uncertainty as to the customs of boroughs in the matter of elections.

[1] See above, p. 413. [2] Prynne, Reg. iii. p. 255. [3] Rot. Parl. iv. 511.

whole order of proceeding rested upon local usage and might be altered by local authority, and that the rule adopted in the municipal elections of the particular town was generally followed. The custom of London in the reign of Edward I, described in a former chapter, was that the election should be made by the mayor, the aldermen and four or six good men of each ward[1]; a method likewise adopted for the election of the mayor himself. In 1346 an ordinance was passed in the city directing that twelve, eight, or six persons from each ward should come to the assemblies for electing the lord mayor, sheriffs and members of parliament. In 1375 another change took place; the elections were to be made by the common councilmen, and the common councilmen were to be nominated by the trading companies. Notwithstanding an alteration made in the appointment of common councilmen, the elections were transacted, from this date to the fifteenth year of Edward IV, by a body summoned by the lord mayor from a number of persons nominated for the purpose by the companies; and in the latter year the franchise was formally transferred to the liverymen of the companies[2].

London elections.

It can hardly be supposed that the smaller chartered cities whose privileges were modelled on those of London would follow these changes, but the earlier custom might very well be followed in places like Oxford. At Bristol, after the town was made a county by Edward III, the election seems to have followed the custom of the county elections; accordingly, when the forty shillings suffrage was established the members were returned by the forty shillings freeholders only[3]; of these from twenty to thirty seal the indentures; it may be inferred that the proceeding was direct and went through only one stage. At York, which was likewise a county, a somewhat similar practice appears as soon as there is any direct evidence, in the

Custom at Bristol.

Elections at York.

[1] See above, vol. ii. p. 234. The London election of 1296 is described in Parl. Writs, i. 49; that of 1300; ib. p. 85. In 1314, the mayor, aldermen, and probi homines of each ward, chose three citizens, out of whom the mayor and aldermen chose two; and the commons three, of whom again they chose two; these four or two of them had full powers given them; ib. II, i. 129: yet only two were summoned in the writ.

[2] See below, ch. xxi; Norton, Commentaries on London, pp. 114, 115, 126.

[3] Prynne, Register, iii. p. 360, 368.

reign of Elizabeth. On October 28, 1584, thirty-six freeholders and commoners appeared and heard the writ in the council chamber; they then went into the exchequer court and voted privately; four names, the result of this conclave, were laid before the assembled freeholders who chose two by a majority of votes; on the 9th of November the names were submitted to and approved by the county court of the city[1]. Traces of the same form may be found in the earlier York records, although in 1484 the proceedings seem to have occupied but one sitting of the council[2] and there is no notice of any approbation of the county court; earlier still, in 1414, the indenture shows that the lord mayor and thirteen 'co-citizens,' having full power from the whole community, chose two citizens[3]. Unfortunately the ambiguity of the word 'community' deprives this and many other similar instances of any great significance. Other instances seem to suggest that the favourite way of making the election was a double one; a small committee or jury of electors was chosen, or otherwise nominated, or a pretaxation was made by the ruling officers of the community. At Leicester, from the time of Edward IV to the Restoration, the mayor and twenty-four chose one member, the commons the other[4]. At Norwich in 1414 an agreement was made that the election should be made by the common assembly and reported in the county court[5]. At Shrewsbury in 1433 it was agreed that the burgesses should be chosen in the same way as the auditors; that is, after three peals of the common bell, by the assembled commons, and not by a bill 'afore contrived in disceit of the said commons[6].' At Worcester in 1466 the rule was that the members should be chosen openly in the Guildhall by the inhabitants of the franchise, 'by the most voice, according to the law and to the statutes in such case ordained, and not privily[7].'

Double process of election at York.

Elections at Leicester, Norwich, Shrewsbury, and Worcester.

[1] Drake, Eboracum, pp. 358, 359.

[2] Davies, York Records, pp. 138, 144, 181, 184. In 1482 the entry is 'Dec. 13, &c. At thys day be the advise of the holl counsell my lord the mair, Richard York, and John Tong war chosyn citizins and knights of the parlement for this honorabill cite and the shir of the same'; p. 138.

[3] Prynne, Reg. iii. 268.

[4] Nichols' Leicestershire, i. 432.

[5] Blomfield's Norfolk, ii. 95.

[6] Rot. Parl. iv. 478; v. 175.

[7] Smith's Gilds, p. 393.

In towns of simple constitution the election may have been transacted by the older machinery of the leet; and the leet jury would elect the members. In others it was very complex. At Lynn in 1384 the members were elected by John a Titleshall and eleven others forming a jury[1]. How this jury was chosen we learn from the Lynn records of 1432 and 1433: the mayor, with the assent of the town meeting, nominated two of the twenty-four, and two of the common council; these four chose four more, two out of each body; and these eight co-opted two more, and the ten two more; these twelve, being sworn according to custom to preserve the liberty of the town, chose two burgesses to go to parliament[2]. A similar rule was adopted at Cambridge, whence probably it had been borrowed by Lynn; in 1426 the members were elected by a select body of eight burgesses; this election by eight is described in the year 1502: the mayor and his assessors nominated one person, and the commonalty another, these two elected eight, and the eight elected the members. The custom had been maintained, and is called the custom of the borough, notwithstanding an ordinance of the corporation made in 1452 directing that the election of the burgesses of the parliament should be chosen 'by the most part of the burgesses in the guildhall at the election, and not one for the bench by the mayor and his assistants and another by the commonalty as of old time hath been used[3].'

Complex elections at Lynn and Cambridge.

Variety of qualification of voters.

These instances are sufficient to prove that the exercise of the local franchise was a matter of local regulation until the cognisance of elections was claimed and recognised as a right and duty of the house of commons. As it is difficult even conjecturally to realise the formal process of the election, it is more difficult to say in whom the right of suffrage in the boroughs

[1] Beloe, Our Borough, p. 25.

[2] '1433, June 17. The king's writ was then publicly read for electing members of parliament. And for electing them the mayor called two of the twenty-four and two of the common council, which four chose two more of the twenty-four and two of the common council, and they chose four others, who all unanimously chose John Waterden and Thomas Spicer to be burgesses in parliament.' 1437, Jan. 7, a similar election was held, the mayor nominating the first two by the assent of the whole congregation: Extracts from the Records of Lynn, Archaeologia xxiv. 320.

[3] Cooper, Annals of Cambridge, i. pp. 173, 205, 272.

was supposed to lie: the whole of our mediaeval history scarcely furnishes more than one or two instances of a contested county election: the town histories are altogether silent. And the differences and difficulties, which arise as soon as political life wakes again in the seventeenth century, show that this obscurity is not new. The franchise, as soon as its value was ascertained, became a subject of dispute between different classes of men, or different candidates for the representation, in every town: the great addition of borough members to the house of commons, caused by the measures of the Tudor sovereigns, brought an influx of strange novelties; the old towns which had never been troubled with a contest had no precedents of custom to allege; in some instances the rules for municipal elections were applied to the parliamentary elections, in others the custom of the county courts was followed, and in others the inhabitants were left to follow their own political instincts of freedom or repression. The increased strength and exclusiveness of the corporations in the chartered towns had in some instances withdrawn the choice of the members altogether from the body of townsmen: in others the weakness of the magistrates had let it slip altogether into the hands of the freemen. In all cases the elections were becoming direct and primary.

Obscurity arising from diversity of qualification.

It is impossible to argue back from the parliamentary judgments of the seventeenth century to the practice of the middle ages: but, as it is improbable that any completely new system of franchise was introduced in the sixteenth century, we may briefly indicate the several theories or customs which are found in working when our knowledge of the subject begins. The most ancient, perhaps, of the franchises was that depending on burgage tenure; this was exactly analogous in origin to the freeholder's qualification in the counties; but as the repressive principle extended, the right of a burgage vote had become in many places attached to particular houses or sites of houses, probably those which were originally liable for a quota of the firma burgi; in others the right still belonged to the whole body of freeholders; and this may be regarded as a second sort of franchise. A third custom placed the right to vote in the

Illustrations from more modern procedure.

Diversities of franchise.

freemen of the borough, or of the guild which was coextensive with the borough; the character of a freeman being personal and not connected with tenure of land or contribution to the public burdens. A fourth gave the electoral vote to all householders paying scot and lot; that is, bearing their rateable proportion in the payments levied from the town for local or national purposes. A fifth lodged the right in the hands of the governing body, the corporation; the constitution of which again varied from comparative freedom in one place to oligarchic exclusiveness in another. The newer the constitution of the town was, the less liberal the constitution seems to have been, and several places, which must in early times have enjoyed fairly free institutions, had, by accepting new charters, lost their liberties, at all events in this particular. As the towns were constantly purchasing new charters, the perpetual changes in their constitutions add a further element of difficulty to our inquiry; but it is obvious that the tendency to restriction set in from the first institution of charters of incorporation in the fifteenth century. The ancient cities of Winchester and Salisbury saw their electoral rights confined to the small body of the corporation, sixty in one and fifty-six in the other[1]. Old Sarum retained the burgage franchise, its desolation saving it from a new charter. Twenty-three persons returned the members for Bath. But for our purpose no further conclusions need be drawn from such premises. The antiquity of the borough was no guarantee for its freedom; its municipal symmetry no security for the soundness of its political machinery. Aylesbury, a new borough of Mary's creation, did not even care to maintain its corporate character, and in the days of Elizabeth the lord of the manor returned the members. Aldborough and Boroughbridge, two boroughs in the same parish, had different franchises; scot and lot gave the right in one, burgage tenure in the other. Both of these were members of the great liberty of Knaresborough, and

Changes in particular places.

Anomalies not to be reduced to rule.

[1] These and the following instances will be found, illustrated by the reports of the election committees of the house of commons upon them, in Browne Willis's Notitia Parliamentaria, in Carew on Elections, in the Appendices to the Royal Kalendars of the last century, and in local histories generally. The primary authority of course is the Commons' Journals.

that town also returned two members and retained the burgage vote. In the Cinque Ports, where at least symmetry might have been looked for, equal variation is found; at Hastings, Dover, Sandwich, Rye and Seaford the constitution was open; at New Romney, Winchelsea and Hythe it was close. These anomalies grew up in the new boroughs as well as in the old ones: the older and larger cities, with the exceptions already noted, maintained their liberties; Norwich, Bedford, Reading, Cambridge, Gloucester, Northampton, Newcastle-on-Tyne, Coventry, and York, retained the scot and lot franchise. But every borough has had a history that was all its own; and some had constitutions and mixtures of franchise as confused as their obscure history.

Every borough has its own constitution.

Cases of early disputed elections.

746. Medieval history records little about contested or disputed elections. In an age when the office of representative was regarded rather as a burden than as a privilege, it is not surprising to find that contested and disputed returns were caused rather by the difficulty of finding candidates than by the rivalry of the competitors themselves. Such was the case in the early days of parliament; in 1321 the mayor of Lincoln writes to the Keeper of the Rolls of parliament, that one of the two elected members, who had gone so far as to assent to his election, would not deign to attend the parliament[1]. But the sheriff was generally the person to blame. In 1319 Sir William Martyn, who had been elected, on the nomination of the bishop of Exeter, knight of the shire for Devon, petitioned the council against the undue return made by the vice-sheriff, who had substituted another name: Martyn obtained a summons for the offending officer to answer for the false return in the Exchequer[2]. In 1323 it was alleged by the grand jury of West Derby wapentake that William le Gentil, when sheriff, had returned two knights of the shire without the consent of the county, whereas they ought to have been elected by the county; he had also levied twenty pounds for their wages, although the county could

The sheriff in fault in Devon,

and Lancashire.

[1] Parl. Writs, II. i. 252. They had elected Henry de Hakethorn and Thomas Gamel; Thomas would 'ne se deygne venir pur riens que nous savons faire'; so they had chosen Alan of Huddleston instead.

[2] Prynne, 4th Inst. p. 31; Hallam, Middle Ages, iii. 109.

Contested elections.

have found two men who would have gone to parliament for ten marks or ten pounds; his predecessor, Henry de Malton, had done the same[1]. In 1362 the county of Lancashire was again in trouble: the king wrote to tell the sheriff that there was a great altercation concerning the last election, and directed him to hold an examination in full county court as to the point whether the two persons named in the return were duly elected; and, if they were, to pay them their wages; if not, to send in the names of the persons who had been so elected. On examination it was found that the two knights whose names had been returned were themselves the lieutenants of the sheriff; they had kept the writ, returned themselves without election, and levied the wages to their own use: the king, puzzled apparently at so impudent a pretension, had to apply to the justices of the peace to ascertain the facts and stop the proceedings of the sheriff[2].

Shaftesbury.

In 1384 the burghers of Shaftesbury petitioned the king, lords and commons, in respect of their election: the sheriff of Dorset had substituted the name of Thomas Camel for that of Thomas Seward, whom, with Walter Henley, they had elected; and they prayed a remedy[3].

Rutland.

In 1404 the county of Rutland elected John Pensax and Thomas Thorpe; the sheriff returned John Pensax and William Ondeby; on a representation made by the house of commons to the king, the lords were directed to examine the parties; Thorpe was declared duly elected; the sheriff was ordered to amend the return and removed from office[4]. The case however which is most closely parallel to more modern usage is that which has been already noticed as illustrating the proceedings at elections.

Huntingdonshire.

In 1450, in Huntingdonshire, the sheriff returned two knights, Robert Stoneham and John Styvecle; but annexed to the indenture of return is a memorial from 124 freeholders, who declare that

[1] Parl. Writs, II, pt. i. p. 315.

[2] Prynne, Reg. iv. p. 259; Hallam, Middle Ages, iii. 109.

[3] Prynne, Reg. iv. p. 1114; Carew, On Elections, p. 118.

[4] Rot. Parl. iii. 530; Hallam, Middle Ages, iii. 110: the other case noticed by Hallam, the election of Camoys a baron and banneret as member for Surrey, and that of Berners, who was elected for Surrey when he was already knight of the shire for Kent, are not cases of disputed election but of the choice of disqualified persons; Prynne, Reg. ii. 118, 119.

they, with more than 300 good commoners of the shire, had voted for Stoneham and Styvecle, whilst seventy others had voted for one Henry Gimber, a man not of 'gentill birth' as the royal writ prescribed; their right was clear, but the under-sheriff having attempted to hold an examination on oath, Gimber's friends had threatened a riot; not knowing how the sheriff would act, they had determined to make the matter sure; fortunately for himself the sheriff had made the right return[1]. No doubt the sheriff frequently had hazardous work; in 1439 no return was made for Cambridgeshire; the sheriff was called up and ordered to publish the writ with a prohibition against the appearance of armed men at the election; it may be fairly inferred that the former election had been prevented by force[2].

Precautions against a false return.

Case of no return made.

These few instances serve to illustrate the more general complaints against the sheriffs which are from time to time made the basis of legislation on this point. They further show that the house of commons had not yet thought of asserting any claim to determine the validity of elections. Until the Act of 1406 the sheriff had to return the writ in full parliament; and the king, in or out of parliament, took direct cognisance of complaints[3]. After that Act the writ was returnable in Chancery, and by the Statute of 1410 the judges of assize were authorised to inquire into the undue returns. But the validity of the return was still, it would seem, a question for the king to consider, with the help of the lords, as in the Rutland case, or with the help of the judges. The right of the commons was first distinctly asserted in 1586[4]: in 1604, in reference to the election for Buckinghamshire, the commons, in the apology addressed to James I, represented the question as one in dispute between their house and the chancery[5]: from the time of the Restoration to the Grenville Act in 1770 election petitions were

Right of determining disputed elections.

Claimed by the house of Commons.

[1] Prynne, Reg. iii. 157.
[2] Prynne, Reg. ii. 139; Hallam, Middle Ages, iii. 110. In 1453 the king had to write to the chancellor of the University not to allow the scholars to impede the election. Cooper, Annals, i. 206.
[3] Prynne, Reg. ii. 119, 122.
[4] Hallam, Constitutional History, i. 274 sq.
[5] Hatsell, Precedents, i. 233.

determined by the whole house; that act provided for the formation and regulation of election committees; and very recent legislation has returned to something like the ancient practice by placing the determination of these disputes, and the infliction of penalties resulting from them, in the hands of select judges.

The persons elected to be resident.

Scarcely any point illustrates the intention of the crown and of the legislature to make the house of commons a really representative body more forcibly than the measures taken both in the writs and by statute to secure the election of persons bonâ fide resident among their constituents. From very early days the writ had ordered that the knights of the shire should be men of the county that elected them. The statutes of Henry IV and V enforced residence as a requisite for electors and elected alike, and that of Henry VI prescribed that the qualification of both must lie within the shire. The same rule applied to the boroughs. And it was for the most part strictly observed; the members were generally 'co-citizens' or 'comburgesses'; for although the more strictly senatorial theory of modern times declared the statute of 1413 unfit to be observed[1], the medieval communities were justly jealous of their relation to their paid representatives. At Lynn, and probably in other places, the members, after the session of Parliament was over, brought down a full account of its proceedings and reported them publicly. It was after the rise of the political jealousies of the Tudor times that strangers began to covet and canvass for the borough membership: and the statute of Henry V was then evaded by admitting them to the free burghership. Thus at Lynn, in 1613, Sir Robert Hitchen and Sir Henry Spelman, two persons foreign to the town, prayed to be elected burgesses[2]. The corporation replied that they intended to act upon the statute of Henry V, and elected two of their neighbours. At Cambridge, in 1460, the magistrates, probably with the intention of warning off political candidates, published an ordinance directing that for the future no non-resident should be elected burgess[3].

The members give account of their work to their constituents.

Strangers excluded from election.

[1] See Hallam, Middle Ages, iii. 119.
[2] Archaeol. xxiv. 372. [3] Cooper, Annales, i. 211.

Other measures of exclusion or restriction, the prohibition of the sheriffs, of lawyers, of maintainers, of ignoble persons, and the like, have been already noticed in our account of the writs; the points of social importance which are connected with them belong to another chapter.

Other restrictions.

747. When the process of election had been completed, provision was made for securing the attendance and competence of the newly-chosen representatives. For each of them manucaptors or bailsmen were provided, who were bound for their obedience to the writ, and the names of the manucaptors were entered in the return. This manucaption was intended to secure the attendance of the members. To assure their full powers, they had letters of commission or of 'ratihabition,' or powers of attorney, such as were usually furnished to proctors or representative officers[1]. After the Act of 1406 the importance of the manucaption was much diminished, the names of the electors entered on the indenture of return being a sufficient warrant for the responsibility of the persons elected; but the indenture likewise contained an equivalent to a power of attorney. Besides this the assembly which elected the members frequently passed a vote determining the sum to be paid to them as travelling expenses or wages. This was done by the citizens of London in 1295 and by those of York in 1483; it may therefore have been continuously regarded as a grant in the power of the represented communities to determine; but the payment was also provided for by a royal writ, issued at the close of the session to the several sheriffs and bailiffs, which fixed the amount to be paid to each according to the number of days of session, the length of the journey, and a fixed rate per diem[2]. The constituents seem in some cases to

Security for the attendance of the members elected.

Vote of wages by the constituents.

[1] The form in which the full powers were given was not always the same: in 1290 the sheriffs of Devon, Lincoln, and Northumberland mention in their returns the bestowal of the 'plena potestas'; Parl. Writs, i. 21–23. See also pp. 39, 41, 59, 60, 66 sq. The mayor and sheriffs of London gave their members a separate commission over and above the return endorsed on the writ, in 1304; Parl. Writs, i. 146; and afterwards; ib. II, i. 7, 30, &c. At Lynn in 1433 the election took place on Jan. 7; the letters of authority were sealed with the common seal, Jan. 16; and generally a few days after the election; Archaeol. xxiv. 321.

[2] See below, p. 483.

have made a bargain with their representatives to do the work for less.

Assembly of the parliament.

748. The newly-elected knights, citizens and burgesses, thus bound over to appear, fully empowered, fairly well provided for, and further invested with the sanctity of ambassadors by the sacred privilege of parliament[1], took their journey to Westminster or the other place of meeting, and presented themselves before the king or his representative on the day fixed. Their writs were produced with them by the sheriff himself or his messenger, and this, with the letters of commission, completed the verification of their powers. At the appointed time and place they met the lords spiritual and temporal, and in the king's presence the parliament was constituted.

Arrangement of the estates in the Parliament Chamber.

The ceremony of opening the parliament generally took place in the Painted Chamber[2] where the king's throne was placed at the upper end; the bishops and abbots were arranged according to their proper precedence on the king's right hand, the lords temporal in their several degrees on the left; at the lower end of the room the knights of the shires and representative citizens and burgesses took their stand. In front of the throne were the woolsacks on which the judges sat, and the table for the clerks and other officers of parliament. Occasionally the session is said to have been opened in the White Chamber, near

[1] See below, p. 494.

[2] The Painted Chamber is first mentioned as the place of meeting in 1340; Rot. Parl. ii. 107, 117: again in 1341, ib. p. 127; cf. vol. ii. p. 387 above. In 1343 the session opened in the Painted Chamber, April 30; the commons met in the same chamber May 12, the lords in the White Chamber; the next day both houses met the king in the White Chamber, ib. pp. 135, 136. The king met the two houses in the White Chamber in 1344, p. 148. In 1351 the two houses met in the 'Chaumbre Blanche pres de la Chaumbre Peynte' where the commission for opening the parliament was read, and afterwards in the Painted Chamber where the causes of summons were declared; ib. p. 225. In 1365 both met in the Painted Chamber where the commons stayed, the king and lords returning to the White Chamber; ib. p. 283: after the lords had deliberated the commons were called in; p. 284: so also in 1366 and 1373; pp. 289, 316. In 1368 the commons sat in the lesser hall, p. 294. In 1382 the meeting was in a chamber 'arraiez pur parlement'; but the opening speech was made in the Painted Chamber; ib. iii. 132. In 1386 the impeachment of Michael de la Pole took place in the Chamber of Parliament; p. 216. In 1383 Nicolas Brember was sentenced in the White Hall; iii. 238.

the Painted Chamber, no doubt the room afterwards used for the House of Lords. Henry VII used the Chamber of the Holy Cross. The king was almost always present in person; when he was not, the commission under which his representative, whether the regent of the realm or some great officer of state, acted, was read before the proceedings commenced[1]. A proclamation to ensure peace was also made in Westminster Hall.

The king generally present.

The first act of the meeting was to call over the names of the elected knights, citizens and burgesses, so as to identify them with those returned by the sheriffs[2]. Possibly the roll of the lords summoned may been called over at the same time. Such was the case in 1315 when they were dilatory in arriving, but the regular adoption of the practice may have been somewhat later. The Statute of 1382[3] ordered an amercement to be laid on all who failed to obey the summons, but both before and after the passing of this act it frequently happened that lords and commons alike showed themselves unpunctual. In 1377, for instance, a few lords met in the White Chamber and waited until the late hour of noon for their brethren; it happened that many

The returns called over.

Fines on absentees.

[1] In 1307 Edward I commissioned the bishop of Lichfield and the earl of Lincoln to open parliament at Carlisle; Parl. Writs, i. 184: in 1313 Edward II empowered the earls of Gloucester and Richmond; Rot. Parl. i. 448: see other cases ib. pp. 450. Instances under Edward III are given by Prynne, Reg. i. 425 sq.; Rot. Parl. ii. 106, 225, &c. In 1316 William Inge, a justice, was ordered by the king to announce the cause of summons on the day of meeting: the proxies were then examined, petitions received, triers and auditors appointed; but the political business was delayed until the earl of Lancaster came; the king's place in the parliament being in the meantime supplied by a commission of lords. When the earl came, the cause of summons was again read and the estates retired to deliberate; Rot. Parl. i. 350, 351. This is important as being the form observed in the first extant Roll.

[2] In the parliament of Lincoln in 1316, the chancellor, treasurer, and a justice were appointed to examine the excuses and proxies of the absent lords, and to report to the king the names of those who had sent none or only insufficient excuses, 'ita quod ipse inde posset percipere quod deberet'; Rot. Parl. i. 350. The names of the lords were called over in 1344 for the king to learn who had come and who not; ib. ii. 147. For the proceedings in 1379, see Rot. Parl. iii. 55; in 1380 the knights of the shire, citizens, and burgesses were called by name, ib. pp. 71, 88; in 1384 it had become an established practice: 'nominatim invocatis prout moris est'; ib. 184.

[3] 5 Rich. II. st. 2. c. 4; Statutes, ii. 25; Rot. Parl. iii. 124. No oaths were taken until 1 Eliz.; Prynne, Reg. i. 406.

Adjournment for fuller attendance.

had not come to town, and some sheriffs had not sent in their returns; the king, who was kept waiting likewise, postponed the ceremony to the next day[1]. This sometimes was done day by day for a week[2]. When however there was a sufficiently large muster, the names were called and the cause of summons[3] declared in a solemn speech by the chancellor, by the archbishop of Canterbury, the lord chief justice, or by some other great officer of state, at the command of the king[4]. The speech, of which many specimens have been given in the foregoing pages, usually began with a text of Scripture or some thesis chosen by the orator himself, and partook more or less of the nature of a sermon; the application of the doctrine came at the close, and generally contained a statement of the royal difficulties, a demand for supplies, and a promise of redress for grievances personal or national; immediately after this promise the king appointed receivers and triers of petitions and the two houses separated. Now and then a second speech was made to the conjoint assembly a day or two later by the chancellor or some officer of the household; and even a third exposition of the cause of summons was occasionally vouchsafed[5]; but more fre-

Opening speech or sermon.

Appointment of triers.

[1] Rot. Parl. iii. 1.

[2] See instances in 1340; and almost every year of Richard II. Rot. Parl. ii. 107, 112, &c.

[3] The first occasion on which the commons are expressly said to be present at the 'exposition' of the cause of summons is in 1339; Rot. Parl. ii. 103; cf. i. 350. In January 1340 the cause is specially declared to the commons; Rot. Parl. ii. 107. In March 1340 the cause is declared first to the lords specially, and then to the lords and commons generally; ib. p. 112. In July 1340 they are again mentioned as present. In April 1341 the cause is declared to the lords and council, but the commons seem to have been there; ib. p. 127.

[4] From 1347 to 1363 the chief justice makes the opening speech; the chief justice of the Common Pleas in 1401; the archbishop of Canterbury in 1344, 1368, 1377, 1399, and 1422; the chancellor in 1343, 1363 (in English) and generally after 1368; the bishop of Winchester in 1410; the bishop of Lincoln in 1453 and 1467, the bishop of Rochester in 1472, and the keeper of the Privy Seal in 1431, supplied the place of the absent chancellor. The longest recorded sermon is that of bishop Houghton in 1377; Rot. Parl. ii. 361; but Michael de la Pole made quite as long an address in 1383; ib. iii. 149, 150. See Elsynge, Ancient Method of holding Parliament, pp. 131 sq.

[5] In 1378, at the Parliament of Gloucester, the chancellor on two different days addressed the whole parliament, and the speaker of the commons had to repeat the main points of the speech to them; Rot. Parl. iii. 35. In 1381 the chancellor made the first statement; a day or two after, the

quently they separated on the first day; the commons being ordered to withdraw to their regular place of meeting and choose a speaker, and both estates being warned that they must get early to work. The morning hours were very precious; in 1373 the commons were directed to meet at the hour of prime; in 1376 and 1378 at eight; in 1397 and 1401 the chancellor fixed ten in the morning for the meeting in the Painted Chamber; in 1406 the commons were ordered to meet at eight, the lords an hour later; in 1413 the commons had to meet at seven and to present their speaker at eight[1]. The apartment to which the commons usually withdrew was the Chapterhouse of Westminster Abbey[2], which is termed in the Rolls their ancient and accustomed place; very often however they met in the Refectory which was specially assigned for their use by Henry V in 1414 and 1416[3]. The Chapterhouse was, until the reign of Edward VI, their withdrawing room or place of separate deliberation. Their communications with the king or lords were held in the Painted Chamber, in the White Chamber, or in the Little Hall of the palace. Edward I, in 1297, is found gathering the knights in his own private chamber to obtain a separate vote of money[4]; the Black Prince, in 1372[5], assembled the borough members in his chamber, when he wanted a vote of tunnage and poundage; and Henry VI, in 1450, after the impeachment of Suffolk, collected the lords 'in his innest chamber with a Gavill window over a

Withdrawal of the Commons.

Their place of deliberation.

Conferences with the king.

treasurer repeated it, and a few days later lord le Scrope, the newly appointed chancellor, made a third exposition; Rot. Parl. iii. 98-100.

[1] Rot. Parl. ii. 316, 321: iii. 33, 338; iv. 9. 34, 495.

[2] The first time that the commons were directed to withdraw to the Chapterhouse seems to be in 1352, when they were told to elect a committee to confer with the lords, and the rest to retire to the Chapterhouse and wait for their companions; they did not comply with the first direction, and so the second was superfluous; Rot. Parl. ii. 237; vol. ii. p. 408. The next time the Chapterhouse is mentioned is in 1376, when the commons, who had met generally in the meanwhile in the Painted Chamber (above, p. 426), were ordered to withdraw 'a lour aunciene place en la maison du chapitre de l' abbe, de Westmostier'; ib. p 322: also in 1377; p. 363, iii. 3. In 1395 they were told to assemble in the Chapterhouse or Refectory to elect a speaker; p. 329: and they met in the Refectory in 1397; ib. 338.

[3] Rot. Parl. iv. 34, 94.

[4] Vol. ii. p. 137.

[5] 'En une chambre pres la Blanche Chambre'; Rot. Parl. ii. 310.

House of Lords.

cloister within his palace of Westminster[1].' But these are exceptional cases, and it is believed that, as a rule, the ordinary place for the session of the lords was the Chamber of Parliament or White Chamber, lying immediately south of the Painted Chamber; and that the Chapterhouse or Refectory was the recognised chamber of the commons.

Historical question as to the division of the two Houses.

749. At how early a date the two houses separated and began to deliberate apart is a question of considerable antiquarian interest, and was once debated with some acrimony[2]. The point looked at in the fuller light of published records becomes one of very small importance. If the proper incorporation of the three estates in parliament be allowed, as it now is, to date from the year 1295, the possible practice of earlier years becomes unimportant by way of precedent. That the baronage, whether assembled in parliament or not, could hold sessions apart from the clergy or the commons, is a fact as clear as that the clergy could and did meet apart from the baronage. On the analogy of the clerical assemblies, it might seem a natural conclusion that the commons, from the year 1295, could meet and deliberate alone. But on the other hand the barons had their own assembly as a great council, and the clergy theirs in synod and convocation; the representatives of the commons had no such collective organisation; they never met but as an estate of parliament. The first place in which the parliament records distinctly notice a separate session is in the rolls of 1332[3], when the prelates, the lords temporal, and the knights of the shire are described as deliberating apart. The deliberations may have

[1] Rot. Parl. v. 182.

[2] See Prynne, Register, i. 233; Coke, 4 Inst. p. 4.

[3] The notices which have been given above (vol. ii. pp. 376, 377) may be recapitulated here: in September 1331 the prelates, earls, barons, and other grantz 'conseilerent pur le mielz, uniement et chescun par lui severalment'; Rot. Parl. ii. 60. In March 1332 the prelates and proctors of the clergy debated by themselves, the earls, barons, and other grantz by themselves; ib. p. 64. In September 1332 the prelates by themselves, the earls, barons, and other grantz by themselves, and the knights of the shires by themselves; ib. p. 66: so also in December 1332; p. 67. In January 1333 a separate section of the lords, probably as the council, sat apart; the rest of the lords, and the proctors by themselves; the knights, citizens, and burgesses by themselves; ib. p. 69. In 1339, and ever after, the division into two houses seems clear enough.

Probability that such division existed from the first incorporation of the Commons.

taken place in one chamber, in Westminster Hall possibly, but it is more probable that each body retired to a room of its own. The fact that money was voted by the different estates in different proportions might suggest even a wider distribution; possibly the prelates and clergy, the lords temporal, the knights of the shire, and the borough members, may have sat in four companies and in four chambers. In 1341 the 'grantz' and the commons seem to have definitely assorted themselves in two chambers[1]; and in 1352 the chapterhouse is regarded as the chamber of the commons[2]. The practice, then, of scarcely forty years is all that is touched by the question before us; and in the absence of any authoritative evidence from documents, together with the proved worthlessness of the *modus tenendi parliamentum*, on which alone the doctrine of the ancient union of the two houses seems to rest, the theory of Prynne that the two never deliberated together is *prima facie* as tenable as that of Coke that they did. If, to go a step further, we give due weight to the influence of custom, and consider that, as soon as we have any evidence at all, we find the estates deliberating apart, we shall incline to the belief that they had done so from the beginning; or, in other words, that it was only in the presence of the king, or to hear a message from him, or when called together for special conferences, that the lords and commons ever formed parts of one deliberative assembly. Their arrangement in the two existing and historical chambers is another point, but the further we look back, more traces of division than of union seem to be discoverable.

Numbers of the two Houses.

750. Of the numbers and special qualifications of the persons who composed what may by a slight anticipation be called the house of lords, not much has now to be added to what has been said in preceding chapters: and that little concerns points of dignity and precedence more than matters of constitutional

[1] 'Ad il chargez et priez en chargeante manere les ditz grantz et autres de la commune, qu'ils se treissent ensemble, et s'avisent entre eux; c'est assaver les grantz de par eux, et les chivalers des counteez, citeyns et burgeys de par eux'; Rot. Parl. ii. 127.

[2] See above, p. 429, note 2.

Ranks among the Lords.

importance. The house consisted of the lords spiritual and temporal, the 'prelatz et autres grantz,' and, more circumstantially, contained the prince of Wales, the archbishops and bishops, the abbots and priors of certain monasteries, the dukes, marquesses, earls, viscounts, and barons. Of these titles some are much more ancient than others, and all have some slight political significance. They may be taken in the order given.

The prince of Wales.

The highest rank after the king himself belonged to the prince of Wales; and throughout medieval English history the prince of Wales is the only person who bears the territorial title of prince. Of the native princes of Wales, who became extinct shortly before the parliament took its permanent form, none is recorded to have been summoned to a council of the barons, although they were cited to do homage, and the last of them, David, the brother of Llewelyn, was tried and condemned before the English baronage. Edward I created his eldest son prince of Wales in 1301[1]. Edward III never bore the title; the Black Prince in 1343 was invested as prince of Wales with a circlet ring and rod: his son Richard, Henry of Monmouth, and the three Edwards, sons of Henry VI, Edward IV, and Richard III, bore the title, in each case by special creation either in parliament or by charter immediately reported to parliament. The eldest son of the king was likewise duke of Cornwall, a title which was created with that special settlement. He was also created earl of Chester, a dignity which since the accession of Henry IV was annexed to the principality. Richard II raised the earldom of Chester into the dignity of a principality to be held with Wales; but the act was repealed by Henry IV[2]. Aquitaine was also constituted a principality for the Black

[1] On Feb. 7, 1301, the king granted to his son his lands in Wales and the earldom of Chester; and on the 10th of May he settled the lands on him and his heirs, by the name of prince of Wales and earl of Chester; Lords' Fifth Report, pp. 9–11. Edward I had himself held under his father Chester and part of North Wales, Perfeddwlad, between the Dee and Conway; the son is to hold his lands by the same service as Edward I had paid to Henry III.

The investiture of the Black Prince is described in the charter 'per sertum in capite et annulum in digito aureum ac virgam argenteam;' Lords' Fifth Report, p. 44; cf. p. 126.

[2] Lords' Fifth Report, p. 120; Rot. Parl. iii. 353.

Prince, but, although he was summoned to parliament by that designation, it can hardly be regarded as an English title. The rank of prince however is not the highest that has been borne by members of the English peerage. John Balliol, as a baron of Yorkshire, but also as king of Scotland, attended an English council in 1294; and Edward Balliol, as king of Scotland, was summoned to the parliaments of 1348 and 1349[1]. The lordship of Man was accounted as a royalty and conveyed within the island itself certain sovereign rights[2]; but, although from the reign of Edward III onwards it was held by an English lord, no lord or king of Man was ever summoned by that title. Henry duke of Warwick was, if we may believe the family chronicle, crowned king of the Isle of Wight, of Jersey and Guernsey, by Henry VI[3]. The only other subjects who bore the sovereign title were Richard, earl of Cornwall and king of the Romans, and John of Gaunt, duke of Lancaster, king of Leon and Castille; both these, as a matter of courtesy doubtless, received their full titles in council or parliament[4].

Scottish kings in parliament.

The lords of Man and Wight.

751. Next in rank among the lords temporal were the dukes. This title, sufficiently well known to the English as the designation of foreign potentates, was first bestowed on a subject in 1337, when Edward III founded the dukedom of Cornwall as the perpetual dignity of the king's eldest son and heir apparent[5]. The dukedom of Cornwall had been known for at least two centuries from the legendary history of Geoffrey of Monmouth. The duchy of Lancaster was founded in 1351 for the younger

The dukes.

Cornwall and Lancaster.

[1] Lords' Report, iv. 58, 577, 579.

[2] Man had been a kingdom, and was, in the hands of its English lords, a separate regality; but the title of king was not borne by them: and the great earl of Derby refused to assume the title of king, though he says that it had been borne by his ancestor the first of the Stanley lords of Man; see Peck's Desiderata Curiosa, pp. 431, 436. Cf. Prynne, 4th Inst. pp. 200–205.

[3] Mon. Angl. ii. 63; from the History of Tewkesbury: 'coronatur a rege in regem de Wight manu regia, et nominatur primus comes totius Angliae.' The truth was that the lordship of the Isle of Wight was a regality, like that of the counties palatine; but the story rests on this evidence only. Coke, 4th Inst. p. 287.

[4] John of Gaunt is summoned under the royal title as well as that of duke; Lords' Report, iv. 708.

[5] See the grants in the Lords' Fifth Report; Cornwall by charter, p. 35; Lancaster for life, by patent, ib. p. 47; Clarence by charter, p. 53; Lancaster, p. 53; Ireland to Robert de Vere, ib. p. 79.

Creation of dukes.

branch of the royal house, and refounded in 1362 in the person of John of Gaunt. In 1362 Lionel was made duke of Clarence. In 1385 the surviving sons of Edward III, Thomas of Woodstock and Edmund of Langley, were made dukes of Gloucester and York; in 1386 Robert de Vere was created duke of Ireland; and in 1397 Richard II created the dukedoms of Hereford, Norfolk, Surrey, Exeter and Aumâle or Albemarle. Of these, Norfolk and Exeter reappear in the later Plantagenet history. Under Henry VI Somerset was made a duchy for the Beauforts, Buckingham for the Staffords, and Warwick for Henry Beauchamp, the king's fellow pupil. In all these cases, except those of Clarence, Ireland, and Aumâle, the title is taken either from a county of England or a county town; of the exceptions the island of Ireland and the honour of Aumâle were distinctly territorial lordships; and the title of Clarence, obscure as it is, bore some reference to the ancient honour of Clare All of them may be termed provincial or territorial designations. The forms of the investiture were not always alike, but it became the rule for a duke to be created by the girding on of the sword, the bestowal of a golden rod, and the imposition of a cap of maintenance and circlet of gold[2]. The duke generally received a pension of forty pounds per annum on his promotion, which was known as creation money[3].

Their territorial designations.

Investiture and creation money.

The dignity of marquess was of somewhat later growth and less freely bestowed. The title derived from the old imperial office of markgrave, 'comes marchensis,' or count of the marches, had belonged to several foreigners who were brought into

[1] The honour of Aumâle consisted of the baronies accumulated by that branch of the house of Champagne which bore the title of count, or earl, of Aumâle, and transmitted the title and honour through females until the middle of the fourteenth century. The chief possession of the house was the lordship of Holderness. The title of Clarence is sometimes, but fancifully and without any real authority, connected with Chiarenza in the Morea. See Finlay's Greece, iv. 192.

[2] John of Gaunt was made duke of Aquitaine 'per appositionem cappae suo capiti ac traditionem virgae aureae'; Lords' Fifth Report, p. 110: so also the dukes made in 1397, ib. p. 118; and the duchess of Norfolk, p. 119; cf. p. 171. The dukes of Warwick and Buckingham, in 1443, have the cap and the gold circlet also, p. 224.

[3] See below, chapter xxi; Rot. Parl. iv. 308.

relation with England in the twelfth century; the duke of Brabant was marquess of Antwerp, and the count of Maurienne marquess of Italy[1]; but in France the title was not commonly used until the seventeenth century, and it is possible that it came to England direct from Germany. Edward III had made the margrave of Jülich earl of Cambridge; Sigismund, the brother of Anne of Bohemia, queen of Richard II, was margrave of Brandenburg, and her elder brother Wenzel had been made a margrave of the empire by his father Charles IV. Richard made Robert de Vere marquess of Dublin[2], and, undeterred by the fate of the first who bore the title, he, in 1397, created John Beaufort marquess of Dorset. Having in 1399 shared the degradation of the dukes created by Richard on the same occasion, John Beaufort, in 1402, declined to be restored to his marquessate on the ground that it was a strange title, unfamiliar and unwelcome to English ears[3]; it was however revived in favour of his son Edmund, who was made marquess of Dorset in 1443; William de la Pole was made marquess of Suffolk in 1444; Edward IV made John Neville marquess of Montague, and gave the marquessate of Dorset to his stepson. The title was not legally and formally given, as it might have been, to the lords marchers or to the earl of March; and the fact that, within a century of its introduction into England, it was used in so unmeaning a designation as the marquess of Montague, shows that it had lost all traces of its original application. The marquesses were invested with the golden circlet and the girding of the sword, and from the year 1470 by the gift of the cap of maintenance. The creation money was thirty-five pounds[4].

Creation of marquesses.

Investiture and creation money.

The ancient dignity of the earl has in former chapters been traced throughout its history. In very few instances was the

The earls.

[1] Selden, Titles of Honour, pp. 758–762. The title of marchio is given by William of Malmesbury to Brian Fitz Count, lord of Wallingford: it was often used loosely for count or duke.

[2] See the charter of creation, Rot. Parl. iii. 210; Lords' Fifth Report, p. 78; and the investiture 'per gladii cincturam et circuli aurei suo capiti impositionem,' ib. p. 77; John Beaufort was made marquess of Dorset 'per cincturam gladii' simply, ib. p. 117; Edmund Beaufort in 1443 has the circlet, ib. p. 241; and the marquess of Suffolk likewise, p. 251. Montague and Dorset have the cap and sword, ib. pp. 378, 403.

[3] Rot. Parl. iii. 488.

[4] Ib. v. 308.

title annexed to a simple town or castle, except in the case of the earldom of Arundel, which probably represents an earldom of the county of Sussex, of which the earl of Arundel received the third penny: the earl of Warenne in the same way was properly earl of Surrey, although he took his title from his Norman lordship; and the earls of Pembroke, of the house of Clare, are frequently called earls of Striguil; otherwise the title throughout medieval history belongs to a county or the county town, although it involved no local authority. The earldom of March, which was the only exception to this rule, was endowed with a pension from the issues of the counties of Stafford and Salop, the latter of which was a march or border county. The earl's creation money, twenty pounds, was a substitute for the third penny of the county, of which little is heard after the thirteenth century; and the retention of this payment probably suggested the bestowal of creation money on those who were raised to the newer ranks of peerage[1]. The earl was created either by charter, or by patent, or by formal act in parliament, and was invested as of old by the girding of the sword[2]. The cap and coronet were late additions.

Their territorial designation.

Creation money. Form of creation and investiture.

The viscounts.

The rank of viscount was a novelty in the fifteenth century; the first English peer who bore the title being the viscount of Beaumont, John, a lineal descendant of that Henry of Beaumont who took so prominent a part in the history of Edward II[3]. It was given him probably, as was the French viscounty which he likewise held, as the representative of the ancient viscounts of Beaumont in Maine, with the intention of securing to him a precedence over the older barons; the lord Bourchier, the next created viscount, was likewise earl of Eu in Normandy;

[1] See grants of the third penny in the Lords' Fifth Report, pp. 1–17; letters patent for the earldom of Carlisle, p. 18; the charter for the earldom of Winchester, p. 18; of March, p. 21; Huntingdon, p. 29; Northampton, p. 30; the last two, by assent of parliament. See above, vol. ii. p. 615. The third penny is mentioned in the grant of the Devonshire earldom to Hugh Courtenay in 1336, ib. p. 27; the creation money by Madox, Bar. Angl. p. 141; Rot. Parl. v. 308.

[2] See for instance the charter of creation of Michael de la Pole, earl of Suffolk, Lords' Fifth Report, p. 69.

[3] Lords' Fifth Report, p. 235; Madox, Baronia, p. 143.

John Talbot was made viscount de l'Isle in 1451, and the lord Berkeley was created viscount in 1481. The title has little or no meaning in English history, and in its Latin form was and is still used as the designation of the sheriffs of town or county.

The barons.

The dignity and title of barony did not during the latter middle ages undergo any change, further than was caused by the superposition of the new dignities of duke, marquess and viscount over it. The method of creation was to some extent affected by the same influences. The year 1295 has been marked as the point of time from which the regularity of the baronial summons is held to involve the creation of an hereditary dignity, and so to distinguish the ancient qualification of barony by tenure from that of barony by writ[1]. As the earls and dukes of the reign of Edward III were created by patent or charter, and generally in parliament, the example was at some distance of time followed in the case of barons. In 1387 Richard II created John Beauchamp of Holt a baron by patent[2], and in 1432 John Cornwall was created baron of Fanhope in parliament, his creation being subsequently confirmed by patent[3]. From the twenty-fourth year of Henry VI barons were generally made by patent[4]. The importance of the distinction seems to lie in the fact that the patent of creation defined the line in which the hereditary peerage was to run, generally to the heirs male of the person promoted, whilst the barony created by ancient writ of summons may descend to heiresses. The political intention of the change has been

Creations by patent.

Importance of the creation by patent.

[1] Vol. ii. pp. 181–184.

[2] Lords' Fifth Report, p. 81; 'in unum parium ac baronum regni.' There was no settled sum of creation money for a baron, nor any distinct form of investiture unless by robes; see Elsynge, Parliament, p. 36.

[3] Lords' Fifth Report, p. 213: Ralph Boteler is made baron of Sudeley by patent in 1441; ib. p. 239: the lord L'Isle is made by charter in 1444; ib. p. 245: Beauchamp of Powick by patent; ib. p. 256: so also Rivers, p. 263.

[4] In the 27 Henry VI Henry Bromflete was created a baron by his writ of summons, which contained the words 'volumus enim vos et heredes vestros masculos de corpore vestro legitime exeuntes barones de Vescy existere'; Prynne Reg. i. 229. In 1444 'by one of the most extraordinary charters on record' the barony of L'Isle of Kingston L'Isle was limited to the person created 'and to his heirs and assigns for ever being tenants of the manor of Kingston L'Isle'; Nicolas, Hist. Peerage (ed. Courthope), p. 291.

Theories as to the creation of barons by patent.

differently interpreted: it has been regarded, on the one hand, as an attempt to establish the right of peerage on more than a mere prescriptive basis, and to control the royal power of continuing or discontinuing the issue of the summons to the heirs of former recipients, a practice tending to make the balance of the house of lords depend on the court party of the moment; on the other hand, it has been regarded as a restraint or limitation of the peerage to a direct line of succession[1]. The two ideas are not incompatible, and the result has certainly been a limitation on the descent of peerages; but it may be questioned whether the advisers of Henry VI, who during the period of the change were playing a very haphazard game, had any deep political object in view. After this, as before, the older baronies descended to heiresses who, although they could not take their places in the assembly of the estates, conveyed to their husbands a presumptive right to receive a summons. Of the countless examples of this practice, which applied anciently to the earldoms also, it may be enough to mention Sir John Oldcastle, who as the husband of the heiress of Cobham was summoned as baron of Cobham; Ralph of Monthermer, husband of the widowed Johanna of Acre, countess of Gloucester, sat as earl of Gloucester during the minority of his stepson; Richard Beauchamp gained the earldom of Warwick as husband of the heiress. The lords Molines, Willoughby, Fitz Walter, and many others whose names occur somewhat confusingly during the wars of the Roses, reached the peerage in this way, and although some royal act of summons, or creation, or both, was necessary to complete their status, the usage was not materially broken down until the system of creation with limitation to heirs male was established. The descent of the peerage through females, and the creation of new titles by patent, alike helped to put an end to the practice of calling the peer by his family name. Even at the accession of Henry VII very few of the ancient baronies by writ were held by the direct representatives in the male line of the barons so summoned by Edward I.

No lady of any rank whatever was ever summoned either in person or by proxy to a full and proper parliament. There are

[1] See Nicolas, Historic Peerage (ed. Courthope), p. xlii.

instances of countesses, baronesses, and abbesses being summoned to send proxies or to furnish their military service, but not to attend parliament as peeresses[1]. The nearest approach to such a summons is that of four abbesses, who in 1306 were cited to the great council held to grant an aid on the knighting of the prince of Wales.

No ladies in parliament.

Although instances occur in which a person not qualified to receive a summons as judge or councillor has been summoned to parliament and yet has not transmitted a hereditary peerage to his descendants, it is not probable that the crown ever contemplated the creation, by such single summons, of a barony for life only[2]. The higher ranks of the peerage were occasionally granted for life; such was the first dukedom of Lancaster, the creation of the duchess of Norfolk in 1397, of Thomas Beaufort duke of Exeter in 1416, of Robert de Vere as marquess of Dublin and duke of Ireland; John of Lancaster was made earl of Kendal and duke of Bedford, and Humfrey earl of Pembroke and duke of Gloucester, in the first instance for life[3]; and in 1377 Guichard D'angle was made earl of Huntingdon for life[4]. No baron however was ever created for life only without a provision as to the remainder, or

Question of life peerages.

Dukes and earls for life.

[1] See above, vol. ii. p. 409. The summonses to furnish military service are numerous and will be found on the parliamentary writs passim. The abbesses summoned in 1306 were those of Barking, Wilton, Winchester, and Shaftesbury. The countesses summoned in 1361 were those who had estates in Ireland; Lords' Report, iv. 628, 630.

[2] In the long lists of barons summoned to parliament between 1295 and 1485 occur a number of names of persons summoned either once only, or irregularly, not hereditarily, although in writs worded exactly like those of the hereditary peers. On these Prynne founds an argument that they were the mere nominees of the king (Reg. i. 232, 233) and combats Coke's doctrine of the hereditary right to the writ. On careful examination Prynne's list shrinks into very small proportions: some of the names are those of judges whose writs have been confusedly mixed with those of the barons; some occur only in lists of summons to councils which were not proper parliaments. In most of the other cases the cessation of the summons is explained by the particular family history; for example, the son is a minor at the time of his father's death, and dies or is forgotten before he comes of age. In others, nothing is known of the later family history, and it must be supposed to have become extinct. The ingenious distinction drawn by Elsynge between barons and peers, the latter including bannerets and life peers, has no foundation.

[3] Lords' Fifth Report, pp. 171, 172.

[4] Ibid. p. 62.

Sons summoned during their fathers' life.

right of succession after his death[1]. The case of a son summoned to the house of lords as a peer in his father's lifetime is not understood as the creation of a new peerage: the first recorded instance of this practice occurs in 1482, when the heir of the earl of Arundel was summoned in his father's barony of Maltravers.

Question as to the title of baron.

It may be observed finally that, although all the 'grantz' summoned in the class of barons were no doubt peers and must have had a right to the title of 'baron' in both the ancient and the modern sense, that title is given in a special way to some few among them[2], the more general denomination being 'seigneur,' 'sieur,' or 'chivaler[3].' The exceptions seem to be the barons of Stafford and Greystoke, who share the designation with the non-parliamentary barons of the two great palatinates of Chester and Durham. This fact has never been explained, and it is the more curious as the title of 'lord' does not in England imply a dignity created by the crown, but is simply a descriptive or honorary appendage to some other dignity[4]. Another curious point, which more directly affects the house of lords, is the dignity of banneret, which has been sometimes regarded as a rank of peerage inferior to a barony[5]. This however was not

Dignity of banneret.

[1] Nicolas, Hist. Peerage, pp. xlv, xlvi. In two cases, the barony of Hay in 1606, and of Reede in 1644, the creation was for life, but it was provided that the bearers of the title should not sit in parliament. One baroness, lady Belasyse in 1674, was created for life; similar creations of higher ranks of the peerage, duchesses, &c., were not uncommon.

[2] Prynne, Reg. i. 220 sq.; Lords' Third Report, ii. 230: so the title of Dominus is said to be given only to Mowbray dominus de Axholm, and Talbot dominus de Furnival, until the reign of Henry VI; ibid.

[3] Madox explains the usage of styling a baron 'chivaler' in the summons to parliament as implying three things, (1) that he was of aetas legitima or aetas tenendi terram, (2) that he was 'extra custodiam,' and (3) that he had taken knighthood; Baronia Anglicana, p. 61.

[4] The puerile dispute about giving the title of lord bishop to colonial and suffragan bishops could not have arisen had this been kept in mind. The title of lord belongs to all bishops in all churches, and not merely to those who possess a seat in the English house of lords: nor has it anything to do with a royal prerogative of conferring titles, not being a recognised grade of peerage.

[5] Prynne, Reg. ii. 117, 118; Madox, Baron. Angl. p. 160; Lords' Report, i. 329, 340, 350, 354; Selden, Titles of Honour, pp. 737, 790. John Cobham, made a banneret by Edward III had 100 marks allowance to maintain his state, 42 Edw. III, Madox, Bar. Angl. p. 161; his father

the case; the rank of banneret was simply a degree of knighthood, superior to that of knight bachelor, but conveying no right of peerage, although of course many peers were in virtue of their degree of knighthood bannerets also. On this point much discussion has arisen; but it is one capable of summary proof; in very many cases barons were also bannerets; but the existence of a single English banneret who is never summoned to parliament would be enough to prove that the dignity conferred no peerage. Sir John Coupland who took king David prisoner at Neville's Cross was made a banneret by Edward III, but never sat in parliament[1]. There are many such instances throughout the whole period during which bannerets are heard of at all: but as the title of baron is, as we have just seen, very sparingly given to the peers, that of banneret or chivaler is frequently bestowed on those who were peers as well[2].

Banneret not a rank of peerage.

At the head of the barons of England, taking a sort of clerical precedence, were the English chiefs of the military orders, the Temple and the Hospital. Of these the Master of the Temple

The priors of the great orders.

and grandfather had sat in parliament as barons, and their barony descended to his daughter. Geoffrey le Scrope in 1340 had a settlement of 200 marks per annum, on himself and his heirs to maintain their estate of banneret, but he died immediately after, and his son was not summoned to parliament until 1350; Lords' Report, i. 354, 355. In this case an hereditary banneretcy must have been contemplated. In 1344 and 1372 bannerets are mentioned on the rolls as present in parliament; Rot. Parl. ii. 147, 309.

[1] Coke, 4th Inst. p. 5; Camden, Britannia (ed. 1600), pp. 138.

[2] This seems to be very conclusive; but Hallam thought the point still unsettled; Middle Ages, iii. p. 126. As however we have the complete lists of summons to identify the hereditary peers, there need really be no further question. The writ of 1378 in which it is stated that John Camoys, being a banneret, could not be elected as knight of the shire for Surrey is explained by the fact that he was also a baron; Prynne, Reg. ii. 117, 118. According to Selden, Titles of Honour, pp. 790–792, a banneret was a person knighted on the field of battle when the king is present or the royal standard displayed; the pennon of a banneret was cut square into the shape of a bannner, whence the name. Of the bannerets in arms in 1322 (Parl. Writs, II. ii. 196 sq.) Sir Warin de l'Isle, Sir Robert de Lidle, Sir Gilbert de Aton, Sir Thomas de Vere, were not barons of parliament. In the Wardrobe Accounts of Edward I, most of the persons receiving pay as bannerets were also barons receiving special summons to parliament; but Sir John Bottetourt who is called a banneret in 1300 is not summoned to parliament until 1305; and among the others are Sir Richard Siward, Sir Simon Fraser, Amanenus de la Bret, Arnold de Gaveston, and Elie de Cavapenna, all of them aliens. It cannot be denied that the subject has some puzzling aspects, but the authority of Selden, Prynne, and the Lords' Report, will probably be sufficient for most investigators.

disappears in 1308, at the suppression of the order; the Prior of S. John's, Clerkenwell, the Master of the Hospitallers of England, took his due place in parliament down to the date of the dissolution of monasteries; although he occupied the seat of a lord temporal, he was summoned among the lords spiritual[1].

Number of lords temporal.

752. The number of the temporal lords varied in almost every parliament; and, from time to time, we have traced the political or other causes of this fluctuation: during the reign of Henry IV the number never exceeded fifty; under Henry V it only once reached forty; under Henry VI, beginning with twenty-three in 1422, it reached fifty-five in 1450; and under Edward IV the maximum was fifty in the year 1466. The variations were caused by extinction, abeyances, minorities and attainders on the one hand, by new creations and restorations on the other. In some cases we may conjecture that the omission of a name from the list of summonses was caused by the neglect of its bearer to

Exemptions from attendance.

obey former citations. There are many instances of barons being relieved from the duty of attending parliament as a privilege due to old age or high favour[3]; without some such licence or other good excuse, and the mission of a proxy, the lords who absented themselves from parliament were liable to a heavy

Fines for non-attendance.

amercement such as was enforced in the parliament of 1454, when archbishops and dukes were subjected to a fine of £100; earls

Resignation of peerage.

and bishops of 100 marks; abbots and barons of £40[4]. The fact of any formal renunciation of the dignity of peerage, on the ground of a want of baronial tenure or other, may well be doubted. In one instance we find a duke, George Neville, of Bedford, degraded by act of parliament as not having sufficient property to maintain his dignity[5]; Lewis of Bruges, created earl of Winchester by Edward IV, resigned his patent to Henry VII[6]: both these are exceptional cases. Henry de Pinkeni, a baron of 1299 and 1301, sold his barony in the latter year to the king, and it was thus

[1] Mon. Ang. vi. 799; the Master of the Gilbertines, or order of Sempringham, ceased to be summoned in 1332. The prior of Clerkenwell sat for the last time in 1536; but was allowed in 1539 to appoint a proxy. He also sat under Philip and Mary.

[2] See above, p. 439 note 2.

[3] See Prynne, 4th Inst. pp. 33–37.

[4] Rot. Parl. v. 248.

[5] Lords' Fifth Report, p. 409; Rot. Parl. vi. 173.

[6] Lords' Fifth Report, p. 392.

extinguished; the earls of Gloucester, Norfolk and Hereford likewise made over their estates and dignities to Edward I in order to obtain a resettlement; and in the case of Norfolk the king took the opportunity of excluding the presumptive heir[1]. But such resignations and resettlements do not amount to a resignation of a right which from the very first was as precious as it was burdensome.

753. The number, degrees and dignities of the spiritual lords require less notice. The two archbishops and the eighteen bishops formed the most permanent element in the house of lords: when a see was vacant, the guardian of the spiritualities was summoned in the place of the bishop, and showed by his compliance with the writ that the seat of the bishop did not depend on the possession of a temporal barony, as was the case with that of an abbot or prior[2]. With respect to this, the second class of lords spiritual, the case was different. The abbots and priors, like the smaller boroughs, felt the burden of attendance to be a severe strain on their resources; and they were satisfied with their position in the spiritual assemblies of their provinces. Hence their attempts, by proving themselves not to be tenants in barony under the crown, to relieve themselves from the burden of peerage. Of these deeds of renunciation many are still extant. In 1318 the abbot of S. James's, Northampton, in 1325 the prior of Bridlington, in 1341 the abbot of S. Augustine's, Bristol, in 1350 the abbot of Osney, in 1351 the abbot of Leicester, declared that they held their estates by no tenure that involved the duty of parliamentary attendance, and they were accordingly relieved. Osney escaped because it was not a royal foundation, Beaulieu because it held in

Number of bishops permanent.

Diminution in the number of abbots and priors.

[1] See above, vol. ii. p. 154.

[2] The house of lords in 1692 resolved 'that bishops are only lords of parliament but not peers, for they are not of trial by nobility'; E. May, Treatise on Parliament, p. 15. Whatever force such a resolution may legally have, it is of no historical authority; for it is certain that from the beginning of the use of the term 'peers' the bishops were recognised as peers, and that it was by one of them, archbishop Stratford, that the right of trial was chiefly won; see above, vol. iii. p. 387–390. The doctrine of ennobled blood, by which this theory has been supported is historically a mere absurdity; it is impossible to regard the blood as ennobled by law, when the nobility of the blood is restricted to the bearer of the title and does not extend even to his younger children.

Gradual diminution of the number of abbots summoned to parliament.

frankalmoign, Thornton because it did not hold in chief or by barony. This process had probably been going on for some time before it is heard of in record. To take, however, only the state of affairs from the reign of Edward I downwards; we find summoned to the normal parliament of 1295 sixty-seven abbots and priors, besides the Masters of the Temple, the Hospital, and the Gilbertines; in 1300 seventy-two abbots and priors; in 1301 eighty; in 1302 forty-four; in 1305 seventy-five; and in 1307 forty-eight abbots. Under Edward II, down to 1319, the number varies between forty and sixty; but from that year the number rapidly declines. Under Edward III, with the exception of the year 1332, when fifty-eight were summoned, the average gradually settles down to twenty-seven, which thenceforward becomes the normal number[1]. The year 1341 seems to be the point from which the permanent diminution dates[2]. A close examination of the list summoned to the last parliament of Henry VI shows that all the Cistercian, Cluniac and Præmonstratensian houses had been relieved from a duty which the extent of their foreign connexions must have made somewhat dangerous; the Master of the Gilbertines is no longer summoned; only two houses of Augustinian canons, Waltham and Cirencester, appear in the list. Of the rest, twenty-three are Benedictine abbeys of royal or reputed royal foundation; one cathedral priory, that of Coventry, still sends its prior; and the prior of Clerkenwell completes the list[3]. Many of these were mitred abbots; that is, abbots who had

The normal number.

[1] The numbers may be verified by reference to the Appendix of the Lords' Report, or to Parry's Parliaments of England under the several dates.

[2] Edward III by letters dated Oct. 20, 1341, and again, June 7, 1347, relieved the abbot of Osney, that house being of the foundation of Robert D'Oilli and not of one of the king's ancestors; Rawlinson, Charters, Bibl. Bodl.; Lords' Report, iv. 554. The petition of the abbot of S. James', Northampton, in 1319, is in Parl. Writs, II. i. 199: the licence for S. Augustine's, Bristol, is in the Lords' Report. iv. 528: and that of the abbot of Thornton, ib. p. 529; both in 1341; that of the abbot of Beaulieu, the same year, ib. p. 533; Crowland, Spalding, p. 535; Thorney, p. 579. See also Prynne, Reg. i. pp. 141–144; Madox, Baronia Angl. pp. 110 sq.; where it is remarked that other onerous services besides parliamentary attendance were escaped by proving that the lands were held in frankalmoign.

[3] The list of parliamentary abbots and priors summoned in 1483 is this: Peterborough, Colchester, S. Edmund's, Abingdon, Waltham, Shrewsbury, Cirencester, Gloucester, Westminster, S. Alban's, Bardney, Selby, S. Benedict of Hulme, Thorney, Evesham, Ramsey, Hyde, Glastonbury, Malmes-

received from the pope the right of wearing the mitre and other vestments proper to the episcopal office; but the mitred and parliamentary abbeys were not identical; and some priors who were mitred were not summoned to parliament. The abbot of Tavistock, who in the reign of Henry VI had received permission to apply to the pope for the mitre, was in the fifth year of Henry VIII made a spiritual lord of parliament by letters patent This is said to have been a unique exercise of prerogative power, but is scarcely to be distinguished in point of principle from the creation of a new temporal barony[1]. The bishops whose sees were created later in the reign had their seats virtually secured by the liberal terms of the legislation which empowered the king to erect the new sees. These prelates had no baronies and cannot be said to have sat in the right of temporal lordships.

Mitred abbots.

Summons of the abbot of Tavistock.

754. The justices and other councillors summoned to assist the parliament completed, with the clerks and other officers, the personnel of the Upper Chamber of parliament. Of these the judges, whatever may have been the intention with which Edward I added them to the parliament, seem to have taken a more or less prominent part in the public business of the house, but not to have succeeded in obtaining recognition as peers, or the right of voting. They were not regular or essential members of the house; their summons did not imply an equality or similarity of functions with that of the peers; they were summoned in varying numbers, and they had no power to appear by proxy[2]. Yet they had very considerable functions as counsellors; in assisting all legislation that proceeded primarily from the king, and in

Judges and councillors.

bury, Crowland, Battle, Winchcomb, Reading, S. Augustine's, S. Mary's York, P. Coventry, P. S. John of Jerusalem. Lords' Report, App. pp. 946, 985. Reyner, Apostolatus Benedictinorum, p. 212, makes twenty-four, adding Tavistock and omitting the Augustinian abbots and the two priors; and adds a list of sixteen, who, although they were not summoned to parliament were counted among the barons. In 1332 Edward III summoned twenty-eight heads of houses, to whom 'non solebat scribi in aliis parliamentis'; Lords' Report, p. 409. See also Prynne, Reg. i. 108 sq., 141 sq., 147.

[1] Monast. Angl. iv. 503; Coke, 4th Inst. p. 45; Prynne, 4th Inst. p. 28; Register, i. 145.

[2] See Prynne, Reg. i. p. 379; Coke, 4th Inst. p. 4; above, vol. ii. pp. 191, 259.

Functions of the judges in the house of lords.

formulating the statutes which proceeded from the petitions of the subject; they were ready to give their opinions on all legal and constitutional questions that came before the parliament; they contributed an important quota to the bodies of receivers and triers of petitions; and on some occasions they may have exercised a right of voting[1]. In our survey of medieval history they have appeared principally as giving or refusing opinions on constitutional procedure; but on certain important occasions one of the chief justices has acted as spokesman for the whole parliament. Whatever was the qualification of Sir William Trussell, who as proctor of the parliament announced the deposition of Edward II, it was a chief justice of the Common Pleas, Sir William Thirning, who declared that Richard II had forfeited his right to the crown. Thirning also opened the parliament of 1401 instead of the chancellor[2].

Clerical assembly in parliament.

755. The position of the clerical proctors summoned under the præmunientes clause has been sometimes regarded as analogous to that of the summoned judges and councillors[3]. For this supposition there does not seem to be any warrant. They were originally summoned to complete the representation of the spiritual estate, with an especial view to the taxation of spiritual property[4]; and in that summons they had standing ground from which they might have secured a permanent position in the legislature. By adhering to their ecclesiastical organisation in the convocations they lost their opportunity, and almost as soon

[1] See Erskine May, Treatise on Parliament, p. 234. In the decision on the claim of the duke of Norfolk in 1425 the advice of the judges is mentioned co-ordinately with that of the lords and commons; Rot. Parl. iv. 274.

[2] See above, p. 38.

[3] Coke, 4th Inst. p. 4.

[4] In the proxy given by the clerical estate in parliament to Sir Thomas Percy in 1397, they describe themselves thus: 'Nos Thomas Cantuariensis et Robertus Eboracensis archiepiscopi ac praelati et clerus utriusque provinciae Cantuariensis et Eboracensis, jure ecclesiarum nostrarum et temporalium earundem habentes jus interessendi in singulis parliamentis domini nostri regis et regni Angliae pro tempore celebrandis, necnon tractandi et expediendi in eisdem, quantum ad singula in instanti parliamento pro statu et honore domini nostri regis, necnon regaliae suae, ac quiete, pace et tranquillitate regni judicialiter justificanda, venerabili viro domino Thomae de Percy militi nostram plenarie committimus potestatem ita ut singula per ipsum facta in praemissis perpetuis temporibus habeantur'; Rot. Parl. iii. 348, 349.

as it was offered them forfeited their chance of becoming an active part of parliament. Although, therefore, the kings continued to summon them to all parliaments, that the pretext of their absence might not be allowed to vitiate the authority of parliamentary acts, they, after a short struggle, acquiesced in the maintenance of convocation as the taxing assembly of the church. Hence, on the occasions on which the clerical proctors are known to have attended, their action is insignificant, and those occasions are very few. We are not told where room was found for their sessions; it would most probably be in some chamber of the abbey, and, if we may argue from the history of Haxey's case, in 1397, in close propinquity to the house of commons. In the year 1547 the lower house of convocation petitioned the archbishop that, 'according to the custom of this realm and the tenour of the king's writ,' 'the clergy of the lower house of convocation may be adjoined and associate with the lower house of parliament.' We have here, possibly, a trace of a long forgotten usage[1].

Continuance of the 'praemunientes' clause.

Clergy in parliament.

756. The questions affecting the personal composition of the house of commons, though more interesting in themselves, demand a less detailed description. They chiefly concern the number and distribution of the borough members. The knights of the shire continue unaltered in number to the close of the middle ages; thirty-seven counties return two knights a piece; Cheshire and Durham retain their palatine isolation, and Monmouth has not yet become an English shire. Monmouth acquired the right of sending two knights in 1536; Cheshire in 1543; and Durham in 1673[2]. The act which gave two members to Monmouthshire gave one each to the Welsh counties. The number of knights in the medieval parliaments was seventy-four. The northern counties seem to have envied the immunities of Durham and Cheshire. In 1312, 1314, and 1327, Northumberland, and in 1295 Westmoreland, allege the danger of the Scottish borders as a reason for neglecting to send

Numbers of knights of the shire permanent.

Later additions.

Attempts to evade the duty of attendance.

[1] Burnet, Reform. ii. 47, app. p. 117: see above, vol. ii. p. 492.

[2] Stat. 27 Hen. VI, cc. 26 and 34; 35 Hen. VIII, cc. 13, 26; Stat. 25 Charles II, c. 9.

knights; they could not afford to pay the wages, and the knights themselves were employed elsewhere [1].

Variation in the number of borough members.

The number of city and borough members fluctuated, but showed a decided tendency to diminish from the reign of Edward I to that of Henry VI. The minimum was reached in the reign of Edward III; and the act of 1382 prevented any further decrease, and all irregularity of attendance. The largest number of parliamentary boroughs is found in the reign of Edward I, when 166 were summoned to send members; from 1382 to 1445 the number was normally ninety-nine, including London [2]. The number of burgesses, including the four members for London, was just two hundred. These were very unequally distributed; from three counties, Lancashire, Rutland, and Hertfordshire, no borough members were sent between the reign of Edward III and that of Edward VI. Fifteen counties sent up, during the same period, only the two representatives of their chief town [3]; and seven of the others contained two parliamentary boroughs each [4]. The remaining

[1] In 1295 the sheriff of Westmoreland writes that his knights cannot possibly attend as they are bound under penalty of forfeiture to appear before the bishop of Durham and the earl Warenne at Emmotbridge two days before that fixed for the parliament; Parl. Writs i. 44. In 1312 the sheriff of Northumberland says that the state of the border is such that the men of the county do not care to send knights or burgesses to the parliament; Prynne, Reg. iii. 165; and in 1327 that they are so impoverished by the Scots that they cannot pay the wages.

[2] The numbers of summoned towns are variously given, the returns being imperfect and confusing: Prynne (Reg. iii. 225) makes 170 towns in all summoned, and 161 occasionally represented. The returns in the reigns of Edward I and Edward II, the period during which the maximum of representation was reached, may be ascertained from the Parliamentary Writs; 166 are mentioned in the former reign, 127 in the latter; but of these many towns although summoned made no return.

[3] The fifteen counties with their chief towns were:—Bedfordshire, Bedford; Buckinghamshire, Wycombe; Cambridgeshire, Cambridge; Cumberland, Carlisle; Derbyshire, Derby; Gloucestershire, Gloucester; Huntingdonshire, Huntingdon; Leicestershire, Leicester; Northamptonshire, Northampton; Northumberland, Newcastle; Nottinghamshire, Nottingham; Oxfordshire, Oxford; Warwickshire, Warwick; Westmoreland, Appleby; Worcestershire, Worcester; to which may be added Middlesex as containing London, and making sixteen in all.

[4] These are:—Essex—Colchester and Malden; Herefordshire—Hereford and Leominster; Kent—Canterbury and Rochester; Lincolnshire—Lincoln and Grimsby; Salop—Shrewsbury and Bridgnorth; Staffordshire—Stafford and Newcastle under Lyme; Suffolk—Ipswich and Dunwich.

twelve counties were more abundantly supplied; Yorkshire, Berkshire, Norfolk, and Hampshire contained each three boroughs[1]; Surrey four; Somerset and Cornwall six each; Devon and Dorset seven; Sussex nine, and Wiltshire twelve[2]. The Cinque Ports altogether returned sixteen members[3]. After the minimum had been reached, Henry VI added eight new boroughs, four of which were in Wiltshire, and one each in Devon, Dorset, Surrey, and Warwickshire. Edward IV added or restored five[4].

Distribution of the parliamentary boroughs.

The causes of this strange distribution are probably to be sought primarily in the amount of maritime or manufacturing industry which had made Devonshire, Dorset, Kent, Wiltshire, and Sussex the wealthiest counties of England. The distance from London was likewise an important element in the consideration of the boroughs themselves, many of which felt the wages of the members as a heavy tax. A third cause might be supposed to be the depopulation of the ancient towns by the Great Plague; and this doubtless did in a small degree affect the returns, but the lowest point of diminution had been reached before the visitation of the Black Death. The most influential cause of this diminution was undoubtedly the desire of the country towns to be taxed with their country neighbours, to be rated to the fifteenth with the shires and not to the tenth with the boroughs.

Possible reasons for the uneven distribution.

[1] Yorkshire—York, Hull, and Scarborough; Berkshire—Reading, Wallingford, and Windsor; Norfolk—Norwich, Lynn, and Yarmouth; Hampshire—Portsmouth, Southampton, and Winchester.

[2] Surrey—Bletchingly, Guildford, Reigate, and Southwark; Somerset—Bridgewater, Taunton, Wells, Bristol, Bath, and perhaps Ilchester; Cornwall—Bodmin, Launceston, Helston, Liskeard, Lostwithiel, and Truro; Devon—Barnstaple, Dartmouth, Exeter, Plympton, Tavistock, Totness, and Torrington (see below); Dorset—Bridport, Dorchester, Lyme Regis, Melcomb, Shaftesbury, Wareham, and Weymouth; Sussex—Arundel, Bramber with Steyning, Chichester, East Grinstead, Horsham, Lewes, Midhurst, Shoreham; Wiltshire—Bedwind, Calne, Chippenham, Cricklade, Devizes, Downton, Ludgarshall, Malmesbury, Marlborough, Salisbury, Old Sarum, and Wilton.

[3] The Cinque Ports, which in 1265 were ordered to send representatives, during the reigns of Edward I and Edward II were directed to elect two barons each; but their actual representation seems to date from 42 Edw. III; see Prynne, Reg. iv. and Willis, Notitia Parl. p. 71. The eight ports were —Dover, Hastings, Sandwich, Hythe, Romney, Winchelsea, Rye, and Seaford. The first five were the original Cinque Ports.

[4] Henry VI added Coventry, Gatton, Poole, Plymouth, Hindon, Heytesbury, Westbury, and Wootton Basset; Edward IV, Grantham, Ludlow, Wenlock, Stamford, and perhaps Ilchester.

The towns avoided sending members that they might be taxed with the shires.

Whilst avoiding the heavier rate, they were also relieved in a perceptible degree in the matter of the members' wages. It was much cheaper for a town to pay its fifteenth and contribute to the payment of the knights than to pay the tenth and remunerate its own burgesses. The petition of the borough of Torrington, in Devonshire, presented to Edward III in 1368, declared that the burden of the members' wages was very grievous, and prayed that the town might be relieved from the duty of representation. Although this town had been represented in the parliaments of the last two reigns, the burgesses declared that, until the 24th year of Edward III, they had not been ordered to send members; and the king having searched the rolls, allowed that no returns could be found before the 21st year. He therefore granted the prayer, and Torrington ceased to be a parliamentary borough[1]. S. Alban's and Barnstaple showed as little regard for truth when, in order to prove themselves free from the demesne rights of their lords, they declared that they had sent members in the days when there were no parliaments, and, in the latter case, from the days of Athelstan[2]. But the petition of Torrington is unique; a much simpler way of evading the duty was to disregard the sheriff's precept, and this was adopted in a large proportion of cases. In others probably the sheriff purposely omitted the smaller towns. On a close examination of the returns, most of the omitted boroughs are found to have made only one or two elections, or to have returned members in only one reign. In the reign of Edward I, 166 boroughs were represented once or twice[3]; of these 33 were not again summoned, and 38 more ceased until they were restored to the list in modern times; about a dozen dropped out in the next two reigns: thus about eighty

Cases of Torrington, S. Alban's and Barnstaple.

Numbers and dates.

[1] See Rot. Parl. ii. 459; Prynne, Reg. ii. 239; iv. 1175, 1176; 4th Inst. p. 32. There are some cases in which permission was granted, for a number of years, to dispense with attendance, but these are unimportant.

[2] On the S. Alban's case see above, vol. ii. p. 222; Rot. Parl. i. 327; Hallam, Middle Ages, iii. 28; and on the Barnstaple case, Hallam, Middle Ages, iii. 32.

[3] These numbers may be verified or corrected by reference to Prynne, or to Browne Willis's Notitia Parliamentaria; but, until the extant returns are all printed, a good deal of uncertainty hangs over the whole calculation.

of Edward's boroughs continued to send members. Under Edward II ten new boroughs appear, some of which made but one return. Edward III added the Cinque Ports and about six short-lived boroughs. The bulk of the borough representation was thus formed by the parliamentary boroughs in which political interest was so strong, or over which the hold of the executive was so firm, that they either would not or could not shake off the burden, but survived to modern times. The number of these at the close of the reign of Edward IV was about 112; two members represented each borough; the city of London had four[1]; these constituencies returned 226 representatives, who, with the 74 knights of the shire, composed an assembly of 300 members[2]. **Amount of borough representation.**

757. The business of parliament was recorded by clerks specially appointed for the purpose. Of these the clerk of the crown superintended the issue of writs and the reception of the returns; he also attested the signature of the king attached to bills when they became statutes. The clerk of the parliament registered the acts of the session; his place was in the house of lords, where he sat at the central table: to this office William Ayremin was specially named and deputed by Edward II in 1315[3]; but some **Clerk of the crown; and of the parliament.**

[1] The representation of London by four members was a matter of historical growth or assumption: originally the writ directed the election of two citizens, but it was very common to nominate four in order to make sure that two would attend. So in 1299 four were returned, in 1312 three, in 1320 four, and in 1318 and 1322, three for two, in 1319 four for three, and in 1326 six for two. In 1315, 1322, and 1324 two were returned. After several other variations, the number was permanently raised to four by the writs from 1378 onwards; see Parl. Writs, i. 80; II, i. 78, 108, 128, &c.; Prynne, Reg. iv. 1041; iii. 369 sq.; Lords' Report, iv. 682. In the year 1483, York elected four citizens for the parliament of Edward V; Davies, York Records, p. 144; this was in compliance with the writ, which must have been unique.

[2] Fortescue states the amount of parliamentary wisdom as 'plusquam trecentorum electorum virorum'; De Laudibus, c. 18. In 1509 there were 296 members; Hatsell, Prec. ii. 413.

[3] 'Memoranda de parliamento . . . facta per Willelmum de Ayreminne clericum de cancellaria praefati regis per eundem regem ad hoc nominatum et specialiter deputatum'; Rot. Parl. i. 350. In the parliament held at Mid-Lent, 1340, the first business done was the appointment of Thomas de Drayton, to be 'clerk du Parlement'; Rot. Parl. ii. 112: in 1347 it is ordered that petitions be delivered to him; ib. p. 202. In 1371 the clerk of the parliament reads the answers to the petitions; Rot. Parl. ii. 304: in 1388 he calls over the names of the receivers and triers; iii. 228.

Clerk of the house of commons.

such official must have been employed from the earliest times; probably the chancellor was allowed to employ any clerk he chose. The clerk of the house of commons, 'the common clerk of the house,' appears in the year 1388 as a person of established position: he was probably an assistant of the clerk of the parliament, and had similar duties in the lower house[1]. Each house had also its serjeant-at-arms, an officer whose duty it was to execute the warrants and orders of the house while in session, and its usher, or ostiarius, who kept the doors of the house and carried messages between the two assemblies. The existence of these offices is shown by occasional mention in the rolls, but the development of their functions, and all matters of constitutional importance connected with them, are of later growth.

Serjeants and ushers.

Receivers and triers of petitions.

As soon as the opening speech of the chancellor was ended, the names of the receivers and triers of petitions were read by the clerk of the crown. The receivers were clerks or masters in chancery; the triers were selected by the king from the list of the lords spiritual, the lords temporal, and the justices. The triers sat in two divisions, in two smaller chambers adjoining the house of lords[2]: they could call to their assistance the chancellor, treasurer, steward, and chamberlain. Of the two committees, one examined the petitions for England, Ireland, Wales, and Scotland; the other for those of Gascony and the foreign possessions of the crown. By them was determined the court to which the particular petitions ought to be referred, and, if any required parliamentary hearing, the triers reported them to the parliament[3].

Election of speaker.

758. The commons, having been directed, in the last clause of the opening speech, to withdraw and choose their speaker, retired as soon as the triers had been nominated, and on the

[1] Rot. Parl. iii. 245; 'le roi . . . granta d'aider Geffrey Martyn clerk de la corone; et granta auxint a la requeste des communes d'aider John de Scardesburgh, lour commune clerk.' The 'modus tenendi parliamentum' makes two chief clerks of parliament and five assistants, one for each of the five grades (bishops, proctors, temporal lords, knights, and burgesses) into which that tract divides the parliament. On the later duties of the clerks see E. May, Treatise on Parliament, pp. 185 sq., 236 sq.

[2] Generally the chamberlain's chamber and Marculf's chamber; Rot. Parl. iii. 323.

[3] These are still appointed; but the lords spiritual are not now nominated to serve; E. May, Treatise on Parliament, p. 542.

same or following day made their election. Although some such officer must have been necessary from the first, the position and title of Speaker becomes settled only in 1377. The silence of records cannot be held to prove that an organised assembly like that of the commons could ever have dispensed with a recognised prolocutor or foreman. It can scarcely be doubted that Henry of Keighley, who in 1301 carried the petition of the parliament of Lincoln to the king, was in some such position[1]. Sir William Trussell, again, answered for the commons in the White Chamber in 1343[2]: Trussell was not a member of the house of commons; he was not a baron, but apparently a counsellor and had in 1342 received a summons to council with the barons. It is possible that the commons employed him as counsel, or chose as prolocutor a person external to their own body, as the clergy did in 1397 when they empowered Sir Thomas Percy to act as their proxy[3], or as the two houses had done on the deposition of Edward II in 1327. Any such irregularity was, however, impossible after 1377. In 1376 Peter de la Mare, a knight for Herefordshire, acted as speaker without the title; but this is given to his successor, Thomas Hungerford, who is said 'avoir les paroles' for the commons[4]; Peter de la Mare is similarly described in 1377; and from that date the list is complete. The speaker was chosen by the free votes of the members, but there is during the middle ages no instance in which any but a knight of the shire was elected. The first exception to this usage is found in the reign of queen Mary; in 1554 Robert Brooke, one of the members

Early cases of the action of a spokesman.

Regular election of speakers.

[1] See above, vol. ii. p. 151. Since the second volume of this work was published I have found that the letter of Edward I on Keighley's imprisonment, which I believed to be new, was long ago published by Madox in the History of the Exchequer, p. 615.

[2] 'Et puis vindrent les chivalers des countees et les communes et responderent par Monsieur William Trussell en la chambre Blanche'; Rot. Parl. ii. 136. Trussell had been an envoy from the king to the parliament in 1340, and had carried messages between them; ib. pp. 121, 122. It is stated in the Historic Peerage that he was summoned to parliament in 1342, but this is a mistake; the summons is to a great council to which ninety-six barons and counsellors were cited; Lords' Report, iv. 537, 538. He was probably son of the William Trussell who acted as proctor for the whole parliament in 1327. See Foss, Biog. Jurid. p. 678.

[3] See above, p. 446.

[4] Above, vol. ii. p. 437; Rot. Parl. ii. 374.

for London, was chosen speaker, and his successor in 1555 was Clement Higham, burgess for West Looe[1].

The speaker-elect is presented to the king.

The day after the election, or the first day of business, the speaker-elect was presented to the king by the commons or some leading member of the house as their chosen 'parlour et procuratour.' The custom was for the speaker to protest his insufficiency for so great an office, but in spite of the protest the king vouchsafed his approval. In the case of Sir John Cheyne, the speaker elected in 1399, the excuse of ill-health was accepted by the king as valid; the clergy had in fact objected to the nomination; Sir John Cheyne withdrew, and John Doreward was chosen in his place[2]. This however is the only case of the kind that occurred before the reign of Charles II; although on more than one occasion, as we have seen in the cases of Peter de la Mare and Sir Thomas Thorpe, the choice of a speaker was in a high degree important. In 1449 Sir John Popham, the speaker-elect, excused himself on the ground of old age and infirmity, and the king admitted the excuse, but in this case there seems to have been no ulterior motive[3]. Generally the excuse was a mere formality.

Excuses generally overruled.

Petition of the speaker for the free customs of the House.

After the royal approval had been expressed, the speaker proceeded to request that his utterances might be regarded as the utterances of the house, that no offence might be taken at his words, that if he omitted to say what he ought to say, or said what he ought not to say, he might have equitable allowance, and other like favours. We have seen in the history of Henry IV that the freedom of language which some of the speakers used on this occasion roused the jealousy of the king; and the whole proceeding, solemn as it was, somewhat later took a settled form: the speaker simply petitioned that he might bring forward and declare all and singular the matters to be brought forward and declared by him in parliament

[1] Browne Willis, Not. Parl. p. 113.

[2] Rot. Parl. iii. 424.

[3] Rot. Parl. v. 171. In 1413 William Stourton had to resign the speakership after he had held it for a week, on plea of illness, and John Doreward again was substituted; ib. iv. 4, 5: in this case there was a political difficulty; the speaker had acted without the authority of the house. In 1437 Sir John Tyrrell resigned on the same plea, after having been speaker for two months; ib. p. 502.

in the name of the commons under the following protest: that if he should have declared any matters enjoined upon him by his companions in any way otherwise than they have agreed, be it in adding or omitting, he might correct and amend the matters so declared by his aforesaid companions; and he prayed that this protest might be entered on the roll of the parliament [1]. The king, by the mouth of the chancellor, returned the equally formal reply, that the speaker should enjoy and have the benefit of such protest as the other speakers had been wont to use and enjoy in the time of the king and his noble progenitors in such parliaments.

Petition of the speaker.

The acceptance of the speaker completed the constitution of the house of commons; in the house of lords the chancellor generally fulfilled the duties of a prolocutor in the absence of the king, and in his presence he acted as his mouthpiece: but his position was in some important respects different from that of the speaker of the commons, who, in addition to the general superintendence of business and his authority as 'procurator'

The chancellor presided in the house of lords.

[1] The following is the form given in the Rolls of 1435 and 1436; Rot. Parl. iv. 482, 496: 'supplicavit quatenus omnia et singula per ipsum ex parte dictorum communium in Parliamento praedicto proferenda sub protestatione posset proferre; ut si quid de sibi injunctis omittendo vel eis addendo, aut aliter quam sibi per eosdem communes injunctum fuerit contigerit declarare, tunc ad praefatos communes resortiri, et se per eorum avisamentum et assensum corrigere posset et emendare, et omnimoda alia libertate gaudere qua aliquis hujusmodi Praelocutor ante haec tempora melius et liberius gavisus est.' In 1406 the speaker asked for leave to send for any bills that required amendment, from the lords; Rot. Parl. iii. 568. The usage given by Sir Erskine May as now and since the sixth year of Henry VIII followed, is for the speaker, 'In the name and on behalf of the Commons, to lay claim by humble petition to their ancient and undoubted rights and privileges; particularly that their persons [estates, *dropped in* 1853] and servants might be free from arrests and all molestations; that they might enjoy liberty of speech in all their debates, may have access to her majesty's royal person whenever occasion shall require, and that all their proceedings may receive from her majesty the most favourable construction'; Treatise on Parliament, p. 65. These claims are not however all so old as the sixth of Henry VIII: the claim for access to the king appears first in the records of 1536 and 1541; Lords' Journals, i. 86, 167; and that for freedom from arrest is described by Elsynge as 'never made but of late days'; Ancient Method of holding Parliaments, p. 173: it is first recorded in 34 Hen. VIII; Hatsell, Precedents, ii. 77.

[2] In 1332 we find Henry de Beaumont acting as foreman or speaker of the lords, possibly of the whole parliament; 'les queux countes barouns et autres grantz puis revinderent et responderent touz au roi par la bouche Monsieur Henri de Beaumont'; Rot. Parl. ii. 64.

and prolocutor of the house, had also to maintain order. This function, which was typified by the mace, was unquestionably attached to the speaker's office from the first, but it receives little or no illustration from medieval records[1].

Discussion of matters mentioned in the opening speech.

759. The two houses being thus constituted, their first duty on proceeding to business was to consider the matters laid before them in the opening speech, generally in the order in which the chancellor had arranged them. Those matters took sometimes the form of questions; they were frequently repeated by the chancellor or some officer of state, or by the speaker himself, to the commons; the answers might either be communicated to the king by the speaker, as soon as the commons had considered them; or they might be made the subject of a conference with the lords; or they might be reported to the lords, and be sent up with the answers of the lords; or they might be kept in suspense till the conclusions of the lords were known, and then be drawn up in concert with or in opposition to them. On this point, which was one of some importance, both opinions and practice differed; the occasions on which those differences illustrate constitutional history have been noticed as we have proceeded. The causes of the calling of parliament were in 1381 repeated to the commons by the lord treasurer in the king's presence, and then at their request explained by the chancellor[2]; in 1382 the bishop of Hereford laid before lords and commons together 'in more especial manner' the occasions of summons[3]; in 1377 Richard le Scrope, steward of the household, repeated the charge to the commons in the presence of the king and bishops[4]; and in 1401 Sir Arnold Savage[5], when admitted as speaker, repeated to the king and lords the matter of the opening speech, 'to assure his own memory, in brief words, clearly and in accordance with its

Special exposition to the commons.

[1] See Hatsell's Precedents, ii. 230–238. The precedents there alleged begin in 1604; see also speaker Popham's speech in 1580; ib. p. 232.

[2] Rot. Parl. iii. 99, 100: in all these points it is needless to give more than a single illustration; the practice from the reign of Edward II to that of Henry V varied so frequently that to attempt a complete classification of instances would be to give an abstract of the whole of the Rolls of parliament.

[3] Rot. Parl. iii. 133.

[4] Rot. Parl. iii. 5.

[5] Rot. Parl. iii. 455.

essence.' When the matter of the questions was thus ascertained, the commons might ask for the nomination of a committee of lords to confer with them: in 1377 we have seen them naming the lords whose advice they desired; in 1381 the lords insisted that the commons should report their advice to them and not they to the commons; in 1378 the lords proposed a conference by a joint committee; and in 1383 the king chose the committee.[1] In 1402 Henry IV made it a matter of favour to allow the communication; but after his concession made, in 1407, that the money grants should be reported to him by the speaker of the commons, the royal objections, which no doubt arose from the wish to balance the two houses against one another in order to obtain larger money grants, were withdrawn. If no question arose upon the subject of the opening speech, the commons sometimes returned an address of thanks to the king for the information given them. This may have been always done, but it is only now and then mentioned in the rolls[3].

Joint deliberations of lords and commons

760. Although the subjects of the royal questions and of the conferences of the two houses would necessarily embrace all matters of policy and administration on which the crown required or allowed itself to be advised, the most frequent and most definite points discussed in them were supply and account. On these points, when the king was present, generalities alone, as a rule, were uttered; it was only in some great strait or in contemplation of some grand design, that figures were mentioned. It would seem to have been usual for the king to send a commissioner or two to discuss his necessities with both houses; just as he communicated with the clerical convocations when he wanted a grant. Thus in 1308 we find Thomas of Lancaster and Hugh le Despenser carrying a message from Edward II to

Money questions discussed privately.

[1] See above, vol. ii. pp. 592, 593.

[2] See Rot. Parl. iii. 486. In 1404 Sir Arnold Savage asked that the king would send certain lords to confer with the commons, and when that was granted, that certain commons might go to confer with the lords; Rot. Parl. iii. 523.

[3] In 1401 the commons (under Arnold Savage) thanked the king for the speech with which Sir William Thirning had opened parliament; Rot. Parl. iii. 455. In 1402 there was an address a few days after the opening of the session, chiefly of gratitude; ib. p. 487.

Financial statements laid before parliament.

the lords[1], in 1343 and 1344 Bartholomew Burghersh, as the king's envoy, and in 1372 Guy Brian, laid the king's financial condition before the lords and commons together[2]. But the most perfect illustration of this proceeding is that of the year 1433, when lord Cromwell made the interesting financial statement from which we learn so much of the nature of the revenue[3]. On the 18th of October, 1433, Cromwell, being then treasurer, laid before the king a petition containing certain conditions on which he had undertaken the office: he explained that the royal revenue was insufficient by a sum of £35,000 for the royal expenditure, but as this fact could not be understood without an examination of the accounts of the exchequer, he prayed that the lords might be charged to examine the accounts and have the record enrolled, and to give diligence that provision should be made for the king's necessities; that he himself should be authorised to give a preference in payment to the debts of the household, the wardrobe, and necessary works; that no grants should be made without information to be laid by the treasurer before the council, and that he should in his office of treasurer act as freely as his predecessors, receive the help of the lords, and incur no hindrance or odium in the discharge of his duties. The king granted the petition: thereupon the accounts were read before the lords: subsequently the treasurer was by advice of the lords charged to lay the state of the kingdom, in the same way, before the commons in their common house on the following day: and this was done[4]. Although the occasion was exceptional, the manner of proceeding was probably customary.

Form of grants of money.

761. The result of the conferences with the lords and with the treasurer on financial questions was the grant of money. On this point we have circumstantial documentary evidence from the very first; both in the writs by which the king, whilst ordering the collection of the taxes, carefully explains the occasion of the grant and states by whom and in what proportions it is granted; and very frequently in the 'form of grant' the

[1] See above, vol. ii. p. 319.
[2] See above, vol. ii. p. 424; Rot. Parl. ii. 137, 157.
[3] See above, pp. 117, 118.
[4] Rot. Parl. iv. 432–439.

schedule of directions for collection which the grantors have drawn up and presented, sometimes as a condition, sometimes as an appendage, to the grant. After the date at which the two houses began to make their grants on one plan, ceasing to vote their money independently, and clothing the gift in the form of tenths and fifteenths, wool, tunnage and poundage, and other imposts which affected all classes alike, the money grant took a more definite form; and from the end of the reign of Richard II all grants were made by the commons with the advice and assent of the lords in a documentary form which may be termed an act of the parliament. Of these we have had many examples; we know them to have been the result of a conference between the lords and commons, but, with the exception of the discussion on the poll-tax in 1377[1] we have very seldom any details of debate upon them, or of the exact steps of the process by which they became law. The practice of three readings in each house, the possible speaking, suggestion of alterations and amendments, all the later etiquette of procedure on money bills, will be sought in vain in the rolls of the medieval parliaments. The practice of thrice reading the bills appears however in the journals of the two houses so early, and is from the very first parliament of Henry VIII regarded so clearly as an established rule, that it must have full credit for antiquity: it was a matter of course[2].

Grants made by the two houses together: by the commons with the consent of the lords.

Money bills thrice read.

762. Scarcely more light is shed on the details of legislative procedure. On this point we have already concluded that both the king and the several members of both houses and the houses themselves had the right of initiation[3]: Edward III of his own good will proposed to remedy the evils of purveyance[4]; the lords proposed the legislation by which peers are entitled to be

Legislative proceedings.

[1] See above, vol. ii. p. 437.

[2] In the first parliament of Henry VIII, on the 23rd day of the session 'adducta est a domo inferiori' 'billa de concessione subsidii quae lecta fuit semel cum proviso adjungendo pro mercatoribus de ly hansa Theutonicorum.' On the 24th day the proviso was read and expedited; on the 27th it was sent down to the commons; on the 29th the bill of the subsidy was delivered to Sir Thomas Lovel and his companions. The plan was thus in full working. Lords' Journals, i. pp. 7, 8.

[3] See above, vol. ii. pp. 588 sq.

[4] Above, vol. ii. p. 414.

Initiation of legislation.

tried by their peers in parliament[1], and on the petition of the commons most of the legislation of the middle ages is founded. The king's projects for the alteration of the law would be laid by the chancellor before the house of lords, and after discussion they would go down to the commons: a similar course was adopted in all cases in which the legislation began in the house of lords or on petition addressed to them. When the act, petition, or bill had reached the requisite stage, that is, as it must be supposed, had been read three times, it was endorsed by the clerk of the parliament 'soit baillé[2] aux communs'; it was then sent down to the lower house by the hands of some of the judges or legal advisers of the parliament, with the message informing the commons of the subject of the bill and asking their advice[3].

Bills sent down from the lords to the commons.

Bills in the house of commons.

The practice of the house of commons was analogous; there also a proposition for the change of the law, or for the remedy of a grievance, might originate in either a private petition of an individual aggrieved, or a proposition by a particular member, or a general petition of the house. The custom of presenting private petitions to the house of commons, desiring them to use their influence with the king, came in first under Henry IV[4]. These petitions would require to be sorted, as did

Private petitions.

[1] Above, vol. ii. p. 389.

[2] See Rot. Parl. Hen. VIII, pp. cxcvii, ccvi, ccix, &c.

[3] See below, p. 472. The form in the Lords' Journals of 1510 was this: 'Jan. 24 Receptae sunt quatuor billae legendae, una pro libertatibus ecclesiae Anglicanae, una pro retornis falsis, &c. Billa pro reformatione ecclesiasticae libertatis bis lecta tradita fuit attornato et sollicitatori regiis reformanda et emendanda, &c.' 'Die 5° Lecta est Billa concernens ecclesiasticas libertates et jam bis lecta; Item, &c.' 'Die 7° Item eodem die lecta est tunc tertia vice billa concernens libertates ecclesiae Anglicanae quae unanimi omnium dominorum tunc praesentium fuit approbata et admissa;' 'Item per dominos datae erat in mandatis clerico parliamenti et attornato et sollicitatori regiis quod crastino in mane deferrent ad domum inferiorem billam de ecclesiasticis libertatibus, &c.' 'Die 8° Billa de libertatibus ecclesiasticis, &c., missae sunt in domum communem; nuncii clericus parliamenti et attornatus regis'; vol. i. pp. 4-6. Bills relating to the crown were sent down by two judges; other messages by masters in chancery; the commons sent up their bills by one member, either the chairman of committee of ways and means or the member in charge of the bill, accompanied by seven others. This was altered in 1817 and 1855; see E. May, Treatise on Parliament, pp. 435-437.

[4] Rot. Parl. iii. 564. Every possible variation is found in the heading of the petitions; some are to the king, others to the king and council,

those addressed to the king and lords; but the house did not yet, so far as can be seen, appoint a committee of petitions; the matter was arranged between the clerk and the whole house. Such private petitions as seemed to merit the consideration of the commons were after examination sent up to the lords with the note prefixed 'Soit baillé aux seigneurs[1],' and there passed through the further stages before receiving the king's assent; 'soit fait comme il est desiré.' All these are of the nature of what are now called private bills; a proceeding half legislative and half judicial; the result may be termed an act of parliament, but it was not a statute, and instead of appearing among the laws of the realm was certified by letters patent under the great seal.

Bills sent up by the commons to the lords.

763. The common petitions of the house were a much more weighty matter. They were the national response to the king's promise to redress grievances. They were the result of deliberation and debate among the commons themselves, whether they originated in the independent proposition of an individual member, adopted by the house as a subject of petition, or in the complaints of his constituents, or in the organised policy of a party, or in the unanimous wish of the whole house. Unquestionably they went through stages of which the rolls contain no indication before they were presented as the 'common petitions[2].' The history of this branch of parliamentary work has already been illustrated as fully as our materials allow; the articles of the barons at Runnymede and at Oxford, the petitions of the whole community at Lincoln in 1301, at Westminster in 1309 and 1310, mark the first great stages of political growth in the nation. They are initiations of legislative reform, as much as the great statutes of Edward I. The common petitions of the fifteenth century, the petty gravamina, the minute details

Common petitions of the house of commons.

to the king, lords, and commons, to the lords and commons, and to the commons alone. The latter request the commons to mediate with the king and council.

[1] See instances in Rot. Parl. iv. pp. 159, 160 sq., and generally from the reign of Henry V onwards.

[2] In 1423 the merchants of the Staple sent in a petition to the lords; 'la quelle petition depuis fuist mande par mesmes les Seigneurs as ditz communes pour ent avoir lour avys, les queux communes mesme la petition rebaillerent come une de lour communes petitions'; Rot. Parl. iv. 250. It is very rarely that we find such an amount of detail.

Parallel drawn from the proceedings of convocation.

of amendments of law, are the later developments of the principles boldly enunciated in those documents: and the statutes based on the common petitions bear on the face evidence of their unbroken descent. It is not improbable that this process was identical with that by which in the discussions of the ecclesiastical convocations the *gravamina* of individuals, the *reformanda* or proposed remedies, and the *articuli cleri* or completed representations sent up to the house of bishops, are and have been from the very first framed and treated[1]. The *gravamina* of individual members of convocation answer to the initiatory act of the individual member in the commons, and the 'articuli cleri' to the 'communes petitiones'; both expressions may be traced back to the earliest days of representative assemblies. In the reign of Henry III we find gravamina and articuli among the clergy; in the reigns of John, Henry III, and Edward I we have *articuli* and occasionally *gravamina* among the laity. From the reign of Edward III the king promises in the opening speech to redress the grievances of his subjects; and from the year 1343 the petitions of the commons are presented in a roll of articles, almost exactly resembling the articuli cleri. Yet here again except for this glimpse of light we are in complete darkness as to the exact steps of proceeding. There was a roll of petitions, on which, as we learn from Haxey's case, it was not very difficult to obtain the entry of a gravamen, which the prudence of the house, were it wide awake, could scarcely have allowed to pass. It cannot be believed that the articles of Haxey's petition, touching the number of ladies and bishops at court, could have been read three times and approved by the house, or, as is the practice in convocation, had been adopted by two-thirds of the members; yet if it were not, it is difficult to understand how the custom of three readings can be regarded as an established rule. By some such process however the common petitions must have been authenticated; they were adopted by the house as its own, and sent up through the

Obscurity of the method of proceeding.

[1] See the standing orders of the lower house of convocation, drawn up it is believed in or about 1722 by bishop Gibson; and Gibson's Synodus Anglicana, cc. xii. xiii.

house of lords to the king. Even this we only learn from the enacting words of the statutes, and from a rare mention on the rolls of the cases in which the lords joined in the king's refusal. The statutes are made by the king with the advice and consent of the lords temporal and spiritual; the petitions are answered 'le roi le veut' or 'le roi s'avisera' with the advice of the lords. Towards the close of our period the form of bill drawn as a statute has begun to take the place of petition. This custom was introduced first in the legislative acts which were originated by the king; the law proposed was laid before the houses in the form which it was ultimately to take. It was then adopted in private petitions which contained the form of letters patent in which a favourable assent was expressed[1]. The form was found convenient by the commons in their grants, and by the king in bills of attainder; it became applicable to all kinds of legislation, and from the reign of Henry VII was adopted in most important enactments[2].

Adoption of the form of bills.

We have already traced the efforts made by the commons to secure the honest reproduction of the words of their petitions in the statutes founded upon them; that object was more perfectly secured by the adoption of the new form, the promulgation of a new law or act in the exact form in which it was to appear, if it passed, eventually in the statute roll. In this form we can more distinctly trace its progress: after the due readings and final adoption by the commons, it was sent up with the inscription 'Soit baillé aux seigneurs,' and was considered and adopted or rejected by the lords[3]. If they accepted it, it was

Process of carrying a bill through the commons.

[1] A good instance is the king's act on purveyance in, 1439; Rot. Parl. v. 7, 8: 'quaedam cedula sive billa communibus praedictis de mandato ipsius domini regis exhibita fuit et liberata sub hac verborum serie.' The act for the attainder of Henry VI and his partisans in 1461 was brought forward as 'quaedam cedula formam actus in se continens'; Rot. Parl. v. 476. Private petitions in this form are found ib. iv. 323, etc.

[2] See Rot. Parl. vi. 138, &c. It is to this form of initiation that the process of readings, committals, and report, are most easily applied; and they appear very early in the Journals; thus 2 Edw. VI Dec. 10, 'The bill for levying of fines in the county palatine of Chester; committed to Mr. Hare.' Jan. 8th: 'To draw a bill for the absence of knights and burgesses of parliament—Mr. Goodrick, Mr. Arundel'; Commons' Journals, i. 5, 6.

[3] The first proofs of the three readings occur in the first Journals of the

Mutual assents.

again endorsed 'Les seigneurs sont assentus and then submitted to the king. The same process was observed in statutes that originated with the lords: the commons recorded their assent, 'Les communs sont assentus,' and the bills went up to the king and his council.

Enacting words of the king.

764. The legislative act, when it had received the final form in which it was to become a part of the national code or statute roll, appeared as the act of the king. The enacting words as they appear in the first statute of Henry VII are these 'The king .... at his parliament holden at Westminster .... to the honour of God and Holy Church and for the common profit of the realm, by the assent of the lords spiritual and temporal and the commons in the said parliament assembled and by authority of the same hath do to be made certain statutes and ordinances .... Be it enacted by the advice of the lords spiritual and temporal and the commons in this present parliament assembled and by the authority of the same[1].'' Sometimes assent as well as advice was again expressed, and the threefold expression of assent, advice, and authority may be regarded as the declaration of the function of the estates in legislation. We have in former chapters dwelt on the importance of these formulae; we have seen how, during the fourteenth century, petition or instance was the word used of the commons' share, and that it expressed the truth that most of the legal changes were suggested by their petitions. Under Richard II the mention of petition drops out,

Commons; the first reading is simply noted; on the second reading follows the direction 'Ingrossetur'; on the third the note 'Judicium'; see Commons' Journals, i. 12, &c. The form however in which the three readings are recorded before the royal assent is given runs thus 'Qua quidem perlecta et ad plenum intellecta eidem per dicta regem &c. &c. fiebat responsio'; Lords' Journal, i. p. 9. This form occurs early in the reign of Henry VI and must be understood to have then the same meaning as in the first of Henry VIII. See Rot. Parl. v. 363: 'Quae quidem petitio et cedulae transportatae fuerunt et deliberatae communibus regni Angliae in eodem parliamento existentibus; quibus iidem communes assensum suum praebuerunt sub hac forma, "a ceste bille et a les cedules a ycest bille annexez les Commyns sount assentuz"; quibus quidem petitione, cedulis et assensu, in parliamento praedicto lectis auditis et plenius intellectis, de avisamento et assensu dominorum spiritualium et temporalium in eodem parliamento existentium, auctoritate ejusdem parliamenti respondebatur eisdem in forma sequenti.'

[1] Stat. 1 Hen. VII, preamble, Statutes, ii. 500.

Introduction of the form 'by authority of the same.'

and occasionally the full equality of the commons is expressed by the form 'assent of the prelates, lords, and commons.' The statutes of Henry IV and Henry V are passed 'by the assent of the prelates, dukes, earls, barons, and at the instance and special request of the commons,' or 'by the advice and assent of the lords spiritual and temporal, and at the prayer of the commons.' The same form is observed during great part of the reign of Henry VI in the statutes; but the assent of the commons is put forward in the act by which the protector is appointed in 1422[1], and in other acts of a less public character: the assent, or advice and assent, of the commons as well as of the lords is likewise expressed in the borrowing powers granted to the council[2]. In the 11th year of this king the expression 'by the authority of parliament' first appears among the words of enactment in the preamble of the statutes[3]. This particular form seems to have been used some years earlier in the separate clauses of statutes, although not in the heading of the roll: and in this way it is found as early as the year 1421[4]: it was also used in petitions, in letters patent drawn up in compliance with private petitions, and in the bills introduced in the form of statutes: thus in 1442 a petition passed the commons for the endowment of Eton College, in which that house was requested to pray the king to grant letters patent under his great seal by the advice and assent of the lords spiritual and temporal in this present parliament assembled, and by authority of the same parliament[5]: in 1439 the bishop of S. David's and the dean and chapter of S. Paul's had letters patent in which the same form was used; in 1423 the executors of Henry V had letters patent under the great seal by the authority of the parliament[6]. From the year 1445 it becomes a regular part of the enacting and ordaining words

[1] Rot. Parl. iv. 174.
[2] Ibid. iv. 276; see above, p. 254.
[3] Statutes, ii. 278.
[4] Rot. Parl. iv. 130.
[5] Rot. Parl. v. 45. Instances of the form in petitions will be found as early as the reign of Henry IV if not earlier; see Rot. Parl. iii. 530, 656; iv. 35, 40, 43, &c., 323, 325, 546. The endorsement on writs 'by authority of the parliament' does not imply that the parliament was sitting at the time, but that the king was acting in virtue of some power bestowed by the parliament by a special act. See Nicolas, Ordinances, &c., vi. p. ccv. and also Elsynge, pp. 282, sq.
[6] Rot. Parl. iv. 206, 207; v. 8, 9, 13.

which head the roll[1]. The form used by Henry VII has lasted with few unimportant variations down to the present day.

Modern procedure on bills.

In modern times—that is, since parliamentary machinery has been matured—a bill before becoming an act has to go through several distinct stages. In the house of commons the proposer asks leave to introduce it, and it is ordered; it passes its first reading, in most cases without being discussed on its merits; it comes to the second reading, is debated clause by clause, receives amendments and passes into committee: it is committed and perhaps recommitted: it is brought up for a third reading, debated again if necessary, read a third time and passed. It goes through a similar process in the house of lords, where however the bills are presented without formal notice. If it has originated in the upper house it does not escape like manipulation in the lower. After the report is brought up it is printed, or, as was until recently the case, ingrossed. After passing both houses it is still subject to the royal veto, although for more than a century and a half that right has not been exercised[2].

Probable antiquity of these processes.

765. Of the minute points of this carefully arranged proceeding some are doubtless of modern growth; but the substance of the programme must be ancient. The three readings of the bills are traceable as soon as the form of bill is adopted; the committees for framing laws find a precedent as early as 1340, when a committee of the two houses was appointed to draw up the statutes framed on the petitions[3]; they are spoken of by Sir Thomas Smith as an essential part of legislative process; 'the committees are such as either the lords in the higher house or the burgesses in the lower house do choose to frame the laws upon such bills as are agreed on and afterwards to be ratified by the same houses;' after the first or second reading the bill is ordered to be ingrossed; it is read a third time, then the question is put, and traces of this procedure are found in the earliest journals of both houses: the silence of the rolls implies nothing as to the novelty of the practice.

1 Statutes, ii. 326; Rot. Parl. v. 70.
2 Sir T. Erskine May, Treatise on Parliament, pp. 468 sq.
3 Rot. Parl. ii. 113; above, vol. ii. p. 382.

We look in vain for illustrations of the rules of debate, and of the way in which order was maintained, or for any standing orders. Yet as soon as the journals begin, order, debate, and the by-laws of procedure, are all found in working. We are compelled to believe that many of them are ancient.

Sir Thomas Smith's account of the session of parliament.

In default then of anything like contemporary evidence, we may accept Sir Thomas Smith's account of the holding of parliament, notwithstanding the strong infusion of Tudor theory with which it is inseparably mixed, as approximately true of the century that preceded: the extract is long, but it needs no apology, and will supply all that is wanted here in respect of the procedure of the two houses :—

Constitution of the parliament.

766. 'The most high and absolute power of the realm of England consisteth in the Parliament: for as in war where the king himself in person, the nobility, the rest of the gentility and the yeomanry are, is the force and power of England; so in peace and consultation where the prince is, to give life and the last and highest commandment, the barony or nobility for the higher, the knights, esquires, gentlemen and commons for the lower part of the commonwealth, the bishops for the clergy, be present to advertise consult and show what is good and necessary for the commonwealth and to consult together; and upon mature deliberation, every bill or law being thrice read and disputed upon in either house, the other two parts, first each apart, and after the prince himself in the presence of both the parties, doth consent unto and alloweth. That is the prince's and whole realm's deed, whereupon justly no man can complain but must accommodate himself to find it good and obey it.

Power of the parliament.

'That which is done by this consent is called firm, stable and sanctum, and is taken for law. The parliament abrogateth old laws, maketh new, giveth order for things past and for things hereafter to be followed, changeth rights and possessions of private men, legitimateth bastards, establisheth forms of religion, altereth weights and measures, giveth form of succession to the crown, defineth of doubtful rights whereof is no law already made, appointeth subsidies, tailes, taxes and impositions, giveth most free pardons and absolutions, restoreth in blood and name,

Representative character. as the highest court, condemneth or absolveth them whom the prince will put to trial. And to be short, all that ever the people of Rome might do either in *centuriatis comitiis* or *tributis*, the same may be done by the parliament of England, which representeth and hath the power of the whole realm, both the head and body. For every Englishman is intended to be there present, either in person or by procuration and attorney, of what pre-eminence, state, dignity or quality soever he be, from the prince, be he king or queen, to the lowest person of England. And the consent of the parliament is taken to be every man's consent.

Judges of parliament. 'The judges in parliament are the king or queen's majesty, the lords temporal and spiritual; the commons represented by the knights and burgesses of every shire and borough town. These all or the greater part of them, and that with the consent of the prince for the time being, must agree to the making of laws.

Officers. 'The officers in parliament are the speakers, two clerks, the one for the higher house the other for the lower [1], and committees.

The speaker. 'The speaker is he that doth commend and prefer the bills exhibited into the parliament, and is the mouth of the parliament. He is commonly appointed by the king or queen though accepted by the assent of the house [2].

The clerks. 'The clerks are the keepers of the parliament rolls and records, and of the statutes made, and have the custody of the private statutes not printed.

Committees. 'The committees are such as either the lords in the higher house, or burgesses in the lower house do choose to frame the laws upon such bills as are agreed upon, and afterward to be ratified by the said houses [3].

Writs of summons. 'The prince sendeth forth his rescripts or writs to every duke, marquess, baron and every other lord temporal or spiritual who hath voice in the parliament, to be at his great council of parliament such a day (the space from the day of the

[1] See above, p. 451.

[2] This is a mark of Tudor innovation. See Coke, 4 Inst. p. 8: 'for avoiding of expense of time and contestation the use is, as in the congé d'eslire of a bishop, that the king doth name a discreet and learned man whom the commons elect.'

[3] See above, p. 466.

writ is commonly at the least forty days[1]); he sendeth also writs to the sheriffs of every shire to admonish the whole shire to choose two knights of the parliament in the name of the shire, to hear and reason and to give their advice and consent in the name of the shire, and to be present at that day; likewise to every city and town which of ancient time hath been wont to find burgesses of the parliament, so to make election, that they might be present there at the first day of the Parliament. The knights of the shire be chosen by all the gentlemen and yeomen of the shire present at the day assigned for the election; the voice of any absent can be counted for none. Yeomen I call here, as before, that may dispend at the least forty shillings of yearly rent of free land of his own. These meeting at one day, the two who have the more of their voices be chosen knights of the shire for that parliament; likewise by the plurality of the voices of the citizens and burgesses be the burgesses elected.

Elections of members.

'The first day of the parliament the prince and all the lords, in their robes of parliament, do meet in the higher house, where, after prayers made, they that be present are written and they that be absent upon sickness or some other reasonable cause, which the prince will allow, do constitute under their hand and seal some one of those who be present as their procurer or attorney, to give voice for them, so that by presence or attorney and proxy they be all there; all the princes and barons, and all archbishops and bishops, and, when abbots were, so many abbots as had voice in parliament[2]. The place where the assembly is, is richly tapessed and hanged; a princely and royal throne, as appertaineth to a king, set in the middest of the higher place thereof. Next under the prince sitteth the chancellor, who is the voice and orator of the prince. On the one side of that house or chamber sitteth the archbishops and bishops each in his rank, on the other side the dukes and barons.

Meeting of parliament.

The parliament house.

'In the middest thereof upon woolsacks sitteth the judges of the realm, the master of the rolls, and the secretaries of state.

Arrangement of the house of lords.

[1] See above, p. 281.

[2] See above, p. 445.

Forms of the house of lords.

But these that sit on the woolsacks have no voice in the house, but only sit there to answer their knowledge in the law, when they be asked, if any doubt arise among the lords: the secretaries do answer of such letters or things passed in council whereof they have the custody and knowledge, and this is called the upper house, whose consent and dissent is given by each man severally and by himself, first for himself, and then severally for so many as he hath letters and proxies; when it cometh to the question, saying only *Content* or *Not Content*, without further reasoning or replying.

Meeting of the commons.

'In this meantime the knights of the shires and burgesses of parliament, for so they are called that have voice in parliament and are chosen (as I have said before), to the number betwixt three and four hundred[1], are called by such as it pleaseth the prince to appoint, into another great house or chamber, by name, to which they answer; and declaring for what shire or town they answer, then they are willed to choose an able and discreet man to be as it were the mouth of them all, and to speak for and in the name of them, and to present him so chosen by them to the prince: which done, they coming all with him to a bar which is at the nether end of the upper house, there he first praiseth the prince, then maketh his excuse of inability, and prayeth the prince that he would command the commons to choose another. The chancellor in the prince's name doth so much declare him as able as he did declare himself unable, and thanketh the commons for choosing so wise, discreet and eloquent a man, and willeth them to go and consult

Choice of speaker.

His admission.

[1] The additions to the representative body made between the time of Smith and that of Fortescue were in Henry VIII's reign the knights of the shire for Cheshire, Monmouthshire, and the Welsh counties; and burgesses for Buckingham, Chester, Berwick, Orford, Calais, and the Welsh county towns; under Edward VI, eight towns in Cornwall, Maidstone, Boston, Westminster, Thetford, Peterborough, and Brackley were added, and S. Albans, Lancaster, Preston, Wigan, Liverpool, Petersfield, Lichfield, Thirsk, Hedon, and Ripon, which had sent members to the early parliaments were revived as parliamentary boroughs: under Mary, Abingdon, Aylesbury, S. Ives, Castlerising, Higham Ferrers, Morpeth, Banbury, Knaresborough, Boroughbridge, and Aldborough were added, and Woodstock and Droitwich revived; under Elizabeth twenty-four new boroughs were added and seven revived. See Browne Willis, Not. Parl. pp. 92–101.

of laws for the commonwealth. Then the speaker maketh certain requests to the prince in the name of the commons; first that his majesty would be content that they may use and enjoy all their liberties and privileges that the common house was wont to enjoy; secondly, that they might frankly and freely say their minds in disputing of such matters as may come in question and that without offence to his majesty: thirdly, that if any should chance of that lower house to offend, or not to do or say as should become him, or if any should offend any of them being called to make his highness' court, that they themselves might, according to the ancient custom, have the punishment of them: and fourthly, that if there come any doubt whereupon they shall desire to have the advice or conference with his majesty or with any of the lords they might do it[1]; all which he promiseth in the commons' names that they shall not abuse but have such regard as most faithful true and loving subjects ought to have to their prince.

Privileges claimed by the speaker.

'The chancellor answereth in the prince's name as appertaineth. And this is all that is done for one day and sometime for two.

'Besides the chancellor there is one in the upper house who is called clerk of the parliament, who readeth the bills. For all that cometh in consultation either in the upper house or in the nether house is put in writing first in paper[2]: which being once read, he that will riseth up and speaketh with it or against it; and so one after another so long as they shall think good. That done they go to another, and so another bill. After it hath been once or twice read, and doth appear that it is somewhat liked as reasonable, with such amendment in words and peradventure some sentences as by disputation seemeth to be amended; in the upper house the chancellor asketh if they will

Process upon bills.

[1] This form does not exactly agree with any of those recorded, but it gives the general spirit of the petition. See above, pp. 454, 455; Lex Parliamentaria, pp. 137, 138; Coke, 4th Inst. p. 8.

[2] Lords' Journals, i. 4: 1510, Jan. 25, 'Billa de apparatu, in papiro, lecta est jam primo et tradita attornato et sollicitatori domini regis emendanda.'

[3] Bills of general pardon, and of clerical subsidies were read but once in each house; Lex Parliamentaria, p. 178.

Form of passing bills

have it ingrossed, that is to say, put into parchment[1]; which done and read the third time and that eftsoones, if any be disposed to object, disputed again among them, the chancellor asketh if they will go to the question. And, if they agree to go to the question, then he saith "Here is such a law or act concerning such a matter, which hath been thrice read here in this house; are ye content that it be enacted or no?" If the Non-Contents be more, then the bill is dashed; that is to say, the law is annihilated and goeth no farther. If the Contents be more, then the clerk writeth underneath "Soit baille aux commons." And so when they see time they send such bills as they have approved by two or three of those which do sit on the woolsacks[2] to the commons; who asking licence and coming into the house with due reverence, saith to the speaker, "Master Speaker, my lords of the upper house have passed among them and think good that there should be enacted by parliament" such an act, and such an act, and so readeth the titles of that act or acts; "they pray you to consider of them and show them your advice:" which done they go their way. They being gone and the door again shut, the speaker rehearseth to the house what they said. And if they be not busy disputing at that time in another bill, he asketh them straightway if they will have that bill, or, if there be more, one of them.

Bills sent down to the commons.

Procedure in the house of commons.

'In like manner in the lower house; the speaker, sitting in a seat or chair for that purpose somewhat higher that he may see and be seen of them all, hath before him, in a lower seat, his clerk who readeth such bills as be first propounded in the lower house, or be sent down from the lords. For in that point each house hath equal authority to propound what they think meet, either for the abrogating of some law made before, or for making of a

[1] See above, p. 463, note. In 1401 the commons pray that the business of parliament may be ingrossed before the departure of the justices; Rot. Parl. iii. 457, 458: and in 1420 that the petitions may not be ingrossed until they have been sent to the king in France; ib. iv. 128. In 1404 they allege that an error had been made in the ingrossing of the grant of subsidy; ib. iii. 556. None of these passages seem to refer to anything like the ingrossing after second reading. See Coke, 4th Inst. p. 25; Lex Parliamentaria, p. 186.

[2] See above, p. 460.

new. All bills be thrice, in three divers days, read and disputed upon, before they come to the question. In the disputing is a marvellous good order used in the lower house. He that standeth up bare headed is understanded that he will speak to the bill. If more stand up, who that is first judged to arise is first heard; though the one do praise the law, the other dissuade it, yet there is no altercation. For every man speaketh as to the Speaker[1], not as one to another, for this is against the order of the house. It is also taken against the order to name him whom ye do confute but by circumlocution, as he that speaketh with the bill or he that spake against the bill and gave this and this reason. And so with perpetual oration not with altercation he goeth through till he do make an end. He that once hath spoken in a bill, though he be confuted straight, that day may not reply, no though he would change his opinion; so that to one bill in one day one may not in that house speak twice, for else one or two with altercation would spend all the time. The next day he may, but then also but once[2]. No reviling or nipping words must be used; for then all the house will cry "it is against the order;" and if any speak unreverently or seditiously against the prince or the privy council, I have seen them not only interrupted, but it hath been moved after to the house and they have sent them to the Tower. So that in such multitude and in such diversity of minds and opinions there is the greatest modesty and temperance of speech that can be used. Nevertheless with much doulce[3] and gentle terms they make their reasons as violent and as vehement one against the other as they may ordinarily, except it be for urgent causes and hasting of time. At the afternoon they keep no parliament. The speaker hath no voice in the house, nor will they not suffer him to speak in any bill to move or dissuade it. But when any bill is read, the speaker's office is as briefly and as plainly as he may to declare the effect thereof to the house. If the commons do assent to such bills as be sent to them first agreed upon

Practice in debates.

Standing orders.

Maintenance of order.

Office of speaker.

[1] Lex Parliamentaria, p. 150.

[2] Ibid. p. 186.

[3] So in the reign of Richard II, the commons urged that the petitions should be 'par amyable manere debatez'; Rot. Parl. iii. 14.

from the lords [they send them back to the lords] thus subscribed "les commons ont assentus"; so if the lords do agree to such bills as be first agreed upon by the commons, they send them down to the speaker thus subscribed "les seigneurs ont assentus." If they cannot agree, the two houses, for every bill from whencesoever it doth come is thrice read in each of the houses, if it be understood that there is any sticking, sometimes the lords to the commons, sometimes the commons to the lords, do require that a certain of each house may meet together and so each part to be informed of other's meaning; and this is always granted. After which meeting for the most part, not always, either part agrees to other's bills.

Cases of difference between the two houses.

Different form of voting.

'In the upper house they give their assent and dissent, each man severally and by himself, first for himself, and then for so many as he hath proxy. When the chancellor hath demanded of them whether they will go to the question after the bill hath been thrice read, they saying only *Content* or *Non-Content* without further reasoning or replying, and as the more number doth agree so it is agreed on or dashed.

No proxies in the commons.

'In the nether house none of them that is elected, either knight or burgess, can give his voice to another, nor his consent or dissent by proxy. The more part of them that be present only maketh the consent or dissent.

Second and third readings.

After the bill hath been twice read and then ingrossed and eftsoones read and disputed on enough as is thought, the speaker asketh if they will go to the question. And, if they agree, he holdeth the bill up in his hand and saith, "As many as will that this bill go forward, which is concerning such a matter, say 'Yea.'" Then they which allow the bill cry "Yea," and as many as will not say "No"; as the cry of yea or no is bigger, so the bill is allowed or dashed. If it be a doubt which cry is bigger they divide the house, the speaker saying "As many as do allow the bill go down with the bill, and as many as do not, sit still." So they divide themselves, and being so divided they are numbered who made the more part, and so the bill doth speed. It chanceth sometime that some part of the bill is allowed, some other part hath much contrariety and doubt made of it; and it is thought

Final question.

if it were amended it would go forward. Then they choose certain committees of them who have spoken with the bill and against it to amend it and bring it in again so amended as they amongst them shall think meet: and this is before it is ingrossed; yea and sometime after. But the agreement of these committees is no prejudice to the house. For at the last question they will either accept it or dash it as it shall seem good[1], notwithstanding that whatsoever the committees have done.

Committals and re-committals.

'Thus no bill is an act of parliament, ordinance, or edict of law until both the houses severally have agreed unto it after the order aforesaid; no nor then neither. But the last day of that parliament or session the prince cometh in person in his parliament robes and sitteth in his state; all the upper house sitteth about the prince in their states and order in their robes. The speaker with all the common house cometh to the bar, and there after thanksgiving first in the lords' name by the chancellor and in the commons' name by the speaker to the prince for that he hath so great care of the good government of his people, and for calling them together to advise of such things as should be for the reformation, establishing, and ornament of the commonwealth; the chancellor in the prince's name giveth thanks to the lords and commons for their pains and travails taken, which he saith the prince will remember and recompence when time and occasion shall serve; and that he for his part is ready to declare his pleasure concerning their proceedings, whereby the same may have perfect life and accomplishment by his princely authority, and so have the whole consent of the realm. Then one readeth the titles of every act which hath passed at that session, but only in this fashion, "An act concerning such a thing," &c. It is marked there what the prince doth allow and to such he saith "Le roy" or "La royne le veult[2]."

Close of the session.

Speeches at the dissolution.

[1] 'Dec. 8. 1548, L. 3. The bill for the assurance of the earl of Bath's lands: 'vacat per majorem numerum super quaestione'; Commons' Journals, i. 5.

[2] The form by which the act of subsidy was authorised ran thus:—'Le roi remercie ses communes de lor boons cuers en faisant les grauntes suisdictz, mesmes les grants accepte, et tout le content en l'endenture avandit especifie graunte et approve, avesque l'act et les provisions a cest indenture annexez'; Lords' Journals, i. 9; Rot. Parl. v. 510. The

Public and private acts.

And those be taken now as perfect laws and ordinances of the realm of England and none other; and, as shortly as may be, put in print, except it be some private cause or law made for the benefit or prejudice of some private man, which the Romans were wont to call privilegia. These be only exemplified under the seal of the parliament and for the most part not printed. To those which the prince liketh not he answereth "Le roy" or "La royne s'advisera," and those be accounted utterly dashed and of none effect.

'This is the order and form of the highest and most authentical court of England[1].'

Judicature of the house of lords.

767. The judicial functions of parliament, including in their widest acceptation the decision of great suits and civil appeals by the house of lords, the trial of lords and others impeached or appealed, the practice used in bills of attainder, and the quasi-judicial action of both houses in the matter of petitions, find ample illustration in the pages of constitutional history: and the minuter details of parliamentary practice in these matters belong to the jurist rather than to the historian. The parliament, and either house of it, was in fact a tribunal of such extreme resort that rules for proceeding must almost necessarily have been framed as each particular case required. On petitions public and private much the same process was used as we have

endorsement on the legislative acts was added after the last act of the session: 'Qua quidem perlecta et ad plenum intellecta eidem per dictum dominum regem de advisamento et assensu dominorum spiritualium et temporalium ac communitatis in parliamento praedicto existentium, auctoritateque ejusdem parliamenti sequens fiebat responsio "Le roi le veult"'; Lords' Journals, i. 9. The process by which the form 'le roi s'avisera' acquired the meaning of refusal, may be worked out on the Rolls: Edward I could say 'rex non habet consilium mutandi consuetudinem . . . nec statuta sua revocanda'; Rot. Parl. i. 51: but he generally gives reasons. Under Edward II we find 'rex habebit advisamentum' in a natural sense, p. 394: 'injusta est,' pp. 393, 408; 'nihil,' p. 435. Edward III has 'le roi s'avisera de faire l'eese a son peuple q'il pourra bonement,' ii. 142; 'soit le roi avise,' p. 169; 'le roi s'avisera queux,' &c., pp. 166, 169; and simply 'le roi s'avisera,' p. 172; 'ce n'est pas resonable,' p. 240; 'est noun resonable,' p. 241; 'les seigneurs se aviseront,' p. 318; after the accession of Richard II it seems to have its modern meaning.

[1] The Commonwealth of England and manner of government thereof; compiled by the honourable Sir Thomas Smith, knight; London, 1589; bk. ii. cc. 2, 3. Sir Thomas died in 1577.

here attempted to trace in the practice of legislation; a bill of attainder went through the same stages as a bill of settlement or of legal reform. The appeal of treason in parliament, always an irregular and tumultuous proceeding, was forbidden by the first parliament of Henry IV[1]. The supreme or appellate jurisdiction of the lords in civil suits is a matter rarely heard of from the time when the complete and matured organisation of the courts of Westminster had been supplemented by the judicial activity of the council, until it was revived and reorganised in the sixteenth and seventeenth centuries[2]. The practice of trial upon impeachment has thus a melancholy prominence in the judicial annals of parliament: and there is no occasion to dwell here on the details which have been given in our narrative chapters. The presumptuous boast of the Merciless Parliament in the case of the appellants of 1388, that parliament is bound by none of the ordinary rules of law, civil or common[3], has not practically met with acceptance even in the extreme cases in which Strafford, Laud, and Charles I were made to feel that a minute adherence to forms is a different thing from the observance of constitutional law. The impeachments as well as the appeals of medieval times are, as has been already remarked, pregnant with warning rather than example.

Appeals of treason.

Appellate jurisdiction of the lords.

Impeachments.

Claim of parliament to be above law.

The Rolls of Parliament afford such scanty glimpses of detail in all points except the results of the session, and so seldom contain any notice of speeches or debates, that it would not be safe to argue from their silence that the kings took a very small share in the deliberative work of the national council. It is

Presence of the kings in parliament.

[1] See above, p. 23.

[2] See May, Treatise on Parliament, p. 53, where the judicial powers of the house of lords are briefly summed up: They have a judicature in the trial of peers, and claims of peerage; a general judicature as a supreme court of appeal from other courts of justice, inherited from the ancient concilium regis. In the seventeenth century they assumed a jurisdiction which has since been abandoned, an original jurisdiction in civil suits; and the like in criminal cases where there was no impeachment by the commons. The appellate jurisdiction in equity has been exercised since the reign of Charles I; and the jurisdiction in cases brought up by writ of error, originally derived from the crown, was confirmed by Stat. 27 Eliz. c. 8; cf. Coke, 4th Inst. p. 20.

[3] See above, vol. ii. p. 480; Rot. Parl. iii. 236; cf. Coke, 4th inst. p. 15.

The king is present at the opening of the parliament.

however quite fair to argue from the position usually occupied by the ministers in the formal transaction of business that it was only on very rare occasions that the king would take part in deliberation, either as a speaker or as a hearer. His presence was deemed necessary at the opening and generally at the close of the session; but most frequently his duty was discharged when he had directed the chancellor to state the causes of summons, and to thank the estates for their attendance. The chancellor was his spokesman in most cases when he approved the election of the speaker. His decision on petitions was expressed by an indorsement which the clerk of the parliament read on

He seldom speaks.

the last day of the session as the king's answer. It was very seldom that he spoke, or was recorded to have spoken; and when it is recorded it is with exceptional solemnity. The imperfection of the records of the reigns of Edward I and Edward II makes it impossible to speak positively with regard to them; Edward I however had probably learned to guard against the garrulity which made his father ridiculous, and Edward II seldom cared even to face his subjects. In 1315 [1] we are told that it was by the king's order that William Inge opened the parliament, but even this slight indication is generally suppressed; and the statement that 'de par le roi' such and such ministers spoke cannot be understood to mean that he gave a

Speeches of Edward III.

verbal direction. Under Edward III, whose popular manners and constant association with his barons make the appearance of silence still more strange, the same course was observed; it is in 1363 [2], after he has been more than thirty years on the throne, that we first distinctly find him making his will known to the commons by his own mouth; they thank him for having done this in the last parliament, from which we infer that he had spoken on the occasion of the dissolution. The parliament of 1362 was that in which the use of English in legal transactions was ordered; that of 1365 was opened with an English speech, and it may be inferred that in giving the estates leave to depart Edward himself had spoken in English, and that where in

[1] Rot. Parl. i. 350.

[2] Ibid. ii. 276.

other cases the address of thanks is not said to have been spoken by the chancellor, it was spoken by the king. In the last interview which he had with his parliament, at Sheen in 1377, the parting words are put in his mouth [1]. The days of serene supremacy passed away with Edward III; Richard II is more than once said to have uttered haughty words in parliament. In 1386 he protested 'par sa bouche demesne' that his prerogative was not impaired by what had taken place in the session; in 1388 he had to declare openly in full parliament that he believed his uncle the duke of Gloucester to be loyal; in 1390 he thanked the lords and commons for their advice and grants. In 1397, in the discussion on Haxey's bill, he allowed the chancellor to complain on his behalf to the lords, but when that was done, administered a reproof and stated his determination in his own words, and in the same way pardoned the commons when they had made their humble apology. But in this and the following parliament Richard played the part of a politician rather than that of a constitutional sovereign; he discussed in a long speech to the commons the foreign policy which he had adopted, and acted as his own minister [2]. In the next session he spoke several times on the accusation against Arundel, and in vindication of his own friends, but these utterances were perhaps judicial: in his last revolutionary session at Shrewsbury he followed the same course, stating with his own mouth at the dissolution that he would annul his pardon recently granted unless the newly voted grants were collected without impediment [3].

His parting speech.

Speeches of Richard II.

The succeeding kings took a still more prominent part in parliament. Henry IV, whose claim to the crown, spoken in English [4], made the occasion an era of constitutional progress, not only signified his wishes to the parliament, but deigned to argue with the commons; he laid himself open to the good advice of the speaker, and condescended on various occasions both to defend himself and to silence his interlocutor: he soon

Speeches of Henry IV.

[1] Rot. Parl. ii. 364.
[2] Ibid. iii. 338, 339.
[3] Ibid. iii. 351, 353, 369.
[4] See above, p. 12.

Discussions of Henry IV with the speaker. learned that his dignity would not survive too great familiarity, and had to reprove the loquacity of the speaker. It is one of the notable features of his policy that he stood, notwithstanding his difficulties, always face to face with his subjects. The records of the next reign are too meagre to illustrate this point; Henry V seems however to have conversed as freely as his father had done with the lords, and perhaps maintained his dignity better. In the minority of his son, the dukes of Gloucester and Bedford are found stating their own quarrels, notwithstanding their dignified place of protector and chief counsellor, and the boy king was very early made to play his part in the formal solemnities of the session. Eloquence of Edward IV. Edward IV, who imitated the more popular usages of the rival house, likewise made speeches to both lords and commons; and in particular, in dissolving his first parliament, addressed the speaker in simple and touching language of gratitude and promise [1]. All these speeches were made by the king either in full parliament, that is, in the presence of both houses, or in the house of lords to the lords who were then and there in attendance upon him. It was fully recognised that Privacy of debate. for anything like consultation the two houses had a right to the utmost privacy; the commons had a right to deliberate by themselves, and the lords by themselves; and when they desired to be private, the king was ill-advised indeed if he listened to any report of their proceedings other than they presented to him [2]. Although, however, a good deal of the business of the lords was no doubt transacted in the king's presence, medieval history affords no instance of his visiting the house of commons whilst they were debating. The question of freedom of debate belongs to another part of our subject.

768. The right of suspending the session by adjournment or prorogation, of countermanding a meeting once called, and of dissolving the parliament itself, was throughout the middle ages vested in the king alone. The distinction between adjournment and prorogation, in so far as the one belongs to the houses and

[1] Rot. Parl. v. 787.

[2] Queen Anne was the last sovereign who attended debates in the house of lords; May, Treatise on Parliament, p. 449.

the other to the crown, is a modern distinction[1]. The necessary adjournment from day to day, as well as the countermanding of a parliament called, and the longer intermission of the session, was known as prorogation[2]: the houses were ordered by the king to meet from day to day until business was finished, and the rule of adjourning at midday originated probably as much in the necessity of dining as in the wish to claim a privilege[3]. The countermanding power is proved by numerous instances: in some cases the king was prevented from attendance at the time fixed, and warned the estates not to assemble; in others they met to be prorogued, as in the case of the parliament of 1454[4], and in several formal sessions of the reign of Edward IV, the political importance of which has been noticed already. The circumstances under which the right was exercised differ widely from those under which in later times the right of prorogation has been regarded as important. It was then, as now, somewhat difficult to keep the members together until business was in a fair way of being finished; but the long continued practice of holding one or more than one new parliament every year was in strong contrast with modern usage. A parliament of Richard II threatens to dissolve itself, but no medieval parliament threatens to sit in permanence. The houses, unlike the clerical convocations, which very unwillingly allowed any interference with their times and places of session, showed an unbounded respect for the king's order in this matter: and the kings showed similar respect for the estates. The long prorogations, when they become usual, are, like the early annual

Royal power of adjourning and proroguing.

[1] See above, vol. ii. p. 473.

[2] The word 'prorogation' is constantly used for countermanding or delaying the day of meeting; see Parl. Writs, i. 33, 120, &c. A parliament is 'revoked' altogether in 1331; Lords' Report, iv. 402.

[3] Under Henry VIII, when the house of lords adjourned, owing to the absence of the prelates in convocation, the adjournment was ordered by royal authority. The growth of the claim of the houses to adjourn themselves may be traced in Hatsell's Precedents, ii. 311 sq. In 1621 Sir E. Coke says 'the commission [of adjournment] must be only declaratory of the king's pleasur but the court must adjourn itself'; ib. p. 311. On the modern law, see May, Treatise on Parliament, p. 50.

[4] See Rot. Parl. v. 238, 497–500, &c.

or terminal sessions, defined by the season of harvest and the church festivals.

Ceremony of dissolving parliament.

769. When the business of the session was finished, the king's questions answered, the petitions heard and decided, the laws ingrossed for final acceptance, and, above all, the money grants agreed upon, all parties were ready and anxious to go home. The session, which, it is scarcely necessary to repeat, was in early times the whole action of the particular parliament, was solemnly closed. Sometimes, as in 1305, the parliament was dissolved by proclamation, sometimes the king in person appeared to take and give leave to depart[1]. The roll of 1365 furnishes a fair instance of the early usage; 'the 17th of February the king, lords and commons being assembled in the white chamber, and the ordinance against those who impugn the rights of the king and his crown being read first, and then the petitions of the commons and their answers, and the grant made to the king of the subsidy of wool, leather, and woolfells being recited to the said lords and commons by the chancellor, the king thanked the said lords and commons heartily for their good council and advice, and the great travail they had had, and also for the aid which they had made and granted him in this parliament, and gave leave to the said lords and commons to depart each where he pleased; and so ended the parliament[2].' Richard II, in 1386, took the opportunity of making a protest on behalf of his prerogative by word of mouth[3]. Henry IV, in 1402, invited both houses to dine with him on the Sunday after the dissolution; but though the king several times spoke in the parliament chamber, the invitation was conveyed by the earl of Northumberland[4]. The Lancastrian kings more than once took leave of the estates in person and with a speech, and Edward IV took particular pains to address the commons at least in his first parliament[5]. It was not always that matters ended so pleasantly;

[1] See the proclamation of dissolution by Edward I in 1305; Parl. Writs, i. 155; Rot. Parl. i. 159.

[2] Rot. Parl. ii. 288.

[3] Ibid. iii. 224.

[4] Ibid. iii. 493: In 1368 Edward III entertained the lords and many of the commons on a like occasion; ib. ii. 297.

[5] Ibid. v. 486.

more than once a committee had to be named to dispatch petitions that had not been fully considered, or to make sure that the common petitions were not altered before they became laws. In 1332 and 1333 the lords were ordered to stay when the commons had leave to go[1]. In 1362 some of the commons were directed to stay for certain business on which the king wished to speak; in 1372 the citizens and burgesses were kept behind and prevailed on to grant tunnage and poundage[2]. In 1376 the king was ill at Eltham, and the three estates went down to take leave of him and to hear his answers to the petitions; in 1377 they went in the same way to Sheen to receive the answers, which were read on the following day in the parliament chamber, and then sat for some days longer[3]. The dissolution was sometimes made an occasion for an oration by the speaker; Sir Arnold Savage furnishes the most conspicuous example, but the announcement of the grant on the last day of the session was a tempting opportunity for compliments on both sides.

Members kept behind.

The parliament was held to be dissolved by the death or deposition of the king in whose name it was called, but this rule was not observed in the case of Edward II, and was evaded in that of Richard II. The parliament of 1413 was dissolved by the death of Henry IV; and this is a solitary example[4].

Dissolution on the king's death.

770. One of the last matters transacted was the issue of the writs to the sheriffs and borough magistrates for the payment of the wages of the representatives in the house of commons. The knights of the shire received each four shillings a day, and the citizens and burgesses each two. This rate of payment was fixed by usage, or possibly by ordinance, in the seventh year of Edward II; and was observed from the beginning of the next reign, the rates of the preceding and intervening years having occasionally varied. These wages were collected by the sheriffs from the 'communities' of the counties and towns represented, and were a frequent matter of petition, in which almost every conceivable plea was alleged in order to escape the obligation[5].

Wages of the members of the house of commons.

[1] Rot. Parl. ii. 65, 69.
[2] Ibid. ii. 275, 310.
[3] Ibid. ii. 330, 364.
[4] Ibid. iv. 9.
[5] See Prynne, Fourth Register, pp. 1-608. Parl. Writs, II. i. 115; cf. pp. 148, 210, &c. The sheriff of Cambridge in 1307 is forbidden to distrain

Disputes about the payment of wages.

It is on the arguments so put forward that some of the erroneous views were formed, which we have seen early obscuring the simplicity of the idea of parliamentary representation. The king's advisers almost invariably decide that the existing custom in the particular county shall be followed. Under Henry VIII the wages of the newly added members were secured by legislation; but until then they were levied under the royal writ, the towns represented being of course at liberty to increase the rate if they pleased. The representatives of London, for instance, in 1296 received ten shillings a day by a vote of the magistrates[1], and the members for York in 1483 were promised eight additional days wages on the occasion of the coronation of Edward V. The sums were paid with due consideration for the time spent on the way, 'in eundo, morando, et redeundo'; this made the burden heavier in the case of the northern counties, and may account in some small measure for their disinclination to send members. In 1421 the people of Ely bought for £200, paid to the county of Cambridge, immunity from this payment which they had previously claimed as tenants of a great franchise: the same county possessed in the reign of Henry VIII a manor, called the shire manor, charged with a payment of £10 a year to the expenses of the knights' wages, the men of Cambridgeshire being thus relieved from direct payments. The

the villeins of John de la Mare for expenses, inasmuch as he attended in person; Parl. Writs, I. 191: so also in Norfolk the villeins of the bishop are free; Parl. Writs, II. i. 259. In 1327 Edward III orders the sheriff of Middlesex to levy the expenses within liberties as well as without, the men of the liberties of Westminster and Wallingford having refused to pay; ib. II. i. 366. On the collection of wages in Gloucestershire from both the liberties and the geldable, see Parl. Writs, I. 95. The sheriff of Kent returns in 1313 that at three county courts the men refused to pay, on the ground that they held in gavelkind; Parl. Writs, II. i. 91. In 1312 the member for Wilts brings an action against the sheriff to recover the difference between 4*s.* and 16*d.*, at which sum he had sent in his account to the sheriff, ignorant of the more liberal tariff; Parl. Writs, II. i. 195.

[1] The parliament of 1296 was at S. Edmund's; Parl. Writs, I. 149: in 1298 the sum fixed is 100*s.* each, ib. p. 72, the parliament being at York. In 1322 the rate is 3*s.* for knights, 20*d.* for burghers; Parl. Writs, II. i. 258. In 1325, 3*s.* for valetti. At Lynn in 1431 the members received 6*s.* 8*d.* a day; Archæol. xxiv. 320: in 1442 it was voted that they should have 2*s.* a day each and no more; ib. p. 322. On the immunity of tenants in ancient demesne, Prynne, Reg. ii. 176.

townsmen of Cambridge passed an ordinance, in 1427, that the wages of their burgesses should be only a shilling a day, and made an agreement with their members to accept half the usual sum[1]. Many curious particulars have been collected upon this point, which has an archaeological as well as a constitutional interest. The refusal of the king, in all cases, to interfere with custom, shows how ancient a right the payment was, and how hazardous a thing to meddle with it. The practice of course vanished as a seat in parliament became an object of more selfish ambition or greater political aspirations.

The king rules in favour of local custom.

771. Although the two houses of parliament had, at least since the accession of the house of Lancaster, been fully recognised as co-ordinate, equal, and mutually independent assemblies, they each retained peculiarities of usage and exclusive rights in special provinces of work to which the names of prerogative or privilege might be given if those names were not otherwise appropriated. At the close of the middle ages the commons were advisers and assentors, not merely petitioners, in matters of legislation, and in matters of political consideration their voice was as powerful as that of the lords; they were no longer, if they had ever been, delegates, but senators acting on behalf of the whole nation[2]. In the other two branches of national business there were distinctions which ran back to the early differences of origin. The lords were the judges of parliament, the commons were the originators of grants; and although the commons were yet a long way from that point at which they were to exclude the lords from all interference with money bills, they had, both in the forms of their grants and in the royal promise to receive information of the grants from the mouth of the speaker alone, won the ground on which their later claim was based. The

Special rights and privileges of the two houses and their members.

Financial right of the commons.

[1] Cooper, Annals of Cambridge, i. 178, 186.

[2] Coke, 4th Inst. p. 14: 'It is to be observed, though one be chosen for one particular county or borough, yet when he is returned and sits in parliament, he serveth for the whole realm, for the end of his coming thither, as in the writ of his election appeareth, is general *ad faciendum et consentiendum hiis quae tunc et ibidem de communi consilio dicti regni nostri, favente Deo, ordinari contigerint super negotiis praedictis*; id est, *pro quibusdam arduis et urgentibus negotiis nos, statum et defensionem regni nostri Angliae et ecclesiae Anglicanae concernentibus*, which are rehearsed before in the writ.' See also Hatsell, Precedents, ii. 76.

Judicial right of the lords.

judicial position of the lords was scarcely better secured, if it were seriously maintained, as it was in the bill of 1414 for the reversal of the judgment against the earl of Salisbury, that judgment by the lords with assent of the king is not lawful, but that it should be given by the king as sovereign judge, and by the lords spiritual and temporal with the assent of the commons in parliament, and not by the lords temporal only[1].' But however this may have been, judicial work was apportioned to the lords, and financial work was ultimately secured to the commons.

Variety of usages.

The difference of usage in the two houses, the difference in the powers of the speaker in each, the different rule of speaking, in the commons to the speaker, in the lords to the whole house, the different way of voting, and the other points in which the custom of the one varied from that of the other, have a history if we only knew it; through the general likeness of procedure minute traces of difference every now and then appear. In the wide and loose application of the word 'privilege,' the privileges or peculiar functions and usages of the house of lords are distinguished from those of the house of commons; the privilege of individual members of the house of lords may be distinguished from the privileges of individual members of the house of commons; both again have common privileges as members of the parliament; and the lords have special privileges as peers, distinct from those which they have as members of a house coordinate with the house of commons.

Different sorts of privilege.

1. Special functions of the two houses.

Of the first of these distinctions no more need be said here than has already been stated; the house of lords had judicial functions which the house of commons disavowed, although those functions could be exercised only during the session of parliament, that is whilst the commons were assembled; and the house of commons developed financial functions which they took care to keep to themselves, although their acts did not become law until they received the assent of the lords. The house of lords had, as the king's great council, an organisation over and above its character as a house of parliament, and a continuity and personal identity which it was impossible for a representative

[1] Rot. Parl. iv. 18.

chamber to secure. But these points are scarcely points of privilege, and they have been sufficiently illustrated already. The house of commons had, at the close of the period, neither raised nor attempted to raise a claim to the right, which afterwards was so fondly cherished, of determining questions of dispute in elections of its own members: the corresponding jurisdiction in the case of the lords was, so far as it was a matter of law at all, within the limits of their existing powers[1].

2. Special rights of the lords.

772. Of the matters that fall under the second head the following are the most important. Every lord had, from the earliest times to a very recent date, when the privilege was voluntarily laid aside[2], the power of appointing a proxy to give his vote. This was done by royal licence, which was very seldom refused. The power of appointing a procurator or proxy was sometimes given and sometimes withheld by the terms of the writ[3]. Thus in the summons of the assembly in which the prince of Wales was knighted in 1306[4], permission is given; in the writ for the parliament of March 1332 proxies are positively forbidden. The usage extended even to the permission for the proxy or power of attorney to be given to a person who was not himself a member of the house; in the parliament of Carlisle in 1307 a baron Reginald de Grey was represented by his attorney, Thomas of Wytnesham. Among the records of the reign of Edward II are numerous letters of proxy from bishops and barons to laymen and clerks, which on some occasions must have reduced the chamber of the lords to the position of a representative assembly[5]. In 1315, for instance, the proxies of both

The right of appointing a proxy.

[1] See the dispute between the earls of Warwick and Norfolk on precedence; Lords' Fifth Report, p. 198: and that between the earls of Devon and Arundel in 1449; Rot. Parl. v. 148. It was in the latter case that the judges declared that such cases belong for decision to the king and the lords.

[2] In 1868; May, Treatise on the Parliament, p. 370.

[3] A list of the occasions on which the permission to appoint proxies is withheld is given by Elsynge, Method and Manner, &c. p. 117; see also Lords' Report, iv. 408.

[4] Parl. Writs, i. 166; the forms of proxy then used are given in the same place.

[5] Proxies for the parliament of York in 1322 are given in Parl. Writs, II. i. 248; cf. pp. 264 sq., 296–299.

Proxies of the lords.

barons and prelates were accepted as a substitute for their personal attendance, and the practice became very common. Originally the permission may have been given merely to bind the absent person to the decisions of those who were present; or to excuse his absence. But it speedily acquired a much greater importance. The earl of Warenne, in 1322, appoints Sir Ralph Cobham and John Dynyeton, clerk, to speak and treat in his place in the parliament of York, and to assent to all that shall be agreed on by his peers for the honour of the king and the benefit of the people. And it was no doubt in such a sense that they were admitted or licenced by the kings[1]. The proxies of the absent lords were read on the day of the opening of parliament[2]. The restriction of the exercise of this power, by limiting the choice of a proxy to members of the house, grew up later, and its history has not been minutely traced. It was however in full use in the sixteenth century.

Proxies not used in the house of commons.

The privilege of appointing a proxy does not seem to have ever belonged to the members of the house of commons, although, if we consider the frequency of such usage in the equally representative house of the clergy, the rule that a delegate cannot make a delegate would hardly exclude the possibility[3]. In the parliament of 1406 the speaker proposed to the king that, as Richard Cliderhow, one of the knights for Kent, had gone to sea as an admiral, his fellow knight, Robert Clifford, should be allowed to appear in parliament in their two names as if they were both present[4]. To this the king agreed, but the

[1] Archbishop Reynolds in 1322 makes two bishops his proctors; Parl. Writs, II. i. 284. In 1347 the earl of Devon is released from the duty of attendance, and allowed to send a proxy to do all that he could have done if he had been present; Lords' Report, iv. 562. See other examples, ib. p. 593; Prynne, Reg. i. 116–120, 214, &c. Madox, in the Formulare Anglicanum, gives two proxies (Nos. 625, 626), one of lord de la Warr, in 21 Hen. VIII, to lord Berkeley 'ad tractandum et communicandum, necnon ad consentiendum vice et nomine meis'; the other given by the abbot of Colchester to two abbots. The proxies of 1322 are 'ad tractandum, providendum et ordinandum.'

[2] See the Roll for 1380, Rot. Parl. iii. 88; and the Lords' Journals for the reign of Henry VIII., vol. i. p. 4.

[3] Instances of proctors appointed with a power of appointing a proxy will be found in Parl. Writs, i. 186.

[4] Rot. Parl. iii. 572.

example was not followed: nor are there instances, except perhaps in the case of the city of London[1], in which the counties or towns elected more than the due number of representatives so that in case of sickness one might take another's place; a practice not unusual in the election of clerical proxies.

Supplementary members.

773. A second important right of the individual lords was that of recording a protest against acts of the house with which they did not agree; no such power has been exercised by the commons. In the upper house the early examples are those of the episcopal protests against the legislation on provisors and praemunire which are recorded in the rolls or even in the statute itself. These again seem to look back to the days when a baron declined to recognise legislation to which he had not personally consented[2]. The more general practice of protests by the lords dates from the seventeenth century. It is difficult to find anything in the powers of members of the lower house which can be set against these practices, of proxy and protest, and it is perhaps a mistake to call them privileges at all.

Right of the lords to record a protest.

774. The third head comprises some very important points; for upon the possession of the common privileges of the houses and their individual members hangs their real independence and the national liberty. Both houses possess the right of debating freely and without interference from the king or from each other. This is secured to the house of commons and to the members collectively by the king's promise to the speaker: and he would have been a bold king indeed who had attempted to stop discussion in the house of lords. Invaluable as the privilege is, it is not susceptible of much historical illustration, and it must suffice to recur to the parliamentary history of the reigns of Richard II and Henry IV. The punishment of Haxey was annulled as a violation of the liberties of the commons[3]: Sir

3. Privileges common to the two houses.

Privilege of debate.

[1] See above, p. 459 note.

[2] See above, vol. ii. p. 245.

[3] 'De volunte du dit roy le dit Thomas estoit adjugez traitour, et forfaita toutz q'il avoit, encontre droit et la curse quel avoit este devant en parlement'; Rot. Parl. iii. 430: it was also 'en anientisement des custumes de lez communes'; ib. p. 434: and the petition requires his restoration 'si bien en accomplissement de droit come pur salvation des libertez

Freedom of discussion. Arnold Savage prayed, but in no very humble tones, that Henry IV would not listen to representations of what the commons were doing; and the king promised to credit no such reports[1]. A few years later, in his undertaking to hear the money grants from the speaker only, he declared that both lords and commons were free to debate on the condition of the kingdom and the proposed remedies[2]. But the very nature of an English parliament repelled any arbitrary limitation of discussion, and the obsequious apology of the commons for allowing Haxey's bill to pass may be said to stand alone in our early annals. The debates were certainly respectful to the kings; of their freedom we can judge by results rather than by details. The commons could speak strongly enough about misgovernment and want of faith; and the strongest kings had to bear with the strongest reproofs. **Never infringed by a hasty dissolution.** Interference with this freedom of debate could only be attempted by a dispersion of parliament itself, or by compulsion exercised on individual members. Of a violent dissolution we have no example; the country was secured against it by the mode of granting supplies. The compulsion of individual members comes under the second sub-division of this head. Of interference of one house with the debates of the other we have no medieval instances.

Security against infringement by compulsion used to particular members. That individual members should not be called to account for their behaviour in parliament, or for words there spoken, by any authority external to the house in which the offence was given, seems to be the essential safeguard of freedom of debate. It was the boon guaranteed by the king to the speaker when he accepted him, under the general term, privilege; and has since the reign of Henry VIII been explicitly demanded on the occasion[3]. The power of the crown to silence or punish a hostile or too independent member, however opposed that power may be to the spirit of the constitution, is better illustrated in medieval precedent than the power of the parliament to resist

de lez ditz communes.' The reference to the commons is not repeated in the act of rehabilitation; p. 430.

[1] See above, p. 29.

[2] See above, p. 61.

[3] See above, pp. 454, 455.

the breach of privilege. Three prominent instances stand out at three important epochs, in which the speaker himself, or the person who fulfilled the duties that afterwards devolved on the speaker was made the scapegoat of the house of commons. In 1301, after the parliament of Lincoln, at which he had been outrageously worried by the opposition of the estates, Edward I sent to the tower Henry Keighley, the knight who had presented to him the bill of articles drawn up in the name of the whole community[1]. We learn from his own letter on the subject that the measure was dictated by policy rather than by vindictive feeling; the prisoner was to be kindly treated and made to believe that mercy was shown him at the instance of the minister whom he had attacked. There is no record of any action taken either in or out of parliament for his release, but he is soon after found in public employment as a commissioner of array and justice of assize. The second case is that of Peter de la Mare, the prolocutor of the good parliament of 1376, who was thrown into prison by John of Gaunt for his conduct in that assembly[2]. The arrest, although prompted by a faction, must have been executed in the form of law. The vindication of Peter de la Mare was undertaken, not by the parliament, which was indeed defunct, but by the citizens of London, who rose in tumult and demanded for him a fair trial; in the succeeding parliament, which was elected under the influence of John of Gaunt, a minority of the knights made an attempt to obtain his release and a legal trial. He remained in prison until the death of Edward III, was released by Richard II, and almost immediately elected speaker in the first parliament of that king. The third case is that of Thomas Thorpe, the speaker of the parliament of 1453; who in consequence of his opposition to the duke of York was prosecuted on a private pretext, cast for damages on the verdict of a jury, and sent to the Fleet during a prorogation of parliament. The imprisonment of Thorpe, like that of Peter de la Mare, was the act of a faction,

Instances of arrest of the speaker.

Henry Keighley.

Peter de la Mare.

Thomas Thorpe.

[1] See vol. ii. p. 151, and above, p. 453.
[2] See vol. ii. pp. 435, 440.

Arrest of Thorpe the speaker.

legally carried into execution, but primarily intended to silence a dangerous enemy. It differed from the former case as occurring during the actual existence of parliament and not after its close. Thorpe was a member, and speaker at the time of his imprisonment, and the privilege of members was directly touched in two points, freedom of speech and freedom from arrest. When the parliament met after prorogation the commons demanded their speaker; they sent to the king and the lords requesting that they might have and enjoy their ancient and accustomed privilege, and in accordance therewith that Thomas Thorpe and Walter Rayle, who were then in prison, might be set free for the dispatch of the business of parliament. The counsel of the duke appeared before the lords to oppose the application; he gave his account of the circumstances of the arrest, and urged moreover that the arrest had been made in vacation. The lords, not intending to 'impeach or hurt the liberties and privileges of the commons,' asked the opinion of the justices, who said 'that they ought not to answer to that question, for it hath not been used aforetime that the justices should in anywise determine the privilege of this high court of parliament; for it is so high and so mighty in its nature that it may make law, and that that is law it may make no law, and the determination and knowledge of that privilege belongeth to the lords of the parliament and not to the justices.' They proceeded however to state that there was no form of 'supersedeas' that could stop all processes against privileged members, but that the custom was, if a member were arrested for any less cause than treason, felony, breach of the peace, and sentence of parliament, he should make his attorney and be released to attend in parliament. The lords declined to suggest this course; they determined that Thorpe should remain in prison; and the commons were ordered in the king's name to elect a new speaker. The case was treated as a simple case of arrest, political reasons were kept out of sight, and the commons found that they had no remedy[1].

Discussion of privilege.

The question shelved.

Besides these instances of arrest of the speaker, two other

[1] See above, pp. 164–166; Rot. Parl. v. 227, 240, 295, &c.; Hatsell's Precedents, i. 31–34.

famous cases are found, in which a similar summary method was adopted for the punishment of other offenders: the case of Haxey in 1397 and that of Yonge in 1455. The former has been frequently adverted to already. He had brought into the house of commons a bill which reflected censure on the king and court; that bill had come to the king's knowledge; he demanded, and the commons with a humble apology gave up, the name of the proposer; how the bill got into the house we do not know, for Haxey was a clergyman, not a member of the house, and although, if he were a clerical proctor, he might have demanded the same privilege as a member, no such claim was raised for him. He was imprisoned, condemned, claimed by the archbishop as a clerk, and pardoned. In this case there is a direct interference of the king with freedom of debate in the commons apart from the question of right of freedom from arrest. The commons did not show, and probably did not see that they ought to have shown, an independent spirit on the occasion.

Arrest of particular offenders.

Haxey's case.

The case of Thomas Yonge or Young, the member for Bristol, who proposed in the parliament of 1451 that the duke of York should be declared heir to the crown, is not free from obscurities of its own[1]. In the records of parliament it appears only in a petition presented by him to the commons in 1455, in which he reminds them of their right that all members 'ought to have their freedom to speak and say in the house of their assembly as to them is thought convenient or reasonable without any manner challenge, charge, or punition therefore to be laid to them in anywise.' Notwithstanding his privilege he had, in consequence of untrue reports to the king, been imprisoned in the Tower, and endamaged to the amount of a thousand marks. He asks the commons to pray the king and lords to procure him compensation. The commons sent up the bill to the lords, and the king ordered that the lords of the council should provide a remedy. Here we have only the complainant's account of the matter; it is no doubt substantially true, but the exact grounds

Case of Thomas Yonge.

[1] See above, pp. 159, 174; Rot. Parl. v. 337.

on which the arrest was made are not stated. Matter of privilege as it was, the prayer is for personal and private indemnity: the commons seem to have no remedy but petition, and no atonement is offered to their injured dignity. So the case stands in the last years of the Lancastrian rule.

Immunity of members from personal molestation and arrest.

775. These instances all really fall on common ground between two great points of privilege—freedom of speech and freedom from arrest. The latter is the guarantee of the former, but it has inevitably a much wider operation, is practically more defensible, and accordingly is technically more definite. What must be said about it here must be confined to the cases of the members of the house of commons: the peers had a similar immunity on other grounds. From the very earliest times the persons of those who were on their way to the king's court and council had a sort of sanctity such as is recognised in an ambassador. By the law of Ethelbert, 'if the king call his "leod" to him, and any one there do them evil,' the offender must make double satisfaction to the injured person and pay a fine to the king[1]. Canute wills, in a law which must have had a still wider application, 'that every man be entitled to grith to the gemot and from the gemot except he be a notorious thief[2].' The laws ascribed to Edward the Confessor recognise a particular immunity for persons going to and from the synods[3]. After the institution of writs there was no occasion for such enactments to be repeated. All members going to or returning from parliament were under the prescriptive protection of the king who summoned them. So long as the parliaments were annual and short the protection secured by this rule was, however important, of no very wide or protracted extent. The early cases of the breach are therefore less important than the later: when a parliament subsisted for great part of a year, or was prorogued at short intervals and for formal sessions, the immunity became personally more valuable. The principle as just stated

[1] Ethelbert, § 1; Select Charters, p. 60.
[2] Canute, § 83; cf. Edw. Conf., § 2; Select Charters, p. 73.
[3] Ll. Edw. Conf. art. 2, cl. 8: this privilege is recognised whether the person in question has been summoned or goes on his own business.

involves two issues: the protection of the member from illegal molestation and the protection of the member from legal arrest. As to the first of these, the special privilege could be asserted only by making the injury done to the individual an injury done to the house of which he is a member, and so visiting the offender with additional punishment. On this point it is not necessary to enlarge; it has been since the reign of Henry IV a matter of law; and that law singularly in concordance with the law of Ethelbert. The Statute of 5 Henry IV, c. 6, lays down the rule in the special case of Richard Chedder, a member's servant, who was beaten and wounded by one John Savage: Savage is to surrender in the King's Bench, and in default to pay double damages besides fine and ransom to the king[1]. By a general enactment, 11 Henry VI, c. 11, the same penalty, which is identical with that of Ethelbert, is inflicted in case of any affray or assault on any member of either house coming to parliament or council by the king's command[2]. Several such cases of violence are reported[3]. The modern importance of this point lies, as a point of privilege, rather in the threat of violence than in the actual infliction.

Members secured from personal molestation.

Chedder's case.

Legislation on the point.

The other point, the protection of the members of parliament and their servants from arrest and distress, from being impleaded in civil suits, from being summoned by subpoena or to serve on juries, and their privilege in regard to commitments by legal tribunals, rests in each particular here enumerated on the supreme necessity of attending to the business of parliament, the king's highest court. The several particulars concern matters of legal detail with which we are not called on to meddle. But some of the leading and most illustrative instances of the prescription are found in medieval records. Some of these have been noticed already in relation to freedom of speech and debate. In 1290 Edward I laid down the rule that it was not becoming for a member of the king's council to be distrained

Protection from legal arrest.

[1] Stat. 5 Hen. IV, c. 6; Statutes, ii. 144; Rot. Parl. iii. 542.
[2] Stat. 11 Hen. VI, c. 11; Statutes, ii. 286; Rot. Parl. iv. 453.
[3] See for instance, Swynerton's case, Rot. Parl. iii. 317; cf. Hatsell, Precedents, i. 16, 26, 73, &c.

Writs of supersedeas. in time of parliament[1]. In 1314 Edward II issued two general writs superseding during the session all writs of taking assizes, juries, and certificates touching any member of either house[2]; and in 1315 he marks the arrest of the prior of Malton on his way from parliament as an act done in contempt of the king, in prejudice of the crown, in damage of the prior and against the king's peace.

Security of members' servants. The immunity was held to extend to the servants of members, and a petition of the commons in 1404 declares that the custom of the realm protects them as well as their masters from arrest and imprisonment, although they pray that such custom may be established by statute. The king's answer is, that there is sufficient remedy in such cases, which seems to amount to a refusal of the petition[3].

Means of enforcing the right. The recognition of the right, however ancient and full the admission may have been, was a very different thing from the power of enforcing it; and the house of commons seems to have had no means of doing this but by petition, or by obtaining a writ of supersedeas. Besides the case of Thorpe, already mentioned, the most prominent cases are those of William Lark in 1429[4], and Walter Clerk, burgess for Chippenham, in 1460[5].

Lark's case. Lark was the servant of William Milrede, member for London, and had been arrested at the suit of Margery Janyns, committed to the Fleet prison by the Court of King's Bench, and there detained for damages. The commons petitioned that in consideration of the privilege of members securing them against arrest except for treason, felony, or breach of peace, Lark might be liberated during the session of parliament; and that the custom claimed for the commons might be established by statute. The king rejected the last petition, but ordered the release of Lark, securing to Margery her rights after the close of the session[6]. In the case of Clerk, who had been arrested for a

[1] See Hatsell, Precedents, i. 3; Coke, 4th Inst. p. 24; Prynne, Reg. iv. 820, &c.

[2] See Rot. Parl. i. 449, 450; Hatsell, Precedents, i. 6, 7.

[3] Rot. Parl. iii. 541; Hatsell, Precedents, i. 13.

[4] Rot. Parl. iv. 357.

[5] Ibid. v. 374.

[6] Hatsell, Precedents, i. 17–22.

fine to the king and damages to two private suitors, and afterwards imprisoned and outlawed, the commons petitioned that the chancellor might order his release by a writ to the warden of the Fleet, saving the rights of the parties after the dissolution. This the king granted[1]. These however are only two out of a large number of like precedents. Another famous case occurred in 1477; that of John Atwyll, member for Exeter, against whom several writs of arrest had been obtained at the instance of a private litigant. The commons petitioned that writs of supersedeas should be issued in each case, saving the rights of the suitor after the close of the session. In this case it is observed that, although the commons claim a right to the suspension of the writ of execution, they do not insist on redress for the impleading of a member during the session as a breach of privilege[2]. The condition of affairs at the end of the reign of Edward IV is thus stated:—'When a member or his servant has been imprisoned, the house of commons have never proceeded to deliver such person out of custody by virtue of their own authority; but, if the member has been in execution, have applied for an act of parliament to enable the chancellor to issue his writ for his release, or if the party was confined only on mesne process, he has been delivered by his writ of privilege to which he was entitled at common law[3].' The privilege was in no case extended to imprisonment for treason, felony, or for security of the peace: it was loosely allowed to the servants in attendance on members, and it was claimed for a period of time preceding and following as well as during the session. The length of this period was variously stated, and has not been legally decided. The general belief or tradition has established the rule of forty days before and after each session.

Case of Walter Clerk.

Atwyll's case.

Statement of the point at the close of the period.

776. The special privileges of peers of the realm were sufficiently numerous, but only those need be noticed here which are connected or contrasted with those of the house of commons. The peers have immunity from arrest, not merely

Privileges of the peers.

[1] Hatsell, Precedents, i. 34–36.
[2] Rot. Parl. vi. 191; Hatsell, Precedents, i. 48–50.
[3] Hatsell, Precedents, i. 53.

Immunities of peerage.

as members of the house, but as barons of the realm; their wives have the same privilege, and, under the statute of 1442, the right to be tried like their husbands by their peers. The duration of the immunity is not limited by the session of parliament, but the person of a peer is 'for ever sacred and inviolable.' Yet this protection is only against the processes of common law, and, notwithstanding the dignity of peerage, instances of imprisonment for political causes and on royal warrants are far more numerous in the case of peers than of members of the house of commons. This then is not a privilege of parliament, and has no relation to any immunity resting on the summons or writ of the king, although, as the peers are hereditary and perpetual counsellors, it has a corresponding validity. The right of killing venison in the royal forests, allowed by the Charter of the Forests, the right of obtaining heavier damages for slander than an ordinary subject[1], and all the rest of the invidious privileges which time has done its best to make obsolete, may be left out of sight. The only other important right of peerage is that of demanding access to the sovereign; a privilege which every peer has, which the ordinary subject has not, and which the member of the house of commons can demand only in the company of his fellow-members with the speaker at their head. There have been times when this right or the suspension of it were important political points: it was by estranging Edward II from the society of his barons that the Despensers brought about his downfall and their own[2]; and Richard II, in the same way, held himself aloof from the men who hated and despised him[3]. This was the right the refusal of which provoked Warwick to fight at S. Alban's and at Northampton[4]. But history in this, as in all the previous instances of privilege, has to dwell on the breach rather than on the observance.

Minute and honorary privileges.

Right of access to the sovereign.

In another chapter we shall have to attempt to trace the social as distinct from the legal and technical working of

[1] 2 Rich. II, c. 5.

[2] See above, vol. ii. p. 347.

[3] See above, vol. ii. p. 473.

[4] See above, pp. 170, 183.

the influences here exemplified in matters of ceremony, form, and privilege; influences which have constantly tended to place the house of commons and its members on a footing of firm and equal solidity with the house of lords, to extinguish invidious and vexatious immunities, and to produce for all political and national purposes something like a self-forgetting and sympathetic harmony of action.

CHAPTER XXI.

SOCIAL AND POLITICAL INFLUENCES AT THE CLOSE OF THE MIDDLE AGES.

777. Plan of the chapter.—778. Variations of the political balance throughout English History.—779. THE KINGS:—popular regard for the Plantagenets.—780. Growth of loyalty.—781. Doctrine of legitimism. 782. Material and legal securities.—783. Extent of the royal estates.—784. Religious duty of obedience.—785. Fealty, homage, and allegiance.—786. Law of Treason.—787. THE CLERGY.—788. Weakness of their spiritual position.—789. Weakness of their temporal position.—790. THE BARONAGE:—their wealth and extent of property.—791. Their territorial distribution.—792. Class distinctions.—793. Livery and maintenance.—794. Heraldic distinctions.—795. Fortified houses and parks.—796. Great households.—797. Service by indenture.—798. Good and evil results of baronial leadership.—799. Baronial position of the bishops. 800. THE KNIGHTS AND SQUIRES.—801. Their relation to the barons.—802. Independent attitude of the knights in parliament.—803. THE YEOMANRY.—804. Expenditure of the squire and tenant farmer.—805. The *valetti* in parliament.—806. The yeomen electors.—807. THE BOROUGHS.—808. The merchant guild and its developments.—809. Constitution of London.—810. Importance and growth of companies.—811. Other municipalities.—812. Politics in the boroughs, and of their representatives.—813. Political capabilities of country and town, merchant, tradesman, and artificer.—814. The life of the burgher.—815. Connexion with the country and with other classes.—816. Artisans and labourers.—817. The poor.—818. The villeins. —819. The chance of rising in the world. Education.—820. Class antagonisms.—821. Concluding reflexions. National character.—822. Transition.—823. Some lessons of history.

Factors of national history.

777. THE great changes which diversify the internal history of a nation are mainly due to the variations in the condition and relations of the several political factors which contribute to that history: their weight, their force and vitality, their mutual

attraction and repulsion, their powers of expansion and contraction. The great ship of the state has its centre of gravity as well as its apparatus for steering and sailing, its machinery of defence, and its lading. And it is upon the working of these factors that every great crisis of national life must ultimately turn. Great men may forestall or delay such critical changes; the greatest men aspire to guide nations through them; sometimes great men seem to be created by or for such conjunctures; and without a careful examination of the lives of such men, history cannot be written. But they do not create the conjunctures: and the history which searches no deeper is manifestly incomplete. In the reading of constitutional history this is a primary condition: we have to deal with principles and institutions first, and with men, great or small, mainly as working the institutions and exemplifying the development of the principles. As institutions and principles, however much they may in the abstract be amenable to critical analysis, can be traced in their operation and development only in the concrete, it is necessary to divide and rule out the design of historical writing by the epochs of reigns of kings and the lives of other great men. A perpetual straining after the abstract idea or law of change, the constant 'accentuation,' as it is called, of principles in historical writing, invariably marks a narrow view of truth, a want of mastery over details, and a bias towards foregone conclusions. In adopting the method which has been used, however imperfectly, in this work, of proceeding historically rather than philosophically, this has been kept in view. We have attempted to look at the national institutions as they grew, and to trace the less permanent and essential influences only so long as they have a bearing on that growth. The necessity of finding one string, by which to give a unity to the course of so varied an inquiry, has involved the further necessity of long narrative chapters and of much unavoidable repetition. The object of the present chapter will be to examine into the condition and relation of the factors which produced the critical changes indicated in the preceding narrative, in those points in which they come less prominently forward, and to take up, as we proceed, some of the most

The causes that produce the changes of national history.

Method of treatment adopted.

Object of the present chapter.

Object of the present chapter. significant aspects of the social history which underlies the political history. The variation of the balance, maintained between the several agencies at work in the national growth, will be regarded as the point of sight in our sketch, but the main object of the chapter will be the examination of the factors themselves; the strength, weight and influence of royalty; the composition, personal and territorial, of the baronage and gentry; their political ideas and education; the growth of the middle class and its relation to those above and below it; and the condition of the lowest class of the nation. It is obvious that only a sketch can be attempted; it is possible that anything more ambitious than a sketch would contain more fallacies than facts.

Various combinations of the national factors in the middle ages. 778. Taking the king and the three estates as the factors of the national problem, it is probably true to say in general terms that, from the Conquest to the Great Charter, the crown, the clergy, and the commons, were banded together against the baronage; the legal and national instincts and interests against the feudal. From the date of Magna Carta to the revolution of 1399, the barons and the commons were banded in resistance to the aggressive policy of the crown, the action of the clergy being greatly perturbed by the attraction and repulsion of the papacy. From the accession of Henry IV to the accession of Henry VII, the baronage, the people, and the royal house, were divided each within itself, and that internal division was working a sort of political suicide which the Tudor reigns arrested, and by arresting it they made possible the restoration of the national balance. In such a very comprehensive summary of the drama, even the great works of Henry II and Edward I appear as secondary influences; although the defensive and constructive policy of the former laid the foundation both of the royal autocracy which his descendants strove to maintain, and of the national organisation which was strong enough to overpower it; and the like constructive and defensive policy of Edward I gave definite form and legal completeness to the national organisation itself. In the struggle of the fifteenth century the clergy, alone of the three estates, seem to retain the unity and cohesion which was proof against the disruptive influences of the dynastic quarrel; but their position, though apparently stronger, had a fatal source of weakness in their alliance with or dependence on a foreign influence; whilst the weakness of the crown and the people was owing to personal and transient causes, which a sovereign with a strong policy, and a people again united, would very soon reduce to insignificance. The crown was a lasting power, even when its wearers were incapable of governing; the nation was a perpetual corporation, in nowise essentially affected by personal or party changes; whereas in the baronage personal and constitutional existence were one and the same thing, and the blow that destroyed the one destroyed the other. Hence during the early days of the Tudor dictatorship, the baronage was powerless; and the clergy and commons, although like the crown they retained corporate vitality, were thrown out of working order by the absence of all political energy in the remains of the other estate. The commons, having lost the leaders who had misled them to their own destruction, threw themselves into other work, and, ceasing to take much interest in politics, grew richer and stronger for the troubled times to come. The clergy, without much temptation to aggression and with little chance of obtaining greater independence, seeing little in Rome to honour and nothing at home to provoke resistance, gradually sank into complete harmony with and dependence on the king. And this constituted the strength of the position of Henry VIII: he had no strong baronage to thwart him; he or his ministers had wisdom enough to understand the interests which were dearest to the commons; the church was obsequious to his friendship, defenceless against his hostility. With the support of his parliaments, which trusted without loving him, and confirmed the acts by which he fettered them, he permanently changed the balance between church and state and between the crown and the estates. He overthrew the monastic system, depriving the church of at least a third of her resources and throwing out of parliament nearly two thirds of the spiritual baronage[1]; he

The Tudor period.

Humiliation of the baronage.

Apathy of the commons.

Dependence of the clergy.

Position of Henry VIII.

[1] The smaller monasteries were dissolved by the Act 27 Hen. VIII, c. 28; after many of the larger houses had surrendered, the rest were

His treatment of the church; broke the union between the English and Roman churches, and declaring himself her head on earth, left the English church[1] altogether dependent on her own weakened resources, and suspended and practically suppressed the legislative powers of convocation[2]. of the nobility; He constructed a new nobility out of the ruins of the old, and from new elements enriched by the spoils of the church: a nobility which had not the high traditions of the medieval baronage, and was by the very condition of its creation set in opposition to the ecclesiastical influences which had hitherto played so great a part. of the parliament; But with the commons Henry did not directly meddle: true he used his parliaments merely to register his sovereign acts; took money from his people as a loan, and wiped away the debt by parliamentary enactment[3]; took for his proclamations the force of laws, and obtained a His dictatorship. 'lex regia' to make him the supreme lawgiver[4]; he arrested and tried and executed those whom he suspected of enmity, demanding and receiving the thanks of the commons for his most arbitrary acts. That by these means he carried the nation over a crisis in which it might have suffered worse evils, is a theory which men will accept or reject according as they are swayed by the feelings which were called into existence by the changes he effected.

Elizabeth carried on the dictatorship which her father had

dissolved by the Act 31 Hen. VIII, c. 13; and the Order of the Hospitallers, by 32 Hen. VIII, c. 24. Colleges, chantries, and free chapels, were given to the king by 1 Edw. VI, c. 14.

[1] This was enacted by 26 Hen. VIII, c. 1: 'That the king our sovereign lord, his heirs and successors kings of this realm, shall be taken accepted and reputed the only supreme head on earth of the Church of England called Anglicana Ecclesia.' The exact terms had been discussed in Convocation as early as 1531, and accepted in a modified form.

[2] By the Act of Submission (25 Hen. VIII, c. 19), and the instrument signed by the clergy, May 15, 1532, it was declared that there should be no legislation in Convocation without the king's licence, and that the existing canon law should be reviewed by a commission of thirty-two persons, half lay and half clerical.

[3] Stat. 21 Hen. VIII, c. 24, and 35 Hen. VIII, c. 12.

[4] Stat. 31 Hen. VIII, c. 8. 'That always the king for the time being with the advice of his honourable council may set forth at all times by the authority of this Act his proclamations . . . and that those same shall be obeyed observed and kept as though they were made by Act of Parliament for the time in them limited unless the king's highness dispense with them or any of them under his great seal.'

won, and which the misgovernment of the intervening reigns had rendered even more necessary than before. In spite of mistakes and under many inevitable drawbacks, she earned her title to the supremacy she wielded, and, so long as she lived, the better side of a strong governmental policy showed itself. She acted as the guide of the nation which she saw strong enough to choose its own course; making herself the exponent of the country's ambition, she ruled the ship of state by steering it; she could not direct the winds or even trim the sails, but she could see and avoid the rocks ahead.

Position of Elizabeth.

James I and his theory of royal power.

The Tudor dictatorship left a sad inheritance to the Stewarts. James I was not content with the possession, without a theory, of supremacy. The power which Henry VIII had wielded he formulated; and challenged the convictions of a people growing more thoughtful as they grew also stronger. His dogmatic theories forced the counteracting theories into premature life: his ecclesiastical policy, the outcome of Elizabeth's, gave a political standing ground to puritanism; and puritanism gave to the political warfare in which the nation was henceforth involved a relentless character that was all its own. He left his throne to a son who had not the power to guide if he had had the chance: whose theory of sovereign right was incompatible with the constitutional theory which, rising as it were from the dead, had found its exposition among the commons. The lords of the new baronage neither loved the clergy nor trusted the people. Divided between the king and liberty, they sank for the time into moral and legal insignificance; and, however singly or personally eminent, ceased for a time to be recognised as an estate of the republic. The clergy, committed to the fatal theory that was destroying the king, had already fallen. The king himself, too conscientious to be politic, scarcely strong enough to be faithfully conscientious; neither trusting nor having cause to trust his people, who neither trusted nor had cause to trust him, fell before the hostility of men for whose safety it was necessary that he should die, and the hatred of fanatics who combined person and office in one comprehensive curse,—a sacrifice to the policy and principles of his enemies, the victim and the martyr to

Charles I unfit to determine the great crisis.

Position of Oliver Cromwell. his own. The place which Cromwell took, when he had wrested the government from the incapable hands that were trying to hold it, was one which he, with his many great gifts and his singular adaptation to the wants of the time, might have filled well, if any man could. But the whole national mechanism was now disjointed, and he did not live long enough to put it together in accordance either with its old conformation or with a new one which he might have devised. So the era of the Commonwealth passed over, a revolution proved to be premature by the force of the reaction which followed it, by the strength of the elements which it suppressed without extinguishing them, and by the fact, which later history proved, that it involved changes far too great to be permanent in an ancient full-grown people.

If the absolutism of the Tudors must in a measure answer for the sins of the Stewarts, and the sins of the Stewarts for the miseries of the Rebellion, the republican government must in like measure be held responsible for the excesses of the Restoration. The Restoration. Both the Rebellion and the Restoration were great educational experiments. The arrogance of puritanism had been almost as fatal to the political unity of the commons, as the doctrine of divine right had been to the king and the church. The Restoration saw the strange alliance of a church, purified by suffering, with the desperate wilfulness of a court that had lost in exile all true principle, all true conception of royalty. Stranger still, the nation acquiesced for many years in the support of a government which seemed to reign without a policy, without a principle and without a parliament. The Revolution. But most strange of all, out of the weakness and foulness and darkness of the time, the nation, church, peers and people, emerge with a strong hold on better things; prepared to set out again on a career which has never, since the Revolution of 1688, been materially impeded. But this is far beyond the goal which we have set ourselves, and would lead on to questions the true bearings of which are even now being for the first time adequately explored, into a history which has yet to be written.

779. Keeping this general outline well in view, but not

guiding our investigation by special regard to it, we may now approach the main subject of the chapter, and come down to details which, however mutually unconnected, have a distinct value, as they help to supply colour and substance to the shadowy impersonations of the great drama.

Strong character of the Plantagenet kings.

Few dynasties in the whole history of the world, not even the Caesars or the Antonines, stand out with more distinct personal character than the Plantagenets. Without having the rough, half Titan, half savage, majesty of the Norman kings, they are, with few exceptions, the strong and splendid central figures of the whole national life. Each has his well-marked individual characteristics. No two are closely alike, each has qualities which, if not great in themselves, are magnified and made important by the strength of the will which gives them expression. There is not a coward amongst them; even the one man of the race who is a careless and incapable king, has the strong will of his race, and a latent capacity for exertion which might have saved him. All of them, or nearly all, lived before the eyes of their subjects; some were oppressively ubiquitous: the later kings from Edward I onwards could speak the language of their people, and all of them doubtless understood it. Whatever there was in any one of them that could attract the love of the people was freely shown to the people: their children were brought up with the sons and daughters of the nobles, were at an early age introduced into public life, endowed with estates and establishments of their own, and allowed, perhaps too freely, to make their own way to the national heart. It can, indeed, scarcely be said that any of the Plantagenet kings after his elevation to the throne enjoyed a perfect popularity. Henry II was never beloved; the Londoners adorned their streets with garlands when Richard came home, but a very slight experience of his personal government must have sufficed them; John hated and was hated of all; Henry III no man cared for; Edward I was honoured rather than loved; Edward II, alone among the race, was despised as well as hated. With Edward III the tide turned; he came to the crown young, and gained sympathy in his early troubles; he took pains to court the

Their doubtful popularity.

Personal popularity of the kings. nation, and in his best years he was a favourite; but, after the war and the plague, he fell into the background, and the nation was tired of him before he died. Richard possessed early, and early forfeited, the people's love; he deserved it perhaps as little as he deserved their later hatred. Henry IV as a subject had been the national champion, and he began to reign with some hold on the people's heart; but the misery of broken health, an uneasy conscience, and many public troubles, threw him early into a gloomy shadowy life of which his people knew little. Henry V was, as he deserved to be, the darling of the nation; Henry VI was too young at his accession to call forth any personal interest, and during his whole reign he failed to acquire any hold on the nation at large; they were tired of him before they came to know him, and when they knew him they knew his unfitness to rule. Edward IV, like Henry IV, came a favourite to the throne, and, without deserving love, retained popularity all his life. Richard III had, as duke of Gloucester, been loved and honoured; he forfeited love, honour and trust, when he supplanted his nephew, and he perished before his ability and patriotism, if he had any, could recover the ground that he had lost.

Growth of a sentiment of loyalty. 780. Notwithstanding this series of failures, we can trace a growing feeling of attachment to the king as king, which may be supposed to form an essential characteristic of the virtue of loyalty. Loyalty is a virtuous habit or sentiment of a very composite character; a habit of strong and faithful attachment to a person, not so much by reason of his personal character as of his official position. There is a love which the good son feels for the most brutal or indifferent father; national loyalty has an analogous feeling for a bad or indifferent king; it is not the same feeling, but somewhat parallel. Such loyalty gives far more than it receives; the root of the good is in the loyal people not in the sovereign, who may or may not deserve it; there is a feeling too of proprietorship: 'he is no great hero but he is our king.' Some historical training must have prepared a nation to conceive such an idea. The name of king cannot have been synonymous with oppression; loyalty itself, in its very name, recals the notion of trust in law, and observance of law; and the race which calls it forth, as well as the nation that feels it, must have been on the whole a law-abiding race and nation. It gathers into itself all that is admirable and loveable in the character of the ruler, and the virtues of the good king unquestionably contribute to strengthen the habit of loyalty to all kings. Once aroused, it is strongly attracted by misfortune; hence kings have often learned the blessings of it too late. Richard II after his death became 'God's true knight' whom the wicked ones slew [1], and Henry VI became a saint in the eyes of the men whom he had signally failed to govern [2]. Yet the growth of loyalty in this period was slow if it was steady. The Plantagenet history can show no such instances of enthusiastic devotion as lighted up the dark days of the Stewarts. Edmund of Kent sacrificed himself for Edward II; and the friends of Richard II perished in a vain attempt to restore him; Margaret of Anjou found a way to rouse in favour of Henry and her son a desperate resistance to the supplanting dynasty; but none of these is an instance of true loyalty unmingled with fear or personal aims. The growth of the doctrine that expresses the real feeling is traceable rather in such utterances as that of the chancellor in 1410, when he quotes from the pseudo-Aristotle the saying, that the true safety of the realm is to have the entire and cordial love of the people, and to guard for them their laws and rights [3].

Its causes.

Slowness of its growth.

Enunciation of the principle.

Thus the growth of loyalty was slow; the feudal feeling intercepted a good deal of it; the medieval church scarcely recognised it as a virtue apart from the more general virtues of fidelity and honour, and, by the ease with which it acquiesced in a change of ruler, exemplified another sort of loyalty of which the king *de facto* claimed a greater share than the king *de jure*. Notwithstanding the sacred character impressed on him by unction at his coronation, notwithstanding oaths taken to him, and perfect legitimacy of title, he is easily set aside when the stronger man comes. Richard II believed in the

How far encouraged by lawyers and clergy.

[1] Political Songs, ii. 267.

[2] See above, p. 131.

[3] See above, p. 239.

virtue of his unction as later kings have believed in the divine right of legitimacy; and, when he surrendered his crown, refused to renounce the indelible characters impressed by the initiatory rite[1].

Doctrine of legitimacy and of the sacredness of hereditary right.

781. If the clergy were disinclined to sacrifice themselves, with archbishop Scrope, for a posthumous sentiment, the lawyers had little scruple in setting up or putting down a legitimate claimant. Yet the idea of legitimacy, the indefeasible right of the lawful heir, was also growing. Edward III in his claim on France; archbishop Sudbury in his declaration that Richard II succeeded by inheritance and not by election[2]; the false pedigree by which the seniority of the house of Lancaster was asserted on behalf of Henry IV[3]; the bold assumption of indefeasible right put forth by duke Richard of York[4]; the outrageous special pleading of Richard III[5]; the formal claim of a just title by inheritance which Henry VII made in his first speech to the commons, not less than the astute policy by which he avoided risking his parliamentary title and acknowledging his debt to his wife[6]—all these testify to the growing belief in a doctrine which was one day to become a part of the creed of loyalty, but was as yet an article of belief rarely heard of save when it was to be set aside.

Personal qualities of the king,

782. Apart from the hold on the people which this growing sentiment gave the king independently of his personal qualifications, rank those individual qualities which, as we have said, the Plantagenet kings, by their public lives, set before the nation: their strength, eloquence, prowess, policy and success. Combined with these were the local influence exercised by the king in his royal or personal demesne, and the legal and moral safeguards sought in the securities of fealty, homage, and allegiance, and in the still more direct operation of the laws of treason.

and his other sources of influence.

[1] See above, p. 13. [2] See above, vol. ii. p. 443.
[3] See above, p. 11. [4] See above, p. 185. [5] See above, p. 224.
[6] 'Subsequenterque idem dominus rex, praefatis communibus ore suo proprio eloquens, ostendendo suum adventum ad jus et coronam Angliae fore tam per justum titulum hereditanciae quam per verum Dei judicium in tribuendo sibi victoriam de suo inimico in campo, &c.'; Rot. Parl. vi. 268: compare the politic silence of the Act of Settlement, Stat. 1 Hen. VII. c. 1.

783. The first of these, the extensive influence exercised by the king as a great landowner, scarcely comes into prominence before the reign of Richard II; for during the preceding reigns the royal demesnes had been so long removed from the immediate influence of the king that they had become, as they became again later, a mere department of official administration. John, who had, before his accession, possessed a large number of detached estates, continued when he became king to draw both revenue and men from them, although by his divorce he lost the hold which he had once had on the great demesnes of the Gloucester earldom. Henry III had given to his eldest son lands in Wales and Cheshire as well as a considerable allowance in money; but Edward I had had no time to cultivate personal popularity in those provinces; and his son, who before his accession had possessed in the principality itself a settled estate of his own, sought in vain, during his troubles, a refuge in Wales. The earldom of Chester, however, which had been settled by Edward I as a provision for the successive heirs apparent, furnished, after it had been for nearly a century in their hands, a population whose loyalty was undoubted. Richard II trusted to the men of Cheshire as his last and most faithful friends; he erected the county into a principality for himself; and the notion of marrying him to 'Perkin's daughter o'Legh,' the daughter of Sir Peter Legh of Lyme[1], was scarcely needed to bring them to his side in his worst days. It was with Cheshire men that he packed and watched the parliament of 1397[2]. Still more did the possession of the Lancaster heritage contribute to the strength of Henry IV. Although the revenue was not so great as might have been imagined, the hereditary support which was given to him, his sons and grandson, was no unimportant element of strength to them. The earldoms of Leicester, Lancaster, Lincoln and Derby, conveyed not merely the demesnes but the local influence which Simon de Montfort, Edmund and Thomas of Lancaster, the Lacys and the Ferrers, had once wielded; and by his marriage with the

Importance of the king as a landowner.

The earldom of Chester.

The duchy of Lancaster.

[1] Chr. Kenilworth, ap. Williams, Chronique de la Trahison, p. 293.
[2] Ann. Ric. p. 208.

The duchy of Lancaster.

co-heiress of Bohun, Henry secured during the whole of his life the supreme influence in the earldoms of Hereford, Essex and Northampton. Part of that influence was lost when Henry V divided the Bohun estates with the countess of Stafford, his cousin[1]; but in the duchy of Lancaster, as it was finally consolidated, he and his son had a faithful and loyal, if somewhat lawless, body of adherents. It was by the Lancashire and Yorkshire men that Beaufort set duke Humfrey at defiance[2]; and by their aid Margaret of Anjou was able to prolong the contest with Edward IV. It was in the halls of Lancashire gentlemen that Henry VI wandered in his helplessness; and in the minster of York that prayers were offered before his image.

A source of strength to the crown.

The estates of the duchy gave the house of Lancaster a hold on almost every shire in England[3]; the palatine jurisdiction of the county of Lancaster, the great honours of Knaresborough, Pomfret, Tickhill, and Pickering in Yorkshire, of Derby, Leicester and Lincoln, the castles and dependencies of Kenilworth, Hertford, Newcastle-under-Lyne, Hinckley, the Peak, and Monmouth, all of them names resonant with ancient fame, were but a portion of the great historical demesne which Edward IV took care to annex, inseparably but distinctly 'amortized,' to the estates of the crown as the personal demesne of the sovereign[4]. The house of Lancaster inherited not only the estates and the principles of the great party of reform, but the personal connexions by marriage and blood with the baronage, of which so much has been said already, and which, if they increased its strength for a time, had the fatal result of dragging down the whole accumulation of family alliances in the fall of the royal house.

784. The elements of strength which the kings both before and after Henry IV derived from the more direct influences of

[1] Rot. Parl. iv. 135 sq.

[2] See above, p. 101.

[3] Some notion of the enormous influence exercised by the house of Lancaster may be derived from an examination of the charters of the duchy, a kalendar of which has been published by the deputy keeper of the Public Records in the 31st and 35th Reports.

[4] See above, p. 245.

personal activity and private wealth were effectual means of bringing home to the subject the better side of the theory of royalty; but they had little connexion with the theory itself. The king who was seen hurrying to and fro at the head of his levies, or who once or twice in the year visited his demesne manors, hunted in his private forests, and brought the mischiefs of purveyance to every man's door, was indeed the king who was God's minister, and wielded the temporal sword for the punishment of evildoers, the king who could do no wrong, against whom no prescription held good, and who never died; but a link was unquestionably wanting to attach the abstract idea to its concrete impersonation. That link was supplied in early times by the clergy, and in later times by the lawyers. The clergy had insisted on the religious duty of obedience, the lawyers elaborated the system of allegiance, fealty, homage, and the penalties of treason. True, the early clergy were supplying the place of lawyers, and the early lawyers were clergymen, but the weapons which they employed were in the first instance drawn from the Scriptures and applied to the conscience; in the latter they were drawn from natural or civil law and applied to the sense of honour and self-preservation. From the time of the Conquest, and still more from that of Henry I, the two lines of influence diverged: the temporal sword came too often into collision with the spiritual—the divine vicegerent at Westminster with the divine vicegerent at Rome; the clergy remembered that there were kings like Saul and Herod, and it was less easy than it had been to determine what things were to be given to Caesar. Hence even the best of the medieval kings were treated by the higher schools of the clergy with some reserve: Edward I was, in spite of his piety and virtue, no ideal king to Peckham or Winchelsey; and, when the unswervingly faithful house of Lancaster came to the throne, they found it fenced about with the statutes of praemunire and provisors which were irreconcileably offensive to the papacy and its supporters. The lawyers had long taken up the burden of a theory which claimed to be equally of divine right; and they had fenced it about with the doctrines of allegiance, and

Theory and reality of kingship.

Religious and legal sanctions.

of treason, with oaths of fealty and acts of homage. This history is not peculiar to England, but it comes into our national institutions somewhat late, and its details are somewhat clearer than they are in the case of the continental nations.

Fealty, homage, and allegiance.

785. The obligations of fealty, homage and allegiance[1], although their result is nearly the same, are founded on three different principles. Fealty is the bond that ties any man to another to whom he undertakes to be faithful; the bond is created by the undertaking and embodied in the oath. Homage is the form that binds the vassal to the lord, whose man he becomes, and of whom he holds the land for which he performs the ceremony on his knees and with his hands in his lord's hands. Allegiance is the duty which each man of the nation owes to the head of the nation, whether the man be a landowner or landless, the vassal of a mesne lord or a lordless man; and allegiance is a legal duty to the king, the state, or the nation, whether it be embodied in an oath or not. But although thus distinct in origin, the three obligations had come in the middle ages to have, as regards the king, one effect. The idea, the development of which has been traced in an early chapter of this work, of making land the sign and sacrament of all relations between ruler and subject, had from the Norman Conquest thoroughly pervaded the law of England. As all land was to be held of the king, all landowners were bound by mediate or immediate homage to him; and as the lord of the land was supreme judge, every man who was amenable to judgment owed fealty and allegiance to the king on that ground; his fealty was not due as an obligation which he had spontaneously incurred, but as the means of certifying his sense of the duty to bear allegiance. And thus, with respect to the king, fealty and allegiance were practically identical; and the act of homage to the king implied and was accompanied by the oath of fealty; the oath recognised that it was the same thing to be 'foial' and 'loial';

Combination of the three in the legal relation between the subject and the king.

[1] On the forms see Madox, Bar. Angl. pp. 270 sq.; Spelman's Glossary, s. vv. Fidelitas, Homagium, Ligantia; Select Charters, pp. 66, 80, 145, &c.; Statutes, i. 226, 227 ('Modus faciendi homagium et fidelitatem'); Digby, Real Property, pp. 62, 63; Bracton, fo. 77 b. 78; lib. ii. c. 35; Glanvill, lib. ix. c. 1; Littleton, Tenures, s. 85–94; Coke upon Littleton, 65 b. sq.

the king's 'fideles' and his 'ligii' were the same, and the closest of all relations with him was expressed by the term 'liege homage.'

Oaths of allegiance.

The oath of allegiance, prescribed to every subject over the age of fourteen[1], was in substance the same as the oath of fealty taken at the time of doing homage, although of course variations of form were admissible[2]; for neither fealty nor homage was confined to the relations subsisting between king and subject, whilst allegiance was due to the king alone; every lord could exact fealty from his servants and homage and fealty from his vassals; if he attempted to get more, he accroached royal power and was amenable to the charge of treason. The words of the oath of allegiance or fealty to the king, taken in the reign of Edward I, ran thus: 'I will be "foial" and "loial" and bear faith and allegiance to the king and his heirs, of life and limb and worldly honour, against all people who may live

[1] 'Voloms nous qe trestouz ceux de xiiii aunz ou plus nous facent serment qe il nous serount feaus et leaus, et qe il ne serount felouns ne a felouns assentauntz'; Britton, lib. i. c. 13; the form is given more fully in c. 31: it is thus translated; 'Hear this, you N. bailiffs, that I, P. from this day forward will be faithful and loyal to our lord E. King of England, and his heirs, and will bear unto them faith and loyalty of life and limb, of body and chattels, and of earthly honour, and will neither know nor hear of their hurt or damage, but I will oppose it to the best of my power, so help me God and the saints.' This is the oath taken on the admission to a tithing or frankpledge. The mention of the 'heirs' has been omitted from the oath since the revolution of 1688; Blackstone, Comm. i. 368.

[2] The oath of fealty taken after homage is given by Britton, lib. iii. c. 4. In case of fealty to the king it is this: 'Hear this ye good people, that I, such a one by name, faith will bear to our lord King Edward from this day forward, of life and limb, of body and chattels and of earthly honour; and the services which belong to him for the fees and tenements which I hold of him, will lawfully perform to him as they become due, to the best of my power, so help me God and the saints.' The oath of fealty to any other liege lord was this: 'Hear you this, my lord John, that I, Peter, from this day forward, will bear you faith of life and limb, saving my faith to the king and his heirs; and the services which belong to you for the fees and tenements I hold of you, lawfully will perform to you, as they become due, to the best of my power, &c.' To any lord not liege, the form was: 'Hear you this, my lord John, that I, Peter, will bear you faith from this day forward, and the services, &c., &c.,' omitting mention of life and limb. See Bracton, ed. Nichols, i. 48, 185; ii. 39, 41. Liege homage is that which is paid by the tenant to the lord 'a quo tenet suum capitale tenementum'; Glanv. ix. 1: the liege lord being 'dominus praecipuus et legitimus quia feoffator primus et propter primum feoffamentum et capitale'; Bracton, fo. 79 b.

and die[1].' Other clauses followed in the case of lords who held lands, and in the case of the private individual the oath of the peace was combined with that of allegiance. The words of homage, which were not sworn, were: 'I become your man, from this day forth, for life, for limb, and for worldly honour, and shall bear you faith for the lands that I hold of you[2].' In liege homage, such as that done by the lords at the coronation, the form is: 'I become your liege man of life and limb and of earthly worship, and faith and troth I shall bear unto you, to live and die, against all manner of folk; so God me help[3].' The kiss of the lord completed the ceremony[4].

The form of homage.

Importance of these obligations.

That these obligations were insufficient to maintain either the peace of the country or the due obedience of the subject, our whole medieval history proves; but that they had a certain and occasionally a strong influence in that direction is proved, once for all, by the history of the parliament of 1460, which, although determined to secure the right of the duke of York to the crown, did not venture to set aside the solemn obligations which its members had undertaken in the repeated oaths sworn to Henry VI. Unhappily in such times the means taken for securing the royal position of the new king sealed the fate of the old king when he had once fallen: no conqueror or victorious faction could afford to be merciful to a person to whom so many honourable men had sworn to be true and loyal. The security which oaths could not give had to be sought by legislation on treason.

Doctrine of treason.

786. The doctrine of treason was the necessary result of the doctrine of oaths and of the duty, moral or religious, of obedience. It appears in germ in Alfred's legislation: 'if a man

[1] Blackstone, Comm. i. 367, 368.

[2] The form given by Britton is this: 'I become your man for the fees and tenements which I hold and ought to hold of you, and will bear you faith of life and limb, of body and chattels, and of every earthly honour against all who can live and die'; lib. iii. c. 4.

[3] See the Coronation Service; and Taylor, Glory of Regality, pp. 204, 205, 353 sq.

[4] 'Then the lord, whoever he may be, whether ourself or another, and whether male or female, clerk or lay, old or young, ought to kiss his tenant, whether he be poor or rich, ugly or handsome, in token of perpetual affiance and obligation of strict friendship'; Britton, lib. iii. c. 4.

plot against the king's life, of himself or by harbouring of exiles or of his men, let him be liable in his life and in all that he has'; and 'he who plots against his lord's life, let him be liable in his life to him and in all that he has[1].' In Glanvill it appears under the Roman name of 'lese-majesty' in the rules for trial of the man who is charged by fame, or by an accuser, touching the king's death, or sedition in the kingdom, or the host[2]. By that time the doctrine of the civil law had leavened the English law, and the sense of betrayal of obligation, which lies at the root of treason, was already lost in the general necessity of securing the king and realm. The general obligation of the subject being recognised, the special plea of treachery, 'proditio,' was a mere rhetorical aggravation of the sin of disobedience.

Early legislation on treason.

The acts that constituted treason, however generally set down in the law books, were not defined by statute until the reign of Edward III. Bracton places in the first class of 'lese-majesty' the case of one who by rash daring has contrived the death of the king, or has done or procured anything to be done to produce sedition against the king or in the army; and the crime involves all who have counselled or consented, even if it has not come to effect[3]. The punishment is to be drawn and to suffer the penalties of felony, death, forfeiture, and corruption of blood. Britton, who more clearly states the idea of 'betrayal' as distinct from that of 'lese-majesty[4],' and includes in treason any mischief done to one to whom the doer represents himself as

Definitions of lese-majesty.

[1] Ll. Alfr. § 4.

[2] 'Crimen quod in legibus dicitur crimen laesae majestatis, ut de nece vel seditione personae domini regis vel regni vel exercitus'; Glanv. lib. i. c. 2; cf. xiv. 1.

[3] Bracton, lib. iii. c. 3: 'Habet enim crimen laesae majestatis sub se multas species, quarum una est ut si quis ausu temerario machinatus sit in mortem domini regis vel aliquid egerit vel agi procuraverit ad seditionem domini regis vel exercitus sui, vel procurantibus auxilium et consilium praebuerit vel consensum, licet id quod in voluntate habuerit non perduxerit ad effectum'; fo. 118 b. 'Continet etiam sub se crimen laesae majestatis crimen falsi, &c.' ibid.; Fleta, lib. i. c. 21. p. 31.

[4] Britton, lib. i. c. 9: 'Tresun est en chescun damage qe hom fet a escient ou procure de fere a cely a qui hom se fet ami . . . graunt tresoun est a compasser nostre mort ou de nous desheriter de noster reaume ou de fauser noster seal, ou de countrefere nostre monee ou de retoundre'; ed. Nichols, i. 40. Compare the general account of treason given in the laws of Henry I. Art. lxxv; Blackstone, Comm. iv. 74–93.

Statute of treasons.

a friend, states the points of high treason to be—to compass the king's death, or to disinherit him of his realm, or to falsify his seal, or to counterfeit or clip his coin. These were among the points established, no doubt under the maxims of the lawyers, by the statute of treasons passed in 1352, which were—the compassing the death of the king, queen, or their eldest son; the violation of the queen or the king's eldest unmarried daughter, or his son's wife; the levying of war against the king in his realm; adhering to the king's enemies, counterfeiting his seal or money, or importing false money, and the slaying of the lord chancellor, treasurer, or judges in the discharge of their duty[1]. New points of possible treason were to be decided by parliament as they arose, and unfortunately this assertion by parliament of its own power was not a dead letter. In 1382, in the alarm which followed the rising of the commons, it was made treason to begin a riot or rumour[2] against the king. In the parliament of 1388 the judges affirmed the illegality of the appeal of treason brought against the king's friends, but the lords decided that, in so high a matter, the question of legality belonged not to the justices but to the lords of parliament, and found the appeal to be good[3]. That great appeal certainly contained many points which could not fairly be treated as treason; but the question decided probably concerned the form only. The power, once asserted, was turned to account by Richard II in his attempt at absolutism; and he prevailed on the parliament of 1397 to declare it to be high treason to attempt the reversal of the acts done in that session[4]. Yet in the very same session the king, by the assent of the lords spiritual and temporal and the commons, defined the four points of treason even more succinctly than they had been defined by the statute of 1352[5]: every one who compasses and purposes the death of the king, or to depose him, or to surrender his liege homage, or who raises the people and rides against the king, to make war in the realm, and is thereupon duly attainted and judged in parlia-

Treasons defined by the act of Edward III.

Additions under Richard II.

Four points defined in 1397.

[1] Stat. 25 Edw. III, st. 5. c. 2; Stat. i. 320; Rot. Parl. ii. 239.

[2] Stat. 5 Rich. II, st. i. c. 6; Stat. ii. 20.

[3] Stat. 21 Rich. II, cc. 3, 4.

[4] Stat. ii. 110.

[5] Rot. Parl. iii. 351; Stat. ii. 98, 99.

ment, is be counted guilty of high treason against the crown. The act of the first year of Henry IV declared appeals of treason in parliament illegal, and repealed the acts of Richard by which new treasons had been created[1]. In the reign of Henry VI the list of treasons was enlarged by the inclusion of some new offences; the man indicted, appealed, or arrested on suspicion of treason, if he escaped from prison, was declared guilty of treason; the burning of houses in execution of a threat to extort money, and the carrying off cattle by the Welsh marauders out of England, were made high treason[2]. These acts however illustrate rather the increasing severity of the law than the doctrine of treason itself, which received little legislative modification during the rest of the period before us. The cruelties and severities of the Wars of the Roses can hardly be held to prove anything as to the accepted doctrine on the point, any more than the attempts made earlier and later to extend the penalties of constructive treasons. Edward IV, greatly to his credit, refused to allow sacrilege to be made high treason[3]. The reign of Henry VIII has, as one point of bad pre-eminence, the multiplication of treasons; and in most of the new treasons the offence against the king's person again becomes the leading idea: the legislation of Mary, however severe on heresy, was more lenient in this respect, and by one act she swept away these monuments of the cruelties perpetrated under her father and brother.

Legislation of Henry IV.

New treasons under Henry VI.

Treason laws of Henry VIII swept away by Mary.

The legislation on treason is not an edifying episode of our history, but it will bear comparison with the practice of other countries which did not possess our safeguards. As an instrument for drawing the people to the king it had little or no result: the severities of the law did not retard the growth of loyalty any more than the legal perfections of the abstract king attracted the affections of the people. The child Richard and the baby Henry might be the object of sincere patriotic attachment to thousands who had never seen them; but the law regarded them as the mainspring of the national

Practical bearing of the legislation on treason.

[1] 1 Hen. IV, cc. 10, 14; Stat. ii. 114, 116.
[2] See Statutes, ii. 226, 242, 318; Rot. Parl. iv. 260, 349; v. 54.
[3] Rot. Parl. v. 632.

The ideal king.

machine. With no more conscious exercise of power than the diadem, or the great seal, or the speaker's mace, they enacted all the laws and issued all the writs on which the welfare and safety of the kingdom hung. In the boy Henry, as his council told him, resided the sum and substance of sovereignty[1]; but the execution of all the powers implied in this was vested in his council. The ideal king could do all things, but without the counsel and consent of the estates he could do nothing. The exaltation of the ideal king was the exaltation of the law that stood behind him, of the strength and majesty of the state which he impersonated. It could be no wonder if now and then a king should mistake the theory for the truth of fact, and, like Richard II, should attempt to put life in the splendid phantom. And when the king arose who had the will and the power, the nation had gone on so long believing in the theory, that they found no weapons to resist the fact, until the factitious theory of the Stewarts raised the ghost of medieval absolutism to be laid then and for ever.

Position of the king at the close of the middle ages.

It is needless to recapitulate here the substance of our former conclusions. The strength of the crown at the close of the middle ages lay in the permanence of the idea of royalty, the wealth of the king, the legal definitions and theory of the supreme power: its position was enhanced by the suicide of the baronage, the personal qualities of the new dynasty, the political weariness of the nation, and the altered position of the kings in the great states of Europe. The place of Henry VII cannot be understood without reference to the events which, in France, Spain and Germany, were consolidating great dynastic monarchies, in the activity of which the nations themselves had little independent participation. But this marks the beginning of the new period, and its historic significance had yet to be divulged.

Influence of the church.

787. Second, but scarcely second, to the influence of the crown was the influence of the church, resulting to a great extent from the same historic causes and strengthened by analogous sanctions. In more ways than one the ecclesiastical

[1] See above, pp. 104, 105.

Territorial influence of the clergy.

power in England was a conserving and uniting element. The possessions of the clergy, the landed estates of the bishops, of the cathedrals, and of the monastic communities, extended into nearly every parish, and the tithes and offerings which maintained the beneficed clergy were a far larger source of revenue than even the lands. The clergy, and the monastic orders especially, had been good farmers; in early days the monks had laboured hard to reclaim the fens; in somewhat later times the Cistercians had clothed the hills and downs with sheep, and thus fostered the growth of the staple commodity of medieval England. The clergy were moreover very mild landlords. Their wealth was greater than the king's; their industrial energy and influence for a long period were unrivalled. To those who knew anything of the political history of the past, the church had great historical claims to honour; her champions had withstood the strongest and most politic kings, and her holiest prelates had stood side by side with the defenders of national liberty. The clergy had a majority of votes in the house of lords, without counting those of such lay lords as were sure to support their spiritual guides. They had also their taxing assembly in the convocation, a machinery which saved them from being directly involved in the petty financial discussions of the parliaments. They furnished the great ministers of state, the chancellors with rare exceptions, and ordinarily the privy seal, who was the chief minister of the council; frequently the treasurer also was a clergyman. Although they may, from their numbers and character, present to modern thought the idea of a class of educated, rather than ordained, ministers, it is certain that they were thoroughly pervaded with class sentiment. Not that they were tempted to assume a position which sectarian jealousy forced upon their successors, for until the close of the fourteenth century their monopoly of spiritual teaching was not imperilled by any serious competition; they had had their struggle with the friars, but the friars had soon become as much a part of the ecclesiastical phalanx as were the endowed clergy themselves. The absence of such rivalry had not had the effect of diminishing the consciousness of corporate unity. However lightly

Their historical claims.

Their constitutional position.

Their personal importance.

Their corporate feeling.

Corporate feeling of the clergy.

the obligations of holy orders lay on the medieval minister of state or official of the chancery, when it came to a question of class privilege or immunity, he knew where and how to take a side with his brethren. Rich, wide-spread, accumulating for centuries a right to national gratitude, working in every class of society, the clergy were strong in corporate feeling and in the possession of complete machinery for public action. To this was added the enormous weight of spiritual influence; if the sense of loyalty to the king was quickened by the arguments of religion, by the obligations of obedience, of fealty, homage, and allegiance, much more strongly and much more directly was the spiritual influence that applied those arguments effective in respect to the church. Nor was the temptation to use this influence to sustain the political and social position of the clergy altogether wanting; for however safe their spiritual pre-eminence might seem, their wealth very early gave occasion for a jealousy which must have proved a strong stimulus to watchfulness. The Lollard attack on the temporalities, which no doubt suggested and prepared the way for the dissolution of the monasteries under Henry VIII, was itself the growth of a long period during which kings and barons had looked askance on the territorial wealth of the religious orders.

Jealousy with which their wealth was viewed.

The national legislation only occasionally clerical.

It would not have been surprising to find that, considering the strength and self-consciousness of the spiritual estate of England, considering the high place and great influence which it had held for so many centuries, the government of the country had become distinctly hierarchical, and that the legislation had shown those marks which are regarded as inseparable signs of clerical domination. There are moreover proofs enough that, when and where there was adequate occasion, the right of the strong will could be asserted even against the right of the strong hand. The legislation against heresy is one great illustration of this; the part taken by archbishops Courtenay and Arundel in the days of Richard II is another; the grasp of political and official power in the hands of cardinals Beaufort and Bourchier is less significant, because in both cases their position was affected by their connexion with the conflicting dynastic parties; and in the last Lancastrian reign the king was a more enthusiastic supporter of church privilege than were his prelates. But on the whole it must be allowed that the ecclesiastical power in parliament was not used for selfish purposes; possibly the clergy regarded themselves as too safe to need the weapons of political priestcraft, possibly they saw that they must not provoke greater jealousy by aiming at more conspicuous power. If we may judge of the class by the character and conduct of the foremost men, they ought to have the full benefit of the admission which their bitterest critics cannot withhold. They worked hard for the good of the nation; they did not forget the good of the church; but they rarely if ever sacrificed the one to the other, whether their guiding line was drawn by confidence or by caution.

Ecclesiastical power not selfishly used.

We have discussed in an earlier chapter the drawbacks which must be taken into account in estimating their real weight in the country; especially the ever-spreading and rankling sore produced by the inquisitorial, mercenary, and generally disreputable character of the courts of spiritual discipline: an evil which had no slight share in making the Reformation inevitable, and which yet outlived the Reformation and did its worst in alienating the people from the church reformed. But neither this nor the jealousy of ecclesiastical wealth, nor disgust at ecclesiastical corruption, nor the dislike and contempt with which men like More viewed the rabble of disreputable and superfluous priests, nor the growth of a desire for purer teaching, would have determined the crisis of the Reformation as it was determined, but for the personal agency of the Tudors, Henry VIII, Mary, and Elizabeth; and the irresistible force of that personal agency proved the weakness of the ecclesiastical position. The clergy had relied too much on Rome, and too much also on the balance of force between the other estates and the crown. 'Rome alone you will have; Rome alone will destroy you,' Ranulf Glanvill had said to the monks of Canterbury[1]; the prophecy was true of the monastic system, and it had a partial application to the whole medieval church system.

Mischief arising from the ecclesiastical courts.

Personal influence of the Tudors in producing ecclesiastical changes.

[1] Gervase, Chron. c. 1544: 'Solam Romam quaeritis; sola Roma destruet vos.'

Injuries done by the church of Rome to the church of England.

788. In the first place the papal policy had taken the innate life and vigour out of the ecclesiastical constitution, and supplied or attempted to supply the place with foreign mechanism: legations, legatine authority, appeals, dispensations, licences; the direct compacts between the crown and the popes to defeat the canonical rights of the clergy in the matters of elections; all the policy which the statutes of praemunire and provisors had been intended to thwart, had fatally impaired the early idea of a self-governing church working in accord with a self-governing nation. The attempt to compel a universal recourse to Rome had destroyed the spiritual independence of the national episcopate; and when the real strength of Rome, her real power to work good and carry into effect her own resolutions, was waning, the more natural and national power of the episcopate was gone beyond recall: it stood before Henry VIII, 'magni nominis umbra'; the monastic system fell at once; the convocations purchased a continued and attenuated existence by an enormous fine: the facilities of doctrinal change and the weakness of the reformed episcopate proved that the religious sanction, which had so long been regarded as the one great stay of the ecclesiastical position, had been tasked far beyond its strength. Nothing in the whole history of the Reformation is so striking, and it is a lesson that ought never to be wasted upon later ages, as the total unconsciousness apparent in even such men as Warham, Tunstall and Fisher, of the helplessness of their spiritual position, the gulf that was opening beneath their feet.

The ecclesiastical position weakened by the connexion.

Weakness of the political position of the clergy.

789. In the second point, that of their political security, the prelates of the sixteenth century were scarcely more upon their guard; although they might have learned to mistrust their political position when they saw the apathy of the commons and the collapse of the baronage. Here they knew that they had no spiritual sanction to fall back upon: their stronghold was that office of mediation which they had so long sustained; the function of mediation ceased when all rivalry had ceased between the forces between which it had acted. When the crown was supreme in wealth, power and policy; when the commons were bent on other work and had lost

their political leaders; when the baronage was lying at the feet of the king, perishing or obsequious; when in other lands absolutism was set up as the model government of a full-grown nationality[1],—the medieval church of England stood before the self-willed dictator, too splendid in wealth, fame and honour, to be allowed to share the dominion that he claimed. It was no longer a mediator, but a competitor for power: the royal self-will itself furnished the occasion for a struggle, and the political claims of the church proved their weakness by the greatness of the fall.

Fall of the church before the king.

Points in the history of the nobility.

790. The historical position and weight of the baronage, the variations of the baronial policy, the changes in the form of qualification, and in the numbers of the persons composing the house of lords, have formed an important part of our last chapter. But some points, such especially as may help to complete our view of the comparative influence exercised by the several powerful elements of society, and their powers of attraction and repulsion as affecting the mass of the nation, may be briefly treated in this place.

Extent of their possessions.

However highly we may be inclined to estimate the extent of royal and ecclesiastical property, it is difficult to overrate the quantity of land which during the middle ages remained in the hands of the great nobles. Encumbered and impoverished, in many instances, it undoubtedly was by the burdens of debt, heavy settlements and the necessities of a splendid expenditure; but these drawbacks only slightly affected the personal influence of the several lords over their tenants and neighbours. Although these estates were unequally distributed, and it would be hazardous to infer from the mere title of earldom or baronage any very definite proportion of property, it may be generally held to be true that there was a wide gap between the poorest of the barons and the wealthiest of the class next below them; and between the earls and the

Difference of rank only partially implies difference of wealth.

[1] 'They blame Lewis XI for bringing the administration royal of France from the lawful and regulate reign to the absolute and tyrannical power and government. He himself was wont to glory and say that he had brought the crown of France *hors de page*, as one would say, out of wardship'; Smith, Commonwealth, bk. i. c. 7.

Pecuniary estimates of the difference in ranks of nobility.

barons, as a rule, there was a very marked difference. The higher ranks in the peerage did not necessarily imply a great superiority in wealth. The history of the fourteenth and fifteenth centuries furnishes many instances in which a pecuniary estimate was set upon the difference of degrees. Thus in 1379, in raising contributions for the maintenance of the garrisons in France, a duke paid a poll tax of £6 13*s*. 4*d*.; an earl £4; barons, bannerets and wealthy knights £2 [1]. In 1454 the fine imposed on a duke or archbishop for non-attendance in parliament was fixed at £100, that of an earl or bishop at 100 marks, and that of a baron or abbot at £40 [2]. The creation money, as we have seen, varied in regular proportion; the duke had an allowance of £40, the marquess £35, the earl £20, and the viscount 20 marks [3]. The substantial endowment secured to the king's sons, and to friends who were suddenly promoted from an inferior rank, affords a better clue to the distinctions made. In 1386 a pension of £1000 per annum was secured to each of the two new dukes of York and Gloucester, until lands of the same annual value could be found for them [4]. In 1322 Sir Andrew Harclay had a similar annuity of 1000 marks on his creation as earl of Carlisle. William Clinton had 1000 marks when he was made earl of Huntingdon in 1336; and there are many other instances [5]. But perhaps the most curious illustration of the point will be found in the document known as the Black Book of Edward IV, in which the arrangements for the households suitable to the several ranks are drawn out

Illustration from the Black Book of Edward IV.

[1] Rot. Parl. iii. 57. [2] Rot. Parl. v. 248.

[3] See above, pp. 434 sq.; proofs will be found in the Acts of Creation given in the Lords' Fifth Report; the duke of Clarence in 1411 has £40, p. 169; cf. pp. 182, 242, 243 sq.; the marquess of Dorset in 1397 has 35 marks, p. 117; in 1443, £35, p. 240; the marquess of Montague in 1473 has £40, p. 378; the earl of Cornwall in 1330 had £20, p. 21; the viscount of Beaumont 20 marks, p. 235, cf. p. 276; Thomas Percy, baron of Egremont, £10, p. 273.

[4] Lords' Fifth Report, pp. 64, 65: see also the case of the duke of Exeter in 1416, ib. p. 182; cf. Madox, Bar. Angl. p. 146.

[5] Lords' Fifth Report, pp. 18, 28. The earl of Stafford has an annuity of 600 marks, p. 146; Guichard d'Angle, earl of Huntingdon, 1000 marks, p. 61; John Holland, earl of Huntingdon, the king's half brother, 2000 marks, p. 83; the earl of Rutland 800 marks, p. 84; Ralph Boteler, baron Sudeley 200 marks, p. 239.

in a tabular form. There the annual outlay of the king on his household is estimated at £13,000, that of a duke at £4000, that of a marquess at £3000, that of an earl at £2000, that of a viscount at £1000, that of a baron at £500, that of a banneret at £200, that of a knight bachelor at £100, that of a squire at £50[1]. In the time of Elizabeth, Sir Thomas Smith estimated the becoming provision for a barony at 1000 pounds or marks a year and the higher grades in proportion[2].

Proportionate expenditure of peers.

These sums however bear very little relation to the real differences in the amount of property and accompanying political interest which existed among the great lords. The duchy of Lancaster grew by the accumulation of royal grants and the marriage of heiresses to an extent rivalling the official demesne of the crown; and the duchy of Norfolk grew in the same way. The fortunes of the Nevilles and Percies were the result of a long series of well-chosen marriages, and were in no way inferior to those of the dukes and marquesses. In the later part of the period the duke of Buckingham rivalled, in the number of his estates and dignities, the honours of John of Gaunt or Henry IV. The kingmaker Warwick was content to remain an earl. The result of the multiplication of dignities was not altogether wholesome; they might not have much meaning as denoting political power or property, but they involved, what in a half barbarous society was almost as precious, certain signs of precedence; and thus they added occasions for personal jealousies and rivalries of which there were too many already. Taken in the aggregate the landed possessions of the baronage were more than a counterpoise to the whole influence of the crown and the other two estates of the realm: fortunately for public liberty their influence was in great measure nullified by personal and family rivalries.

Territorial acquisitions of the great houses.

Result of the multiplication of ranks.

791. It would be an easy task, if we possessed a map of

[1] Published by the Society of Antiquaries among the Ordinances of the Royal Household, pp. 15-35.

[2] Commonwealth, book i. c. 17: 'In England no man is created a baron except he may dispend of yearly revenue one thousand pounds or one thousand marks at the least; viscounts, earls, marquesses, and dukes, more according to the proportion of the degree and honour.'

A medieval map wanted.

feudal or medieval England, to determine the amount of local influence possessed by the great houses, and to see how the line taken in the hereditary and dynastic quarrels was affected and illustrated by their relations to one another. In default of such a guide we must content ourselves with generalities[1]. Of the earls as they were at the beginning of the fifteenth century, the titles in many cases still point to their chief centres of interest. The strength of the Courtenays lay in Devon, that of Arundel in Sussex, that of the earl of Salisbury in Wiltshire and Dorsetshire, that of the earl of Warwick in Warwickshire. But this rule was not without exceptions; the strength of the earl of Oxford was in Essex, and that of the earl of Kent in the lordship of the Wakes in Yorkshire and Lincolnshire. Nor was the local influence of the earls at all confined to their chief seats of power; the Percy was dominant not only in Northumberland, but in Yorkshire, and in Sussex also, where the lord of Petworth was a match for the lord of Arundel. In Essex again the earl of Oxford was strong, but the earldom of the Bohuns was strong also. There was a marked difference between the stronger earldoms like those of the Bohuns, the Clares and the Bigods, on which the dukedoms were founded, and the smaller accumulations of the Veres and Montacutes of Oxford and Salisbury; and no doubt similar influences affected the baronies, although in less conspicuous degrees.

Local influences of the earldoms.

Stronger and weaker earldoms.

Local distribution of the great lordships.

Of all the counties, Yorkshire, as might be expected, contained the greatest number of the great lordships: there, not to mention minor cases, were Richmond the chief seat of the Breton earls; Topcliffe the honour of the Percies, Thirsk of the Mowbrays, Tanfield of the Marmions, Skipton of the Cliffords, Middleham of the Fitz-Hughs and Nevilles, Helmsley of the Roos, Masham and Bolton of the two Scropes, Sheffield of the Furnivals and Talbots, and Wakefield of the duke of York; there too were numerous castles and honours that united to form the great Lancaster duchy. In Lincolnshire were the homes of Cromwell, Willoughby and Wells. Further north Cumberland supplied the

[1] These statements may be verified by Dugdale's Baronage and the 'Inquisitiones post mortem,' published by the Record Commission.

baron of Greystoke, Durham the lords of Lumley and Raby, besides its palatine bishop, to the list of Northern lords. The southern counties were thickly sown with smaller lordships; Sussex was the home of Camoys, Dacre, and la Warr; from Kent came the lord of Cobham, from Gloucester Berkeley, from Cornwall Botreaux and Bonneville, from Somerset Hungerford, Beauchamp, Montacute. Along the Welsh march the greater English earldoms long retained their old fighting grounds; the lords of Lancaster at Monmouth and Kidwelly, the Bohuns at Brecon and Hereford, the Mortimers at Chirk and Wigmore. In the middle of England the baronage was less strong; the crown and the duchy of Lancaster were very powerful: and with the exception of the duchy of Buckingham the other lordships were neither many nor large. On the east the duke of Norfolk, gathering in the Mowbray dignities of Nottingham and the Marshallship, was almost supreme, and before the battle of Bosworth field had acquired the earldom of Surrey. Although both the great earldoms and the more important baronies retained a sort of corporate identity derived from earlier times, almost all the elder historic families had, as we have seen already, become extinct in the male line, before the Percies and Nevilles came into the van of the baronage. The representation of the Clares and Bohuns as well as that of the Lacys, the Ferrers, the Bigods, and many others, had fallen into the royal family. The Mowbrays of Norfolk and the Staffords of Buckingham derived their importance rather from their marriage with heiresses of royal blood than from the elder Mowbrays and Staffords; and this was one of the causes that gave peculiar horrors to the dynastic quarrel. But even this short sketch leads into inquiries that are too remote from constitutional history.

Local distribution of the great lordships.

Early extinction of the greater families.

Besides territorial competition and family rivalries, hereditary politics contributed to the weakening of the baronage as a collective estate. The house of Lancaster with its hereditary principles had its hereditary following. Bohun and Bigod were consistent, for generations, in opposition to the assumptions of the crown; and when John of Gaunt failed to support adequately the character of the house he represented, Henry IV

Hereditary politics.

learned from the Bohuns and Arundels the lessons that led him to the throne. To develop however this side of the subject would be to recapitulate the history of the fifteenth century.

Factitious sources of strength.

792. If we pass thus summarily over the points in which faction and personal rivalry weakened the baronage internally, and turn to those in which class feeling gave them a false strength, and set them apart from the classes next below them, we shall find additional reasons for doubting their substantial influence and for believing that their great period of usefulness was coming to an end But more than one of the points to be noted are common to the nobility and the higher gentry or knightly body; and causes which tended to divide the one from the other, tended, in a similar though less effective way, to sever the interests and sympathies of the gentry from those of the inferior commons. Chief amongst these causes were the customs of livery and maintenance, the keeping of great households and flocks of dependents, the fortification of castles and manor-houses, the great value set on heraldic distinctions, and the like. These matters are not all of the same importance, and have not all the same history. The old feudal spirit which prompted a man to treat his tenants and villeins as part of his stock, and which aspired to lead in war, and to judge and tax, his vassals without reference to their bond of allegiance to the crown, had been crushed before the reign of Edward III; but the passions to which it appealed were not extinguished, and the pursuits of chivalry continued to supply some of the incentives to vanity and ambition which the feudal customs had furnished of old. The baron could not reign as king in his castle, but he could make his castle as strong and splendid as he chose; he could not demand the military services of his vassals for private war, but he could, if he chose to pay for it, support a vast household of men armed and liveried as servants, a retinue of pomp and splendour, but ready for any opportunity of disturbance; he could bring them to the assizes to impress the judges, or to parliament to overawe the king; or he could lay his hands, through them, on disputed lands and farms, and frighten away those

Survival of feudal instincts.

Great retinues of the lords.

who had a better claim. He could constitute himself the champion of all who would accept his championship, maintain their causes in the courts, enable them to resist a hostile judgment, and delay a hazardous issue. On the seemingly trifling pomp and pretence of chivalry, the mischievous fabric of extinct feudalism was threatening gradually to reconstruct itself.

Origin of the usage of livery.

793. Livery was originally the allowance (liberatio) in provisions and clothing which was made for the servants and officers of the great households, whether of baron, prelate, monastery or college [1]. From the rolls of accounts and household books of such families it is possible to form a very exact notion of the economy of the medieval lords. The several departments were organised under regular officers of the buttery, the kitchen, the napery, the chandlery and the like; every inmate had his fixed allowance for every day, and his livery of clothing at fixed times of the year or intervals of years. The same custom was practised in the reception of guests; the king of Scots, when he came to do homage to the king of England, had his allowance of wax and tallow candles, of fine and common bread, measured out like any servant, and the due delivery of all was secured by a formal treaty [2]. The term livery was however gradually restricted to the gift of clothing, the gift of food and provisions being known as allowances or corrodies: the clothing took the character of uniform or badge of service; as it was a proof of power to have a large attendance of servants and dependents, the lords liberally granted their livery to all who wished to wear it, and the wearing of the livery became a sign of clientship or general dependence. It was thus a bond between the great men, who indulged their vanity, and the poorer, who had need of their protection, sometimes by force of arms, but generally in the courts of law: it was a revival, or possibly a survival of the ancient practice, by which

Its practical evils.

[1] The customs of livery and allowances are still maintained in some of the colleges of the Universities, and in many respects these institutions furnish most important illustrations of what in the middle ages was the domestic economy of every large household. At Oriel, for instance, every fellow has his daily allowance whilst in residence, and, every other year, a payment for livery, if he has resided the fixed number of days.

[2] See Hoveden, iii. 245.

every man was bound to have a lord, and every lord had to represent his men or be answerable for them in the courts.

The mischief of maintenance.

The English of the middle ages were an extremely litigious people; it was one of the few qualities which their forefathers had shared with their Norman masters; and it was that side of the national character which was most mischievously developed by the judicial institutions of Henry I and Henry II. Litigation was costly, at least to the poor; and it was far easier for a man who wished to maintain his own right, or to attack his neighbour's, to secure the advocacy of a baron who could and would maintain his cause for him on the understanding that he had the rights of a patron over his client. This practice of maintenance, the usage of the strong man upholding the cause of the weak, was liable to gross perversion; and the maintainers of false causes, whether they were barons or lawyers, became very early the object of severe legislation. Edward I, in the statute of Westminster the First, forbad the sheriffs and other officers of his courts to take any part in quarrels depending in the courts[1]. By a statute of 1327 it is forbidden that any member of the king's household, or any great man of the realm, by himself or by another, by sending letters or otherwise, or any other in the land, great or small, shall take upon him to maintain quarrels or parties in the country to the let and disturbance of the common law[2]; in 1346, in an act which marks by its wording the growth of the practice in the higher classes, prelates, earls, barons, the great and small of the land, are all alike forbidden to take in hand or maintain openly or privately, for gift, promise, amity, favour, doubt or fear, any other quarrels than their own[3]. The long list of statutes in which the evil practice is condemned shows how strong it had become; sheriffs are forbidden to return to parliament the maintainers of false suits[4]; the lawyers and the barons are alike struck at in petition and statute; and the climax is reached when Alice Perrers, the king's mistress, takes her seat in the law courts and urges the

Legislation against maintenance.

[1] Stat. Westm. i. cc. 25, 28, 33; Statutes, i. 33, 35.
[2] 1 Edw. III, st. 2. c. 14; Statutes, i. 256.
[3] 20 Edw. III. cc. 4, 5, 6; Statutes, i. 304. 305.
[4] See above, p. 399.

quarrels of her clients[1]. In the condemnation of maintainers pronounced by the Good Parliament, ladies as well as lords come in for general reprobation[2]. The support given by John of Gaunt and Henry Percy to Wycliffe at St. Paul's was a gross act of maintenance[3].

The abuse of maintenance for the purpose of increasing the estates of the maintainer, by a compact in which the nominal plaintiff shared the profits of victory with his patron, or the patron secured the whole, was one very repulsive aspect of the custom. Another, and that more directly connected with the giving of liveries, was the gathering round the lord's household of a swarm of armed retainers whom the lord could not control, and whom he conceived himself bound to protect. In the former aspect the law regarded maintenance as a description of conspiracy; in the latter as an organisation of robbers and rioters; but the difficulty of restraining the abuse was very great; the lords were themselves the makers of the law, and the source of their local power lay in these very retinues which disgraced them. The livery of a great lord was as effective security to a malefactor as was the benefit of clergy to the criminous clerk. But livery, apart from maintenance of false quarrels, involved a political mischief.

Maintenance and champerty.

Riotous households.

794. Under the auspices of Edward I and Edward III there was a great development of heraldic splendour; heraldry became a handmaid of chivalry, and the marshalling of badges, crests, coat-armour, pennons, helmets, and other devices of distinction, grew into an important branch of knowledge. The roll of knights who attended Edward I at Caerlaverock is one of the most precious archives of heraldic science[4]. The coat-armour of every house was a precious inheritance, which descended, under definite limitations and with distinct differences, to every member of the family: a man's shield proved his gentle or noble birth, illustrated his pedigree, and put him on his honour

Importance of heraldry.

[1] Vol. ii. p. 431. [2] Rot. Parl. ii. 329; iii. 12. [3] Vol. ii. p. 438.

[4] It was published by Sir Harris Nicolas in 1828. Other Rolls are printed in the Parliamentary Writs, i. 410-420; ii. pp. 2, 196-200; Excerpta Historica, pp. 50, 163, 314, &c., and in the ordinary books on heraldry.

not to disgrace the bearings which his noble progenitors had worn. The office of the Earl Marshall of England was empowered to regulate all proceedings and suits of heraldry, and it had a staff of busy officers[1]. The great suit between Scrope and Grosvenor[2], for the right to bear the bend or on the field azure, is one of the *causes celèbres* of the middle ages; it dragged on its course from 1385 to 1390; a vast mass of evidence was brought up on both sides, and the victory of Scrope was one of the first facts that brought before the notice of the baronage the antiquity claimed for the house of Grosvenor. Scarcely less famous was the contest between lord Grey of Ruthyn and Edward Hastings, the heir by half blood of the Hastings barony[3]: Grey of Ruthyn succeeded in gaining the arms; both competitors assumed the title to which neither had a right. Regular visitations were held by the heralds, who kept courts in every county, where the claimants of heraldic honours were bound to appear under the penalty of being declared ignoble. The institution of the Order of the Garter by Edward III marks another step of this history: it was the erection of a new sort of nobility by livery; a body of exalted pretensions in chivalry, whose mark was the collar, mantle, jewel and garter of the Order of S. George. The king had numerous imitators; the heraldic devices of lords and ladies were pressed into the service of chivalry; and 'livery of company' became a fashionable practice. It was no longer a mere mark of service to wear the badge of a lord; the lords wore one another's badges by way of compliment; Richard II greatly offended the earl of Arundel by wearing the collar of his uncle's livery; the livery of John of Gaunt was severely criticised as being scarcely distinguished from that of the king[4]. Worse evils followed: liveries became the badges of the great factions

Court of the Earl Marshall.

Herald's visitations.

Orders of knighthood.

Livery of company.

[1] See Coke, 4th Inst. pp. 123 sq.; Prynne, 4th Inst. pp. 59 sq. The jurisdiction of the Earl Marshall was defined by Stat. 13 Rich. II. c. 2; and the College of Arms was incorporated by Richard III; Coke, 4th Inst. p. 125.

[2] See Prynne, 4th Inst. pp. 62, 63. The whole proceedings in this case were edited by Sir Harris Nicolas in 1832.

[3] Nicolas, Historic Peerage, p. 239; Rot. Parl. iii. 480.

[4] Rot. Parl. iii. 313.

of the court, and the uniform, so to speak, in which the wars of the fifteenth century were fought.

Acts of parliament on the subject of livery.

Livery in these two aspects, in connexion that is with illegal maintenance and with dynastic faction, occupies no insignificant place in the statute book and rolls of parliament. In 1377 the commons petitioned against 'the giving of hats by way of livery for maintenance,' and the justices were directed to inquire into cases of abuse[1]; in 1389 a royal ordinance was founded on the petition that no one should wear the badge of a lord[2], and that no prelate or any layman below the rank of banneret should give such livery of company: dukes, earls, barons, or bannerets might give livery, but only to knights retained for life by indenture, and to domestic servants. A very long list of petitions, and a proportionate number of statutes, all of the same tendency, prove that the evil was ineradicable by mere measures of restriction.

Classes allowed to give livery.

In the parliament of 1399 it was enacted that the king alone might give any livery or sign of company; and the lords only livery of cloth to their servants and counsellors[3]; in 1401 the prince of Wales was allowed the same privilege as the king[4]; in 1411 the right was conceded to guilds and fraternities founded for a good intent[5]; in 1429 further allowances are made, livery of cloth is not forbidden to the lord mayor and sheriffs of London, to the serjeants-at-law, or the universities; in time of war the lords may give liveries of cloth and hats, but such livery may not be assumed without leave[6]; and in 1468 Edward IV confirmed the previous legislation on the point[7].

Abuses of the licence.

Proofs of the abuse are not wanting; in 1403 the Percies had given liveries to the rebels[8]; the permission to give livery of cloth only rendered the offence more difficult of detection, and the penalty on giving such livery beyond the prescribed limits, 'the pain to make fine and ransom at the king's will' was not sufficiently definite

[1] Rot. Parl. iii. 23. [2] Rot. Parl. iii. 265; St. 13 Rich. II, c. 3.
[3] Stat. 1 Hen. IV, c. 7; Statutes, ii. 113.
[4] Stat. 2 Hen. IV, c. 21; Statutes, ii. 129, 130.
[5] Stat. 13 Hen. IV, c. 3; Statutes, ii. 167.
[6] Stat. 8 Hen. VI, c. 4; Statutes, ii. 240, 241.
[7] Stat. 8 Edw. IV, c. 2; Statutes, ii. 426, 428. [8] Rot. Parl. iii. 524.

Mischiefs arising from the custom of giving livery.

to be effective; the statutes of Henry VI and Edward IV direct a more distinct form of process. Viewed as a social rather than a legal point, whether as a link between malefactors and their patrons, a distinctive uniform of great households, a means of blunting the edge of the law, or of perverting the administration of justice in the courts—as an honorary distinction fraught with all the jealousies of petty ambition, as an underhand way of enlisting bodies of unscrupulous retainers, or as an invidious privilege exercised by the lords under the shadow of law or in despite of law,—the custom of livery forms an important element among the disruptive tendencies of the later middle ages. It resuscitated the evils of the old feudal spirit in a form which did not furnish even such security for order as was afforded in the older feudal arrangement by the substantial guarantee found in the tenure of land by the vassal under his lord. Livery and maintenance, apart or together, were signs of faction and oppression, and were two of the great sources of mischief, for the correction of which the jurisdiction of the Star Chamber was erected in the reign of Henry VII[1].

Fortified houses of the great lords.

794. Somewhat akin to the practice of livery of servants was the usage of fortifying the manor houses of the great men: a usage which went a long way towards making every rich man's dwelling-place a castle. The fortification or crenellation of these houses or castles could not be taken in hand without the royal licence: a matter, it must be supposed, of ancient prerogative, as it does not rest upon statute, and must be connected with the more ancient legislation against adulterine castles.

Licences for crenellation.

A great number of the licences to crenellate or embattle dwelling houses are found among the national records from the reign of Henry III onwards[2]; in the majority of cases the licence is granted to a baron or to some prelate or knight nearly approaching baronial rank; a few to the magistrates of towns for town walls. Between 1257 and 1273 Henry III granted twenty such licences; on the rolls of Edward I appear

[1] See Stat. 3 Hen. VII, c. 1; Lambarde, Archeion, pp. 183, 190.

[2] The list of licences from 1257 was printed by Mr. Parker in the first volume of the New Series of the Gentleman's Magazine, 1856, vol. i. pp. 208 sq., and from it the numbers given in the text are taken.

44; on those of Edward III 58; the long reign of Edward III furnished 180 cases, and that of Richard II 52. In a parliamentary petition of 1371 the king was asked to establish by statute that every man throughout England might make fort or fortress, walls and crenelled or embattled towers, at his own free will, and that the burghers of towns might fortify their towns, notwithstanding any statute made to the contrary. The king replied, that the castles and fortresses might stand as they were, and refused to allow the re-fortification of the towns[1]. Any such measure would have been a mark of impolicy, and opposed to the interest of both king and commons. From the accession of Henry IV the number of licences diminishes; only ten are on the rolls of his reign, one on those of Henry V, five on those of Henry VI, and three on those of Edward IV; but it does not seem certain that the diminution resulted from any change in the royal policy. In the proposition for the resumption of gifts, which was urged on Henry IV in 1404, the commons declared that they had no wish to restrain any subject from applying for licence either to fortify his castle or to enclose his park[2]. But however freely this was done, the age of Edward III would seem to have been the period of greatest activity in this respect.

Petition on the subject.

Discussion on fortified houses.

The licence to crenellate occasionally contained the permission to enclose a park, and even to hold a fair. The first of the two points must be interpreted to show that the royal jealousy of forest rights was much less strongly felt than it had been in the early Norman and Plantagenet times, when forest administration was an important constitutional question. Edward I had indeed granted that a writ 'ad quod damnum' should issue out of chancery to any who wished to make a park; the permission, after due inquiry, was to be granted on the payment of a reasonable fine[3]: so that the increase of parks perhaps may have kept pace with the multiplication of fortified houses. It was an important privilege, whether looked at as an extension of forest liberties, or as an encroachment, as it

Enclosure of parks.

[1] Rot. Parl. ii. 307.
[2] Rot. Parl. iii. 548.
[3] Rot. Parl. i. 56; Statutes, i. 131.

Effect of the enclosure of parks. often was, on the waste or common lands of the manors. But land was cheap and plentiful, and little heartburning seems to have been produced by it among the classes that could make their voices heard in parliament. On the class which was likely to produce trespassers and poachers the hand of the law was heavy. Offenders against the game laws. The statute of Westminster the First[1] classed such offenders with those found guilty of open theft and robbery, if they are convicted of having taken any game; the trespasser was liable to three years' imprisonment, to pay damages, and make a fine with the king; and in the parliament of 1390 it was enacted that no one possessing less than forty shillings a year, and no priest or clerk worth less than ten pounds a year, should keep a dog, 'leverer, n'autre chien[2].' This early game-law was primarily intended to stop the meetings of labourers and artificers, and has little permanent importance besides.

Baronial establishments. 796. In their great fortified houses the barons kept an enormous retinue of officers and servants, all arranged in well-distinguished grades, provided with regular allowances of food and clothing, and subjected to strict rules of conduct and account[3]. A powerful earl like the Percy, or a duke like the Stafford, was scarcely less than a king in authority, and much more than a

[1] Statutes, i. 32. See also an ordinance of 1293; ib. p. 111.
[2] Stat. 13 Rich. II, c. 13; Statutes, ii. p. 65.
[3] The following table is an abstract of the estimates given in the Black Book of Edward IV on this point:—

Person.	Income.	Knights.	Clerks.	Squires.	Yeomen.	Secondary clerks.	Grooms.	Stablemen.	Total.
King	£13,000	16	24	160	240	20	16	40	516
Duke	4000	6	..	60	100	..	40	24	230
Marquess	3000	4	..	60	100	..	60	..	224
Earl	2000	..	..	30	60	..	40	..	130
Viscount	1000	..	..	20	40	..	24	..	84
Baron	500	..	..	4	16	..	6	..	26
Banneret	200	..	..	..	3	..	6	..	24
Knight	200	..	..	..	..	..	..	..	16
Squire	50	..	1	..	2	..	2	2	16

The columns do not exactly coincide. The whole number of inmates of the Percy household in the reign of Henry VIII was 166; See Northhumberland Household Book, p. x, and the valuable note of Hume, Hist. Engl., vol. ii. note Z.

king in wealth and splendour within his own house. The economy of a house like Alnwick or Fotheringay was perhaps more like that of a modern college than that of any private house at the present day. Like a king, too, the medieval baron removed from one to another of his castles with a train of servants and baggage, his chaplains and accountants, steward and carvers, servers, cupbearers, clerks, squires, yeomen, grooms and pages, chamberlain, treasurer, and even chancellor. Every state apartment in the house had its staff of ushers and servants. The hall had its array of tables at which the various officers were seated and fed according to their degree. The accounts were kept on great rolls, regularly made up and audited at the quarter days, when wages were paid and stock taken. The management of the parks, the accounts of the estates, the holding of the manorial courts were further departments of administration: every baron on his own property practised the method and enforced the discipline which he knew and shared in the king's court; he was a man of business at home, and qualified in no small degree for the conduct of the business of the realm. And this is a point that enables us to understand how it was possible that men like the earl of Arundel of Henry V's time, or lord Cromwell of Henry VI's, could be called to the office of treasurer at a moment's notice: they had been brought up and lived in houses the administration of which was, on a somewhat reduced scale indeed, but still on the same model, the counterpart of the economy of the kingdom itself[1].

Great trains of servants.

Household economy.

797. When the baron went to war, he collected his own contingent for the royal army, frequently at his own cost, but always with the expectation of being paid by the king. And this is one of the points in which the later medieval practice is most curiously distinguished from the earlier. The old feudal institutions, which, for the purposes of war, long retained a vitality which in other respects they had lost, were

The baron's military service.

[1] Several volumes of Household books have been printed; Bishop Swinfield's, by the Camden Society in 1854 and 1855; the Northumberland Household Book, by Bishop Percy and Sir H. Nicolas; those of the duke of Norfolk by the Roxburghe Club, in 1844; and that of the duke of Buckingham by the Abbotsford Club.

Service by indenture.

now replaced by a combination of chivalric sympathy with mercantile precision. This reflects very distinctly the two sides of the policy of Edward III, who must have introduced the practice when he found that for foreign service the feudal organisation of the army was absolutely useless, and had to attempt to utilise on the one hand the chivalry and on the other the business-like astuteness of his subjects. Armies were no longer raised for the recovery of the king's inheritance by writs of summons, but by indenture of agreement. The great lords, dukes, earls and barons, bound themselves by indenture, like the apprentices of a trade, to serve the king for a fixed time, and with fixed force, for fixed wages[1]. Beyond their wages the great men reckoned on the ransom of their prisoners, the poorer on the plunder of the battle-field or the foraging raid. As the lords bound themselves by indenture to the king to serve in the field or to act as constables of castles or governors of conquered provinces, so the lower ranks of knights and squires bound themselves to the baronial leaders, took their pay and wore their livery. When John of Gaunt went to Castille he took with him by indenture some of the noblest knights of England. John Neville, the lord of Raby, bound himself to serve him for life at wages of 500 marks a year[2]. When duke Richard of York or Edmund of Somerset governed Normandy, the terms of their appointment, service and remuneration, were set out in a like indenture of service. This document sometimes determined also the lord's share in the winnings of his retainers[3].

Money speculation in war.

[1] For example, in 1380 Thomas of Woodstock agreed to serve the king in Brittany, by indenture; Rot. Parl. iii. 94; in 1381 the names of all who had agreed to serve the king in his wars, with indentures and without indentures, were to be enrolled; ib. p. 118. The haggling about indentures of service during the minority of Henry VI is one of the most curious points brought out in Ordinances of the Privy Council.

[2] Calendar of the Patent Rolls, p. 186; a long list of knights who had entered into the same engagement was used by Sir H. Nicolas on editing the Scrope and Grosvenor Roll.

[3] See for example the indenture by which John de Thorpe Esquire binds himself for life to serve Ralph Neville, earl of Westmoreland, in peace and war; Madox, Formulare, p. 97; an indenture between the earl of Salisbury and his own sons, touching the lieutenancy of Carlisle, ib. p. 102; and an indenture between the earl of Warwick and Robert Warcop, p. 104.

When accordingly, in the troubled times of Richard II and Henry VI, the necessities of private defence compelled the great households to revive the practices of private war, the service by indenture and the wearing of livery were familiar methods of enlistment; and the barons, besides their hosts of menial servants, had trains of armed and disciplined followers. If to these we add the council of the duke or earl, the personal or official advisers who attended him when he had anything like public business to manage, the lawyers who held his courts, the clerks who kept his accounts, and the chaplains who sang and celebrated the sacraments in his chapels, we shall see that, with all its drawbacks and disadvantages, its dangerous privileges and odious immunities, the position of a powerful baron was one which enabled him to draw classes of society together in a way which must be regarded as beneficial for the time. His house was a school for the sons of neighbouring knights and squires, a school of knightly accomplishment and of all the culture of the age. By the strictest bonds of friendship and interest he could gather his neighbours about him. His bountiful kitchen and magnificent wardrobe establishment linked him to the tradesmen and agriculturists of the towns and villages round him. His progresses from castle to castle, and his visits to the court, taught his servants to know the country and spread public intelligence, whilst it made men of distant counties acquainted with one another. It was thus doubtless that men like Warwick maintained their hold on the country; thus duke Richard of Gloucester was able to cultivate popularity in the north; and thus in some degree the barons were qualified to act, as they acted so long, the part of guides and champions of the commons. For good or for evil, it linked together the classes which possessed political weight. The Speaker of the house of commons was not unfrequently a bound officer of some great lord whose influence guided or divided the peers. In 1376 Peter de la Mare was steward of the earl of March[1], Thomas Hungerford was steward of the duke of Lancaster[2]; they were the Speakers in two strongly-contrasted parliaments. Such was the

The great retinues of the nobles served in some measure to draw classes together.

[1] See vol. ii. p. 430. [2] Vol. ii. p. 437.

relation of Sir William Oldhall to duke Richard of York in 1450; he had been his chamberlain in Normandy, and was still one of his council[1].

Questionable benefit of baronial leadership.

798. It is obvious that such a state of things can be beneficial only in certain stages of political growth; and that it has a tendency to retain dangerous strength long after the period of its beneficial operation is over. Whilst the liberties of England were in danger from the crown, whilst the barons were full of patriotic spirit, more cultivated and enlightened than the men around them, whilst they were qualified for the post of leaders, and conscious of the dignity and responsibility of leading, this linking of class to class around them was productive of good. When the pride of wealth and pomp took the place of political aspirations, personal indulgence, domestic tyranny, obsequious servility followed as unmitigated and deeply-rooted evils. Of both results the later middle ages furnish examples enough; and yet to the very close the manly and ennobling sense of great responsibilities lights up the history of the baronage. They were not the creatures of a court; they were not the effete and luxurious satellites of kings like those who ruled on the other side of the Channel. They were ambitious, covetous, unrelenting, with little conscience and less sympathy; but they were men who recognised their position as shepherds of the people. And they were recognised by the people as their leaders, although the virtue of the recognition was dimmed by servile and mercenary feelings on the one side, and by supercilious contempt on the other. When the hour of their strength was over, the evil leaven of these feelings remained, and, under the new nobility of the Tudor age, became more repulsive than it had been before. The obsequious flattery of wealth, however acquired, and of rank, however won and worn, is a stain on the glories of the Elizabethan age as of later times, and does not become extinct even when it provokes an equally irrational reaction.

Real greatness of the medieval baronage.

799. Much that has been said of the great temporal barons may be held to apply also to the great prelates in their baronial

[1] See above, p. 158.

capacity. The two archbishops maintained households on the same scale as dukes, and the bishops, so far as influence and expenditure were concerned, maintained the state of earls. They had their embattled houses, their wide enclosed parks, and unenclosed chaces; they kept their court with just the same array of officers, servants, counsellors and chaplains; they made their progresses with armed retinues and trains of baggage[1], and took their audits of accounts with equal rigidity. In one point, that of military service, they exercised less direct authority; but in other respects they possessed more. Besides their religious vantage ground, they had a stronger hold on inherited loyalty, and possessed longer and higher personal experience. The ecclesiastical estates remained far more permanently in the hands of the prelates than the lay estates in those of the lords. Many of the bishops possessed manors which had been church lands from the time of the heptarchy; few of the lay lords could boast of ancestry that took them back to the Norman Conquest, without many changes of rank and tenure. And in personal experience few of the barons could compete with the prelates. The life of a lay lord in the middle ages was, with rare exceptions, short and laborious: the life of a great prelate, laborious as it was, was not liable to be shortened by so many risks. Kings seldom lived to be old men; Henry I and Edward I reached the age of sixty-seven; and Elizabeth died in her seventieth year: until George II no king of England lived over seventy. Simon de Montfort, 'Sir Simon the old man,' may have been over sixty when he died; the elder Hugh le Despenser was counted wondrously old, a nonagenarian at sixty-four; the king-maker died a little over fifty. But forty years of rule was not a rare case among the prelates: William of Wykeham, Henry Beaufort, and William Waynflete, all bishops, chancellors, and great politicians, filled the see of Winchester for a hundred and seventeen years in succession; Beaufort was forty-nine years a bishop;

Episcopal households.

Influence of territorial loyalty.

Personal experience.

Long life.

[1] Machin writes of the great bishop Tunstall, when he came up to London to be deprived and to die in 1559: 'The 20th day of July the good old bishop of Durham came riding to London with threescore horse'; Diary, p. 204.

Hard work. Arundel thirty-nine; Bourchier fifty-one; Kemp thirty-four; and all were men of some experience before they became bishops. Like most medieval workers they all died in harness, transacting business, hearing suits, and signing public documents until the day of their death. Both the early industry of the barons, and the long-protracted labours of the prelates, convey the lesson that life was not easy in the middle ages, except perhaps in the monasteries, where the ascetic practices and manual labour of early days no longer counteracted the enervating influences of stay-at-home lives. They teach us, too, how strange a self-indulgent idle king must have seemed in the eyes of men who were always busy, and how a king who shunned public work must have repelled men who lived and died before the world, whose very houses were courts and camps.

The body of knights and squires. 800. The knights and squires of England, on a smaller scale, and with less positive independence, played the same part as the great lords; their household economy was proportionately elaborate; their share in public work, according to their condition, as severe and engrossing. There was much, moreover, in their position and associations that tended to ally them politically with the lords. They had their pride of ancient blood and long-descended unblemished coat armour; they had had, perhaps, as a rule, longer hereditary tenure of their lands than those higher barons who had played a more hazardous game and won larger stakes. What attendance at court, the chances of royal favour, high office, the prizes of war, were to the great lord, the dignity of sheriff, justice, knight of the shire, commissioner of array, were to the country gentleman. He was in some points equal to the nobleman; in blood, knightly accomplishment, and educational culture, there was little difference, and need be none; the gentleman was brought up in the house of the nobleman, but with no degrading sense of inferiority, and with a thorough acquaintance with his character and ways. He might have constituted, and perhaps in many instances did constitute, an invaluable link of union betwixt the baron and the yeoman.

In this class of gentry, including in that wide term all who possessed a gentle extraction, the 'generosi,' 'men of family, of worship, and coat armour,' are comprised both the knight, whether banneret or bachelor, and the squire. The attempts of the successive kings to enforce upon all who held land to the value of a knight's fee the obligation of becoming belted knights seem to have signally failed; the fines and licences by which men of knightly estate were allowed to dispense with the ceremony of the accolade were more profitable to the crown than any services which could be exacted from an unwilling class; and few became knights who were not desirous of following the profession of arms. Hence the difficulty of enforcing the election of belted knights as representatives of the shires[1]. It is not easy to account for this prevalent dislike to undertake the degree of chivalry, unless it arose from a desire to avoid the burden of some public duties that belonged to the knights. Exemption from the work of juries and assizes was coveted under Henry III[2]; the reluctance to take up knighthood was increased by the somewhat exorbitant demands for military service which were made by Edward I and Edward II for the Scottish wars: all who possessed the knightly estate were summoned for such service, and, even if they served for wages, their wages we may suspect were not very regularly paid. The fines and licences were in use before the Scottish wars began, but the diminution in the knightly rank, which embarrassed county business even in the reign of Henry III, had increased very largely under Edward III. After the middle of the fourteenth century, and the development of courtly chivalry, the rank of knight recovered much of its earlier character and became again a military rank. But the class of squires had then for all practical purposes attained equality with that of knights, and all the functions which had once belonged exclusively to the

Reluctance of the smaller landowners to become knights.

Revival of the military spirit of knighthood.

[1] See above, p. 400.

[2] This was the ground of the complaint made by the barons against Henry III in the parliament of 1258: 'Quod dominus rex large facit militibus de regno suo acquietantiam ne in assisis ponantur, juramentis vel recognitionibus'; Ann. Burton, p. 443; Select Charters, p. 378. Of course it was easier and cheaper to avoid taking knighthood than to purchase such an immunity.

Increase of the class of squires.

knights were discharged by the squires. A large and constantly increasing proportion of knights of the shire were 'armigeri,' and the Speaker as often as not was of the same order. There were, notwithstanding this, many families in which the head was always a knight, and in which the title signified rank as well as the profession of arms. Such, for instance, were the families sprung from the old minor barons, who had under Edward I been summoned by special writ to military service but not to parliament, and in which the assumption of the knightly title was really the continued claim to rank with the magnates of the county: the great legal families also maintained the same usage[1].

Different origin of the classes of knights and squires.

So wide a class contained, of course, families that had reached their permanent position by different roads. Some were the representatives of old land-owning families, probably of pure English origin, which had never been dispossessed, which owned but one manor, and restricted themselves to local work. Others had risen, by the protection of the barons or by fortunate marriages, from this class, or from the service of the great lords or of the king himself, and, without being very wealthy, possessed estates in more than one county, and went occasionally to court. A third class would consist of those who have just been mentioned as being of semi-baronial rank. The two latter classes in all cases, and the first in later times, would have heraldic honours. From the second came generally the men who undertook the offices of sheriff and justice. All three occasionally contributed to the parliament knights of the shire: the humbler lords of manors being forced to serve when the office was more burdensome than honourable, the second class being put forward when political quarrels were increasing the importance of the office, and the highest class undertaking the work only when political considerations became supreme.

An examination of the lists of sheriffs and knights leads to this general conclusion, although there are of course exceptions. The

[1] The absence of the knightly title is marked especially in the case of Thomas Chaucer, who although closely connected with the baronage, and even with the royal house, and a very rich man, continued to be an esquire.

earlier parliaments of Edward I are largely composed of the highest class of knights, but that soon ceases to be the rule; and from the beginning of the fourteenth century they are filled with men of pure English names, small local proprietors, whose pedigrees have more charm for the antiquary than for the historian [1]. Towards the middle of the fourteenth century come in the better-known names of families which have risen on the support of the dynastic factions; quite at the close of the middle ages are found the men of the baronage [2]. A single example will suffice: In Yorkshire the first stage is marked by the election of a Balliol and a Percy, Fitz-Randolf, S. Quentin, Hotham, Ughtred and Boynton; the second by names like Barton, Thornton, Clotherholm, Bolton, Malton, with a sprinkling of Nevilles and Fairfaxes; the third, beginning half-way in the reign of Edward III, includes Scrope, Pigot, Neville, Hastings, Savile, Bigod, Grey and Strangways. In Yorkshire the knightly element continued strong enough to hold the representation until modern times; the Saviles, Fairfaxes, Constables and Wentworths succeeded one another generation after generation, and before the sixteenth century closed these families had won a place of equality with the titular nobility.

Illustrations from the lists of knights of the shire.

The same conclusion may be drawn from the lists of sheriffs; and, in fact, from the time at which the annual appointment of new sheriffs was forced upon the crown, the two lists are of very much the same complexion. The Act of Henry VI, in 1446, requiring the election of 'notable squires, gentlemen of birth, competent to become knights,' attests the high importance which the ruling class was setting on the county representation; but as a matter of fact it did not change the character of the elected knights. It

From the lists of sheriffs.

[1] I must give a general reference for these particulars to Prynne's Writs, Reg. ii, iii, and iv. It is one of the marvels of our constitutional indifferentism that the ancient returns have never been collected and properly edited. The lists of sheriffs are still to be found only in the several county histories, or in Fuller's Worthies. For a few counties complete lists of members were printed by Browne Willis, who also published full lists from the reign of Henry VIII to that of Charles II. But his collections for the earlier parliaments are mostly in MS. still.

[2] The first recorded precedent for the heir apparent of a peerage sitting in the house of commons, is that of Sir Francis Russell, son of the earl of Bedford, in 1549; Hatsell, Precedents, ii. 18.

Rise of the knightly class to nobility.

is in the second class of the gentry that we find the more notable cases of a rise to nobility through long political labours: a Bourchier is chancellor to Edward III; his descendant becomes a viscount under Henry VI, partly by prowess, mainly by a lucky marriage: a Hungerford is speaker in 1377; his house becomes ennobled in 1426; but the promotion to the rank of baronage is very slow; and most of the families which have furnished sheriffs and county members in the middle ages have to wait for baronies and earldoms until the reigns of the Tudors and Stewarts, to whom they furnish the best and soundest part of the new nobility.

Household of a country gentleman.

801. The household of the country gentleman was modelled on that of his great neighbour; the number of servants and dependents would seem out of proportion to modern wants; but the servants were in very many cases poor relations; the wages were small, food cheap and good; and the aspiring cadet of an old gentle family might by education and accomplishment rise into the service of a baron who could take him to court and make his fortune[1]. In the cultivation of his own estate the lord of the single manor found employment and amusement; his work in the county court, in the musters and arrays, recurred at fixed times and year by year; he prayed and was buried in his parish church; he went up once in his life perhaps to London to look after the legal business which seems to have

[1] The estimate of the outlay of the knight and squire, in the Black Book of Edward IV, shows how largely both were expected to live on home-grown produce. In the knight's house are drunk twelve gallons of beer a day, and a pipe of wine in the year; fourteen oxen are allowed for beef, sixty sheep for mutton, and sixteen pigs for bacon: these are bought. Out of the home stock are required twenty pigs, thirteen calves, sixty piglings, and twenty lambs, besides twelve head of deer, taken by my lord's dogs, which cost more than they bring in. Geese, swans, capons, pullets, herons, partridges, peacocks, cranes, and smaller fowls, either kept at home or taken in hawking, and a hundred rabbits, are required; Ordinances of the Household, p. 34. The squire's household is more thrifty: for every day are required eighteen loaves of household bread, eight gallons of mean ale, cyder without price; fivepence a day is allowed for beef, twopence for mutton, sixpence for an immense variety of things produced at home; bacon, veal, venison, lamb, poultry, eggs, milk, cheese, vegetables, wood, coal, candles, salt, and oatmeal. In all twentypence a day. Fish-days must have come very often, by 'help of rivers and ponds, &c.; Item to make verjuice themselves, &c.'; p. 46. See more particulars below, p. 554.

been a requisite of life for great and small. His neighbour, somewhat richer, had a larger household, a chaplain, and a steward to keep his courts; he himself acted as sheriff or knight of the shire, and was often a belted knight; if he were fortunate in the field he might be a banneret; he built himself a chapel to his manor-house or founded a chantry in his parish church: he looked out for a great marriage for his sons, and portioned off his daughters into nunneries; he mingled somewhat of the adventurer with the country magnate, and, although he did not crenellate his houses or enclose large parks, he lived on terms of modest equality with those who did; he could act as steward to the neighbouring earl, whose politics he supported, and by whose help he meant to rise. Above him, yet still in rank below the peerage, was the great country lord who, in all but attendance in parliament, was a baron; the lord of many manors and castles, the courtier, and the warrior. There was no insuperable barrier between these grades; and many influences that might lead them to combine.

Life of the richer gentleman.

The greater knights.

The political attitude of the knights of the shire.

802. It may be asked to what cause we are to attribute the attitude of opposition in which, during the more bitter political contests, we find the knights of the shire in parliament standing with respect to the lords, the church and the crown, if the gradations of class were so slight and the links of interest so strong. The reply to the question must be worked out of the history through which we have made our way[1]. It is too much to say that the knights as a body stood in opposition or hostility to the crown, church and lords; it is true to say that, when there was such opposition in the country or in the parliament, it found its support and expression chiefly in this body. It must be remembered that the baronage was never a united phalanx. Throughout the really important history of the fourteenth and fifteenth centuries it was divided from head to foot by the hereditary political divisions in which the house of Lan-

[1] The first trace of this is seen in the Good Parliament of 1376: 'Magna controversia inter dominos et communes'; Mon. Evesham, p. 44. The same writer in 1400 represents the 'plebeii' clamouring for the execution of the degraded lords, but resisted by the king; p. 165.

Attitude of the commons liable to change from year to year.

caster was set against the crown, or the dynastic opposition against the Lancastrian king. When the nation was with the constitutional baronage against the court, the knights of the shire were strong in supporting, and were supported by, the constitutional baronage: but the court was strong too, and a little dealing with the sheriffs could change the colour of the parliament from year to year. The independent knights were a majority in the parliament of 1376; they were reduced to a dozen in that of 1377. There were subservient as well as independent parliaments; the subservient parliaments make little figure in history, but their members were drawn from the same class, perhaps the same families, as the independent parliaments. County politics, as we know so well from the Paston Letters, were not less troubled and not less equally balanced than were the national factions; and many of the local rivalries that originated in the fourteenth century waxed stronger as they grew older, until the competitors were matched against one another in the great war of the Rebellion. It is true then that what was done in parliament for the vindication of national liberties was mainly the work of the knights, but it is not true that their policy was an independent or class policy, or that their influence was always on the right side.

Illustration from the history of the Wycliffites.

In one remarkable struggle, that of the Wycliffite party for the humiliation of the clergy, this conclusion should be carefully weighed. There was no point in which the proposals of a distinct policy were more pertinaciously put forward than that of the confiscation of the temporalities of the clergy: so at least we are told by the historians, and the same may be gathered from the controversial theology of the time. It cannot be doubted that session after session the project was broached; yet it never once reached the stage at which it would become the subject matter of a common petition of the house; that is, it never once passed the house of commons or was carried up to the lords. It is easy to judge how it would have fared in the upper house, where the lords spiritual formed a numerical majority; but it never was presented to them. Nor ought it to be argued that, because it never appears on the Rolls of Parliament, it was excluded by ecclesiastical trickery: a house of commons such as that of which Arnold Savage was the spokesman, a body of justices of whom Gascoigne was the chief, could not have endured dishonest ecclesiastical manipulation of their records; such interference on the king's part was one of the points which contributed to the fall of Richard II. Arundel might persuade the king to decline a speaker like Cheyne, but he could not have falsified or mutilated a record of the house of commons. The conclusion is simply that the Wycliffite knights were a pertinacious minority, never really strong enough to carry their measure through its first stages.

The influence of the clergy not to be overrated.

803. Next after the gentry, in respect of that political weight which depends on the ownership of land, was ranked the great body of freeholders, the yeomanry of the middle ages, a body which, in antiquity of possession and purity of extraction, was probably superior to the classes that looked down upon it as ignoble. It was from the younger brothers of the yeoman families that the households of the great lords were recruited: they furnished men at arms, archers and hobelers, to the royal force at home and abroad, and, settling down as tradesmen in the cities, formed one of the links that bound the urban to the rural population.

Importance of the yeoman class.

As we descend in the scale of social rank the differences between medieval and modern life rapidly diminish; the habits of a modern nobleman differ from those of his fifteenth century ancestor far more widely than those of the peasantry of to-day from those of the middle ages, even when the increase of comfort and culture has been fairly equal throughout. But to counterbalance this tendency to permanence in the lower ranks of society, comes in the ever-varying influence arising from the changes of ownership; the classes of nobility, gentry and yeomanry, having their common factor in the possession of land, expand and contract their limits from age to age. When personal extravagance is the rule at court, the noble class, and the gentry in its wake, gradually lose their hold on the land; great estates are broken up; the rich merchant takes the place of the old noble, the city tradesman buys the manor of the impoverished squire; and in the next generation the merchant

Permanent usages in the lower ranks of life.

Change in the balance of land-owning classes.

Transmutation of classes.

has become a squire, the tradesman has become a freeholder; both, by acquiring land, have returned to strengthen the class from which they sprang. On the other hand, when the greed for territorial acquisition is strong in the higher class, the yeoman has little chance against his lordly neighbour: if he is not overwhelmed with legal procedure, ordered to show title for lands which his fathers have owned before title deeds were invented, driven or enticed into debt, or simply uprooted with the strong hand, he is always liable to be bought out by the baron who takes advantage of his simplicity and offers him ready money. So in many cases the freeholder sinks into the tenant farmer, and the new nobles make up their great estates.

Check arising from the restraints on the alienation of land.

This rule of expansion and contraction was in the middle ages somewhat restricted in its operation by the difficulty of alienating land: but the ingenuity of lawyers seldom failed to overcome that difficulty when might or money was concerned in the overruling of it. As the freeholding class possessed in itself greater elements of permanence than either the nobility or the gentry, was less dependent on personal accomplishments, and less liable to be affected by the storms of political life, the balance of strength turned in the long run in favour of the yeomanry.

Freeholders recognised as the electoral body in the counties.

There are traces amply sufficient to prove their importance from the reign of Henry II onwards, but the recognition of their political right grows more distinct as the middle ages advance; and the election act of 1430, whatever its other characteristics may have been, establishes the point that the freeholders possessing land to the annual value of forty shillings were the true constituents of the 'communitas comitatus,' the men who elected the knights of the shire. They were the men who served on juries, who chose the coroner and the verderer, who attended the markets and the three-weeks court of the sheriff, who constituted the manorial courts, and who assembled, with the arms for which they were responsible, in the muster of the forces of the shire.

After the economical changes which marked the early years of the fifteenth century, the yeoman class was strengthened by the addition of the body of tenant farmers, whose interests

Growth of the class of tenant farmers.

were very much the same as those of the smaller freeholders, and who shared with them the common name of yeoman. These tenant farmers, succeeding to the work of the local bailiffs who had farmed the land of the lords and of the monasteries in the interest of their masters, were of course less absolutely dependent on the will of the landlord than their predecessors had been on the will of the master: they had their own capital, such as it was, and, when the rent was paid, were accountable to no one. They were also free from many of the burdens in the shape of legal obligation to which the freeholder was liable, and, whatever may have been their position before the statute of 1430, they were, unless they also possessed a freehold, excluded by that act from the county franchise. They contributed however to the taxes in very much the same proportion[1], being assessed 'in bonis' whilst the freeholder was assessed 'in terris'; their rank and comforts were the same. Their personal weight and influence depended, as always, rather on the amount of capital and extent of holding, than on the exact nature of the tenure. Under the older system the pampered bailiff could safely look down on the poor freeholder; under the newer the wealthy tenant was far more independent than the man whose all was in the few fields to which he was as much bound by his necessities as was the legal villein by the condition of

[1] This distinction became very important after the adoption of the later form of 'subsidy' in taxation, a measure which does not fall within our period, but deserves some notice here as a sequel to our inquiries into the earlier taxes. The custom of granting a round sum had already appeared in the reign of Edward IV, in 1474; see above, p. 213; and particular methods of levying the money were devised in such cases. Under Henry VIII the sums were much increased; the grant in 1514 was £160,000, which was raised on an elaborately graduated calculation of lands, goods, and rents. Under queen Mary the name of subsidy, like that of tenths and fifteenths, acquired a technical sense, and meant a tax raised by the payment of 4*s.* in the pound for lands, and 2*s.* 8*d.* for goods; aliens paying double. Each of these brought in a sum of about £70,000; and the clerical subsidy £20,000 more. The taxes were then granted in the form of one subsidy and one or two tenths and fifteenths; the latter being likewise fixed sums of about £29,000; in the 31st of Elizabeth, the parliament voted an unparalleled grant, two subsidies and four tenths and fifteenths; Coke, 4th Inst. p. 33. How these sums were locally raised we learn from the Subsidy Rolls, some of which have been printed by the Yorkshire and other Archaeological Societies; and especially from Best's Farming Book (Surtees Society), pp. 86, 87–89, where will be found some invaluable hints for the history of local administration.

Gradations in the yeoman class.

birth and tenure. But it would be a mistake to argue as if all the freeholders were owners of forty-shilling freeholds, and all the tenant farmers were rich men. The gradations of wealth and poverty were the same throughout; the political franchise linked the poor freeholder on to the gentry and nobility; community of habits and a common liability to suffer by the caprices of the seasons, good and bad harvests and the like, linked him on to the villein class. The tenant farmer was not so linked to the gentry, and was not so tied to the land. In other respects the two classes were companions and equals.

Economy of the squire's household.

804. The Black Book of Edward IV describing the domestic economy of the squire who can spend fifty pounds a year, may be compared with Hugh Latimer's often-quoted account of his father's yeoman household. Of his £50 the squire spends in victuals £24 6*s*; on repairs and furniture £5; on horses, hay and carriages £4; on clothes, alms and oblations £4 more. He has a clerk or chaplain [1], two valletti or yeomen, two grooms, 'garciones,' and two boys, whether pages or mere servants; and the wages of these amount to £9; he gives livery of dress to the amount of £2 10*s*., and the small remainder is spent on his hounds and the charges of hay-time and harvest [2]. Hugh Latimer's father was not a freeholder, but farmed land at a rent of from £3 to £4; from which he 'tilled so much as kept half a dozen men.' His wife milked thirty kine; he had walk for a hundred sheep. He was able and did find the king a harness with himself and his horse, until he came to the place of muster where he began to receive the king's wages: this of course was a rare piece of occasional service. He could give his daughters at their marriage £5 or 20 nobles each. He sent his son to school, and gave alms to the poor: 'and all this he did of the same farm; where he that now [in 1549] hath it payeth £16 by the year or more, and is not able to do anything for

Compared with that of the yeoman.

[1] 'Clericus' at 40*s*. wages. The ordinary fee of a chaplain which gave him a title for holy orders was fixed by a constitution of archbishop Zouch at a maximum of 6 marks (£4). In 1378 the choice was given between 8 marks and 4 marks with victuals; see above, vol. ii. p. 446; Johnson, Canons, ii. 405.

[2] Ordinances of the Household, p. 46.

his prince or for himself or for his children, or give a cup of drink to the poor[1].' The balance of comfort in this comparison is in favour of the yeoman.

Comparison of squire and yeoman.

The wills and inventories of the well-to-do freeholder and farmer furnish similar evidence of competency[2]; and these are an irrefragable answer to the popular theories of the misery and discomfort of medieval middle-class life: all the necessaries of living were abundant and cheap, although the markets were more precarious owing to there being no foreign supplies to make up for bad harvests, and the necessary use of salted provisions during great part of the year was an unwholesome burden which fell heavily on this class; the supply of labour was fairly proportioned to the demand; the life of the country was almost entirely free from the evils that in modern times have resulted from the overgrowth or unequal distribution of population. The house of the freeholder was substantially but simply furnished, his stores of clothes and linen were ample, he had money in his purse and credit at the shop and at the market. He was able in his will to leave a legacy to his parish church or to the parish roads, and to remember all his servants and friends with a piece of money or an article of clothing. The inventory of his furniture, which was enrolled with his will, enables the antiquary to reproduce a fair picture of every room in the house: there were often comforts and even luxuries, although not such as those of later days; but there was generally abundance. It is of course to be remembered that only the fairly well-to-do yeoman would think it worth while to make a will; but also it was only the fairly well-to-do yeoman who could contribute to the political weight of his class.

Comparative comfort of the yeoman class.

805. If the 'vadlettus' of the reign of Edward II distinctly answered to the 'vadlettus' of 1446, we should have in him a certain link between the 'liberi homines' and 'libere tenentes'

The 'valetti' as yeomen.

[1] First sermon before King Edward, cited in the Preface to the Northumberland Household Book, p. xii.

[2] No evidences on social matters are half so convincing as wills and inventories; and fortunately large selections of medieval wills are now in print or accessible: seven volumes of Yorkshire and Durham wills have been issued by the Surtees Society.

Return of valetti to parliament.

of Henry II and the yeomen of the fifteenth century. In 1311 Rutland returned two 'homines' to parliament because there were no knights, and in 1322 several counties returned 'valletti' in the same capacity[1]: this was doubtless done on the principle according to which Henry II allowed 'legales homines,' in default of knights, to act as recognitors. But it would seem more probable that the class which furnished the 'valletti' of 1322 was that of the squires, and that they themselves would have been a few years later called 'armigeri.' On the other hand, the 'valletti' of 1446, whom the sheriffs are forbidden to return as knights, are certainly yeomen. The statute enumerates the classes who may be chosen, notable knights, or notable squires,—gentlemen of birth, and excludes those who are 'en la degree de vadlet et desouth[2].' But, as has been already stated, very little can be inferred from this act; for although it is distinctly aimed at the exclusion of persons of inferior rank from the body of knights of the shire, it does not appear to have caused any change in the character of the persons returned. In every county the same family names recur before and after the passing of the act, and it can only be conjectured that the statutory change was called for by the occurrence of some particular scandal the details of which have been forgotten. As it stands, however, it proves that the position of a knight of the shire was not farther removed from the ambition of a well-to-do yeoman, than it is from that of the tenant farmer or gentleman farmer of the present day. The precedent of 1322, if it applies at all, is weakened by the fact that there was a strong reluctance in the knights to undertake the task of representation, and a consequent anxiety on the part of the sheriff to return any one who was willing to attend.

Valetti are yeomen in 1446.

The act of 1446 did not materially affect the representation.

Political influence of the yeomanry.

806. It is not then in the point of eligibility to serve in parliament, but in the collective weight given by the right of franchise, that we must look for the real political influence which the yeomanry exercised. What was the exact state of affairs which the forty-shilling franchise was intended to remedy, can only be conjectured, for plain as the words of the statute seem,

[1] See above, p. 397.

[2] See above, pp. 401, 402.

they are met by what seems equally conclusive evidence in the lists of the knights returned. By the existing law the elections were to be made by all who were present at the county court; according to the popular interpretation of that law, as the statute informs us, they were made by persons of little substance and no value[1], that is, by the medley multitude that held up their hands for or against the nominees of the hustings. It is a natural inference from the changes which had been going on since 1381 to suppose that the self-enfranchised villeins may have formed a formidable part of these assemblies; or that the Wycliffite or socialist mobs that rose under Jack Sharp, a year later[2], attempted in certain cases to turn the election in favour of unworthy candidates. But these are mere conjectures. It happens fortunately that the returns for both 1429 and 1431 are extant; and a careful scrutiny of the lists of the two parliaments will show that there is no difference whatever in the character and position of the knights elected. In both parliaments they are almost exclusively members of families which furnished knights to both preceding and succeeding parliaments, and out of whose number the sheriffs were selected. The alteration of the franchise made no change in this; and the necessary inference from the fact is that the words of the statute, describing the character of the elective assemblies with a view to their reform, must not receive a wider interpretation than literally belongs to them; the county courts were disorderly, but it does not follow that unfit persons were elected, or that any great constitutional change was contemplated.

The statute on the franchise intended to secure order not to alter the balance of representation.

Illustrations from the returns to parliament.

Into the status of the forty-shillings' freeholder it is impossible to inquire with complete certainty; that sum was the qualification of a juror and was probably for that reason adopted as the qualification of an elector. But on any showing, if £50 was the annual expenditure of a small country squire, an act which lodged the franchise in the hands of the forty-shilling freeholder cannot be regarded as an oligarchic restriction The later effects of the change in the law cannot have been within the contemplation of its authors.

Less clear in the later acts.

[1] See above, p. 412.

[2] See above, p. 112,

General inference on the subject.

With the more distinct evidence of the act and writs of 1446 and 1447 it is less easy to deal, for the returns of previous years are incomplete, and it must be allowed that unfit persons had probably made their appearance as knights of the shire. But the act of 1446 did not alter the franchise, it merely attempted the more complete regulation of the elective assemblies, and the exclusion of members who were below the customary rank; in this point following the precedents of the earlier reigns. These considerations then do not much qualify our general conclusion that both before and after the act of 1430 the franchise was in the hands of the substantial freeholders, and that both before and after 1446 the representation of the counties was practically engrossed by the gentry; the election of a yeoman knight of the shire was not impossible or improbable, but no proof of such election having been made is now forthcoming. It may be remarked by the way that in 1445 political feeling was already rising, and that in 1447 it had risen to a dangerous height. Duke Humfrey, whose overthrow was contemplated in the parliament of the latter year was, however undeservedly, a favourite with the commons, and it would not have been a strange weapon in the hands of political agents to term the leaders of the opposing party yeomen, ignoble, neither knights nor gentlemen.

Condition of the commons in the boroughs.

807. From the condition of the commons of the shires we turn to a much more intricate subject, the condition of the commons of the boroughs, and the questions touching town constitutions generally, which have arisen since we left them in an earlier chapter, just achieving municipal independence. The difficulty of this investigation consists in the fact that whilst certain general tendencies can be traced throughout the whole of the borough history, the details of their working vary so widely, and the results are so divergent.

Absence of any law of progress.

It is possible to detect a certain development, now towards liberty, now towards restriction, and to account for local struggles as resulting in definite steps one way or the other; but it is not easy to combine the particulars into a whole, or to formulate any law of municipal progress. It is possible that, had there been any such law, or had there been more decided concert between the several boroughs, the influence of the town members in the house of commons would have been more distinctly apparent. Throughout the middle ages it scarcely can be detected at all except in two or three very narrow points; a tendency to precision in mercantile legislation, a somewhat illiberal policy towards the inhabitants of towns who were not privileged members of the town communities[1], and an anxiety to secure local improvements; the only important act attributed to any borough member is that for which the member for Bristol, Thomas Young, was imprisoned, in 1450, the proposal to declare the duke of York heir to the crown; and the only distinct act of the borough members as a body is the grant of tunnage and poundage, at the request of the Black Prince.

Insignificance of town members in parliament

The two limits of municipal change, between the reign of Henry III and that of Henry VII, may be simply stated. In 1216 the most advanced among the English towns had succeeded in obtaining, by their respective charters and with local differences, the right of holding and taking the profits of their own courts under their elected officers[2], the exclusion of the sheriff from judicial work within their boundaries, the right of collecting and compounding for their own payments to the crown, the right of electing their own bailiffs and in some instances of electing a mayor; and the recognition of their merchant guilds by charter, and of their craft guilds by charter or fine. The combination of the several elements thus denoted was not complete; the existence of bailiffs implies the existence of a court leet and court baron or court customary of the whole body of townsmen; the existence of the merchant guild implies an amount of voluntary or privileged association which in idea,

General estimate of municipal change during the period.

[1] See vol. ii. p. 463.

[2] In many of the towns which are called 'hundreds' in Domesday, and doubtless in others, the right of holding their own courts was already established (vol. i. pp. 94, 408). In other cases, as at Dunwich, 'sac and soc' were given by charter (Select Charters, p. 303). In towns like Beverley, which were under a great lord, the jurisdiction remained with him, and the courts were held by his officers, the merchant guild confining itself to the management of trade and local improvements. For the completion of municipal judicature, it would appear that these three points were necessary, the holding of the courts, the reception of the fines, and the election of the bailiffs or mayor.

Condition of towns at the close of the period.

whatever may have been the case in fact, is in contrast with the universality and equality of the courts leet; the relations of the craft guilds to the merchant guild are by no means definite; and the character of a *communa*, which is symbolised by the title of the mayor, is not clearly reconcileable either with the continued existence of the ancient courts, or with the restrictive character of the merchant guild. Such in very general terms is the condition of affairs at the starting-point. At the close of the period the typical constitution of a town is a close corporation of mayor, aldermen and council, with precisely defined numbers and organisation, not indeed uniform but of the same general conformation; possessing a new character denoted by the name of corporation in its definite legal sense; with powers varying in the different communities which have been modified by the change, and in practice susceptible of wide variations. Between these two limits lies a good deal of local history which it is scarcely possible even briefly to summarise.

Points to be examined.

808. The most important preliminary points to be determined are these: the first, at what date does the chief magistracy pass from the old bailiffs or praepositi to a mayor, whose position gives to the town constitution a unity which is not apparent before; the second, what is the precise relation of the merchant guild to the craft guild on the one side and to the municipal government on the other; and thirdly, how were those bodies finally created and constituted to which charters of incorporation were granted.

Office of mayor.

The first historical appearance of the office of mayor is in London [1], where the recognition of the communa by the national council in 1191 is immediately followed by the mention of Henry Fitz-Alwyn as mayor: he retained the office for life, and in 1215, three years after his death, John granted to the citizens, or recognised, the right of electing their mayor annually [2]. In

[1] In the lists of mayors of other places, e.g. Oxford and York, there are names much earlier than 1191, but no reliance can be placed upon the lists, and if the persons designated really bore the name, it must be regarded as an imitation of continental usage which has no further constitutional significance.

[2] Select Charters, p. 306; Rot. Chart. p. 207.

the year 1200, twenty-five citizens had been chosen and sworn to assist the mayor in the care of the city[1]; if these twenty-five jurats are the predecessors of the twenty-five aldermen of the wards, the year 1200 may be regarded as the date at which the communal constitution of London was completed. The more ancient designation of barons, with 'sac and soc' in the several franchises, would gradually disappear. The title of alderman had been applied in the reign of Henry II to the head of a craft guild[2]; early in the reign of Henry III the twenty-five wards appear; and, as the name 'Aldermaneria' seems to be used exchangeably with 'Warda,' thus much of the municipality was already in existence. Before the end of John's reign, York, Winchester and Lynn, and many other towns, had their mayors; possibly by special grants or fines in each case, but more probably by a liberal interpretation of the clause inserted in their charters, by which they were entitled to the same liberties as London. In those towns in which there was no mayor the presidency of the local courts remained with the bailiffs, whether elected by the townsmen or nominated by the lord of the town. The development however of the idea of municipal completeness as represented by a mayor and aldermen may be placed at the very beginning of the thirteenth century[3].

Institution of aldermen.

[1] 'Hoc anno fuerunt xxv electi de discretioribus civitatis et jurati pro consulendo civitatem una cum majore'; Lib. de Antt. Legg. p. 2. There are now twenty-six wards, two of them sub-divisions of older wards. One, 'Cordwainer,' retains the name of a guild; Castle Baynard that of a magnate, Portsoken that of the ancient jurisdiction of the Cnihtengild and Portreeve. All the rest are local divisions. Faringdon Without was created in 1394; Rot. Parl. iii. 317. In 1229 the Aldermanni acted with the 'magnates civitatis' in framing a law; Lib. de. Antt. Legg. p. 6. These must have been the aldermen of the wards, the magnates being the lords of franchises, such as the lord of Castle Baynard, and the ecclesiastical dignitaries who joined in the government of the city, such as the Prior of Trinity Aldgate.

[2] See Madox, Hist. Exch. p. 490. Of the wards there mentioned all are designated by the name of the alderman of the time except the 'Warda Fori,' or Cheap, Portsoken, and Bassishaw; Michael de S. Elena was probably the alderman of Bishopsgate ward. Under Edward II the wards had all acquired the names which they still bear; ib. p. 694: Firma Burgi, p. 30. In a list of aldermen of adulterine guilds in 1180, three appear as aldermen of the Gilda de Ponte.

[3] The following towns are mentioned as having mayors in the Rolls of John: Bristol, York, Ipswich, London, Lynn, Northampton, Norwich, Oxford, and Winchester.

Relations of the guilds.

Importance of the struggle for class privilege.

The history of the merchant guild, in its relation to the craft guild on the one hand, and to the municipal government on the other, is very complex. In its main features it is a most important illustration of the principle which constantly forces itself forward in medieval history, that the vindication of class privileges is one of the most effective ways of securing public liberty, so long as public liberty is endangered by the general pressure of tyranny. At one time the church stands alone in her opposition to despotism, with her free instincts roused by the determination to secure the privilege of her ministers; at another the mercantile class purchase for themselves rights and immunities which keep before the eyes of the less highly favoured the possibility of gaining similar privileges. In both cases it is to some extent an acquisition of exclusive privilege, an assertion of a right which, if the surrounding classes were already free, would look like usurpation, but which, when they are downtrodden, gives a glimpse and is itself an instalment of liberty. But when the general liberty, towards which the class privilege was an important step, has been fully obtained, it is not unnatural that the classes which led the way to that liberty should endeavour to retain all honours and privileges which they can retain without harm to the public welfare. But the original quality of exclusiveness which defined the circle for which privilege was claimed still exists; still it is an immunity, a privilege in its strict meaning, and as such it involves an exception in its own favour to the general rules of the liberty now acquired by the community around it; and if this is so, it may exercise a power as great for harm as it was at first for good. Such is one of the laws of the history of all privileged corporations; fortunately it is not the only law, and its working is not the whole of their history. It applies however directly to the guild system.

Antiquity of the guilds.

The great institution of the 'gilda mercatoria' runs back, as we have seen, to the Norman Conquest and far beyond it; the craft guilds, the 'gilda telariorum,' the 'gilda corvesariorum' and the like, are scarcely less ancient in origin, but come prominently forward in the middle of the twelfth century. The 'gilda mercatoria' may be regarded as standing to the craft guilds either inclusively or exclusively; it might incorporate them and attempt to regulate them, or it might regard them with jealousy, and attempt to suppress them. Probably in different places and at different stages it did both. It would be generally true to say that, when and where the merchant guild continued to exist apart from the judicial machinery of the town, as a board for local trade and financial administration, it incorporated and managed the craft guilds; but, when and where it merged its existence in the governing body of the town, identifying itself with the corporation and only retaining a formal existence as the machinery for admitting freemen to a participation of the privileges of the town, it became an object with the craft guilds to assert their own independence and even to wrest from the governing body judicial authority over their own members.

Relation of the *gilda mercatoria* to the craft guilds.

The charter granted by Henry II to Oxford distinctly lays down the principle that the merchant guild has an exclusive right of regulating trade except in specified cases [1]; it is provided that no one who is not of the guildhall shall exercise any merchandise in the town or suburbs, except as was customary in the reign of Henry I, when, as we know from the Pipe Rolls, the craft guilds of weavers and cordwainers had purchased their freedom by fines [2]. We may infer from this that, wherever such exceptions had not been purchased, the merchant guild possessed full power of regulating trade. In the charter granted to the city of Worcester by Henry III a similar provision is inserted, and at Worcester as late as 1467 we find the citizens in their 'yeld merchant' making for the craft guilds regulations which imply that they had full authority over them [3].

Power of the merchant guild to regulate trade.

When the merchant guild had become identified with the corporation or governing body, its power of regulation of trade passed, together with its other functions and properties, into the

The merchant guild merged in the corporation.

[1] Select Charters (2nd ed.), p. 167; Peshall's Oxford, p. 339. So also the Charter granted by Henry III to Worcester; Madox, Firma Burgi, p. 272; and other instances noted above, vol. i. p. 417.

[2] In the charter of Oxford the exceptions are 'nisi sicut solebat tempore regis Henrici avi mei'; in that of Worcester 'nisi de voluntate eorundem civium.'

[3] Smith's English Gilds, pp. 371–412.

same hands. It is probable that this is true in all cases except where the towns continued to be in the demesne of a lord who exercised the jurisdiction through his own officers, as the archbishop of York did at Beverley. In that town the merchant guild administered the property of the town, regulated trade, and exercised most of the functions which the 'local boards' of modern towns now possess; it elected the twelve governours of the town annually; but the courts were held in the archbishop's name and by his bailiffs, down to the reign of Henry VIII[1]. But as a rule it was otherwise: the ancient towns in demesne of the crown either possessed a hundredal jurisdiction at the time of the Conquest or obtained 'sac and soc' by grant from the crown[2]; as soon as they obtained the exclusion of the sheriffs and the right of electing their magistrates, they were municipally complete; and then the merchant guild merged its existence in the corporation. In some cases it dropped altogether out of sight; at York for instance it had either been forgotten, or newly organised as a merchants' company, one among many craft guilds, at the beginning of the fifteenth century[3]: and at London it is uncertain whether any primitive merchant guild ever existed. But, even where the name was suppressed, the function of admitting freemen was discharged in such a way as proved that the powers exercised by the corporation were those of the old merchant guild. At York the right of freedom was acquired by birth, apprenticeship or purchase: the admission of apprentices was subject to the jurisdiction of eight chamberlains[4], who were no doubt anciently guild officers; and, as all apprenticeship was transacted through the members of the craft guilds, the older relation between the

Cases in which the merchant guild was not the governing body of the town.

Union of the merchant guild with the leet jurisdiction.

The office of chamberlain.

[1] See Scaum s Beverlac, passim, and below, p. 583.

[2] As for example Dunwich; Select Charters, p. 303; Worcester, Nash's Worcestershire, vol. ii. App. p. cx; the Cnihtengild of London, Madox, Firma Burgi, p. 23.

[3] So also at Beverley there is a Mercers' guild, pp. 254, 255; at Coventry a new merchant guild is instituted in 1340; Smith's Gilds, p. 226.

[4] Drake, Eboracum, pp. 187, 199. One of the earliest custumals in which freedom of the town is mentioned is that of Newcastle-upon-Tyne, where it is said 'si burgensis habeat filium in domo sua ad mensam suam, filius ejus eandem habeat libertatem quam et pater suus'; Acts of Parl. of Scotland, i. 33, 34.

two institutions must be regarded as continuously subsisting. In Leicester the connexion is still more clear; for there the admission to freedom was distinctly designated as admission to the merchant guild[1]. At Oxford the freemen were admitted to the guild and liberty of the whole city. In other places, such as Preston in Lancashire, where, owing to some ancient custom or endowment, the idea of the guild had been kept prominently in view as furnishing occasion for a splendid pageant, the name was still more permanent, and the powers of the guild were more distinctly maintained. But in all these cases it may be said that the 'gilda mercatoria' had become a phase or 'function' of the corporation; where there was no ancient merchant guild, or its existence had been forgotten, the admission of freemen to a share in the duties and privileges of burghership was a part of the business of the leet[2]. Whether apart from, or identified with, the governing body of the borough, the relation of the merchant guild to the craft guilds may on this hypothesis be regarded as corresponding with the relation subsisting at Oxford and Cambridge between the University and the Colleges with their members. Lastly, in some places probably, as at Berwick, the several craft guilds having united to form a single town guild, all trade organisation and administration was lodged, by a reverse process, in the governing body of the town[3].

Merchant guilds at Leicester and Preston.

When the merchant guild had acquired jurisdiction or merged its existence in the corporation, the communa or governing body, the guild hall became the common hall of the city, and the 'port mote,' for that seems to be the proper name for the court of the guild, became the judicial assembly of the freemen and identical with the leet; the title of alderman which had once belonged to the heads of the several guilds was transferred to the magistrates of the several wards into which the town was divided, or to the sworn assistants of the mayor in the cases in which no such

Results of the union of the merchant guild with the governing body.

[1] Nichols, Leicestershire, i. 375, 377, 379 sq. At Beverley the governours admitted the freemen; see Scaum, p. 163. At Winchester, the admission to the merchant guild constituted freedom, persons not taking up their freedom paid 6*s*. 8*d*., half to the bailiffs, half to the chamber; Woodward, Hampshire, i. 270 sq.

[2] As at Huntingdon; Merewether and Stephens, pp. 1714, 2186.

[3] Vol. i. p. 418.

division was made; the property held by the merchant guild became town property and was secured by the successive charters.

The craft guilds. The craft guilds, both before and after the consolidation of the governing bodies, aimed at privileges and immunities of their own, and possessed, each within the limits of its own art, directive and restrictive powers corresponding with those claimed by the merchant guilds. Restriction on craft guilds. Consequently under Henry II they are found in the condition of illegal associations, certainly in London, and probably, in other towns. The adulterine guilds, from which heavy sums were exacted in 1180, were stigmatised as adulterine because they had not purchased the right of association, as the older legal guilds had done[1], and had set themselves up against the government of the city which the king had recognised by his charter. The later development of the contest must be looked at in connexion with the general view of municipal development. The most important features of the history are still found in London, where the craft guilds, having passed through the stages in which they purchased their privileges year by year with fines, obtained charters from Edward III. Growth of the craft guilds into trading companies. The guilds thus chartered became better known as companies, a designation under which they still exist. An act of 1364 having compelled all the artisans to choose and adhere to the company proper to their own craft or mystery, a distinction between greater and smaller companies was immediately developed. The more important companies, which were twelve in number, availed themselves of the licence reserved to them in the acts against livery to bestow livery on their members, and were distinguished as the livery companies. Between these and the more numerous but less influential and lesser companies the old struggle for privilege and equality was renewed. Classes within the trading companies. And lastly, within the livery companies themselves a distinction was

[1] 'Quia constitutae sunt sine waranto'; Madox, Exch. p. 391.

[2] Brentano (in Smith's Gilds, p. cli) describes the state of these bodies in the sixteenth century: 'The gild members were divided into three classes, the livery to which the richer masters were admitted, the householders to which the rest of the masters belonged, and the journeymen,' yeomanry, bachelors, or simple freemen. From the middle of the century the management of the companies was engrossed by the courts of assistants; Herbert, i. 118.

made between the liverymen and the ordinary freemen of the craft, the former being entitled to share in all the privileges, proprietary and municipal rights in the fullest degree, and the latter having a claim only to the simple freedom of the trade. Unfortunately the details of these two processes are very obscure, and only very wide limits can be fixed as dates between which the great companies engrossed the municipal power, and the more powerful men in each constituted themselves into the body of liverymen, excluding the less wealthy members of the company as mere commonalty or ordinary freemen.

The liverymen of London.

The third point, referred to above, the growth of the governing bodies which in the fifteenth and succeeding centuries were incorporated by charter, will be cleared up as we proceed: there is great diversity in the results, and accordingly considerable diversities must be supposed to have coloured the history which produced them; in some towns the new constitution was simply the confirmation of a system rooted in municipal antiquity, in others it was the recognition of the results of a movement towards restriction or towards greater freedom; in all it was more or less the establishment, by royal authority, of usages which had been before established by local authority only, which had grown up diversely because of the loose language in which the early charters of liberties were worded. In the following brief sketch of municipal history it will not be necessary to call attention to the diversities and multiplicities of legal usages, such as the courts of law or their customs. These vary widely in different places, and, although in some parts of the earliest constitutional investigations they illustrate the continuity of ancient legal practice, they lose their interest from the period at which they become a merely subordinate part of the machinery of civic independence. The election of magistrates, and the municipal arrangements by which such elections are determined, are on the other hand matters of permanent constitutional interest, not only in themselves and in their social aspect, but in the light they throw on the political action of the towns. The modes of electing members of parliament varied directly with the municipal usages.

Diversity of growth in the different towns.

Importance of the municipal history of London.

809. London claims the first place in any such investigation, as the greatest municipality, as the model on which by their charters of liberties the other large towns of the country were allowed or charged to adjust their usages, and as the most active, the most political and the most ambitious. London has also a preeminence in municipal history owing to the strength of the conflicting elements which so much affected her constitutional progress.

London in the thirteenth century.

The governing body of London in the thirteenth century was composed of the mayor, twenty-five aldermen of the wards, and two sheriffs. All these were elective officers; the mayor was chosen by the aldermen, or by the aldermen and magnates of the city, and required the approval of the crown; the aldermen were chosen by the citizens or commons of their respective wards[1], and the election of the sheriffs, which was a point much disputed, was probably transacted by the mayor and aldermen, with a body of four or six 'probi homines' of each ward. The sheriffs, like the mayor, were presented to the king for his approval. The term for which both mayor and sheriffs were chosen was a year; but the mayor was generally continued in office for several years together until 1319, after which date a change was annually made[2]. The sheriffs, by a by-law passed in 1229, were not allowed to hold office for more than two years together[3]. In the administration of their wards the aldermen were assisted by a small number of elected councillors who are said to make their appearance first in 1285[4].

Common councillors.

Struggles with the crown.

The supremacy of the governing body was constantly endangered from two sides. On the one hand, the kings, especially Henry III and Edward I, frequently suspended the city constitution for some offence or on some pretext by which money might be exacted[5]; a custos was then substituted for the mayor, and the

[1] A.D. 1248: 'Homines illius wardae accepta licentia eligendi elegerunt . . . Alexandrum le Ferrun . . . qui postea veniens in hustingo . . . admissus est aldermannus'; Liber de Antt. Legg. p. 15.

[2] See Liber de Antt. Legg. p. 22; Liber Albus, p. 22.

[3] 1229: 'Omnes aldermanni et magnates civitatis per assensum universorum civium'; Liber de Antt. Legg. p. 6.

[4] Norton, Commentaries on London, p. 87; quoting Liber Albus, fo. 116.

[5] In 1239 the king attempted to appoint a sheriff; Lib. de Antt. Legg.

whole independence of the municipality remained for the time in abeyance. On the other side the body of the citizens, or a large portion of the less wealthy and more excitable 'commons,' begrudged the authority exercised by the mayor and aldermen, demanded a share in the election of officers and something more than the right to hear and consent to the proceedings of their rulers in the Guildhall. In 1249, when the mayor and aldermen met the judges at the Temple for a conference on rights claimed by the abbot of Westminster, the populace interfered, declaring that they would not permit them to treat without the participation of the whole 'Communa[1].' In 1257 the king attempted to form a party among the commons by charging the mayor and aldermen with unfair assessment of tallage[2]. In 1262 Thomas Fitz-Thomas the mayor encouraged the populace to claim the title of 'Communa civitatis' and to deprive the aldermen and magnates of their rightful influence; by these means he obtained a re-election by the popular vote in 1263, the voices of the aldermen being excluded: in 1264–5 he obtained a reappointment. But his power came to an end after the battle of Evesham; he was imprisoned at Windsor and the citizens paid a fine of £20,000 to regain the royal favour which they had lost by their conduct in the barons' war[3]. Although at this price they recovered the right of electing a sheriff, the city still remained under him as custos and the mayoralty remained in abeyance. The commons at the election of the new sheriff declared that they would have no mayor but Thomas Fitz-Thomas, and the king had to put down a riot. Another change was made the next year; the citizens were allowed to elect two bailiffs instead of a custos: the election was dispatched in the guildhall before all the people[4]. When the earl of Gloucester seized the city in 1267 the dominant party was again humbled; when he submitted, they recovered their power[5]. But the king did not trust the Londoners again; and, although they were allowed to

Struggles between the magnates and the commons.

Thomas Fitz-Thomas.

Disputes after the barons' war.

p. 8: in 1240 he refused to accept the mayor elect; ibid.: in 1244 he took the city into his own hands, and exacted £1000 before he gave it up; see also the years 1249, 1254, 1255; ibid. pp. 9, 21, 23 sq.

[1] Lib. de Antt. Legg. p. 17.
[2] Ibid. p. 32.
[3] Ibid. pp. 29–86.
[4] Ibid. p. 88.
[5] Ibid. pp. 90–93.

elect bailiffs, there was no mayor until 1270, when at the intercession of Edward, and on condition of an increase in the ferm, Henry was induced to restore the recognised constitution of the city[1]. The communal or popular faction was not however crushed. On the feast of S. Simon and S. Jude in 1272 there was a contested election to the mayoralty. The aldermen and more 'discreet' citizens chose Philip le Taylur, the populace, 'vulgus,' chose the outgoing mayor, Walter Hervey. The aldermen betook themselves to the king, and explained to him that the election of mayor and sheriffs rightly belonged to them; the mob declared that they were the Communa of the city and that the election was theirs by right. The arguments of the aldermen are important as showing that their opponents were not an organised body of freemen, but simply the aggregate of the populace. They urged that the election of the mayor belonged to them; the commons were the members, they were the heads; they also exercised all jurisdiction in lawsuits set on foot within the city; the populace contained many who were neither owners of lands, rents or houses in the city, who were 'the sons of diverse mothers,' and many of them of servile origin, who had little or no interest in the welfare of the city. As the king was on his deathbed his court endeavoured to mediate; it was proposed that both candidates should be withdrawn and a custos appointed until a unanimous choice could be made; five persons were to be elected by each party, and they were to choose a mayor. Before the election could be made the king died, and the earl of Gloucester, who was the leading man among the lords, seeing that the majority of the Londoners were determined to force Walter Hervey into office, prevailed on the royal council to advise the aldermen to submit. They agreed thereupon that he should be mayor for a year. The next year Henry le Waleys was chosen, apparently by the aldermen; he was speedily involved in a quarrel with his predecessor, obtained an order for his arrest, and with the permission of the council removed him from the office of alderman. Thus ended, not without much complication with national

Contests for the office of mayor of London.

[1] Lib. de Antt. Legg. p. 124.

politics, one phase of the communal quarrel [1]. The aldermen, in alliance with the king and council, had overcome the party of the commons, the leaders of whom had certainly been in alliance with Simon de Montfort and Gloucester.

The city during the reign of Edward I.

The condition of the city during the next reign was anything but easy: and the relations of the magistracy with the king seem to show that the popular party had now got a hold on the municipal government, or else that the reforms which Edward had introduced into legal procedure had offended the jealous conservatism of the governing body; from 1285 to 1298 the liberties of the city were in the king's hands, owing to an attempt made by the mayor to defy or to elude the jurisdiction of the justices in Eyre: the king appointed a custos and exacted a heavy fine when he relaxed his hold. The election of a new mayor after so long a period of abeyance was made by the aldermen with twelve men selected by them from each ward [2]; an important change from the old and closer system of election by the aldermen alone, and especially interesting as it coincides in point of time with the earliest elections of members of parliament. The efforts of Thomas Fitz-Thomas and Walter Hervey bore, it would appear, fruit thus late. Up to this time however no trace is discovered of trade disputes underlying the political rivalry; the struggle has been between the two political parties, the magnates on the one side and the commons on the other.

Arrangement for the election of mayor.

Expansion of the system of government.

It is probable that two new points which now emerge are connected with a relaxation of the close government by the mayor and aldermen. In 1285 the aldermen began to act with the aid of an elected council in each ward; and under Edward II we find distinct traces of the creation of a body of freemen other than the resident householders and house-owners who had until now engrossed the title of citizens. An article of the charter granted by Edward II to London lays down very definite rules as to the admission of freemen; no alien is to be admitted

Admission of freemen.

[1] Lib. de Antt. Legg. pp. 142 sq., 164 sq.

[2] Norton, Commentaries, p. 87; quoting Liber B. fol. 38; Fabyan, pp. 389, 400.

except in the hustings court, and native traders only on the manucaption or security of six good men of the mystery or guild[1]: all so admitted are to pay lot and scot with the commoners. To the same reign belongs the great quarrel between the weavers' guild and the magistracy, one of the first signs of that change in the constitution of London which placed the supreme influence in the hands of the craft guilds or city companies.

Quarrel of the weavers' guild.

Growth of the weavers' guild.

810. The weavers' guild was the oldest, or one of the oldest, of the trade communities; it could look back to the twelfth century, and perhaps even further, for Robert the London citizen, who in 1130 accounted for sixteen pounds paid by this guild, was son of Leofstan, who had been the alderman of the still more ancient cnihtengild. The weavers had obtained from Henry II a very important privilege, which placed in their hands the exclusive control of their craftsmen, and confirmed to them the liberties which they had enjoyed under his grandfather. Their payments for the royal protection appear regularly in the Pipe Rolls: the annual sum of two marks of gold, or twelve pounds of silver, fixed by their charter[2]. With some of the other wider crafts, the bakers in particular, they managed by these means to elude the royal jealousy which fell so heavily on the unauthorised or adulterine guilds. On the establishment of the communal authority under Henry Fitz-Alwyn, the weavers' guild ran some risk of destruction, for in 1202 the citizens offered the king sixty marks 'pro gilda telaria delenda ita ut de cetero non suscitetur[3].' The guild however outbid the citizens, and the king confirmed their privileges, raising their annual payment to twenty marks of silver. In 1223, in fear that the citizens would seize and destroy their charter, they lodged it in the treasury of the Exchequer. Notwithstanding these perils they grew stronger and more independent, obtained a fresh charter from Edward I, elected bailiffs to execute their regulations[4], and going beyond the letter of their privilege,

It is viewed with jealousy by the body of the citizens.

[1] Liber Albus, i. pp. 142, 143.

[2] Pipe Rolls of Henry I, p. 144; Hen. II. p. 4; Madox, Exch. p. 231; Firma Burgi, pp. 191, 192, 284; Herbert, Livery Companies, i. 17–21; cf. Liber Albus, i. p. 134; Liber Custumarum, i. pp. 33, 48, 417.

[3] Madox, Exch. p. 279.

[4] Liber Custumarum, i. p. 126.

established courts and passed by-laws, which they enforced to the hurt of public liberty; in particular, they persecuted the guild of burrillers, a sort of clothworkers, who interfered with their interests, and attempted to punish offenders against their rules by a verdict of twenty-four men of the guild[1] Although there is no positive evidence to connect them and their fellow-guildsmen with the factions of Thomas Fitz-Thomas and Walter Hervey, or with the later troubles under Edward I, it is not at all unlikely that their struggle with the governing body was a continuous one. Edward I seems to have encouraged the development of the guild jurisprudence, and may have been induced to do so by his hostility to the magnates of the commune; under his son the whole case came before the royal courts. In the 14th year of Edward II, on a plea de quo warranto, the citizens, before Hervey de Staunton and his companion judges, called on the weavers to show by what authority they exercised the right of holding courts, trying offenders, enforcing their sentences, and assuming, as they did, complete independence of administration. The guildsmen produced their charter, and the verdict of the jury, impannelled to determine the question of fact, was, that they had gone beyond their charter 'ad damnum et dispendium populi[2].'

Usurped rights.

The lawsuit between the city and the weavers' guild.

It is possible that this trial was only one sign of the growing importance of the trades. In the regulations for the government of the city, confirmed by Edward II in 1318, occurs an order that no native merchant of certain mystery or office shall be admitted to the freedom of the city except on security given by six good men of certain mystery or office[3]. This order may be construed as implying either that the trades had such hold on the city as to exclude all claimants of the freedom who were not able to produce six sureties belonging to a craft, or that the governing body was so jealous of admitting any tradesman to the freedom that it

Freedom of the city acquired on the security of members of crafts.

[1] Herbert, Livery Companies, i. 20.

[2] Liber Custumarum, i. 416–424; Madox, Firma Burgi, p. 285. This is only one of the contests waged by the weavers' guild for the control of trade and exclusion of foreign workmen; others occurred in 1352, and 1409; ibid. pp. 192 sq., 283 sq.; Rot. Parl. iii. 600, iv. 50.

[3] Liber Albus, i. p. 142.

Victory of the trading companies.

required six sureties for his good behaviour. But this obscurity does not long embarrass the subject; the article, with another of the same code ordering the annual election of the aldermen, soon acquired a very definite application; for before the end of the reign of Edward III the victory of the guilds or companies was won; but it was won by the greater guilds for themselves rather than for the whole body of the tradesmen.

Multiplication of trading companies.

The guilds had increased and multiplied since Henry II had crushed the 'adulterine' aspirants to independence. There were now forty-eight, and of these the weavers were not in the first class: the grocers, mercers, goldsmiths, fishmongers, vintners, tailors and drapers being evidently richer and more influential bodies [1]. All had been liberally inclined towards the king, and he probably saw that, in allowing them to remodel the city constitution in their own way, he would gain strength in the city and make friends in that class from which all through his reign he had contrived to raise supplies.

Representative councils in the city.

By an ordinance of 1346 the deliberative council of the city had been made strictly representative: each ward, in its annual moot, was to elect, according to its size, eight, six, or four members, who were to be summoned to consult on the common interests; and all elections were to be made by a similar select number of twelve, eight, or six, specially summoned [2]. The deliberative council was thus a standing body of citizens, the elective courts were composed of persons summoned for the occasion. The qualification for membership of the council, or for the electoral summons, was simply freedom or citizenship, although that freedom may already have been closely connected with guild-membership. The plan did not work well, and was superseded in 1375. The governing body had summoned the representatives of the wards to both councils and elections very

[1] The twelve great companies, later called the Livery Companies, are the Mercers, Grocers, Drapers, Fishmongers, Goldsmiths, Skinners, Merchant Taylors or Linen Armourers, Haberdashers, Salters, Ironmongers, Vintners, and Clothworkers. Of these only the Fishmongers have charters as early as the reign of Edward I. They were however of much greater antiquity as guilds.

[2] Norton, Commentaries, p. 114, quoting Liber F. ultimo fol. 5 b.

much as they pleased: it was now established that the common councilmen should be nominated by the trading companies and not by the wards; and that the same persons so nominated, and none others, should be summoned to both councils and elections[1]. The considerable body of citizens who were not members of the companies were thus altogether excluded from municipal power, although they retained the right of choosing their aldermen; and to this they were not disposed to submit.

The trading companies obtain exclusive power in the councils.

We can but regret that we have no information as to the part played by Philipot, Walworth and John of Northampton in these changes; we know however that political and party spirit ran high during these years in London, and the history of John of Gaunt, Wycliffe, and Wat Tyler, shows that the factions were fairly balanced. The history and fate of Nicholas Brember, who forced himself into the mayoralty to further the designs of Richard II and Michael de la Pole, assume the importance of a constitutional episode[2].

Possible connexion with political events.

In 1384 another change was made: the election of the deliberative council was given back to the wards, but the choice of the electoral bodies was left to the companies[3]. From this date the greater companies appear to engross the power thus secured to the traders. In 1386 Nicholas Brember was elected to the mayoralty 'by the strong hand of certain crafts' in opposition to the great body of the freemen. The mercers, cordwainers, founders, saddlers, painters, armourers, embroiderers, spurriers and bladesmiths, petitioned the king and parliament against the violence with which the election had been conducted, and alleged that the election of the mayor ought to be 'in the freemen of the city by good and peaceable advice of the wisest and truest.' Brember was supported by the grocers, who numbered at the time not less than sixteen aldermen in their company[4]. His fall in 1388 probably prevented any judicial proceedings which might have put a stop to the usurpations of the greater companies. The

Further changes.

The stronger companies and Nicolas Brember.

[1] Norton, Commentaries, p. 115, quoting Liber Leg. fol. 25 b.
[2] See above, vol. ii. p. 447.
[3] Norton, Commentaries, p. 116, quoting Liber H, fol. 173.
[4] Rot. Parl. iii. 225, 226.

Final victory of the companies.

growth of their pretensions is however as yet unchronicled; their final victory was gained in the reign of Edward IV.

One further change, and this nearly at the close of the period, completes this curious chapter of history. Edward IV had found good friends among the Londoners; his father had succeeded to the popularity of duke Humfrey, and Henry VI had had none to lose. Edward too had the instincts of a merchant, and sympathised, as much as he could sympathise with anything, with the interests of trade. It is however unnecessary to suppose that he had any personal share in the alteration, which may have been desired simply in the interests of order. The usage which had prevailed in the elections had left the number of electors quite indeterminate; it was necessary, according to the idea of the time, that the number should be fixed, and it was certainly inexpedient to leave the mode of summons and the exercise of the right at the discretion of the officials. In the seventh year of Edward IV it was enacted that the election of the mayor and sheriffs should be in the common council, together with the masters and wardens of the several mysteries; in the fifteenth year of the same king this body was widened by an act of the common council, who directed that the masters and wardens should associate with themselves the honest men of their mysteries, and come in their last liveries to the election[1].

Progress under Edward IV.

Supremacy of the livery.

The discretionary power of the mayor or presiding officer in summoning electors was thus taken away, and the election lodged altogether in the hands of the liverymen. The liverymen were those on whom, under the saving clause of the act of Henry IV[2] already mentioned, the several guilds were allowed to bestow their livery, which was done, and still is done, according to the rules of the several companies. The election of members to parliament was in all these proceedings treated in the same way as that of the mayor. The result may be briefly stated: the mayor, sheriff, other corporate officers, and members of parliament, were elected by the livery and common council. The aldermen were elected by the citizens of the wards for life;

[1] Norton, Commentaries, pp. 126, 127.
[2] Statutes, ii. 156.

the common council annually by the wards, four from each. The position of freemen, the right to which might be based on birth or inheritance, which might be given as a compliment, or acquired by purchase, was generally obtained by apprenticeship under one of the companies; it simply gave the right to trade; the freeman who became a resident householder, and took the livery of his company, entered into the full enjoyment of civic privilege.

Position of freemen of the city.

Such then was the medieval constitution of London in the point which most nearly touches national politics; and such the tendency of all the changes through which it passed, from the unorganised aggregation of hereditary franchises, of which it seems in the eleventh century to have been composed; through the communal stage in which magnates and commons conducted a long and fruitless strife, to a state of things in which the mercantile element secured its own supremacy. It was on this condition of things that the charter of Edward IV, which allowed the city to acquire lands by purchase and in mortmain, conferred the complete character of a corporation[1]. Most of the essential features of such a body London already possessed; the city had long had a seal, and had made by-laws: the other three marks which the lawyers have described as constituting a corporation aggregate are the power to purchase lands and hold them, 'to them and their successors' (not simply their heirs, which is an individual and hereditary succession only); the power of suing and being sued, and the perpetual succession implied in the power of filling up vacancies by election. Into the possession of most of these London had grown long before the idea was completed or formulated: and it would be difficult to point to any one of its many charters by which the full character was conferred. It is accordingly regarded as a corporation by prescription[2]; and in this respect, as in some others, takes its place rather as a standard by which the growth of other similar communities may be tested than as a model for their imitation in details.

Stages of municipal history.

Charter of Edward IV.

Prescriptive character of the corporation.

811. The growth of municipal institutions in the other

[1] Norton, Commentaries, pp. 75, 379.
[2] Coke, 2 Inst. p. 330; Blackstone, Comm. i. 472.

Country corporations.

towns follows at long distances and in very unequal stages the growth of London. Even those cities whose charters entitle them to the privileges of the Londoners, and which may be supposed to have framed such new usages as they adopted upon the model of the capital, very soon lose all but the most superficial likeness: they had early constitutions of their own, the customs of which affected their later development quite as much as any formal pattern or exemplar could; and they were much more earnest in acquiring immunities of trade and commerce which they were to share with London than in reforming their own domestic institutions.

Municipal history of York.

York was the second capital of the kingdom; it retained in the twelfth century vestiges of the constitutional government by its lawmen which had existed before the Conquest; it had also its merchant guild and its weavers' guild; its citizens attempted to set up a communa, and were fined under Henry II; but it had achieved the corporate character and possessed a mayor and aldermen under John[1]. Under Henry III the citizens of York were more than once in trouble on account of the non-payment of their ferm; Edward I kept the liberties of the city for twelve years in his own hands, and settled an appeal, which came before him on account of the renewal of an ancient guild, in favour of the guildsmen[2],—a fact which perhaps denotes that in York as well as in London the party most dangerous to royal authority was the old governing body, the mayor and aldermen. Under Edward III, in 1371, we find a contested election between John Langton and John Gisburn for the mayoralty, in which the king's peace and the safety of the city were endangered, and the bailiffs and 'probi homines' were directed to proceed to a new election, from which both the competitors should be excluded[3]. John Langton had already been nine times mayor, and John Gisburn had been member of parliament for the city. Gisburn retained the mayoralty for two years, and was again, in 1380, involved in an election quarrel which came before the parliament which was sitting

Disputes with the crown.

Contests for the mayoralty.

[1] See vol. i. pp. 395. 412, 418. [2] Rot. Parl. i. 202.
[3] Drake, Eboracum, App. p. xxvi.

at the time at Northampton. He had been duly elected and held office until the 27th of November, on which day the common people of the city had risen, broken into the Guildhall, and forced Simon of Whixley into the mayor's place. The earl of Northumberland was, by the direction of parliament, sent down to confirm Gisburn in possession and to arrest the offenders; but the next year Simon of Whixley was chosen, and held the office for three years running; and in 1382, by a fine of a thousand marks, the citizens purchased a general pardon for all their offences against the peace[1]. It is not impossible that these troubles may have had a direct connexion with the rising of the commons in 1381; but it certainly appears, from the circumstances recorded, that the chief magistracy was made the bone of contention between two factions, one of which was the faction of the mob, while the other was supported by royal authority. The result of this state of things was, that Richard bestowed by charter a new constitution on the city. He had, in 1389, presented his own sword to the mayor, who thenceforward was known as the lord mayor; and in 1393 had given the lord mayor a mace. In 1396 he made the city a county of itself, annexing to it the jurisdiction of the suburbs, and substituting two sheriffs for the three bailiffs who had hitherto assisted the mayor; the sheriffs were to be chosen by the citizens and community, and to hold their county court in the regular way[2]. The favour shown by Richard II to the city won the affection of the citizens, in so far at least as to implicate them in the revolt of the Percies in 1405, when their liberties were again seized for a short time.

Contested election of mayor.

New constitution given by Richard II.

The corporate body at this time consisted of the lord mayor and twelve aldermen, but the city was not divided into wards until the reign of Charles II: the aldermen represented either the ancient aldermen of guilds, or the more ancient lawmen of Anglo-Saxon times. The freemen of the city were made as usual by service, inheritance or purchase; and the great number

Character of the corporation.

[1] Drake, Eboracum, App. p. xxvi; Rot. Parl. iii. 96.

[2] Drake, Eboracum, pp. 205, 206; Madox, Firma Burgi, pp. 246, 247, 293.

of companies, thirteen greater and fifteen smaller, proved the importance of the craft-guilds.

Charter of Henry VI.

After an important exemplification and extension of their privileges by Henry VI[1], in which the circle of their county jurisdiction was extended over the wapentake of the Ainsty, and which accounts in some measure for the reverence with which his memory was regarded, succeeded a period during which the Yorkist kings carefully cultivated the friendship of the citizens. Edward IV, in 1464, issued directions for the election of mayor which show that he was inclined to assimilate the constitution of the city to that of London in one more point of importance, and which possibly imply that the old disputes about the elections had again arisen amid the many other sources of local division. He directed that the searchers or scrutators of each craft should summon the masters of the trades to the guildhall, where they should nominate two of the aldermen, one of whom should be selected by the upper house of aldermen and assistants to fill the vacant office[2]. The plan was soon modified. During the short restoration of Henry VI, in 1470, a new scheme is said to have been proposed in parliament, and a lord mayor was appointed by royal mandamus[3]; and almost immediately after the restoration of Edward IV, the restriction of the elective power to the masters of the trades was abolished; the searchers were directed to summon the whole body of the citizens and to elect an alderman as mayor without any interference from the upper house[4]. As the aldermen of York retained the power of filling up vacancies in their own body, and the twenty-four assistants were men who had served the office of mayor, this proceeding left a fair share of power to both houses; and the constitution underwent no further change until Henry VIII instituted the common council composed of two representatives for each of the thirteen greater and one for each of the smaller companies; the election of the mayor was then given to the common council and senior searchers, who presented three candidates to the aldermen for their final choice[5].

Attempts to throw the elections into the hands of the trades.

Final arrangement under Henry VIII.

[1] Madox, Firma Burgi, p. 293. [2] Ibid. p. 33; Rymer, xi. 529.
[3] Drake, Eboracum, p. 185. [4] Ibid. p. 185. [5] Ibid. p. 207.

Although we have these details of changes, we sadly want a clue to the interpretation of them. In the earlier part of the period the city does not seem to have been disturbed by political disputes; the influence of the archbishops and of the neighbouring lords was great but not provokingly strong, and the citizens acted fairly well together. In the later part there was no doubt a party of the White Rose as well as of the Red, and the increased weight given to the trade organisations by both Edward IV and Henry VIII is a distinct recognition of their supreme influence. As York was not divided into wards before the reign of Charles II, we must trace the existence of the aldermanate either to the ancient guild system, or the combination of the merchant guild with the leet jury. The connexion of the freemen with the craft-guilds is not distinctly stated; but as these guilds were so numerous, and as no master craftsman was allowed to trade unless he were a freeman, such a connexion must necessarily have existed: the lord mayor and the eight chamberlains constituted a court which took cognisance of all apprenticeships, and which must have fulfilled the functions of the merchant guild, if it were not the merchant guild itself in a new form.

Difficulty of understanding these changes.

General conclusions.

The constitution of Leicester may be taken as a type of a large class of borough forms, which retained the older names of local institutions, and thus maintained a more distinctly continuous history. There the chief court of the town, after it became consolidated, was the portman-mote, in which the bailiff of the lord continued to preside until the middle of the thirteenth century; and there was likewise a merchant guild, at the head of which were one or two aldermen. From the year 1246 a mayor took the place of the aldermen, and gradually edged out the bailiff, but the portman-mote and the merchant guild retained their names and functions; the latter as the means by which the freemen of the borough were enfranchised, whilst the former was the court in which they exercised their municipal functions. Under this merchant guild were the craft guilds; the tailors' guild paid ten shillings to the merchant guild for every new master tailor enfranchised, and doubtless the other trades were under similar obligations. In 1464 Edward IV recognised the position of

Municipal history of Leicester.

Portman-mote and merchant guild.

Municipal constitution of Leicester. twenty-four comburgesses or mayor's brethren, and a court of common council who, in 1467, were empowered to elect the mayor. In 1484 the twenty-four took the title of aldermen, and divided the town into twelve wards; and in 1489 the mayor, twenty-four and forty-eight councillors formed themselves into a strictly close corporation; took an oath by which all the other freemen were excluded from municipal elections, and obtained an act of parliament to confirm their new constitution: a new charter was granted in 1504[1].

Constitution of Worcester; At Worcester, the merchant guild maintained a still stronger vitality, and was indeed the governing body of the city, the bailiffs, twenty-four and forty-eight being the livery men of the guild; but the constitution is more liberal at Worcester than at Leicester[2]. Shrewsbury; At Shrewsbury, on the other hand, although the constitution to some extent resembles that of Worcester, there is no mention of the guild in the act which created the corporation[3]. Exeter; At Exeter, where the merchant guild was not one of the privileges originally granted, we find the mayor and burgesses exercising or attempting to exercise supreme authority over the craft guilds[4]. Bristol. At Bristol, there had been a merchant guild, but there, as at York, it had merged its existence in the communal organisation; in the year 1314, there was an association of fourteen of the greater men of the city, who Political troubles at Bristol. were stoutly resisted by the community; the quarrel between the two bodies was one of the minor troubles of the reign of Edward II, and was rather of a political than of a municipal character, although the oligarchy of fourteen strengthened themselves by alliance with the royal officers, and the commonalty, with the covert assistance of the opposition, carried on a local war for some four years. Bristol was now the third, if not the second, town in the kingdom, and it was probably with a view of consolidating its constitution, as well as by way of

[1] Nichols, Leicestershire, i. pp. 374, 380, 383, 385.
[2] Nash, Worcestershire, ii. pp. cx sq.; Green, Hist. Worcester, ii. 31 sq.; Smith s Gilds, pp. 370 sq.
[3] Rot. Parl. iv. 476, v. 121.
[4] Izaack's Exeter, pp. 89, 91; Smith's Gilds, pp. 297 sq.

compliment, that Edward III in 1373 gave it a shire organisation[1].

In some towns which were part of the demesne or franchises of prelates, the relation between the lord and the municipal organisation gave a peculiar colour to the whole history. Two or three such cases may be mentioned here. Beverley was an ancient possession of the see of York; there the archbishop retained his manorial jurisdiction until the Reformation, when he exchanged the manor for other estates. But although he retained jurisdiction, the townsmen in their guild, erected under archiepiscopal charter and with royal licence, administered the property and regulated the trade of the town, by a body of twelve governours; on one or two occasions they attempted, during vacancies of the see, to have some of their governours appointed justices of the peace, but in this they were defeated by the new archbishops. The constitution of a council of twenty-four to assist the twelve was ratified by the archbishops, and became a permanent part of the constitution, which, after the town became a royal borough, was completed by the addition of a mayor and aldermen. In Beverley the rights of the archbishop were older than that of the merchant guild[2]. In Ripon, another franchise of the archbishop, there was no chartered merchant guild; the jurisdiction was exercised by the bailiffs in the manorial courts, and the elective wakeman, an official of very ancient origin and peculiar to this town, had certain functions in the department of police. In both places there was generally harmony between the lord and the town. At Reading it was otherwise[3]. Reading had an ancient merchant guild which claimed existence anterior to the date at which the town was given to the abbey by Henry I. There was in consequence a perpetual conflict of jurisdiction between the mayor with his guild and the abbot with his courts leet and baron. In 1253 there was open war between the two bodies; the abbot had seized the merchant guild and destroyed

Towns in demesne of prelates.

Constitution of Beverley;

of Ripon;

of Reading.

[1] See Seyer's Charters of Bristol, p. 39.
[2] See Scaum's Beverlac, i. pp. 149–321.
[3] Coates, History of Reading, pp. 49–56.

Municipal troubles at Reading.

the market; under royal mediation the townsmen bought their peace, their guild and corporate property, the abbot being allowed to nominate the warden of the guild. In 1351 the mayor, and the commons who had chosen the mayor, insisted on their right to appoint constables; this the abbot claimed as appurtenant to his manor; this dispute ran on to the reign of Henry VII. The election of the mayor himself was another bone of contention. The abbot had chosen the warden of the guild from three persons selected by the brethren; in 1460 the abbot chose the mayor 'cum consensu burgensium.' But in 1351 the right of choosing the mayor was claimed as an immemorial privilege of the burghers. An end was put to these contests by the charter of Henry VII, which divided the town into wards and prescribed the rights of the guildsmen. Similar difficulties marked the earlier history of Winchester and other towns where the bishops claimed not the whole, but a distinct quarter. But these instances must suffice.

No general law of growth to be traced in detail.

The first and perhaps the only distinct conclusion that can be drawn from these details is that the town constitutions reached the stage at which they were recognised by charters of incorporation, rather by growth than by any act of creation. Where the constitution of the guild had been insufficient for the administration of the borough, or where there had been no guild, some plan of electing a permanent or annual committee of councillors to assist the mayor or the bailiffs had sprung up. In the same way, where the ancient machinery of court-leet and court-baron had worn itself out, the want of magisterial experience or authority had been supplied by an elected council. Such in their origin were the 'twenty-four' in corporations like Cambridge and Lynn, where they acted as a common council; the 'twenty-four' at York, who were the aldermen that had passed the chair, the name bearing no reference to the existing number; such were too the mayor's brethren at Leicester. The constant recurrence of the number of twenty-four in this connexion may possibly imply an early connexion with the jury system, and the 'jurati' of the early communes, which again must have been connected with the system of the hundred court,

The town councils of twenty-four.

as exhibited in the East Anglian counties. The division of the larger towns into wards can scarcely be accounted for upon any one principle applicable to all cases; for it took place at very different times in different towns; the simplest way of accounting for it is to suppose that it was intended to supply a more efficient police system. The connexion of the aldermanship with the ward varies in different towns; in some it is a result, as in London, of the coalition of several jurisdictions; in others, as in Winchester, of the sub-division for the purposes of police; in others, as in York, it is of late origin, and simply a measure of local reform. Finally, in all the cases cited, there is a common tendency towards the general type of an elective chief magistrate, with a permanent staff of assistant magistrates, and a wider body of representative councillors—in other words, to the system of mayor, aldermen, and common council, which with many variations in detail was the common type to which the charter of incorporation gave the full legal status.

Division into wards.

Office of alderman.

General type.

The several marks of a legal corporation, which were impressed, conferred, or perpetuated by the charter of incorporation, are five in number: the right of perpetual succession, to sue and be sued by name, to purchase lands, to have a common seal, and to make by-laws[1]. The first involved, in the case of towns and collective organisations generally, the right of perpetuating its existence by filling up vacancies as they occur; and this right was exercised by all the organised communities, whether by guild or leet, or by mere admission to civic privileges, from the earliest times. It is true that the early charters were granted to the burghers and their heirs, but although the form implied simple inheritance, the power of admitting new members, a power of very primitive antiquity, involved the idea of succession, and secured it. In the same way a town could be sued or sue, could be fined or otherwise punished by royal authority as a whole, long before charters of incorporation were granted. Again, the ancient guilds could hold property; the towns themselves, whether as organised guilds or as ancient communities of land-owners like the village

Legal idea of corporations.

Prescriptive rights of the boroughs.

[1] Blackstone, Comm. i. 475.

Right of acquiring land.

communities, could hold land in common; and although in the latter case the basis of the common ownership was inheritance, the grants of land to the burghers and their successors were sufficiently early to prove that there was no recognised bar to the possession of corporate property even in the fourteenth century. It was in the reign of Richard II that the acquisition of land by guilds was first made subject to a licence of amortization, a fact which proves that the power of acquiring without such licence had not as yet been limited by law. The common seal and the right to make by-laws had been enjoyed by the boroughs from time immemorial, the latter by the original borough charter, if not earlier, the former from the date at which public seals came into common use. Thus viewed, all the ancient boroughs of England, or nearly all, must have possessed all the rights of corporations and have been corporations by prescription long before the reign of Henry VI; and the acquisition of a formal charter of incorporation could only recognise, not bestow, these rights.

Common seal and by-laws.

Grants of charters of incorporation.

These new charters were, however, required in many instances to give firmness and consolidation to the local organisations which had been up to this time a matter of spontaneous and irregular growth; they gave to the local by-laws the certainty of royal authorisation, and they served to bring up the general status of the privileged communities to the point at which the lawyers had fixed the true definition of incorporation. Before the complete charter was devised, some towns, Shrewsbury for instance, had procured an act of parliament to secure their local constitutions; it was on the whole easier to procure a royal charter. From the reign of Henry VI these charters were multiplied, and they contained both a recognition of the full corporate character of the town and some scheme of municipal constitution[1]. As time advanced these schemes were made more and more definite, and contained more precise rules for proceeding. The charter of Henry VI to Southampton mentions only a mayor, bailiffs, and burgesses,

Increase of definiteness in the chartered corporations.

[1] The charter of Hull, 18 Hen. VI is said to be the first charter in which incorporation is distinctly granted to a town; Merewether and Stephens, p. xxxiv.

and that of Edward IV to Wenlock only a bailiff and burgesses; in such cases the corporate government already existing was merely confirmed or recognised. A century later the number of aldermen and councillors is often prescribed; and a century later still, in the reign of Charles II and onwards, alterations are made in the constitution of the several bodies, not only by royal nomination of individual aldermen and councillors, but by varying the numbers and functions of the several bodies that formed the corporations. More exact organisation.

These changes for the most part lie a long way beyond the point at which our general view of the social state of England must now stop, but the later development of the corporation system serves to illustrate a tendency which is already perceptible in the fifteenth century. Much of the freedom of the town system was inseparable from the idea of growth; with the definite recognition conferred by the charters of incorporation comes in a tendency towards restriction. The corporate governing body becomes as it were hardened and crystallised, and exhibits a constantly increasing disposition to engross in its own hands the powers which had been understood to belong to the body of the burghers. The town property comes to be regarded as the property of the corporation; the corporation becomes a close oligarchy; the elective rights of the freemen are reduced to a minimum, and in many cases the magistracy becomes almost the hereditary right of a few families. The same tendency exists in the trading companies also. The highest point of grievance is reached when by royal charter the corporation is empowered to return the members of parliament. And this power, notwithstanding the legal doctrine that such a monopoly, although conferred by royal charter, could not prejudice the already existent right of the burgesses at large, was in many cases, as we have noted already, exercised by the municipal corporations until it was abolished by the Reform Act of 1832. Irregularity a mark of growth. Tendency towards restriction. Oligarchic corporations. Exclusive political rights.

The highest development of corporate authority had in some few instances been reached, a century before the charter of incorporation was invented, in the privileges bestowed on some of the large towns when they were constituted counties, with Towns made counties.

Shire constitution of large towns.

sheriffs and a shire jurisdiction of their own. This promotion, if it may be so called, involved a more complete emancipation than had been hitherto usual, from the intrusion of the sheriff of the county; the mayor of the privileged town was constituted royal escheator in his place, and his functions as receiver and executor of writs devolved on the sheriffs of the newly constituted shire; a local franchise, a hundred or wapentake, was likewise attached to the new jurisdiction, in somewhat the same way as the county of Middlesex was attached to the corporation of London. After London, to which it belonged by the charter of Henry I, the first town to which this honour was granted was Bristol, which Edward III in 1373 made a county with an elective sheriff. In 1396 Richard II conferred the same dignity on York, constituting the mayor the king's escheator, instituting two sheriffs in the place of the three primitive bailiffs, and placing them in direct communication with the royal exchequer. Newcastle-on-Tyne was similarly promoted in 1400, Norwich in 1403, Lincoln in 1409, Hull in 1440, Southampton in 1448, Nottingham in 1449, Coventry in 1451, and Canterbury in 1461. At later periods, Chester, Exeter, Gloucester, Lichfield, Worcester, and Poole were added to the number of 'counties corporate[1].'

Political importance of town history.

812. It is by no means easy to ascertain the definite amount of political consciousness which underlay the municipal struggles of medieval England; or even to determine the direction in which the influence of municipal feeling helped the national advance. On the other hand it is very easy to speculate on the affinities and analogies of continental town history and to draw a picture of what may have been. Some speculation indeed is necessary, but it must be guarded with many provisoes and hedged in with stubborn facts. It has been already remarked more than once that the battle of the medieval constitution, so far as it was fought in the house of commons, was fought by the knights of the shire. This fact is capable of two explana-

[1] I must content myself here with a general reference to Merewether and Stephens on the History of Corporate Boroughs, where most of the details given above may be found.

tions; it may imply the hearty concurrence of the town representatives, or it may imply their neutrality and insignificance. As they are seldom even mentioned in connexion with the greater struggles of the fourteenth century, it is impossible to determine from any positive evidence which was really the case. But there are some reasons for doubting whether political foresight was to any considerable extent developed in the towns. In parliament, throughout the fourteenth century, the presence of the borough members is only traceable by the measures of local interest, taken on petitions which we must infer to have been presented by them, local acts for improvement of the towns, paving acts, diminution of imposts in consideration of the repair of walls, and the redress of minor grievances. Outside the parliament, the merchant interest of England is seen to have been nourished, utilised, and almost ruined by Edward III; conniving at and profiting by his acts of financial chicanery and enabling him, by supplying money as long as it was forthcoming, to disregard the wishes of the nation expressed in the parliament. As the town members must have been in many cases the great merchants of the country, the only conclusion that we can draw from their conduct is that they thought it more profitable and more prudent to negotiate in private or half public assemblies with the king, than to support his claims for increased grants of money in parliament; out of parliament they were his pliant instruments, in parliament they were silent or acquiescent in the complaints of the knights. In another point, which affects the history of the following century, the inaction of the town members is remarkable: there is scarcely a vestige of an attempt to reform or even to regulate the borough representation. There is no trace whatever, except in the statute of 1382, of any interest felt on this point. There is a long string of petitions and statutes touching the shire representation, from the year 1376 to the year 1445; but, with the exception of a single complaint against the sheriffs in 1436, nothing answering to it on the part of the towns. Yet, as we have seen, the town franchise was in a very anomalous condition, subject generally to the manipulation of the governing bodies of the

Insignificance of the towns in parliament.

Action of the mercantile interest under Edward III.

Subservience to the king.

towns, whilst custom was nowhere so strong or so uniform as to have presented any obstacle to a general project of reform.

Absence of political wisdom in the towns.

In these two points must be read distinctly an insensibility in the represented classes of the towns as to the great questions at stake between the king and the nation, and as to the line on which political liberty was ultimately to advance. This absence of political insight may be explained in more ways than one: and in some ways which, although in themselves contradictory, may have been true in reference to different parts of the country. In some counties the towns followed with a good deal of sympathy the politics of their great neighbours, who also led the shires; in others there was no doubt a rivalry, in England as elsewhere, between town and country. In some towns the family factions of the royal house, or of the neighbourhood, were reproduced and intensified, and the two representatives would be the nominees of two rival parties. In most of the towns however the members would almost certainly be the nominees of the local magistrates rather than of the great body of the commons; and the facility or difficulty with which this result was secured would be the only index of any political aspiration in the inferior body. Traces of any such difficulty in the matter of parliamentary elections are, as we have seen, extremely rare; but they are not altogether absent, and they have their reflexions in the proceedings of parliament.

How this may be accounted for.

Internal jealousies in the towns.

In the reign of Richard II several petitions were presented in parliament which show that the strife between the governing bodies and the craft guilds was not yet decided; possibly the statute which subjected the guild lands to the restraints of the mortmain acts owed its acceptance to this jealousy; and, more distinctly, the proposal to limit the right of the towns to enfranchise villeins, speaks of an intention in the represented classes to hold fast their power[1]. The most offensive of these proposals were rejected by the king, but they were made in the most subservient parliaments of the reign, and by that party no doubt which might have reckoned most securely on the king's support. But Richard had probably conceived the idea of appealing to the

[1] See above, vol. ii. pp. 463, 485.

lower stratum of the nation in order to crush the baronial opposition; and with all his weakness he was clever enough to see that, in the class which had risen against his ministers in 1381, there was a power which it would be foolish to oppress, and which it might be wise to propitiate. He would defend the villein against the burgher, the burgher against the knight, the knight against the baron, but it was that he himself might profit by the overthrow of all. And this has to be borne in mind in reading the whole of his most instructive history. There were many points in his policy which were, in themselves, far more liberal than the policy of the barons; yet it was on the victory of the barons that the ultimate fate of the constitution hung. Richard, very early in his career, would have saved the villeins when the parliament revoked the charters; he refused to sanction later restrictive measures against them; his court, if not himself, was strongly inclined to tolerate the Wycliffites; many of the wisest measures against the papacy were passed during the time of his complete supremacy; the barons and knights of the shire may be represented as a body of self-seekers and oppressors in these very points, and they certainly were in the closest alliance with the persecuting party in the church. Yet they were the national champions, and their victory was the guarantee of national progress. If Richard had overcome them England might have become the counterpart of France, and, having passed through the ordeal, or rather the agony, of the dynastic struggle and the discipline of Tudor rule, must have sunk like France into that gulf from which only revolution could deliver her.

Possible alliance between Richard II and the towns.

In the fifteenth century the towns seem to have shared pretty evenly the sympathies of the dynastic parties; but they do not play, either in or out of parliament, an important part in the struggle. They were courted by the kings as a counterpoise to the still overpowering baronage, and by the aspirants to power against its actual possessors; they were courted by Henry IV as against the party of Richard, and by the Yorkists against Henry VI; and it was the absence of any popular qualities in Henry, as compared with the gallant and popular manners of the rival princes, which,

The politics of the towns under the Lancaster kings.

Relation of the house of York to the towns.

far more than any questions of deeper import, placed him at a disadvantage regarding them. But the facility with which the Tudor succession was welcomed proved that there was no real affection felt for the house of York, and proves further that the towns as well as the nation at large were weary of dynastic politics. From that time the municipal organisation is strengthened and hardened, still with that tendency towards restriction which betrays a want of political foresight: the victory of the trading spirit once won, the trading spirit shows itself as much inclined to engross power and to exclude competition as any class had done before.

Work of different classes of society in the securing general progress towards liberty.

813. It cannot be too carefully borne in mind, especially as we approach more modern times and have to look at questions more or less akin to those which divide modern opinion, that political progress does not advance in a single line, and political wisdom is the heirloom of no one class of society. There is an age of ecclesiastical prevision, an age of baronial precaution, an age of municipal pretension; of country policy, of mercantile policy, of trade policy, of artisan aspiration: all, one after the other, putting forth their best side in the struggle for power, showing their worst side in the possession and retention of it. But in spite of selfish aims and selfish struggles for the maintenance of power, each contributes to the great march of national wellbeing, and each contributes an element of its own, each has a strong point of its own which it establishes before it gives way to the next. The church policy of the earlier middle ages was one long protest against the predominance of mere brute strength, whether exemplified in the violence of William Rufus, or in the astute despotism of Henry I: the baronial policy, which from the reign of John to the accession of Henry IV shared or succeeded to the burden of the struggle, was directed to the securing of self-government for the nation as represented in its parliament: and the country interest, as embodied in the knights, worked out in the fifteenth century the results of the victory: the other influences are only coming into full play as the middle ages close; but we can detect in them some signs of the uses that they are still to serve. The country interest has still to con-

tinue the battle of self-government; the mercantile spirit to inform and reform the foreign policy; the trade influence to remodel and develop national economy; the manufacturing influence to improve and to specialise in every region of national organisation. Such has been the result so far; it is vain and useless to prophesy. But it would seem that the peculiar tendencies which are encouraged by the habits and trains of thought which these pursuits severally involve, have worked and are working their way into real practical influence as the balance of national power has inclined successively to the several classes which are employed on these pursuits. The churchman struggled for moral against physical influence, as for the cause of the spirit against the flesh; he forgot sometimes that the very law of the spirit is a law of liberty. The baron struggled for national freedom against royal encroachment; the habits of the warrior and the hunter, the judge and the statesman, were all united in him; the medieval baron was a wonderful impersonation of strength and versatility, and combined more great qualities, for good or for evil, than any of the rival classes; but in the idea of corporate freedom the idea of individual and social freedom was too often left out of sight: the whole policy of the baronage was insular and narrowed down to one issue. The mercantile influence tended to widen the national mind; it grew under the Tudors to great importance and power, but it did not directly tend to the increase of liberty. The national programme of liberation had to be taken up under the Stewarts in a condition scarcely more developed than when it was laid down under the Lancastrian kings: only the nation had learned in the meantime more of the world, of diplomacy, of the balance of nations, and of the bearing of commercial alliances on domestic welfare. The economical and administrative reforms for which trade and manufacture train men until the balance of national power falls to them, are matters which we ourselves have lived to witness. What organic changes the further extension of political power to the labourer in town and country may bring, our children may live to see.

Influence of social pursuits on political life and progress.

To return however to the special point. One fact remains to

The borough representation was no adequate representation of a class.

be considered, which must to a great extent modify all conclusions on the subject. The town members in parliament during the middle ages represented only a very small proportion of the towns, and those selected by the merest chance of accident or caprice. They were, as we have seen, very unequally distributed, and were in no way, like the knights of the shire, a general concentration of local representation. In so far then as they represented an interest at all, they represented it very inadequately; and if, as we have supposed, they represented chiefly the governing bodies among their constituencies, they are still further removed from being regarded as the true exponents of any element of the national will. And this consideration will account in great measure for their insignificance in action and their obscurity in history.

Hence its insignificance.

Social life of the townsman.

813. Of the social life and habits of the citizen and burgher we have more distinct ideas than of his political action. Social habits no doubt tended to the formation of political habits then as now. Except for the purposes of trade, the townsman seldom went far from his borough; there he found all his kinsmen, his company, and his customers; his ambition was gratified by election to municipal office; the local courts could settle most of his legal business; in the neighbouring villages he could invest the money which he cared to invest in land; once a year, for a few years, he might bear a share in the armed contingent of his town to the shire force or militia; once in his life he might go up, if he lived in a parliamentary borough, to parliament. There was not much in his life to widen his sympathies; there were no newspapers, and few books; there was not enough local distress for charity to find interest in relieving it; there were many local festivities, and time and means for cultivating comfort at home. The burgher had pride in his house, and still more perhaps in his furniture; for although, in the splendid panorama of medieval architecture, the great houses of the merchants contribute a distinct element of magnificence to the general picture, such houses as Crosby Hall and the Hall of John Hall of Salisbury must always, in the walled towns, have been exceptions to the

rule, and far beyond the aspirations of the ordinary tradesman; but the smallest house could be made comfortable and even elegant by the appliances which his trade connexion brought within the reach of the master. Hence the riches of the inventories attached to the wills of medieval townsmen, and many of the most prized relics of medieval handicraft. Somewhat of the pains, for which the private house afforded no scope, was spent on the churches and public buildings of the town. The numerous churches of York and Norwich, poorly endowed, but nobly built and furnished, speak very clearly not only of the devotion, but of the artistic culture, of the burghers of those towns. The crafts vied with one another in the elaborate ornamentation of their churches, their chantries, and their halls of meeting; and of the later religious guilds some seem to have been founded for the express purpose of combining splendid religious services and processions with the work of charity. Such was one of the better results of a confined local sympathy. But the burgher did not either in life or in death forget his friends outside the walls. His will generally contained directions for small payments to the country churches where his ancestors lay buried. Strongly as his affections were localised, he was not a mere townsman. Nine-tenths of the cities of medieval England would now be regarded as mere country towns, and they were country towns even then. They drew in all their new blood from the country; they were the centres for village trade; the neighbouring villages were the play-ground and sporting-ground of the townsmen, who had, in many cases, rights of common pasture, and in some cases rights of hunting, far outside the walls. The great religious guilds just referred to, answered, like race meetings at a later period, the end of bringing even the higher class of the country population into close acquaintance with the townsmen, in ways more likely to be developed into social intercourse than the market or the muster in arms. Before the close of the middle ages the rich townsmen had begun to intermarry with the knights and gentry, and many of the noble families of the present day trace the foundation of their fortunes to a lord mayor of

Comfort and wealth of the burgher.

Town churches.

Country interests.

Religious guilds.

Intermarriages with the country folk.

London or York, or a mayor of some provincial town. These intermarriages, it is true, became more common after the fall of the elder baronage and the great expansion of trade under the Tudors, but the fashion was set two centuries earlier. If the adventurous and tragic history of the house of De la Pole shone as a warning light for rash ambition, it stood by no means alone. It is probable that there was no period in English history at which the barrier between the knightly and mercantile class was regarded as insuperable since the days of Athelstan, when the merchant who had made his three voyages over the sea and made his fortune, became worthy of thegn-right: even the higher grades of chivalry were not beyond his reach, for in 1439 we find William Estfeld, a mercer of London, made Knight of the Bath[1]. As the merchant found acceptance in the circles of the gentry, civic office became an object of competition with the knights of the county; their names were enrolled among the religious fraternities of the towns, the trade and craft guilds, and as the value of a seat in parliament became better appreciated, it was seen that the readiest way to it lay through the office of mayor, recorder, or alderman of some city corporation.

No barrier between trade and gentry.

Absence of 'professional' classes.

814. Beside these influences, which without much affecting the local sympathies of the citizen class joined them on to the rank above them, must be considered the fact that two of the most exclusive and 'professional' of modern professions were not in the middle ages professions at all. Every man was to some extent a soldier, and every man was to some extent a lawyer; for there was no distinctly military profession, and of lawyers only a very small and somewhat dignified number. Thus, although the burgher might be a mere mercer, or a mere saddler, and have very indistinct notions of commerce beyond his own warehouse or workshop, he was trained in warlike exercises, and he could keep his own accounts, draw up his own briefs, and make his own will, with the aid of a scrivener or a chaplain who could supply an outline of form, with but little fear of transgressing the rules of the court of law or

[1] Ordinances of the Privy Council, vi. 39.

of probate. In this point he was like the baron, liable to be called at very short notice to very different sorts of work. Finally, the townsman whose borough was not represented in parliament or did not enjoy such municipal organisation as placed the whole administration in the hands of the inhabitants, was a fully qualified member of the county court of his shire, and shared, there and in the corresponding institutions, everything that gave a political colouring to the life of the country gentleman or the yeoman.

Variety of employment.

Many of the points here enumerated belong, it may be said, to the rich merchant or great burgher, rather than to the ordinary tradesman and craftsman. This is true, but it must be remembered always that there was no such gulf between the rich merchant and the ordinary craftsman in the town, as existed between the country knight and the yeoman, or between the yeoman and the labourer. In the city it was merely the distinction of wealth; and the poorest apprentice might look forward to becoming a master of his craft, a member of the livery of his company, to a place in the council, an aldermanship, a mayoralty, the right of becoming an esquire for his life and leaving an honourable coat of arms for his children. The yeoman had no such straight road before him; he might improve his chances, as they came; might lay field to field, might send his sons to war or to the universities; but for him also the shortest way to make one of them a gentleman was to send him to trade; and there even the villein might find liberty and a new life that was not hopeless. But the yeoman, with fewer chances, had as a rule less ambition, possibly also more of that loyal feeling towards his nearest superior, which formed so marked a feature of medieval country life. The townsman knew no superior to whose place he might not aspire; the yeoman was attached by ties of hereditary attachment to a great neighbour, whose superiority never occurred to him as a thing to be coveted or grudged. The factions of the town were class factions and political or dynastic factions, the factions of the country were the factions of the lords and gentry. Once perhaps in a century there was a rising in the

Difference of class in towns mainly a difference in wealth.

Different position of the country yeoman.

Town struggles.

country; in every great town there was, every few years, something of a struggle, something of a crisis, if not between capital and labour in the modern sense, at least between trade and craft, or craft and craft, or magistracy and commons, between excess of control and excess of licence.

Artisans and labourers.

815. In town and country alike there existed another class of men, who, although possessing most of the other benefits of freedom, lay altogether outside political life. In the towns there were the artificers, and in the country the labourers, who lived from hand to mouth, and were to all intents and purposes 'the poor who never cease out of the land.' There were the craftsmen who could or would never aspire to become masters, or to take up their freedom as citizens; and the cottagers who had no chance of acquiring a rood of ground to till and leave to their children: two classes alike keenly sensitive to all changes in the seasons and in the prices of the necessaries of life; very indifferently clad and housed, in good times well fed, but in bad times not fed at all. In some respects these classes differed from that which in the present day furnishes the bulk of the mass of pauperism. The evils which are commonly, however erroneously it may be, regarded as resulting from redundant population, had not in the middle ages the shape which they have taken in modern times. Except in the walled towns, and then only in exceptional times, there could have been no necessary overcrowding of houses. The very roughness and uncleanliness of the country labourer's life was to some extent a safeguard; if he lived, as foreigners reported, like a hog, he did not fare or lodge worse than the beasts that he tended. In the towns, the restraints on building, which were absolutely necessary to keep the limited area of the streets open for traffic, prevented any very great variation in the number of inhabited houses; for, although in some great towns, like Oxford, there were considerable vacant spaces which were apt to become a sort of gypsey camping-ground for the waifs and strays of a mixed population, most of them were closely packed; the rich men would not dispense with their courts and gardens, and the very poor had to lodge outside the walls. In the country townships again, there

The poorer classes.

Not overcrowded;

except in walled towns.

was no such liberty as has in more modern times been somewhat imprudently used, of building or not building cottage dwellings without due consideration of place or proportion to the demand for useful labour. Every manor had its constitution and its recognised classes and number of holdings on the demesne and the freehold, the village and the waste; the common arable and the common pasture were a village property that warned off all interlopers and all superfluous competition. So strict were the barriers, that it seems impossible to suppose that any great increase of population ever presented itself as a fact to the medieval economist; or, if he thought of it at all, he must have regarded the recurrence of wars and pestilences as a providential arrangement for the re-adjustment of the conditions of his problem. As a fact, whatever the cause may have been, the population of England during the middle ages did not vary in anything like the proportion in which it has increased since the beginning of the last century; and there is no reason to think that any vast difference existed between the supply and demand of homes for the poor. Still there were many poor; if only the old, the diseased, the widows, and the orphans are to be counted in the number. There were too, in England, as everywhere else, besides the absolutely helpless, whole classes of labourers and artisans, whose earnings never furnished more than the mere requisites of life; and, besides these, idle and worthless beggars, who preferred the freedom of vagrancy to the restrictions of ill remunerated labour. All these classes were to be found in town and country alike.

Villages not over-peopled.

Population of the country varied very slowly.

Classes of poor.

816. The care of the really helpless poor was regarded both as a legal and as a religious duty from the very first ages of English Christianity. S. Gregory, in his instructions to Augustine, had reminded him of the duty of a bishop to set apart for the poor a fourth part of the income of his church; and some vestiges of the usage, which does not seem ever to have been generally adopted, are found in the ecclesiastical legislation of the fourteenth century: in 1342 archbishop Stratford ordered that in all cases of impropriation a portion of the tithe should be set apart for the relief of the poor. The neglect of

Religious duty of providing for the poor.

Legislation for the care of the poor.

the poor was alleged as one of the crying sins of the alien clergy[1]. The legislation of the witenagemotes of Ethelred bore the same mark; a third portion of the tithe that belonged to the church was to go to God's poor and to the needy ones in thraldom; it was enjoined on all God's servants that they should comfort and feed the poor. Even in the reign of Henry I the king was declared to be the kinsman and advocate of the poor. On such a point it is needless to multiply proof; almsdeeds were always regarded as a religious duty, whether as an act of merit or as an act of gratitude. The dispensation of alms was as a rule left to the clergy, just as the duty of inculcating almsgiving was chiefly left to them. The beneficed clergy in their parishes, the almoners of the monasteries, and the hosts of mendicant friars, to some extent fulfilled the task, and certainly kept the duty of almsgiving prominently before men's eyes. The guilds too, in each of their aspects, whether they were organised for police, for religious, social, or trade purposes, made the performance of this duty a part of their regular work. In the frith guild of London the remains of the feasts were dealt to the needy for the love of God; the maintenance of the poorer members of the craft was, as in the friendly societies of our own time, one main object in the institution of the craft guilds; and even those later religious guilds, in which the chief object seems at first sight, as in much of the charitable machinery of the present day, to have been the acting of mysteries and the exhibition of pageants, were organised for the relief of distress as well as for conjoint and mutual prayer. It was with this idea that men gave large estates in land to the guilds which down to the Reformation formed an organised administration of relief. The confiscation of the guild property together with that of the hospitals was one of the great wrongs which were perpetrated under Edward VI; and, whatever may have been the results of the stoppage of monastic charity, was one unquestionable cause of the growth of town pauperism. The extant regulations and accounts of the guilds show how this duty was

A duty of the clergy.

Fulfilled by the guilds.

Confiscation of guild property.

[1] Johnson, Canons, ii. 364; Rot. Parl. iv. 290.

carried into effect; no doubt there was much self-indulgence and display, but there was also effective relief; the charities of the great London companies are a survival of a system which was once in full working in every market town.

Side by side with the organisations for the relief of real poverty must be set the measures for the restraint of idleness and begging. These formed a part of the legislation on labour which was attempted from the middle of the reign of Edward III, and which has been regarded by political economists as one of the great blemishes of medieval administration. The same principle of combination, which had its better side in the charity of the guilds, had, if not its worst, at least its most dangerous side, in the associations of the artisans for the purpose of enforcing a higher rate of wages. The great plague of 1348 caused such a terrible diminution of the population that the land was in danger of falling out of cultivation; labour was extremely scarce, and excessive wages were immediately demanded by those who could work; excessive wages at once produced improvidence and idleness. As early as 1349, in the first ordinance on labour, it was found necessary not only to fix the amount of wages, and to press all able-bodied men into the work of husbandry, but to forbid the giving of alms to sturdy or valiant beggars[1]. The quick succession of enactments on this point shows the urgency of the evil and the inadequacy of the remedy sought in the limitation of wages and the prices of victuals, and in peremptory interference between the employers and the employed. The ordinance of 1349 was followed by the statute of 1351 which, among other enactments, provided a regular machinery by which the excess of wages paid to the labourers could be recovered from them by process before justices assigned for the purpose, the proceeds of these actions being appropriated, where the masters did not sue for it, to the relief of the local contributions towards the national taxes[2]. In 1357 the money so recovered was assigned to the lords of franchises on the understanding that they should contribute

Legislation against begging.

Statutes of labourers.

[1] Statutes, i. 307.

[2] Statutes, i. 311, 312.

Statutes and petitions on labour.

to the expenses of the justices[1]. An almost immediate result of this over-repression was seen in the formation of conspiracies among the carpenters and masons, the flight of labourers from their native counties, and the crowding of the corporate towns with candidates for enfranchisement. All these practices were attacked by the statute of 1362, but ineffectually, as the results showed[2]. The statutes of 1349 and 1351 were confirmed in 1368 on the prayer of the employers of paid labourers, 'la commune que vivent par geynerie de lour terres ou Marchandie[3],' who have no lordships or villeins to serve them. In almost every parliament petitions were presented for the enforcement of the statutes, or for the increase of their stringency; but their chief result was the spread of disaffection and disorder. From the paid artificers the dread of servitude and the desire of combination spread to the villeins, against whose conspiracies for constraining their masters a statute was passed in 1377, and who were thus drawn or driven into participation with the rebellion of 1381, for which at the time they suffered so heavy retribution. Although the events of that year tended to bring the employers to a more just sense of their relation to the employed, petitions every now and then emerge, showing that the lesson had not been completely learned, and from this time the cause of the villein and the artisan is one. Besides the petitions for the enforcement of the statutes, which are presented as late as the year 1482, statutes were passed in 1388, 1427, and 1430 confirming or amending the acts of Edward III[4]. As early as 1378 the commons had petitioned that agricultural labourers might not be allowed to be received into towns, there to become artisans, mariners, or clerks; in 1391 occurs the famous petition that villeins may not be allowed to send their children to the schools; in the first parliament of Henry IV the same feeling is displayed in a request that they may no longer be enfranchised by being received into a market town[5]. All attempts however either to compel the artisans

[1] Statutes, i. 350.
[2] Statutes, i. 375.
[3] Rot. Parl. ii. 296.
[4] Statutes, ii. 63, 233, 244.
[5] Rot. Parl. iii. 294, 296, 448.

to work at husbandry, or to prevent the villeins from becoming artisans, failed; the land went rapidly out of cultivation; pasturage succeeded tillage; poverty in the labouring class became a growing evil, and the laws against the beggars grew more and more stringent. Deficiency of labour.

It is to the legislation of 1388 that England owes her first glimpse apparently of a law of settlement and organised relief. The act by which the statute of labourers was confirmed and amended contained a clause which forbad the labourer to leave his place of service or to move about the country without a passport. Another clause directed that impotent beggars should remain in the places where they were at the passing of the statute, and that, if the people of those places would not provide for them, they were to seek a maintenance in other townships within the hundred or wapentake, or in the places where they were born, within forty days after the proclamation of the statute, there to remain during their lives[1]. The same intention appears in the acts of 1495 and 1504, which were no doubt an expansion of the statute of 1388, and which direct that beggars not able to work are to be sent to the place where they were born or have dwelt or are best known, to support themselves by begging within the limit of the hundred[2]. All these acts refer to mendicancy as if it were a recognised profession, in which both pilgrims and poor scholars of the Universities were included, and such as was practised in Germany by both apprentices and students in much later times. It is probable, and indeed certain, that for the poor who remained at home no such legislation was needed: in the towns the guilds, and in the country the lords of the land, the clergy, and the monasteries, discharged the duty, whether on legal or religious grounds, of providing for the settled poor without putting them to unnecessary shame. First appearance of a law of settlement. Legislation for vagrant poor.

817. One class of the poor, the villein class, has engrossed almost the whole of the interest which the sympathy of historical students can furnish for the medieval poor; and in our former chapters we have attempted to gather from the extremely The villeins.

[1] Statutes, ii. 58.

[2] Statutes, ii. 569, 656.

Early villenage.

obscure statements of legal writers, and in spite of the diversities of local customs, some slight notion of their condition at different periods of our history. We have seen how in Anglo-Saxon times the relation of the landless man to his lord placed him under a protection which was liable to be merged in total dependence, whilst between him and the bondslave there still existed a difference so wide as to be really a difference in kind; and how under the Norman government the differences of rank in the lower classes of the native population were probably confused; the bondman possibly gained, whilst the villein for the time as certainly lost. Both were 'rustici' or 'nativi,' both had land on customary conditions, both were so far 'ascriptitii glebae,' that they could not leave their land without losing their all, or escape from the claims of their lord without the risk of being brought again into bondage. There was no doubt a strong tendency to make the servile relation altogether dependent on the tenure of land, and to put an end even to the forms of personal servitude, the disabilities which were attached to the blood as well as to the territorial status of the villein.

Acts of manumission.

By acts of emancipation or manumission the 'native' was made a freeman, even though with the disabilities he lost the privileges of maintenance which he could claim on the land of his lord. And acts of emancipation were regarded by the church as meritorious. The old law books drew a distinction between the villein regardant and the villein in gross, and Sir Thomas Smith remarks that the distinction subsisted in his own time, although villenage was then altogether vanishing away. The villein regardant was a villein who laboured under disabilities in relation to his lord only; the villein in gross possessed none of the qualities of a freeman. It has been doubted whether the villein in gross is not altogether a figment of the lawyers, and English sentiment has always been adverse to considering any man of native blood as less than free. Until we have a much more thorough investigation of the manorial records than has been yet attempted, no decision can be arrived at on this point; but it appears certain from known instances that there were, down to the close of the middle ages, and perhaps longer, bondmen on many manors, to whom the definition of villein regardant would not apply. Possibly these were the survivors of the peasant population which had been servile before the Conquest; or, possibly they had been depressed by the very definitions of the law which they are found to illustrate. All that is certain is that they were disqualified from all the functions of political life, and were, owing to their depressed social state, the objects of much pity. It is from the acts of manumission that we learn what little we know of their legal status; and some of those acts of manumission are, in language at least, creditable to the age that encouraged them.

Bondmen on manors.

'Whereas,' writes bishop Sherborne of Chichester in 1536, quoting the Institutes of Justinian, 'at the beginning nature brought forth all men free, and afterwards the law of nations placed certain of them under the yoke of servitude; we believe that it is pious and meritorious towards God to manumit them and to restore them to the benefit of pristine liberty;' and on this consideration he proceeds to liberate Nicolas Holden, a 'native and serf,' who for many years has served him on his manor of Woodmancote and elsewhere, from every chain, servitude, and servile condition, by which he was bound to the bishop and his cathedral church; 'and, so far as we can,' he adds, 'we make him a freeman; so that the said Nicholas, with the whole of the issue to be begotten by him, may remain free, and have power freely to do and exercise all and singular the acts which are competent to free men, just as if he had been begotten by free parents[1].' All acts of manumission, it is true, are not worded like this; but it is obvious that, in such an act, something more was done than the mere release of the villein from the services that were due by reason of his lord's right over the land which he occupied, and that the native so emancipated laboured under other disqualifications than those from which he could have delivered himself by obtaining his lord's leave to quit his holding. On whatever the hold of the lord over his 'native' was originally based, there were at the date of the Reformation,

A manumission of a bondman.

[1] From Bishop Sherborne's Register at Chichester; folio 150. Other forms will be found in Madox, Formulare Anglicanum, pp. 416–420.

Importance of manumission.

and after it, whole families who were liable to be sold as well as to be emancipated. Against this is to be set the fact that the sums for which the villein and his whole family and chattels were transferred from one owner to another were so small as to prove that the rights thus acquired, however heavy the disabilities of the villein may have been, were worth little to the master; and from this it may be inferred that the act of manumission itself was intended rather to prove that the emancipated person was not disqualified for holy orders or for knighthood, than to give him the ordinary powers of a freeman. We may conjecture that the villein regardant had fallen into villenage by occupying some of the demesne of the lord on servile conditions, and that the villein in gross was a chattel of the lord whom he paid or maintained by a similar allotment of land; that the former class could not be alienated without the land which they occupied, but were in most other respects free, whilst the latter might be sold from one manor to another, and were by reason of villein blood incapable of most legal acts; that the condition of the former was ameliorated and perhaps altogether made free by the substitution of rents for services from the tenant, and by the institution of copyhold titles, in which the custom of the manor fettered the will of the lord; whilst the lot of the latter remained unimproved, except by separate manumissions, until the country was ashamed of such servitude, and thought it best to forget that it had ever existed. But, as has been already said, the obscurity of the question, and the certain diversities of usage, prevent us from offering any mere conjecture like this as a possible solution of the difficulty.

Grades of villenage.

No barriers between classes.

818. Whatever theoretical conclusion may be drawn touching the condition of the poor, and there is no occasion that either way it should be exaggerated by false sentiment, there is very little evidence to show that our forefathers, in the middle ranks of life, desired to set any impassable boundary between class and class. The great barons would probably, at any period, have shown a disinclination to admit new men on terms of equality to their own order, but this disinclination was overborne by the royal policy of promoting useful servants, and the

baronage was recruited by lawyers, ministers, and warriors, who in the next generation stood as stiffly on their privilege as their companions had ever done. The country knight was always regarded as a member of the noble class, and his position was continually strengthened by intermarriage with the baronage. The city magnate again formed a link between the country squire and the tradesman; and the tradesman and the yeoman were in position and in blood close akin. Even the villein might, by learning a craft, set his foot on the ladder of promotion. But the most certain way to rise was furnished by education. Over against the many grievances which modern thought has alleged against the unlearned ages which passed before the invention of printing, it ought to be set to the credit of medieval society that clerkship was never despised or made unnecessarily difficult of acquisition. The sneer of Walter Map, who declared that in his days the villeins were attempting to educate their ignoble and degenerate offspring in the liberal arts, proves that even in the twelfth century the way was open. Richard II rejected the proposition that the villeins should be forbidden to send their children to the schools to learn 'clergie'; and even at a time when the supply of labour ran so low that no man who was not worth twenty shillings a year in land or rent was allowed to apprentice his child to a craft, a full and liberal exception was made in favour of learning; 'every man or woman'—the words occur in the petition and statute of artificers passed in 1406,—'of what state or condition that he be, shall be free to set their son or daughter to take learning at any school that pleaseth them within the realm[1].' What, it may be asked, was the supply that answered to a demand so large as this? It would be very unfair to underrate the debt which England owes to the statesmen who, after the dissolution of monasteries, obtained in the foundation of grammar schools a permanent, free, and to some extent independent, source of liberal education for the people, or to object to the claim made by that liberal education to have been higher in character and value than anything

Blending of society by intermediate classes.

Education the best means for rising.

Education not restricted by legislation.

[1] Rot. Parl. iii. 602; Statutes, ii. 158.

Education furnished by the monastic and other schools.

that had preceded it. Yet it must be remembered that the want which it supplied was one which had been to a great extent created by the destruction of the religious houses and other foundations in which the middle ages had cultivated a modicum of useful learning. In a former chapter attention has been called to the fact that absolutely unlettered ignorance ought not to be alleged against the middle and lower classes of these ages; that in every village reading and writing must have been not unknown accomplishments, even if books and paper were so scarce as to confine these accomplishments practically to the mere uses of business. Schools were by no means uncommon things; there were schools in all cathedrals; monasteries and colleges were everywhere, and wherever there was a monastery or a college there was a school. Towards the close of the middle ages, notwithstanding many causes for depression, there was much vitality in the schools. William of Wykeham at Winchester and Henry VI at Eton set conspicuous examples of reform and improvement; the Lollards taught their doctrines in schools; the schools of the cathedrals continued to flourish. The depression of education was recognised but not acquiesced in. In 1447 four parish priests of London, in a petition to parliament, begged the commons to consider the great number of grammar schools 'that sometime were in diverse parts of the realm beside those that were in London, and how few there be in these days;' there were many learners, they continued, but few teachers; masters rich in money, scholars poor in learning; they asked leave to appoint schoolmasters in their parishes, to be removed at their discretion; and Henry VI granted the petition, subjecting that discretion to the advice of the ordinary[1]. Learning had languished, as may be inferred from the fact that the decline of the universities had only been arrested by the rapid endowment of the new colleges, and that the restriction of the church patronage of the crown to university men had been offered as an inducement to draw men to Oxford and Cambridge. But the great men of the land, ministers and prelates, were

Attempts to remedy the depression of education.

[1] Rot. Parl. v. 137.

devoting themselves and their goods liberally to prevent further decline, and their efforts were not unappreciated in the class they strove to benefit. In this, as in some other matters, it is probable that the invention of printing at first acted somewhat abruptly, and by the very suddenness of change stayed rather than stimulated exertion. Just as men ceased for the moment to write books because the press could multiply the old ones to a bewildering extent, the flood of printing threatened to carry away all the profits of teaching and most of the advantages which superior clerkship had included. It is true the paralysis of literary energy in both cases was short, but it had in both cases the result of giving to the revival that followed it the look of a new beginning. The new learning differed from the old in many important points, but its novelty was mainly apparent in the fact that it sprang to life after the blow under which the old learning had succumbed. So it was with education generally: the new schools for which Colet and Ascham and their successors laboured, and the new schools that Edward VI, Mary, and Elizabeth founded out of the estates of the chantries, were chiefly new in the fact that they replaced a machinery which for the time had lost all energy and power. It is not improbable that the fifteenth century, although its records contain more distinct references to educational activity than those of the fourteenth, had experienced some decline in this point, a decline sufficiently marked to call for an effort to remedy it. But however this may have been, whether the foundation of Winchester and Eton, and the country schools that followed in their wake, was the last spark of an expiring flame, or the first flicker of the newly lighted lamp, the middle ages did not pass away in total darkness in the matter of education; and it was not in mockery that the parliament of Henry IV left every man, free or villein, to send his sons and daughters to school wherever he could find one. For anything like higher education the Universities offered abundant facilities and fairly liberal inducements to scholars; every parish priest was bound to instruct his parishioners in a way that would stimulate the desire to learn wherever such a desire existed. Lollardism would have been,

First effects of the invention of printing.

Character of the educational revival.

Existence of earlier schools.

if not innocuous, still incapable of anything like secret propagandism, if the faculty of reading had not been widely diffused. But it is impossible now to discuss at any length a subject, the importance of which is at least equalled by its difficulty.

Strength of class jealousies.

820. Great facilities for rising from class to class in the social order are not at all inconsistent with very strong class jealousies and antipathies and broad lines of demarcation. So, although we may readily grant that it was not impossible or even rare for the son of a yeoman to reach the highest honours in the church, or for the son of a merchant to reach the highest grade of nobility, it would be wrong to shut our eyes to the estranging and dividing influences by which interest was set against interest, estate against estate. The relation of the clergy to the laity was, as to some degree it always must be, an obstacle to any perfect identity of class interests. The legal and social immunities which belonged to the former, were begrudged and watched jealously by the latter. Between the landowning and landless classes there were similar grounds of division; for, although the actual value of land, as property, was neither so great nor so highly appreciated as in later times, the privileges which the possession of it included were even greater, politically and socially, than they are at the present day. A lower rate of taxation, the possession of the county franchise and of a considerable share of the borough franchise also, the legal protection with which the ownership of land had been guarded from the earliest times, and the strictness of the land-law framed upon feudal ideas, were benefits which were not shared by even the wealthiest of the mercantile classes. The landowner had a stake in the country, a material security for his good behaviour; if he offended against the law or the government, he might forfeit his land; but the land was not lost sight of, and the moral and social claims of the family which had possessed it were not barred by forfeiture. The restoration of the heirs of the dispossessed was an invariable result or condition of every political pacification; and very few estates were alienated from the direct line of inheritance by one forfeiture only. With the

Clergy and laity.

Landowners and landless.

merchant, it was not so; if he offended, all his material security was at once swallowed up by the forfeiture; a record might be kept of the profits, but they were not to be recovered; as he had risen, so he fell, unless he had in good time invested some part of his fortune in land. In the lower classes, again, the distinctions of interest in land, and varying views as to the employment of it, caused great heart-burnings and social discontents. As the freeholder engrossed the county franchise, the political divisions in the agricultural class scarcely rose to the level of parliament; but out of parliament they were the causes of much discontent, which found vent in the popular risings, and a welcome sympathy in the social doctrines of Lollardy. The burdens of the copyhold and customary tenures, the heavy heriots and fines, the unpaid services of villenage, the difficulty of obtaining small holdings on fair terms, combined with the equally important questions between tillage and pasturage to divide the agricultural class against itself. The price of wool enhanced the value of pasturage, the increased value of pasturage withdrew field after field from tillage; the decline of tillage, the depression of the markets, and the monopoly of the wool trade by the staple towns, reduced those country towns which had not encouraged manufacture, to such poverty that they were unable to pay their contingent to the revenue, and the regular sum of tenths and fifteenths was reduced by more than a fifth in consequence. The same causes which in the sixteenth century made the enclosure of the commons a most important popular grievance, had begun to set class against class as early as the fourteenth century, although the thinning of the population by the Plague acted to some extent as a corrective. To these deeply seated sources of division, the invidious laws on apparel and sumptuary legislation were small matters of aggravation, but they served to bring more prominently before mens' eyes the outward marks of inequality.

In the lower classes.

Tillage and pasturage.

That these causes were at work during the fifteenth century, as well as those which preceded and followed it, there is no doubt. The great dynastic quarrel gave more prominence to

Connexion of class grievances with the dynastic quarrel.

local and personal faction than to class distinctions and separations; the great crisis of the constitutional history turned, or seemed to turn, on points rather of dynastic than of social importance. But whilst town and country, clergy, nobles, and commons, were alike divided, house against house, family against family, bishop against bishop, man against wife, we can see in the attempts made by the two rival factions to turn the social divisions to account, that the social divisions were scarcely less deep and wide than they had been in the days of Wat Tyler and Jack Straw. The anti-Lancastrian party in the reign of Henry IV courted the Lollards in and out of parliament; the Lancastrian House fortified itself in the support of the clergy, until the duke of York, by appointing Bourchier to the primacy, divided the camp of the bishops. The Mortimer interest was put forward as an excuse for popular disturbances as well as for court intrigues and political conspiracies, in so much that, even when the duke of York had united in his own person the claims of indefeasible hereditary right and popular championship, the name of Mortimer continued to be the watchword of disaffection. It is true that, like almost everything else but dynastic hatred, these causes worked with diminished strength in the general attenuation and exhaustion of national vitality. But they certainly subsisted, and exercised a secondary influence, widening, perhaps, and deepening unseen, in preparation for the ages in which they would work with greater intensity and with fewer extrinsic incumbrances. A nation that seems to be perishing takes less heed of the minor causes of ruin, although they may be still acutely felt by individuals and classes of sufferers.

Close of the middle ages.

821. And here our survey, too general and too discursive perhaps to have been wisely attempted, must draw to its close. The historian turns his back on the middle ages with a brighter hope for the future, but not without regrets for what he is leaving. He recognises the law of the progress of this world in which the evil and debased elements are so closely intermingled with the noble and the beautiful, that, in the assured march of good, much that is noble and beautiful must needs

share the fate of the evil and debased. If it were not for the conviction that, however prolific and progressive the evil may have been, the power of good is more progressive and more prolific, the chronicler of a system that seems to be vanishing might lay down his pen with a heavy heart. The most enthusiastic admirer of medieval life must grant that all that was good and great in it was languishing even to death; and the firmest believer in progress must admit that as yet there were few signs of returning health. The sun of the Plantagenets went down in clouds and thick darkness; the coming of the Tudors gave as yet no promise of light; it was 'as the morning spread upon the mountains,' darkest before the dawn.

Marks of a period of transition.

The natural inquiry, how the fifteenth century affected the development of national character, deserves an attempt at an answer; but it can be little more than an attempt; for very little light is thrown upon it by the life and genius of great men. With the exception of Henry V, English history can show throughout the age no man who even aspires to greatness; and the greatness of Henry V is not of a sort that is peculiar to the age or distinctive of a stage of national life. His personal idiosyncrasy was that of a hero in no heroic age. Of the best of the minor workers none rises beyond mediocrity of character or achievement. Bedford was a wise and noble statesman, but his whole career was a hopeless failure. Gloucester's character had no element of greatness at all. Beaufort, by his long life, high rank, wealth, experience and ability, held a position almost unrivalled in Europe, but he was neither successful nor disinterested; fair and honest and enlightened as his policy may have been, neither at the time nor ever since has the world looked upon him as a benefactor; he appears in history as a lesser Wolsey,—a hard sentence perhaps, but one which is justified by the general condition of the world in which the two cardinals had to play their part; Beaufort was the great minister of an expiring system, Wolsey of an age of grand transitions. Among the other clerical administrators of the age, Kemp and Waynflete were faithful, honest, enlightened, but quite unequal to the difficulties of their position; and besides them there are absolutey

Little light on national character.

No great ministers.

Warwick the type of baronial greatness.

none that come within even the second class of greatness as useful men. It is the same with the barons: such greatness as there is amongst them,—and the greatness of Warwick is the climax and type of it,—is more conspicuous in evil than in good. In the classes beneath the baronage, as we have them pourtrayed in the Paston Letters, we see more of violence, chicanery and greed, than of anything else. Faithful attachment to the faction which from hereditary or personal liking they have determined to maintain, is the one redeeming feature, and it is one which by itself may produce as much evil as good; that nation is in an evil plight in which the sole redeeming quality is one that owes its existence to a deadly disease. All else is languishing: literature has reached the lowest depths of dulness; religion, so far as its chief results are traceable, has sunk, on the one hand into a dogma fenced about with walls which its defenders cannot pass either inward or outward, on the other hand into a mere war cry of the cause of destruction. Between the two lies a narrow borderland of pious and cultivated mysticism, far too fastidious to do much for the world around. Yet here, as everywhere else, the dawn is approaching. Here as everywhere else, the evil is destroying itself, and the remaining good, lying deep down and having yet to wait long before it reaches the surface, is already striving toward the sunlight that is to come. The good is to come out of the evil; the evil is to compel its own remedy; the good does not spring from it, but is drawn up through it. In the history of nations, as of men, every good and perfect gift is from above; the new life strikes down in the old root; there is no generation from corruption.

General decline in literature and religion.

Charm of medieval history.

822. So we turn our back on the age of chivalry, of ideal heroism, of picturesque castles and glorious churches and pageants, camps, and tournaments, lovely charity and gallant self-sacrifice, with their dark shadows of dynastic faction, bloody conquest, grievous misgovernance, local tyrannies, plagues and famines unhelped and unaverted, hollowness of pomp, disease and dissolution. The charm which the relics of medieval art have woven around the later middle ages must be resolutely, ruthlessly, broken. The attenuated life of the later middle ages is in

thorough discrepancy with the grand conceptions of the earlier times. The thread of national life is not to be broken, but the earlier strands are to be sought out and bound together and strengthened with threefold union for the new work. But it will be a work of time: the forces newly liberated by the shock of the Reformation will not at once cast off the foulness of the strata through which they have passed before they reached the higher air: much will be destroyed that might well have been conserved, and some new growths will be encouraged that ought to have been checked. In the new world, as in the old, the tares are mingled with the wheat. In the destruction and in the growth alike will be seen the great features of difference between the old and the new.

Features of a gradual transition.

The printing press is an apt emblem or embodiment of the change. Hitherto men have spent their labour on a few books, written by the few for the few, with elaborately chosen material, in consummately beautiful penmanship, painted and emblazoned as if each one were a distinct labour of love, each manuscript unique, precious, the result of most careful individual training, and destined for the complete enjoyment of a reader educated up to the point at which he can appreciate its beauty. Henceforth books are to be common things. For a time the sanctity of the older forms will hang about the printing press; the magnificent volumes of Fust and Colard Mansion will still recal the beauty of the manuscript, and art will lavish its treasures on the embellishment of the libraries of the great. Before long printing will be cheap, and the unique or special beauty of the early presses will have departed; but light will have come into every house, and that which was the luxury of the few will have become the indispensable requisite of every family.

Illustration from the printing press.

With the multiplication of books comes the rapid extension and awakening of mental activity. As it is with the form so with the matter. The men of the decadence, not less than the men of the renaissance, were giants of learning: they read and assimilated the contents of every known book; down to the very close of the era the able theologian would press into the service of his commentary or his summa

Illustration from literature.

Transition in learning

every preceding commentary or summa with gigantic labour, and with an acuteness which, notwithstanding that it was ill-trained and misdirected, is in the eyes of the desultory reader of modern times little less than miraculous: the books were rare, but the accomplished scholar had worked through them all. Outside his little world all was comparatively dark. Here too the change was coming. Scholarship was to take a new form; intensity of critical power, devoted to that which was worth criticising, was to be substituted as the characteristic of a learned man for the indiscriminating voracity of the earlier learning. The multiplication of books would make such scholarship as that of Vincent of Beauvais, or Thomas Aquinas, or Gerson, or Torquemada, an impossibility. Still there would be giants like Scaliger and Casaubon, men who culled the fair flower of all learning, critical as the new scholars, comprehensive as the old; reserved for the patronage of sovereigns and nations, and perishing when they were neglected like the beautiful books of the early printers. But they are a minor feature in the new picture. The real change is that by which every man comes to be a reader and a thinker; the Bible comes to every family, and each man is priest in his own household. The light is not so brilliant, but it is everywhere, and it shines more and more unto the perfect day. It is a false sentiment that leads men in their admiration of the unquestionable glory of the old culture to undervalue the abundant wealth and growing glory of the new.

Diffusion of light.

Illustration from architecture and mechanical inventions.

The parallel holds good in other matters besides books. He is a rash man who would with one word of apology compare the noble architecture of the middle ages with the mean and commonplace type of building into which by a steady decline our churches, palaces, and streets had sunk at the beginning of the present century. Here too the splendour of the few has been exchanged for the comfort of the many; and, although perhaps in no description of culture has the break between the old and the new been more conspicuous than in this, it may be said that the many are now far more capable of appreciating the beauty which they will try to rival, than ever the few were to comprehend the value of that which they were losing. But it is needless to multiply illustrations of a truth which is exemplified by every new invention: the steam plough and the sewing machine are less picturesque, and call for a less educated eye than that of the ploughman and the sempstress, but they produce more work with less waste of energy; they give more leisure and greater comfort; they call out, in the production and improvement of their mechanism, a higher and more widely-spread culture. And all these things are growing instead of decaying.

Emblems of new growth.

823. To conclude with a few of the commonplaces which must be familiar to all who have approached the study of history with a real desire to understand it, but which are apt to strike the writer more forcibly at the end than the beginning of his work. However much we may be inclined to set aside the utilitarian plan of studying our subject, it cannot be denied that we must read the origin and development of our Constitutional History chiefly with the hope of educating ourselves into the true reading of its later fortunes, and so train ourselves for a judicial examination of its evidences, a fair and equitable estimate of the rights and wrongs of policy, dynasty, and party. Whether we intend to take the position of a judge or the position of an advocate, it is most necessary that both the critical insight should be cultivated, and the true circumstances of the questions that arise at later stages should be adequately explored. The man who would rightly learn the lesson that the seventeenth century has to teach, must not only know what Charles thought of Cromwell and what Cromwell thought of Charles, but must try to understand the real questions at issue, not by reference to an ideal standard only, but by tracing the historical growth of the circumstances in which those questions arose: he must try to look at them as it might be supposed that the great actors would have looked at them, if Cromwell had succeeded to the burden which Charles inherited, or if Charles had taken up the part of the hero of reform. In such an attitude it is quite unnecessary to exclude party feeling or personal sympathy. Whichever way the sentiment may incline, the truth,

Concluding reflexions on the study of history.

A training for the study of controversial history.

Respect for sincerity on both sides.

the whole truth and nothing but the truth, is what history would extract from her witnesses: the truth which leaves no pitfalls for unwary advocates, and which is in the end the fairest measure of equity to all. In the reading of that history we have to deal with high-minded men, with zealous enthusiastic parties, of whom it cannot be fairly said that one was less sincere in his belief in his own cause than was the other. They called each other hypocrites and deceivers, for each held his own views so strongly that he could not conceive of the other as sincere. But to us they are both of them true and sincere, whichever way our sympathies or our sentiments incline. We bring to the reading of their acts a judgment which has been trained through the Reformation history to see rights and wrongs on both sides; sometimes see the balance of wrong on that side which we believe, which we know, to be the right. We come to the Reformation history from the reading of the gloomy period to which the present volume has been devoted; a worn-out helpless age, that calls for pity without sympathy, and yet balances weariness with something like regrets. Modern thought is a little prone to eclecticism in history: it can sympathise with puritanism as an effort after freedom, and put out of sight the fact that puritanism was itself a grinding social tyranny, that wrought out its ends by unscrupulous detraction and by the profane handling of things which should have been sacred even to the fanatic if he really believed in the cause for which he raged. There is little real sympathy with the great object, the peculiar creed that was oppressed; as a struggle for liberty the Quarrel of Puritanism takes its stand besides the Quarrel on the Investitures. Yet like every other struggle for liberty, it ended in being a struggle for supremacy. On the other hand, the system of Laud and of Charles seems to many minds to contain so much that is good and sacred, that the means by which it was maintained fall into the background. We would not judge between the two theories which have been nursed by the prejudices of ten generations. To one side liberty, to the other law, will continue to outweigh all other considerations of disputed and detailed right or wrong: it is enough for each to look at them as the actors themselves looked

Training supplied by study of earlier history.

Two parties in the reading of later history.

at them, or as men look at party questions of their own day, when much of private conviction and personal feeling must be sacrificed to save those broader principles for which only great parties can be made to strive.

The historian looks with actual pain upon many of these things. Especially in quarrels where religion is concerned, the hollowness of the pretension to political honesty becomes a stumblingblock in the way of fair judgment. We know that no other causes have ever created so great and bitter struggles, have brought into the field, whether of war or controversy, greater and more united armies. Yet no truth is more certain than this, that the real motives of religious action do not work on men in masses; and that the enthusiasm which creates Crusaders, Inquisitors, Hussites, Puritans, is not the result of conviction, but of passion provoked by oppression or resistance, maintained by selfwill, or stimulated by the mere desire of victory. And this is a lesson for all time, and for practical life as well as historical judgment. And on the other hand it is impossible to regard this as an adequate solution of the problem: there must be something, even if it be not religion or liberty, for which men will make so great sacrifices.

Political dishonesty.

The best aspect of an age of controversy must be sought in the lives of the best men, whose honesty carries conviction to the understanding, whilst their zeal kindles the zeal, of the many. A study of the lives of such men will lead to the conclusion that, in spite of internecine hostility in act, the real and true leaders had far more in common than they knew of; they struggled, in the dark or in the twilight, against the evil which was there, and which they hated with equal sincerity; they fought for the good which was there, and which really was strengthened by the issue of the strife. Their blows fell at random: men perished in arms against one another whose hearts were set on the same end and aim; and that good end and aim which neither of them had seen clearly was the inheritance they left to their children, made possible, and realised not so much by the victory of one as by the truth and self-sacrifice of both.

The lives of the best men illustrate the great lesson of history.

At the close of so long a book, the author may be suffered to moralise. His end will have been gained if he has succeeded in helping to train the judgment of his readers to discern the balance of truth and reality, and, whether they go on to further reading with the aspirations of the advocate or the calmness of the critic, to rest content with nothing less than the attainable maximum of truth, to base their arguments on nothing less sacred than that highest justice which is found in the deepest sympathy with erring and straying men.

THE END.

INDEX.

Lightning Source UK Ltd.
Milton Keynes UK
UKOW042150130313

207601UK00001B/24/P